HANDS-ON
PHYSICS
ACTIVITIES
WITH REAL-LIFE
APPLICATIONS

Easy-to-Use Labs and Demonstrations
for Grades 8-12

JAMES CUNNINGHAM

NORMAN HERR

JOSSEY-BASS
A Wiley Imprint
www.josseybass.com

Published by Jossey-Bass
A Wiley Imprint
989 Market Street, San Francisco, CA 94103-1741   www.josseybass.com

Jossey-Bass books and products are available through most bookstores. To contact Jossey-Bass directly call our Customer Care Department within the U.S. at 800-956-7739, outside the U.S. at 317-572-3986 or fax 317-572-4002.

Jossey-Bass also publishes its books in a variety of electronic formats. Some content that appears in print may not be available in electronic books.

Library of Congress Cataloging-in-Publication Data

Cunningham, James B.,
    Hands-on physics activities with real-life applications : easy-to-use
  labs and demonstrations for grades 8-12 / James Cunningham,
  Norman Herr.
      p. cm. – (Physical science curriculum library ; v. 1)
    Includes index.
    ISBN0-87628-845-X
    1. Physics–Study and teaching (Elementary) I. Herr, Norman.
  II. Title. III. Series.
  QC30.C86 1994
  530'.071'2–dc20   93-47374

FIRST EDITION
HB Printing 10 9 8 7

DEDICATION

To the memory of my sister, Susan Mary Cunningham,
and my brother, Peter Michael Cunningham.

JAMES CUNNINGHAM

To my wife, Roberta,
and our children Christiana, Stephen, and John.

NORMAN HERR

ABOUT THE AUTHORS

James Cunningham is professor of science and computer education at California State University, Northridge where he serves as Chair of the Department of Secondary Education. He received his Ph.D. in Science Education from Syracuse University and previously served as Chair of the Departments of Science and Mathematics at Brainbridge Island and Trout Lake High Schools in the state of Washington. Dr. Cunningham is author of *Teaching Metrics Simplified* and co-author of *BASIC for Teachers* and *Authoring Educational Software*. He is currently co-authoring *Hands-On Chemistry Activities* with Norman Herr.

Norman Herr is associate professor of science and computer education at California State University, Northridge. He received his Ph.D. from the University of California, Los Angeles and has worked as a chemist, a community college science instructor, and consultant for the College Board. He served as chair of the Science Department at Maranatha High School in Sierra Madre, California. Dr. Herr has written numerous articles in the field of science education and is currently co-authoring *Hands-On Chemistry Activities* with James Cunningham.

ABOUT THIS RESOURCE

This resource contains intriguing investigations designed to provide an activity-oriented approach to learning science and to engage students in a genuine pursuit of science. It also serves as a resource book for teachers and students. Each set of activities is preceded by a concise introduction giving students a foundation on which to build their understanding, including a discussion of major concepts related to the activities.

The activities provide meaningful interactions between students and their world in a manner encouraging sound scientific reasoning. Many of the activities produce unexpected or dramatic results that capture student interest. Thought-provoking questions follow each set of activities. Following the questions is a section developed especially for the teacher in which concepts are explained in greater detail and directions are provided for converting some of the student activities into impressive classroom demonstrations. Also included in this section are clear and concise answers to the questions. Because students often have difficulty seeing the relevance of science, we discuss applications of the investigated principles to their everyday lives.

Activities included in the book have been successfully implemented and tested in the classroom by experienced and novice science teachers. These activities, coupled with the explanation of the underlying concepts, show that science is composed of two dimensions — content and process. Science is not merely something a scientist does in the laboratory or a rhetoric of conclusions to be gleaned from a textbook or lecture and soon forgotten. The book emphasizes the "process-dimension" of science. Without processes such as observing, measuring, and hypothesizing, there would be no scientific facts, theories, or laws.

Most of the activities can be performed with materials commonly found in the students' everyday environment. Some require equipment found in the typical science classroom or inexpensive equipment available from scientific supply houses.

Every effort has been made to ensure teachers and students will enjoy the activities so they will become meaningfully engaged in the processes of science. Consequently, they will acquire knowledge and understanding of basic science concepts and the application and relevance of these to their everyday lives.

James Cunningham
Norman Herr

California State University, Northridge

ACKNOWLEDGMENTS

We are grateful to Connie Kallback, Editor; Eve Mossman, Production Editor; Barbara Palumbo, Manager, Electronic Production; and Audrey Kopciak, Electronic Production Editor for their editorial expertise, patience, and diligence in producing this book. In addition we wish to thank the science teacher candidates at California State University, Northridge for field testing the activities and offering suggestions for improvement. Finally we wish to express deep gratitude to our families for their support and encouragement while this book was being written.

CONTENTS

ABOUT THE AUTHORS   IV

ABOUT THIS RESOURCE   V

UNIT ONE: MEASUREMENT
1

1.1 UNITS   2

    1.1.1 Dimensions (Units)   3

1.2 INDIRECT MEASUREMENT   13

    1.2.1 Indirect Measurement of Distance   14
    1.2.2 Indirect Measurement of Volume: 17
    1.2.3 Indirect Measurement of Mass: 19

1.3 SCALING   27

    1.3.1 Ratios   28
    1.3.2 Surface-Area-to-Volume Ratio   30
    1.3.3 Scaling in Biological Systems   36

UNIT TWO: MOTION
39

2.1 CENTER OF MASS   40

    2.1.1 Center of Mass   41
    2.1.2 Stability   43
    2.1.3 Center of Mass of Composite Objects   47
    2.1.4 Motion of the Center of Mass   49

2.2 INERTIA   56

2.2.1 *The Effect of Inertia*   57

2.2.2 *Newton's First Law*   58

2.2.3 *Linear Inertia*   60

2.2.4 *Inertia of Liquids*   62

2.2.5 *Rotational Inertia*   63

2.2.6 *Distribution of Mass and Rotational Inertia*   65

2.3 VELOCITY AND ACCELERATION   73

2.3.1 *Acceleration Due to Gravity*   76

2.3.2 *Accelerometer*   78

2.3.3 *Centripetal Acceleration (Motion in a Horizontal Circle)*   80

2.3.4 *Centripetal Acceleration (Motion in Vertical Circle)*   82

2.3.5 *Acceleration Greater than Gravity*   83

2.3.6 *Projectile and Target*   84

2.4 PERIODIC MOTION   95

2.4.1 *Simple Pendulums*   96

2.4.2 *Physical Pendulums*   98

2.4.3 *Determining the Acceleration of Gravity*   100

2.4.4 *Foucault Pendulum*   102

UNIT THREE: FORCE
113

3.1 FORCE   114

3.1.1 *Vectors and Scalars*   115

3.1.2 *Resultant and Equilibrant Forces*   117

3.1.3 *Newton's Second Law (Law of Acceleration)*   119

3.1.4 *Newton's Third Law (Law of Interaction)*   122

3.1.5 *Centripetal Force*   124

3.1.6 *Gravity*   126

3.2 BUOYANT FORCE   134

3.2.1 *Archimedes' Principle*   136

3.2.2 Regulation of Buoyancy   137

3.2.3 Calculating Buoyant Force   139

3.2.4 Buoyancy and Newton's Law of Interaction   141

3.2.5 Fluid Density and Buoyancy   143

3.2.6 Specific Gravity   145

3.3 FRICTION   151

3.3.1 Center of Mass and Friction   153

3.3.2 Ranking Frictional Forces   155

3.3.3 Static and Sliding Friction   157

3.3.4 Factors Affecting Friction   159

3.4 TORQUE   167

3.4.1 First-Class Levers   171

3.4.2 Second-Class Levers   174

3.4.3 Third-Class Levers   176

3.4.4 Levers in Everyday Life   179

UNIT FOUR: PRESSURE
187

4.1 AIR PRESSURE   188

4.1.1 The Magnitude of Air Pressure   190

4.1.2 Pressure Equation   192

4.1.3 Pascal's Law   194

4.1.4 Pressure Differentials   196

4.1.5 Air Pressure and Breathing   198

4.1.6 Measuring Barometric Pressure   199

4.2 VAPOR PRESSURE   212

4.2.1 Energy and Vaporization   213

4.2.2 Atmospheric Pressure and Boiling   216

4.2.3 The Influence of Surface Area on Vaporization   219

4.2.4 Molecular Structure and Vaporization   221

4.2.5 Vapor Pressure of Solutions   223

4.2.6 Determining Relative Humidity   225

4.3 FLUID PRESSURE   234

4.3.1 Siphons   236
4.3.2 Hou Does Water Pressure Vary with Depth?   238
4.3.3 Pascal's Principle   240

4.4 FLUIDS IN MOTION   247

4.4.1 Bernoulli's Principle   249
4.4.2 Lift   252
4.4.3 Streamlines and Air Drag   255

UNIT FIVE: ENERGY AND MOMENTUM
265

5.1 WORK AND POWER   266

5.1.1 Measuring Work   268
5.1.2 Measuring Power   270
5.1.3 Reading Your Electric Meter   272
5.1.4 Conserving Electricity   275

5.2 POTENTIAL AND KINETIC ENERGY   282

5.2.1 Magnetic Potential Energy 285
5.2.2 Kinetic Energy   287
5.2.3 Conversion of Potential and Kinetic Energy   289
5.2.4 Conservation of Energy   290
5.2.5 Linear and Rotational Kinetic Energy   293

5.3 MOMENTUM   304

5.3.1 Linear Momentum   306
5.3.2 Elastic and Inelastic Collisions   308
5.3.3 Conservation of Linear Momentum   310
5.3.4 Impulse and Momentum   314
5.3.5 Conservation of Angular Momentum   316
5.3.6 Precession   319

5.4 MACHINES   330

    5.4.1 Levers   332

    5.4.2 Wheel and Axle   334

    5.4.3 Pulleys   336

    5.4.4 Inclined Plane, Wedge, and Screw   339

    5.4.5 Gears, Chains, and Belts   342

    5.4.6 Compound Machines   344

UNIT SIX: WAVES
353

6.1 WAVES   354

    6.1.1 Wave Characteristics   355

    6.1.2 Transverse and Longitudinal Waves   357

    6.1.3 Superposition   359

    6.1.4 Standing Waves   362

    6.1.5 Wave Propagation and Interactions   365

6.2 SOUND   376

    6.2.1 Sound Is Caused by Vibration   378

    6.2.2 Sympathetic Vibrations   379

    6.2.3 Sound Is a Form of Energy   381

    6.2.4 Psychological and Physical Definitions of Sound   382

6.3 TRANSMISSION OF SOUND   387

    6.3.1 Can Sound Travel in a Vacuum?   389

    6.3.2 Determining the Speed of Sound in Air   391

    6.3.3 Sound Transmission in Solids and Liquids   393

    6.3.4 Speed of Sound in Different Media   395

    6.3.5 Locating the Source of Sound   396

6.4 FREQUENCY AND WAVELENGTH OF SOUND   403

    6.4.1 Vibrational Frequency and Pitch   405

    6.4.2 Doppler Effect   407

    6.4.3 Determining the Wavelength of Sound   409

6.4.4 Resonant Frequency and Pitch   412
6.4.5 Laws of Strings   414

6.5 WAVE PROPERTIES OF SOUND   420

6.5.1 Reflection of Sound   421
6.5.2 Diffraction of Sound   423
6.5.3 Interference of Sound   425
6.5.4 Refraction of Sound   427

UNIT SEVEN: LIGHT
433

7.1 REFLECTION   434

7.1.1 Law of Reflection   436
7.1.2 Creating Illusions with Reflections   438
7.1.3 Multiple Images   439
7.1.4 Total Internal Reflection   441
7.1.5 Fiber Optics   443

7.2 REFRACTION   449

7.2.1 Refraction   451
7.2.2 Index of Refraction   453
7.2.3 Refraction and Distortion   455
7.2.4 Total Internal Reflection   456
7.2.5 Magnification   457
7.2.6 Refraction and Transparency: Disappearing Act   458

7.3 INTERFERENCE AND DIFFRACTION   464

7.3.1 Interference in Thin Films   466
7.3.2 Single Slit Diffraction   469
7.3.3 Diffraction by Gratings and Particles   471

7.4 POLARIZATION   478

7.4.1 Cross Polarization   480

7.4.2 Polarization by Reflection 482

7.4.3 Polarization by Scattering 484

7.4.4 Polarization by Refraction 486

7.4.5 Analyzing Physical Stress with Polarized Light 487

7.4.6 Polarization of AM Radio Signals 489

7.5 OPTICS 497

7.5.1 Law of Rectilinear Propagation 499

7.5.2 Magnification 501

7.5.3 Real Versus Virtual Images 503

7.5.4 Focal Length 504

7.5.5 Practical Uses of Lenses 506

7.6 COLOR 514

7.6.1 The Visible Spectrum 516

7.6.2 Infrared Radiation 518

7.6.3 Absorption and Transmission 520

7.6.4 Primary Colors 522

7.6.5 Complimentary Colors 524

7.6.6 Scattering of Light 526

7.6.7 Determining the Wavelength of Light 527

UNIT EIGHT: ELECTRICITY AND MAGNETISM
537

8.1 ELECTROSTATICS 538

8.1.1 Electroscopes 540

8.1.2 Electric Charges 542

8.1.3 Electrostatic Attraction 544

8.1.4 Induction 546

8.1.5 Distribution of Charge 549

8.1.6 Electrostatic Separators 551

8.1.7 Electric Potential 553

8.1.8 Capacitance 555

8.2 CIRCUITS   564

  8.2.1 Electric Current   565
  8.2.2 Electrical Energy from Chemicals   568
  8.2.3 Electric Energy from Heat   571
  8.2.4 Cells in Series and Parallel   574
  8.2.5 Ohm's Law   576
  8.2.6 Heating Effects   578
  8.2.7 Series and Parallel Circuits   581

8.3 MAGNETISM   590

  8.3.1 Magnetic Domains   592
  8.3.2 Magnetization   594
  8.3.3 Magnetic Poles   597
  8.3.4 Magnetic Fields   599
  8.3.5 Magnetic Force   602
  8.3.6 Magnetic Shielding   605
  8.3.7 Geomagnetism   607

8.4 ELECTROMAGNETISM   617

  8.4.1 Electromagnetic Fields   618
  8.4.2 Electromagnets   620
  8.4.3 Electromagnetic Induction(Generators)   624
  8.4.4 Motors   627
  8.4.5 Mutual Inductance (Transformers)   630

**APPENDIX
641**

  TABLE 1: Physical Quantities and Their Units   642
  TABLE 2: Metric System Prefixes   643
  TABLE 3: Greek Alphabet   643
  TABLE 4: SI and Customary Units and Conversions   644
  TABLE 5: Common Conversions   644
  TABLE 6: Units of Pressure   645
  TABLE 7: Relative Humitidy from Wet and Dry Bulb Thermometer   646
  TABLE 8: Writing Style Guidelines   647

INDEX OF CONCEPTS TO INVESTIGATE   649

UNIT ONE

Measurement

1.1 Units

1.2 Indirect Measurement

1.3 Scaling

1.1 UNITS

In the early 1980s a "hacker" illegally obtained access to a computer that controlled much of the government payroll. Using his computing expertise, the hacker made a slight change to the payroll program to divert fractions of a cent from all workers' paychecks into his own account. Thus, if a workers' paycheck was $523.236, a check for $523.23 was sent to the worker, and the remaining $0.006 (six tenths of a cent) was illegally redirected to the hacker's account. The hacker's scheme went undetected for months, and he soon became quite rich. No one suspected any problems until a worker observed that his paychecks were always rounded down to the nearest penny, and he wondered where the remainder was going. His careful observation led to an investigation that resulted in the apprehension of one of the most notorious computer hackers of all time.

Observational skills are of great benefit in everyday life and are essential in science. Observations may be either qualitative or quantitative. Using one's finger to test the temperature of water represents a qualitative observation, while measuring with a thermometer represents a quantitative observation. Quantitative observations provide more information than qualitative observations. As the English physicist William Thomson (Lord Kelvin) wrote, "When you can measure what you are speaking about, and express it in numbers, you know something about it."

Every measurement must specify a unit or dimension. To state that an object has a height of 6.5 is meaningless. We are left to ask: Six-and-a-half what? 6.5 centimeters? 6.5 inches? 6.5 fathoms? 6.5 feet? 6.5 meters? 6.5 miles? 6.5 kilometers? 6.5 light-years? While stating that the height of a person is 6.5 is meaningless, stating that the person is 6.5 feet tall (6 feet, 6 inches) tells us that the person is of above average height. Similarly, to say that a container has a volume of 2 is meaningless. Two what? 2 liters? 2 milliliters? 2 quarts? 2 cups? While stating that a soft drink container has a volume of 2 is useless, stating that it has a volume of 2 liters indicates that it has the size of a large-size soft-drink container.

Measuring an object means comparing it to a selected unit (such as a meter) and expressing it as a multiple or fraction of that unit (e.g., 2 meters, 1/2 meter, 1.3 meters). Accuracy of measurement refers to the discrepancy between the true or actual value and the result obtained by measuring. Precision refers to the agreement among repeated measures of the same quantity or object. To understand the difference between precision and accuracy, suppose you use a meter stick to measure the length of a table and get these results: 2.31 m, 2.32 m, 2.30 m. The spread of the measurements is only 0.02 m, which indicates good precision. If, however, the meter stick itself were not graduated correctly, and was actually 1.04 meters in length, then the marks on the stick would be slightly farther apart than they should be. Consequently, although the measurements are precise, they are not accurate because they do not represent the true value of the length of the table. Thus, measurements can have high precision but low accuracy. Can measurements have high accuracy but low precision?

1.1.1 Dimensions (Units)

Concepts to Investigate: Dimensions (units), measurement, accuracy, precision.

Materials: None required.

Principles and Procedures: We use units every day, often without even realizing it. In the statements that follow, you will find a wide variety of interesting facts, but each is missing a crucial piece of information—the dimensions. All the statements are meaningless until you supply the appropriate units. On the basis of your experiences, try to determine the appropriate units from the list provided. Units may be used more than once or not at all.

Possible Units for Questions in (a)–(t)

bushels	centimeters	days	degrees Celsius	degrees Fahrenheit
feet	grams	hours	inches	kilocalories
kilometers	kilowatt hours	meters	miles	miles per hour
milligrams	minutes	percent	persons	pounds
seconds	square miles	stories	terms	yards

(a) The world's tallest building (Sears Tower in Chicago) is 110 ___ high. *stories*

(b) The Empire State Building in New York is 1,250 ___ high. *feet*

(c) The Nile is the world's longest river. It is 4,180 ___ long. *miles*

(d) The Amazon River in South America is ___ 6,296 long. *kilometers*

(e) Alaska has the lowest recorded temperature of any state. In 1981 the temperature was recorded at -81 ___. *degrees fahrenheit*

(f) The highest recorded temperature in the United States was in Death Valley, California, when the mercury reached 57 ___. *degrees celcius*

(g) The world-record rainfall occurred in Cherrapunji, India, where 1,042 ___ of *inches* rain fell in one year. In the United States, the record is held by Kukui, Hawaii, where 739 ___ (or 1,878___) fell in 1982. *inches, cm*

(h) The largest recorded hailstone ever to fall landed in Coffeyville, Kansas, in 1979. It had a diameter of 44.5 ___ (17.5 ___). *cm, in*

(i) The longest punt in NFL history was by Steve O'Neal of the New York Jets. He kicked the football 98___. *yards*

(j) Big fish don't always get away: In 1953 A. C. Glassel caught a marlin that weighed in at 1,560___. *pounds*

(k) The dimensions of a professional basketball court are 94___ by 50___. *feet feet*

(l) In 1986, Bobby Rahal won the Indianapolis 500 averaging a speed of 170.722 ___ for all 500___. *miles per hour, miles*

(m) In August 1989, the U.S. spacecraft *Voyager* passed the planet Neptune at a time when the planet was 2.8 billion ___ from the sun. By contrast, the Earth averages only 93 million ___ from the sun. *miles, miles*

(n) The temperature of the core of the Earth is estimated to be 11,000____. *degrees F*

(o) The world's fastest aircraft was the Lockheed SR-71 A/B Blackbird. Before being retired, it clocked a record speed of 2,193.67____. *mph*

(p) Iowa is the biggest corn producer in the country. Each year it averages over 1.6 million ____. *bushels*

(q) One large cooked egg yields an average of 6 ____ fat and 274____ cholesterol. *grams, mg*

(r) A 16-year-old male requires an average of 2,800 ____ of energy per day while an average 16-year-old female requires only 2,100____. *kilocalories* *kcal*

(s) Before its breakup, the world's largest country was the Union of Soviet Socialist Republics. It had an area of 8,649,496 ____, compared to only 3,615,105 _____ for the United States. *square miles, square miles*

(t) The United States produces and consumes more electric energy than any other nation. Each year we produce over 2,500 billion ____ while the entire nation of China produces only about 400 billion ____. *kilowatt hours, kilowatt hrs*

Questions

(1) Why is it essential that all measurements be accompanied by appropriate units?

(2) When you measure an object with a measuring instrument such as a ruler, there is always some uncertainty in the measurement. Explain.

(3) Distinguish between accuracy and precision in a measurement.

(4) Give an example of how measurements may have high precision and yet have low accuracy.

FOR THE TEACHER

Most students are introduced to the concept of a variable when they take algebra. Unfortunately, they rarely see units placed on these variables, and as a result they often feel as though units are superfluous when solving science problems. Encourage the mathematics teachers at your school to use units when teaching algebra so students will get into the habit of using them when they study science.

Although the activity in this section introduced students to the importance of units, it did not illustrate their value in problem solving. In this section we present two related techniques that are invaluable when solving problems in the physical or life sciences, both of which make use of units. We strongly encourage you to introduce both techniques and use them throughout the course.

Factor-Label Method: The factor-label method (dimensional analysis) is a technique that assists in performing and checking scientific calculations. This method employs unit factors (ratios equal to one) that are cancelled leaving the desired unit. Some examples of unit factors are: 1 km/1000 m, 1 m/1000 cm, 1 in/2.54 cm, 1 mile/5280 ft. Since the numerator and denominator express the same value, each fraction has a value of one.

Suppose we want to convert 132 km to cm. It is easy to set the problem up using ratios equal to one:

$$132 \text{ km} \times (1000 \text{ m}/\text{km}) \times (100 \text{ cm}/\text{m}) = 1.32 \times 10^7 \text{ cm}$$

Although this setup is correct, it is difficult to visualize the ratios. It is perhaps better to set the problem up using blocked fractions as follows.

$$132 \text{ km} \times \frac{1000 \text{ m}}{\text{km}} \times \frac{100 \text{ cm}}{\text{m}} = 1.32 \times 10^7 \text{ cm}$$

Contrasted with the above setups is one called the "straight line." The straight-line setup often makes the problem easier to visualize.

$$\begin{array}{c|c|c} 132 \text{ km} & 1000 \text{ m} & 100 \text{ cm} \\ \hline & \text{km} & \text{m} \end{array} = 1.32 \times 10^7 \text{ cm}$$

Which setup do you find easiest to use and interpret? Whatever the case, note that all the units cancel except the units that must appear in the final answer. It is important that you draw a line through each cancelled unit so you can inspect the final result. If the desired unit does not appear in the final answer you can be certain that something is wrong with the setup of the problem. Upon investigation you may note errors in logic such as the use of incorrect ratios (that is, 1 m / 1000 km). When using any of these setups always reduce complex fractions such as

$$\frac{3/9 \text{ kg/s}}{9/6 \text{ m} \times 2/3 \text{ s}}$$

to simple fractions as you set up the problem:

3 kg	6	3
9 s	9 m	2 s

The following example may help you see how dimensional analysis works: The speed of light is approximately 300,000,000 meters per second, written in scientific notation as 3.0×10^8 m/s. How many meters does light travel in one year?

3.0×10^8 m	60 s̶	60 m̶i̶n̶	24 h̶	365 d̶	=	9.5×10^{15} m
s̶	m̶i̶n̶	h̶	d̶	y		y

You can see that all units are cancelled except meters in the numerator and years in the denominator. Since we wanted to determine the number of meters per year, the units (m/y) are correct and we can be confident that our setup is correct.

Dimensional analysis is a very powerful tool in solving problems in science. Although this book focuses on physics, you should show your students that dimensional analysis applies to every discipline where calculations are made using values that have been determined by measurement. The following example from chemistry may be useful in clarifying the simplicity of the "straight line" setup when dealing with problems involving many ratios.

Let us determine the volume of dry hydrogen collected over water at 27° C and 75.0 cm mercury as produced by the reaction of 3.0 g zinc metal within an excess of sulfuric acid. The following is a summary of the information :

$$Zn_{(s)} + H_2SO_{4(aq)} \longrightarrow ZnSO_{4(s)} + H_{2(g)}$$

1 mole of Zn = 65 g Zn
1 mole of Zn is consumed for every mole of H_2 produced
1 mole H_2 of occupies 22.4 liters at STP

The problem is set up as shown below. The student must make sure that all units (dimensions) are canceled appropriately to leave just the desired unit, which in this case is liters of hydrogen gas. You will notice that what may seem like a rather complex problem is reduced to a simple series of multiplications and divisions. Virtually all the problems encountered in secondary science classes may be reduced to a simple "straight-line format" that helps students structure their thinking as they solve problems. With a little practice your students will find the factor-label method is easy and convenient to use and is a help in eliminating errors. If the desired unit does not appear in the final answer, your students can be sure that something is amiss and can immediately proceed to locate any errors in logic.

3.0 g Zn	1 mole Zn	1 mole H_2	22.4 liters H_2	300 K	760 mm Hg	=	1.19 liters H_2
	65 g Zn	1 mole Zn	1 mole H_2	273 K	723.3 mm Hg		

Fundamental units: There are 26 letters in the English alphabet, yet with these letters it is possible to construct all the words in the English language. In a similar way, there are 7 "letters" in the "language of measurement" of which all units of scientific measurement are composed. These 7 "letters" are length, mass, time, electric charge, temperature, amount, and luminous intensity. They are known as the fundamental units because they cannot be expressed in a simpler fashion. Velocity is not a fundamental unit because it can be expressed as a ratio of two other units, namely distance and time $v=d/t$. Because velocity can be derived from distance and time, it is known as a derived unit. By contrast, time and distance are fundamental units because they cannot be expressed in any simpler terms.

Every derived unit is composed of fundamental units. Acceleration is considered to be a derived unit because it can be expressed in terms of velocity and time. By examining the units of acceleration (m/s^2), one can see its relationship to velocity (m/s) and time (s):

$$a = \frac{m}{s^2} = \frac{m}{s} \times \frac{1}{s} = \text{velocity} \times \frac{1}{\text{time}} = \frac{\text{velocity}}{\text{time}}$$

Thus, by examining the units (dimensional analysis), it appears that acceleration is a ratio of velocity to time. This discovery, by dimensional analysis, is consistent with the definition of acceleration as the change in velocity per change in time.

Dimensional analysis works just as well with more complex units. A farad is a measure of electrical capacitance (the ability to store charge) and can be expressed in fundamental terms as:

$$\frac{C^2\, s^2}{kg\, m^2}$$

where C represents charge in coulombs, s represents time in seconds, kg represents mass in kilograms, and m represents length in meters. If we know how a quantity may be expressed in fundamental terms, we can discover relationships between it and other phenomena. For example, knowing the fundamental units of capacitance C; potential difference V, and charge Q, we can see the relationship between them (C = coulombs, s = seconds, kg = kilograms, m = meters):

$$C = \text{capacitance} = \text{farad} = \frac{C^2 \cdot s^2}{kg\, m^2}$$

$$V = \text{potential difference} = \text{volt} = \frac{kg \cdot m^2}{C \cdot s^2}$$

$$Q = \text{charge} = \text{coulomb} = C$$

By examination of the fundamental units, it can be seen that capacitance is very similar to the inverse of potential difference:

$$\frac{1}{V} = \frac{C \cdot s^2}{kg\ m^2} \quad \text{is similar to capacitance:} \quad C = \frac{C^2 \cdot s^2}{kg\ m^2}$$

If we multiply the inverse of potential difference by charge (measured in coulombs, C), then the units are the same as capacitance:

$$\frac{1}{V}Q = \frac{Q}{V} = \frac{(C)\ C \cdot s^2}{kg \cdot m^2} = \frac{C^2 \cdot s^2}{kg \cdot m^2} = C$$

Thus, by examining the fundamental units of capacitance, charge and potential difference, we have discovered a fundamental relationship: Capacitance is equal to ratio of charge to potential difference $C = Q/V$.

Additional Activities

If you want to give your students exercises similar to this, you may provide them with the following two tables. The first table shows the most commonly used units and shows how they may be expressed in fundamental terms. The seven fundamental units are shown at the top of the table in bold typeface. The second table lists sets of physical quantities that are related. By examining the fundamental units of these quantities, students can determine the relationship and express it mathematically. It is not necessary that students understand what the terms mean to be able to come up with the desired relationships. If students master this technique, they will be better able to understand the meaning of these relationships when they are introduced later in the course. The relationships in the second table are as follows: $C = Q/V$; $V = IR$; $P = IV$; $P = I^2R$; $P = W/t$; $E = Fd$; $E = W$; $E = 1/2\ mV^2$; $E = mAd$. These equations are important equations in physics. After deriving these relationships by dimensional analysis, students will have a better understanding of what these units represent and will be better able to solve problems that use a variety of units.

Physical Quantities and Their Units

Physical Quantity	Quantity Symbol	Measurement Units	Unit Symbol	Unit Dimensions
length (distance)	*l (d)*	**meter**	**m**	**m**
mass	*m*	**kilogram**	**kg**	**kg**
time	*t*	**second**	**s**	**s**
electric charge	*Q*	**coulomb**	**C**	**C**
temperature	*T*	**kelvin**	**K**	**K**
amount of substance	*n*	**mole**	**mol**	**mol**
luminous intensity	*l*	**candela**	**cd**	**cd**
acceleration	*a*	meter per second squared	m/s^2	m/s^2
area	*A*	square meter	m^2	m^2
capacitance	*C*	farad	F	$C^2{\cdot}s^2/kg{\cdot}m^2$
density	*D*	kilogram per cubic meter	kg/m^3	kg/m^3
electric current	*I*	ampere	A	C/s
electric field intensity	*E*	newton per coulomb	N/C	$kg{\cdot}m/C{\cdot}s^2$
electric resistance	*R*	ohm	Ω	$kg{\cdot}m^2/C^2{\cdot}s$
emf	*ξ*	volt	V	$kg{\cdot}m^2/C{\cdot}s^2$
energy	*E*	joule	J	$kg{\cdot}m^2/s^2$
force	*F*	newton	N	$kg{\cdot}m/s^2$
frequency	*f*	hertz	Hz	s^{-1}
heat	*Q*	joule	J	$kg{\cdot}m^2/s^2$
illuminance	*E*	lux (lumen per square meter)	lx	cd/m^2
inductance	*L*	henry	H	$kg{\cdot}m^2/C^2$
luminous flux	*F*	lumen	lm	cd
magnetic flux	*φ*	weber	Wb	$kg{\cdot}m^2/C{\cdot}s$
magnetic flux density	*B*	tesla (weber per square meter)	T	$kg/C{\cdot}s$
potential difference	*V*	volt	V	$kg{\cdot}m^2/C{\cdot}s^2$
power	*P*	watt	W	$kg{\cdot}m^2/s^3$
pressure	*p*	pascal (newton per square meter)	Pa	$kg/m{\cdot}s^2$
velocity	*v*	meter per second	m/s	m/s
volume	*V*	cubic meter	m^3	m^3
work	*W*	joule	J	$kg{\cdot}m^2/s^2$

Fundamental Units (rows 1–7)

Derived Units (rows 8–end)

Determining Relationships by Dimensional Analysis

Derived Unit	*Expressed as Fundamental Units*	*Complete the Equation*	*In Terms of*
farad (capacitance, C)	$\dfrac{C^2 \cdot s^2}{kg\, m^2}$	$C = Q/V$	potential difference V charge Q
volt (potential difference, V)	$\dfrac{kg \cdot m^2}{c\, s^2}$	$V =$	current I resistance R
watt (power, P)	$\dfrac{kg \cdot m^2}{s^3}$	$P =$	current I potential difference V
watt (power, P)	$\dfrac{kg \cdot m^2}{s^3}$	$P =$	current I resistance R
watt (power, P)	$\dfrac{kg \cdot m^2}{s^3}$	$P =$	work W time t
joule (energy, E)	$\dfrac{kg \cdot m^2}{s^2}$	$E =$	force F length l
joule (energy, E)	$\dfrac{kg \cdot m^2}{s^2}$	$E =$	work W
joule (energy, E)	$\dfrac{kg \cdot m^2}{s^2}$	$E =$	mass m velocity v
joule (energy, E)	$\dfrac{kg \cdot m^2}{s^2}$	$E =$	mass m acceleration a length l

1.1 Dimensions

Discussion: It is critical that all measurements be expressed with appropriate units or dimensions. Students were asked to give the units for various measurements in which the units were purposely omitted. The fact that students might find this a difficult task highlights the importance of always attaching units to measurements, no matter how obvious they may seem. Some of the questions have been designed in a seemingly contradictory fashion simply to get students to think. For example: question (a) states that "The world's tallest building (Sears Tower in Chicago) is 110 ___ high," while question (b) states that "The Empire State Building in New York is 1,250 ___ high." Students should realize that this "contradiction" is resolved if they realize that the heights of these buildings are measured in different units (stories versus feet). This activity is intended to illustrate that units are used not only in science, but in every endeavor where humans attempt to measure something.

Answers to this activity, a-t: (a) stories, (b) feet, (c) miles, (d) kilometers, (e) degrees Fahrenheit, (f) degrees Celsius, (g) inches; inches, cm, (h) cm; inches, (i) yards, (j) pounds, (k) feet; feet, (l) miles per hour; miles, (m) miles, miles, (n) degrees Fahrenheit, (o) miles per hour, (p) bushels, (q) grams, milligrams, (r) Kcal (Cal), Kcal (Cal), (s) square miles, square miles, (t) kilowatt hours, kilowatt hours.

Answers to questions 1 - 4: (1) A "measurement" without units is not a measurement at all. It is simply a number that has no scientific meaning. (2) Measurement is a comparison between a standard unit (for example, the standard meter stick in the Louvre museum in Paris) and the object being measured. Uncertainty is introduced by the following: inexact replicas of the standard unit (inaccurately constructed meter sticks), human error in measurement (parallax, poor vision) and the inability to resolve minute differences (the smallest unit of measure marked on a meter stick is the mm, which is insufficient to resolve micrometer differences). (3) Accuracy is a measure of how close measurements are to the true value while precision is a measure of how close measurements are to each other. (4) In Figure A the marksman is precise because the hits are consistent, but not accurate because the hits are far from the bull's-eye.

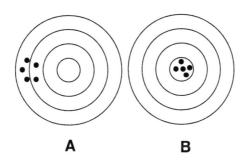

A   **B**

Applications to Everyday Life

Business: Everything that is bought or sold has dimensions. A land investor needs to know if a tract is measured in acres, hectares, square feet, or square miles. A commodities broker needs to know if soy beans are priced by the bushel, peck, kilogram, liter, cubic foot, or cubic yard. A building contractor needs to know whether a developer has given him a concrete order in cubic yards or cubic feet. It would be nearly impossible to run a successful business without knowledge of the units of the trade.

Retooling: In the 1980s, much of the American automobile industry switched from the English system of measurement to the metric system of measurement. Changing the measurement units required a massive amount of retooling. For example, where a one-inch bolt was previously used, a 2.5-cm bolt was substituted. Because of the slight differences in size, it became necessary to buy new tool sets to work on these cars.

Home Economics: Recipes always specify measurements in units. You need to know whether your recipe is measured in tablespoons, teaspoons, cups, quarts, gallons, milliliters, or liters! When cooking dinner, it is essential that you know whether directions were written for a stove calibrated in Celsius or Fahrenheit. When comparing the rates of competing long-distance carriers, it is necessary to know the unit on which the billing rate is set.

International Trade: Each country has its own monetary system. Although countries may use the same unit, each unit may have a different meaning. A Canadian dollar is not worth the same as an American dollar, neither is a Japanese yen worth the same as a Chinese yuan. The full name of the unit should be specified whenever doing calculations. In other words, it is necessary to specify an American dollar, not just a dollar.

Measurement: It is important that you know the meaning of the units by which something is measured. On business reports you may hear the price of a particular commodity quoted. Although they may say that it costs a $1,000 per ton, the question remains, are they quoting the price per long ton (1.016 metric tons), per short ton (0.97 metric tons), or per metric ton? To understand the world around us, it is necessary to know how things are measured, and what the units they are measured in represent.

1.2 INDIRECT MEASUREMENT

On a cold winter night in 1930, the astronomer Clyde Tombaugh discovered Pluto, the smallest and most distant planet in our solar system. Since Tombaugh's discovery, we have learned that Pluto orbits the Sun at an average distance of 5.9 billion kilometers (3.7 billion miles), approximately 39 times farther than the Earth. Since it is so far from the Sun, it takes a long time to orbit—284.4 times as long as the Earth. Thus, if a tree were 284.4 years old on Earth, it would be only 1 Pluto-year old if grown on Pluto. Since Pluto is so far away from the Sun, it is extremely cold. In fact, it is so cold that a frozen layer of methane (natural gas) covers the Plutonian landscape. Pluto is very small compared to the Earth. It has a diameter of 2,200 km (1,367 miles), approximately the distance between Denver and Detroit or between London and Berlin. Pluto is very small and has very little mass, only 1/500 that of Earth. Since gravity is proportional to mass, a truck that weighs 4,000 pounds on Earth would weigh only 8 pounds on Pluto.

Do you really believe all this data? Who has ever been to Pluto? Pluto is small, distant, and barely visible through powerful telescopes, yet scientists confidently report data about it. Who has ever taken a tape measure and determined its diameter? Besides, who has a tape measure 2,200 km long? Who has ever watched to make sure that Pluto orbits the Sun in 284.4 Earth-years? Pluto was discovered only in 1930, so no one could possibly have watched to see how long it takes to complete an orbit. Astronomers say that the surface of Pluto is covered with frozen natural gas, but no space probes have ever landed on Pluto to run tests on its environment. The gravity on Pluto is purported to be only 1/500 of that on the Earth, but who has ever weighed anything on Pluto?

There are many things that are either very difficult or impossible to measure directly. No one can weigh an electron directly, and yet science textbooks report it has a mass of 9.1083×10^{-28} grams. No one can weigh a blue whale directly, but the record books report weights in excess of 200 tons. No one was present when a bristlecone pine by the name of Methuselah sprouted in the White Mountains of California, but botanists claim it to be nearly 4,700 years old. No one can see X-rays, but physics books report they have a wavelength of 10^{-10} meters.

Although it is impossible or impractical to measure many quantities directly, it is often possible to do so indirectly. In this chapter you will use the principle of similar figures and similar ratios to learn how we can measure things such as those just mentioned.

1.2.1 Indirect Measurement of Distance

Concepts to Investigate: Similar ratios, similar triangles, indirect determination of distance.

Materials: Book, ruler, measuring tape or meter stick.

Principles and Procedures

Part 1. Thickness of a sheet of paper: Suppose we want to measure the thickness of the page in a book. It is impossible to measure the thickness of a page directly with your ruler because the thickness is much less than the distance between the mm markings. We can, however, obtain an indirect measurement. Use a ruler to measure the width of all the pages together (not counting the back and front covers). Divide the result by the total number of sheets. For example, if a book of 800 pages length (400 sheets) has a width of 40 mm, then the thickness of one sheet is 0.10 mm (40 mm/400 sheets). Compute the thickness of sheets in this book and compare them with those from another book of your choice.

Part 2. Height of a tree: On a hiking trip you have discovered a very tall tree. How tall? You can find out using the following procedure and an understanding of similar triangles. Two triangles are similar if they contain equal angles as in Figure B. If two triangles are similar their corresponding sides are proportional. Since the triangles in Figure B are similar, the corresponding sides bc and ec, ab and de, and ac and *dc* are proportional as shown:

© 1994 by John Wiley & Sons, Inc.

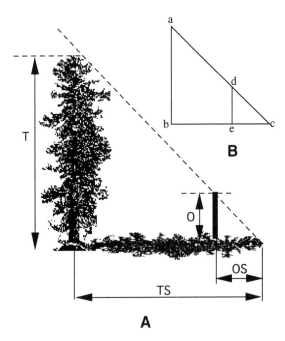

$$\frac{bc}{ec} = \frac{ab}{de} = \frac{ac}{dc}$$

We can use proportions to find the length of an unknown side if we know the lengths of the other sides. When using similar triangles and proportions, you have to choose the sides that form the ratios necessary to solve the problem. For example, if side ab is not known, but sides bc, de, and ec are known, you can solve for side ab as shown here:

$$ab = \frac{de \times bc}{ec}$$

Suppose the length of bc is 58 cm, ec is 34 cm, and de is 29 cm. Substituting these values in the equation:

$$ab = \frac{29\text{ cm} \times 58\text{ cm}}{34\text{ cm}} = 49\text{ cm}$$

Now let's find the height of that tall tree without climbing it. First, position an object of known height (e.g., meter stick, book, yourself) in such a way that the shadow of the object ends at exactly the same point as the shadow of the tree (Figure A). You can easily measure the following distances: *TS* (tree's shadow), *OS* (object's shadow), and *O* (height of the object casting the shorter shadow). Because the triangles formed by the tree and the stick are similar, we can solve for the height of the tree T using the following proportion:

$$\frac{T}{TS} = \frac{O}{OS} \qquad\qquad T = \frac{O \times TS}{OS}$$

Now it is your turn to determine the height of some trees, buildings, or other objects. Using a meter stick, measuring tape, or your pace, measure the length of the tree's shadow *TS*. Now measure the height of the object you will use to cast the second shadow (a meter stick is a convenient object). Move the object until its shadow ends at the same place and then measure the length of its shadow. Complete the following table.

Indirect Measurement of Tall Objects

Object Being Indirectly Measured	(TS) Length of Tree's (Tall Object's) Shadow	(O) Height of Object Casting Shorter Shadow	(OS) Length of Object's Shadow	(T) Height of Tree (Building, Flagpole, etc.)

Questions

    (1)   Will you obtain a more accurate measure of the thickness of a page from a new or used book? Explain.

    (2)   How could you measure the height of a tree at noon when the sun is directly overhead and the tree casts no shadow?

    (3)   How could you determine the distance to the moon, knowing only its diameter, and having only a meter stick and a pen?

1.2.2 Indirect Measurement of Volume

Concepts to Investigate: Displacement method of measuring volume, indirect measurement of volume.

Materials: Eye dropper or pipette, graduated cylinder, milk carton or similar container.

Principles and Procedures

Part 1. Determining the volume of a single drop: Suppose you want to find the volume of one drop of water from a small eye dropper. If you place one drop of water in a calibrated measuring container you will find that it can hardly be seen. Can you think of a method of making an indirect measurement? Use the dropper to fill a 10-ml graduated cylinder, counting the number of drops required to completely fill the container to the 10 ml mark. In measuring volume always use the meniscus (bottom of the curve) as shown in Figure C. Divide the volume of water by the number of drops to find the volume of one drop. For example, suppose 200 drops are required to fill the cylinder to the 10-milliliter mark. The volume of one drop is: 10 ml/200 drops or 0.05 ml per drop. Now try it yourself with the liquids shown in the following table. Why do you think the size of a drop varies from liquid to liquid? What does the size of the drop tell you about a liquid?

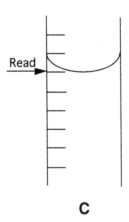

Read

C

Indirect Measurement of the Volume of a Drop

Liquid	Number of Drops to Fill 10 ml	Volume of a Single Drop
Water	_____	_____ ml
Water with detergent	_____	_____ ml
Rubbing alcohol	_____	_____ ml
Salad oil	_____	_____ ml

Part 2. Determining the volume of an irregular object: Two substances cannot occupy the same space at the same time. If you place your hand in a bowl that is filled with water, some of the water spills over the edge because your hand and the water can't occupy the same space. Let's put this important idea to use to find the volume of one of your hands. Obtain a half-gallon milk carton or similar container. Cut off the top and cut a spout as shown in Figure D. Fill the container with water until the water pours from the spout. Once the water has stopped dripping, place a beaker, graduated cylinder, or kitchen measuring cup under the spout. Carefully submerge your hand to the wrist and wait until the displaced water flows into the container. The amount of water in the collection container represents the volume of your hand. Repeat three times, making certain your hand is submerged to the same depth each time. What is the average value of the volume of your hand? Find an object that you think has approximately the same volume and measure its volume by the displacement of water as before.

D

© 1994 by John Wiley & Sons, Inc.

Questions

(1) Which is larger, a drop of fresh water or a drop of soapy water? What does this tell you about soap's ability to help water penetrate fabrics?

(2) How could you measure the volume of an irregularly shaped object such as a wrench?

(3) In part 2 we measured the volume of an irregularly shaped object by measuring the volume of water displaced. Is this technique a form of direct or indirect measurement? Explain.

(4) How could you determine if a gem is authentic or artificial, having nothing more than a sensitive balance and an accurate graduated cylinder?

1.2.3 Indirect Measurement of Mass

Concepts to Investigate: Indirect measurement of mass, ratios.

Materials: Sand, rice, goggles, large rock, geologist's hammer, string, meter stick or tape.

Principles and Procedures

Part 1. Estimating the mass of a very small object: Although the mass of a single grain of sand or rice is too small to register on a standard classroom balance, we can use a balance to estimate the mass using indirect measurement. Count out 100 grains of sand and use a classroom balance to mass them to the nearest tenth of a gram. Divide this mass by 100 to determine the average mass of an individual grain of sand. Repeat this procedure with rice to determine the mass of an individual grain of rice.

Part 2. Estimating the mass of a very large object: Suppose there is a boulder that is too large to be picked up and massed on a balance. How could you find the approximate mass of this boulder using indirect measurements? Find a large rock that is relatively round. Put on goggles and use a geologist's hammer to carefully chip off a small piece from the rock. Determine the mass of this piece using a classroom balance and its volume using a graduated cylinder. (The volume of the rock chip is equal to the difference in volume of the water before and after the rock chip is submerged.)

Wrap a string around the middle of the rock. Straighten the string out and lay it next to a measuring tape to obtain a measure of the rock's circumference. Wrap the string around the rock in two additional directions and determine the average circumference. Although the rock is not spherical, this technique produces fairly good results for rocks that are relatively round. Since the circumference of a circle is, $c = 2\pi \times r$, we simply solve for the radius r as follows: $r = c/(2\pi)$, where π is approximately 3.14. The formula for computing the volume of a sphere is: $V = (4/3)\pi r^3$. Now we use the following proportion (equal ratios) to complete the problem:

$$\frac{\text{mass of rock}}{\text{volume of rock}} = \frac{\text{mass of piece of rock}}{\text{volume of piece of rock}}$$

$$\text{mass of rock} = \frac{(\text{mass of piece of rock}) \times (\text{volume of rock})}{(\text{volume of piece of rock})}$$

Since the other three quantities are known, we can estimate the mass of the rock without lifting it. Now it is your turn. Follow the procedure mentioned above and determine the approximate mass of a rock that is too large to be massed on your balance:

Indirect Measurement of the Mass of a Large Rock

	Equation	Trial 1	Trial 2
Average circumference of rock	$c_{(rock)} = (c_1 + c_2 + c_3)/3$	_____ cm	_____ cm
Radius of Rock	$r_{(rock)} = c_{(rock)}/2\pi$	_____ cm	_____ cm
Volume of rock	$V_{(rock)} = (^4/_3)\pi r^3$	_____ cm³	_____ cm³
Mass of piece of rock	$m_{(piece\ of\ rock)}$	_____ g	_____ g
Volume of water displaced by piece of rock	$V_{(piece\ of\ rock)}$	_____ cm³	_____ cm³
Mass of rock	$m_{(rock)} = m_{(piece\ of\ rock)}\dfrac{V_{(rock)}}{V_{(piece\ of\ rock)}}$	_____ kg	_____ kg

We will investigate one additional problem to show the power of the indirect measurement concept. Suppose someone has loaned us a moon rock brought back by one of the Apollo astronauts. We will use this rock to estimate the mass of the moon, but first we make some assumptions: the moon is a sphere of radius 1,738 km, it is composed of the same kind of rock as our sample; and the density of this rock does not change with depth due to pressure (a rather naive assumption). We place the moon rock on our balance and find its mass to be 33.3 g. We use a graduated cylinder to find that its volume is 10.0 cm³. The solution is as follows:

$$\text{volume of moon in km}^3 = 4/3 \times 3.14 \times (1738\ \text{km})^3 = 22,000,000,000\ \text{km}^3$$

$$1\ \text{km}^3 = 1,000,000,000,000,000\ \text{cm}^3$$

$$\text{volume of moon} = 22,000,000,000,000,000,000,000,000\ \text{cm}^3$$

$$\text{mass of moon} = \frac{(\text{mass of moon rock})\ (\text{volume of moon})}{(\text{volume of moon rock})}$$

$$\text{mass of moon} = \frac{(33.3\text{g})\ (22,000,000,000,000,000,000,000,000\ \text{cm}^3)}{10.0\ \text{cm}^3}$$

$$\text{mass of moon} = 73,300,000,000,000,000,000,000,000\ \text{g} = 7.33 \times 10^{25}\ \text{g (approximate)}$$

Questions

(1) The most massive tree in the world is the General Sherman giant redwood in Sequoia National Park, California. It has been estimated to have a weight of 2,756 tons. How might such an estimate be made?

(2) An ounce of grass pollen contains approximately 6 billion grains of pollen. Approximately how much does one grain of pollen weigh?

(3) The world's smallest commercial fish is the sinarapan. If you ordered one kilogram of sinarapan, you would receive approximately 154,000 fish. Approximately how much does each fish weigh?

FOR THE TEACHER

It is often necessary to use an indirect technique when measuring the mass, length, or volume of something that is either very large or very small. When dealing with very large or very small numbers, it is best to use scientific notation. We introduce scientific notation to you at this point, so you can share it with your students when appropriate. As a beginning, you could show students how to use scientific notation to solve the mass of the moon problem after they have tackled the problem directly using those really large numbers!

Scientific notation is a method that simplifies the writing of very small and very large numbers and computations involving these. In scientific notation, numbers are expressed as the product of a number between 1 and 10 and a whole-number power (exponent) of 10. The exponent indicates how many times a number must be multiplied by itself. Some examples follow: $10^1 = 10$, $10^2 = 10 \times 10 = 100$, $10^3 = 10 \times 10 \times 10 = 1000$.

Exponents may also be negative. For example, $10^{-1} = 1/10 = 0.1$. Also, $10^{-2} = 1/100 = 0.01$ and $10^{-3} = 1/1000 = 0.001$. Following are some examples of numbers written in scientific notation:

$30 = 3 \times 10^1$ $150 = 1.5 \times 10^2$ $60{,}367 = 6.0367 \times 10^4$

$0.3 = 3 \times 10^{-1}$ $0.046 = 4.6 \times 10^{-2}$ $0.000\,002 = 2 \times 10^{-6}$

Writing a number in scientific notation involves successively multiplying the number by the fraction 10/10 (which is equal to 1). Multiplying a number by one does not change the value of that number. For example:

$$142 = 142 \times \frac{10}{10} \times \frac{10}{10} = 1.42 \times 10^2$$

It is certainly not necessary to use the above formal procedure to write a number in scientific notation. After some practice you and your students will be doing it in your head. You may wish to think as follows: to write 142 in scientific notation, move the decimal point two places to the left (which is dividing by 10^2), and multiply by 10^2 to get 1.42×10^2. To write 0.013 in scientific notation, move the decimal point two places to the right (which is multiplying by 10^2), and divide by 10^2 to get 1.3×10^{-2}.

Computations involving numbers written in scientific notation are easy to perform. To multiply numbers written in scientific notation, multiply the whole-number parts and add the powers (exponents). To divide numbers written in scientific notation, divide the whole-number-number parts and subtract the powers (exponents). Following are some examples:

$$(3 \times 10^4) \times (5 \times 10^3) = 15 \times 10^7$$

$$\frac{6 \times 10^8}{3 \times 10^3} = 2 \times 10^5$$

$$(5 \times 10^2) \times (2 \times 10^3) \times (1.5 \times 10^{-4}) = 1.5 \times 10^2$$

$$\frac{6 \times 10^{-2}}{2 \times 10^{-4}} = 3 \times 10^2$$

Scientific notation makes it possible to unambiguously indicate the number of significant digits in a measurement. Suppose a student reports a measurement of the length of an object as 230 cm. How many significant digits are contained in this measurement? We don't know. The digits 2 and 3 are obviously significant, but what about the zero? Is it just a place holder or did the student actually estimate the length to the nearest cm? Scientific notation can help the student and us answer this important question. Carefully inspect the following:

$$230 = 2.3 \times 10^2$$

$$230 = 2.30 \times 10^2$$

The first measurement 2.3×10^2 indicates that there are only two significant digits in the measurement. That is, the student did not measure to the nearest cm—the zero is only a place holder. The second measurement 2.30×10^2 indicates that the student did measure to the nearest cm—the zero is a significant digit.

1.2.1 Indirect Measurement of Distance

Discussion: Ask your students if they have any ideas concerning how to estimate the distance to the moon given its diameter (3,480 km; 160 miles) and nothing more than a pen and a meter stick. The following is a method to accomplish this (see figure E). Hold one end of the meter stick carefully alongside your eye with the end in approximately the same plane as the retina of your eye. Place the cylindrical pen next to the side of the stick. Now push the pen away from your eye until the diameter of the pen just blocks your view of the moon. Measure the distance from your eye to the pen in millimeters. Now carefully measure the diameter of the pen in millimeters. We can use our knowledge of similar triangles to compute the distance to the moon as follows.

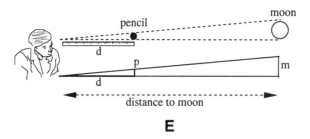

E

$$\frac{\text{distance to moon}}{\text{diameter of moon}} = \frac{\text{distance to pencil}}{\text{diameter of pencil}}$$

$$\text{distance to moon} = \frac{(\text{distance to pencil}) \times (\text{diameter of moon})}{(\text{diameter of pencil})}$$

The distance to the moon varies from 356,000 km (221,000 miles) at its perigee (nearest point) to 407,000 km (253,000 miles) at its apogee (farthest point). Your students may obtain more accurate measurements by using an object of greater diameter than a pen.

Answers (1) After a book has been used, there will be more air between the pages, and the indirect measurement technique will produce greater than the actual values. (2) You could use the same technique used in determining the distance to the moon (see discussion section). (3) See discussion section.

1.2.2 Indirect Measurement of Volume

Answers (1) Fresh water forms larger drops. Soap reduces the surface tension of water, allowing it to form smaller drops that more easily penetrate small pores in fabrics. (2) Pour water into a graduated container until it is deep enough to submerge the object. Place the object in the water and measure the change in volume. (3) This is a form of indirect measurement because we measure the water displaced, not the volume of the object itself. (4) Each type of gem has a unique density, or mass to volume ratio. Using the balance, you could determine the mass, and using the cylinder, you could determine the volume. If the density of the "gem" did not correspond to accepted values, you could assume it was counterfeit.

1.2.3 Indirect Measurement of Mass

Answers (1) Determine the density of a few samples of wood and foliage from the tree. Using these, calculate an average density for each. Make a scale model of the tree and determine the volume of this model by the water displacement technique. To obtain a rough estimate of the mass of the tree, use the ratio technique. (2) 1.67×10^{-7} ounce. (3) 6.5×10^{-6} kg (6.5×10^{-3} g).

Applications to Everyday Life

Astronomical Distances: The star nearest Earth is Alpha Centauri, at a distance of 4 light years, or the distance that light travels in four Earth-years time. Since light travels 299,792 km/s and there are 31,557,600 seconds per year, Alpha Centauri is at a distance of 37.8 trillion miles from Earth. Without indirect measurement, there would be absolutely no way to measure even short astronomical distances.

Subatomic Particles: Chemistry books report the mass of an electron as 9.1083×10^{-28} grams. Since the finest balances are sensitive only in the microgram range, it is obvious that the masses of subatomic particles must be measured by indirect means.

Surveying: In 1867, Congress authorized a survey of the western United States. To help fulfill this mission, John Wesley Powell conducted a survey of the Rocky Mountains and prepared detailed maps showing accurate elevations of numerous mountains. Powell and his team obtained such measures using a triangulation method similar to that used to measure the height of a tree as described in this chapter.

Zoology: Zoology texts report the weights and dimensions of creatures that are too large to measure directly. Using techniques similar to those introduced in section 1.2.3, zoologists have determined that certain blue whales (*Balaenoptera musculus*) weigh over 200 tons!

The Circumference of the Earth: The first relatively accurate measurement of the Earth's circumference was made indirectly by Eratosthenes of Cyrene in the third century B.C. Eratosthenes noticed that the noon sun reflected off the water in a deep well in the city of Syene in southern Egypt on the longest day of the year (summer solstice), indicating that the well was on a direct line between the sun and the Earth's center. During a subsequent year, he was in Alexandria in northern Egypt on the summer solstice and noted that the sun was south of the vertical by an angle equal to approximately 1/50 of a full circle. Because of the great distance to sun, Eratosthenes assumed that the sun's rays were essentially parallel when they struck the Earth, and that the difference in the angle of the sun's rays in these two cities resulted from the difference in the angle between the center of the Earth and the two cities. He therefore measured the distance between Alexandria and Syene and multiplied by 50 to calculate the circumference of the Earth. His indirect measurement was within 15 percent of the currently accepted value, which is 40,075 km (24,902 mi).

1.3 SCALING

In the sixth century A.D., the bubonic plague swept across the Middle East, Europe, and Asia, claiming the lives of an estimated 100 million people. Approximately 800 years later the plague spread again, killing approximately 75 million people. In Europe alone, an estimated one third of the population died from the second wave of the "Black Death." The bubonic plague is an acute infection caused by the bacterium *Yersinia pestis*. This bacterium infects not only humans, but also rodents, particularly rats. When a flea feeds on the blood of an infected rat, the ingested plague bacteria multiply in the flea's digestive tract. When the flea then feeds on human blood, some of the regurgitated bacteria enter the person's blood stream, thereby spreading the infection. People in the fourteenth century realized that rats spread the plague. The fourteenth-century German legend of the Pied Piper of Hamelin tells the story of a man who lured rats away from a town through the playing of his magical pipe. Once the rats were gone, there were fewer fleas and less chance of contracting the plague. Although the bubonic plague still exists, modern antibiotics and sanitation procedures have kept it in check.

Because fleas spread a variety of serious diseases, entomologists (those who study insects) are interested in their behavior. One of the characteristics that allows the flea to spread disease from one animal to another is its amazing ability to jump. The flea is able to jump 130 times its height. Proportionately, a human would have to jump over 750 feet high (equivalent to a 55-story building) to match the flea's accomplishment, but the world's record is only 8 feet. What allows the flea to jump so much higher relative to its height than a human?

Although the flea is a rather amazing organism, it is not alone in its ability to perform feats that would be impossible for animals of a larger scale. An ant can carry an object many times its own weight while a human may barely lift his or her own weight. The click beetle (*Athous haemorrhoidalis*) accelerates at 400 g's when jumping into the air to escape predators, while a human accelerates at less than 2 g's when jumping. The tiny insect known as a midge (*Forcipomyia*) beats its wings more than 130,000 times per minute, while the African marabou stork, with a wing span in excess of 11 feet, can't even beat its wings 60 times per minute. An insect known as a water strider walks across the surface of water, while larger organisms sink. The concept of scaling can explain all these phenomena.

A scale is a ratio between the dimensions of a representation (map, model, blueprint, or diagram) and the object it depicts. A road map may have a scale of "1 inch = 1 mile," while an architectural model of a skyscraper may have a scale of "1 millimeter = 1 meter." Scaling, sometimes referred to as scaling-up or scaling-down, is an increase or reduction in linear dimensions according to a fixed ratio. For example, to find the distance from your city to another, you can consult a map that has a scale of a given number of centimeters per kilometer. You measure the distance between the two cities on the map in centimeters and use the scale to convert to kilometers. If the scale is 1 cm = 15 km, and your measurement is 10 cm, then the actual distance between the cities is 150 km.

Although the ratio of the external dimensions of an object remain constant when it is scaled up or down, the ratio of its surface area to volume does not. The surface area of a sphere is $4\pi r^2$, while its volume is $(4/3)\,\pi r^3$. If a sphere is scaled up by a factor of two, the surface area increases by a factor of four ($r^2 = 4$ when $r = 2$; area = $4\pi r^2$), and the volume increases by a factor of 8 ($r^3 = 8$; when $r = 2$; volume = $(4/3)\pi r^3$). Thus, when scaled up by a factor of two, the surface area to volume ratio is cut in half.

If, however, the radius of the sphere is cut in half, its surface area is reduced to one fourth ($r^2 = 1/4$ when $r = 1/2$), and its volume to one eighth ($r^3 = 1/8$ when $r = 1/2$). Thus, when the scale is cut in half, the surface area to volume ratio doubles. In summary, the surface area to volume ratio is high in small-scale objects, but low in similarly shaped large-scale objects. By performing the following activities, you can learn how this principle helps us to understand how fleas can jump so high, how cockroaches can survive a 100-story fall, and why emphysema patients are always short of breath.

1.3.1 Ratios

Concepts to Investigate: Ratios, scaling up.

Materials: No materials required.

Principles and Procedures: Large shopping malls and college campuses post maps so visitors can find their way around. To understand the scales of such maps, people note the distance between themselves and a local landmark and then compare this with the distance on the map between the "you are here" marker and the landmark. In making this comparison, the visitor develops an intuitive scale for the map and is able to judge the distance required to travel to the desired shop or building. In this activity you will develop a scale for a world map and will then use this to estimate the distances between major cities.

The map provided in Figure A shows the locations of a number of major cities in the world. The table, however, includes only the distance between Washington,

A

D.C., and Berlin, Germany (6,713 km). Use this information to develop a scale for the map and estimate the distances between Washington, D.C., and the other cities specified on the map. If necessary, use an atlas to identify the locations of the cities specified.

Determining Distances Using a Scale
Scale of Map: 1 mm = ? km

	Distance from Washington, D.C., USA (mm)	*Distance from Washington, D.C., USA (km)*
Beijing, China	_____ mm	_____ km
Berlin, Germany	_____ mm	6,713 km
Bombay, India	_____ mm	_____ km
Buenos Aires, Argentina	_____ mm	_____ km
Cape Town, S. Africa	_____ mm	_____ km
Lagos, Nigeria	_____ mm	_____ km
Los Angeles, U.S.A.	_____ mm	_____ km
London, England	_____ mm	_____ km
Mexico City, Mexico	_____ mm	_____ km
Sydney, Australia	_____ mm	_____ km
Vancouver, Canada	_____ mm	_____ km

Questions

(1) In general, would calculations of distance made from a map or a globe be more accurate? Explain.

(2) Besides distance, what other values can be measured using a scale? Look in an atlas that includes thematic maps (that is, population density, climatic data, agricultural products, etc.) and identify three different scales.

1.3.2 Surface-Area-to-Volume Ratio

Concepts to Investigate: Surface area to volume ratio, scaling up, scaling down.

Materials: No materials required.

Principles and Procedures: Phytoplankton are microscopic algae that live in the surface waters of the world's oceans. Although these organisms are quite small, they are extremely important to life on earth and account for approximately 90 percent of all food production that occurs in oceans and approximately one third of all oxygen production in the world. For phytoplankton to produce food, they must be near the surface because the food-producing process of photosynthesis requires light. If phytoplankton were less dense than water, they would float to the surface, but in reality, they are considerably denser than water so we might, therefore, expect them to sink to the ocean depths. Knowing that they have no fins or flippers, what keeps these tiny organisms near the surface where they can capture light?

The force of gravity is proportional to an object's mass $F = mg$, while the resistance to sinking (drag) is proportional to its surface area. Given constant density, the mass of an object is directly proportional to its volume. If an object has a high volume-to-surface-area ratio, then the force of gravity acting on it will be much greater than its drag and the object will readily sink. If, however, the volume-to-surface-area ratio is low (high surface-area-to-volume ratio), the drag force will be significant. Thus, a skydiver will fall rapidly when his or her chute is folded because the surface-area-to-volume ratio is low, but will descend slowly when the parachute opens and the surface-area-to-volume ratio is high.

Does the surface-area-to-volume ratio change with the scale of an object? Phytoplankton stay suspended in the upper layers of the ocean, but if a 1000 × scale model of a single plankton were placed in the ocean, would it also float, or sink? In

© 1994 by John Wiley & Sons, Inc.

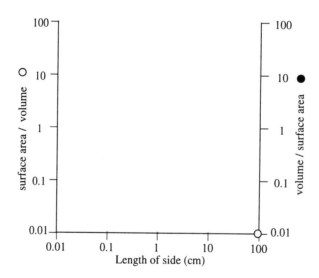

B

this activity you will investigate how the surface-area-to-volume ratio of an object changes as a function of its scale.

You are going to investigate a cube to see how changes in a linear dimension affect its surface area and volume. For each cube, compute both the surface area and the volume and write your answers in the table provided. Then use these results to compute the ratio of surface area to volume and the ratio of volume to surface area. Plot these ratios on the graph provided in Figure B.

Length of Edge l	*Surface Area* l^2	*Volume* l^3	$\dfrac{Surface\ Area}{Volume}$	$\dfrac{Volume}{Surface\ Area}$
0.01 cm	_____ cm²	_____ cm³	_____ $\dfrac{1}{cm}$	_____ cm
0.1 cm	_____ cm²	_____ cm³	_____ $\dfrac{1}{cm}$	_____ cm
1 cm	_____ cm²	_____ cm³	_____ $\dfrac{1}{cm}$	_____ cm
10 cm	_____ cm²	_____ cm³	_____ $\dfrac{1}{cm}$	_____ cm
100 cm	_____ cm²	_____ cm³	_____ $\dfrac{1}{cm}$	_____ cm

Questions

(1) As the cube gets smaller, does the ratio of surface area to volume increase or decrease? As the cube grows larger does the ratio of surface area to volume increase or decrease?

(2) Phytoplankton are very small and often contain numerous spines. Explain how these features help keep them near the surface.

(3) In animals, heat production is proportional to mass. Heat loss is proportional to surface area. If all other factors are equal, will a baby or an adult be more susceptible to getting chilled?

(4) If the amount of heat lost through the skin of an animal is directly proportional to its surface area, what might you conclude about the relative heat loss of a very small animal to a very large animal? Which animal would find it easier to keep warm in the winter, and which animal would find it easier to keep cool in the summer?

1.3.3 Scaling in Living Systems

Concepts to Investigate: Surface-area-to-volume ratio in animals, scaling up, scaling down.

Materials: No materials required.

Principles and Procedures: Carefully inspect Figure C, which shows three fictitious humans. The center human we will call Standard Stan, the larger we will call Towering Tom, and the smaller we will call Minuscule Mike. Stan's height is 170 cm, which is approximately 5 feet 7 inches. We will scale by a factor of 10. That is, each linear dimension of Towering Tom is exactly 10 times that of Standard Stan, and each linear dimension of Minuscule Mike is exactly 1/10 that of Standard Stan. Consequently, Tom's height is 1,700 centimeters, which is about the height of a 5-story building, and Mike's height is 17 centimeters, which is about the length of a small rat. Tom's arms and legs are 10 times those of Stan, and Mike's arms and legs are 1/10 those of Stan. Using the concept of scale, we will investigate whether persons such as Tom and Mike could actually exist in our world, and if so, what particular problems or advantages each might have in adapting to the environment.

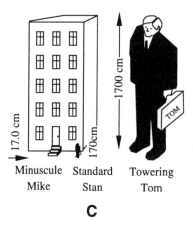

Minuscule   Standard   Towering
Mike   Stan   Tom

C

Let us compare Stan with Tom and then Stan with Mike. These comparisons will help to show that for every animal there is a convenient or right size, and that a change in size may necessitate a change in form (shape). Before we begin with the comparisons, you will be required to do a little work to help us. Refer to the table, which shows certain characteristics of Stan, Tom, and Mike. Remembering that the scaling is by 10 for Tom and 1/10 for Mike, complete the table and inspect the results.

Part 1. Scaling up: Tom's height is ten times that of Stan. Since the ratios of Tom's dimensions are exactly like those of Stan, every one of his linear dimensions is ten times Stan's corresponding dimensions. Consequently, the bodies of Stan and Tom are exactly similar in cross-sectional shape.

The strength of Tom's bones is proportional to their cross-sectional area, which is 10^2 or 100 times the cross-sectional area of Stan's bones (see your results in the table), so his bones will be 100 times as strong as Stan's. Tom's weight is proportional to his volume. Since his volume is 10^3 or 1,000 times Stan's, his weight is 1,000 times that of Stan. Thus, Tom's bones have a strength-to-weight ratio one tenth that of Stan. That is, every square centimeter of Tom's bones must support 10 times the weight of an equal area of Stan's bones. Tom would most surely break his bones just by walking.

If you compare similar animals, you will notice that larger animals are not scale models of smaller ones. A tiger is not a scaled-up house cat. Rather, its legs are wider than one might expect from a proportionately scaled-up house cat. The gigantic spider in a monster movie may appear 100 times the size of a normal tarantula, but in reality it simply could not move on the legs as shown. The cross-sectional area of its legs would be insufficient to support its weight.

Scaling

	Minuscule Mike	Standard Stan 5′7″	Towering Tom
Height h	17.0 cm	170 cm	1700 cm
Diameter of femur d	0.400 cm	4.00 cm	40.0 cm
Radius of femur r	0.200 cm	2.00 cm	20.0 cm
Cross sectional support area of femur πr^2	_____ cm^2	12.6 cm^2	_____ cm^2
Volume of entire body V	_____ cm^3	60,000 cm^3	_____ cm^3
Mass of entire body m assuming density = 1 g/cm^3	_____ kg	60 kg	_____ kg
Weight w = mass(kg) × 9.8 m/s^2	_____ N	588 N	_____ N
Pressure on bones (Weight/support area)	_____ N/cm^2	47 N/cm^2	_____ N/cm^2
Surface area	_____ cm^2	17,000 cm^2	_____ cm^2
Surface area / Volume	_____ cm^2/cm^3	3.5 cm^2/cm^3	_____ cm^2/cm^3

Part 2. Scaling down: If we scale down by a factor of 10 (see your results in the table), the surface area of Mike will be $(1/10)^2$ or 1/100 times that of Stan, while his volume and weight will be only $(1/10)^3$ or 1/1000 of Stan. In other words Mike's surface area is 100 times less than Stan's surface area but his volume and weight are 1,000 times less than Stan's, so now things are working the other way around. Whereas when scaling up to larger sizes the volume or weight overshadows the strength and surface area, when scaling down, it is the surface area that overshadows the volume and weight. So what are some consequences of scaling down?

The air resistance on a falling object is proportional to its surface area and speed while the force of gravity on it is proportional to its mass. So what does this mean for objects or animals that fall from great heights? If the animal is small, such as an ant, the force of air resistance soon becomes equal to the force of gravity and the animal moves slowly toward the ground at a constant speed and simply walks away after landing. A mouse may be able walk away from a 10-story fall because of its high-surface-area-to-weight ratio, but a human being would not because his or her speed on impact would be too great. How would Stan, Tom, and Mike look after falling 900 meters? Let's examine another problem related to the ratio of surface area to weight. If Stan should happen to fall into a pool of water, he should experience little difficulty climbing out. The film of water on his skin is nearly proportional to the surface area of his body, having a mass of about 0.5 kg, or approximately equivalent to a large glassful. Certainly this mass of water when compared to Stan's is minimal, and he could easily climb out of the pool. But what would happen to Mike? Since he is 1/10 the height of Stan, his weight is 1/1000 and his surface area 1/100 of Stan. The amount of water he carries out of the pool is proportionally 10 times as much as Stan carries out, which would be equivalent to wearing several layers of heavy clothing. Mike might get out of the pool, but it would not be easy. For this reason, small insects find it difficult, if not impossible, to climb out of water.

Let's consider another significant problem relating to scaling down. Bodies lose heat mainly through the skin, and it can be shown that the rate of heat loss is proportional to the surface area, all other factors being constant. Since food provides the heat necessary for an animal to keep warm and mobile, food requirements are proportional to surface area. Consequently, smaller animals with greater surface-area-to-weight ratios require proportionally more food to survive. Mike would require a volume of food only 1/100 as great as Stan, even though he has only 1/1000 the weight of Stan. Hence, proportionate to his body size, Mike would have to eat 10 times as much food as Stan. To do this, Mike would spend much of his time eating, which is exactly what humming birds and other small warm-blooded animals do.

Questions

(1) Explain how a whale can weigh 40 times more than an elephant, yet have bones that are no thicker. Why does a beached whale generally suffer from broken ribs?

(2) Small animals, such as insects, have no problem with gravity and can walk up walls and across ceilings with ease. But larger animals must maintain a great respect for gravity. Explain.

FOR THE TEACHER

An understanding of ratios and scaling is requisite to an understanding of many phenomena in the physical and biological world, yet few textbooks give much attention to this issue. For example, many textbooks will state that the metabolic rate of a mammal increases as its body weight decreases, but few explain that this rate increase is a necessary consequence because the ratio of the smaller animal's surface area to volume is much greater than a larger animal's. Thus the animal loses heat rapidly and must have a high metabolic rate to maintain its proper body temperature. Although most biological and physical structures are not cubic or spherical, the basic principles drawn from such simple geometric solids apply to irregularly shaped objects as well. The surface area of an object increases as a square, and its volume as a cube of its linear dimensions. Thus, the surface-area-to-volume ratio is always greater in a small-scale object than in a large-scale object of the same shape.

1.3.1 Ratios

Discussion: Since it is impossible to accurately portray a three-dimensional object in two dimensions, all maps have an imperfect scale. Certain projections, such as the Mercator projection found on many wall maps, are extremely inaccurate because they keep all longitude lines parallel, when in fact these lines converge at the poles. The projection used in this exercise is better than most, but it too will produce errors. You may want to ask your students to repeat this activity comparing a Mercator projection, an equal-area projection, and a globe. The globe will produce the best results, and the Mercator Projection the worst. The distances in kilometers between Washington, D.C., and the cities specified are as follows: Beijing (11,133), Berlin (6,701), Bombay (12,845), Buenos Aires (8,393), Cape Town (12,713), Lagos (8,726), Los Angeles (3,694), London (5,886), Mexico City (3,036), Sydney (15,702), Vancouver (3,781).

Student answers should be within 10 percent of these values.

Answers (1) Maps are inherently less accurate than globes because they represent a three-dimensional landscape using just two dimensions. (2) There are many possible responses. For example, when representing agricultural production, a cartographer may use a scale such as "one dot = 100,000 bushels of wheat per year." When representing population a map may state "one dot = 1,000,000 people."

1.3.2 Surface-Area-to-Volume Ratio

Discussion: It is important that you help your students interpret the graph in Figure D. Note that the axes are scaled logarithmically. In other words, the scales are based upon multiples and sub-multiples of 10, allowing you to draw the graph in a reasonable amount of space. Ask your students how the graph would appear if the scales were linear, and why the logarithmic scale is advantageous in situations like this.

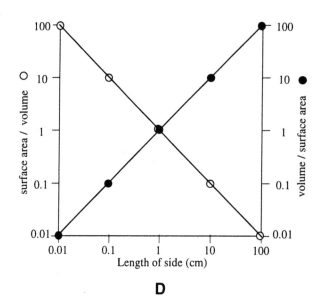

D

Answers (1) The surface-area-to-volume ratio increases as the size of the cube decreases, and decreases as the size of the cube increases. (2) The surface-area-to-volume ratio of smaller-scale objects is much greater than that of larger scale objects. Since mass is directly proportional to volume, the surface-area-to-mass ratio of smaller objects is much greater than that of larger-scale objects. Thus, the drag forces, which are dependent upon surface area, are proportionately greater on smaller objects such as plankton than on larger objects such as fish. The presence of spines further increases the surface-area-to-mass ratio and provides additional resistance to sinking. Since the rate of sinking is extremely slow, small upwelling currents in the ocean are sufficient to hold phytoplankton near the surface. (3) Babies are more likely than adults to get chilled because they have a relatively high surface-area-to-volume ratio. To help compensate for this, they also have a higher metabolic rate. (4) The relative heat loss from a small animal will be much greater than that from a large animal. Therefore, it is easier for a large animal such as a polar bear to keep warm in the winter than it is for a small animal such as a rat.

1.3.3 Scaling in Biological Systems

Discussion: A gazelle is a small, fast, graceful antelope with long thin legs. Ask your students if a gazelle could walk if it were scaled up 10 times. Look at the front leg bones shown in Figure E. The smallest bone is from a gazelle and the largest bone is from a bison. Both animals are members of the *Bovidae* family. If we simply enlarge the gazelle's bone to the same length as the bison's bone to create a larger gazelle, we have the bone shown in the middle. However, this bone will not have the strength to support the larger gazelle. You can see that the bone of the bison is much thicker (has a greater diameter) in comparison to its length than does the gazelle's. The larger

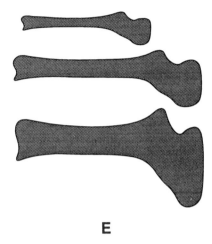

E

gazelle's bone must be increased in thickness in greater proportion than its length in order to be comparably stronger, otherwise the gazelle's legs will break under its own weight. One way to increase the size of a gazelle is to make its legs short and thick such as those of a rhinoceros, or long and really thick such as those of an elephant. However, if the gazelle had legs like an elephant, it would not be a gazelle. Our point is that you cannot scale up an organism without changing its form. The larger gazelle would have bones that are much thicker compared to their length than the small gazelle; hence the two animals could not look the same.

Answers (1) Much whale's weight is supported by the buoyant force of water. The weight of a beached whale must be supported by its bones, many of which would soon break under the animal's weight. (2) Friction is proportional to surface area, while the force of gravity is proportional to volume (weight). Thus, the high surface-area-to-volume ratio of small insects gives them proportionately a greater friction-to-weight ratio than that of larger animals and allows them to hang on surfaces where larger animals could not.

Applications to Everyday Life

Breathing: The alveoli (air sacs) of lungs must have appropriate radii to insure maximum diffusion of oxygen into the blood. If they were too large, their surface-area-to-volume ratio would be too low and there would be insufficient diffusion of gases because of reduced surface contact between the tissues and the air. By contrast, if they were too small, the cross-sectional area of the alveoli and bronchioles would be too small and would restrict gas flow.

Emphysema: Emphysema, a condition that often accompanies smoking, results in a breakdown of the walls between alveoli in the lungs. In emphysema, a few large air sacs exist where many small sacs previously existed, dramatically decreasing the lungs' surface-area-to-volume ratio and thereby reducing the contact surface between blood vessels and air. As a result, people with emphysema can breath deeply, yet assimilate little oxygen.

Powdered Milk: When you pour powdered milk into a container of water, it forms a heap on the bottom. By stirring the solution, you increase the surface-area-to-volume ratio of the powder. Where particles were once imbedded in a heap, they now come in contact with the water and dissolve. A cube of sugar will dissolve more slowly than an equal amount of powdered sugar because it has a low surface-area-to-volume ratio.

Evaporation: The surface-area-to-volume ratio of a liquid is critical in determining how fast it will evaporate. Water in a cup takes a much longer time to evaporate than the same amount of water spread out on a table. The surface-area-to-volume ratio in the glass is relatively low, while the surface-area-to-volume ratio of the spilled liquid is high.

Animal Behavior: Smaller animals have a large surface-area-to-volume ratio and therefore lose proportionately more heat energy to the surrounding environment than larger animals do. To compensate, small homeotherms (warm-blooded animals) such as the hummingbird or shrew consume proportionately more food than larger animals like a hawk or a bear. The hummingbird, for example, may consume an amount of food equivalent of its entire weight in one day, while a bear may do the same over a period of one to two months.

Elephant Ears: The surface-area-to-volume ratio decreases as the scale of an organism increases. Consequently, larger animals have more difficulty dissipating heat energy than do smaller animals, and are more prone to overheating. The large ears of elephants dramatically increase the surface area of the elephant, allowing it to dissipate heat on warm days.

UNIT TWO

Motion

2.1 Center of Mass

2.2 Inertia

2.3 Velocity and Acceleration

2.4 Periodic Motion

2.1 CENTER OF MASS

For centuries, wrestling has been practiced in various forms throughout the world. Sumo is the national wrestling sport of Japan and the major tournaments attract international attention. A sumo ring is 3.66 m in diameter and made of sand and clay. The objective of sumo is to either throw the opponent to the ground or to force him out of the ring. Sumo has no weight classes, and participants often weigh more than 160kg (353 pounds). Sumo wrestlers have large stomachs, which lowers their center of mass and makes them more stable when attacked. Without such a physique, the quick opening charge could topple the wrestler and send him careening out of the ring in the first seconds of the match.

The center of mass of an object is that point at which the entire mass may be considered to be concentrated. The center of mass is a point fixed relative to that object, but does not necessarily lie inside the material of the object. If the object is located in the gravitational field created by a star, planet, or other astronomical body, it also has a center of gravity at which the entire weight of the body may be considered as concentrated. *The center of mass and the center of gravity are the same point,* and in this book we use these two terms interchangeably. The center of mass helps us understand when objects will be stable or unstable. *An object has greatest stability when its base is as wide as possible, its center of mass is as low as possible, and its center of mass is positioned directly over or under the base of support.* By contrast, a high center of mass, a center of mass beyond the base of support, and a small base of support, all contribute to instability.

Many objects, such as a ball or meter stick, have sufficient symmetry so there is an obvious geometrical center at which the center of mass lies. If a body is supported at the center of mass, the body will be in equilibrium and will balance. For example, the center of mass of a meter stick is at the 50-cm mark. If you support the stick at this point, it will be in equilibrium and will balance. If you support the stick at any point to the left or right of the center of mass, it will rotate and fall (Figure A). In the activities that follow you will find out how the center of mass helps us understand many phenomena in the world around us.

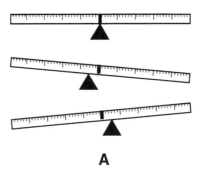

A

2.1.1 Center of Mass

Concepts to Investigate: Geometric center, internal center of mass, external center of mass.

Materials: Nails or pencils, cardboard, scissors, coat hanger or horseshoe.

Principles and Procedures

Part 1. Estimating the center of mass: If an object is constructed of a uniform material, then the center of mass will reside at the geometric center. Although it is easy to locate the geometric center of a circle or sphere, it is more difficult to locate the geometric center of an irregularly shaped three-dimensional object. Inspect each of the objects shown in Figures B to I and use a pencil or pen to place an x on the spot that you think is the center of mass. Using a series of xs, draw the trajectory of the center of mass of the sky rocket from the point it explodes to the point at which it hits the ground.

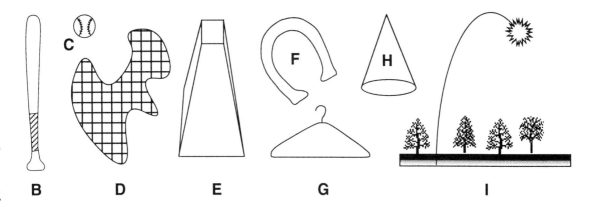

Part 2. Center of mass of irregular objects: How can we find the center of mass of irregularly shaped objects such as the piece of cardboard, coat hanger, and map shown in Figures J, K, and L? From a cardboard box, cut an irregular shape such as shown in Figure J. Use a nail or pencil to punch three holes in the perimeter of the cardboard. Slightly enlarge these holes so the cardboard can rotate freely. Place a nail or pencil in one hole and hang a weighted piece of string from it. Swing the cardboard and when it comes to rest, draw a line on the cardboard showing the position of the string. The cardboard swings back and forth as a pendulum until the center of mass comes to rest directly below the point of support. This position represents the state of least energy for the body, and all bodies move toward a position of minimal energy. Repeat, using the other two holes. Attempt to balance the cardboard at the intersection of the three lines. If this point is the center of mass, then it should be possible to balance the cardboard. What is the fewest number of lines necessary to locate the center of mass? To determine the center of mass for the coat hanger or horseshoe,

tape a piece of paper in the middle as shown in Figure K and repeat the procedure just described, drawing the lines on the paper. Where is the center of mass?

As you travel you may pass through towns that claim to be the geographic center of a particular state, province, or country. Such claims can be verified by the same technique used to locate the center of mass of other irregular objects. Glue a map of a particular state, country, or continent to a piece of cardboard, cut along the borders, and punch three holes in the perimeter as before. Draw lines of hanging weights as before and locate on the map where all three lines intersect (Figure L). The center of mass of the cardboard cut-out represents the geographic center. What is the geographic center of your state or province, country, and continent?

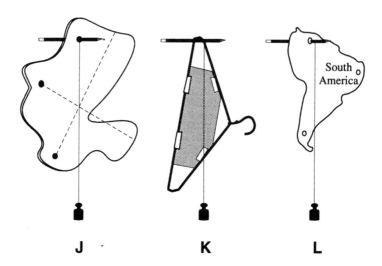

J   K   L

Questions

(1)   Will the position of the center of mass of a body ever be different from the position of its center of mass?

(2)   Name several solid objects in which the center of mass lies outside the body.

(3)   If you are in a space station and move from one side to the other, do you change the position of the center of mass about which the space station rotates? Explain.

(4)   A horizontal nonuniform bar 3 m long is supported at its ends by vertical cords attached to spring balances. If the balances read 4.6 newtons and 3.2 newtons, what is the weight of the bar and where is its center of mass?

2.1.2 Stability

Concepts to Investigate: Stability, base of support, center of mass.

Materials: Large rectangular blocks of wood, nails, washers, paper, scissors, Erlenmeyer flask, salt, straw.

Principles and Procedures: Inspect the sphere, cone, and rectangular box shown in Figure M. The dotted arrows show the force acting on the center of mass. The bold lines at the bottom indicate the bases of support. The sphere demonstrates neutral stability in that its center of mass always remains over the point of support when the object is resting on a level surface. The sphere will remain in any position placed. When the cone is resting on its side, it also demonstrates neutral stability in that it will remain in any position placed. The cone is stable on its bottom base and unstable on its tip. Try balancing the tip of a cone or a pencil on your finger. It is not easy because the slightest motion will cause the center of mass of the cone or pencil to fall outside the point of support and the object will topple. You have probably seen a seal balance a ball on its nose and noticed that the seal had to move its head from side to side to keep the ball balanced. You may have also seen a person walking a tightrope and swinging his or her arms or a balancing pole to maintain balance. Indeed, the whole idea behind a balancing act is to keep the center of mass above the point of support. The acrobat moves his or her arms or the balancing pole to keep the center of mass over the point of support.

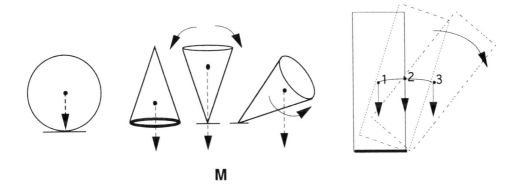

M

The rectangular box (Figure N) is stable when resting on its base, but if tipped too far will become unstable and topple. As long as the center of mass remains above the base, the box is stable. Even if the box is pushed and pivoted at one of its ends, when released it will return to its original position as long as the center of mass is over the base at the point of greatest rotation. Although the center of mass rises when the box is tipped (Figure M), when released it will be pulled back to its original position (position 1) unless the center of mass has risen to the point directly over the pivot (position 2). The box is unstable at this point and may fall either way. If the center of mass moves beyond the base (position 3), the box will topple because the center of mass is no longer over the base of support.

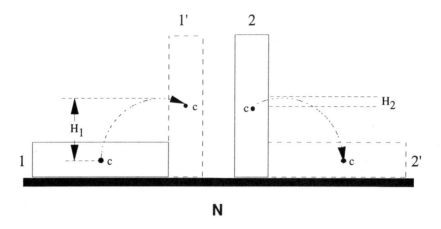

N

Part 1. Center of mass and base of support: The center of mass of a truck varies with the amount of cargo it carries. If the truck illustrated in Figure O has a center of mass at C_1 will it remain upright or topple? What will happen if the heavy cargo is at the top so the center of mass is at C_2? Draw a vertical line from each center of mass to see if it falls outside the wheel base of the truck.

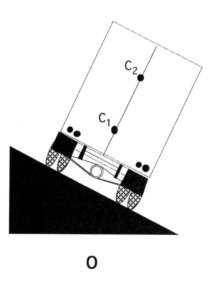

O

Take two or three blocks of wood, and using a heavy marker, draw diagonals on one of the large faces of each of these blocks. Place nails at the points where the diagonals intersect. Using heavy paper or other suitable material, fashion arrows that will hang on the nails as illustrated in Figure P. Place a washer behind the arrows to minimize friction between the arrow and wood. Tilt the block so the arrow is nearly in line with a diagonal. Which way will the block fall if the arrow is to the right of the diagonal? Which way will it fall if it is to the left of the diagonal? Try it.

Part 2. Center of mass of humans: Horses learn to walk very soon after birth while humans usually require about a year. The center of mass of humans is in the

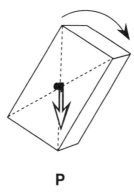

P

abdomen, and when one stands upright the abdomen must be carefully positioned over a narrow base of support, the two feet. By contrast, the center of mass of four-legged animals is much lower, and the base of support is much broader since there are four feet rather than two. Given these facts, it is obvious that four-legged animals should have an easier time learning to walk and maintaining their stability.

Place a pencil on the floor near your feet and attempt to pick it up without bending your knees or moving your feet. Most people can do this. Now stand with the backs of your shoes touching the wall and try to pick up the pencil. You probably will not be able to do it! When standing upright your center of mass is located near your waist, above your feet, which are the supporting base. When you bend over with your feet away from the wall you are able to lean your legs and buttocks backward, shifting the center of mass backward and allowing you to compensate for any forward movement of the center of mass resulting from the forward movement of the top part of your body.

Part 3. Balancing an object over a point of support: An Erlenmeyer flask can be balanced on an edge as shown in Figure Q if the center of mass is directly above the point of support. Fill an Erlenmeyer flask approximately two thirds full with water. Pour a pile of salt on the table top and then balance the flask, using the salt as a support. Place a rag below the flask to soften the impact if it topples. The cubic crystals of salt brace the flask in the same way that wooden blocks placed in front of car tires brace the tires and prevent the car from rolling. Once the flask is balanced, use a straw to gently blow the salt away from beneath the flask. It is fairly easy to blow away all the salt except two crystals, one on each side of the flask. Keep trying until it balances with just two crystals. If there are no vibrations, the flask can stand in this position for days.

Questions

(1) When you carry a large object at your side, you must lean in the opposite direction. When you carry a backpack, you must lean forward. Explain.

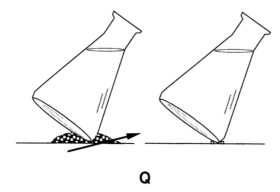

Q

(2) In which sports is it particuluarly important to have a low center of mass? Why?

(3) Why is a double-decker bus less stable than a regular bus?

(4) A flamingo has very long legs and a very long neck but is easily able to stand and sleep on one leg. Explain.

2.1.3 Center of Mass of Composite Objects

Concepts to Investigate: Composite bodies, center of mass, center of mass below point of support, stability.

Materials: Belt, piece of wood, saw, hammer, hinge, boards, clamp, potato, toothpick, two heavy forks.

Principles and Procedures

Part 1. Composite bodies: If two or more objects are fastened to each other, a composite body is formed with a center of mass of its own. Cut a notch into a block of wood as illustrated in Figure R. Place the block on a table and locate the position of the center of mass by moving the block to the last point at which it will remain balanced. Mark this point on the block. By adding another object to the block, it is possible to shift the center of mass. Place a belt in the slot, and after positioning it so it once again balances, place another mark on the wood to see where the new center of mass is. How does the belt affect the center of mass of the composite object?

Part 2. Center of mass below point of support: Cut a small piece from the end of a potato and stick a toothpick in the center as shown in Figure S. Try to balance the potato on the toothpick on top of a post or inverted glass. The potato is difficult to balance because the center of mass (c_1) is above the point of support and the base of support (diameter of toothpick) is very small.

Now stick two forks in the potato such that the majority of the fork is below the bottom of the toothpicks and again try to balance the potato, adjusting the forks if necessary. The potato balances because the center of mass has been shifted and is now located below the point of support as shown by the c_2. When the center of mass is below the point of support, the object is stable. After any small disturbances, the object rotates so the center of mass returns to its position under the point of support. Grasp one of the forks and give it a slight push. The center of mass will move, but gravity will then pull it down to its original position under the point of support.

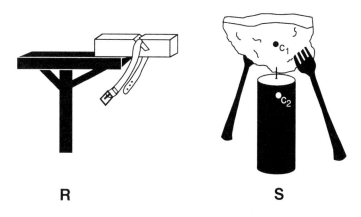

R   S

Questions

    (1)   Describe the experimental procedure you would use to find the center of mass of a three-dimensional object such as a cone or the potato-toothpick-fork combination.

    (2)   A tram suspended from a cable is stable but a person walking above on the same cable is not. Explain.

2.1.4 Motion of the Center of Mass

Concepts to Investigate: Motion of irregular objects.

Materials: Lollipop, horseshoe, baseball bat, coat hanger, large outdoor field.

Principles and Procedures: An object can undergo two kinds of motion, translational and rotational. Translational motion is motion along a line. Rotational motion is motion about a point acting as a pivot. Inspect Figures T-V. The object shown in Figure T shows translational motion only. The object shown in Figure U shows rotational motion only. The object shown in Figure V shows both translational and rotational motion. The pivot point is the center of mass. *Any freely rotating object always rotates (spins) about its center of mass.*

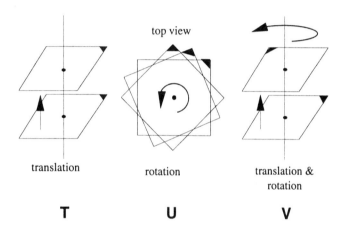

translation · rotation · translation & rotation

T   **U**   **V**

top view

As a horseshoe is tossed, its center of mass (which is located in space) travels in a curved path called a parabola. The horseshoe rotates around the center of mass as the center of mass travels along the parabolic path. Larger objects such as our galaxy, the Milky Way, also rotate around their centers of mass as their centers of mass travel through space.

For safety, perform the following activities outside the classroom and well away from other people. Grasp a lollipop by the end of the stick and give it a twirl as you toss it. Throw a horseshoe, giving it a flip as you release it. Grasp a baseball bat by the end of the handle and give it a twirl as you throw it in an arc. Give a metal coat hanger a twirl as you toss it and watch its motion. For all objects, draw their trajectories in the same way as the trajectory of the lollipop illustrated in Figure W. If you watch these moving objects closely you will see that each rotates around its center of mass as it moves through the air. Also, the center of mass follows a parabolic trajectory showing the translational motion of the object.

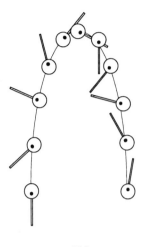

W

Questions

(1)   Describe the path traveled by the center of mass of a horseshoe after it has been tossed. What path is traveled by the center of mass of a baseball bat as it tumbles after being accidently thrown by a batter after a swing.

(2)   Of what advantage is the concept of center of mass to a diver or gymnast?

FOR THE TEACHER

Calculus is required to show that the center of mass of a body is the point at which all the weight of the body is concentrated. However, we can provide a rather intuitive approach to help you explain the concept of center of mass to your students. Consider the boulder to be made up of an infinitesimal number of particles. Each of these particles has weight and is attracted by the Earth. All downward forces on these particles are parallel. The actual weight of the boulder is the resultant of these separate parallel forces, and the point of application of this resultant force is called the center of mass. If you attach a rope to the boulder directly above the center of mass, you can lift it without any rotation.

Some students have difficulty understanding the difference between center of mass and center of gravity. Explain that these are actually one point that has no physical substance. It is simply a point where all the weight and mass of an object appears to be located. An object always has a center of mass. If, however, it is located at a position, such as somewhere in deep space, where a gravitational field is almost nonexistent, then it can be considered to have no center of gravity. The distinction between center of mass and center of gravity is important because it helps students understand the difference between the terms mass and weight, which many students find difficult.

Be sure students understand that the stability of a body resting on a surface depends on the size of its base and the position of its center of mass. If the base is large and the center of mass is low and positioned over the base of support, the body will be stable. Students must also understand that the center of mass of an object doesn't always lie within the object. The activities using the coat hanger and horseshoe clearly demonstrate this.

2.1.1 Estimating the Center of Mass

Discussion: The center of mass of the baseball is located at its geometrical center in the material from which the ball is constructed. The same is true for the tapered box. The center of mass of the cone is inside and closer to the base than the tip. The center of mass of the baseball bat is located toward the fatter part away from the handle. Baseball players refer to this as the "sweet spot" in the bat because it transfers the greatest energy to the ball when the ball is hit. If they hit the ball outside or inside this point, the bat will tend to rotate about the center of mass and cause strong vibrations in the hands of the batter. The center of mass of the remains of the skyrocket will continue on a parabolic trajectory until it hits the ground.

Answers (1) No. The center of mass is always at the same point as the center of gravity. (2) Such objects as donuts, motorcycle helmets, and steel pipes have external centers of gravity. (3) The space station is a composite object made of the station and its contents, and its center of mass will change as the astronauts move about. (4) The weight of the bar is 7.8 kg, the sum of the forces measured by the balances. Since the bar is not rotating, we know that the clockwise torque around the center of mass of the bar must be equal to the counterclockwise torque. This is accomplished when the center of mass is 1.23 m from the heavy end, and 1.77 m from the light end.

2.1.2 Stability

Discussion: The concept of work is discussed in a later chapter, but you may want to introduce it here so that students can understand the concept of stability. Work is defined as the product of force and distance. Work must be performed to raise an object against the force of gravity. The greater the distance, the more work that must be performed. Inspect the two identical bricks shown in Figure N labeled 1 and 2, one lying on its side and one lying on its end. The letter *c* indicates the center of mass of each brick. Which brick, 1 or 2, has the lower center of mass? Which brick has the larger base? After brick 1 is tipped to position 1' and brick 2 is tipped to position 2', which brick has the lower center of mass? Which has the larger base? The stability of an object is determined by the amount of work that must be done to rotate it to the point where its center of mass is outside its base of support. This work is determined by the object's weight and the distance the center of mass must be raised. The brick in position 1 has the lowest center of mass and the largest base of support. It requires more work to turn this brick on end because the center of mass must be lifted a distance H_1 while to turn brick 2 on its side requires that the center of mass be lifted only the short distance H_2.

   Many students find it difficult to understand that the center of mass need not be in the object. For example, although the center of mass of a baseball is in its solid core, the center of mass of a basketball is in the air inside the ball. As students determine the center of mass of a coat hanger and a horseshoe, as requested, they may obtain a better understanding of this difficult concept.

Answers (1) You must lean to the opposite side to ensure that the center of mass of the composite object (you and the object you are carrying) remains over the base of support (your feet). (2) In many combative sports (wrestling, sumo, boxing, and football), it is important to keep a low center of mass so as to maintain stability when colliding with opponents. (3) A double-decker bus is less stable than a regular bus because it has a high center of mass that is more easily moved outside of the base of support (see discussion section). (4) A flamingo moves its neck and feathers the way an acrobat uses a balancing pole to position the center of mass directly over the point of support, its feet.

2.1.3 Center of Mass of Composite Objects

Discussion: The demonstration in Part 1 produces counter-intuitive results, because students expect that the addition of weight to the end of the board will cause it to fall. The following is a similar counter-intuitive activity that works well as a teacher demonstration.

A board attached to another board by a hinge will rotate downward when there is no weight added, as shown in Figure X. Most students will assume that the addition of weight to the freely moving board will move the center of mass outward and cause it to rotate downward even faster. If, however, an object is added to the freely moving board such that the center of mass for the new composite body is inside and below the pivot point, the reverse will happen, creating an unexpected result.

Using a rope or strap, position a hammer so it is supported by the board and the center of mass of the composite body is directly below the hinge (Figure Y). The board remains stationary because the center of mass is directly below the point of support. Consequently, there is no net torque on the composite body. Now move the hammer so the center of mass of the composite body is inside and below the hinge. The board rotates upward because there is a net upward torque on the composite body. Reposition the hammer so the center of mass is outside and below the hinge. The board rotates downward because there is a net downward torque on the composite body. The concept of torque is explained in greater detail in a later chapter.

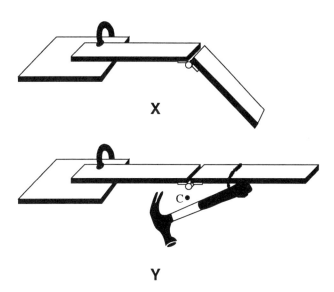

X

Y

Some students are mystified when they see those composite bodies such as the potato-toothpick-forks combination balance because they were not able to balance the simple potato-toothpick combination. It is important that you point out the essential difference in each case. In the potato-toothpick combination the center of mass is above the point of support. To keep the center of mass directly over the point of support, which is the end of the toothpick, the student must constantly move the support to compensate for the movement of the center of mass outside this small base. However, in the potato-toothpick-fork combination, the addition of the forks moves the center of mass to a position below the point of support. If the center of mass is below the point of support the object is stable.

Answers (1) Tape a thread or string to one side of the object and let it hang. Draw an imaginary extension of the thread through the object. Tape the thread to another location and repeat. The intersection of the two imaginary extensions indicates the center or mass. Students may propose alternative techniques. (2) The tram is stable because its center of mass is directly below the point of support. A person standing on the cable is unstable because his or her center of mass is high above a narrow base of support.

2.1.4 Motion of the Center of Mass

Discussion: Knowing the center of mass of a composite body can greatly simplify the description of the motion of the body. No matter how complicated the structure of the composite body may be, its motion and other attributes can be explained by considering the motion of its center of mass.

Answers (1) The centers of mass of both these objects will follow parabolic trajectories. (2) As divers and gymnasts perform midair flips and turns, they rotate about their center of mass. By moving their arms and legs, they can reposition their center of mass as necessary to get the desired motion.

Applications to Everyday Life

Animals: Four-legged animals have a lower center of mass and a larger base of support relative to their height than do two-legged animals such as birds and humans. The lower center of mass and larger base of support gives them greater stability. The pit bull, for example, has a very low center of mass and a wide base of support, making it an excellent fighting dog. By contrast, a bird resting on a wire must constantly move its tail in order to keep its center of mass over the wire.

Tree Growth: Although it is common to see short trees growing at an angle, it is very unusual to see tall trees such as redwoods growing at an angle. If the center of mass of a tall tree is positioned outside its base of support, it will likely topple in a strong wind.

Bicycles: Smaller wheels such as those found on the "dirt" bikes are more maneuverable and lower the bicycle's center of mass, making it easier to stay upright and perform tricks on uneven terrain.

Motorcycles: Motorcycles used in racing have a low-slung chassis, short handlebars, and footrests near the rear wheel, which keeps the center of mass low. In addition, the rider sits behind a streamlined windshield in a tight crouch, which lowers the center of mass even more. The low center of mass of the motorcycle makes it more stable as it negotiates the oval or irregular tracks with straightaways that permit the bikes to achieve speeds of about 300 kilometers (185 miles per hour).

Javelin Throw: The javelin is a shaft of wood or metal shaped like a spear with a metal tip at one end and a grip bound around the shaft at the center of mass. The javelin must be grasped at the center of mass when thrown so it will not tumble in its trajectory.

Rotation of the Earth and Moon: You have been told that the moon revolves around the Earth, but this is not entirely correct because the Earth also revolves around the moon. The Earth and the moon represent a composite body held together by gravitational attraction. This composite body has a center of mass about which the Earth and the moon rotate. Because the Earth is much more massive than the moon, the center of mass of the composite body is located inside the Earth about 3,000 miles from the earth's center. The Earth and the moon system revolves around this center of mass about once a month.

Binary Stars and Black Holes: A binary star is a star that has a companion. The two stars revolve around the center of mass between them. Astronomers have observed systems in which only one visible star orbits around some unseen companion. By examining the path of the visible star, it is possible to locate the center of mass of the binary system and predict the mass of the unseen object, whether it is a white dwarf, neutron star, or black hole. Many scientists believe that a black hole is a star that is so massive and compact that its strong gravitational field prevents anything, including light, from escaping. Data on the center of mass of binary systems have led astronomers to postulate that such astronomical bodies exist.

2.2 INERTIA

Skiers hurtling down a mountain slope out of control sit on their backsides in an attempt to stop. Skateboarders whisking down a path drag a foot to slow their speed. A girl standing in a crowded bus grabs the rail as she lurches forward when the driver makes a sudden stop. Your friends struggle to push your motionless automobile that is stalled in a parking lot. A book sits on your desk unread. All these objects possess linear inertia. If an object is moving, a force is required to stop it. If an object is not moving, a force is required to set it in motion. *The property of an object to resist change in its linear state of motion is called linear inertia.*

A door stands ajar until closed by the wind. Ice skaters twirling in a tight circle extend their arms to slow the rotation and pull them in to rotate faster. A raw egg spun on a table top wobbles and soon stops while a hard-boiled egg spins rapidly. A top spins and remains upright until the rotational speed decreases and it finally topples. All these objects possess rotational inertia. If an object is rotating, a torque is required to stop it. If an object is not rotating, a torque is required to set it rotating. *The property of an object to resist change in its rotational state of motion is called rotational inertia (also called moment of inertia).*

Sir Isaac Newton stated as his first law of motion: *Every body persists in its state of rest or of uniform motion in a straight line unless it is compelled to change that state by forces impressed on it.* When a body is in a state of rest or when it is moving at a constant speed in a straight line, its velocity is constant. The velocity of an object does not change unless an unbalanced (external) force acts on the object. The velocity of an object is changed when we speed it up, slow it down, or change the direction in which it moves. An unbalanced force accelerates an object. Stated in simple terms, Newton's first law is: Matter resists any change in its velocity (speed or direction). Only an unbalanced force (push or pull) can change an object's speed or direction. Inertia is the resistance to a change in the velocity of matter. *A body at rest tends to remain at rest and a body in motion tends to remain in motion.*

Imagine you are in a spacecraft in outer space and there are no stars, planets, or other bodies in your vicinity. If the spaceship is weightless, is any force required to move it? Yes! The spacecraft is composed of matter, has mass, and therefore has inertia. *Mass is the amount of matter in a body and is a measure of inertia.* Suppose you ignite the rocket engines of the spaceship that is at rest. The engines supply the force required to accelerate the spacecraft. The longer the engines burn the greater the velocity (speed in a given direction) of the ship. Suppose you cut the engines. Will the ship come to a stop? No. Inertia will cause it to continue indefinitely at its present velocity until some external force acts to slow and stop it.

2.2.1 The Effect of Inertia

Concepts to Investigate: Inertia, weight, mass.

Materials: Block of wood (approximately 1 kg), string or thread, screw eyes.

Principles and Procedures: Attach two screw eyes to two ends of a block of wood as shown in Figure A. Use one piece of thread to suspend the object from a suitable support such as a hook. The thread should be barely strong enough to support the object when it is suspended. Attach another piece of the thread to the bottom and pull steadily until one of the threads breaks. Again support the object, as shown in Figure A. Grasp the bottom thread, but this time give it a quick jerk rather than a steady pull. Repeat the procedure 5 times. Which thread breaks when you pull slowly? Which thread breaks when you pull rapidly? Why?

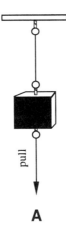

A

© 1994 by John Wiley & Sons, Inc.

Questions

(1) Explain why the top thread breaks when the bottom string is pulled slowly but the bottom string breaks when you jerk the bottom string.

(2) If a massive object such as a blacksmith's anvil is placed on the stomach of a person lying on the floor and a second person strikes the anvil hard with a sledge hammer, the reclining person is unhurt. However, if the anvil were not on the stomach, the person would certainly have been injured by the blow. Explain. (*Note:* Don't attempt this activity.)

(3) Suppose you have a hammer with a loose head. Although you could strike the hammerhead with a solid object to secure it on the handle, an easier method to secure it is to grasp the handle of the hammer and repeatedly strike the butt (end opposite the handle) on a solid surface. Explain in terms of inertia.

(4) Imagine you are in deep space holding a large boulder in your hands. You would find it quite difficult to move this boulder back and forth even though it has no weight. Explain.

2.2.2 Newton's First Law

Principles and Procedures: Newton's first law, linear inertia.

Materials: Marble, pie pan.

Principles and Procedures: Use a hacksaw or hefty scissors to cut a section from a pie pan, as shown in Figure B. Place a marble inside the pan as shown and give the marble a quick push in the direction shown by the arrow. The inside edge of the pan will force the marble to move in a circular path. This force exerted by the side of the pan on the marble is called centripetal force because it is a force that holds the object toward the center of the pan. But what will happen when the marble leaves the confining side of the pan? Will the marble follow path 1, 2, or 3? Try it and explain the results.

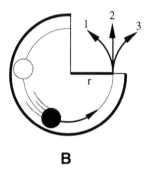

B

The crux of the question is this: What external forces act on the marble when it leaves the pan? Gravity acts on the marble in a downward direction, but produces no effect on the horizontal direction of the marble as it leaves the confines of the pan. The direction of the marble at the edge as it leaves the pan is tangential to the radius *r* as shown by arrow 2. That is, the direction is in a straight line shown by 2. Remember Newton's first law of motion: Every body persists in its state of rest or of uniform motion in a straight line unless it is compelled to change that state by forces impressed on it. Since no constraining force acts on the marble after it leaves the pan it will travel in a straight line as shown by 2. The marble could not possibly travel in the direction shown by arrow 1 because there is no centripetal force to compel it to do so. Also, the marble could not travel on the course shown by arrow 3 because there is no force to move (push) it in that direction.

To help clarify the marble-in-the-pan activity let us consider the revolution of the moon around the Earth. The moon remains in a rather circular orbit around the Earth because the gravitational force of the Earth provides the required centripetal force. If one could suddenly cut the gravitational force between the Earth and the moon, the moon would move off in a straight line just as the marble moved in the direction shown by arrow 2 when it left the pan and there was no longer any centripetal force to keep it moving in its original circular path.

Questions

(1) Describe centripetal force and explain how it keeps the marble moving in a circular path while in the pan.

(2) In what direction does the marble move after leaving the pan? Why?

(3) Suppose you are swinging a weight on the end of a rope around your head. The rope is suddenly cut. In what direction will the weight move?

(4) You are in a car rapidly rounding a corner and a friend sitting next to you states that centrifugal force is trying to push you out of the car. Another friend watching your car from the corner states that there is no such thing as centrifugal force, and that the only force you feel is the force of the car pushing against you to keep you moving in a circular path. With which friend do you agree? Explain.

2.2.3 Linear Inertia

Concept to Investigate: Linear inertia.

Materials: 3" × 5" card, coin, glass or cup, glass with a smooth base filled with water, smooth tabletop, overhead transparency or handkerchief.

Principles and Procedures

Part 1. Place a 3" × 5" card over the mouth of the glass and then place the coin on the center of the card (Figure C). Your goal is to put the coin in the glass without lifting the card. Grasp the card by one edge and pull it slowly away from the mouth of the glass and note the results. Reposition the card and coin and flick the card with your finger in a horizontal direction and note the results.

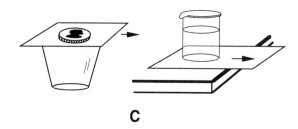

C

Part 2. Spread a handkerchief or overhead transparency on a small table or desk. Place a plastic container of water on it. Grasp the overhead transparency or hand-kerchief by an edge and pull it slowly to one side and observe the motion of the glass of water. Repeat, but this time pull very quickly (jerk) and observe the glass of water. Place an empty container of water next to the full container, and see if you can pull the sheet such that the full glass remains stationary while the empty one moves. Why would there be such a difference in the motion of the full and empty glasses?

Questions

(1) When the card was pulled slowly the coin moved with it, but when the card was flicked (moved quickly) the coin dropped in the glass. Explain.

(2) Make a stack of five coins (use pennies if you are on a tight budget) on a smooth, flat surface. Place another coin on the surface a short distance from the stack. Use a finger to quickly flick this coin against the stack (Figure D). Does the entire stack move or does just one coin in the stack move? Explain in terms of inertia.

(3) When the cloth is pulled very slowly, the glass moves with the cloth. When the cloth is pulled faster, the glass topples. If the cloth is pulled very rapidly, it moves from under the glass and the glass remains in place. Explain in terms of inertia and torque.

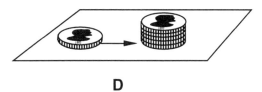

D

(4) Place a collection of unbreakable items on a tablecloth that is covering a smooth tabletop. Grasp the tablecloth firmly by an edge and pull slowly in a horizontal motion. Replace the tablecloth and items. Grasp the cloth by an edge and pull very quickly. The items remain in position on the table after the cloth is pulled from beneath them. Explain in terms of inertia.

(5) When you want to tear a paper towel from a roll, you make a sharp jerk rather than a slow pull. Explain.

2.2.4 Inertia of Liquids

Concepts to Investigate: Inertia of liquids, viscosity, inertia of fluid/solid systems.

Materials: Large glass, pepper, water, syrup, raw egg, cooked egg.

Principles and Procedures

Part 1. Inertia of liquids: Pour water into a glass until about half full. Sprinkle some pepper or other insoluble substance on the surface of the water so you will be able to note any movement of the water. Allow the container to sit until the water is still. Grasp the container by the rim and give it a very slow twist in a clockwise direction (Figure E). The container rotates. Does the water at the edge rotate? Does the water toward the center rotate? Repeat the activity several times, rotating the container in both a clockwise and a counterclockwise direction at various speeds. Is there any difference in the movement of the pepper when the glass is spun rapidly compared to when it is spun slowly? Repeat the process using syrup instead of water.

Part 2. Inertia of fluid/solid systems: Obtain a hard-boiled and a raw egg. Place each egg on its side on a flat surface, spin rapidly, and note the results (Figure F). How does the spinning of the cooked egg differ from that of the raw egg? Spin them again and stop each in the midst of its spinning and then immediately release each. Which, if either, starts to spin again? Why do the two eggs behave differently?

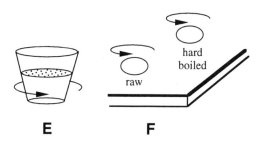

E   F

Questions

(1) What force between the inside of the glass and the water touching this glass causes the water to rotate?

(2) Why is there less rotation of water nearer the center of the glass?

(3) Syrup has a higher viscosity than water, meaning that it provides more resistance to flow when pressure is applied. Was there more or less rotation when the water was replaced with syrup? Explain your findings.

(4) Explain why the raw egg wobbled and spun slowly while the cooked egg spun rapidly.

(5) The raw egg may resume spinning but the cooked egg will not. Explain.

2.2.5 Rotational Inertia

Concepts to Investigate: Rotational inertia, angular velocity, angular acceleration.

Materials: Two rolls of adding-machine tape (one of the rolls should be complete, the other half full), ring stands, dowel, large hinge-type paper clip.

Principles and Procedures: Racing bicycles used in road competitions are made of lightweight alloys and often weigh less than 20 pounds (9.1 kg). Sprinting bicycles, used in track competitions are even lighter than racing bicycles, weighing only 11–15 pounds (5.0–6.8 kg). Although it is important to minimize the weight of the entire racing or sprinting bicycle, it is particularly important to minimize the weight from the moving parts. All parts of the bicycle contribute to its linear inertia, but the moving parts also contribute to rotational inertia. Racers are therefore particularly interested in new alloys or synthetic materials that make it possible to minimize the weight of the wheel rims and the gears. The less massive the rotating parts, the faster the racer will be able to accelerate.

As its name implies, rotational inertia is the property that resists change in rotational motion. If the rotational inertia of a stationary object is great, it will be difficult to spin it. If the rotational inertia of a spinning object is great, it will be difficult to bring it to a stop. The greater the rotational inertia, the greater force required to spin. The angular velocity of an object is the rate at which it spins and is measured in radians per second, where a radian is 57.3°. (A radian is the angle formed by an arc whose length is equal to the radius and is the same for all circles.) Rotational inertia is the resistance of an object to changes in its angular velocity. The angular acceleration of an object is directly proportional to the torque that is applied T, but inversely proportional to the rotational inertia I. $\alpha = T/I$. This equation is analogous to the equation for linear acceleration: $a = F/m$ (where a = acceleration, F = force, and m = mass).

It is difficult to start or stop the rotation of an object if it has a large rotational inertia. What factors influence the rotational inertia? Place two different-sized rolls of adding-machine tape or other rolled paper on the dowel, as shown in Figure G. Attach heavy clips to the rolls and hold so they cannot unwind. Release the rolls at the same time and note which unrolls most rapidly. Which roll has the greatest rotational inertia? Experiment with different diameters to determine the size that unrolls the fastest.

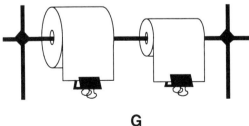

G

Questions

(1) The torque created by the weight of the clip on the larger roll is greater, but the smaller roll unwinds more rapidly. Explain.

(2) Shorter legs have less rotational inertia than longer legs. How would this affect the stride of a dachshund compared to a horse?

(3) When you run you do not keep your legs straight but bend them. What advantage does this have?

2.2.6 Distribution of Mass and Rotational Inertia

Concept to Investigate: Rotational inertia.

Materials: Meter stick, two cans of soup, heavy-duty tape.

Principles and Procedures: Tape cans of soup or other similar objects an equal and short distance from the center of a meter stick, leaving room for your hand to grasp the stick at its center (Figure H). Apply torque to the stick by twisting it back and forth and note the effort required. Move the objects to the ends of the meter stick and tape them. Is it easier or more difficult to rotate the stick?

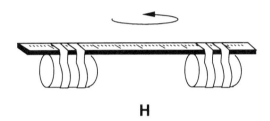

H

    Although the mass of the objects and stick remain constant, the torque required to twist the stick increases as the distance of the masses from the axis of rotation, which in this case is the center of the stick, increases. Rotational inertia, also referred to as moment of inertia I depends not only on the mass of an object m, but also on the distribution of this mass about the axis of rotation. Distance from the axis is the greater contributor to rotational inertia because moment of inertia is proportional to the mass and to the square of the distance r of the mass from the axis of rotation: $I = mr^2$. Suppose we neglect the mass of the stick and consider the mass of the objects to be one unit. If the objects are initially 10 cm from the axis of rotation (at 40 cm and 60 cm on the meter stick) and are moved to 20 cm from the axis (at 30 cm and 70 cm on the meter stick), the distance r is doubled and the rotational inertia is therefore increased by a factor of four, meaning that four times as much torque (twisting force) is necessary to rotate it.

Questions

   (1)   Explain why the stick was easier to twist when the weights were located closer to the axis of rotation.

   (2)   If the mass of each object is doubled and the distance from the axis of rotation of each is tripled, by what factor is the rotational inertia increased?

   (3)   Suppose you grip the stick at the 25-cm mark and twist it with the weights hanging at the ends. Is the torque greater than that required when you twist at the 50-cm mark?

FOR THE TEACHER

Inertia is not a difficult concept for students to understand or appreciate, but some of the manifestations of inertia are at times perplexing or seemingly contrary to intuition. It is these discrepant events that generate interest and motivate students to pursue science. For example, many students are amazed that a raw egg will only wobble when spun but the same egg when cooked will spin rapidly. Likewise, students are usually perplexed by the fact that the string above a mass will break as a steady force is applied to the thread below the mass but that the bottom string will break if a quick jerk is applied to the bottom thread. While factors other than inertia may be involved in these demonstrations, we suggest that you keep it simple and deal with only one concept at time.

These activities illustrate that in a given situation a force acting for different amounts of time may cause different results. In addition, they show that a rotating body has the same tendency to maintain its state of rotational motion as has a body moving in a straight line to maintain its linear motion.

2.2.1 The Effect of Inertia

Discussion: Students often mistakenly assume that the strain (tension) in the strings above and below the mass are the same. Use the following analogy to show that this is not true. Suppose a student is hanging from the branch of a large tree. Further suppose that another student is hanging from the legs of the top student and that a third student is hanging from the legs of the second. Now suppose a fourth student tugs slowly on the legs of the bottom student. The tension will be greatest on the top student because he or she has to support the weight of everyone below. As a result, each student will release his or her grip in the same way the top string broke when the bottom string was pulled rapidly. Now suppose the fourth student pulled (jerked) quickly on the legs of the third student. The inertia of the first two students would resist this pull and consequently the third student would probably be the first to let go. In a similar manner, the inertia of the block resists motion, and as a result the bottom string will snap first when jerked.

The threads used in this activity are assumed to be weightless (massless), but a real rope has mass. Suppose you suspend a very long and thick rope from the top of a tall building. Further suppose you are strong enough to pull the bottom of this rope hard enough to break it. Where would the rope break? The center of mass (gravity) of the rope is in the middle and may be considered the same as the mass between the two threads. Consequently, if the bottom of the rope is pulled slowly the rope will break somewhere above the center of mass, probably near the top point of attachment. However, if the rope is jerked quickly at the bottom it will break somewhere below the middle due to the rope's inertia acting at the center of mass.

When pulling the bottom string slowly you are putting both the force of your pull and the weight of the object (remember that weight is the force of gravity on an object) on the top string. Since the force on the top string is greater than that on the bottom string, the top string breaks. When you jerk the bottom string, the inertia of the object restricts the strain to the thread below the object. Since the strain on the bottom string is greater than that on the top string, it breaks first.

Answers (1) When pulled slowly, the strain on the top string is greatest and it breaks because it is supporting both the weight of the block and the force of your pull. When the bottom string is jerked quickly, it breaks because the inertia of the block resists the pull and little tension is transmitted to the upper thread. (2) The mass of the anvil is great and its inertia resists the motion imparted by the impact of the hammer. Consequently, the acceleration of the anvil is small and its impact on the body is small. If the anvil were not present, the kinetic energy of the hammer would do great harm to the body on contact. (3) When the butt of the handle is moved rapidly toward the ground the inertia of the hammerhead is great. After the handle strikes the surface it stops, but the inertia of the hammerhead keeps it moving in the same direction thus seating it snugly on the end of the handle. (4) Although the boulder does not have weight because it is not located in a significant gravitational field, it has mass and therefore possesses inertia. A force is required to overcome inertia and set a stationary body in motion as well as to stop it if it is moving.

2.2.2 Newton's First Law

Discussion: The authors never cease to be amazed by the predictions of both secondary-school students, college students, and lay people concerning the direction the marble will take after leaving the pan. Some say that centrifugal force will fling the marble in a path directly outward from the center. Convince your students that centrifugal force is actually a fictitious force—it simply does not exist when the observer is outside the moving frame of reference. The only horizontal force acting on the marble is the force of the side of the pan (centripetal force) directed toward the center of the pan. Students invent centrifugal force to explain the force they feel when they are in the rotating frame of reference. For example, suppose you are riding in an automobile rounding a tight curve. You feel the side of the car pressing on your body and interpret this force as one attempting to push your body out of the car in a direction away from the car. A person outside the car in a stationary frame of reference interprets this same force differently. He or she sees it as a centripetal force exerted by the car on your body that compels it to move in a curve. So whether we speak of centrifugal or centripetal force depends on the frame of reference.

Those students who predict that the marble will continue in a circular path after it leaves the pan do not understand that an external force must act on an object to change its speed or direction. Show them an analogous situation in which you swing an object on the end of a string around your head. Ask what would happen if the string were cut. Convince students that the object would continue in a straight line perpendicular to the string at the point the string was cut because at this point the string exerts no external force on the object and Newton's first law states that an object will remain in motion in a given direction unless acted upon by an external force. When the string is cut or the marble leaves the edge of the pan, an external force is no longer acting to change the direction of the ball or marble and they continue in a straight line perpendicular to the point at which centripetal force ceased to act.

Understanding centripetal force is important because this force plays an important part in everyday phenomena experienced by students such as the revolution of the moon around the Earth and the revolution of the Earth around the sun.

Answers (1) Centripetal (center seeking) force is exerted by the pan on the marble just as a string exerts a centripetal force on an object tied to one end when you swing the object around in a circle. (2) The marble will move in the direction shown by arrow 2 because upon exiting the pan there is no centripetal force exerted on the marble and it thus continues to move in a direction perpendicular to the line from the center of the pan to the edge at which point the marble exited. (3) The weight will continue to move in a straight line perpendicular to the string at the point the string was cut. (4) Centrifugal force is actually a fictitious force we invent to make explanations easier. It all comes down to the frame of reference from which we are making observations. If you are in a rotating frame of reference such as the car rounding a corner (same as sitting on the edge of a rotating merry-go-round) centrifugal force is a real force to you. For example, if you sit on the outer edge of a merry-go-round and your friend spins it rapidly you will definitely feel a force that you interpret as pushing you outward just as you do when sitting in the car, but this is only because you are part of the rotating frame of reference. Your friend standing on the ground and observing your motion either in the car or on the merry-go-round sees a completely different situation. To him or her you are revolving around a center just as an object revolves around your head when you spin it on a piece of string. To your friend, who is an observer outside your rotating frame of reference, the only force acting on you is that of the car's door or the outside rail of the merry-go-round, which act toward the center to keep you moving in a circle. Think carefully about the important concept of frames of reference.

2.2.3 Linear Inertia

Discussion: Moving the card (part 1) slowly will allow the frictional force between card and the coin to act for a sufficient amount of time so the coin will move with the card. However, if the card is moved very rapidly (flicked) then the frictional force between card and coin cannot act for a sufficient amount of time to overcome the inertia of the coin: The coin remains essentially at rest and drops into the cup after the card is pushed from beneath it.

If the overhead transparency or cloth in part 2 is pulled slowly, friction between it and the container will act for a sufficient amount of time that the container will move with the cloth. If the cloth is pulled quickly, friction will not be able to act for a sufficient time on the bottom of the container and the inertia of the glass will keep it stationary while the cloth moves below it. You should ask students if the results would be the same if the glass were empty. If the cloth is jerked very suddenly the results will be the same, but if not, the empty glass will probably travel with the cloth because the inertia of the empty glass is much less than that of the filled glass. Also ask students if a tall glass with a small base would produce the same results as a short glass with a wide base. If the glass is quite tall with a narrow base it will have a higher center of mass and a small base of support. Consequently, the torque produced by the frictional force of the cloth on the bottom of the glass may be sufficient to topple the glass.

Answers (1) Pulling the card slowly allows friction to act for enough time to drag the coin. Flicking the coin does not provide enough time for friction to act and the inertia of the coin keeps it over the mouth of the glass. (2) All the coins in the stack possess the same inertia. The moving coin imparts energy directly to the bottom coin, sufficient to overcome its inertia and set it in motion. Only the bottom coin will move because the friction between this coin and the one above does not act long enough to set the coins above in motion. (3) When pulled slowly there is sufficient time for friction to act between glass or object and cloth, and the glass moves with the cloth. When pulled slightly faster the torque produced by the friction of the cloth on the bottom of the glass topples the glass. If the cloth is pulled rapidly, frictional forces act for only a short time and the inertia of the glass keeps it in place. (4) The explanation is the same as for number 3. However, if some of the items are tall with small bases such as a tall glass filled with water, they may topple because of torque produced by the cloth. (5) With a quick jerk, the inertia of the roll keeps it in position and a towel separates just as a quick jerk breaks the thread below a heavy mass as described in Activity 2.2.1. A slow pull unrolls the paper.

2.2.4 Inertia of Liquids

Discussion: Both activities can easily be performed as a teacher demonstration and viewed by the entire class if the glass is placed on an overhead projector. Figure I shows the top of the glass of water from Part 1. When considering the inertia of a liquid it is helpful to consider the liquid as composed of a very large number of layers (columns) of which we show a few. When the glass is rotated very slowly the friction of the inside of the glass on the layer of water adjacent to the glass is sufficient

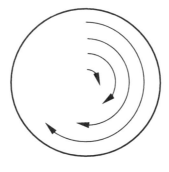

I

to set this layer in motion as can be seen by the movement of the pepper on the surface of the water. If the rotation is slow enough, this layer will set the second layer of water in motion. If the glass is rotated very rapidly, the frictional force between the glass and the first layer of water will not be sufficient to set this layer in motion (rotate it). Consequently, the glass rotates but the water does not.

The explanation of the motions of the raw and hard-boiled eggs in part 2 is similar to the explanation for part 1. Consider the liquid substance of the raw egg to be composed of layers as in a glass of water. When one attempts to spin the raw egg rapidly, the initial motion of the shell is so fast that the inner layers of the liquid (albumin) inside the egg slip on the outer layers and the friction of this slipping changes part of the energy of rotation into heat. The decrease in the energy of rotation allows the egg to soon stop spinning. When the raw egg is stopped briefly the liquid inside the egg continues to move because of its inertia. Its movement now causes the shell to resume spinning when released. Since the hard-boiled egg is essentially solid throughout, it rotates as a solid object and continues to spin until the friction between the shell, the supporting surface, and air causes it to stop. When a hard-boiled egg is stopped in the midst of its spinning it will not resume spinning because all material in the egg is brought to a stop. In other words, when the raw egg is stopped, there is still inertia of motion of the material inside, but when the cooked egg is stopped, there is no inertia of motion.

Answers (1) Frictional force between glass and water causes water to rotate. (2) Frictional force between layers of water decreases as you move toward the center. (3) The viscosity of syrup is greater than water. This creates more friction between layers and consequently more rotation of syrup. (4) In the raw egg, much of the applied energy goes into frictional heating of the inner fluid, while in the cooked egg, nearly all goes into rotation. (5) When the raw egg is stopped in the midst of spinning, the liquid inside continues to move, causing the egg to resume spinning when released.

2.2.5 Rotational Inertia

Discussion: Torque is directly proportional to the radius of the roll r but the moment of inertia I is directly proportional to r^2. The moment of inertia of the larger roll is much greater than that of the smaller. Consequently, the smaller roll unrolls faster. Challenge students to design and construct the fastest unrolling tape. Have students demonstrate their tapes in a demonstration before the class.

Answers (1) To simplify the explanation, we consider each roll to be solid with the dowel as the axis of rotation. The moment of inertia I of a solid cylinder is $1/2mr^2$, where r is the radius from the axis of rotation and m is the mass. The larger cylinder has both greater mass and radius and hence a greater moment of inertia, which means it has the greater tendency to resist a change in rotation. Although the torque produced on the larger cylinder by the weight of the clip is greater than that produced on the smaller because of the difference in the radii, the r^2 term in moment of inertia offsets this difference and the smaller cylinder unwinds more rapidly. Not only is it more difficult to accelerate the large roll, it is also more difficult to decelerate it as well. (2) The dachshund would have a much quicker stride than the horse, just as a short pendulum has a shorter period than a long pendulum. (3) One advantage of bending your legs when running is that it reduces their rotational inertia so you can move (rotate) back and forth more rapidly.

2.2.6 Distribution of Mass and Rotational Inertia

Discussion: The following teacher demonstration provides an interesting introduction to significance of the distribution of mass when determining the rotational inertia of an object. Obtain two equal lengths (about a meter each) of PVC pipe. (Polyvinyl chloride, PVC, is a plastic pipe used in plumbing.) Use packing material, popcorn, or paper to secure two pieces of round metal bar in the center of one pipe, and two identical pieces at the ends of the second pipe. Adjust the amount of packing material as necessary so that both bars weigh the same. Seal the ends of the pipe with PVC caps. Have your students rotate each bar at its center. They will find that one pipe is much more difficult to rotate than is the other. Ask them to hypothesize why the two pipes respond differently. After confirming that the weight and length of both are the same, the only remaining variable is the distribution of the mass. At this point you can describe how the pipes were constructed and introduce the importance of the distribution of mass when determining rotational inertia.

Although the mass of an object may remain constant, the rotational inertia of this object can change depending on the axis of rotation chosen. A greater torque is required to rotate a meter stick about one of its ends than is required to rotate the same stick at its center point. Following are some values for moment of inertia I for the same objects rotated on different axes: thin rod of length r rotated about axis through center perpendicular to length $I = mr^2/12$, thin rod of length r rotated about axis through one end $I = mr^2/3$; hoop of radius r rotated about cylinder axis $I = mr^2$, hoop of radius r rotated about any diameter $I = mr^2$, hoop of radius r rotated about any tangent line $I = 3mr^2/2$. The following is a listing of the moments of inertia for some other objects: solid sphere of radius r $I = ^2/_5\, mr^2$, thin spherical shell of radius r about any diameter $I = 2\,mr^2/3$, annular cylinder about cylinder axis $I = ^1/_2\, m\, (r_1{}^2 + r_2{}^2)$, rectangular plate of length a and width b rotated about axis through center $I = ^1/_{12}\, m\, (a^2 + b^2)$.

Answers (1) The moment of inertia of the stick with weights close to axis of rotation was less and consequently required torque was less. (2) If the mass is doubled the rotational inertia is doubled. If the distance is tripled the rotational inertia is increased by a factor of nine. Consequently, the rotational inertia is increased by a factor of 2×9 or 18. (3) The torque is greater when the axis of rotation is at 0.25-m mark. The rotational inertia may be calculated as $I = mr^2$. Assume the mass is 1 kg. At 0.50-m mark the rotational inertia is: $1\text{kg}((0.50\ \text{m})^2 + (0.50\ \text{m})^2) = 0.50\ \text{kg·m}^2$. At 0.25-m mark the rotational inertia is: $1\text{kg}((0.25\ \text{m})^2 + (0.75\ \text{m})^2) = 0.625\ \text{kg·m}^2$.

Applications to Everyday Life

Amusement-Park Rides: When riding a roller coaster the bar across the legs keeps the rider from leaving the seat when the coaster reaches the top of the track and then begins to descend rapidly. Without the constraint of the bar your body would continue moving upward out of the seat due to your body's inertia. When riding in an octopus or a tilt-a-whirl, the inertia of the riders would soon send them spinning through space were it not for the constraining belts and bars.

Seat Belts, Air Bags, and Helmets: Sometimes we must protect ourselves from our own inertia. Many states in the United States have laws concerning the use of helmets when riding motorcycles and the use of seat belts when riding in an automobile. The inertia of a passenger in the front seat of a rapidly moving automobile involved in a head-on collision could propel that person through the windshield were it not for the constraint of the seat belt or air bag. The inertia of the head of a motorcycle rider involved in a collision or fall might shatter that head on impact with a nonmovable object such as pavement were it not for the cushioning effect of the padded helmet. The padded head rest in automobiles prevents whiplash that would otherwise occur due to the inertia of your head when rear-ended by another automobile.

Locomotives, Freighters: Massive objects such as locomotives and ocean freighters have great inertia and require great forces to set them in motion when they are at rest and to stop them when they are moving. When a freighter is moving rapidly forward on the surface of the ocean it may take one mile or more for the ship to come to a stop even with the engines and propeller in full reverse.

Earth, Moon, and Other Planetary Bodies: Our moon revolves around our Earth just as other moons revolve around other planets. These moons are massive, and their great inertia would cause them to leave their orbits around the planets and move in a straight-line path were it not for the gravitational force (centripetal force) of each planet on its moon.

Flywheel: Engines in cars and other vehicles contain pistons that move up and down. A massive flywheel is attached to the crankshafts in these engines to provide the rotational inertia to keep the engine running smoothly as the pistons rapidly change from an upward to a downward motion.

Bicycle Wheels: The further mass is from the axis of rotation, the greater its contribution to rotational inertia $I = mr^2$ for a ring. When manufacturing bicycle wheels, it is therefore more important to remove weight from the rims than from the hubs.

2.3 VELOCITY AND ACCELERATION

Could you withstand a force of three times your weight pressing against your body? Eight times? Loads from 3 to 8 times the weight of a person may be experienced by occupants of rockets that lift off from the Earth's surface. Members of the crew of the space shuttle experience forces much greater than their weight during launch. Such forces are described in terms of "*g*" loads where *g* is the acceleration of gravity at the Earth's surface—one *g* is your weight, 2 *g*'s are twice your weight, and so on. On launch, the crew is placed in a reclining position so the "*g*" loads are experienced in the chest-to-back position rather than in a standing position where the *g* loads would act in a head-to-foot position. The human body can withstand much higher "*g*" loads in a reclining position. During reentry the crew of the space shuttle experience a force of about 1.5 *g* in the feet-first position, which causes blood to move toward their feet. To keep blood from pooling, the crew wears suits that produce pressure on the lower part of their bodies.

You may have seen a drag-racing event. These dragsters accelerate rapidly and the occupants experience significant *g* loads. You experience a *g* load when in a car rounding a corner at high speed or when moving in one of the many rides at an amusement park such as the tilt-a-whirl, octopus, or roller coaster. You will learn about acceleration and other types of motion in this section.

Linear motion: A car that starts from rest and moves 200 meters in a straight line in 5 seconds has an average speed of 100m\5s or 20 meters per second (m/s). Velocity is speed in a particular direction. If the car is moving directly north, its velocity is 20m/s north. Instantaneous velocity is the velocity of an object at any particular time. The symbol for velocity is sometimes written with a small arrow above to indicate it is a vector quantity: $\vec{v}$. If the velocity of an object is constant, the distance traveled can be determined using the relation, $d = vt$, where d is distance, v is velocity, and t is time. For example, a power boat moving at 30 km/h for 30 minutes will cover a distance of 30 km/h × 0.5 h = 15 km.

If, however, that power boat is crossing a river with a current of 5 km/h, the net velocity of the boat will be the vector sum of the boat's movement across the river (30 km/h) and the current (5 km/h). Since the current is at right angles to the motion of the boat, we can use the Pythagorean Theorem to calculate the resulting velocity of the boat to be 30.4 km/h (Figure A) at an angle that is 9.5° downstream. As a result, the boat will hit the opposite bank 1/3 of a km downstream from where it began (Figure B).

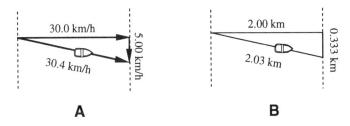

A   **B**

Acceleration is the rate of change of velocity. When you press on the gas pedal your car accelerates and when you press on the brakes it decelerates. A car that goes from 0 km/h to 40 km/h in 8 seconds has a greater average acceleration than a car that goes from 0 km/h to 80 km/h in 20 seconds. The average acceleration of the first car is 40 km/h divided by 8 seconds or 5 km/h per second, meaning it changes its velocity 5 km/h every second. The average acceleration of the second car is 80 km/h divided by 20 seconds or 4 km/h per second. An acceleration in the direction an object is moving will increase the object's velocity whereas an acceleration in an opposite direction will decrease the velocity.

Nonlinear motion: An object moving in a curved path exhibits nonlinear motion. If you throw a baseball from first base to a player standing on second base and disregard air resistance, the ball travels in a curved path (trajectory) called a parabola. The ball has a horizontal component of motion without acceleration (constant velocity) and a vertical component of motion with acceleration caused by gravity. These two components are completely independent—one has no influence on the other. Adding the two components (velocities) gives the resultant velocity that determines the path of the ball over time as show in Figure C. As the ball leaves the hand at point 1, it has constant horizontal velocity, maximum velocity upward, and moves along the curve as shown by the resultant. At point 2 the horizontal velocity remains the same but the upward component is now less because gravity has decelerated the ball. At point 3 the upward velocity is zero, horizontal velocity is still the same, and the ball has reached the top of its trajectory. Gravity increases the downward velocity and by point 5 the ball is moving with the same speed as at point 1 but its velocity is different as shown by the resultant.

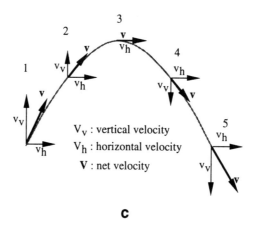

V_v : vertical velocity
V_h : horizontal velocity
V : net velocity

c

Motion in a circular path is an important type of nonlinear motion. If you swing an object about your head at a constant rate as shown in Figure D, it experiences a constant acceleration toward the center even though its speed does not change. Although the speed of the object is constant, its velocity is changing because velocity is speed in a particular direction and the object's direction is continuously changing. Such acceleration toward the center is known as centripetal (center-seeking) acceleration. If you swing the object at an increasing rate of rotation, then the object experiences two types of acceleration: centripetal and tangential. Tangential acceleration is acceleration along the circular path. According to Newton's second law, $F = ma$, part of the force you impart to the object goes into centripetal acceleration a_c and part goes into tangential acceleration a_t, which are the components of the resultant acceleration of the object shown as "a" in Figure E. Tangential acceleration is caused by a change in magnitude of the velocity while centripetal acceleration is caused by a change in the direction of the velocity.

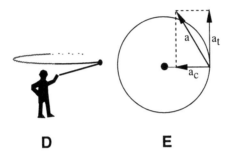

D   **E**

2.3.1 Acceleration Due to Gravity

Concepts to Investigate: Constant acceleration, gravity, free fall.

Materials: Wooden molding with a recessed groove, steel ball or marble of appropriate size for groove, protractor, stopwatch; an assortment of balls (e.g., Styrofoam ball, golf ball, tennis ball, baseball, basketball).

Principles and Procedures

Part 1. Motion down inclined plane: Galileo wished to study the motion of freely falling objects, but he lacked a suitable timing device for measuring such rapid motion, so he used an inclined plane to slow the motion. He was able to study acceleration by successively increasing the angle of the plane. As the angle increased, so did the component of gravity necessary to move the ball. By examining Figure F, you can see that when the plane is level, there is no force F to move the ball parallel to the ramp. As the angle increases, the force increases, and so must the acceleration ($F = ma$).

Place a 2 meter section of grooved molding on a table, raise one end 5°, place the ball in the groove, release and record the time to reach the table top. Increase the angle by increments of 5° and repeat the activity (Figure F). As the angle increases, the component of gravitational force acting on the object increases until the force is equal to that of gravity when the plane is in a vertical position. What are your conclusions concerning angle of elevation and acceleration of the ball?

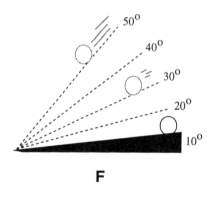

F

Part 2. Freely falling objects: Station a person at the top and bottom of a high wall, preferably two stories or higher. The person at the top should release a golf ball and a basketball at the same time, and the person at the bottom should determine if they strike the ground at the same or different times (Figure G). Repeat with pairs of different balls including steel balls, marbles, golf balls, tennis balls, basketballs, baseballs, and Styrofoam balls. Galileo said that, in the absence of air friction, all objects fall at the same rate. Discounting minor differences that may result from air friction, do your results support Galileo's conclusions? Why did the Styrofoam ball strike the ground after the other objects?

Activities such as you investigated in this section, when carried out in a quantitative manner, show the following relationships between linear acceleration, velocity, time, and distance when acceleration is constant:

G

Velocity equals acceleration multiplied by time:

$$v = at$$

Distance equals one-half acceleration multiplied by the square of the time:

$$d = \tfrac{1}{2}at^2$$

Velocity equals the square root of two times acceleration times distance:

$$v = \sqrt{2ad}$$

If the objects are freely falling bodies, substitute g, the acceleration of gravity, for a:

$$v = gt;\ d = \tfrac{1}{2}gt^2;\ v = \sqrt{2gd}$$

Questions

(1) The acceleration of the ball increased as the angle of the incline increased. Explain.

(2) When you dropped objects from the same height, all but the Styrofoam ball hit the floor at approximately the same time. Explain.

(3) A car travels 300 km in 5 h. What was the average speed of the car?

(4) Starting from rest, a ball rolls down an incline at a constant acceleration of 2.0 m/s². What is the velocity of the ball after 10 seconds? What distance does the ball roll in 10 seconds?

(5) An object is projected vertically upward with a velocity of 80 m/s. To what height will it rise? What time will be required for the ascent? What will be the total elapsed time before it strikes the ground?

2.3.2 Accelerometer

Concepts to Investigate: Acceleration, centripetal acceleration, accelerometer.

Materials: Large glass container (gallon jug, quart jar, wide-mouth jar, etc.), lid or screw cap, gasket to fit lid, cork, string.

Principles and Procedures: An accelerometer is a device for measuring acceleration. Follow these instructions to construct a simple accelerometer as shown in Figure H. Cut the string to a length slightly less than the height of the container. Remove the cardboard gasket from the lid of a jar and punch a small hole in the center. Pass one end of the string through the hole in the gasket and secure with a knot. Replace the gasket in the cap. Use a tack to secure the other end of the string to the cork. Fill the container with water. Screw the cap on the container and invert. The cork should float at the end of the string just below the bottom of the container.

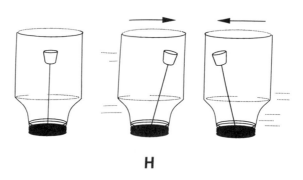

H

Hold the container securely and move it quickly to one side, noting the direction the cork moves relative to the container. Move the container quickly in the opposite direction and note the cork's direction. Hold the container at arm's length in front of you and then rotate your body in a circle. Note the cork's direction.

The behavior of the cork seems odd to most people. We expect the cork to experience "whiplash" the way we might in a rapidly accelerating car, but instead it lunges forward. If suspended in air, the cork would experience whiplash, but water is denser than the cork, and therefore has greater inertia. When the water experiences "whiplash," it forces the cork out of its way, giving the appearance that the cork is lunging ahead in the direction of acceleration (Figure H).

The cork moves in the direction of acceleration. When the jar is accelerated to the left, the inertia of the water makes the water pressure on the right side of the cork higher than on the left side, causing the cork to move to the left. In circular motion the cork moves toward the center of the circle for the same reason. The inertia of the water is greater than the inertia of the cork, and therefore it tends to collect on the side of the jar away from you. The water displaces the cork back toward the center of rotation. The string's angle with a vertical line from the center of the cap of the container indicates the magnitude of the acceleration. While holding the jar securely, move it in a circle so that the angle is 45°. Under such conditions, the cork experiences 1 *g*.

Acceleration may also be measured using the device illustrated in Figure I. When the pole is swung in a horizontal circle above your head, the magnitude of the centripetal acceleration is equal to the acceleration of gravity multiplied by the tangent of the angle: $a = g \tan \theta$. At 45° the magnitude of centripetal acceleration is equal to the acceleration due to gravity: $a = g \tan (45°) = g$. One student should carefully swing the pole at a rate such that the angle is 45°. How many revolutions per minute produces a centripetal acceleration of 1 g? At NASA's training centers, astronauts experience the sensation of 8 g's when placed in rotating chambers. How fast must such chambers rotate to produce such centripetal acceleration? Can you produce 8 g's using your accelerometer device? Use the acclerometer on an amusement park ride to determine the maximum accelerations encountered.

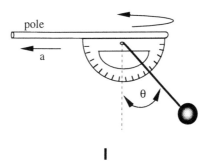

I

Questions

(1) What is an accelerometer and what is its purpose?
(2) When the jar was moved to the left, the cork moved to the left. Explain.
(3) Motion in a curved path with constant speed is accelerated motion. Explain.
(4) Why does the accelerometer point to the center when rotated at a constant rate?

2.3.3 Centripetal Acceleration
(Motion in a Horizontal Circle)

Concepts to Investigate: Centripetal force, centripetal acceleration, *g*'s.

Materials: Piece of glass or plastic tubing, collection of metal washers, one-hole rubber stopper, nylon fishing line or strong string, paper clips.

Principles and Procedures: An object accelerates if its velocity changes. Because velocity is a vector quantity, acceleration occurs whenever the speed *or* direction of an object change. Thus, your car accelerates as it speeds up from a stop light, or when it turns a corner. In a similar manner, the Earth is constantly accelerating as it orbits the sun because its direction is constantly changing. The acceleration of a turning or orbiting object is known as centripetal acceleration, and the force responsible for this acceleration is known as centripetal force.

You can use the swinging stopper apparatus (Figure J) to verify that the centripetal acceleration is equal to the square of the velocity of the cork in its circular path divided by the radius of the circle: $a = v^2/r$. Since *a* is constant for an object rotating at constant speed, the ratio of v^2 to *r* should be constant for given rates of rotation and associated values of *r*.

J

© 1994 by John Wiley & Sons, Inc.

Cut a piece of glass tubing about 15 cm in length. Heat one end in a Bunsen burner flame until the walls of the tube are smoothly rounded. Hang one end of a one-meter section of fishing line to a two-holed rubber stopper and thread the other end through the tube. Tie approximately 50 grams of metal washers from the line as shown. These washers provide the centripetal force that is exerted through the line to keep the stopper rotating in a circle. The magnitude of the centripetal force can be calculated by multiplying the mass tied to the line by the acceleration due to gravity: $F_c = mg$.

Using a stopwatch or other timing device, swing the stopper at a constant rate. Be certain to adjust the line so the distance from the top of the tube to the stopper is equal to the chosen radius, and attach a paper clip to the line above the weights to use as an indicator to check that the circular motion is steady. If the clip remains stationary, the radius and speed of rotation are constant. The velocity *v* can be computed by dividing the circumference of the circle by the period of rotation: $v = (2\pi r)/T$, where r is radius and T is the time required for a rotation. It is easiest to determine the period of rotation by measuring the time required for ten rotations and then dividing by ten. Calculate the centripetal acceleration acting upon the stopper. Repeat, using a larger radius. Does the speed of the cork change as the radius changes? Does acceleration change as the radius changes?

Radius r	Circumference $2\pi r$	Period T	Velocity v	Centripetal Acceleration (v^2/r)
_____ m	_____ m	_____ s	_____ m/s	_____ m/s²
_____ m	_____ m	_____ s	_____ m/s	_____ m/s²
_____ m	_____ m	_____ s	_____ m/s	_____ m/s²
_____ m	_____ m	_____ s	_____ m/s	_____ m/s²
_____ m	_____ m	_____ s	_____ m/s	_____ m/s²

Questions

(1) Why is an unbalanced force required to produce circular motion?

(2) In the above activity the ratio of squared velocity to radius was a constant. In other words, the centripetal acceleration did not change as the radius changed. Explain.

(3) A rubber stopper of mass 0.014 kg is swung at the end of a string 0.95 m long with a period of 0.75 s. Compute the centripetal force exerted on the stopper.

(4) The moon revolves about the Earth in a trajectory that is very nearly a circle of radius $r = 384{,}401$ km (239,000 miles) or 12.6×10^8 feet, and requires 27.3 days (23.4×10^5 seconds) to make a complete revolution. What is the acceleration of the moon toward the Earth?

(5) In an amusement-park ride called the spinout, riders are positioned against the inside wall of a rotating drum. The drum begins to rotate and after a certain rotational speed is reached, the floor is lowered and the riders remain in position and do not fall. The diameter of the chamber is 4.3 meters and the period of rotation is 1.7 seconds. What is the centripetal acceleration of the rider? Approximately how many g's does the rider experience?

2.3.4 Centripetal Acceleration
(Motion in A Vertical Circle)

Concepts to Investigate: Motion in a vertical circle, weightlessness.

Materials: Strong string, strong rope, block of wood, bucket with strong handle, spring balance.

Principles and Procedures: Gravity has no effect on the tangential velocity of an object revolving in a horizontal circle. If you rotate the object in a vertical circle, however, gravity acts to accelerate the object when it moves downward and to decelerate the object when it moves upward, which means that the velocity of the object in its circular path is not constant. The velocity of the object is a minimum at the top of the circle and a maximum at the bottom.

Attach a rope securely to a block of wood or other heavy object. Rotate the block in a vertical circle at various rates and note the force of the rope acting on your hand. When is the force greatest? When is it least?

Using a less massive object, tie a spring balance in line and record the average force at the top and bottom of the rotation. Where is acceleration the greatest? Practice rotating the object until the scale registers no force. Describe the conditions necessary to achieve this situation of "weightlessness." The critical velocity is the velocity below which an object moving in a vertical circle will no longer move in a circular path. The critical velocity can be calculated as $\sqrt{rg}$, where r is the radius and g is the acceleration due to gravity.

Pour water into the bucket until about half full. Grip the bucket's handle firmly with one hand and swing the bucket rapidly in a vertical circle. The water remains in the bucket. Slow your rotation of the bucket and the water begins to drop from the bucket on your head. At this point you have dropped below the critical velocity.

Questions

(1) Gravity affects the motion of an object moving in a vertical circle but does not affect the tangential velocity of an object moving in a horizontal circle. Explain.

(2) A rope is tied to a pail of water and the pail is swung in a vertical circle of radius 1.3 m. What must be the minimum velocity of the pail at the highest point of the circle if no water is to spill?

(3) Explain how "critical velocity" could be used in developing an amusement-park ride.

(4) In a roller-coaster ride called the revolution, the car moves from a high point on the track to the bottom and then moves upward in a circular path that, at the highest point, has the riders in an inverted position. We can refer to this ride as "looping the loop." If the height of the top of the loop is 16.2 meters, what would be the required speed of the car to keep it and the rider on the track assuming the car did not have any mechanical devices holding it to the track or restraining devices holding the passengers inside the car?

2.3.5 Acceleration Greater than Gravity

Concepts to Investigate: Center of mass, acceleration due to gravity.

Materials: Two boards each about 1m long and 8 cm wide, marble, small plastic or paper cup, hinge, drill, nail, small screws to fit holes in hinge, screwdriver.

Principles and Procedures: In the town of Pisa, Italy, stands a world-famous eight-century old landmark known as the Leaning Tower of Pisa. The top of this cathedral bell tower is inclined 5 meters (16 ft) from the perpendicular, giving the appearance that the tower is ready to fall. Galileo is said to have conducted his experiments on gravity from the top of this tower and discovered the principle that, in the absence of wind resistance, all objects fall to the ground with the same acceleration. Although Galileo's findings have been verified repeatedly, the device that you will make in this activity appears to contradict Galileo's principle.

The gadget shown in Figure K is easily constructed. Place one side of the hinge on one board, mark the position of holes with a pencil, drill small holes or punch with a nail, and attach the hinge with screws. Attach hinge to the second board in the same manner. Use the screwdriver to gouge a small rounded depression deep enough to hold a marble or small ball in place when the board is elevated at 30°. Use scissors to trim a paper cup so it is only 4 cm high. Attach the cup approximately 5 cm away from the ball on the side of the hinge. Use a pencil or short stick to hold the top board in position after it is raised. Quickly jerk the stick from between the boards. Keep practicing until the ball consistently lands in the cup. For the ball to land in the cup, it is necessary that the board (and cup) be accelerating faster than the ball. How can this be?

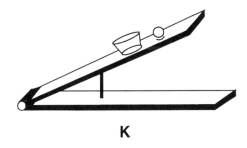

K

Questions

(1) Disregarding friction of air, all objects fall toward the Earth with the same acceleration. Explain.

(2) The marble fell into the cup, which means the acceleration of the cup was greater than the marble. Explain.

2.3.6 Projectile and Target

Concepts to Investigate: Parabolic trajectories, influence of gravity upon projectile motion.

Materials: Large piece of wood with smooth surface, saw, double-sided tape, two large steel balls, plastic or wood corner molding or other suitable *v*-shaped material, small rectangular piece of wood or plastic.

Principles and Procedures: Objects such as an arrow shot from a bow, a baseball tossed by a player from third to second base, a shell fired from a gun, or a sky diver jumping from an aircraft are called projectiles. Any object that is given an initial velocity and that subsequently follows a path determined by the gravitational and frictional forces acting on it is called a projectile. A projectile fired from the Earth's surface, if air friction is neglected, follows a trajectory (path) called a parabola. The "gun and target" demonstration that follows is useful in examining projectile motion.

In the usual demonstration, a gun is pointed directly at a target as shown in Figure L. At the instant the projectile leaves the gun, the target starts to fall. Neglecting air friction for any angle of elevation of the gun, any initial velocity of the projectile (assuming the velocity is great enough to reach the target), and any distance to the target, the projectile will always hit the target. Sound intriguing? In this activity you will "launch" a projectile and drop a target simultaneously. The ramp apparatus shown in Figure M will proportionally decrease the effect of gravity on the projectile and target (two balls) and consequently the speed of each, making the simultaneous release of the balls and examination of their trajectories easier.

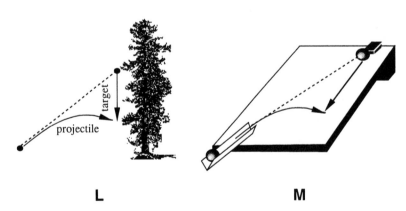

L   **M**

Obtain a piece of wood about 1.5 cm thick with a smooth surface, and use a saw to cut a piece about 25 cm by 30 cm. Tape a 5-cm rectangular piece of wood to the upper right corner to act as a release for the "target" ball. Cut an 8-cm-long piece of plastic or wood corner molding (*v*-shaped) to serve as the "gun" and tape it so that it is "aimed" directly at the other ball as shown in Figure M.

Use a 3-cm block of wood to elevate one end of the board. Use your left hand to hold one ball in the *v*-shaped groove and your right hand to hold one ball just below the small piece of wood. Make certain the groove is pointed directly at the tar-

© 1994 by John Wiley & Sons, Inc.

get ball. Propel the ball from the groove at different velocities while simultaneously releasing the other ball. The balls should collide. Reposition the small piece of wood slightly to the left, realign the groove so it points at the target ball, and again launch both balls. They should collide. Practice until you always hit the target, regardless of the angle of trajectory, angle of the board, velocity of the projectile, or distance. Why do we get such results?

Questions

(1) The greater the elevation of the board, the more difficult it is to coordinate the launching of the balls. Explain.

(2) If you were careful to simultaneously launch the balls, they collided regardless of the launch velocity, the angle of elevation, or the distance to the target. Explain.

FOR THE TEACHER

Speed is not a difficult concept for students to understand, but velocity (speed in a given direction) and acceleration (time rate of change of velocity) often are. You will have to spend time explaining how vectors are used to represent velocity and acceleration, and how they can be added to produce resultants. Since velocity is a vector quantity, it may change as a result of a change of magnitude (speed), a change in direction, or both. Acceleration is the time rate of change of velocity. Make certain students understand that an object moving at constant speed in a curved path is experiencing centripetal acceleration as a result of its constantly changing direction. An acceleration timer can be purchased at minimal cost from most scientific supply houses to provide quantitative results in determining velocity and acceleration. The timer works like a clock and produces precisely 60 dots per second on a paper strip that is attached to a moving object. Students can measure the intervals between the dots and calculate accurate values for velocity and acceleration. Make certain students are aware of the wide range of possible speeds in their environment. The speed of light is about 300,000 km/s (186,000 miles per second) while the speed of the common garden snail is 0.000014 km/s (0.0000087 miles/s).

Your students can experience some exciting and unique methods of being accelerated if you take them on a field trip to a carnival or amusement park. Since there is a great deal of physics involved in these rides, students can have fun and learn important science concepts at the same time. Students can construct and carry accelerometers on various rides and measure linear and centripetal accelerations. Centripetal forces exerted on riders can be determined, such as those exerted on riders positioned against the inside wall of a spinning cylinder (drum) in which the supporting floor is lowered once the riders are "sticking" to the wall.

2.3.1 Acceleration Due to Gravity

Discussion: The inclined plane (molding) slows acceleration so students can see that the objects rolling down the incline increase their velocity (accelerate) over time. If molding is unavailable, you may substitute rulers with grooves, but the results will be more difficult to observe because the distances traveled will be shorter. The accelerometers introduced in the next section provide more quantitative observations of acceleration. If you wish students to obtain some accurate quantitative results on motion and acceleration, use acceleration timers available from scientific supply companies.

Answers (1) When the plane is horizontal (Figure N) the normal force F_n counters the gravitational force F_w. When the ball is placed on an incline (Figure O), these vectors no longer cancel. As shown by Figures P and Q, the vector sum creates a force F that increases as the angle increases. (2) As the mass of an object increases, the force of gravity also increases proportionally, imparting the same acceleration to all objects. For the Styrofoam ball, however, air friction is significant because it has a high surface area to mass ratio. Thus, the force of friction, which depends upon surface area, is relatively high, while the force of gravity, which depends upon mass, is relatively

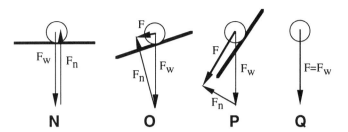

N   **O**   **P**   **Q**

low. (3) $v = d/t = 300$ km$/5$ h $= 60$ km/h. (4) $v = at = 2.0$ m/s$^2 \times 10$ s $= 20$ m/s. d $= \frac{1}{2}$ $at^2 = \frac{1}{2} \times 2.0$ m/s$^2 \times (10$ s$)^2 = 100$ m. (5) Since $v = \sqrt{2ad}$, $v^2 = 2ad$, and $d = v^2/2a = (80$ m/s$)^2/(2 \times 9.8$ m/s$^2) = 327$ m. Since $v = gt$, $t = v/g = (80$m/s$)/(9.8$ m/s$^2)= 8.2$ s. Total time elapsed = time up + time down = 8.2 s + 8.2 s = 16.4 s.

2.3.2 Accelerometer

Discussion: You may wish to have your students construct a simple device for measuring vertical accelerations using a spring scale calibrated from 0 to 5 N from which a mass m of 100 grams is attached (Figure R). According to Newton's second law, the reading of the scale F should equal the force due to gravity mg plus the vertical forces ma: $F = mg + ma$. In upward motions, the scale reading equals the weight of the object when a is zero, exceeds it when a is positive, and is less when a is negative (scale is decelerating). The vertical acceleration a of the mass and, consequently the person holding the scale, can be computed using the reading of the scale: $a = F/m - g$. You may request your students measure the acceleration of a rapidly accelerating elevator using such a device (Figure R). Students can use the accelerometers described to measure the vertical and centripetal (radial) accelerations exerted on them when they visit an amusement park and experience some of the rides.

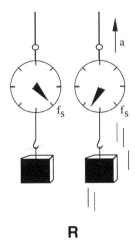

R

Answers (1) An accelerometer is a mechanical or electromechanical instrument that measures the components of linear or centripetal acceleration. (2) When the jar is accelerated to the left, the water appears to move to the right due to inertia. This water displaces the cork, pushing it to the left. (3) Although the speed of the object along the curved path is constant, the velocity is not. Centripetal force produces centripetal acceleration, which continuously changes the direction of the object. (4) A rotating object is constantly accelerating toward the center of rotation.

2.3.3 Centripetal Acceleration (Motion in a Horizontal Circle)

Discussion: The centripetal force exerted by the hanging weight should equal the product of the mass of the stopper and its centripetal acceleration: $F_c = ma_c$. This force is provided by the hanging weights. You may wish to have your students confirm that the centripetal acceleration calculated as the product of the mass of these weights times g is equal to the centripetal force calculated as the product of the centripetal acceleration times the mass of the stopper.

Encourage students to minimize frictional forces by beveling the edge of the tube. To obtain good results, timing must be accurate. Small discrepancies in measuring the velocity of the stopper will be compounded in calculating centripetal acceleration because the velocity term is squared. Students should practice rotating the stopper and timing it before actually taking measurements.

Answers (1) There must be an unbalanced force because it is this force that produces the acceleration keeping the object moving in a curved path. If forces are balanced, there can be no acceleration. (2) The hanging washers provide a constant centripetal force. Since the mass of the stopper remains constant, as the radius increases the velocity must increase such that the ratio v^2/r remains constant. $F_{constant}/m_{constant} = a_{constant} = (v^2/r)_{constant}$ (3) The velocity of the stopper is $v = (2\pi r)/T$, where r is radius and T is period: $v = (2 \times 3.14 \times 0.95 \text{ m})/0.75 \text{ s} = 8.0 \text{ m/s}$. $F_c = mv^2/r$ $= (0.014 \text{ kg} \times (8.0 \text{ m/s})^2)/0.95 \text{ m} = 0.94 \text{ N}$. (4) T of 27.3 days $= 2.36 \times 10^6$ s. $v = 2\pi r/T$. $V = 2 \times 3.14 \times 385,000 \text{ km}/2.36 \times 10^6 \text{ s} = 1.025 \text{ km/s} = 1025 \text{ m/s}$. $a = v^2/r = (1.025 \text{ m/s})^2/3.85 \times 10^8 \text{ m} = 0.00273 \text{ m/s}^2$ (5) $v = 2\pi r/T$, where r is radius and T is period: $v = 2 \times 3.14 \times 2.15$ m. $a_c = v^2/r = (2\pi r/T)^2/r = 4\pi^2 r^2/T^2 r = 4\pi^2 r/T^2 = (4 \times (3.13)^2 \times (2.15 \text{ m}))/(1.7 \text{ s})^2 = 29.3 \text{ m/s}^2$. $(29.3 \text{ m/s}^2)/(9.8 \text{ m/s}^2) =$ approximately 3 "g"s.

2.3.4 Centripetal Acceleration: (Motion in a Vertical Circle)

Discussion: Motion in a vertical circle in which gravity acts on the object is useful in explaining important phenomena. Consequently, we present here a concise description of such motion which you may wish to pass on to your students.

Figure S shows an object attached to the end of a piece of string of length r moving in a vertical circle about a fixed point O. The motion of the object is circular, but not constant, because gravity acts to increase the speed downward and to decrease the speed upward. The speed of the object is minimum at the top of the circle and maximum at the bottom. The forces acting on the object are its weight mg and the tension T in the string. Resolve the weight into a normal component of magnitude

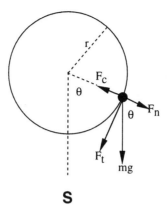

S

$mg \cos \theta$, and a tangential component of magnitude $mg \sin \theta$. The tangential force is, $F_t = mg \sin \theta$. The normal force is $F_n = T - mg \cos \theta$. From Newton's second law, the tangential acceleration is

$$a_t = \frac{F_t}{m} = g \sin \theta$$

The radial (normal) acceleration, $a_n = v^2/r$, is

$$a_n = \frac{F_n}{m} = \frac{T - mg \cos \theta}{m} = \frac{v^2}{r}$$

The tension in the cord is therefore

$$T = m(\frac{v^2}{r} + g \cos \theta)$$

At the lowest point of the circle, $\theta = 0°$, $\sin \theta = 0$, and $\cos \theta = 1$. There is no tangential acceleration, only radial acceleration. The magnitude of the tension is:

$$T = m(\frac{v^2}{r} + g)$$

Rearranging, we get: $mv^2/r = T - mg$ or centripetal force = tension - weight of object.
At the highest point in the circle, $\theta = 180°$, $\sin \theta = 0$, and $\cos \theta = -1$. There is no tangential acceleration, only radial acceleration. The magnitude of the tension is

$$T = m(\frac{v^2}{r} - g)$$

Rearranging we get: $mv^2/r = T + mg$ or centripetal force = tension + weight of object. When an object moves in a vertical circle, there is a certain velocity below which the object will not follow a circular path (the string becomes slack). This critical velocity can be determined by setting the tension T equal to zero at the highest point of the circle:

$$0 = m(\frac{v_c^2}{r} - g)$$

$$v_c = \sqrt{rg}$$

Note that critical velocity depends only on the acceleration of gravity and the radius of the vertical circle. Critical velocity does not depend on the mass of the object describing the motion.

Answers (1) When an object swings in a horizontal circle, gravity acts perpendicular to the direction of motion and has no effect. However, gravity acts in the direction of motion of a vertically swinging object, accelerating the object in its downward path and decelerating the object in its upward path. (2) v_c = critical velocity = $\sqrt{rg}$ = $\sqrt{1.3 \text{ m} \times 9.8 \text{ m/s}^2}$ = about 3.6 m/s. (3) Critical velocity would be involved in any ride that becomes inverted, such as a roller coaster that moves down an incline and then into a vertical loop. It is important to make sure your customers don't fall out. (4) The radius of the loop is 16.2 m/2 = 8.1 m. Critical velocity $v_c = \sqrt{8.1 \text{ m} \times 9.8 \text{ m/s}^2}$ = about 9 m/s.

2.3.5 Acceleration Greater than Gravity

Discussion: This activity is an excellent discrepant event since students generally expect the cup to fall at the same rate as the ball. When the ball lands in the cup, they are often quite surprised because such results seem to contradict Galileo's principles. All objects have a center of mass, and gravity acts on the center of mass to accelerate the object. The center of mass of the marble is at the center of the marble. The center of mass of the falling board is at the center of the board. Consequently, every point on the board beyond the center of mass, including the cup, will experience an acceleration greater than that of gravity, while every point on the hinge side of the center of mass will experience an acceleration less than that of gravity. Since the acceleration of the cup is greater than 9.8 m/s², while that of the free-falling ball is 9.8 m/s², the cup lands before the ball, allowing the ball to fall into it.

Answers: (1) The force gravity exerts on objects is proportional to their masses. As the mass increases, the force of gravity increases proportionally, imparting the same acceleration to each mass. (2) The center of mass of the marble and the center of mass of the board both experience the same acceleration. However, because the board is hinged, the acceleration of the free end on which the cup is attached must exceed g.

2.3.6 Projectile and Target

Discussion: The fact that the two balls collide is a discrepant event for many students. A simple method of understanding is to assume there is no acceleration due to gravity. Then the target ball would not fall and the propelled ball would move along the line of sight directly into the target ball. The effect of gravity is to cause each ball to accelerate down at the same rate from the position it would otherwise have had (see Figure T). Therefore, in a given amount of time t the projected ball will fall a distance $(1/2)gt^2$ from the position it would have had along the line of sight, and the target ball will fall the same distance from its starting position.

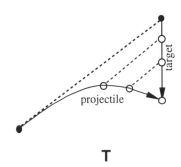

projectile

T

The following is a more rigorous treatment of the relations describing the motion of a projectile that you can pass on to your students who may be interested. A projectile such as a shell shot from a gun has an initial velocity and follows a path determined by the gravitational force acting on it and the frictional resistance of the atmosphere. Suppose a cannon is aimed at an angle θ to the horizontal. The upward velocity of the cannon ball decreases (the ball decelerates) under the influence of gravity. The velocity of the ball in the horizontal direction is constant if we neglect the frictional force of the atmosphere. The path (trajectory) traced by a projectile that accelerates only in the vertical direction while moving at a constant horizontal velocity is a parabola, as we shall show. Let x indicate the horizontal direction, y the vertical direction, and v_o the initial velocity of the projectile. We assume the velocity in the horizontal direction is constant and $v_{xo} = v_x$. The horizontal velocity is therefore $v_{xo} = v_o \cos \theta$. The initial velocity in the vertical direction is $v_{yo} = v_o \sin \theta$. Since the vertical acceleration is "$-g$," the vertical velocity after time t is $v_y = v_{yo} \sin \theta - gt$. The x (horizontal) position of the ball is given by $x = t v_o \cos \theta$, and the y (vertical) position is given by $y = t v_{yo} - 1/2\, gt^2$. The preceding two equations are parametric equations for a parabola and give the equation of the trajectory in terms of the parameter t. We can eliminate t and give the equation in terms of x and y:

$$y = (tan\ \theta_o)x - \frac{g}{2v_o^2 cos^2\theta}\, x^2$$

Because v_o, $\cos \theta_o$, $\tan \theta_o$, and g are constants, the equation can be written as $Y = c_1 x - c_2 x^2$, which is the equation for a parabola.

The "gun-and-target" demonstration is useful in clarifying the applications of these equations. In the demonstration, a gun is pointed directly at a target. At the instant the projectile leaves the gun, the target starts to fall, as shown earlier in Figure L. Neglecting air friction, for any angle of elevation of the gun, any initial velocity (assuming it is great enough to reach the target) of the projectile, and any distance to the target, the projectile will always hit the target. It seems unlikely, but the analysis to confirm the collision is not complicated. The angle θ_o is the angle of departure of the projectile. Since $tan\theta_o = y/x$, $y = x(tan\ \theta_o)$. The initial elevation of the target is thus $x(tan\ \theta_o)$. In time t the target falls a distance of $1/2gt^2$. Upon collision its elevation is $y = x(tan\ \theta_o) - 1/2gt^2$. But in the same time t, the elevation of the projectile is also $x(tan\ \theta_0)\ -1/2\ gt^2$, which can easily be determined by substituting $(tv_0\ cos\ \theta_0)^2$ for x^2 in the equation for y above. Actually, if the frictional force of air on the projectile is considered, the vertical and horizontal components would not be independent and the projectile would probably not hit the target.

Answers (1) As the elevation of the board increases, so too does the acceleration of the balls. The balls move more slowly at lower elevations and give you more time to coordinate the "drop" and "launch" of the balls. (2) Because gravity accelerates both balls equally, their movement due to gravity can be neglected. If the "gun" were aimed directly at the target, both balls would collide just as if there were no gravity acting.

Applications to Everyday Life

Speed of Things: Compare and contrast the following speeds: the speed of light is about 1,080,000,000 km/h (669,600,000 miles per hour); Earth's average speed in orbit around the Sun is about 107,000 km/h (66,600 mi/h); speed of artificial satellite in orbit around Earth is approximately 29,000 km/h (18,000 mi/h); speed of moon in orbit is approximately 3,690 km/h (2290 mi/h); the Concord supersonic transport jet cruises at a speed of approximately 2,230 km/h (1,450 mi/h); speed of sound in air at a temperature of 20°C is about 1,200 km/h (746 mi/h); speed of peregrine falcon, fastest creature on the wing, reaches 350 km/h (220 mi/h) when stooping; speed of ball in Jai Alai, said to be the fastest of all ball games, reaches 310 km/h (190 mi/h); speed record for single-rider bicycle is about 105 km/h (65 mi/h); fastest land animal is the cheetah, which can run 105 km/h (65 mi/h); tropical cockroaches, the fastest moving insects, move at 4.7 km/h (2.9 mi/h); the three-toed sloth moves 0.16 km/h (0.098 mi/h); common garden snail moves 0.05 km/h (0.03 mi/h).

Weightlessness: Sky divers or parachutists experience free fall before their chutes open. As they fall, the frictional force of air continues to increase until it equals the force of gravity, at which point there is no further acceleration. A falling body reaches a terminal velocity of 180 to 250 km/h (110 to 155 mi/h), depending on its orientation. Free fall is motion determined solely by gravitational forces and occurs, not only when an object is dropped, but also when an object is in space, despite the fact that it may not actually be falling toward any celestial body. Your weight is defined as the force you exert against the supporting floor—you are as heavy as you feel. In an elevator accelerating downward, the supporting force of the floor on you is less and, hence, you weigh less. If the elevator is in free fall, the floor provides no support and your apparent weight is zero. Astronauts experience a similar sensation in orbit as they would in an elevator that is in a state of free fall. Although astronauts in orbit are in a weightless environment, they are still under the influence of gravitational force that constantly changes their direction to follow the closed orbital trajectory. True weightlessness could be achieved only if the astronauts were in deep space away from the gravitational attractions of celestial bodies.

Drag Racing: Drag racing has become an increasingly popular sport. It is an acceleration event in which vehicles compete on a short track of about 0.4 km (0.25 miles) to determine which can achieve the greatest acceleration and hence the greatest speed at the end of the track. In the fastest classification of dragsters, parachutes are required to stop the vehicles, which can reach maximum speeds approaching 400 km/h (250 mi/h).

Accelerometer: An accelerometer is a mechanical or electromechanical instrument that measures both translational and angular acceleration. Accelerometers are used to measure acceleration of industrial machinery, vehicles, and seismic phenomena such as earthquakes.

Wind Patterns and Ocean Currents: The Coriolis effect describes the circular motion of fluids (ocean currents, winds, water going down a drain) moving in a rotating system such as the Earth. The Coriolis effect arises because of the acceleration inherent in the moving reference system. The motion of a water northward along the Earth's surface in the Northern Hemisphere reduces the distance of the water from the Earth's axis, increasing its angular velocity, and forcing the water to move eastward. As a result, ocean currents in the Northern Hemisphere move in a clockwise direction, while those in the Southern Hemisphere move in a counterclockwise direction.

Amusement-Park Rides: An amusement park is a great place to safely experience linear and centripetal acceleration. The popular octopus and tilt-a -whirl provide both linear and centripetal accelerations. A ride called free fall allows riders to fall freely for a vertical distance before turning in a sharp curve to move horizontally with the ground and coming to rapid halt. In a ride called the evolution, a train quickly descends a track and then moves through a vertical loop. In a ride called spinout, passengers stand against the inside wall of a large rotating drum, and after the drum reaches maximum rotational speed the floor is lowered and passengers remain in place against the wall due to centripetal force.

Satellites: A satellite, such as the space shuttle or a communications satellite, is a projectile in a constant state of free fall, falling around the Earth rather than vertically into it. Other Earth satellites, such as our moon, also fall around the Earth rather than into it. (The satellite does not move closer to the Earth in terms of the common definition of falling.) The speed of a satellite must be great enough to ensure that the horizontal distance it travels compensates for the vertical distance it falls. A speed of 29,000 km/h or 18,000 miles/h is required for a satellite to orbit the Earth and follow its curvature. As the altitude of the satellite increases, its velocity decreases and the period required to circle the Earth increases. A satellite that has a period of 24 hours, which is the same as the period of rotation of the Earth, is called a geosynchronous satellite.

Space stations: It is conceivable that in the future people may be living in space stations such as those depicted in movies. In order to provide a sense of gravity these stations must rotate on their axes. Since centripetal force and centripetal acceleration vary as a function of distance from the axis, there will be an appropriate radius at which point the centripetal acceleration caused by the rotation may be the same as the acceleration of gravity on Earth and the people will feel as if they were on the Earth's surface.

2.4 PERIODIC MOTION

A pendulum is a body suspended from a fixed point such that it is free to swing (vibrate) in a vertical plane under the influence of gravity. The word *pendulum* comes from the Latin word "pendulus," which means "hanging." Important types of pendulums are physical pendulums, simple pendulums, and Foucault pendulums. Pendulums are used to keep time, to measure the acceleration of gravity, and even to show that the Earth spins on its axis. The longest-running timepiece is the pendulum clock on the Salisbury Cathedral in Wiltshire in the United Kingdom. The Salisbury clock ticked more than 500 million times for nearly 500 years before it was restored in 1956.

A simple pendulum consists of a mass called the bob supported by a wire or thread (Figure A). When the bob is held to one side and then released, the pendulum exhibits periodic motion. *Periodic motion is one in which the motion of a body is repeated in each of a succession of equal time intervals.* The vibrations of strings on a guitar, the vibrations of air columns in the pipes of an organ, the oscillation of a suspended mass on a spring, and even the regular vibrations of bridges and buildings illustrate periodic motion. In this section we will focus on pendular motion as an example of periodic motion.

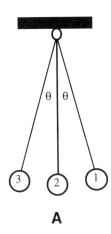

A

2.4.1 Simple Pendulums

Concepts to Investigate: Amplitude, frequency, period, periodic motion, factors affecting simple pendulums.

Materials: Strong thread or monofilament fishing line, collection of large metal washers of the same size, support for pendulum, meter stick or measuring tape, stopwatch or watch with a second hand.

Principles and Procedures: What factors influence the swing of a simple pendulum? Inspection of a pendulum suggests that the mass of the bob and the length of the string might affect the swing. Before you investigate these possibilities, we must define a few terms. Inspect Figure A. The rest point of a pendulum (position 2) is the lowest point in the swing and is located directly below the point of support. The amplitude of a pendulum is the angle of displacement of the bob from its rest point, shown in Figure A as theta (q). The further the pendulum is pulled back from its rest point the greater the amplitude. The period of a pendulum is the time required to complete one cycle, from position 1 to position 3 and back to position 1. The frequency of a pendulum is the number of cycles completed per second. You can see that period and frequency are related. If a pendulum completes two cycles in one second its frequency is 2 cycles/s and its period is 1/2 s. The period is the reciprocal of the frequency: $T = 1/f$.

Attach a plank of wood to the top step of a stepladder or other support with a clamp or strong tape so the plank extends over free space. Attach an eye hook to the piece of wood. Thread the line through the hook. At the other end of the line, attach a large hook on which you will hang the washers one at a time. Now you are ready to investigate the possible effects of mass and length on the period of a pendulum. Why is it important to change only one factor (variable) at a time and not both when you do this?

Place one washer on the hook and adjust the length of the thread through the supporting eye hook until the length from supporting hook to center of washer (measure to center of hole in washer) is 1 meter. Pull back the washer to a position where the angle of displacement, theta, is somewhere between 10 degrees and 15 degrees. In other words, the arc of the swing should be small. If the amplitude is kept small, a simple pendulum executes simple harmonic motion.

Release the washer and simultaneously start the stopwatch. You may want to practice this a few times to perfect the timing. Record the time required for the washer to complete 10 cycles. Divide the time by 10 to determine the period. Add washers, one at a time, and repeat the procedure for up to six washers. It is not necessary to mass the washers. We can assume that the mass of each is the same and we will call this mass *washer*. Record the results in the table. Does the mass of the pendulum affect the period?

Let's see if the length affects the period. Place five washers on the hook. Adjust the string so the length is one meter. Using the procedure described earlier, record the time required for the pendulum to complete 10 cycles. Repeat the procedure using the following lengths: 100 cm, 80 cm, 60 cm, 40 cm, and 20 cm. Record your results in the table. What can you determine about the effect of mass and length on the period of a pendulum?

Mass	Period (seconds)
1 washer	———————
2 washers	———————
3 washers	———————
4 washers	———————
5 washers	———————

Length	Period (seconds)
100 cm	———————
80 cm	———————
60 cm	———————
40 cm	———————
20 cm	———————

Effect of length?
Effect of mass?

Questions

(1) Is the motion of the pendulum periodic? Explain.

(2) Which factors affect the period of a pendulum?

(3) If you sit on a swing (a swing is a pendulum) at rest and pump, you will not be able to get the swing moving. However, if you touch the ground with your feet and give the swing a push, you can then get the swing moving by pumping. Explain.

(4) Pendulum 1 has a mass of 500 g and a length of 64 cm. Pendulum 2 has a mass of 1,000 g and a length of 16 cm. Compare the periods of these pendulums.

2.4.2 Physical Pendulum

Concepts to Investigate: Physical pendulums; comparison of simple and physical pendulums; periods of pendulums.

Materials: Meter stick with small hole as close to one end as possible, nail, support for pendulum.

Principles and Procedures: A rigid pendulum, such as the familiar clock pendulum, is called a physical pendulum. In a physical pendulum, the entire mass can be considered as located at the center of mass of the pendulum. A physical pendulum, like a simple pendulum, executes simple harmonic motion if the amplitude is small. A physical pendulum may have a regular shape, such as the pendulum in a grandfather clock, or an irregular one such as the one illustrated in Figure B. The length of this physical pendulum is the distance d from the pivot point p to the center of mass c. If the cardboard is rotated so the center of mass is moved from below the pivot point, gravity will act on the center of mass to rotate the pendulum. The pendulum will continue to swing back and forth until frictional forces bring it to a stop.

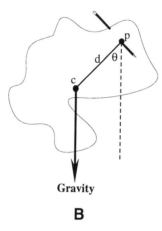

Gravity

B

© 1994 by John Wiley & Sons, Inc.

A meter stick pivoted at one end is a physical pendulum (Figure C). In a physical pendulum, the entire mass can be considered as located at the center of mass of the pendulum. In the case of a meter stick, the center of mass is exactly in the center of the stick at the 50-cm mark. Swing the pendulum on the nail, keeping the amplitude less than 15° as in the previous activity. Pull the stick away from its rest position and use a stopwatch to determine the frequency and period of this pendulum. Compare the period of this physical pendulum to the periods of the simple pendulums in the previous activity. Which of the simple pendulums has a period closest to the physical pendulum? Record this information in the table on the following page. Is the period of a pendulum dependent upon the total length or the length to the center of mass?

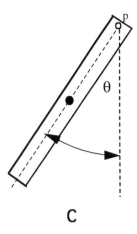

C

Pendulum Type	Period T	Total Length of Pendulum L_1	Length to Center of Mass L_2
Simple	_____ s	_____ cm	_____ cm
Physical	_____ s	_____ cm	_____ cm

Questions

(1) What length of a simple pendulum has the same period as a 1.0-meter physical pendulum (meter stick). Explain.

(2) Will a grandfather clock that is not properly adjusted gain or lose time as its environment grows colder in the winter? Will it gain or lose time during warming summer days? There is an adjustment screw at the bottom of the pendulum that can be turned to effectively lengthen or shorten the pendulum. What adjustment should be made as the days grow colder? Warmer?

2.4.3 Determining the Acceleration of Gravity

Concepts to Investigate: Pendulum equation, calculating *g*.

Materials: Strong thread or monofilament fishing line, collection of large metal washers of the same size, support for pendulum, meter stick or measuring tape, stopwatch or watch with second hand.

Principles and Procedures: When a body accelerates, its velocity (speed) changes over time. For example, if you drop a ball from the top of a tree, gravity pulls on the ball and causes it to move faster and faster toward the ground. Likewise, a sky diver accelerates toward the Earth after jumping from an airplane. If a body has an acceleration of 9.8 meters per second (9.8 m/s^2) this means that its velocity is increasing at the rate of 9.8 meters per second every second. After one second the body would have a velocity of 9.8 m/s, after two seconds a velocity of 19.6 m/s, after three seconds a velocity of 29.4 m/s, and so on.

Gravity is the force that causes the pendulum to accelerate and swing back and forth. We can use a simple pendulum to find the magnitude of the acceleration of gravity because the simple pendulum executes simple harmonic motion. The period of a simple pendulum, when the amplitude is small, is given by the following formula where *T* is the period of the pendulum, *l* is length of the pendulum, and *g* is the acceleration of gravity:

$$T = 2\pi\sqrt{l/g}$$

Notice that there is no term for mass in the formula, indicating that the period is independent of mass. We can use this formula to experimentally determine the acceleration of gravity. Pull the pendulum back 10–15° and release. Measure the time required for the pendulum to swing ten times, and divide by ten to find the average period *T*. Substitute this value and the measured length of the pendulum *L* into the following equation, and solve for *g*:

$$g = \frac{4\pi^2 l}{T^2}$$

Record your results in the table. Repeat with three different lengths, and calculate an average value of *g*. The accepted value for the acceleration due to gravity at the Earth's surface is 9.8 meters per second per second (9.8 m/s^2).

Experimental error may involve errors made by the experimenter or errors resulting from limitations of laboratory equipment. *Absolute error is defined as the difference between the value obtained by experiment and the accepted value.* A more useful quantity is *relative error, which is defined as the absolute error divided by the accepted value, expressed as a percentage.* Relative error expresses the magnitude of the error relative to the accepted value. For example, if the accepted value for gravity is 9.8 m/s^2, and by measurement you obtain a value of 9.9 m/s^2, then the relative error is calculated as follows:

$$\text{relative error} = \frac{(\text{observed-accepted})}{\text{accepted}} \times 100\% = \frac{9.9\text{-}9.8}{9.8} \times 100\% = 1.0\%$$

Calculate the relative errors of your values of g.

Trial	Period T	Length l	Acceleration of gravity g	Accepted g	Relative Error
1	___ s	___ m	___ (m/s^2)	___ 9.8 m/s^2	___ %
2	___ s	___ m	___ (m/s^2)	___ 9.8 m/s^2	___ %
3	___ s	___ m	___ (m/s^2)	___ 9.8 m/s^2	___ %
average	___ s	___ m	___ (m/s^2)	___ 9.8 m/s^2	___ %

Questions

(1) What was your average value for g?

(2) Compare the period of a simple pendulum on Earth with the period of the same pendulum on the moon where the gravity is approximately one sixth that on Earth.

2.4.4 Foucault Pendulum

Concepts to Investigate: Foucault pendulum, rotation of Earth, determination of latitude.

Materials: Ring stand, mass, monofilament fishing line or other string.

Principles and Procedures: Jean Foucault was born in 1819, the son of a French publisher. Foucault was adept at setting up and performing interesting and important physical-science investigations. One of his most intriguing demonstrations used a simple pendulum to demonstrate that the Earth rotates on its axis. Scientists before Foucault's time believed that the Earth rotated on its axis but could not actually demonstrate this rotation.

Foucault's first demonstration of the Earth's rotation was in the cellar of his home. His second demonstration was in the Paris Observatory using a pendulum 36 feet (11 m) in length, and the third, in 1851, was in the Pantheon, a building in Paris, where a 220-foot (67 m) pendulum with a 60-pound (27 kg) metal bob was suspended from the center of the dome in the building.

If you visit the Smithsonian Institution in Washington, D.C., you can see a Foucault pendulum that is about 70 feet (21 m) in length with a bob weighing about 240 pounds (109 kg). Longer pendulums with heavy bobs minimize the problem of air friction. On the floor beneath the pendulum is a large design over which the pendulum swings that shows the movement of the Earth as it rotates. Air resistance (friction) will eventually bring any pendulum to a stop. Consequently, electromagnets and other devices are used to keep those pendulums swinging.

You need not travel to Washington, D.C., to study and understand the operation of a Foucault pendulum. You can do it in your classroom or even at home. Study Figure D, which shows a simple pendulum attached to a clamp that is attached to a ring stand. Suppose we pull the pendulum back from its rest position and release it. The pendulum will swing in an arc. Now suppose we grasp the ring stand at its base and slowly rotate the entire stand in a counterclockwise or clockwise direction. Will the pendulum follow? That is, will the pendulum turn with the ring stand? Try it.

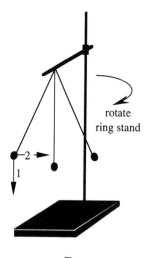

rotate
ring stand

D

The pendulum does not turn with the ring stand, but rather continues to swing in the same plane in which it began swinging. You can watch the base of the ring stand turn under the swinging pendulum. Why does the pendulum continue to swing in the same plane? To answer this question we must understand Newton's first law: *"Every object continues in its state of rest or of uniform motion in a straight line unless compelled to change that state by forces impressed on it."* That is, a body will remain at rest or in motion unless acted upon by external forces. An external force is a force outside the body. Gravity is a force that acts on a pendulum and is external to it, but it cannot force the pendulum to rotate with the ring stand because it acts only in a downward (vertical) direction. This downward force is what causes the pendulum to swing in an arc. Gravity does not act in a sideways (lateral) direction. Consequently, there is no force to push the pendulum in a sideways direction. That is, there is no force to make it rotate. The pendulum continues to swing in a straight line (the same plane) as the base of the ring stand turns under it.

The turning of the base of the ring stand under the swinging pendulum is analogous to the turning of the floor under a Foucault pendulum. The building is attached to the Earth and thus rotates with it. The pendulum is attached to the building but does not rotate with it because there is no external force acting on the pendulum to change its lateral direction. Let's consider three Foucault pendulums at three positions on the Earth's surface (Figure E). One pendulum is located at 90° North latitude (the North Pole), another is at 45° N, and the last is at 0° (on the equator). *The latitude of a location on the Earth's surface is its angular distance from the equator.* In the northern hemisphere the latitudes are North latitudes. In the southern hemisphere the latitudes are South latitudes.

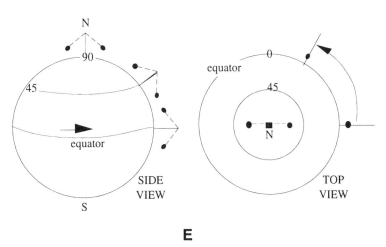

E

At the North Pole the pendulum will appear to turn (twist) 360° after one rotation of the Earth. Since one rotation of the Earth requires 24 hours, the apparent rotation of the pendulum will be 360°/24 h, or 15° per hour. We use the term "apparent rotation" since it is actually the Earth that is rotating, not the pendulum. Because the Earth rotates in a counterclockwise direction when viewed from above the North Pole, the apparent rotation of the pendulum is in a clockwise direction.

The pendulum at the equator will travel eastward along with its point of attachment but there will be no turning motion of the Earth under it. That is, there will be no rotational motion of the Earth under the pendulum (see Figure E).

Consequently, there will be no turning motion of the pendulum under its point of support, and the apparent rotation of the pendulum will be 0° per hour.

What about the pendulum at 45° north? This pendulum will travel eastward as does the pendulum on the equator, but there will also be some rotation of the Earth under the pendulum. How many degrees per hour will the pendulum appear to rotate? The answer to this question is not obvious because there is simultaneous "twisting" and "traveling" of the pendulum. The number of degrees of apparent rotation per hour ($Rot_{(h)}$) is given by the formula:

$$Rot_{(h)} = 15° \times \sin (latitude)$$

Remember that latitude is an angle. Multiplying by 24 gives the apparent rotation in 24 hours or one day ($Rot_{(d)}$):

$$Rot_{(d)} = 15° \times \sin (latitude) \times 24 = \sin (latitude) \times 360°$$

If a Foucault pendulum is located in Anchorage, Alaska (61° N), its apparent rotation in 24 hours will be:

$$Rot_{(d)} = \sin (61°) \times 360° = 0.875 \times 360° = 315°$$

We can use a Foucault pendulum to find the latitude of any place in the world by measuring the apparent rotation of the pendulum at that location for a 24-hour period and solving for sine of the latitude:

$$\sin (latitude) = Rot_{(d)}/360°$$

Suppose we find that a pendulum located in a certain city has an apparent rotation of about 200° in 24 hours. What is the approximate latitude of this city?

$$\sin (latitude) = Rot_{(d)}/360° = 200°/360° = 0.555$$

The angle with a sine of 0.555 is 33.7° (arc sin 0.555 = 33.7°). Therefore, the latitude of this city is approximately 33.7°. Can you name a large city in the United States at this latitude? The following table shows data from Foucault pendulums at different locations around the world. Use a table of sines, and an almanac, map, or globe to complete the table.

Rot_d	$Rot_d/$ $360°$	Angle with this sine	Direction	Latitude	City or geographic feature at this latitude
360°			clockwise		North Pole
360°			counter		South Pole
222°			clockwise		Athens, Greece
141°			counter		
298°			clockwise		
284°			clockwise		
202°			counter		

Questions

(1)   You are in a large building in either Los Angeles or Washington, D.C., but you can't see outside. Knowing that the apparent daily rotation of your trusty Foucault pendulum is 226°, determine the city in which the building is located.

(2)   What causes the plane of the Foucault pendulum to appear to move?

FOR THE TEACHER

It is important that students understand that a body that exhibits periodic motion, such as a pendulum, does not necessarily exhibit *simple harmonic motion*. When performing the pendulum experiments, we cautioned students to avoid using large amplitudes, but we did not explain why. In this section we will explain why small amplitudes are necessary if accurate and meaningful results are to be obtained. All pendulums exhibit periodic motion, but periodic motion is not necessarily simple harmonic motion. The two terms are sometimes used interchangeably, but they are not the same.

We gave the following formula to students for use in computations and deliberations concerning simple pendulums:

$$T = 2\pi \sqrt{l/g}$$

This formula is derived using the assumption that a pendulum exhibits simple harmonic motion. Simple harmonic motion is a rectilinear motion in which the magnitude of the acceleration is proportional to the magnitude of the displacement of the particle (the bob in the case of our simple pendulum), and the direction of the acceleration is always opposite to that of the displacement. The further the bob is from its rest position the greater the force pulling it back toward its rest position.

Inspect Figure F showing a simple pendulum of mass m and length l, displaced at an angle θ from the rest point. The forces acting on the bob are F_1 (the weight of the bob, equal to mg), and F_t (the tension in the cord supporting the bob). F_1 can be resolved into two components. F_2 is the radial component that supplies the necessary force to keep the bob moving in a circular arc, and F_3 is the tangential component that is the restoring force acting to return the bob to its rest position. The mag-

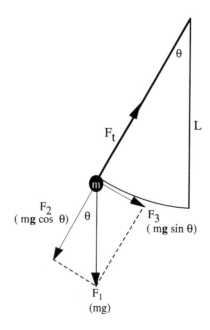

F

nitude of the restoring force is *mg sin* θ, and is written as *-mg sin* θ to indicate that the acceleration of the bob is in a direction opposite to its displacement. That is, when the bob is moving in a clockwise direction, its acceleration is in the counter-clockwise direction. The important thing to note is that the restoring force is not proportional to the angular displacement θ, as is required for simple harmonic motion. Instead it is proportional to *sin* θ.

When θ (a measure of the amplitude or angular displacement) is small, then *sin* θ is very nearly equal to θ (measured in radians). To understand what we mean by saying that *sin* θ is almost equal to θ, study Figure G, which shows three circles with central angle θ becoming successively smaller and smaller. The arc of the circle subtended by the angle θ is the measure of the angle θ in radians. The chord subtended by the angle θ is the value of *sin* θ, assuming a radius of 1. You can see that as θ becomes smaller, the length of the arc approximates the length of the chord. At small values of θ the length of the arc and chord are essentially equal, and θ and *sin* θ can be considered to be equal.

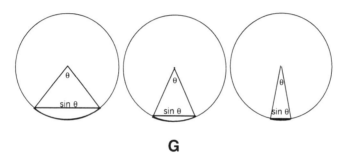

G

Thus for small angular displacements, the restoring force is proportional to the displacement and opposite in direction, so the pendulum exhibits simple harmonic motion. Consequently, the formula $T = 2\pi \sqrt{l/g}$, which is derived under the assumption that a body exhibits simple harmonic motion, can be used to describe the motion of a simple pendulum when the amplitude is small. The percentage difference between the values of θ and *sin* θ for an amplitude of 15° is about 1, so displacements from 0° to 15° can be used in the activities and the simple pendulum can be considered to exhibit simple harmonic motion for these displacements.

2.4.1 Simple Pendulums

Answers: (1) Motion is periodic if it is repeated in a succession of even time intervals. The pendulum exhibits such motion, and we characterize its "period" as the time required to complete a swing. (2) The period of the pendulum is affected by length, but not by mass. This dependence upon length can be seen in the equation for the period of a pendulum ($T = 2\pi \sqrt{l/g}$). (3) A force is required to set a stationary object in motion. When you push against the ground, the ground pushes back on you (Newton's third law), and sets the swing in motion. Once in motion, the swing can be "pumped" higher by redistributing the center of mass. (4) The longer pendulum will exhibit a greater period. If we use the formula for the period of a pendulum ($T = 2\pi \sqrt{l/g}$) we see that the 64-cm pendulum will have twice the period of the 16-cm pendulum.

2.4.2 Physical Pendulums

Answers: (1) A 1.0-m physical pendulum should have the same period as a 0.67-m simple pendulum. (2) Metals contract when they cool. As a result, the rigid pendulum in a grandfather clock will become shorter in the winter, and its period will therefore decrease. Consequently, the clock will tick faster than it should (gain time). The reverse occurs during warm summer weather. During the winter, the adjustment screw should be moved out to increase the length between the pivot and the center of mass to compensate for the contraction of the metal. During the summer the screw should be moved in so as to shorten the length of the pendulum to compensate for the expansion of the metal.

2.4.3 Determining Acceleration of Gravity

Discussion: In this activity, students calculated *g* using a simple pendulum. You may wish to have your students determine *g* using a physical pendulum. The formula to compute the acceleration of gravity with a physical pendulum is more complicated than for a simple pendulum because the simple pendulum is an ideal case in which only the bob is considered to have mass. However, if a physical pendulum has a uniform shape, such as a meter stick, then the formula for its motion is more easily determined. For a meter stick pivoted at one end, the formula is:

$$T = 2\pi \sqrt{2l/3g}$$

Solving the equation for *g*:

$$g = \frac{8\pi^2 l}{3T} = \frac{2}{3}\frac{4\pi^2 l}{^2 T^2}$$

The formula for the period of a simple pendulum is,

$$g = \frac{4\pi^2 l}{T^2}$$

By comparing these two formulas, it can be seen *that the period of the physical pendulum (meter stick) is two thirds the period of a simple pendulum of the same length.*

Answers (1) Answers will vary, but they should be within 5 percent of 9.8 m/s². (2) The moon has only about one sixth the gravity of the Earth. As a result, the period of a pendulum on the moon would be approximately two and a half times as long as on Earth.

2.4.4: Foucault Pendulum

Discussion: If you want to construct an accurate Foucault pendulum, perform the following procedure. Attach a universal joint (such as a fishing line swivel) to the ceiling of a large room such as a gymnasium or auditorium. Attach one end of a heavy-duty fishing line to the universal joint and the other to a 15-kg sack of fine-grain dry sand. Puncture a tiny hole in the sack so that a very fine trickle of sand flows onto the floor. The bag should be positioned as close to the floor as possible. Pull the bag back approximately 15° and let it swing. As the bag swings, it will leave trails of sand on the floor. As the Earth rotates, the apparent angle of these trails will change. Students can determine the apparent rotation per day and use it to calculate their latitude using the technique described in the activity. As a result of friction, the amplitude of the pendulum will decrease significantly as the day progresses, but the apparent angle of rotation can still be used to calculate latitude. If your pendulum experiences significant damping, measure the apparent rotation in 3 hours and multiply by 8 to determine the apparent rotation per day.

Rot_d	$Rot_d/360°$	*Angle with this sine*	*Direction*	*Latitude*	*City or geographic feature at this latitude*
360°	1	90°	clockwise	90° N	North Pole
360°	1	90°	counter	90° S	South Pole
222°	.617	38°	clockwise	38° N	Athens, Greece
141°	.392	23°	counter	23° S	
298°	.828	56°	clockwise	56° N	
284°	.789	52°	clockwise	52° N	
202°	.561	34°	counter	34° S	

Answers (1) Washington, D.C. (2) Newton's law of inertia states that an object will remain in a given state unless a force acts upon it. As the Earth turns, it exerts a force upon the building, causing it to turn with it. Because the fishing line is not rigid, little lateral force is transferred to the pendulum bob. As a result, the orientation of the Earth underneath the pendulum changes, while the pendulum remains constant. Since we view things from the perspective of the Earth, the plane in which the pendulum swings appears to have changed.

Applications to Everyday Life

Clocks: Grandfather clocks are driven by the periodic motion of a pendulum. The longest pendulum clock in the world is nearly 74 feet (23 meters) long. It keeps time on the Shinjuku building in Tokyo, Japan.

Latitude Determination: Foucault pendulums may be used to determine latitude using the methods described in the preceeding activity.

Metronomes: A metronome is used to maintain a tempo for music. It is an inverted pendulum with an adjustable weight that slides on a calibrated pendulum rod. The entire unit, powered by a spring or electricity, is in the shape of a pyramid. Moving the weight up or down the rod changes the period of the pendulum. During each period it emits one or two audible beats to help the musician maintain the proper tempo.

Ballistic Pendulums: Although guns were ubiquitous in the early eighteenth century, no acceptable method of measuring the muzzle velocity of these guns (firearms) was available until the ballistic pendulum was invented in 1740. A ballistic pendulum consists of a large wooden block hanging vertically by two cords (see Figure H). A bullet is fired into the block, causing the block and embedded bullet to swing upward as one unit. The velocity of the bullet can be determined from the known masses of the block and bullet and the amplitude of the swing using basic laws of physics related to energy and momentum.

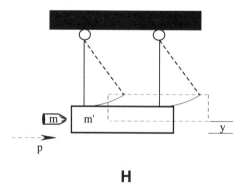

H

Battering Rams: A battering ram was a military siege weapon consisting of a large wooden beam, often with a head of iron. It was used to break down walls by repeatedly striking them. Battering rams were suspended by ropes from a wheeled vehicle and swung like a pendulum. Battering rams of more than 30 m (100 feet) in length, operated by up to 100 men, were used in medieval Europe. The battering ram became obsolete after gunpowder was introduced into warfare.

Springs and Shock Absorbers: The suspension systems of most modern automobiles employ helical springs on the front wheels and leaf springs on the rear axles. These springs cushion the chassis of the car and make the ride smoother. However, springs, like pendulums exhibit simple harmonic motion and will continue to oscillate long after a wheel has hit a pothole or bump. To minimize this oscillation, automobile manufacturers install shock absorbers.

Light: The electrical and magnetic fields of light vibrate in a periodic fashion. If the period is short, the frequency is high, and if the period is long, the frequency is low. X-rays, gamma rays, and ultraviolet rays have a short period (high frequency), while radio waves and microwaves have a long period (low frequency).

Sound and Music: When a guitar string is plucked, it oscillates in a periodic fashion, generating sound waves. A periodic vibration of 256 cycles per second will create a sound we identify as "middle C."

Biological Clocks: Most organisms demonstrate periodic changes in physiology on a cycle of approximately 24 hours. Such circadian rhythms can operate even in the absence of light. The leaves of many plants, for example, rise and fall on a regular 24-hour cycle, even when kept in complete darkness.

Cepheids: Cepheids are variable stars that expand and contract in a periodic fashion. The brightness of cepheids increases as the star expands, and diminishes as the star contracts. Cepheids help us determine intergalactic distances.

Pulsars: Pulsars are believed to be neutron stars that are spinning rapidly and emitting electromagnetic radiation in a highly periodic fashion. Bursts of radio waves are emitted in highly regular intervals ranging from 0.0015 to 4 seconds, depending on the star.

UNIT THREE
Force

3.1 Force

3.2 Buoyant Force

3.3 Friction

3.4 Torque

3.1 FORCE

On the morning of June 30, 1908, reindeer herders in remote regions of central Siberia witnessed a brilliant blue-white fireball in the sky. The fireball descended and then exploded with the strength of a 12-megaton blast—a force equivalent to 12 million tons of TNT. No one is sure what caused the blast, but many scientists now believe the Tunguska explosion was caused when the head of a small comet disintegrated upon entering the Earth's atmosphere. (Some scientists now believe that dinosaurs became extinct after an earlier comet struck the Earth, sending enough dust into the air to change the global climate and make the environment hostile to the giant reptiles.) The Tunguska comet exploded with tremendous force, destroying trees within a 30 kilometer radius and creating a rumble that was heard 1,000 kilometers away.

Everyone would agree that the Tunguska comet exerted great force upon the environment of central Siberia, but not everyone could define what the term "force" means. You have probably used the term "force" often in describing your everyday activities: "I will use force if necessary! Don't force me to eat that lousy cereal! He forced his way to the goal line! May the force be with you!" The word *force* is commonly used to denote an influence that tends to produce a change in the state of affairs. In science, *a force is that which affects the motion of a body.* Our intuitive idea of force is the push or pull necessary to change an object's motion. Some forces require direct contact, while others do not. The Earth does not need to touch the moon to keep it in orbit, nor does a magnet need to touch a nail to attract it! Forces such as gravity and magnetism, which act through a distance without physical contact, are still not well understood.

All known physical interactions of matter occur through four fundamental forces: gravitation, electromagnetism, strong nuclear force, and weak nuclear force. The most pervasive force is gravitation, in that every particle of matter attracts every other particle. Without gravity you would have no weight, objects would float in midair, the Earth would slowly disintegrate, and our solar system and galaxy would fly apart. Electromagnetic forces exist between those particles that have electric charge and/or a magnetic moment. Electromagnetic forces are responsible for electricity, magnetism, and light. In addition, they control the way atoms interact and are the bases for all chemical reactions, both in living and nonliving systems. Muscle action, the explosions in an automobile engine, and the adhesion of glues are but a few of the many expressions of electromagnetic forces. The nuclear forces are crucial for the existence of matter as we know it. Strong nuclear forces hold neutrons and protons together in nuclei while the weak nuclear forces are involved in many nuclear decay processes. Without nuclear forces, atoms, the building blocks of matter, could not exist. In this chapter we will investigate force and Newton's laws, which describe the effects and interactions of force.

3.1.1 Vectors and Scalars

Concepts to Investigate: Vectors, scalars, vector addition.

Materials: Metric rulers, pencil, protractor, paper.

Principles and Procedures: Physical quantities such as length, area, volume, mass, time, and temperature can be expressed in terms of magnitude alone. A distance measurement of 27 meters or a time measurement of 19 seconds gives you complete information regarding distance or time. Quantities that can be fully expressed in terms of their magnitude are known as scalars. Scalar comes from the Latin word "scala" meaning magnitude.

Other physical quantities such as velocity, force, and momentum, which specify both magnitude (how much) and direction (which way), are known as vector quantities. The term vector is derived from the Latin word meaning "carrier." Force is a vector quantity because its magnitude and direction are required to describe it completely. A small arrow is often written above a variable to indicate that it is a vector $\vec{F}$.

"A picture is worth a thousand words." For this reason, vector quantities such as a force are depicted graphically as arrows, with the length representing the magnitude of the force and the orientation representing its direction. The net force resulting from two or more concurrent (meeting at the same point and occurring at the same time) forces is known as the resultant. The resultant is a single force that, if substituted for the component forces, would produce the same effect.

Multiple forces may act on the same point in the following ways: parallel and in the same direction (Figure A); parallel and in opposite directions (Figure B); or at an angle to each other (Figure C). Here are some basic rules for adding vectors. When two or more vectors act at the same point and in the same direction, the magnitude of the resultant is the algebraic sum of the magnitude of the components and is in the same direction. When two or more vectors act at the same point and in opposite directions, the magnitude of the resultant is the algebraic difference between the magnitudes of the components and has the same direction as the larger component. When two or more vectors act at the same point, but at different angles, the resultant can be found by placing the components head to tail. The resultant vector extends from the tail of the first vector to the tip of the last vector.

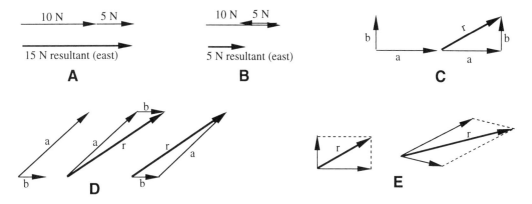

Study the vectors and resultants shown in Figure D. We get the same resultant *r* if we add vector *b* to the tip of vector *a* or if we add vector *a* to the tip of vector *b*. Vector problems can be solved trigonometrically or graphically using a ruler and a protractor as shown here. To solve vector problems, you must remember that the magnitude is represented by the length, and the direction by the angle of the arrow. Suppose we agree that 1 cm in length represents a force of 10 newtons. Then an arrow 5 cm in length pointing north would represent a force of 50 newtons directed north.

A convenient method of finding the resultant of two forces is called the "parallelogram of force" method. The two forces are represented to scale at the indicated angle. The parallelogram is completed as shown by the dotted lines in Figure E. The diagonal is the resultant *r*. Use a ruler and protractor to find the resultant in the vector addition problems that follow.

Questions

(1) Define the following terms: vector, component, resultant.

(2) Two basketball players exerted forces simultaneously on a ball at the tip-off to a game. One exerts a force of 50 N toward the sidelines, while the other exerts a force of 100 N toward one of the goals. Draw a diagram to determine the resultant force on the ball.

(3) A force of 50 N acts on a rock directly east while a force of 100 N acts simultaneously on the same rock directly west.

(4) A person pushes on the handle of a lawn mower with a force of 140 newtons at an angle of 30 degrees to the grass (horizontal). What is the magnitude of the horizontal component of force moving the mower?

3.1.2 Resultant and Equilibrant Forces

Concepts to Investigate: Resultant, equilibrant, vector addition, equilibrium.

Materials: Table, spring scales, paper, washers, fishing line or string.

Principles and Procedures: While earlier we investigated vector addition using pencil and paper, in this activity we will study it directly. Place a mark in the center of a piece of paper and tape this paper in the center of a level desktop. Tie three spring scales to a washer using fishing line or string. Tie additional string to the other ends of the spring scales and hang weights of your choice, as shown in Figure F. Adjust the positions of the scales so the center of the ring is over the center of the board. Using an appropriate scale, record on the paper the direction and magnitude of each of the three forces. Complete a parallelogram using any two of the forces and draw the diagonal between them. The magnitude and direction of the diagonal should be equal and opposite to the third force. This force is called the *equilibrant* because it keeps the system in static equilibrium—a condition where nothing moves because forces are balanced. Determine the resultant vectors for each pair of forces. Is the equilibrant always equal and opposite to each resultant? Repeat the process using different weights and different angles. Is the net force on the washer always zero? How do you know?

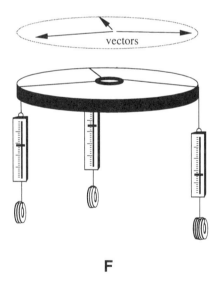

F

Questions

(1) When three scales are attached to the board and adjusted until the ring is centered, how should the reading of any one scale compare to the readings of the others?

(2) Attach a scale to a wall or other fixed support. Attach a second scale to the first and a third scale to the second. Pull on the third scale and note the reading on each of the three scales. Explain your findings.

(3) What is an equilibrant and how is it related to the resultant?

(4) The resultant of two forces is 150 N. The two components that produce this resultant act at an angle of 90 degrees and the magnitude of one component is 80 N. Use the Pythagorean theorem to find the second component.

(5) What is the net force on the washer if it is not moving?

3.1.3 Newton's Second Law
(Law of Acceleration)

Concepts to Investigate: Newton's second law, $F = ma$, acceleration, deceleration, resting weight.

Materials: Spring scales, weights.

Principles and Procedures: If a car in which you are riding changes velocity you feel these changes and shift backward or forward in your seat. The faster the velocity changes the greater the effect on you! Acceleration is the rate of change of velocity and, for motion in a straight line, is equal to the change in velocity divided by the time required for that change. Using the symbol Δ to indicate "change in," we can define acceleration: $a = \Delta v/\Delta t$. For example, suppose you are riding in a car that goes from 20 km per hour to 60 km per hour in 5 seconds. The average acceleration is (60 km/h - 20 km/h divided by 5 seconds) = 8 km/h·s = 0.002 km/s² = 2 m/s², which means the velocity of the car changes 2 meters per second each second.

If you pull on an object with a constant force, the object will accelerate. If you double the force, the acceleration will double showing that acceleration is directly proportional to force. If you keep the force constant but double the mass of the object, the acceleration of the object is halved, showing that acceleration is inversely proportional to the mass. Newton stated these results concisely in his second law: *The acceleration of a body is directly proportional to the resultant external force acting on the body, is inversely proportional to the mass of the body, and has the same direction as the resultant force.* Stated in other terms, as the force increases the acceleration increases. As the mass increases the acceleration decreases. Newton's second law can be summarized using an equation: $F = ma$, where F is force, m is mass, and a is acceleration. Force can be measured by the acceleration it imparts to a given mass. When more than one force acts on an object, it is the net force that causes the acceleration. For example, if the acceleration of an object of mass 16 kg is 4 m/s², the net force on this object is 16 kg × 4 m/s² = 64 kg·m/s² = 64 N. Given any two quantities in the equation, $F = ma$, we can compute the third. If the force is gravity, then $F = mg$. The acceleration of gravity g is 32 ft/s² or 9.8 m/s².

Tie enough washers to one end of a spring scale so that the indicator is in the middle of the scale. Tie a string to the other end of the scale and loop it over a dowel or pulley that is at least 2 meters above the scale (Figure G). Hold the free end and record the weight. Pull the washers up at a steady velocity and record their weight. Now tie an object that is 5 times as massive as the washers to the other end of the string and release (Figure H). One student should record the greatest weight observed as the washers accelerate, while a second records the least weight observed as they come to a stop. Because the scale is moving, you will be able to make only approximate measurements. Perform this procedure until you obtain consistent values, and record these in the table. Repeat, substituting with a mass 10 times as great. Are the maximum and minimum weights any different?

According to Newton's second law, the scale reading should equal $mg + ma$, where g is the acceleration of gravity and a is the acceleration of the object. When the

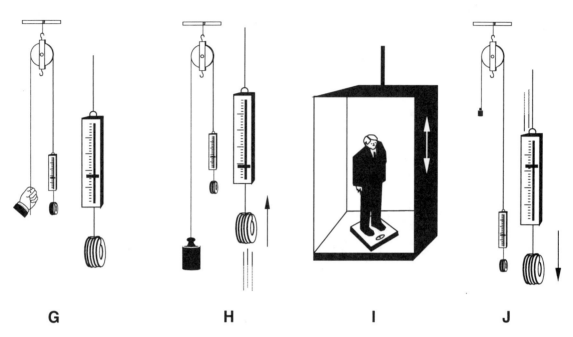

G   **H**   **I**   **J**

scale is moved upward at constant velocity there is no acceleration and $a = 0$, in which case the reading should be the same as the resting weight of the washers mg. When the washers accelerate upward, a has a value greater than 0 so the weight should be greater than the resting weight. When the washers decelerate as the object lands on the ground, the value of a is negative, and the scale reading should be less than the resting weight.

	Accelerating Force	
	5x	10x
Weight at rest	_____	_____
Weight at constant velocity	_____	_____
Maximum weight when accelerating	_____	_____
Minimum weight when decelerating	_____	_____

Questions

(1) Explain why the reading of the scale was less than the actual weight of the mass when the scale was decelerating and was greater when the scale was accelerating.

(2) Describe Newton's second law of motion and give examples.

(3) On one of the lunar missions, an American astronaut dropped a feather and a rock from the same height. Do you think they hit the surface at the same time? Explain.

(4) A rocket engine imparts a constant force while its mass decreases as fuel is consumed. Describe the acceleration of the rocket as a function of time.

(5) Suppose you are standing on a scale resting on the floor of an elevator (see Figure I). How would the reading of the scale compare to your actual weight as the elevator accelerates upward? How would the reading compare as you move upward at constant speed? As you decelerate to stop? How much would you weigh if the cables of the elevator were cut and the elevator fell freely? (Test your hypothesis using the apparatus shown in Figure J.)

3.1.4 Newton's Third Law
(Law of Interaction)

Concepts to Investigate: Newton's third law, interaction, opposite and equal forces, propulsion.

Materials: Long cylindrical balloon, tape, plastic straws or round pencils, 2-liter plastic soda bottle, cork or stopper to fit bottle, baking soda, vinegar.

Principles and Procedures: Newton's third law states that for every action there is an equal but opposite reaction. Stated in another way, when one body exerts a force on another, the second body exerts on the first a force of equal magnitude in the opposite direction. When standing on the floor your body exerts a force on the floor equal to your weight and the floor exerts an upward force on your body equal to your weight. If the floor did not exert an equal force on your body you would fall through it. Unaccompanied forces do not exist in nature—they always come in pairs. For example, a rotating lawn sprinkler moves in one direction when the jets of water move in the opposite direction. A rocket moves in one direction while the exhaust gases move in the opposite direction. Newton's third law is valid whether an object is moving or stationary. If you attempt to step from a rowboat to a dock, you exert a force on the boat and the boat exerts an equal and opposite force on you. The force you exert will cause the boat to move (accelerate) in one direction and the force exerted by the boat will cause you to move in the opposite direction, hopefully with enough acceleration to place you on the dock and not in the water!

Part 1. Balloon rocket: Inflate a balloon fully and hold the opening closed with your fingers. Tape a straw to the balloon parallel to its length. Place a long piece of string or fishing line through the straw and tie both ends in a room to opposite walls, about two meters from the floor. Hold the inflated balloon close to one wall and then release it (Figure K). Alter the design as necessary to get maximum propulsion. See if you can get the balloon to move all the way across the room. What causes the balloon to move?

Part 2. Carbon dioxide rocket: When vinegar (acetic acid) reacts with baking soda (sodium hydrogen carbonate), carbon dioxide is produced. If this gas is produced in a closed container, the pressure increases. Once a vent is opened, the carbon dioxide will rush out, forcing the container in the opposite direction. Pour approximately 200 milliliters of fresh vinegar into a 2-liter plastic soft-drink container. Place a rubber stopper in the mouth of the container and then position it on round pencils or straws, as shown in Figure L. Use aluminum foil to make a trough short enough to fit into the container as shown. Fill the trough with baking soda, and then carefully insert the baking soda into the mouth of the bottle, being careful not to spill any of it into the vinegar. While the trough is balanced above the vinegar, carefully seal the bottle with a rubber stopper. Make sure that no one is in front or in back of the container. Stand to the side and then rotate the bottle so the baking soda and vinegar mix. Carbon dioxide will be produced immediately, and in a short time the stopper will fly out of the mouth with great speed (Figure M). What causes the container to move backwards when the cork flies forward?

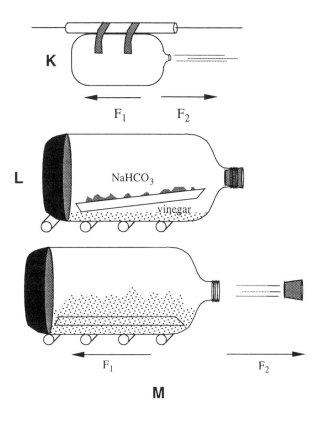

Questions

(1) State Newton's third law of motion in your own words and give examples other than those discussed in this section.

(2) The forward motion of a bullet shot from a gun causes a recoil of the gun, just as the jumping of a person from a rowboat to a dock causes the boat to be pushed backward. Explain.

(3) If the reaction is of equal magnitude to the action, why don't you observe your Ping-Pong paddle recoil when it strikes the Ping-Pong ball?

(4) During an interaction between a 12-kg object and a 4-kg object, the 12-kg object experiences an eastward acceleration of 2.5 m/s^2. What is the acceleration of the 4-kg object?

3.1.5 Centripetal Force

Concepts to Investigate: Newton's second law, centripetal force, orbital velocity.

Materials: Piece of glass or plastic tubing, collection of metal washers, one-hole rubber stopper, nylon fishing line or strong string, alligator clips or paper clips.

Principles and Procedures: What force holds the moon in orbit around the Earth and the Earth in orbit around the sun? What force causes a passenger in a car that is rounding a corner to move in a curved path with the car? What force causes a stone attached to a rope and swung around your head to move in a circular path? When an object moves in a curved or circular path, the turning force is always perpendicular to the object's path and points in the direction of the center of the curve or circle. This force is called *centripetal* force, which means "center-seeking."

Part 1. Centripetal force and orbital velocity: Cut a piece of glass tubing about 15 cm in length. Heat one end in a Bunsen-burner flame until the walls of the tube are smoothly rounded. Tie a two-holed rubber stopper to one end of the line and thread the other end through the tube. Hang six or more iron washers from a paper clip tied to the end of the line (See Figure N.) Adjust the line so that the distance from the top of the tube to the cork is 1.0 meter. Attach a paper clip to the line above the weights to use as an indicator to check that the circular motion is steady. Walk outside the classrom where there is plenty of room. Grip the tube and swing it in a small circle above your head so the rubber stopper moves in a horizontal circle. The weight of the washers, acting through the tension in the string, provides the force necessary to keep the stopper moving in a circle. Double the number of washers and record the velocity required to keep the stopper moving in a path of radius 1 meter. The velocity of the stopper can be calculated from the following equation: $v = (2\pi r)T$; where r is the radius of orbit, $2\pi r$ is the circumference of the orbit, and T is the time required to complete one orbit. The period T can be determined by dividing 60 seconds by the number of revolutions completed in one minute. On the basis of your observations, is greater force required to keep an object in a slow orbit or a rapid one? Remove the extra washers and repeat the procedure. Are your results the same? Record your findings in column 1 of the table. What is the relationship between centripetal force and the orbit?

© 1994 by John Wiley & Sons, Inc.

N

Part 2. Mass and centripetal force: Use the same set-up used when you started Part 1 (radius of 1.0 meters, same number of washers). Double the mass of the "satellite" by adding a duplicate stopper to the end of the line. Add washers until the stopper orbits at the same velocity and radius as before. Record your results in column 2 of the following table. What is the relationship between mass and centripetal force?

Centripetal Force

Mass: Constant Value of _____ g	*Mass: Variable*
Radius: Constant value of 1.0 m	Radius: Constant value of 1.0 m
Velocity: Variable	Velocity: Constant value of _____ m/s
Velocity _____ m/s Centripetal Force: _____ N	Mass: _____ g Centripetal Force: _____ N
Velocity _____ m/s Centripetal Force: _____ N	Mass: _____ g Centripetal Force: _____ N

Questions

(1) Given constant radius, the greater the frequency of revolution, the greater the number of washers required. Explain.

(2) If the velocity is held constant, a decrease in the radius requires an increase in the number of washers. Explain.

(3) If the velocity of the stopper is doubled, what is the effect on centripetal force?

(4) A centrifuge rotates test tubes at very high velocities causing denser components to move away from the axis of rotation (toward the bottom of the tube), while less dense components move toward the axis of rotation (toward the top of the tube). Is more centripetal force required to rotate a full test tube or an empty one?

(5) The equation for centripetal force is $F_c = mv^2/r$, where F_c is the centripetal force, m is the mass of the object, v is its velocity, and r is the radius of its orbit. Explain how your data either support or contradict this equation.

3.1.6 Gravity

Concepts to Investigate: Gravity, air resistance, independence of gravitational acceleration and weight.

Materials: Paper, aluminum foil, test tube, vacuum pump, small feather (goose or duck down), small ball bearing, ruler, coins.

Principles and Procedures: If you look up in the night sky late in the year 2061, you may be treated to a view of a Haley's comet, a mass of rock and luminescent vapor that "visits" us every 76 years. Isaac Newton proposed that the force causing an apple to fall to the ground is the same force that keeps such comets orbiting the sun and the moon orbiting the Earth. Of the four fundamental forces, gravity was the first one to be studied by scientists.

Until Galileo, people thought gravity accelerated heavier objects faster than lighter objects because most daily observations tend to support this view. A bowling ball accelerates toward the ground faster than a feather. Galileo argued that gravity accelerates all objects at the same rate, but that the counteracting force of friction does not. In other words, the acceleration caused by gravity is independent of mass and shape, while acceleration caused by interaction with the air is not.

Part 1. Air resistance: Obtain three square sheets of aluminum foil, 30 cm on a side. Fold one of the sheets into as tight a ball as possible, using a vice if available. Crumple the second sheet into a loose ball and leave the third sheet as you found it. Drop all three items from a height of at least 3 meters and rank them in terms of the time required to strike the ground. Is air resistance proportional to surface area? Repeat the process using paper instead of aluminum.

Part 2. Independence of gravitational acceleration and weight: Galileo said that all objects should fall to the earth at the same rate in the absence of air friction. Place a small ball bearing and a light feather from a pillow or down garment in a large, strong, thick-walled test tube equipped with a one-hole stopper as shown in Figure O. Invert the tube and observe the motion of the ball bearing and feather. Do they fall at the same or at different rates? Attach a vacuum pump to the test tube assembly, evacuate the air, and repeat the process. Do they fall at the same or at different rates? Do your data support Galileo's conclusion that the acceleration of gravity is independent of mass?

Part 3. Independence of gravity and other forces: Position a ruler or other stick on the edge of a table, as shown in Figure P. Place a penny on one end of the ruler as indicated, and place another penny on the edge of the table as shown. Quickly pivot the ruler about its other end and one penny will drop straight down while the other will be hit by the ruler and move in a horizontal and a vertical direction simultaneously. Listen for the clicks as each penny hits the floor. Do they hit the floor at the same or at different times? Repeat the activity using different sizes of coins and different heights. Does the motion in the horizontal direction influence the motion in the vertical direction? Explain.

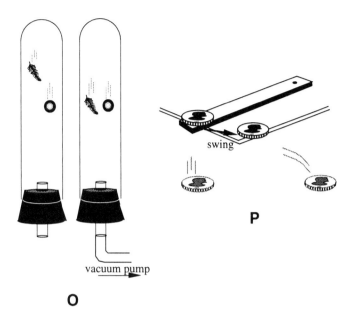

vacuum pump

O

P

Questions

(1) Based upon your findings from Part 1, is air resistance on all objects the same? Explain.

(2) Based upon your findings from Part 2, is acceleration due to gravity independent of mass. Explain.

(3) What would be the result if flat and wadded sheets of paper were dropped from the same height on the moon?

(4) Based upon your findings from Part 3, does acceleration in a horizontal direction affect the acceleration due to gravity?

(5) When you rotated the ruler rapidly in Part 3, one penny fell vertically to the floor while the other was struck and moved in a parabolic path, but both hit the floor at the same time. Explain.

(6) Newton's universal law of gravitation states that the gravitational force between two objects is proportional to the product of their masses and inversely proportional to the square of the distance between them. If the distance between two objects is tripled, what is the decrease in the gravitational force?

FOR THE TEACHER

Forces are ubiquitous in your students' everyday lives. If the forces on an object are balanced then the net force is zero and no acceleration of the object occurs. If the net force is not zero, the object accelerates according to Newton's second law. An object moving in a curved path may experience two kinds of acceleration—tangential acceleration in the direction of motion tangential to the curve, and centripetal acceleration toward the center of the curve. Make certain students understand the difference between velocity and acceleration. Although both can be represented as vectors, velocity is the speed of an object in a given direction while acceleration is the rate of change of speed in a given direction.

Of the four fundamental forces, students are most familiar with gravity. Surprisingly, the other forces are substantially stronger than gravity. Weak nuclear force is 10^{35} times stronger, electromagnetism is 10^{38} times stronger, and strong nuclear force is 10^{40} times stronger! You can use this information to help students understand why there is significant force in an electromagnet when the current is flowing, but virtually none when the current is off. The magnetic attraction between the electromagnet and the iron is much greater than the gravitational attraction.

What causes gravity and magnetism to act without contact? Nobody really knows. Scientists talk about gravitons as particles that cause gravity, but no one has yet discovered a graviton. Gravitation has no known distance limitations so its effects are easily observed in the behavior of large objects on the Earth and in the motions of celestial bodies.

3.1.1 Vectors and Scalars

Discussion: Some students find the parallelogram method for finding the resultant of two vectors easier than the tip-to-tail method, but it becomes cumbersome when there are more than two component vectors. If components are at right angles the Pythagorean theorem can be used to find the magnitudes: The square on the hypotenuse is equal to the sum of the squares on the sides: $C^2 = A^2 + B^2$. Show students how to use this formula to compute the resultant given the components, or to compute one of the components given the resultant and the other component. If students have a knowledge of trigonometry, have them use it to solve vector problems.

Answers: (1) A vector is a quantity that has both magnitude and direction. A component is one of several vectors that can be combined to yield a resultant vector. A resultant is a vector that has the same effect as two or more vectors applied simultaneously at the same point. (2) 112 N at an angle of 26.6 degrees from the goal. (3) 50 N west. (4) In a 30° - 60° right triangle, the side opposite the 30° angle is half the hypotenuse so the vertical component is 70 N. Hence, the horizontal component is $\sqrt{(140\ N)^2 - (70\ N)^2} = 121$ N.

3.1.2 Resultant and Equilibrant Forces

Discussion: To perform this activity without spring balances, simply measure forces in "washer units." Since most spring balances are not very sensitive, best results will be obtained when readings are midscale. When drawing force vectors, make certain students select a scale appropriate to the range of the spring scales being used. To give students an everyday reference for force, explain that an ordinary flashlight battery (size D) has a mass of about 100 grams and weighs approximately 1 newton. Depending on the dimensions of your force table, a scale of 1 cm = 1 N, or 2 cm = 1 N may be appropriate. Emphasize that the resultant of two forces *decreases* as the angle between them *increases*.

To make a force table for use on an overhead projector, cut a 20-cm circular disk from a sheet of clear Plexiglas. Mark a spot in the center and place a washer or key ring over the spot as before. Attach three pieces of string to the ring and attach various numbers of identical iron washers to each string, adjusting the angles among the strings until the ring is centered directly over the mark. Each washer can be considered to be a unit or force. Since the washers may be out of students' sight, it may be necessary to indicate on the overhead the number of washers tied to each string. If, for example, two strings are at 90 degrees and 3 washers hang from one and 4 from the other, then 5 washers should be required for the resultant to keep the ring centered.

Answers (1) The reading of each scale should be equal to the resultant of the other two scales but opposite in direction. The force on each string is the equilibrant to the other two. (2) Each scale will read the same value because, according to Newton's third law, each exerts an equal and opposite force on the other. (3) The equilibrant is equal in magnitude to the resultant but opposite in direction. (4) Magnitude of second component = $\sqrt{(150\text{ N})^2 - (80\text{ N})^2} = 126.9$ N. (5) If there is no movement, the net force must be zero.

3.1.3 Newton's Second Law (Law of Acceleration)

Discussion: A vivid demonstration of Newton's second law is possible if you use a demonstration scale (see Figure Q) that can be read by students throughout the room. Demonstrate the following four motions: (1) moving upward at constant speed, (2) moving downward at constant speed, (3) moving upward while accelerating, (4) moving downward while decelerating. The scale reading should be equal to the resting weight in 1 and 2, be greater than the resting weight in 3 and be less in 4. According to Newton's second law, $F = mg + ma$. When there is no acceleration, as in cases 1 and 2, $a = 0$, and $F = mg$, the resting weight. When the object is accelerating, the scale reading should exceed the resting weight because a is positive. When decelerating, the scale reading should be less than the resting weight because a is negative.

Answers: (1) See discussion. (2) Answers will vary, but should include a discussion of the following: An object accelerates in the direction of the net force. The acceleration of an object is directly proportional to the net force exerted on it and is inversely proportional to the mass of the object being accelerated. (3) Yes. The acceleration due to gravity is constant, regardless of the shape or size of an object, and since there

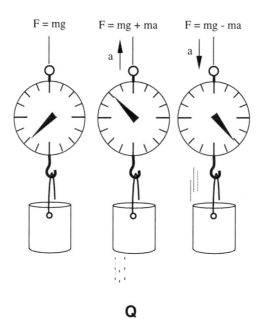

$F = mg$ $F = mg + ma$ $F = mg - ma$

Q

is no atmosphere on the moon, there are no frictional forces to mask this effect. (4) If force remains constant while mass decreases, acceleration increases: $a = F/m$. (5) The scale would register a greater weight as you accelerate upward, the same weight as you traveled at constant velocity, a lower weight as you decelerated while moving up, and no weight when in free fall.

3.1.4 Newton's Third Law (Law of Interaction)

Discussion: To add some excitement to your class, stage balloon-rocket races between lab teams. A rocket is propelled by the ejection of a portion of its mass. The forward movement of the rocket is the reaction to the force of the ejected material on the rocket. In the case of the balloon, the thrust (reaction force) is equal to the product of the mass and acceleration of the escaping gasses $(F = ma)$. Make sure your students understand that an action always produces a reaction, but not necessarily motion. A book lying on a desk pushes on the desk with a force equal to the force exerted by the desk on the book (forces are in equilibrium and there is no motion).

Answers (1) Answers will vary but should reflect an understanding that an action produces a reaction. (2) The action of the bullet produces a reaction known as recoil. Likewise, the action of a person jumping from a rowboat produces a reaction as the boat moves in the opposite direction. (3) The paddle has much greater mass than the ball, so although it moves, its movement is almost imperceptible compared to the movement of the Ping-Pong ball. (4) $F_1 = m_1a_1$ and $F_2 = m_2a_2$. Since action must equal reaction, $F_1 = F_2$. Then, $m_1a_1 = m_2a_2$, and $a_1 = m_2a_2/m_1 = (12\text{kg})(2.5\text{m/s}^2)/(4\text{kg}) = 7.5$ m/s^2.

3.1.5 Centripetal Force

Discussion: The centripetal (center seeking) force is provided by the weight of the washers. Given constant radius, the faster the rate of rotation of the stopper, the more washers required (the greater centripetal force required). Increasing the speed, while holding the radius constant, requires an increase in the number of washers (increase in centripetal force). The relationship between centripetal force F_c, radius r, mass of stopper m, and velocity v is: $F_c = mv^2/r$, where $v^2/r = a$ (centripetal acceleration). This activity can be used to show that $a = v^2/r$ and to demonstrate angular momentum. As the stopper is pulled toward the center, the momentum decreases. Hence, its rate of revolution increases.

The word *centripetal* is often used as an adjective, conveying the notion that there is some difference in nature of centripetal and other forces, which of course is not true. Centripetal forces, like other forces, are pushes and pulls exerted by such things as strings, walls, or gravity. The term "centripetal" refers to the effect of the force in changing the direction of the object. Centripetal force is "center-seeking," continually redirecting the object toward the center. Centrifugal ("center-fearing") force is a fictitious force invented to explain why you feel you are being pushed against the door of your car when turning a corner. In reality, the car door pushes against you as your body attempts to continue in a straight line.

Answers (1) Newton's second law states that $F = ma$, where a is acceleration. In an orbiting stopper, the centripetal acceleration is equal to v^2/r, where v is the velocity of the stopper along the circular path and r is the distance from the center of revolution to the stopper: $F_c = mv^2/r$. If the radius is held constant and the velocity is increased, the centripetal force must increase. (2) If the velocity is held constant, a decrease in the radius causes an increase in the centripetal force because centripetal force is inversely proportional to radius: $F_c = mv^2/r$. (3) Doubling the velocity quadruples the centripetal force. (4) $F_c = mv^2/r$. Therefore, an increase in mass requires an increase in centripetal force. (5) Answers will vary.

3.1.6 Gravity

Discussion: Gravity is universal and always attracts, distinguishing it from the other fundamental forces. Although gravity is a long-range interaction and is the dominant force in the universe, it is also the weakest of the fundamental forces. *Newton's law of universal gravitation states that every body in the universe attracts every other body with a force directly proportional to the product of their masses and inversely proportional to the square of the distance between them.* When considering a solid body such as the Earth, we can treat its mass as if concentrated at its center. The law of universal gravitation can be summarized in the following equation where G is the universal gravitation constant, m_1 is the mass of one object, m_2 is the mass of the other object, and d is the distance between their centers of mass:

$$F = G\frac{m_1 m_2}{d^2}$$

Gravity increases as the mass of the bodies increase and decreases as the distance between the bodies increases. G is the *universal gravitation constant* and has the value of 6.67 x 10⁻¹¹ N·m²/kg². The very small value of G indicates that the force of gravity is an extremely weak force.

The moon and all artificial satellites such as the space shuttle and communication satellites are actually falling objects, but because of their tangential speed, they fall around the Earth rather than into it. An orbital speed of approximately 17,000 miles per hour (27,000 km/h) is required to keep a satellite in orbit at a distance of 100 to 200 miles (160-320 km) above the Earth's surface, while an orbital speed of only approximately 2,300 miles per hour (3,680 km) is required to keep the moon in orbit at an average distance of 240,000 miles (384,000 km). A speed of 25,000 miles per hour (40,000 km/h) is required to escape the Earth's gravitational field. In 1968, Frank Borman, William A. Anders, and James A. Lovell became the first humans to do this as their craft, the *Apollo 8*, left Earth to orbit the moon.

Answers (1) Air resistance is dependent upon surface area. The larger the surface area, the more air resistance, and the slower the object falls. (2) Acceleration due to gravity is independent of mass. Both the feather and the ball bearing fall at the same rate in the evacuated test tube. (3) There is no atmosphere on the moon, so they would fall at the same rate. (4) Motion in a horizontal direction does not affect the vertical acceleration due to gravity. (5) The vertical and horizontal components of motion for each penny are independent, meaning that the motion in the vertical direction has no effect on the motion in the horizontal direction. Since the force of gravity is identical on both pennies, each experiences the same vertical acceleration and strikes the floor at the same time. (6) The gravitational force will be cut to one ninth its original value.

Applications to Everyday Life

Forces: One cannot escape forces. According to Newton's Law of Universal Gravitation, every body in the universe, from the smallest atomic particle to the largest galaxy, attracts every other body. The larger the object the greater the force of gravity.

Four Fundamental Forces: All known physical interactions of matter occur through four fundamental forces: gravitation, electromagnetic, strong nuclear, and weak nuclear. Gravity and the electromagnetic force act over long distances and are relatively easy to observe. However, the range of nuclear force is limited to subatomic distances and can be investigated using only highly specialized instrumentation.

Tides on the Earth: Tide-generating forces arise from the gravitational action of the moon and sun, the moon's effect being about twice that of the sun. At most places in the ocean and along the coasts, sea level rises and falls in a regular manner, with two high tides and two low tides daily. *Spring tides* occur when the Earth, the moon (new or full phase), and the sun are in alignment, producing higher-than-average high tides and lower-than-average low tides. *Neap tides* occur when the moon is halfway between a new moon and a full moon. In this position, the moon and sun are about 90° apart in our sky, which means the attraction due to the moon and sun partially cancel each other. High neap tides are lower than usual and low neap tides are higher than usual.

Weightlessness: Astronauts in orbit around the Earth experience weightlessness because they are not supported by anything—everything in the spacecraft is falling around the Earth as fast as the astronauts. Astronauts experience the same sensation in orbit you would experience in a freely falling elevator. Near the Earth's surface weightlessness can be produced for periods of only 30 to 40 seconds when aircraft fly in special parabolic patterns.

Space Vehicles: Millions of newtons of thrust are required to lift a space vehicle from Earth! The most powerful rocket ever constructed was the *Saturn V*, which was used for manned flights to the moon. The first stage included a cluster of five engines developing a combined thrust exceeding 33 million newtons. The *Saturn V* is an awesome sight and is on display at the Kennedy Space Center in Florida.

Unified Field Theory: James Clerk Maxwell demonstrated that electricity and magnetism are different aspects of the same phenomenon. Some physicists believe that all four "fundamental" forces are really different aspects of the same force. Although several physicists have proposed grand unification theories, none has yet been validated.

3.2 BUOYANT FORCE

In 1912, the largest and most luxurious ship ever built set sail on its maiden voyage from Southampton, England, enroute to New York. Unfortunately, the steel hull of the *Titanic* was ripped open when it hit the submerged portion of an iceberg. On board were over 2,200 passengers, 1,500 of whom perished when the "unsinkable" *Titanic* sank in the frigid Atlantic Ocean. Icebergs are notoriously hazardous for large boats, because 87 percent of their mass lies out of sight, below the ocean surface. If a ship does not leave sufficient clearance as it passes an iceberg, it may damage its hull on submerged ice.

The *Titanic* was constructed of steel, a carbon alloy of iron approximately 8 times denser than water. It is easy to see how the *Titanic* could sink once its steel hull was ripped open, but can you explain how it was ever able to float in the first place? Prior to the third century B.C., most people thought it would be impossible for a boat made of iron to float. An iron nail dropped overboard would surely sink, so wouldn't a large boat made from iron also sink?

Archimedes, a third-century B.C. resident of Sicily, is credited with discovering the natural law of buoyancy that proved the common thinking incorrect. Archimedes stated that *any object submerged or floating in a fluid is buoyed upward by a force equivalent to the weight of the fluid it displaces.* For an object to float, the water must exert an upward force equivalent to the weight of the object. A floating object is in equilibrium—the buoyant force upon it equals its weight, and the net force on it is therefore zero. Archimedes suggested that a boat made of iron would float if it was designed to displace (push aside) a volume of water with weight equal to its own. Today, nearly all large commercial ships are made of steel. If these ships were solid, like a nail, they would immediately sink, but because they have hollow hulls, they can float. The largest boat ever to sail, the *Hellas Fos* of Greece, weighs 611,000 tons. For this giant tanker to float, the ocean must exert an upward force of 611,000 tons to counter its weight. According to Archimedes' principle, the ocean exerts this force when 611,000 tons of water have been displaced by the boat. Figure A illustrates that the forces are equal and opposite when the ship floats. The net force is zero and the ship is in equilibrium.

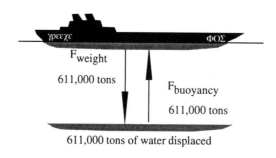

F_{weight}

611,000 tons

$F_{buoyancy}$

611,000 tons

611,000 tons of water displaced

A

Although Archimedes suggested that iron-hulled ships could float, ship builders did not put this idea into practice for approximately 2,000 years. A major turning point in ship construction occurred in 1862, when the Union's U.S.S. *Monitor* engaged in battle with the Confederate's C.S.S. *Virginia (Merrimack)* in an early battle of the American Civil War. This encounter was the first battle between two iron-clad warships and demonstrated the nautical and strategic value of iron. The battle of the *Monitor* and the *Merrimack* helped usher out the days of wooden-hulled ships and usher in the age of steel.

Archimedes' principle applies to all liquids and gasses. A helium balloon rises because the weight of air displaced by the balloon exceeds the weight of the balloon and the helium it contains. You don't rise like a balloon because the weight of the air you displace is significantly less than your own weight. The first balloon to carry passengers was a hot-air balloon invented by the Montgolfier brothers of France in 1783 and traveled for a distance of 5 miles (8 km). In 1981, a team of Americans and Japanese set the record for a hot-air balloon, traveling 5,208 miles from Japan to California. These balloons float because the weight of the balloons, baskets, and the hot air they contain is less than the colder air they displace.

In this section you will investigate Archimedes' principle of buoyancy.

3.2.1 Archimedes' Principle

Concepts to Investigate: Archimedes' principle, displacement.

Materials: Sheet metal and tin snips (or aluminum foil and scissors) and caulking.

Principles and Procedures: The Netherlands is a tiny nation in Northern Europe. Due to a shortage of land, the Dutch have made great efforts to reclaim some of the shallow coastal waters for agricultural purposes. The Zuider Zee project, completed in 1932, reclaimed 200,000 hectares (500,000 acres) of land from the sea by the use of massive sea dikes. These walls are constructed of concrete blocks shaped like boats, which were floated into position and then sunk by opening holes in the bottoms. According to Archimedes' principle, an object will float when it displaces a weight of water equal to its own weight. Many people find it surprising that some commercial boats are made of concrete. Yet even concrete, like steel, will float if shaped appropriately, as the Dutch have shown.

A flat piece of heavy-gauge sheet metal (Figure C) will sink because its weight exceeds the buoyant force. If, however, the metal is bent, as illustrated in Figure B, it will displace more water and be subject to a greater buoyant (upward) force. Using pliers and caulking, build and test your own sheet-metal boat. If you do not have sheet metal, you may investigate the same principles using aluminum foil.

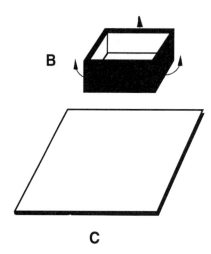

Questions

(1) Using Archimedes' principle, explain why your boat will sink if placed on its side.

(2) Explain how concrete boats are able to float.

(3) The density of lead is 11.3 times the density of water. How would you modify the design of your boat if it were made of lead?

3.2.2 Regulation of Buoyancy

Concepts to Investigate: Buoyancy, neutral buoyancy, ballast, swim bladders, Cartesian diver.

Materials: Eye dropper, permanent marker, 2-liter flexible soft-drink container.

Principles and Procedures: If you observe fish in an aquarium, they appear to maintain constant depth with virtually no effort. By contrast, you must support a bowling ball to keep it from sinking and must restrain a basketball under water to keep it from rising to the surface. If an object remains suspended in a fluid, there is no net force on that object—the force of gravity is countered by an equal and opposite buoyant force. This condition of "weightlessness" is known as "neutral buoyancy."

Approximately 50 percent of all species of fish maintain neutral buoyancy through use of a swim bladder, a gas-filled sac located in the upper portion of the body cavity. The gas in the bladder helps to establish neutral buoyancy by countering the heavier tissues of the fish. By regulating the amount of gas in the bladder, fish can regulate their buoyancy and the depth at which they remain while resting. In this activity you will make a device known as a Cartesian diver to study the principles of buoyancy.

Use a permanent fine-tipped marker to draw a scale on an eyedropper in 5-millimeter increments. Fill approximately one fourth to one third of the eyedropper with water and place it in a flexible, plastic soft-drink container that is completely filled with water. Once the eyedropper is floating with its tip down, seal the container and measure the height of the water in the eyedropper (Figure D). Squeeze the walls of the container and watch the eyedropper descend (Figure E). If the eyedropper sinks before pressure is applied, there is too much water in the dropper. If it does not descend when pressure is applied to the container, there is not sufficient water in the dropper. Record the height of the water in the eyedropper when it is at the bottom and when it is suspended in the middle, and compare these values with the height when it is floating on the surface. According to Archimedes' principle, the

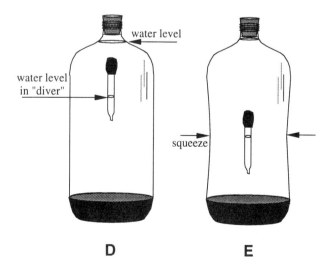

D   **E**

eyedropper is buoyed up by a force equivalent to the weight of the water it displaces. Do your data confirm Archimedes' principle?

Questions

(1)   Explain why the "diver" descends when pressure is applied to the system.
(2)   Is more or less water displaced when the "diver" is on the bottom? Explain.
(3)   How might a submarine regulate its depth?
(4)   The National Aeronautics and Space Administration (NASA) requires astronauts in training to have experience in a weightless environment. How might such an environment be simulated here on Earth? Explain.

3.2.3 Calculating Buoyant Force

Concepts to Investigate: Determining buoyant force, buoyancy of different materials, water displacement.

Materials: Beaker, spring balance, graduated cylinder or other container, metal and wooden weights of equal mass.

Principles and Procedures: Archimedes' principle states that the buoyant force is equal to the weight of the fluid displaced or pushed aside by an object. Thus, the weight of a submerged object should be less than its weight in air by an amount equal to the weight of the water it displaces. Perform the following investigation to see if this is correct.

Suspend a metal object in air from a spring balance, as illustrated in Figure F, and record its weight in the table (1 kg weighs 9.8 N; 1 g weighs 0.0098 N). Fill a beaker with water until it overflows. Once water has stopped flowing, place a dry graduated cylinder or other container beneath the spout of the beaker. Hang the object from the scale and slowly immerse it in the beaker such that all of the displaced water flows over the spout and into the graduated cylinder. Record the new weight of the submerged object (Figure G). The weight of water displaced can be measured by collecting and weighing all the water that overflows from the beaker. If you do not have a triple-beam balance, you can determine the weight of water simply by measuring the volume in a graduated cylinder. The volume in milliliters will be the same as the mass in grams since the mass of one milliliter of water is one gram (the density of water is 1 g/ml). Repeat the activity with a block of wood of equal mass. Analyze the results recorded in the table. Is the weight of the displaced water equal to the difference in the weight of the object when measured in air in water?

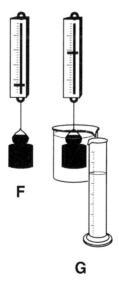

F

G

Object	Weight in air	Weight in water	Difference in weight	Weight of water displaced
metal	_____ N	_____ N	_____ N	_____ N
Wood	_____ N	_____ N	_____ N	_____ N

Questions

(1) What is the buoyant force on the metal and wood objects in this activity? Explain.

(2) What was the weight of the wood when resting in the water? Explain.

(3) Would an object weigh more or less if there were no atmosphere on Earth? Explain.

(4) If a block of metal and a block of wood of identical mass were submerged, would the buoyant force on both be the same? Why or why not?

(5) An average-sized adult human has a volume of approximately 68,000 cm³. If air weighs 1 newton per cubic meter, what is the buoyant force of the atmosphere on such an individual?

3.2.4 Buoyancy and Newton's Law of Interaction

Concepts to Investigate: Buoyancy, Newton's third law (law of interaction), weight.

Materials: Beaker, balance, spring scale, metal object.

Principles and Procedures: In some areas of the world, expensive liquids such as natural oils and perfumes are sold by weight in open-air markets and bazaars. Suppose a customer orders 1 kg of kiwi-seed oil, and the vendor weighs it, stirring the liquid with a spoon while adjusting the balance. The customer complains that the spoon is making the weight of the oil appear larger than it really is, while the vendor defends himself by showing that he is supporting the spoon and claims it therefore can't add weight to the pot. Newton's third law states that if one object exerts a force upon a second object, the second object exerts a force of equal magnitude but opposite direction on the first object. On the basis of Newton's third law, do you think the vendor is cheating the customer? Perform the following activity to find out.

Determine the weight of a beaker two thirds full of water and record in the table. Suspend a metal mass from a spring scale and record its weight. Submerge the weight in the middle of the beaker as illustrated in Figure H, being careful not to allow the mass to touch the side or bottom of the beaker. Again measure the weight of the beaker and hanging metal object. Analyze your results and determine if the customer or the vendor was correct.

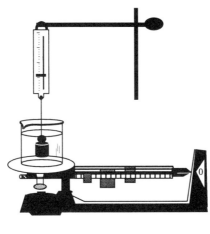

H

	Weight	
	Separate	*Submerged*
Object	———— N	———— N
Beaker	———— N	———— N

Questions

(1) Does the weight of the beaker increase, decrease, or remain the same as the object is submerged? Explain.

(2) Does the weight of the metal object increase, decrease, or remain the same as it is submerged? Explain.

(3) Was the vendor cheating the customer? Explain.

3.2.5 Fluid Density and Buoyancy

Concepts to Investigate: Density, buoyancy, Archimedes' principle.

Materials: Salt, eggs, beakers.

Principles and Procedures: Salmon are one of the most economically important fish of the Pacific Northwest. They spend much of their lives in the ocean, but swim up major rivers to spawn. When swimming from the ocean into rivers, will salmon find the water more or less buoyant? Major cargo ships sail up the Saint Lawrence Seaway from the Atlantic Ocean to the Great Lakes. If their ballast tanks are not adjusted, will the ships ride higher or lower when they move from the ocean to the freshwater seaway? To answer these questions we first need to determine if the density of a fluid affects the buoyancy of objects immersed in it.

Density is the mass to volume ratio of a substance. If the density of an object is less than the density of the fluid in which it is placed, the object will float. If the density of the object is greater than the density of the fluid, it will sink. Because of the presence of dissolved salts, salt water has greater density than freshwater. Archimedes' principle states that an object is buoyed by a force equivalent to the weight of the water it displaces. Knowing this, what will happen to a ship or fish as it moves from salt water to fresh water or vice versa?

Place a fresh egg in a beaker of tap water and record its position. Slowly stir salt into the beaker until the egg rises and is suspended above the bottom of the beaker but below the surface of the water (Figure I). What should be added to raise the egg to the surface? What should be added to cause the egg to sink to the bottom once again? Try it.

I

Questions

(1) Should more solute (salt) or solvent (water) be added to raise a submerged egg to the surface? What should be added to cause the egg to sink? Explain.

(2) Why did the egg rise when salt was added to the system?

(3)   Will a ship ride higher in an ocean or a lake?

(4)   Icebergs pose a threat to navigation because the majority of their mass is submerged and hidden from view. Will more or less of an iceberg be submerged if it is floating in fresh water?

(5)   Petroleum geologists and engineers often flood oil wells with salt water to increase production. Why?

3.2.6 Specific Gravity

Concepts to Investigate: Density, specific gravity.

Materials: Plastic drinking straw, modeling clay or paraffin, sand, beaker, glycerin, olive oil, milk, salt.

Principles and Procedures: Buoyancy is dependent upon the density of a fluid. The denser a fluid, the greater the buoyant force per unit volume displaced. Since the density of ocean water is 1.025 g/ml, while that of fresh water is only 1.000 g/ml, an equal displacement of salt water will produce a greater buoyant force than fresh water. For this reason, boats float slightly higher in salt water.

Since the buoyancy of an object is dependent upon the density of the fluid in which it is floating, it is possible to make an instrument that measures fluid density on the basis of how high the instrument floats. Such an instrument is known as a hydrometer and can be constructed from a plastic drinking straw, as illustrated in Figure J. Seal one end of a straw by plugging it with modeling clay and paraffin (hot candle wax) as shown. Hold the straw upright in water while you pour a small amount of sand into the open end of the straw. Add enough to stabilize the straw, but not enough to sink it. Carefully note the water line and mark this as 1.00 with a fine-tipped permanent marker, since the density of water is 1.00 g/ml. To provide another reference point, float the hydrometer in olive oil and mark the level as 0.92. The density of olive oil is 0.92 g/ml, or 92 percent the density of water, so we say it has a specific gravity of 0.92. The specific gravity is merely the ratio of a substance's density relative to water. Using these two points you should be able to generate an approximate scale of specific gravity. Using your hydrometer, determine the approximate specific gravity of glycerin and milk. If you do not have these liquids, you may still observe how the hydrometer works by slowly adding salt to the beaker and watching it rise.

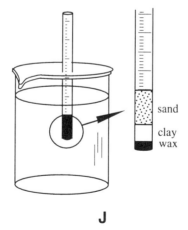

J

	Specific Gravity
Water	1.00
Olive oil	0.92
Glycerin	
Milk	

Questions

(1) Which liquid is densest?

(2) Hydrometers are used to determine the density of water in car radiators. Since density varies as a function of the amount of antifreeze (ethylene glycol) added, it is possible to determine the percentage of antifreeze in the radiator and the temperature at which it would freeze. Knowing the specific gravity of ethylene glycol to be 0.958, would a radiator containing fluid with a specific gravity of 0.976 or of 0.989 be better prepared for cold weather?

(3) How could you make your hydrometer more accurate?

FOR THE TEACHER

Buoyancy and Archimedes' principle can be explained as a pressure differential of the fluid on a floating or submerged object. The explanation is simplified using a regularly shaped object such as a cube. Suppose a cube 10 centimeters on an edge is submerged so its top is at surface level. According to Archimedes' principle, the buoyant force on the object is equal to the weight of the water displaced. The volume of water displaced is 1,000 ml (10 cm × 10 cm × 10 cm = 1,000 cm³ = 1,000 ml), which has a mass of 1 kilogram and a weight of 9.8 N.

The pressure exerted by a fluid on a submerged object is $P = \rho gh$, where P is pressure, ρ is fluid density, and h is depth of the fluid. The buoyant (upward) force on the cube can be calculated as $F = PA$, where P is the pressure exerted on the bottom surface of the cube and A is the area of the bottom surface of the cube. Thus, $F_{buoyant} = PA = \rho ghA = (1 \text{ kg}/0.001\text{m}^3)(9.8 \text{ m/s}^2)(0.10 \text{ m})(0.01\text{m}^2) = 9.8$ N. Since there is no fluid above the top surface of the cube, the pressure differential between the top and bottom surfaces is 9.8 N, the same value derived by direct application of Archimedes' principle.

3.2.1 Archimedes' Principle

Discussion: Aluminum foil may be substituted for sheet metal in this activity. When aluminum foil is rolled up in a ball, it will sink, but when fashioned into a small boat it floats.

Answers (1) When placed on its side, water will fill the space once occupied by air, and the only water displaced will be that displaced by the metal. Since metal has a greater density than water, the boat will sink. (2) Concrete boats will float if their hulls are shaped to displace an amount of water greater than or equal to their own weight. (3) To make the boat out of lead, it may be necessary to increase the size of the hull to displace a greater amount of water. This can be done by making the hull longer and thinner.

3.2.2 Regulation of Buoyancy

Discussion: This activity serves as an excellent inquiry-based demonstration. Perform the demonstration without telling the students how you are regulating the depth of the eyedropper and have them generate and test hypotheses.

Answers (1, 2) As pressure increases, the volume of air inside the eyedropper decreases $(V = {}^{nRT}/P)$, reducing the amount of water displaced. Thus, the buoyant force is reduced while the force of gravity remains constant, and the net downward force upon the eyedropper causes it to sink. (3) Submarines dive by allowing outside water into ballast tanks. By releasing compressed air into these ballast tanks, water is forced out, causing the submarine to rise because the buoyant force now exceeds the submarine's weight. (4) Using giant aquariums and specially designed neutral buoyancy suits, astronauts are able to experience a weightless environment here on Earth.

3.2.3 Calculating Buoyant Force

Discussion: Many students fail to recognize weight as a force. While some spring balances are calibrated in units of mass, measurements should be converted to units of force to help students see the forces involved. Newton's second law states that force is equal to the product of the mass and acceleration of an object: $F = ma$. When acceleration is due to gravity, $a = g = 9.8\text{m/s}^2$, the force on a 1-kg mass is 9.8 N: $F = (1\text{kg})(9.8\text{m/s}^2) = 9.8 \text{ kg·m/s}^2 = 9.8 \text{ N}$.

Answers (1) Student answers will vary, but the buoyant force should equal the weight of the water displaced, which is equivalent to the difference of the weight of the object in air and water. (2) The apparent weight of the wood in water is zero because the buoyant force is equal and opposite to the weight of the wood. The spring balance has nothing to support and registers a weight of zero. (3) It would weigh more because there would be no buoyant force from air. The buoyant force or air exerted on an individual is equivalent to the weight of the air the person displaces. (4) The buoyant force on wood exceeds the buoyant force on metal because the wood has lower density, occupies more space, and therefore displaces more water when fully submerged. (5) 0.068 N.

3.2.4 Buoyancy and Newton's Law of Interaction

Discussion: *Newton's third law states: "If one body exerts a force on another body, then the second body must exert a force equal in magnitude but opposite in direction on the first body."* As the water exerts a buoyant force upon an object, then the object must exert a force of equal magnitude upon the water.

Answers (1) The weight of the beaker increases due to the force of the object upon the liquid. This force is equivalent to the weight of the water displaced by the object. (2) The weight of the suspended object, as registered by the spring balance, decreases as the buoyant force counteracts gravity. (3) The vendor was cheating the customer because the spoon contributed to the weight, making it appear as though more oil were present.

3.2.5 Fluid Density and Buoyancy

Discussion: Fluid density has a significant influence upon buoyancy. The air around us provides a buoyant force equivalent to the weight of the air our body displaces, but this force is very small because the density of air is very low. When an equivalent volume of water is displaced the buoyant force is greater because the density of water is greater.

Answers (1) To bring the egg to the surface, add more salt. This increases the density of the water and increases the buoyancy of objects floating or submerged in it. To sink the egg, dilute the solution by adding more fresh water. If there is insufficient space in the beaker, it may be necessary to first remove some of the salt water. (2) A submerged egg displaces the same amount of salt water as it does fresh water, but since salt water is denser, the submerged egg displaces a greater weight of salt water than fresh water. According to Archimedes' principle, it therefore experiences greater buoyant force when submerged in salt water. (3) A ship will ride higher in the ocean because salt water is denser than fresh water and therefore provides greater buoyancy. Many ships have ballast tanks to provide greater stability in the ocean. Ballast tanks are filled with ocean water to lower the center of mass of the boat and increase stability. (4) A greater percentage would be submerged because fresh water is less dense than salt water. (5) Salt water is denser than oil and sinks to the bottom of the well. It creates a buoyant force that subsequently helps lift the oil to the surface.

3.2.6 Specific Gravity

Discussion: If a liquid has a density of 0.95 g/ml, its specific gravity (density relative to water) is 0.95 (water has a density of 1.000 g/ml). This hydrometer will produce reliable qualitative data on the relative densities of liquids, but is not capable of generating precise quantitative data. The specific gravity of glycerin is 1.26 and whole milk is 1.03. You may wish to demonstrate the specific gravity of acetone (fingernail-polish remover) since it is so low (0.79), but don't allow the students to handle it.

Answers (1) The hydrometer should ride highest in the glycerin because it has the highest density (1.26 g/ml). (2) A specific gravity of 0.976 shows a higher percentage of ethylene glycol, which means the coolant in the radiator will have a lower freezing point and be less likely to freeze in cold weather. (3) The hydrometer can be made more accurate by altering its shape. The base of the hydrometer should be large and contain weights to keep it stable. The rest of the hydrometer should be very thin, so slight changes in fluid density will produce significant changes in the amount of tubing submerged.

Applications to Everyday Life

Balloons: Balloons filled with helium are buoyed by a force equivalent to the weight of air they displace. At high altitudes, the buoyancy of balloons decreases as the density of air decreases.

Submarines: Submarines adjust ballast tanks to maintain a specific depth in the ocean. To dive, the submarine crew allows water into ballast tanks, thereby decreasing the amount of water displaced and reducing the buoyant force (increasing the density of the submarine). To rise to the surface the crew releases compressed gas into the ballast tanks, forcing water out, increasing the buoyancy (decreasing the density of the submarine), and allowing the submarine to rise.

Swimming: It is much easier to float on your back in the ocean than in a lake due to the greater density of salt water. The Dead Sea in Israel, at 1,290 feet below sea level, is one of the saltiest and densest bodies of water on Earth. It is therefore very easy to float in the Dead Sea.

Fish: Many fish contain swim bladders to regulate the depth at which they swim. These gas-filled chambers reduce the net density of the fish and allow it to have neutral buoyancy.

Hydrometers: Hydrometers measure the density (specific gravity) of a liquid. The scale on a hydrometer can be adapted to read a variety of units including percentage sugar (saccharimeter), the percentage of fat in milk (lactometer), or percentage alcohol (alcoholmeters).

Airships: The German company Luftschiffbau Zeppelin built a number of rigid airships between 1900 and 1940. The *Graf Zeppelin II* was capable of carrying a payload of 30 metric tons across the Atlantic Ocean. Like blimps, balloons, fish, submarines, or boats, the *Zeppelin* could rise only when the weight of the air it displaced was greater than its own weight. The Zeppelin company accomplished this by using helium, the second lightest gas known. Because there was a shortage of helium in the 1930s, the company substituted hydrogen (the lightest gas) for helium. Unfortunately, hydrogen will combust if ignited in the presence of oxygen, which is what happened in the infamous Hindenburg explosion of 1937.

Oil Spills: Oil has lower specific gravity than water, and as a result, it floats on the surface of the ocean. On the surface it kills marine animals that get stuck or are poisoned or suffocated by it. One of the worst spills of all times was that of the *Ixtoc 1*, which ruptured in Campeche Bay off the Mexican coast, releasing approximately 530 million liters of oil into the ocean.

3.3 FRICTION

Figure skating is one of the most popular events in the Winter Olympics. As skaters trace a figure on the ice, they are judged according to balance, control, and precision. To accurately execute their jumps, spins, and flips, skaters must perform on a surface that is nearly frictionless. Under proper conditions, the pressure of the skate blade melts the ice, allowing the skater to glide along on a nearly frictionless layer of water. If, however, the ice is too cold, it will not melt. Ice provides much greater friction than liquid water, and this may cause blades to stick to the ice and interfere with the performance.

Although it is easy to walk on dry pavement, it can be dangerous to walk on ice. Both surfaces are hard but have different friction. Friction is a force that resists motion and opposes the sliding or rolling of one object over or through another. When walking on dry pavement there is friction between your feet and the pavement, which acts in a direction opposite your horizontal motion. When you attempt to walk on wet ice, the small frictional force may not be sufficient to allow you to move forward.

The frictional force between two objects depends on the materials from which they are constructed and the force with which they are pressed together. Contact between irregularities on the surfaces of objects obstructs motion. Even very smooth polished surfaces, when viewed microscopically, have irregular surfaces (Figure A). Atoms and molecules on one surface may cling to those on the other until they snap apart, allowing the object to slide. If you push horizontally on a box resting on the floor you will find it takes more force to start the box sliding (Figure B) than to keep it sliding at constant speed (Figure C). This shows that *kinetic (sliding) friction is less than static (at rest) friction. Static friction is a force tangential to the surfaces, exerted by one surface on another when the two surfaces are not sliding past each other. Kinetic friction is similar, but occurs only when the two surfaces are sliding past each other.*

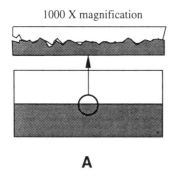

A

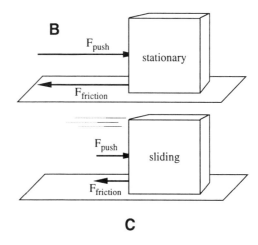

C

Friction can be a hindrance or help, depending on the situation. Skiers in the Winter Olympic Games want to minimize friction to increase their speed. Since friction between their skis and the snow is very small, the main drag on speed is the wall of air in front of them. To reduce air friction, skiers maintain a tight tuck position, use boot buckles that are flush with their boots, and use poles that curve around the body so the baskets hide behind them.

While minimal friction is desirable in the giant slalom, it is not desirable on the road. Icy roads are treacherous because there may be insufficient friction between car tires and the road, and wet brakes can be hazardous because water decreases the friction between brake linings and discs necessary to stop the automobile.

Does friction depend upon the type of surface? Is sliding friction greater or less than static friction? Is friction dependent on the area of contact between the surfaces? Is friction dependent on the force pressing two surfaces together? You will investigate these questions in the following activities.

3.3.1 Center of Mass and Friction

Concepts to Investigate: Center of mass, sliding friction, static friction.

Materials: Meter sticks, weights or rocks, baseball bat.

Principles and Procedures: A tire wears as a result of friction between the tire and the road. The greater the friction, the greater wear upon the tire. Despite the fact that they are attached to the same vehicle, the tires on a car do not all wear at the same rate. In many cars, particularly those with front-wheel drive, the front tires wear out much faster than the rear tires. After performing the following activity, determine what might cause front tires to wear out sooner.

Hold a cylindrical pen in each hand and rest a meter stick on them as shown in Figure D. Slowly move the pens toward each other. At what point do they meet? Reposition the pens at any two points on the meter stick and again move them toward each other and record where they meet. Repeat the procedure using your fingers instead of the pen. Why do your fingers or pens always meet at the 50-centimeter mark?

Place a mass of approximately one kilogram at the 25-centimeter mark, securing it with tape if necessary. Position the meter stick as before and move the pens or your fingers together, recording the position where they meet. Is this point different from the previous points? When a weight is placed on the stick, the center of gravity of the combination is moved in the direction of the weight. What is the relationship between the center of mass and the location where the fingers or pens meet?

Position your fingers under a baseball bat and move them toward each other and record the position where they meet. Do they meet near the neck, the sweet spot, or the head of the bat?

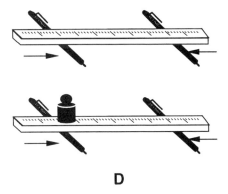

D

Questions

(1) Where do the pens or fingers meet when there is no weight on the meter stick?

(2) Where do your fingers or pens meet when the meter stick is supporting a weight at the 25-cm point? Explain why this occurs.

(3)   The "sweet spot" of a baseball bat is located at its center of mass. Baseball players try to hit the ball here because it transfers greatest energy to the ball and minimizes the vibrations felt by the hands. In this activity, why do your fingers end up under the sweet spot of the bat?

(4)   Why do the front tires of most cars wear out before the rear tires?

(5)   Under what conditions would the rear tires of a car wear out before the front tires?

3.3.2 Ranking Frictional Forces

Concepts to Investigate: Coefficient of static friction, surface interactions, angle of slip, ranking frictional forces.

Materials: Block of wood, fine and rough sandpaper, plastic bag, cotton cloth, aluminum foil, piece of smooth plate glass with no sharp edges, wood inclined plane, tape, protractor.

Principles and Procedures: In this activity you will use an inclined plane to rank the coefficients of static friction μ_s for various materials. Rather than pulling on the object, you will use gravity to provide the force to move the object down an incline. Place a block of wood on a board and slowly raise one end of the board. As the board is raised, the block remains stationary until a certain angle θ is reached, at which point it slides down the board.

When the weight of the block F_w is resolved, it can be seen that part acts to move the block down the board F_A, and part acts to hold the block against the board F_B. The normal force F_N is of equal magnitude to the force holding the block against the board F_B. When the board is horizontal, there is no force pulling the block down the board and the normal force is equal to the weight of the block (Figure E). As the end of the board is raised, the component of the weight pulling the block down the board increases while the normal force decreases (Figure F). When the board is vertical, the force pulling the block down the board is equal to the weight of the block and there is no normal force (Figure G).

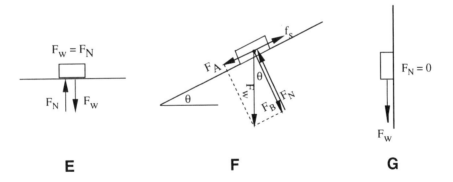

E   F   G

Examine the surfaces of the materials listed in the table and predict the rank of each in terms of their coefficients of friction. A rank of 7 would indicate the greatest friction (greatest μ_s) while a rank of 1 would indicate the lowest friction (lowest μ_s).

Test your predictions. Place the block on a smooth wooden board and slowly raise one end until the block begins to slide. This angle is known as the angle of slip or the angle of repose. Use a protractor to measure this angle. The angle of slip is proportional to the frictional interaction and the coefficient of friction. Secure other materials to the bottom of the block and repeat this procedure. Determine the rank order of the coefficients of friction for each of the seven materials using a scale of 1 to 7, 7 being greatest. How accurate were your predictions?

Material	Angle of slip (°)	Your Prediction (1–7)	Coefficient μ_s ranking (1–7)
Wood on wood			
Aluminum on wood			
Plastic on wood			
Cotton on wood			
Glass on wood			
Fine sandpaper on wood			
Coarse sandpaper on wood			

Questions

(1)   Which material had the greatest coefficient of friction? The smallest?

(2)   What kinds of applications require a material with a high coefficient of friction? A low coefficient of friction?

(3)   A sky diver jumps from a plane and plummets toward the earth. His or her speed does not increase indefinitely but reaches a terminal speed of 120 miles per hour (193 km/h). Explain.

3.3.3 Static and Sliding Friction

Concepts to Investigate: Coefficient of static friction, coefficient of sliding friction, surface interactions.

Materials: Block of wood, fine and rough sandpaper, plastic bag, cotton cloth, aluminum foil, glass plate, spring scale, tape.

Principles and Procedures: Attach a spring balance to a block of wood using tape or a screw eye as shown in Figure H. Pull horizontally and measure the minimum force required to set the block sliding. This force is equal in magnitude, but opposite in direction to the force of static friction. Record this value as the magnitude of static friction in the table. Measure the force required to keep the block moving at a constant velocity. This force is equal in magnitude, but opposite in direction to the force of kinetic friction. Record this value as the magnitude of kinetic friction in the table.

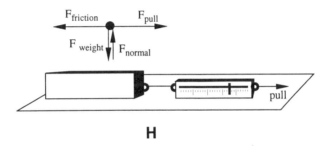

H

Wrap the block in aluminum foil, making certain the foil is smooth on the sliding surface. Pull the block with the scale and measure static and kinetic friction as before. Repeat, using a plastic bag, a cotton cloth, a glass plate or small mirror, fine sandpaper, and rough sandpaper. You will need to use double-stick tape or glue to get these materials to stick to the wood. Report your results in the table.

Since the surface and the block are horizontal and the block is not moving in a vertical direction, the normal force F_{normal} is equal to the weight of the block F_{weight}. The coefficient of friction, represented by the Greek letter μ (pronounced mu), is the ratio of the force of friction to the normal force pressing the surfaces together. For example, assume a box resting on the floor has a weight of 10 N. If you push horizontally on the box and after exerting a force of 5 N, the box begins to move, then the coefficient of static friction μ_s is 5 N/10 N or 0.5. If it requires only 2 N to keep it moving at a constant rate, the coefficient of kinetic friction μ_k is 2 N/10 N or 0.2. Note that the coefficients of static and kinetic friction have no units.

Use your scale to determine the weight of the block. If your scale reads in kilograms, multiply your value by 9.8 to obtain the force expressed in newtons. Compute μ_s and μ_k for each case and enter these values in the table.

	Static Friction f_s	Sliding Friction f_k	Block weight $F_n = F_w$	μ_s f_s/F_n	μ_k f_k/F_n
Wood on wood	N	N	N		
Aluminum on wood	N	N	N		
Plastic on wood	N	N	N		
Cotton on wood	N	N	N		
Glass on wood	N	N	N		
Fine sandpaper on wood	N	N	N		
Coarse sandpaper on wood	N	N	N		

Questions

(1) Which material had the greatest static friction? The least?
(2) Leather, rather than rubber, is generally recommended for the soles of toddlers' shoes. Why?
(3) Sand is often scattered on roads during snowstorms and icing. Why?
(4) If there were no friction would it be possible to tie a knot in a piece of string or rope? Would the knot hold? Explain.
(5) Knowing that the static friction for a rubber tire on a concrete road is 1.0 while the kinetic (sliding) friction is only 0.7, explain why a driver should not jam on the brakes and lock the tires when making an emergency stop.

3.3.4 Factors Affecting Friction

Concepts to Investigate: Friction equation, coefficient of static friction, coefficient of sliding friction, independence of surface area and friction.

Materials: Wood blocks, spring scale, tape or screw eyes.

Principles and Procedures

Part 1: Does weight affect friction? Attach a spring balance to a rectangular block of wood using tape or a screw eye. Pull horizontally and measure the magnitude of static friction as the force required to set the block sliding. After the block begins to move measure the magnitude of kinetic (sliding) friction as the force required to keep it moving at a constant velocity. Repeat these procedures using two, three, and four blocks (Figure I). (If your scale reads in kilograms, multiply your value by 9.8 to obtain the force expressed in newtons.) Graph your results, using weight as the independent variable (x axis), and friction as the dependent variable (y axis). What can you conclude from your results concerning the relationship of weight and friction?

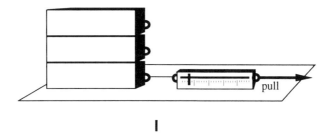

I

The friction equation states: $\mu = F_f/F_N$, where F_f is the force of friction, and F_N is the normal force. Solving for the frictional force, $F_f = \mu F_N$. This is the equation of a straight line with a slope equal to the coefficient of friction μ. Thus, a graph of friction as a function of weight should produce a straight line with a slope equal to the coefficient of friction. Does a graph of your data produce a straight line? Determine the coefficient of friction by measuring the slope.

Part 2: Does surface area affect friction? Using the method described in Part 1, measure the static and kinetic friction of a block resting on different faces (Figure J). Based upon your observations, does surface area affect friction?

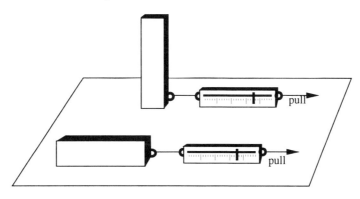

J

Part 1 Does Weight Affect Friction?				Part 2 Does Surface Area Affect Friction?			
Blocks	Weight (N)	Static Friction (N)	Sliding Friction (N)	Surface	Area of Face (cm²)	Static Friction (N)	Sliding Friction (N)
1				Side			
2				Edge			
3				End			
4							

Questions

(1) Inspect your results in the table and describe the relationship between weight and static friction, and between weight and sliding friction.

(2) Will the soles of your boots wear out faster when hiking or backpacking? Explain.

(3) On the basis of your findings in Part 2, does surface area of contact affect friction? Explain.

(4) If friction between a tire and the road is the same whether the tire is wide or narrow, what is the advantage of having wide tires on your vehicle?

(5) Mountain bicycles use wide tires, while racing bicycles use narrow tires. Explain.

FOR THE TEACHER

Friction is a very complicated phenomenon. In fact, there is no exact theory of dry friction. The laws of friction have been determined empirically, and predictions from these laws are approximate. For all practical purposes, the force of friction between two surfaces depends only upon the roughness of the surfaces and the forces pressing them together. Friction is relatively independent of the area of contact between the surfaces.

Increasing the speed with which two dry bodies slide over each other does not greatly increase the amount of friction. However, increasing the speed with which an object moves through a fluid does increase friction. When you run, air around your body creates friction, which retards your motion. For slow speeds this friction is almost unnoticed, but for higher speeds it can be significant. Some Olympic sprinters have worn special aerodynamic caps specifically to minimize such air friction. Similarly, automobiles are given an aerodynamic shape to reduce air friction and boost performance and gas mileage.

Fluid friction depends on speed and area of contact. A boat moving through water, or a plane through air, will encounter more friction at high speeds because they must push aside more fluid in a given amount of time. At low velocities the frictional force exerted by a fluid on an object is directly proportional to the relative velocity of the liquid and object. As the relative velocity increases, friction increases disproportionately due to increased turbulence. When the force of friction equals the weight of a falling object, the object reaches a terminal velocity. The terminal velocity of a sky diver ranges between 180 to 250 km/h (110 to 155 mph), depending on the orientation of the diver's body.

The normal force F_N and the weight hold surfaces together. If a block rests horizontally on a surface, the normal force exerted by the surface on the block is equal to the weight of the block. If one begins to push or pull horizontally on the block there is a maximum force f_{max} beyond which the block will begin to move. The coefficient of static friction μ_s is defined as f_{max}/F_N, the quotient of the maximum force of friction just before movement and the normal force. For example, if a horizontal force of 125 N is required to set a table that weighs 375 N in motion, the coefficient of static friction is 125 N/375 N = 0.33. After the block begins moving, there is a minimum force f_{min} required to keep it moving at constant velocity. The coefficient of kinetic friction μ_k is defined as f_{min}/F_N. For example, if a horizontal force of 75 N is required to keep the table moving at a constant velocity, then the coefficient of kinetic friction is 75 N/375 N = 0.20.

Figure K shows a block resting on an inclined plane. The frictional force increases as the inclination of the plane (angle θ) increases. The weight of the block F_w can be resolved into two components as shown. While the block does not move, $F_N = F_w\cos\theta$ and $f_s = F_w\sin\theta$. Thus, the force of static friction f_s increases as the inclination θ of the plane increases. The inclination cannot exceed a certain value θ_{max} or the block will slide because the maximum value of static friction is exceeded. When the block is on the point of slipping, $f_{max} = F_w\sin\theta_{max} = \mu_s F_N$, and $F_w\cos\theta_{max} = F_N$. Dividing the first equation by the second gives $\tan\theta_{max} = \mu_s$. The plane can be raised to an angle

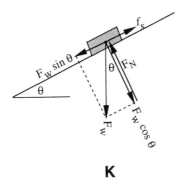

K

of inclination whose tangent is μ_s before the block starts to slip. This limiting angle is called the angle of slip or the angle of repose. You may wish to have your students empirically determine the angle of repose for various surfaces.

3.3.1 Center of Mass and Friction

Discussion: Remind students that the center of gravity (mass) of the meter stick is the point at which all the weight (mass) of the stick can be considered to be concentrated. To emphasize this important concept, place one finger under the stick at any point other than the 50-cm mark and attempt to lift it. Then place your finger directly below the 50-cm mark and lift the stick. When the stick is resting on two fingers there is a greater weight (downward force) on the finger closest to the center of gravity. Consequently, the frictional force between the stick and this finger is greater than the frictional force between the stick and the other finger. The outer finger begins moving first. Just at the point where one finger stops moving and the other starts moving, the force of static friction of the fixed finger equals the force of kinetic friction of the moving finger. The sliding will continue to alternate between one finger and the other until the fingers meet at the center of gravity. Placing a weight on the meter stick changes the position of the center of gravity, but regardless of its position, both fingers should always end up there.

Answers (1) The fingers or pens always meet at the 50-cm point, which is the center of mass of the meter stick. (2) The fingers meet at the center of mass, which is close to the object. See discussion for explanation. (3) See discussion. (4) In many cars, the engine is in the front. Since the engine is heavy, greater weight is placed upon the front tires. Since friction is a function of the force between two surfaces, the front tires will experience greater friction. (5) The rear tires may experience greater wear if the engine is in the rear or if the vehicle is towing a heavy trailer.

3.3.2 Ranking Frictional Forces

Discussion: Comparison of the results obtained in this activity with those in the subsequent activity will help students understand the difference between qualitative and quantitative observations. Observations of frictional forces in the subsequent activity are quantitative in that each contains a measurement. It is therefore possible to state that the static friction of one substance is so many units greater than another. For example a *μs* of 0.50 is twice that of a *μs* of 0.25. The results obtained in this activity were qualitative, meaning there was no magnitude attached. Consequently, students could rank substances in order of *μs* but could not say how much greater or less the coefficient of static friction of one substance was than another. Quantitative observations contain more information than qualitative observations because they contain a measurement. Ask students to compare the results of both activities. The authors obtained the following ranking of *μs* from highest to lowest: rough sandpaper, fine sandpaper, cotton, plastic bag, wood, aluminum foil, glass.

Answers (1) Rough sandpaper had the greatest coefficient of friction while glass had the smallest. (2) There may be many legitimate responses. For example, a high coefficient of friction is required between brake linings and drums while a low coefficient of friction is required between the moving parts of a car's engine. (3) The frictional force of air on the diver increases as the speed of the diver increases because the diver collides with more molecules in the same period of time. When the frictional force is equal to the weight of the diver, the net force on the diver is zero so there is no additional acceleration and the speed remains constant at about 200 km/h.

3.3.3 Static and Sliding Friction

Discussion: Students have an intuitive feel for friction in that they realize the type of surface (rough or smooth) will contribute to frictional forces. Rougher surfaces have more protuberances and irregularities and will exhibit greater frictional forces than smoother substances.

Answers (1) Rough sandpaper has the greatest static friction (highest *μk*) while glass has the lowest static friction (least *μk*). (2) Soles made of rubber offer much more friction than soles made of leather and may cause a young child to fall forward on his or her face. (3) Sand increases friction between wheels and road and thus increases traction. (4). One could tie the knot, but it would not hold because there would be no friction between pieces of the rope to prevent slipping. (5) Rolling tires exhibit static friction because the tire is not sliding over the road. However, when tires lock, they slide over the road and the point of contact moves. Because static friction is greater than sliding friction, the car can come to a stop sooner if the brakes are not locked.

3.3.4 Factors Affecting Friction

Discussion: In this activity, students learn that friction is directly proportional to the force pressing two surfaces together. Be certain they understand what "directly proportional" implies. If the force pressing two surfaces together is doubled, the force of friction between them is doubled. If the force is cut in half, the force of friction between them is cut in half.

Students will understand why friction is independent of the area of contact between surfaces if they understand the difference between pressure and force. Pressure is force per unit area. Since the weight of the block is constant, the pressure it exerts on the smooth surface is directly proportional to the area of contact. Pressure is greatest when the block rests on an end, less when it rests on a small side, and even less when it rests on a large side. An increase in surface area is accompanied by a reduction in pressure. The difference between pressure and force is graphically illustrated if a woman walks across a soft linoleum floor wearing high-heeled shoes and then walks across it wearing flat-heeled shoes. Although the force is identical, the pressure is much greater when wearing high heels, and consequently the floor is more easily dented.

In this activity we introduced the concept of independent and dependent variables. The dependent variable responds to changes in the independent variable, but the independent variable does not respond to changes in the dependent variable. Thus, the dependent variable is dependent upon the independent variable, while the independent variable is independent of the dependent variable. In this activity, students observed how friction changed in response to weight. Friction was the dependent variable because it depended upon weight.

Answers (1) The force of friction is directly proportional to the weight. Doubling the weight doubles the force of friction, tripling the weight triples the friction. (2) Wear is proportional to friction, and friction is proportional to weight. Thus, when greater weight is exerted on your boots, as when backpacking, they will experience greater wear. (3) No. The same force was required to move the block, regardless of which face it was placed upon. (4) The greater contact area of a wide tire does not increase friction between the tire and ground, but it does reduce pressure, and thus helps reduce heating and wear. (5) Although friction is independent of surface area, the pressure exerted by a tire on the ground is not. Wider tires distribute weight over a larger area, exert less pressure on the ground, and thus do not sink into the dirt as far as narrow tires do.

Applications to Everyday Life

Walking: The simple acts of walking and running would not be possible were it not for friction. However, if your shoes do not fit properly, friction may stimulate the formation of painful blisters or corns.

Holding Things Together: A knot tied in a string or rope could not hold without friction. Nails, screws, and bolts would be useless without friction.

Lubricants: Oil is used in engines to reduce friction between moving parts and prolong the engine's life. If you fail to change oil regularly, it becomes dirty, offers more friction, and causes greater wear on the engine. Chemists have developed synthetic oils that bond to the metal in engines providing an "oil-carpet" that stays in place even when the engine is shut off, protecting the engine from wear when it is restarted.

Brakes: A brake is a device that uses friction to slow or stop a vehicle. Brake shoes and pads are lined with a heat-resistant friction material that presses against rotating disks or drums to convert kinetic energy into thermal energy.

Anti-lock Brakes: When a tire rolls, it experiences static friction (its surface is pressed against the road), but when it skids it experiences sliding friction. Since static friction is greater than sliding friction, a car will stop sooner if its tires roll, rather than skid, to a stop. Anti-lock brakes are designed to prevent locking and thereby provide the shortest stopping distance.

Traction: When accelerating or climbing hills, engineers release sand on the tracks in front of the driving wheels of a locomotive. The sand increases the friction between the wheels of the train and the track and keeps the train from spinning its wheels. In winter, sand is placed on icy streets to increase friction between automobile tires and the ice.

Starting Fires: Native Americans used a wooden rod and bow to start fires. The rounded end of the rod was placed into a small indentation in a block of wood, and the string of the bow was wrapped around the rod. When the bow was pulled rapidly back and forth, the rod would spin. Friction at the point of the spinning rod provided sufficient heat to ignite grass and twigs. The first practical friction matches were invented by the Englishman John Walker in 1827. These matches were tipped with potassium chlorate and antimony sulfide and were ignited when rubbed against a rough substance.

Meteors: Any object that moves through the air is subject to air resistance, commonly called "drag." Drag increases with speed and the density of the surrounding fluid. In outer space there is no air and hence no friction on moving objects, but when a meteor enters the atmosphere, friction between the meteor and air increases rapidly generating great heat. Meteors become "shooting stars" when they enter the atmosphere, encounter air friction, and burn. If there were no friction, numerous meteorites would strike the surface of the Earth and our terrain would look like the moon's.

Reentry of Satellites and Shuttles: The space shuttles have a shape that reduces friction on reentry into the atmosphere. In addition, their lower surfaces are covered with special ceramic tiles that are especially designed to dissipate the tremendous heat generated by friction on reentry into the atmosphere.

Erosion: The frictional force generated by wind provides an erosive force that can remove topsoil and render land incapable of producing and sustaining vegetation. From 1934 to 1937, a severe drought struck the panhandles of Oklahoma and Texas. Wind eroded soil loosened by poor agricultural practices, creating the infamous Dust Bowl.

3.4 TORQUE

In 1483, Leonardo da Vinci proposed the idea of a hovering aircraft that would derive its lift by rotating horizontal blades. Approximately 450 years after da Vinci's proposal, the first practical helicopter was developed by Louis Breguet and Rene Dorand of France. Today, it is common to see helicopters seemingly defying gravity as they collect traffic reports, pursue criminal suspects, or carry patients to trauma wards. The rotor above a helicopter acts like the wing of a conventional airplane by providing the required lift. The blades of the rotor can also be tilted to provide the thrust necessary to move the helicopter forward and backward. When the large lifting rotor rotates in one direction it creates a torque (a turning force) that acts to rotate the fuselage in the opposite direction. This torque would produce an unnerving spinning ride were it not countered by the opposite torque of the small tail rotor. Some helicopters have two lifting rotors rotating in opposite directions. The opposite rotations counteract each other so that no small tail rotor is required to keep the fuselage from rotating.

The word *torque* comes from the Latin word *torquere*, which means twist, and that is exactly what a torque produces. A torque can set an object spinning or twisting, or can keep it stable by countering an opposite torque. You often use torque without thinking about it—opening a door, prying the lid from a can, throwing a Frisbee, twirling a baton, up-righting an overturned object, turning the pages of a book, using a fishing pole to land a fish, painting, and rowing a boat. How many activities can you identify that do not involve torque in some way at some time?

What exactly is torque? Let's find out by investigating a common event—opening a door (Figure A). To open a door do you apply force at point *x* or *y*? You may be thinking that the answer is obvious: "Pull at point *x* because that is where the doorknob is." But why is the doorknob at point *x* and not at point *y*? If the knob were at point *y* would you be able to open the door? You are probably saying no. But can you explain? If you apply an external force at point *x* the door will open, but if you apply the same external force at point *y* the door will not open. There must be more to opening a door than merely applying a force at the appropriate point and in the appropriate direction.

A

The torque about a given axis or fulcrum is the product of the force (F) and the lever arm (L). This product is called the moment of the force. The lever arm of a force is the perpendicular distance from the axis of rotation to the line of force. The greater the force the greater the torque. The greater the lever arm the greater the torque. The customary unit of torque is foot-pound (ft·lb) and the metric unit is newton-meter (N·m). You are able to open the door by applying a force at point x because this produces a torque of magnitude $F \cdot L$. You cannot open the door by applying a force at point y because there is no lever arm ($L = 0$) upon which this force can act, and hence the torque is zero ($F \cdot L = 0$). You can open the door by applying a force at a point between x and y, but it will never be as easy as when applying the force at point x. Why?

Figure B shows a 40-pound bar, 4 feet in length with the fulcrum f at the left end. If a force of ten pounds is applied perpendicularly to the right end of the bar as shown, the bar experiences a torque of 40 foot-pounds in a clockwise direction ($T = F \cdot L = 10\text{lb} \cdot 4\text{ft} = 40$ ft·lb). In addition, the bar experiences an 80 ft·lb ($T = 40\text{lb} \cdot 2\text{ft} = 80$ ft·lb) clockwise torque due to its own weight acting at the center of mass. Thus, the total clockwise torque on the bar is 120 foot-pounds. If the applied force is not perpendicular (Figure C), then the torque is found by multiplying the perpendicular distance to the line of force by the magnitude of the force. For example, if the angle θ shown in Figure C is 45 degrees, then the lever arm is 2.8 feet and the applied torque is 2.8 feet x 10 pounds or 28 foot-pounds (total clockwise torque is 80 ft·lb + 28 ft·lb = 108 ft·lb). As the angle between the force and the bar decreases, so too does the lever arm and the torque. When the angle between the line of force and the lever arm is zero, there is no torque.

Figure D shows a lever being used to lift a heavy boulder. For purposes of explanation we assume the lever is weightless. The effort force is the person's force on the end of the lever and produces a torque in the counterclockwise direction. The resistance force is the weight of the boulder, which produces a torque in the clockwise direction. To lift the rock, the counterclockwise torque must exceed the clockwise torque. If the boulder weighs 330 pounds, the torque in the clockwise direction

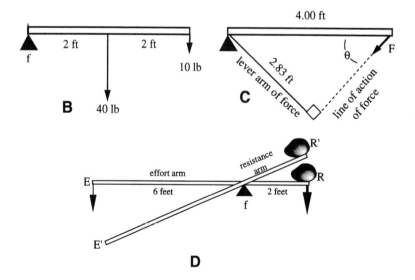

is 2 feet multiplied by 330 pounds, or 660 ft·lb. Since the effort arm is 6 feet in length we can compute the force needed to balance the boulder:

$$\text{effort force} = \frac{660 \text{ ft·lb}}{6 \text{ ft}} = 110 \text{ pounds}$$

If 110 pounds will balance the boulder, any force greater than 110 pounds will lift the boulder. But how can a force of 110 pounds lift a weight (counteract a force) of 330 pounds? Notice that the distance moved by the effort is greater than the distance moved by the resistance. In fact, the distance moved by the effort is three times the distance moved by the resistance. This lever multiplies force, but divides distance. The force was magnified by a factor of three, but the distance moved was only one third as great. In other words, you don't get something for nothing. A lever can be used to multiply force at the expense of distance, or to multiply distance at the expense of force.

Levers may be used to gain speed, to gain force, or to change direction. The distance moved by the effort *E* and resistance *R* forces are proportional to the lengths of the lever arms upon which they act.

$$\frac{\text{distance moved by effort}}{\text{distance moved by resistance}} = \frac{\text{effort arm}}{\text{resistance arm}}$$

The mechanical advantage of a simple machine is defined as the ratio of the force exerted by the machine to the force applied to the machine. Stated in another way, mechanical advantage is the ratio of the output force (resistance) to the input force (effort). It can also be expressed as the ratio of the distance through which the input force moves to the distance through which the output force moves. Thus, the mechanical advantage of a lever can be found either by dividing the resistance by the effort or by dividing the distance the effort moves by the distance the resistance moves:

$$\frac{\text{resistance}}{\text{effort}} = \frac{330 \text{ pounds}}{110 \text{ pounds}} = \text{mechanical advantage of 3}$$

$$\frac{\text{distance moved by effort}}{\text{distance moved by resistance}} = \frac{6 \text{ feet}}{2 \text{ feet}} = \text{mechanical advantage of 3}$$

A simple machine such as a lever does not change the amount of work you must do, but it allows you to do the work using a smaller force. The scientific definition of work is discussed in Section 5.1.

When you use a pair of scissors to cut an article from a newspaper, a wheelbarrow to carry a load of bricks, or a broom to sweep the kitchen floor, you are using torque. The scissors, wheelbarrow, and broom represent three different types of levers. In a first-class lever such as scissors, the fulcrum is always between the effort and the resistance (Figure E). *A first-class lever may be used to gain speed, to gain force, or to change direction.* In a second-class lever, such as a wheelbarrow, the resistance is always somewhere between the fulcrum and the effort (Figure F). *The mechanical advantage of a second-class lever is always greater than one, but a second-class lever cannot be used to gain speed or change direction.* In a third-class lever such as a broom, the effort is always between the fulcrum and the resistance (Figure G). *A third-class lever can be used only to gain speed.*

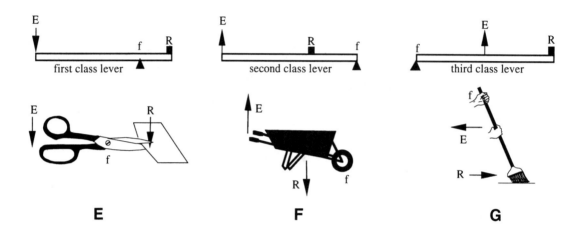

3.4.1 First-Class Levers

Concepts to Investigate: First-class levers, fulcrum, effort, resistance, equilibrium, balanced torque, multiplying force with levers, multiplying speed with levers, mechanical advantage.

Materials: Meter stick, finishing nails, drill, spring scales, wood to make meter stick support, string.

Principles and Procedures: In this and subsequent activities, you will investigate levers using the apparatus shown in Figure H. Holes are drilled every ten centimeters along the length of a wooden meter stick. The stick is allowed to pivot when hung at one of these points on a finishing nail, which is hammered partway into the side of the support.

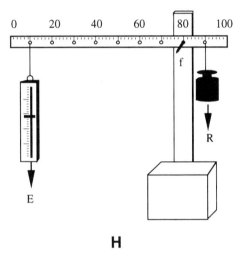

H

In a first-class lever, the fulcrum is always located between the effort force and the resistance. Pivot the meter stick on the nail at the 80-cm (0.80 m) mark, as shown in Figure H. The stick should pivot freely. Obtain an object such as a balance-weight and find its weight in newtons. Attach this weight at the 90-cm (0.90 m) mark. The distance from the weight to the fulcrum is 10 cm (0.10 m). The torque in the clockwise direction created by the weight is computed by multiplying the magnitude of the weight by the lever arm, 0.10 m. Record this torque in the table. Now attach the scale at the 20-cm (0.20-m) mark and pull straight down on the scale until the meter stick is horizontal. Record the force shown on the scale in the table. Since the distance from the point of attachment of the scale to the fulcrum is 0.70 m (0.70 m), the torque in the counterclockwise direction is computed by multiplying the force shown on the scale by the lever arm, 0.70 m. You will find that the torques are not equal because the lever itself has weight. Many books simply state that one should neglect the weight of the lever, but this is not practical if the lever is massive. For example, you could not use a first-class lever to lift a large boulder if you were not able to lift and position the lever itself.

The weight of the stick can be considered as concentrated at the center of gravity (0.50-m mark) of the stick. Remove the meter stick from the stand. Attach the stick to the scale and find its weight in newtons. The torque in the counterclockwise direction caused by the weight of the stick is computed by multiplying the weight of the stick in newtons by the distance from the center of mass to the point of support, 0.30 m. When added together, the torque in the clockwise direction should approximately equal the torque in the clockwise direction. Do the clockwise and counterclockwise torques balance each other? What factors may contribute to slight differences between them?

Try different positions of the fulcrum on the meter stick and different combinations of weights and distances and record your results in the table. Calculate the mechanical advantage of each lever as the ratio of the output force (resistance) to the input force (effort). Under what conditions is the mechanical advantage greatest?

First-Class Levers								
	1	2	3	4	5	6	7	8
Weight of object (resistance force) *N*								
Lever arm of object *m*								
Torque of object *N·m*								
Direction of object's torque *clockwise or counterclockwise*								
Weight of meter stick *N*								
Lever arm of meter stick *m*								
Torque of meter stick *N·m*								
Direction of meter stick's torque *clockwise or counterclockwise*								
Weight of effort (effort force) *N*								
Lever arm of effort *m*								
Torque of effort *N·m*								
Direction of effort's torque *clockwise or counterclockwise*								
Total clockwise torque *N·m*								
Total counterclockwise torque *N·m*								
Mechanical advantage *resistance force/effort force*								

Questions

(1) Under what conditions can a first-class lever be used to magnify force? Give an example.

(2) Under what conditions can a first-class lever be used to gain speed? Give an example.

(3) Draw diagrams of the following first-class levers. Indicate the resistance R, fulcrum f and effort E: teeter-totter (see-saw), bumper jack, wrench.

(4) Rocks used to build the great pyramids of Egypt had to be moved great vertical distances. Suggest how torque may have been used to accomplish the feat.

(5) Name five activities in your everyday life that do not involve torque.

(6) Under what conditions is the mechanical advantage of a lever greatest?

3.4.2 Second-Class Levers

Concepts to Investigate: Second-class levers, fulcrum, effort, resistance, equilibrium, balanced torque, multiplying force with levers.

Materials: Meter stick, finishing nails, drill, spring scales, wood to make meter stick support, string.

Principles and Procedures: Construct the apparatus shown in Figure I according to the procedure mentioned in the previous activity. Pivot the meter stick on the stand at the 80-cm (0.80 m) mark as shown. Attach an object of known weight to the stick at the 70-cm (0.70 m) mark. The distance from the weight to the fulcrum is 10 cm (0.10 m). The torque in the counterclockwise direction created by the weight is computed by multiplying the magnitude of the weight by the lever arm, 0.10 m. Record this torque in the table. Also record the counterclockwise torque caused by the weight of the stick as the product of the weight of the meter stick acting at its center of mass. Now attach the scale at the 20-cm (0.20 m) mark and pull straight up until the meter stick is horizontal. Record the force shown on the scale in the table. Since the distance from the point of attachment of the scale to the fulcrum is known, and the effort force is known, the torque of the effort may be calculated. Try different positions of the fulcrum, effort, and object as well as different weights of the object. Do clockwise and counterclockwise torques always balance?

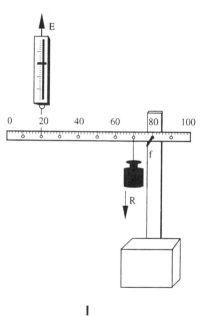

I

Questions

(1) Do second-class levers always magnify force? Explain.
(2) Give some examples of tools that are second-class levers.
(3) Draw a diagram of a paper cutter and indicate the effort, resistance, and fulcrum. Is it a second-class lever?
(4) The molars are those teeth set farthest back in the jaw. Explain why they are particularly useful in crushing hard food.

Second-Class Levers								
	1	2	3	4	5	6	7	8
Weight of object (resistance force) N								
Lever arm of object m								
Torque of object N·m								
Direction of object's torque *clockwise or counterclockwise*								
Weight of meter stick N								
Lever arm of meter stick m								
Torque of meter stick N·m								
Direction of meter stick's torque *clockwise or counterclockwise*								
Weight of effort (effort force) N								
Lever arm of effort m								
Torque of effort N·m								
Direction of effort's torque *clockwise or counterclockwise*								
Total clockwise torque N·m								
Total counterclockwise torque N·m								
Mechanical advantage *resistance force/effort force*								

3.4.3 Third-Class Levers

Concepts to Investigate: Third-class levers, fulcrum, effort, resistance, equilibrium, balanced torque, multiplying speed.

Materials: Meter stick, finishing nails, drill, spring scales, wood to make meter stick support, string, Ping-Pong balls or suitable substitute, large cooking spoon.

Principles and Procedures: In a third-class lever, the effort is applied between the fulcrum and the resistance. You may investigate third-class levers using the device illustrated in Figure J.

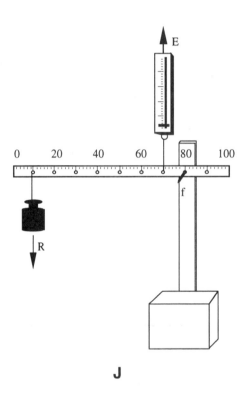

J

Part 1. Equilibrium: Use a nail to pivot the meter stick on the stand at the 80-cm (0.80 m) mark. The stick should pivot freely. Obtain an object such as weight or set of washers, hang from your scale, and find its weight in newtons. Attach this object to the other end of the stick at the 10-cm (0.10 m) mark. The distance from the weight to the fulcrum is 70 cm (0.70 m). The torque in the counterclockwise direction created by the hanging object is computed by multiplying the magnitude of the weight by the lever arm, 0.70 m. Record this torque in the table. Don't forget to consider the

© 1994 by John Wiley & Sons, Inc.

counterclockwise torque caused by the weight of the stick when calculating the total counterclockwise torque. Now attach the scale at the 70-cm (0.70 m) mark and pull straight up until the meter stick is horizontal. Record the force shown on the scale in the table. Try different combinations of weights and distances and record your results in the table. Does clockwise torque always equal counterclockwise torque when the meter stick is in equilibrium (balanced)?

Part 2. Multiplying speed with a third-class lever: You may have noticed that third-class levers arc incapable of multiplying force, but do multiply the distance that the resistance moves. Thus, third-class levers are particularly suitable when a wide range of motion or an increase in speed is desired. Catapults were used by ancient armies to hurl rocks, darts, or arrows at an enemy fortress. As a third-class lever, a catapult is capable of sending projectiles rapidly, but only if they are relatively small. To investigate the ability of a third-class lever to multiply speed, place a Ping-Pong ball or similar object in a large serving spoon, as illustrated in Figure K. Use one hand to hold the end of the spoon while you hold the handle with the other. Use your thumb to apply pressure on the back of the handle and then release your hand from the end of the spoon and allow the ball to fly. Note the location of your thumb and the distance the ball travels when released. Repeat the procedure, using the same pressure, first applying it closer to the pivot point (end of the handle) and then farther from the pivot point. Does the ball travel farther when the pressure is applied close to or far from the pivot point? What do you sacrifice when you multiply speed?

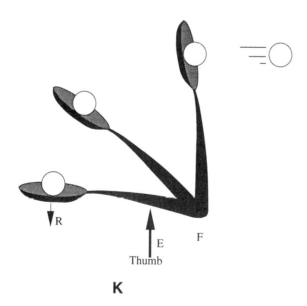

K

Third-Class Levers								
	1	2	3	4	5	6	7	8
Weight of object (resistance force) *N*								
Lever arm of object *m*								
Torque of object *N·m*								
Direction of object's torque *clockwise or counterclockwise*								
Weight of meter stick *N*								
Lever arm of meter stick *m*								
Torque of meter stick *N·m*								
Direction of meter stick's torque *clockwise or counterclockwise*								
Weight of effort (effort force) *N*								
Lever arm of effort *m*								
Torque of effort *N·m*								
Direction of effort's torque *clockwise or counterclockwise*								
Total clockwise torque *N·m*								
Total counterclockwise torque *N·m*								
Mechanical advantage *resistance force/effort force*								

© 1994 by John Wiley & Sons, Inc.

Questions

(1) Are third-class levers capable of multiplying force? Explain.

(2) Are third-class levers capable of multiplying speed or range of motion? Explain.

(3) Most of the levers in the arms and legs of a human body are third-class levers. What advantages do third-class levers have compared to second-class levers?

(4) Draw a picture of a pair of tweezers and explain why they are third-class levers.

(5) The elbow and knee joints are third-class levers. Draw pictures to indicate the resistance R, fulcrum f, and effort E at both these joints.

3.4.4 Levers in Everyday Life

Concepts to Investigate: Comparison of first-, second-, and third-class levers; identification of fulcrum, resistance, and effort; uses of levers in everyday life.

Materials: No materials needed.

Principles and Procedures: When you use pliers to grasp an object you are using a first-class lever, with the fulcrum between the effort and the resistance (Figure L). When you use a nutcracker to crack a nut you are using a second-class lever, with the resistance between the effort and the fulcrum (Figure M). When you use a shovel to lift dirt you are using a third-class lever, with the effort between the resistance and the fulcrum (Figure N). Study the levers shown in Figures L–N and then study the tools, objects, or body parts listed below. Draw a simple diagram of each, indicating the location of the fulcrum *f*, resistance *R*, and effort *E*. Note the distances moved by the resistance and effort forces and classify each lever appropriately as a first-, second-, or third-class lever.

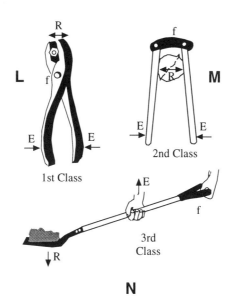

a. Manual can opener punching a hole in a can
b. Oars of a rowboat pushing against water
c. Wire strippers cutting wire on the handle side of pivot
d. Screwdriver prying lid off a paint can
e. Your lower jaw when biting food
f. Your lower jaw when chewing food with your molars (teeth in back)
g. Claw hammer pulling a nail out of a block of wood
h. Your arm when throwing a baseball
i. Ice tongs picking up an ice cube
j. Paddle of canoe pushing water

Questions

(1)   Which type of lever is most versatile? Explain.

(2)   What are the advantages of a second-class lever compared to a third-class lever? Explain.

(3)   What are the advantages of a third-class lever compared to a second-class lever? Explain.

FOR THE TEACHER

Virtually every task we perform involves torque, but few stop to think about its significance. Students will appreciate the importance of torque if you bring in a variety of tools that illustrate the principles of leverage. You may illustrate first-class levers using a crowbar, automobile jack, hand can opener, the claw on a hammer, or the oars of a rowboat. There are a variety of double first-class levers including lopping sheers, scissors, wire cutters, and pliers. You may illustrate second-class levers using a wheelbarrow, paper cutter, or a door. A nutcracker is an example of a double second-class lever. To illustrate third-class levers, you may use a pitchfork, golf club, tennis racket, mousetrap, catapult, broom, baseball bat, fishing pole. Tweezers and ice-cube tongs are examples of double third-class levers.

Even pendulums rely on torque to move (see Figure O). We can consider the motion of the pendulum as the rotational oscillation of a rigid body about a horizontal axis through *P*, the fixed point of support. The equilibrium position of the pendulum is the position in which the center of gravity of the bob is directly below the point of support. When the pendulum is displaced from this position gravity acts on the lever arm to produce a torque that tends to pull the bob down. The greater the displacement of the bob from the rest position the greater the lever arm and the greater the restoring torque. As the pendulum moves down, the lever arm decreases in length and the velocity and momentum of the bob increase. At the rest position there is no lever arm and, consequently, there is no torque. But the bob is moving in an arc at the rest position and has momentum that carries it past the rest position. As the bob moves in an upward arc past the rest position, gravity acts on the lever arm on this side of the swing to produce a torque that retards the upward motion of the bob. We refer to this as giving the bob a negative acceleration. Soon the bob comes to a stop and gravity provides a torque to pull it in the opposite direction. This back-and-forth motion continues until frictional forces eventually bring the bob to a stop.

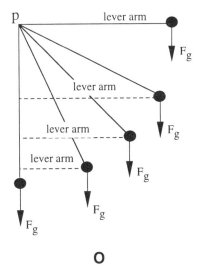

O

We informed students that if the force applied to a bar is not perpendicular (Figure P), the torque is found by multiplying the perpendicular distance to the line of force by the magnitude of the force. We will explain to you how to calculate the lever arm so you can pass it on to your students when appropriate. The explanation requires a bit of simple trigonometry using the sine function. In a right triangle such as shown in Figure P, the sine of an angle is defined as the ratio of the length of the side opposite the angle to the length of the hypotenuse. The length of the bar (B) is the hypotenuse, and the length of the lever arm (L) is the length of the side opposite angle theta. If the magnitude of the angle and the length of the bar are known, then the length of the lever arm can be determined using the following relationship:

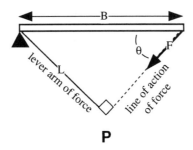

P

$$\sin\theta = L/B \therefore L = B \sin\theta$$

For example, if the angle between the line of force and the bar is 30° and the length of the bar is 3.4 m, then the length of the lever arm is computed as follows:

$$L = 3.4 \text{ m} \times \sin 30° = 3.4 \text{ m} \times 0.5 = 1.7 \text{ m}$$

To compute the torque, simply multiply the force by the length of the lever arm. If the force is 30 newtons then the torque is:

$$30 \text{ newtons} \times 1.7 \text{ m, or } 51 \text{ newton-meters}$$

3.4.1 First-Class Levers

Discussion: Make certain students understand the significance of the relative positions of the fulcrum (pivot point), effort (applied force, input force), and resistance (output force) for a first-class lever. The fulcrum is always somewhere between the effort and the resistance. When performing the activities, students will notice that the effort and resistance move over different distances depending on their relative positions from the fulcrum. By using different positions for the fulcrum together with different weights and lever arms, students should be able to discover that a first-class lever may be used to gain speed, to gain force, or to change direction, and that the distances moved by the effort and resistance forces are proportional to the lengths of the lever arms upon which they act.

The principles of torque and first-class levers can be demonstrated to the entire class using a long, strong board and a wooden pivot point as illustrated in Figures Q–T. Figure Q illustrates the equilibrium condition when clockwise and counterclockwise torque balance each other because forces and torque arms are equal. Although the torque arms in Figure R are equal, the forces are not, and so the plank rotates. In Figure S, the counterclockwise force is greater than the clockwise force, but because the torque arm of the clockwise force is much greater, the clockwise torque exceeds the counterclockwise torque and the plank rotates in a clockwise direction. In Figure T, the clockwise force is able to balance more than twice the counterclockwise force because of a significantly longer torque arm. Students may be surprised to see one student balancing two or more of his or her peers on the board.

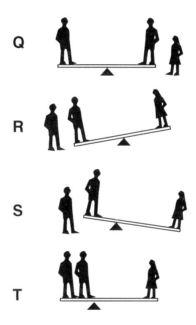

Answers (1) A first-class lever will magnify force if the effort arm is longer than the resistance arm. A crow bar is an example of such a lever. (2) A first-class lever can be used to gain speed if the resistance arm is longer than the effort arm. (3) Make sure that the fulcrum on student diagrams is always between the effort and the resistance. (4) Rocks of great mass may be lifted using long effort arms. (5) Student answers will vary. Some possible examples include thinking, dreaming, etc. (6) The mechanical advantage will be greatest when the ratio of the effort arm to resistance arm is maximized.

3.4.2 Second-Class Levers

Discussion: Make certain students understand the significance of the relative positions of the fulcrum, effort, and resistance for a second-class lever. The resistance is always somewhere between the fulcrum and the effort force. By using different positions for the fulcrum together with different weights and lever arms, students should be able to discover that a second-class lever may be used to gain force, but not to change direction or speed, and that the distance moved by the effort and resistance are proportional to the lengths of the lever arms upon which they act.

Answers (1) By definition, the effort arm of a second-class lever is longer than the resistance arm. Therefore, it must magnify force. (2) Student answers will vary, but may include such things as wheelbarrows, paper cutters, nutcrackers, and doors. (3) Student diagrams should indicate the paper providing a resistance between the blade's pivot and the end of the handle. (4) The jaw can be a second- or a third-class lever depending upon the location of the food. When food is in the rear of the mouth, the jaw is a second-class lever. Unlike third-class levers, second-class levers always multiply force, giving you the ability to crush hard foods.

3.4.3 Third-Class Levers

Discussion: Make certain students understand the significance of the relative positions of the fulcrum, force, and resistance for a third-class lever. The effort force is always somewhere between the fulcrum and the resistance. By using different positions for the fulcrum together with different weights and lever arms, students should be able to discover that a third-class lever may be used only to gain speed, but not to gain force or change direction. They should also realize that the distance moved by the effort force and resistance are proportional to the lengths of the lever arms upon which they act

Answers: (1) No. The resistance arm of a third-class lever is always longer than the effort arm, making it impossible to multiply force. (2) Yes. The resistance arm of a third-class lever is longer than the effort arm, so it will move through a greater distance when pivoted. Since the resistance travels through a greater distance in a given amount of time than the effort, it travels faster. (3) The limbs are third-class levers, allowing you to run rapidly and throw things rapidly. If the limbs were second-class levers, they would be stronger, but too slow to be of much use, particularly in activities such as throwing, running, and typing. (4) Make sure students label the resistance at the end of the tweezers and the effort in the middle. (5) Check to see that students have identified the center of mass of the moving bone as the location of the resistance, and the point of muscle attachment as the location of the effort force. The joint itself should be identified as the fulcrum or pivot point.

3.4.4 Levers in Everyday Life

Discussion: A machine is a device for multiplying forces, multiplying speed, or changing the direction of forces. Levers are examples of simple machines. Some students mistakenly believe that one "gets something for nothing" when using a lever. Remind students of the scientific definition of work. Work is the product of a force multiplied by the distance through which the force acts. When we do work on one end of a lever the other end of the lever does work on the load (resistance). If we neglect friction, work input must equal work output. Consequently, the product of the input force and the distance through which it moves must equal the product of the output force and the distance through which it moves. For example, when using a bumper jack to lift a car, you must move the handle up and down many times (through a large distance) in order to lift the car a small vertical distance. By exerting a small force through a large distance we are able to produce a large force acting through a small distance and lift the car.

You may at this time wish to introduce the concept of machine efficiency. If friction forces are not neglected, work done by a lever cannot equal work done on the lever, because some of the input work is changed to heat by frictional forces. Efficiency is the ratio of useful work to the total work. For example, when using a lever, if 10 ft·lb of work are input and 9.8 ft·lb are output, then the efficiency of the lever is, 9.8 ft·lb/10 ft·lb or 98 percent.

For the activity, students should draw diagrams of the tools listed, carefully identifying the effort, resistance, and fulcrum. The answers to the activity are as follows: (a) first, (b) first, (c) second, (d) first, (e) third, (f) second, (g) first, (h) third, (i) third, (j) third.

Answers (1) The first-class lever is the most versatile. Because the fulcrum is between the effort and resistance, it is possible to have an effort arm that is longer than a resistance arm and thereby multiply force, or a resistance arm that is longer than an effort arm and thereby multiply speed. (2) Second-class levers multiply force. (3) Third-class levers multiply speed or distance.

Applications to Everyday Life

Making Life Easier: Torque makes our everyday life easier. By applying torque to a handle you can open or close windows and doors. The torque you apply to a bumper jack makes it possible for you to lift a heavy car. The torque you apply to a spoon or fork helps you bring food to your mouth. The simple acts of walking, talking, and smiling involve torque. It is difficult to name an everyday activity that does not involve torque in some way.

Sports Activities: Torque is used by athletes in every sport. In any running game such as football, baseball, soccer, or tennis, the players' muscles must provide torque in their thighs and legs to allow them to run. Good surfers, skate boarders, and skiers are able to position their bodies so their weight will provide the proper torque to move the boards or skis in the desired direction. A sumo wrestler crouches low to minimize the torque his opponent may apply when trying to topple him. Great baseball pitchers, football quarterbacks, and tennis players have a knack for placing the proper torque on the ball to make it travel in the correct direction to produce a strike, touchdown, or point. A rower in a shell uses an oar as a first-class lever to produce a torque to move the shell quickly over the surface of the water.

Machines and Tools: A mechanic uses a torque wrench to provide the proper amount of torque to a bolt as it is tightened on the engine of your vehicle. When you pull the starting rope on a lawnmower, chain saw, outboard engine, or other machine you are applying the torque required to start the engine. Machines that you see every day, such as power shovels, street sweepers, automobiles, and airplanes generate torque necessary to move dirt, pick up debris, or move passengers.

Switches and Levers: You are applying torque when you pull the lever to move the front seat of your vehicle backward or forward. You use torque to flip a light switch, turn off a circuit breaker, set the parking brake in your car, or use the turn indicator.

Games: Many arcade games require the use of torque on a joystick to position players or vehicles on the screen. The simple act of moving a piece from one part of the board to another in checkers or chess involves torque.

Occupations: Occupations, regardless of their nature, require torque. A carpenter uses torque to drive a nail with a hammer. A banker uses torque when moving a pen to sign a contract. You use torque when working in the home—lifting pans off the stove, pushing the vacuum cleaner, ironing clothes, and turning on the stereo. A race-car driver uses torque to turn the steering wheel. A reader uses torque to turn the pages of a book.

Leisure-time Activities: Swings and seesaws require the application of torque for their operation. When sitting on a motionless swing, you must push on the ground with your foot to provide the torque required to set the swing in motion. Knitting and crocheting require not only a knowledge of the art but also torque to keep the needles moving in the correct manner.

UNIT FOUR

Pressure

4.1 Air Pressure

4.2 Vapor Pressure

4.3 Fluid Pressure

4.4 Fluids in Motion

4.1 AIR PRESSURE

Imagine playing a game of football and having 65 players pile on top of you after being tackled. Such pressure would be deadly, yet the atmosphere exerts an equivalent pressure on your body 24 hours a day. How can this be? Air is so light! How can it exert great pressure? Why aren't we crushed by it? Performing the following activities will answer these and many other intriguing questions.

Pressure is defined as the amount of force applied per unit area. For example, if a 1 pound weight rests on 1 square inch of surface area, the pressure is 1 pound per square inch, abbreviated as PSI. Inspect the side of an automobile tire and you may see a warning such as "Do not inflate above 40 PSI" or "Do not inflate above 276 kPa". This means that the pressure inside the tire should be less than that created by a 40-pound weight resting on 1 square inch of surface area.

Pressure can be measured with many different units. Although many people prefer to measure pressure in PSI, most scientists use a unit known as the Pascal. A Pascal (Pa) is defined as the pressure exerted by a one-newton weight resting on an area of 1 square meter. (A newton is the weight of a 1-kg mass at the Earth's surface.) Because the Pascal is a very small unit, it is often more convenient to measure pressure in a kilopascal (kPa), which is defined as 1,000 newtons of force per square meter.

Just as water exerts pressure on you when you swim below the surface, the atmosphere exerts pressure on everything immersed in it. The atmosphere is a sea of air that is pulled by gravity toward the center of the Earth. Air pressure increases with depth, just as water pressure does. With the exception of a few locations, such as California's Death Valley, the "deepest" you can be in the atmosphere is sea level, identified as zero meters. Figure A shows that the atmosphere presses down on you, and at sea level this is equivalent to 101.3 kPa, or 14.7 pounds per square inch.

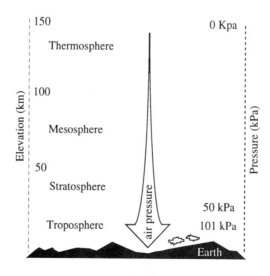

A

We are not crushed by the air surrounding us for the same reason fish living in the depths of the ocean are not crushed by the water surrounding them. Fish are permeable to water, meaning water can move relatively easily into and out of the fish. As a result, the pressure inside fish becomes the same as the pressure surrounding them. Similarly, humans are relatively permeable to air and hence our internal pressure stays the same as the pressure of the surrounding air. Thus, while the atmosphere exerts 14.7 pounds of force per square inch on our bodies, our bodies counter with an equivalent pressure in the opposite direction.

The only time most people are aware of air pressure is when it changes. You may have noticed a change in air pressure in your ears when driving on a mountain road. As you ascend, atmospheric pressure decreases. While air pressure outside drops, the pressure in your middle ear may remain constant, causing a pressure differential (Figures B and C). This difference in pressure causes your eardrums to bulge and may produce pain, which may be relieved by yawning (Figure D). Yawning opens the small Eustachian tubes between your ear and pharynx allowing air to rush out of the middle ear and into the atmosphere through the nose or mouth. Your ear "pops" when the eardrum snaps back into its normal position as pressure is equalized.

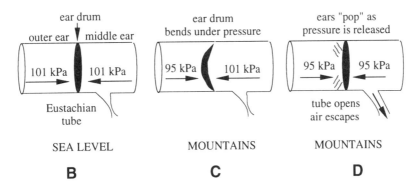

Although the atmosphere exerts a significant amount of pressure on everything in our environment, we notice its effect only when a difference in air pressure (pressure differential) exists. In the following activities you will create pressure differentials in order to study the influence of air pressure.

4.1.1 The Magnitude of Air Pressure

Concepts to Investigate: Definition of pressure, pressure equation, implosions, atmospheric pressure.

Materials: Balance, meter stick, graph paper, soft-drink can, beaker tongs or equivalent, large beaker or bucket, packing tape.

Principles and Procedures

Part 1. How great is atmospheric pressure? Atmospheric pressure at sea level is 14.7 lb/in² (101.3 kPa). Is this a large pressure or a small pressure? To understand the magnitude of atmospheric pressure, you must relate it to something with which you are familiar. In this activity you will compare atmospheric pressure to the pressure you exert on the floor, or a book exerts on a table. Since pressure is defined as the ratio of force to area $p = F/A$, we can calculate the pressure an object exerts if we know its weight (which is its force of gravity on the object) and the surface area of contact. To complete the following table, it will be necessary to measure the contact area of your feet. Draw the outline of your shoe on a piece of graph paper and count the number of squares inside the figure. Multiply the number of squares by the area of an individual square to determine the approximate surface area of the bottom of your feet. Complete the table using the following conversion factors as needed.

$$1 \text{ cm}^2 = 0.0001 \text{ m}^2$$
$$1 \text{ lb} = 0.454 \text{ kg}$$
$$1 \text{ in}^2 = 6.45 \text{ cm}^2 = 0.000645 \text{ m}^2$$
$$1 \text{ Pa} = 1.45 \times 10^{-4} \text{ lb/in}^2$$
$$1 \text{ kg mass weighs } 9.8 \text{ N}$$

Object	mass (kg)	weight (N)	area (m²)	pressure (Pa)	pressure (lb/in²)
Textbook (lying on front cover)					
Textbook (standing upright)					
You (standing on both feet)					
You (standing on one foot)					
Atmospheric pressure (sea level)				1.01×10^5	14.7
Atmospheric pressure (Mt. Everest)				3.40×10^4	4.9

Part 2. The collapsing can: Obtain a large beaker or bucket and fill with water. Pour water into an aluminum soft-drink can to a depth of approximately 1 cm and place it on a hot plate until the water boils. Do not allow the can to boil dry. As soon as the water begins to boil, remove the can from the heat source and place it in an

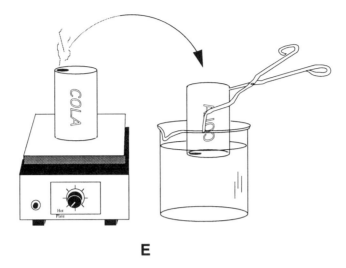

E

upright position on the table top. Is there any change in the can? Repeat the process, only this time invert the can and submerge the opening in the water, as illustrated in Figure E. Is there any change in the can? Draw a diagram of the experimental setup and indicate where the pressure must be highest with an *H* and where it must be lowest with an *L*.

When one milliliter of water boils (vaporizes) it changes into 1,000 milliliters of steam. As water in a soft-drink can boils, it displaces air that was originally in the can. When the can is sealed and cooled, the steam condenses to liquid water, but now occupies only 1/1000th the volume it occupied as steam! In other words, for every milliliter of water that condenses inside the can, 999 milliliters of vacuum are left behind. The air pressure outside the can remains the same while the pressure inside drops, creating a difference in pressure that collapses the can.

Questions

(1) On the basis of your calculations in Part 1, what is the relative magnitude of atmospheric pressure at sea level compared to the pressure you exert when standing on two feet?

(2) Under what conditions does the can collapse in Part 2? Explain.

(3) In the introduction to this chapter we explained why your ears "pop" when you drive up a steep mountain road. Using diagrams, explain why your ears also "pop" when you travel down the same road.

(4) Airline companies pressurize the cabins of aircraft so passengers do not experience rapid changes in air pressure. On at least one occasion, however, an airplane's pressurization system failed and a passenger lost her hearing. Explain how the depressurization of the cabin may have caused this hearing loss.

(5) Why may it be painful to travel into the mountains if you have a head cold?

4.1.2 Pressure Equation

Concepts to Investigate: Pressure equation, force, pressure, surface area.

Materials: Newspaper, notebook paper, thin wooden slat, hammer.

Principles and Procedures: Archaeological evidence suggests that sails have been used to propel boats for more than 4,000 years. Sailing reached its height in the middle of the nineteenth century when large clipper ships such as the *Sovereign of the Seas* routinely traveled across the Atlantic Ocean in 15 days or less. In 1871 the British christened the H.M. Battleship *Sultan*, with a record 49,400 square feet of sails. For 75 years this gargantuan ship sailed the oceans of the world. Why do large boats like the *Sultan* require large sails? As long as the sails are exposed to the same wind, they experience identical pressure regardless of size, so what is the advantage of having large sails? See if you can answer this question after performing the following activity.

Pressure is the ratio of force to area $p = F/A$, while force is the product of pressure and area $F = pA$. At a given elevation, the pressure the atmosphere exerts upon objects is equal, but the force is not if the surface areas upon which the atmosphere is pressing are different sizes.

Position a thin slat of wood such as a ruler or paint stirrer on a table so approximately 20 cm hangs over the edge. Place two sheets of notebook paper on the slat and press against the table until the paper is as flat as possible. Strike the overhanging portion of the slat with a hammer, as shown in Figure F. Repeat this procedure using two pieces of unfolded newspaper and record your results in the table provided. What is the magnitude of the force holding the slat down on the table in each case?

F

	Notebook Paper	*Unfolded Newspaper*
Area of paper	_____ m²	_____ m²
Atmospheric pressure	101,300 N/m²	101,300 N/m²
Force upon paper	_____ N	_____ N
Does wood break?	_____	_____

Questions

(1) Is the air pressure on a sheet of notebook paper and the newspaper the same? Is the force upon them the same? Explain.

(2) Did the wood break when placed under the notebook paper? When placed under the newspaper? Explain.

(3) Realizing that air pressure is independent of surface area, why do large ships require large sails?

4.1.3 Pascal's Law

Concepts to Investigate: Pascal's law, fluid, fluid pressure.

Materials: Jar, overhead transparency or 3″ × 5″ card, plungers (plumber's helpers), light grease.

Principles and Procedures: In addition to his brilliant works in mathematics, engineering, and theology, the French thinker Blaise Pascal helped establish the foundations of hydrostatics, the study of fluids at rest. In 1653 Pascal discovered that *the force exerted by a confined fluid acts at right angles at every point on a submerged object.* In other words, a point-object submerged in a fluid experiences the same pressure on the bottom surface as on the side or top. A fluid is a substance that flows easily and takes the shape of the container in which it is enclosed. Since air is a fluid, Pascal's law should apply to objects immersed in the atmosphere. Let's find out.

Part 1. Hanging water upside down: You may have noticed that it is possible to hold water in a straw simply by covering the top with your finger while withdrawing it from a liquid. When the top is sealed, water cannot leave because air pressure outside pushes against the water through the open end of the straw. If water were to fall out of a covered straw, a vacuum would be created in the region vacated by the water. However, since a vacuum has no pressure (0 kPa) while the atmosphere does (101.3 kPa at sea level), the pressure differential keeps the water in the straw against the force of gravity. According to Pascal's principle, this pressure acts against the open end of the straw the same way as it works down against the tabletop (Figure G). When you remove your finger from the end of the straw the force of gravity will drain the water since there is no longer a pressure differential. (A pressure of 101.3 kPa exists on both sides of an open straw, as shown in Figure H.) Would the same result occur when using containers with larger diameters? To find out, fill a jar or flask completely with water. Cover the mouth of the container with a piece of an overhead transparency, a 3″ × 5″ card, or other suitable material, as shown in Figure I.

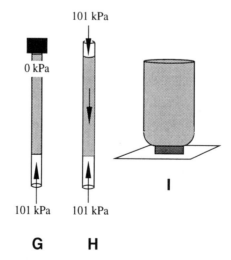

G   H

Keeping one finger on the cover, invert the container. Carefully remove your finger. Slowly rotate the container through a complete circle so the mouth faces up and then down again. Does the card remain in place regardless of the orientation? Are your observations consistent with Pascal's principle?

Part 2. Magdeburg hemispheres: The tremendous pressure exerted by air can be demonstrated in a dramatic fashion using two drain plungers. When two plungers are pressed together to form a tight seal, it becomes very difficult to pull them apart. Cover the adjoining surfaces of two plungers with a light grease so a good seal will form and push them together, as illustrated in Figure J. As the plungers collapse, air escapes, and if a good seal forms, no air will reenter when pressure is released. When you stop pushing on the plungers, the rubber or neoprene in the head of the plunger will expand due to internal restoring forces. As the heads expand, a partial vacuum is created, causing the formation of a pressure differential between the outside and the inside of the plungers. Go outside on a lawn and try to pull the plungers apart. Can you do it? If not, how can you separate the plungers? Pascal's law says that the pressure on the plungers is the same regardless of their orientation. Are your data consistent with this? Explain.

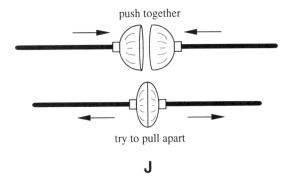

J

Questions

(1) Are your data consistent with Pascal's principle? Explain.
(2) Gasoline cans that are used to fill the tanks of lawn mowers and other gasoline-powered machines generally contain a vent in addition to the pouring spout. Explain.
(3) Would it be more difficult to separate large Magdeburg hemispheres than small ones? Explain.
(4) How can the plungers be separated if you are unable to pull them apart?

4.1.4 Pressure Differentials

Concepts to Investigate: Pressure differentials, fluid flow, "suction."

Materials: Shallow dish; candle, matches, flask or drinking glass, hard-boiled egg, paper, Erlenmeyer flask.

Principles and Procedures

Part 1. "Suction" from candles? Light a candle and stand it upright in the middle of a pan and secure it with melted drippings. Fill the pan half full with water. While the candle is still burning, place a narrow glass or graduated cylinder over the candle (Figure K). Carefully observe the base of the container, the water level in the container, and the flame. Record your observations in the table. When does the water level in the jar rise (Figure L)? Why does it rise? Indicate on Figure L where the pressure must be higher and where it must be lower to cause the results you observed.

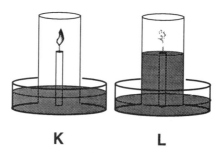

Time	Base of Jar	Water Level	Flame

Part 2."Suction" from burning paper? Find a flask or jar that has a mouth slightly smaller than the diameter of an egg. Peel the shell from a hard-boiled egg. Crumple a piece of notebook paper and after lighting it on fire, quickly stuff it in the flask. Immediately place the egg over the mouth of the flask and observe, paying particular attention to the egg when it is first placed on the flask (Figure M). When does the egg enter the flask or bottle? Why does it enter? To remove the egg from the bottle, invert the bottle so the egg settles in the neck. Gently heat the flask with a candle or

alcohol burner until the egg is forced out by expanding air. Light a second piece of paper and place it inside a flask. While holding the flask with a hot mitt, quickly place the egg in the neck and invert the bottle while holding the egg in place. Does the egg rise into the flask against gravity? Explain.

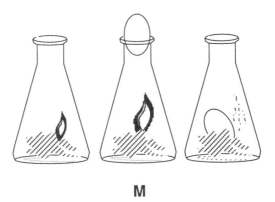

M

Questions

(1) Was the water in Part 1 pushed or pulled into the bottle? Was the egg in part 2 pushed or pulled into the flask? Explain.

(2) The air pressure inside the containers in Parts 1 and 2 must have been reduced to allow the water to rise. What are two factors that would lead to a reduction in air pressure?

(3) Explain how a syringe withdraws blood. Draw a diagram and indicate regions of higher and lower pressure.

(4) In rural areas, some people use manual lift pumps to withdraw water from wells. When the handle of the pump is depressed, a vacuum in the cylinder inside the pump is created and air pressure pushes water from the water table below, up into the cylinder, and eventually out the spout. If air pressure can lift water only to a maximum height of 10.3 meters (34 feet), how can lift pumps work when a well is greater than 34 feet deep?

(5) How does a vacuum cleaner work? Draw a diagram and indicate regions of higher and lower pressure.

(6) Are fluids pushed (by pressure differentials) or pulled (by "suction")?

4.1.5 Air Pressure and Breathing

Concepts to Investigate: "Negative pressure," breathing, pressure differentials.

Materials: Bell jar, balloons, glass tubing, one-holed stopper, twine.

Principles and Procedures: Inhalation is the process whereby air is delivered to the lungs, where it is then absorbed into the blood. In mammals, inhalation is dependent upon a pressure gradient that pushes air into the lungs. When inhaling, the diaphragm (a muscular membrane at the bottom of the chest cavity) is pulled down while the rib cage is pulled up and out. As a result of such movement, the lungs expand like a bellows. As a result of this expansion, a partial vacuum is created inside the lungs and air from the outside is pushed in.

The action of lungs can be demonstrated using the apparatus illustrated in Figure N. To simulate the lungs, place a balloon over the ends of a glass tubing fitted into a rubber stopper. Stretch a sheet of rubber from a large balloon over the base of the bell jar to simulate the diaphragm. Secure the rubber diaphragm with heavy tape or twine so it will not slip off when pulled. Carefully pull the rubber diaphragm down, as shown in Figure O, and observe the inflation of the balloon (lungs).

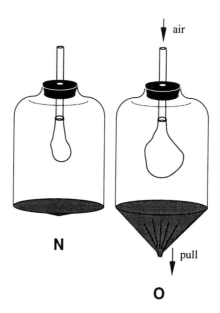

© 1994 by John Wiley & Sons, Inc.

Questions

(1) Some textbooks state that mammalian lungs operate on the principle of "negative pressure." Is this statement accurate? Explain.

(2) Frogs use a "positive pressure" pump to inflate their lungs after using a "negative pressure pump" to draw air into their mouths. Describe how this might work.

(3) Explain how a drinking straw works. Draw a diagram and indicate regions of higher and lower pressure.

4.1.6 Measuring Barometric Pressure

Concepts to Investigate: Measuring atmospheric pressure, water barometers, aneroid barometers, weather forecasting.

Materials: Clear plastic tubing, food coloring, bucket, clamps, wide-mouth jar, broom straw or drinking straw, mylar balloon, adhesive, rubber bands.

Principles and Procedures: Weather forecasters make their predictions on the basis of meteorologic data such as wind speed, barometric pressure, relative humidity, and temperature. Meteorologists have found that one of the most valuable pieces of information in making predictions is atmospheric (barometric) pressure, and this is why weather maps such as Figure P often include isobars, lines that connect points of equal barometric pressure. A fall in barometric pressure is often accompanied by the entrance of a cold front that may bring inclement weather. A rise in barometric pressure generally indicates that skies will become or remain fair. In this section you will make two different barometers for measuring barometric pressure.

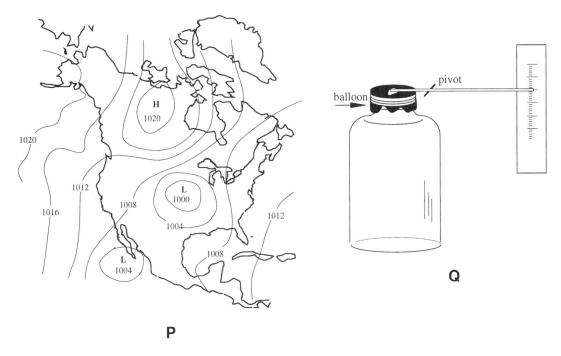

P

Q

Part 1. Water barometer: Obtain a 12-m section of clear plastic tubing and immerse it in a bucket of water colored with food coloring. Massage the tubing until all the air escapes and it is completely filled with the colored water. Clamp both ends of the tubing with screw clamps and hang it out of a third-story window so that it dangles freely and one end nearly touches the ground. A second student should remove the clamp at the bottom of the tubing while the clamp at the top remains fixed. The water will start to drain out and then will come to a sudden stop. Why? Using a fine-tipped permanent marker, note the location of the meniscus, and measure the height of the water column that is supported.

If possible, suspend the tubing in a permanent location and record the barometric pressure in millimeters of water throughout the month. The bottom end of the tubing should be submerged in a bucket filled with water. The height of the column, which indicates the barometric pressure, is read from the surface of the water in the bucket to the meniscus in the tube. Observe the barometer throughout the month and determine if there is a correlation between barometric pressure and weather patterns as indicated in the introduction to this activity.

Part 2. Aneroid barometer: A simple aneroid barometer (Figure Q) can be made from household materials and used to observe changes in air pressure. Although not as accurate as the water barometer, it is more convenient to use if you don't have access to a three-story building. Obtain a wide-mouthed empty jar and seal it with a sheet of mylar. Mylar is used in aluminized party balloons, is relatively impermeable to gas, and thereby allows balloons to remain inflated much longer than balloons made of latex or rubber. Stretch a sheet of mylar until it forms a tight drum over the top of the jar and use heavy rubber bands to hold it in place. Place a small piece of chewing gum or other adhesive in the center of the membrane and attach the end of a spaghetti noodle, broom straw, or appropriate filament to the gum. The needle can pivot on the edge of the jar, or you may use another pivot point such as a nail. As atmospheric pressure decreases, the pressure inside the jar will exceed the external pressure and force the membrane to bulge up and the needle to move down. Conversely, if the atmospheric pressure increases, the membrane will bend inward and the needle will swing up. To calibrate your barometer, tune your radio to a local station that reports barometric pressures. When a pressure reading is given, write that pressure adjacent to the point on your scale where the needle is pointing. Repeat this procedure when the pressure is significantly different. Although your barometer may not be very accurate, you should be able to observe major changes in barometric pressure. Observe your barometer over a one- or two-week period and determine if there is a relationship between changes in barometric pressure and changes in weather.

Questions

(1) Mercury is 13.6 times denser than water. Would a mercury barometer be taller or shorter than a water barometer? Explain.

(2) Why is it essential that material used to seal the aneroid barometer be impermeable to air? Are common party balloons permeable to air? Explain.

(3) The air pressure at the summit of Mount Everest, the tallest mountain in the world (29,028 ft.; 8,848 m), is only about one third that at sea level. Explain.

FOR THE TEACHER

One of the most confusing aspects about pressure is the wide variety of units used to measure it. It is conceivable some students may have heard pressure referred to in units of torrs (torr), millimeters mercury (mm Hg), millimeters water (mm H_2O), inches mercury (in Hg), inches water (in H_2O), pounds per square inch (PSI), pounds per square foot (lb/ft^2), Pascals (Pa), kilopascals (kPa), millibars (mb), barye (dynes/cm^2), newtons per square meter (N/m^2), or atmospheres (atm). It is no wonder students may be confused when studying pressure. When different units are used to indicate pressure, students may think a different quantity is being measured. It is important that students realize all these terms are simply different ways of measuring the same thing, namely the ratio of force to area. The SI unit for pressure is the Pascal (Pa), defined as 1 newton of force per square meter of surface area. Although we encourage use of Pascals or kiloPascals whenever possible, each discipline has its own preferred units, and it is therefore important to be familiar with these. For your convenience we have prepared a table of the important units of pressure and their SI equivalents.

Units of Pressure
and Their Equivalents in Pascals

Unit	Definition	Pascal Equivalents	When It Is Used
Pascal (Pa)	N/m^2	1	Standard SI Unit. When mass is measured in kg and area in meters.
kiloPascal (kPa)	1000 N/m^2	1000	Practical metric unit of measuring gaseous, fluid or mechanical pressure (Pa is generally too small).
bar	10,000 N/m^2	100,000	Practical metric unit of measuring atmospheric pressure. One bar is approximately 1 atmosphere.
millibar (mb)	100 N/m^2	100	Weather reports. Note: Some weather maps drop the first two digits (e.g., 1013.3 mb may be reported as 13.3)
barye (dyne/cm^2)	0.1 N/m^2	0.1	Standard CGS unit. When measurements are made in centimeters and grams.
torr	1/760 of standard atmospheric pressure	133.3	When pressure is measured with a mercury manometer or barometer.

mm Hg	Pressure required to support a column of Hg 1 mm in height	133.3	Blood pressure measurements. Standard blood pressure is 120/80 (systolic/diastolic).
cm H$_2$O	Pressure able to support a column of water 1 cm in height	98.1	When pressure is measured using simple water barometer or manometer.
atmosphere (atm)	Atmospheric pressure at sea level	101,325	When a comparison to standard atmospheric pressure is desired.
PSI	lb/in^2	6,894	Common measurement in mechanical and structural engineering. Tire pressures are rated in PSI.

4.1.1 The Magnitude of Air Pressure

Discussion: Before heating, the pressures inside and outside the soft-drink can in part 2 are the same. Since the can does not deform while being heated, one can assume pressures on both sides remain the same. The air that escapes from the can is gradually replaced by water vapor until the internal atmosphere is composed almost exclusively of water vapor. The vapor pressure of water drops dramatically when it is allowed to cool. The vapor pressure decreases from 101.3 kPa at 100° C to about 5 kPa at room temperature (Figure R). Thus, as the temperature drops to room temperature, the pressure inside the can drops 95 percent. If the can is open to the atmosphere, air will flow back into the can as the water condenses. If the opening to the can is submerged, the vapor in the can will not equilibrate with the atmosphere. Water rapidly removes heat from the surroundings and thus lowers the temperature of the atmosphere inside the can. The water vapor quickly condenses, creating a pressure differential of nearly 96 kPa (13.9 lb/in^2). Water is forced in to fill this partial vacuum, but before it does, air pressure on the walls implodes the can. Note that the collapsed can contains water, indicating water entered at the same time the walls collapsed.

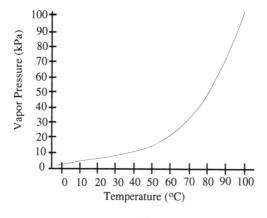

R

Teacher demonstration—Collapsing sealed can: Air pressure can be illustrated in a very dramatic manner by using a resealable metal can such as those used to package ditto fluid or paint solvents. The instructor should make certain the can is completely clean prior to the demonstration or dangerous fumes might enter the atmosphere. Seal the can and ask a student to try crushing the can with his or her hands. It will be very difficult for the student to do much more than slightly dent the can. Now add water to a depth of 1 centimeter and heat <u>without the lid</u> until it boils (Figure S). NEVER HEAT A SEALED CONTAINER! Using pot holders, remove the can from the heat and seal it with its lid (Figure T). Do not reseal the can while it is being heated or an explosion may occur. As the can is allowed to cool on a bench top, it will gradually collapse as the water vapor condenses and the internal pressure drops to approximately 5 percent of atmospheric pressure (Figure U). Cooling the outside of the can with water or a damp cloth will speed this process. Students can calculate the force upon the can by first calculating the surface area and then solving the equation $F = pA$ where $p = 101 \text{ N/m}^2$.

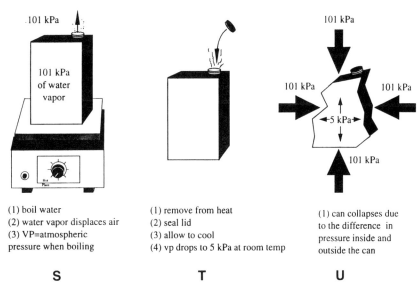

(1) boil water (2) water vapor displaces air (3) VP=atmospheric pressure when boiling	(1) remove from heat (2) seal lid (3) allow to cool (4) vp drops to 5 kPa at room temp	(1) can collapses due to the difference in pressure inside and outside the can
S	**T**	**U**

Answers (1) Student answers will vary depending upon their weight and the surface area of the bottoms of their feet. In general, students should find that air pressure is approximately five times as great as the pressure they exert on the floor when standing on both feet. (2) The can will collapse only if it is not open to the air. If it is open, air will rapidly rush in while the can is cooling and a pressure differential will not develop. (3) Student diagrams should show the eardrum bending in under increasing atmospheric pressure. When the Eustachian tubes open, air rushes into the middle ear and the ears "pop." (4) If the passenger had a cold, her Eustachian tubes may have been blocked, making it impossible to equilibrate pressure across the eardrum. Following cabin depressurization, the pressure inside her ears greatly exceeded the external pressure, and her eardrums bulged out and eventually burst. (5) See the answer to the previous question.

4.1.2 Pressure Equation

Discussion: The wood should snap when placed under the newspaper, but not when placed under the notebook paper. You may need to experiment with various thicknesses of wooden slats before finding a thickness that breaks consistently. The newspaper has a much greater surface area than the notebook paper, and since force is a function of surface area $F = pA$, more force must be used to lift it. The notebook paper is small enough that the wood can lift it without breaking. By contrast, the force exerted by the atmosphere on the newspaper is sufficiently great to restrain the stick when hit with the hammer. Since the covered end cannot move, the wood breaks.

Answers (1) See discussion. (2) See discussion. (3) Newton's second law states that an object will accelerate only when there are unbalanced forces applied to it. Although pressure is independent of surface area, force is not $F = pA$. If you wish to increase the force of wind on a sailboat, you must increase the surface area of the sails.

4.1.3 Pascal's Principle

Discussion: This activity provides a dramatic illustration of air pressure and works well as a classroom demonstration. A classic experiment was performed in which two teams of horses were harnessed to a pair of evacuated metal Magdeburg hemispheres. Despite their efforts, the horses were unable to overcome air pressure and separate the hemispheres. Many scientific supply houses sell steel or brass Magdeburg hemispheres, which may be evacuated with a vacuum pump. These are much more dramatic than the plungers, and come equipped with valves used to adjust the vacuum.

Answers (1) The card should stay on the cup regardless of orientation, showing that air pressure is exerted on the card from the top, the side, and the bottom as Pascal's law states. (2) Gasoline cans contain vents so air will enter the can, equalizing internal and external pressure and allowing gasoline to flow out. If unvented, little gasoline will flow for the same reason water does not flow out of a straw when one end is covered. (3) Force is dependent upon surface area $F = pA$. The larger the surface area, the larger the force. Thus, it would be much more difficult to separate large Magdeburg hemispheres than small ones. (4) Slide the plungers sideways until an opening is created and air enters.

4.1.4 Pressure Differentials

Discussion

Part 1: The rise of water will be greater if the candle is inverted under a narrow flask or cylinder rather than a wide jar. If performing this activity as a classroom demonstration, put food coloring in the water to make the rise more noticeable from the back of the room. Water rises in the container due to an imbalance in pressure. Many people refer to this as "suction," but this is misleading since nothing is pulling water into the container. Rather, water is pushed in because the pressure outside is greater than inside. Two factors cause the reduction of pressure in the container: 1. The flame heats the air in the container and causes it to expand, thus forcing air out from around the base. As the flame starts to die, the gasses inside the container cool and contract, but air does not enter because water seals the mouth of the jar. Since gas has escaped, the pressure in the container will now be less than outside. 2. Paraffin is a long chain alkane hydrocarbon (C_nH_{2n+2} where n ranges between 26 and 30). When a 30-C paraffin molecule burns it produces 62 molecules of carbon dioxide and 60 molecules of water vapor for every 91 molecules of oxygen consumed:

$$2C_{30}H_{62} + 91O_2 \text{ (g)} \longrightarrow 60CO_2 \text{ (g)} + 62H_2O \text{ (g)}$$

The molecules of water vapor quickly condense, leaving only carbon dioxide in the atmosphere of the container. Thus, for every 91 gaseous molecules that exist prior to combustion, only 60 exist following combustion. Since pressure is dependent upon the number of gaseous molecules, the pressure will drop.

The following are key observations and interpretations that students should have made. Gas inside the container heats and expands causing bubbling around the base. As oxygen inside the container diminishes, the flame gets cooler and so does the air. Cool air contracts resulting in a pressure drop. Water starts to move into the container. When the candle is extinguished, the temperature in the flask drops, causing a further reduction in pressure and a further rise in the water level. Finally, water vapor produced by combustion condenses and can be seen on the inside of the jar. This further reduces internal pressure and allows water to be pushed even higher.

Part 2: As the flame burns, it heats the air. As the temperature increases, the pressure inside the container increases causing some air to escape, as can be seen by a slight wobbling of the egg. As the flame dies, the air inside the container cools. Since there is less air in the container than there was initially, the pressure decreases. The egg is positioned so that it acts as a one-way valve. Because it is flexible and creates an excellent seal, air is allowed to escape from the container when heating, but is not allowed to enter during cooling. There is now a difference in pressure in the air inside and outside the flask. The greater pressure outside the flask pushes the egg inside. Although this demonstration is designed to demonstrate air pressure, it also illustrates the operation of one-way valves. Although designs vary, one-way valves have a wide variety of biological and industrial applications including the valves in the heart and veins as well as the valves of basketballs and volleyballs. Although the egg is easily removed from the flask by heating, you may also remove it by first inverting the flask so that it settles in the neck of the container. If you now blow into the flask the egg will once again act as a one-way valve and allow the air to pass by into the flask. When you stop blowing, however, the egg creates a seal because the air pressure inside the flask is now greater than the atmosphere outside. This pressure differential pushes the egg toward the neck. If you blow hard enough you will be able to create enough pressure in the flask so that it will force the egg out once you stop blowing. A little water or cooking oil may be used to lubricate the egg and keep it from breaking as it travels through the neck of the flask.

Teacher demonstration—Air pressure fountain: (Materials: ring stand, support ring, round-bottom or strong Erlenmeyer flask, one-hole stopper, glass tubing, heat source, food coloring.) Air pressure can be used to do work as is demonstrated by making the fountain described here. Fill a 500-ml beaker with water and add a few drops of food coloring to improve visibility. Place approximately 20 ml of clear water in a 500-ml Erlenmeyer or round-bottomed flask and heat uncovered (Figure V). NEVER HEAT A SEALED CONTAINER! As soon as the water boils, remove the flask from the heat source and place a one-hole stopper that has been fitted with a hollow glass tube in the mouth of the flask. Quickly invert the flask and support it on a ring stand, as illustrated in Figure W. The glass tubing should extend deep into the water. As the flask cools, the water vapor inside will condense and the pressure will drop considerably. Although the pressure inside the flask drops, the pressure outside the flask remains constant, creating a pressure differential. As a result of this pressure differential, water slowly rises up the tube into the flask. Once it enters the partially evacuated flask, it sprays cool water, thereby further cooling the internal atmosphere. Now vapor condenses rapidly, pressure drops quickly, and a strong jet of water is pushed into the flask to fill the void. This is a very dramatic demonstration, particularly if you use a long tubing so the water rises a great distance.

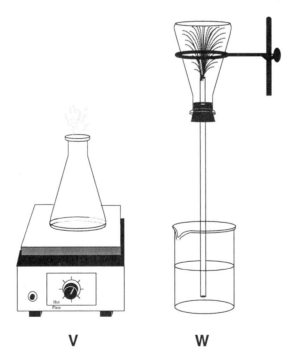

V   W

Teacher Demonstrations—Lift pumps: (Materials: Plexiglas tubing, sheet rubber, screws, rubber stoppers fitted to Plexiglas tubing, threaded metal rod, valve grease.) For many years, people living in rural areas have relied upon manual lift pumps to extract water from wells. When the piston is lifted, the pressure inside the cylinder drops. The magnitude of the atmospheric pressure acting on the water in the bottom of the well is sufficient to push the water up 10.3 meters (34 feet). When the piston is forced down, the one-way valve at the bottom closes while the valve within the piston opens, allowing water to travel into the upper portion of the cylinder where it then flows out the spout and is collected. Air pressure can be used to extract water from deeper wells when pumps are used in tandem. A demonstration pump can be made using Plexiglas tubing for the cylinder, rubber for the valves, rubber stoppers for the pistons, and valve grease as a lubricant. The rubber flaps should be secured to the stoppers with screws, as shown in Figure X. A threaded metal rod is needed to serve as the shaft of the piston. Place bolts on both sides of the rubber stopper so that it is secured to the piston shaft.

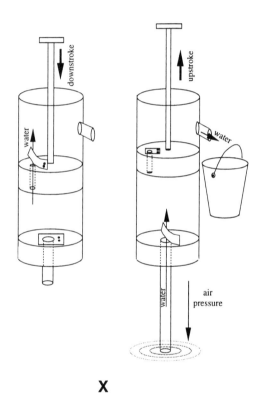

X

Answers (1) Both the water and the egg were pushed into the containers because the pressure outside the containers was greater than the pressure inside. (2) See discussion. (3) When the piston in a syringe is retracted, the volume in the cylinder increases and the pressure decreases. As a result of the pressure differential, blood is pushed into to the barrel. (4) A series of lift pumps can be used to bring water up from depths greater than 34 ft. Water exiting the first pump enters a second pump and is pushed higher. (5) An electric fan pumps air out of the machine, thereby reducing internal pressure. Due to the resulting pressure differential, debris is forced into the cleaner. (6) Fluids are pushed by pressure differentials. "Suction," as a pulling force, is an erroneous concept.

4.1.5 Air Pressure and Breathing

Discussion: If you do not have access to a bell jar such as illustrated in Figure N, it is possible to make your own by cutting the bottom out of a large jug such as is frequently used to carry apple cider. Glass cutters are available at many hobby and craft stores.

Answers (1) Pressure is defined as the ratio of force to surface area. For pressure to be negative the force must be negative since it is not possible to have a negative area. Force is generally considered to be negative when an object is pulled, and positive when it is pushed. As discussed in the previous activity, air is always pushed, and never pulled, so the discussion of "negative pressure" is misleading. (2) "Negative pressure" (pressure lower than atmospheric) is created in the mouth of the frog when the floor of its mouth drops, and air is pushed through the nostrils into the mouth. The frog then closes its nostrils, raises the floor of its mouth and forces air into the lungs using positive pressure (pressure that is greater than atmospheric). (3) Pressure inside your mouth is reduced when the floor of the mouth is dropped, and water is forced up the straw due to the resulting pressure differential.

4.1.6 Measuring Air Pressure

Discussion: If performed at sea level, the water level in the water barometer will drop until the column is 10.3 meters (34 feet) high. The top portion of the tube may or may not collapse depending upon the strength of the walls of the tubing. You may use the conversion factors listed in the beginning of the teacher section to convert your readings to the pressure units used in the weather reports appearing in your local newspaper. In general, most maps report values in millibars, but often drop the first two digits. For example a 1013.3 mb may be reported as 13.3. The water barometer should produce very accurate measures of barometric pressure providing there are no air bubbles in the tube. An interesting variation to this activity is to fill the tube, cap one end, and attach the capped end to the rope of a flagpole. While keeping the open end of the tube submerged in a bucket, slowly raise the tubing and watch the water column stop at 34 feet even as the tubing is raised higher.

Answers (1) Since mercury is much denser than water, it is not lifted as high by air pressure. As a result, a mercury barometer does not need to be as tall as a water barometer. (2) It is essential that the seal on an aneroid barometer be air tight, otherwise air would cross the membrane and it wouldn't move and deflect the needle. Normal party balloons deflate within a few days, indicating that their walls are permeable to air molecules. (3) Air pressure is dependent upon depth with the "sea of air" known as the atmosphere. The higher you are in this sea, the less air above you and the lower the atmospheric pressure.

Applications to Everyday Life

Weather Forecasting: Most students have seen weather maps either in the newspaper or on the television weather report. These maps generally have isobars (contours of equivalent pressure) that are very helpful in predicting weather patterns (Figure P). High-pressure zones are generally accompanied by fair weather while low-pressure zones are often associated with stormy weather. The phrase "the barometer is falling" is a familiar reference indicating approaching inclement weather. In the Northern Hemisphere, surface winds tend to move in a clockwise direction around high-pressure zones (anti-cyclones) but counterclockwise around low-pressure zones (cyclones). Wind patterns are reversed in the Southern Hemisphere due to the Coriolis effect. Students can estimate the locations of high- and low-pressure zones using Buys Ballot's Rule: If you are in the Northern Hemisphere and stand with the wind at your back, a zone of low pressure is to your left while a zone of high pressure is to your right.

Winds: Pressure differentials cause winds. Air moves from regions of higher pressure to regions of lower pressure. For example, on-shore breezes occur on summer afternoons at the beach when warm air on the land rises and leaves a partial vacuum that is filled by the cooler air off the water. Winds tend to flow from regions of high pressure to regions of low pressure. The Coriolis effect, caused by rotation of the Earth, modifies wind patterns. Because the Coriolis effect is minimal at low latitudes, the rotation of the Earth does not complicate the prediction of wind patterns at these latitudes. However, the prediction of wind patterns at higher latitudes is more complicated because of this effect.

Altimeter: The most common method of measuring altitude uses the altimeter, which is generally an aneroid barometer that measures atmospheric pressure. While barometers are calibrated in millibars, altimeters are generally calibrated in meters or feet. A mountain climber or pilot sets the barometer to correspond to a known elevation. As he or she goes up in elevation, the barometer will detect a decrease in pressure that is registered as an increase in elevation. Such altimeters are obviously susceptible to air pressure changes associated with weather changes. The following table records standard pressures for specified elevations.

Altitude (m)	Pressure (kPa)	*Point of Comparison*
0	101.3 kPa	Sea level; at the beach
500	95.5 kPa	On top of World Trade Tower, New York City
1000	89.9 kPa	Mount Davis, highest point in Pennsylvania
1500	84.6 kPa	Denver, Colorado (1700m)
2000	79.5 kPa	Mount Mitchell, North Carolina; highest point in eastern U.S. (2193m)
3500	65.8 kPa	La Paz, Bolivia; highest major city in the world (3800m)

4500	57.8 kPa	Mount Whitney, CA; highest mountain in lower 48 states (4418m)
6500	44.1 kPa	Mount McKinley, AK; highest mountain in U.S. (6193m)
9000	30.8 kPa	Mount Everest, Nepal; highest mountain in the world (8848m)
12000	19.4 kPa	Cruising altitude for commercial jets
95000	0.0001 kPa	Record height for aircraft (X-15 rocket plane; Robert White, USAF)

Altitude Sickness: Many hikers and backpackers become easily exhausted when they hike at higher elevations because the air pressure is significantly lower at these elevations than at their homes in the cities. Our atmosphere is composed of approximately 21 percent oxygen. Thus, the partial pressure of oxygen at sea level is 21.3 kPa (21 percent of 101.3 kPa). At the top of Mount Whitney in California, the barometric pressure is approximately 60 percent of the pressure at sea level. Consequently the partial pressure of oxygen is approximately 12.8 kPa. As one climbs, the net outside pressure forcing oxygen into the blood in the lungs decreases. For example, at sea level the external oxygen pressure is 21.3 kPa and the oxygen pressure of the blood in the lungs is 5.4 kPa. Consequently, there is a net pressure of 15.9 kPa forcing oxygen into the blood. At higher altitudes, such as on top of Mt. Whitney, the partial pressure of oxygen is only 12.8 kPa and the net pressure (12.8-5.4 kPa) is only 7.4 kPa, which is significantly less than that at sea level. This reduction in oxygen pressure can cause a reduction in respiration and metabolism and may stimulate the nausea, dizziness, and shortness of breath associated with altitude sickness.

Vacuum-Packed Foods: The flavor and quality of many foods degenerate rapidly upon exposure to oxygen. For this reason food manufacturers often "vacuum pack" their products. You may have noticed that the lid of a jelly jar pops up when you crack the seal. This popping is a result of the rapid increase in air pressure in the jar that occurs when air rushes in to fill the partial vacuum.

Inhaling and Exhaling: Inhalation results from a pressure differential that is created by the muscles of the thorax. The brain sends messages that cause the diaphragm, intercostal, and levator scapuli muscles to contract so that the volume of the thorax increases. As volume of the thorax increases, the pressure in the lungs decreases. Since atmospheric pressure remains constant, air is pushed into the lungs.

Speech: Phonation, the process of producing voiced sound, is dependent upon air pressure changes in the larynx (voice box). As one exhales, the volume of the lungs decreases, which creates an increase in pressure. This increased pressure forces the vocal cords in the larynx apart. Simultaneously, a partial vacuum is created between the vocal cords due to the rapidly moving air which pulls the cords together again. This process is repeated, causing the vocal cords to vibrate and create sounds associated with speech.

Vacuum Cleaners: An electric motor drives a fan that pushes air out the back of the cleaner, leaving a partial vacuum in the dust bag. Outside air pressure pushes dirt and other debris into the bag.

Drinking Straws: When a person sucks on a drinking straw, the pressure inside the straw decreases, and the atmosphere pressing down upon the liquid's surface forces the fluid up the straw.

4.2 VAPOR PRESSURE

Tibetans live on the high plateaus of the Himalayan mountains in central Asia. If you were to join a Tibetan family for dinner, they might serve you tsaumpa, a food made of tea, yak butter, and barley. If you put a thermometer in the tsaumpa while it was boiling in an open pot, you would notice that the temperature of the mixture was only about 89°C. When your hostess adds salt to the pot, the temperature rises to 92°C, and when she puts a lid on the pot it rises to 96°C. Finally, you notice that the temperature rises to 103° when a rock is placed on the lid of the tsaumpa pot. Upon departing, your hostess gives you some tsaumpa with the recommendation that you reduce the cooking time at your home in the flatlands. How does elevation influence the temperature at which liquids boil, or the amount of time required to cook foods (Figure A)? How does salt increase the temperature at which liquids boil? How does the addition of a lid increase the boiling temperature of a liquid? In this section you will discover that these questions can be answered by understanding the concepts of vapor pressure and vaporization.

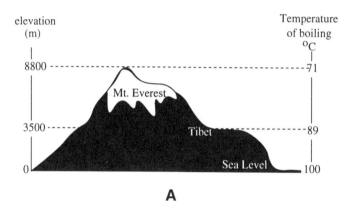

A

If a liquid is placed in an evacuated chamber (no atmosphere present), random molecules will escape from the liquid as vapor. Eventually, a dynamic equilibrium is reached in which the number of molecules escaping from the liquid is equal to the number of molecules returning to the liquid. The pressure exerted by the vapor at this point is known as the vapor pressure of the liquid and is dependent only upon temperature. The vapor pressure of water is 3.2 kPa at room temperature and 101.3 kPa at 100°C.

Liquids will not boil if they are at temperatures where their vapor pressure is less than the atmospheric pressure. *When heated to the point where the vapor pressure equals the restraining atmospheric pressure, molecules throughout the liquid spontaneously vaporize in a process known as boiling.* The bubbles that rise to the surface in a boiling pot of water are not composed of air, but are composed of steam. *Vaporization is influenced by energy, barometric pressure, surface area, molecular nature, the quantity of dissolved solutes, and the concentration of similar molecules already in the atmosphere.* In the following activities we will investigate each of these variables.

4.2.1 Energy and Vaporization

Concepts to Investigate: Energy and vaporization, evaporative heat loss.

Materials: Celsius thermometer, cotton cloth.

Principles and Procedures: Temperature is a measure of the average kinetic energy of molecules. Given constant barometric pressure, a rise in temperature indicates that molecules are increasingly active and more likely to escape the liquid phase and enter the vapor phase. Figure B shows that the vapor pressure above water at 0°C is only 0.6 kPa. As the water is heated to 50°C, the vapor pressure increases to 12.3 kPa. At 100°C, the vapor pressure is 101.3 kPa, equal to the atmospheric pressure and molecules of water enter the vapor phase in great numbers. This process is known as boiling. Figure B shows how the vapor pressure of water increases as temperature increases under standard atmospheric pressure.

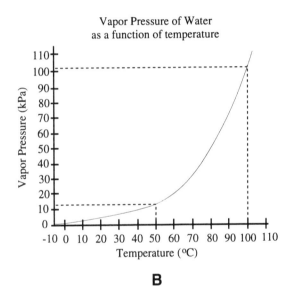

B

For water to vaporize, molecules must gain enough energy from their environment to overcome the intermolecular forces that keep them bound in the liquid phase. When water is heated it boils because energy has been added. But why does water evaporate from a bowl sitting on a countertop at room temperature? Where is the energy source that causes these molecules to vaporize? If the water molecules are gaining their energy from the environment, then the environment should cool as the water evaporates. To investigate this, we will examine the influence evaporation has upon the temperature of the surface from which it is evaporating.

Obtain two identical thermometers and wrap the bulb of one with a piece of fabric, securing it with thread. Place both thermometers in a beaker of water at room temperature. After recording this temperature remove the thermometers and quickly dry the one without the fabric. Place both in front of a fan as illustrated in Figure C and record the lowest temperatures observed. (If you do not have a fan, you may

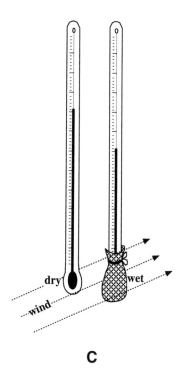

C

carefully wave the thermometer bulb back and forth in the air.) A drop in the temperature of the thermometer indicates energy was removed from the liquid in the thermometer. If energy is used to evaporate water, then the temperature of the wet bulb should be significantly lower than the temperature of the dry bulb. Is this what you observed? Record your results in the table.

When your body temperature rises, vessels in your skin dilate, increasing blood flow to your sweat glands and consequently increasing the amount of sweat produced. Heat from your body is used to evaporate sweat on your skin, just as heat from a thermometer is used to evaporate water on its surface. As sweat evaporates, body heat is lost, keeping your body temperature within a safe range. When exercising in very dry environments, it is possible to lose so much water that your body no longer produces sweat. What will happen to your body temperature in such situations?

	Initial Temperature	Lowest Temperature	Change in Temperature	Time in Front of Fan
Wet	_____ °C	_____ °C	_____ °C	_____ s
Dry	_____ °C	_____ °C	_____ °C	_____ s

Questions

(1) Which thermometer experiences the greatest drop in temperature? Why?

(2) Assuming water in a swimming pool is at the same temperature as the air, will you feel cooler immediately after climbing out of the pool or after you have dried off? Explain.

(3) Explain how sweating influences body temperature.

(4) Explain why physicians often recommend that you dampen your skin with water when you are suffering with a high fever.

4.2.2 Atmospheric Pressure and Boiling

Concepts to Investigate: Barometric pressure, boiling, vacuum.

Materials: Erlenmeyer flask, one-hole stopper, thermometer, hot plate or burner, ring stand, clamp, ice (optional). *Note:* Use goggles, lab coat, and hot mitts when performing this investigation.

Principles and Procedures: Imagine living on a planet where cooling a liquid caused it to boil. How would life be different? Would life as we know it be possible? Surprisingly, you live on a planet where this occurs. You don't believe it? Well, perform the following investigation and see for yourself.

A liquid will boil if its vapor pressure is equal to or greater than the pressure of the atmosphere. At sea level, the vapor pressure must equal 101.3 kPa for the liquid to boil (Figures D–F). If the atmospheric pressure is increased (Figure G), the liquid will not boil until heated to the point where its vapor pressure equals the new atmospheric pressure (Figure H). If the barometric pressure is decreased using a vacuum pump, liquid will boil at much lower temperatures (Figure I).

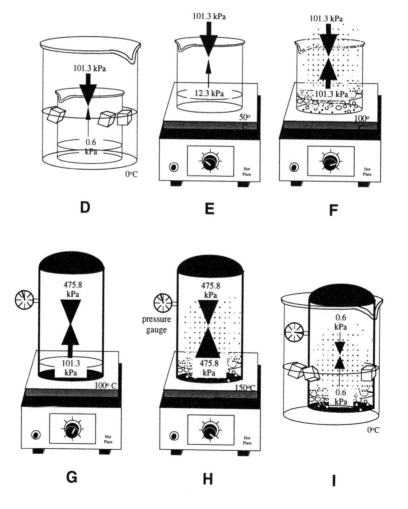

Apply glycerol or another suitable lubricant to the end of a thermometer and gently push through a rubber stopper with a slow twisting motion. Fill a flask to approximately 25 percent of its capacity with tap water and heat without the stopper until the water begins to boil (Figure J). NEVER HEAT A SEALED CONTAINER! Using hot mitts or tongs, remove the flask from the hot plate and then quickly place the thermometer-stopper assembly in the mouth of the flask. Using hot mitts, position the flask in a ring support as illustrated in Figure K. Place a container under the flask to collect water that will be poured over the flask. Using a beaker or cup, pour tap water over the flask and watch the water inside the flask boil. When tap water no longer causes the water to boil, use ice water and see if it will start boiling again. Why does water boil when it is cooled?

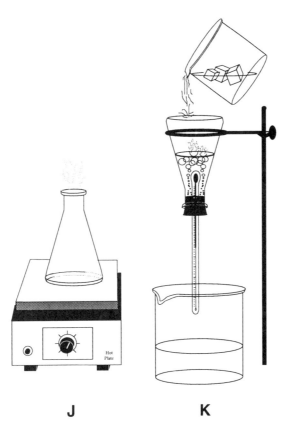

J   K

Record the lowest temperature at which the water will boil, and record the pressure that must be present in the flask, using the information in the table provided. To express pressure in kilopascals or millibars, multiply by 0.133 or 1.33 respectively. What percentage of standard atmospheric pressure remains in the flask at this temperature? (The percentage of atmospheric pressure remaining in the flask can be calculated by dividing by standard atmospheric pressure (760 mm Hg) and then multiplying by 100 percent.)

Temperature of Water (from Thermometer)		Barometric Pressure (from Table)		Percent Atmospheric Pressure(Calculated)	
	°C		mm Hg		%

Temperature °C	-5	0	5	10	15	20	25	30	35	40	45	50
Pressure (mm Hg)	3	5	7	9	13	18	24	32	42	55	72	93

Temperature °C	55	60	65	70	75	80	85	90	95	100	105
Pressure (mm Hg)	118	149	188	234	289	355	434	526	634	760	906

Questions

(1) Why did the water in this activity boil when cooled? Would the water have boiled if the cooling flask were open to the atmosphere? Explain.

(2) It was shown that water will boil at temperatures far below 100°C if the pressure on the water's surface is reduced sufficiently. Given this information, explain why many recipes recommend increased cooking time at high altitudes.

(3) Unlike normal pots, pressure cookers have lids that lock securely to their pots and allow for a significant increase in pressure. Explain the advantage of using such cookware.

4.2.3 The Influence of Surface Area on Vaporization

Concepts to Investigate: Surface area and vaporization, surface-area-to-volume ratio, phase boundaries.

Materials: Petri dish, test tube, 50-ml beaker, heat lamp.

Principles and Procedures: Vaporization occurs at the boundary between a liquid and gas. The greater the surface area, the greater the amount of evaporation. To minimize water loss due to evaporation, engineers and hydrologists prefer to build dams in deep, narrow canyons rather than in broad wide ones. A deep and narrow reservoir has less surface area than a broad flat one of the same volume and therefore loses less water to evaporation. This is particularly important in hot, dry regions of the world. In this activity you will investigate the relationship between the surface-area-to-volume ratio of a liquid and evaporation.

Pour 5 ml of water into a Petri dish, a 50-milliliter beaker, and a test tube. Calculate the surface area of each using the formula $A = \pi r^2$ where π is 3.14, and r is the radius of the circle (Figure L). Place all three containers under a heat lamp and record the time required for the water to evaporate. If you do not have access to a heat lamp, place the containers in a sunny location on a hot day. Draw a graph showing the relationship between the surface-area-to-volume ratio and the evaporation rate. The surface-area-to-volume ratio is the independent variable and should be plotted on the x axis. The evaporation rate is the dependent variable and should be plotted on the y axis. What happens to the evaporation rate of a given volume of liquid as the surface-area-to-volume ratio increases? Explain.

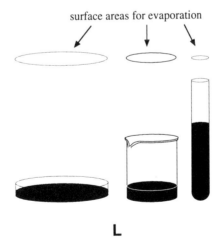

surface areas for evaporation

L

	Petri Dish	*50-ml Beaker*	*Test Tube*
Radius	___ cm	___ cm	___ cm
Surface area	___ cm²	___ cm²	___ cm²
Surface-area-to-volume ratio	___ cm²/ml	___ cm²/ml	___ cm²/ml
Time required for water to evaporate	___ min	___ min	___ min
Evaporation rate	___ g/min	___ g/min	___ g/min

Questions

(1) Interpret your graph of evaporation rate as a function of the surface-area-to-volume ratio.

(2) A swamp cooler is an inexpensive alternative to an air conditioner. Water evaporates from the surface of the cooler, removing energy from the surface of the cooler and subsequently lowering its temperature. As a result, air circulated through the cooler loses energy and cools. How would you design the evaporative surface of a swamp cooler to ensure maximum cooling? Draw a picture.

(3) The leaves of desert plants are generally quite small. On the basis of the principles discussed in this section, why don't you find plants with large leaves growing in deserts?

4.2.4 Molecular Structure and Vaporization

Concepts to Investigate: Molecular size, vaporization, volatility.

Materials: 2-propanol (rubbing alcohol), acetone (fingernail-polish remover, white gasoline (camping fuel), salad oil (vegetable oil). *Note:* Acetone, rubbing alcohol, and white gasoline are hazardous substances and should only be used under direct teacher supervision in well-ventilated areas, away from any flames or sparks.

Principles and Procedures: Gasoline is very volatile; that is, it vaporizes readily at normal temperatures and pressures. However, the crude oil from which gasoline is made is not volatile and vaporizes very slowly. Differences in volatility are due in part to differences in intermolecular forces. If the attractive forces between molecules are very small, then the material will be volatile like gasoline. If, however, the intermolecular forces are strong, as in oil, molecules will attract one another and stay in the liquid phase for a greater length of time.

Each substance has unique vapor pressure characteristics. A material with a high vapor pressure will evaporate more quickly than one with a low vapor pressure. Thus, you can rank the vapor pressures of liquids on the basis of the time required to evaporate. Determine the relative vapor pressures of water, salad oil, rubbing alcohol (2-propanol), fingernail-polish remover (acetone), and gasoline by dispensing 1 ml of each from a pipette into a Petri dish in a sunny, outdoor location and recording the time required for each to evaporate (Figure M). The substance that evaporates the most rapidly has the highest vapor pressure.

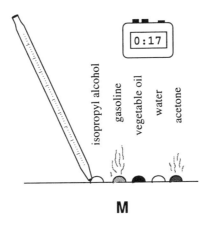

M

One factor influencing vapor pressure is molecular size. The larger a molecule, the greater its inertia and the less likely it is to escape from the liquid phase. All other factors being equal, the vapor pressure of substances with low molecular weight will be greater than the vapor pressure of substances with high molecular weight. Stated another way, if two substances have relatively similar structures, the one with the highest vapor pressure (the most volatile) is most likely the one with the smaller sized molecules. Knowing this, predict the relative molecular size for the following substances using a scale of 1 to 5, where 1 is the smallest and 5 is the largest.

Substance	Common Uses	Relative Molecular Size
2-propanol	rubbing alcohol	_____
Acetone	fingernail-polish remover	_____
Paraffin	candle wax	_____
Oleic acid	olive oil	_____
Natural gas; methane	fuel used in stoves and ranges	_____

Questions

(1) On the basis of your experimental data, rank the following liquids in terms of their vapor pressure: water, salad oil, rubbing alcohol, acetone, and gasoline. Explain your ranking.

(2) When applying rubbing alcohol you may have noticed that your hands feel cold. If you have spilled acetone (fingernail-polish remover) on your skin, it feels even colder. Explain why these liquids produce a short-lived cold sensation.

4.2.5 Vapor Pressure of Solutions

Concepts to Investigate: Vapor pressure of solutions, boiling-point elevation, solute, solvent, solution.

Materials: Salt (NaCl), accurate thermometer.

Principles and Procedures: A solution is made when a solute, such as salt, is dissolved in a solvent, such as water. The solute is the substance dissolved and the solvent is the substance in which it is dissolved. Water is the most common and important solvent. When solutes are added to a solvent, they lower the vapor pressure by getting in the way of those solvent molecules at the surface that might otherwise escape from the liquid. Figure N shows molecules of a pure liquid escaping the liquid phase. Figure O shows how molecules of a solute block the escape paths of some solvent molecules, thereby reducing the number that escape into the vapor phase, and consequently reducing the vapor pressure.

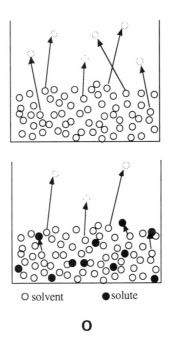

O solvent   ● solute

O

Fill three 500-ml beakers with 100 ml of water. Bring beaker #1 to a boil and record the temperature at which pure water boils. Read the temperature to the nearest tenth of a degree if possible. Bring beaker #2 to a boil, and then add 3 g of salt, mixing the solution until all of the salt is dissolved. Record the time required to bring this solution to a boil again, as well as the temperature of the new boiling point. Repeat this procedure adding 6 g of salt to beaker #3. Based upon the information you have collected, describe the relationship between solute concentration and boiling. How can boiling points be used to determine the purity of liquids?

Beaker #	1	2	3
Solvent	100 g H$_2$O	100 g H$_2$O	100 g H$_2$O
Solute	none	3 g NaCl	6 g NaCl
Boiling Pt. °C	_____ °C	_____ °C	_____ °C
Additional time required to boil	_____ s	_____ s	_____ s

Questions

(1) Is there a change in the boiling point as the concentration of solute particles increases?

(2) Some cooks add salt to water in which they are boiling food. Will this affect the total cooking time required?

(3) Will mineral water boil at the same temperature as distilled water? Explain.

4.2.6 Determining Relative Humidity

Concepts to Investigate: Psychrometry, absolute humidity, relative humidity.

Materials: Two thermometers, cotton fabric, thread.

Principles and Procedures: The Pharaohs of ancient Egypt were buried in special tombs in the sides of cliffs or within grandiose monuments like the great pyramids. The insides of their tombs were often decorated with detailed paintings depicting the everyday life of the deceased. In 1922, British archaeologist Howard Carter discovered the fabulously arrayed tomb of King Tutankhamen (King Tut). Most of the artifacts in Tutankhamen's tomb were in excellent condition, even though they were made in approximately 1350 B.C. The artifacts remained in excellent condition in part due to the very dry conditions of the Egyptian desert. In a humid environment, metals would have corroded, woods would have rotted, and pigments within paints would have reacted and degraded. Today, the curators of art museums are aware of the potentially damaging influence of humidity and maintain art museums at constant relative humidity of approximately 50 percent. What is humidity and how can it be measured? Perform the following investigation to find out.

    Absolute humidity is defined as the water vapor content of the atmosphere. If one cubic meter of air contains 6 grams of water, the absolute humidity is defined as 6 g/m³. By contrast, relative humidity is a measure of the degree of saturation of the atmosphere at any given temperature. *Relative humidity is the ratio of the amount of water air contains to the maximum amount it can contain at that temperature.* Air at 0°C is saturated (relative humidity = 100 percent) if it contains 6 grams of water per cubic meter. If the temperature of this air is raised to 20°C, the absolute humidity remains unchanged, but the relative humidity drops to 33 percent since air at 20° is capable of holding 18 g/m³ ((6 g/m³)/(18 g/m³) = 0.33). When the relative humidity is high, you may feel clammy because your sweat does not evaporate. When the relative humidity is low, evaporation occurs readily and you feel cooler. Heat stroke is more common in warm, humid environments than equally warm, dry environments because humidity inhibits evaporative cooling and the body can overheat. The relative humidity of the atmosphere can be determined by measuring the amount of evaporation that occurs, which in turn can be measured by the amount of evaporative cooling that occurs. If no evaporation occurs, then there will be no cooling, and it can be assumed that the relative humidity is 100 percent.

    Tie a small piece of thin cotton cloth around the bulb of a thermometer and soak the cloth in water at the same temperature as the air. Place this thermometer next to a dry one in front of a fan as shown in Figure C in 4.2.1 Energy and Vaporization. Record the temperature of the wet bulb and the dry bulb and use these temperatures to determine the relative humidity of the atmosphere by referring to table 7 in the appendix. Note that the greater the drop in temperature of the wet bulb (Δt), the lower the relative humidity. If there is no difference in the temperatures between wet and dry bulbs, no evaporative cooling has occurred because the air is already fully saturated (100 percent relative humidity). Plot changes in relative humidity throughout the week.

Questions

(1) Would a swamp cooler (evaporative cooler) be more useful in a humid or a dry environment? Explain.

(2) You are more likely to suffer heat exhaustion by exercising excessively in Atlanta, Georgia, in the summer (average July temperature = 79°F (26°C); high relative humidity) than in Albuquerque, New Mexico (average July temperature = 79°F; very low relative humidity). Explain.

(3) Respiratory water loss (water lost by breathing) is greatest on cold, dry days. Explain.

FOR THE TEACHER

Vapor pressure is one of the most important physical properties of liquids. It is used in a variety of thermodynamic calculations as well as in several methods for determining the molecular weights of dissolved solutes. Vapor pressure is the pressure exerted by a vapor in dynamic equilibrium with its liquid form. It has a unique, consistent value, dependent only upon temperature and the nature of the substance. Students often confuse vapor pressure, as previously defined, with the pressure of a vapor. Vapors can exert a wide range of pressures when they are not in equilibrium with their liquid states. Thus, the pressure exerted by steam in a steam engine will increase dramatically if a piston reduces the volume of a cylinder because the steam does not rapidly establish equilibrium with the liquid phase.

At room temperature (25°C), water has a vapor pressure of 23.8 mm Hg (3.17 kPa). As the temperature is increased to 50°C, the vapor pressure increases to 92.5 mm Hg (12.3 kPa). Although water is evaporating under both conditions, the rate of evaporation at 50°C is nearly four times as great. When water is heated to 100°C in an open container, it boils. Boiling is a special case of vaporization. Although water at 50°C vaporizes, it is generally a slow process in which molecules on the surface occasionally escape into the liquid phase. When water is heated to 100°C, the vapor pressure is equivalent to the atmospheric pressure and molecules enter the vapor phase throughout the liquid. Many students believe that these bubbles are air, when in fact they are water vapor. The goal of this series of activities is to illustrate that vaporization is dependent upon temperature, atmospheric pressure, surface area, molecular properties, dissolved solutes, and concentration of molecules already in the vapor form.

4.2.1 Energy and Vaporization

Discussion: Students may have difficulty identifying the energy source involved in the evaporation of water at room temperature. Most people think about heat only as something that is added to matter rather than something that is inherent to matter. A thermometer at room temperature has energy that may be used to vaporize water. As water in the fabric wick evaporates, it extracts energy from the thermometer, lowering its temperature. Since the heat of vaporization of water is 580 cal/g, each gram of water removes 580 calories of heat energy from the environment as it evaporates.

Answers (1) The wet thermometer experiences the greatest drop in temperature. As water evaporates, it withdraws energy from its surrounding environment. As a result, wet surfaces will cool as water evaporates. (2) As water evaporates from your skin, energy is removed and your body temperature drops. Therefore, you will feel cooler when you are wet. (3) As sweat evaporates, energy is removed from your body, keeping your body within a safe temperature range. (4) Heat energy is removed from the body as water evaporates, hopefully keeping your temperature within a reasonable range. Body temperatures in excess of 105°C may cause tissue damage, and temperatures above 112°C are usually fatal because they cause irreversible damage to the nervous system.

4.2.2 Atmospheric Pressure and Boiling

Discussion: Everyday experience indicates that removal of heat inhibits boiling, and yet in this activity it causes it. The counterintuitive results of this activity will pique student curiosity. Although heat is essential to produce the phase change, its effect is masked by the influence of the reduction in air pressure that occurs as the flask is cooled. At sea level, the pressure exerted by the atmosphere is equivalent to 101.3 kPa (760 mm Hg, or 14.7 PSI). The vapor pressure of water does not reach 101.3 kPa until the water is heated to a temperature of 100°C, which is why 100°C is the boiling temperature of water at standard pressure. As pressure is reduced, the boiling point of water drops (Figure P).

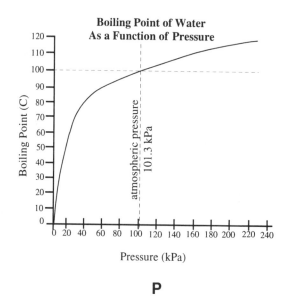

P

    Prior to heating, the air inside the flask is in equilibrium with the atmosphere with respect to pressure and composition (Figure Q). When heated, air expands and leaves, and is replaced by water vapor (Figure R). The pressure remains constant because the flask is open to the atmosphere. After the flask is removed from the heat source and sealed it is no longer an open system (Figure S). When the flask is cooled, its temperature drops and water condenses. As condensation continues, the pressure drops because there are fewer molecules in the gaseous state. As the pressure drops the boiling point of water decreases.

Answers (1) See discussion. (2) At high altitudes, water boils at a lower temperature and foods don't get as hot. To ensure that foods get fully cooked, it is necessary to heat them for a longer period of time at this lower temperature. (3) Under normal atmospheric conditions, water will not get hotter than 100°C because it turns into vapor at this temperature. In a pressure cooker the boiling point of water is substantially higher (see Figure H), and foods cook faster. In open cookware, the energy from the burners goes into vaporizing the water, while in a pressure cooker, a larger percentage of the energy is used to cook the food. The following table shows how the boiling point of water increases as a function of pressure.

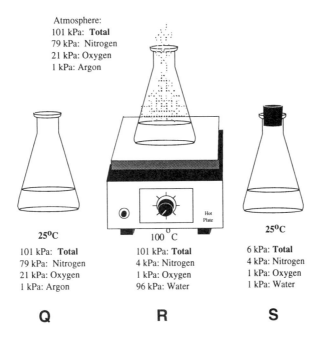

Boiling Point as a Function of Pressure										
Pressure (mm Hg)	760	788	816	845	875	906	937	970	1004	1039	1075
Temperature °C	100	101	102	103	104	105	106	107	108	109	110

4.2.3 The Influence of Surface Area on Vaporization

Discussion: Students will find that water evaporates much more quickly when the surface area is large as it is in the Petri dish as opposed to when it is small as in the test tube. You may also illustrate the significance of surface area by boiling an equal amount of water in both a small- and a large-diameter beaker. Although the temperature in all containers is 100°C, the water will boil off fastest in the large-diameter beaker because it has the largest air/water interface.

Answers (1) For a given volume of liquid, evaporation will be greatest when the surface-area-to-volume ratio is highest. (2) It is important that the swamp cooler have a large air/water interface. The larger the surface area of contact between the air and water, the greater the evaporation and the resulting cooling. (3) Large leaves have a large surface area across which water may evaporate. Consequently, such plants generally die quite rapidly in the desert due to water loss unless they are growing near an oasis or other water source.

4.2.4 Molecular Structure and Vaporization

Discussion: Intermolecular attractions have a significant influence on vapor pressure. Although water has a weight of only 18 g/mole, its boiling point is 100°C, while methane, with a weight of 16 g/mole has a boiling point of only –163°C. Water has an exceptionally high boiling point because it is polar, having one end that is negative and another that is positive. The hydrogen/oxygen covalent bond in water is a polar because the oxygen atom has a greater affinity for electrons than the hydrogen does. The negative end of one molecule is attracted to the positive end of the next one, creating a phenomenon known as hydrogen bonding. Hydrogen bonding acts as a glue to keep water molecules close to one another in the liquid phase, thereby resisting vaporization. If water were not polar, it would have no hydrogen bonding to keep it in the liquid phase and thus would boil at extremely cold temperatures. Ask your students to predict how the world would be different if water were not polar.

Molecular size also plays a role in determining the volatility of a liquid. Kinetic energy is defined as: $E_k = 1/2mv^2$, where m is mass and v is velocity. Temperature is a measure of the average kinetic energy of molecules. If two substances are at the same temperature, but have different molecular sizes, their molecules must have different velocities. Small molecules will have greater velocities than large molecules, and will therefore be more likely to escape the intermolecular forces that hold them in the liquid state. As a result, substances with small molecular size have higher vapor pressures and boil at lower temperatures. The following table shows the relationship between molecular size and the vapor pressure of various hydrocarbons. The larger the molecule, the lower the vapor pressure of the liquid.

Answers (1) Gasoline evaporated fastest, followed by acetone, 2-propanol, water, and salad oil. As a result we can infer that gasoline has the highest vapor pressure, followed by acetone, 2-propanol, water, and salad oil. (2) Rubbing alcohol and acetone are very volatile and evaporate rapidly, removing heat from your skin and leaving you with a cold sensation.

Substance	Common Uses	Boiling Point °C	Molecular Formula	Relative Molecular Size
2-propanol	rubbing alcohol	83	C_3H_8O	3
Acetone	fingernail-polish remover	57	C_3H_6O	2
Paraffin	candle wax	>300	$C_{30}H_{62}$	5
Oleic acid	olive oil	286	$C_{18}H_{34}O_2$	4
Natural gas; methane	fuel used in stoves and ranges	–163	CH_4	1

4.2.5 Vapor Pressure of Solutions

Discussion: The French chemist F. M. Raoult discovered that dissolved solutes reduce the vapor pressure of solvents. Raoult stated that the vapor pressure of the solvent above a solution is equal to the product of the vapor pressure of the pure solvent and its mole fraction in solution. The higher the concentration of solute molecules or ions, the lower the mole fraction of solvent molecules and the lower the vapor pressure.

Vapor pressure lowering is a colligative property—one that is dependent only on the number of particles, and not on the type of particle. Thus, a 1-molal solution (1 mole of solute/kg solvent) of sucrose will behave the same way as a 1-molal solution of fructose. (Sodium chloride is an ionic substance, so one mole of sodium chloride will produce two moles of solute particles when dissociated in water.) You can calculate the boiling point elevation using the following equation:

$$\Delta T_b = K_b m$$

where ΔT_b is the elevation in the boiling point, K_b is the boiling point constant for water ($0.51°C/m$), and m is the molality of the solution. Because the boiling point elevations are very small, it may be difficult for students to accurately measure them, but they can easily measure the time required to resume boiling after a solute has been added, and this measurement may serve as a qualitative measure of the boiling-point elevation. You may wish to demonstrate how solutes affect vapor pressure by adding successive quantities of solute to boiling water. Students will note the water temporarily stops boiling after each addition. When three grams of salt are added to 100 grams of water, the boiling point increases to $100.5°C$. When 6 grams are added, the boiling point increases to $101.0°C$.

Answers (1) The boiling point increases as the solute concentration increases $\Delta T_b = K_b m$. (2) Adding salt will increase the temperature at which water boils, and will thereby decrease the amount of cooking time required. (3) Mineral water will boil at a higher temperature due to the presence of dissolved solutes.

4.2.6 Determining Relative Humidity

Discussion: In cold climates, the relative humidity inside buildings in the winter is often very low because external cold air is transported into buildings and heated. Cold air holds little moisture, so when it is warmed the relative humidity drops although the absolute humidity remains constant. By contrast, the relative humidity inside air-conditioned buildings in warm environments is often high because warm outside air is cooled and no longer holds as much water. As a result, water condenses on the walls inside air-conditioned buildings and may cause mildew or other water-related damage.

Answers (1) A swamp cooler will work only if water evaporates. When the relative humidity is high, water cannot evaporate and the swamp cooler ceases to remove much heat from the building. (2) Sweat evaporates most rapidly when the relative humidity is low. In humid environments, such as Atlanta, sweat does not evaporate rapidly and thus little heat is removed from the body and you are more likely to suffer heat exhaustion. (3) Cold air holds less water than warm air (absolute humidity is less). When cold air is inhaled, it is warmed and humidified by the warm, wet surfaces of the lungs. When you exhale, this water is lost. The condensation of your breath in cold weather is evidence that water is lost each time you exhale.

Applications to Everyday Life

Sweating: Mammals possess sweat glands that allow for evaporative cooling under conditions of high temperature or exertion. For every gram of water that evaporates, one calorie of heat is removed from the body and the air immediately surrounding it.

Swamp Coolers: Swamp coolers are designed to remove heat from houses or buildings by the evaporation of water. For every gram of water that evaporates, one calorie of heat is removed from the structure. Swamp coolers are not effective in humid environments because water does not evaporate fast enough.

Engine Cooling Systems: Because liquids conduct heat more effectively than gases, it is necessary to keep water as a liquid within engine cooling systems. Such systems are pressurized, thereby increasing the boiling point and ensuring that water stays in a liquid form. It is dangerous to remove a radiator cap from a car when its engine is hot because the water in the radiator is significantly higher than 100°C and will instantly become steam when pressure is released.

Cooking at High Elevations: It is necessary to cook food longer at higher elevations because water does not get as hot as it does at lower elevations. While water boils at 100°C at sea level, it may boil at only 95°C in the mountains. Cooking for longer lengths of time helps compensate for lower water temperature.

Pressure Cookers: When cooking in an uncovered pot, temperatures do not rise above 100°C because at that point all additional energy goes into vaporizing the liquid. By closing the system, the pressure will continue to build. Increased pressure prevents the water from boiling and will allow the temperature of the water to increase greatly, thereby cooking food faster.

Drying Clothes: After washing clothes, people don't normally dump them in a heap and expect them to dry by evaporation. The reason that this won't work is that the surface area between liquid and gaseous phases is too small. Hanging clothes on a line increases the surface area of the phase boundary between water and air and facilitates evaporation.

Odors: In order to "smell" a substance, molecules of that substance must be vaporized and diffuse to the olfactory bulb inside your nose. One can smell dirty feet because the vapor pressure of butyric acid ($C_4H_8O_2$; the offending chemical) is high and the molecules rapidly diffuse. Similarly, one can smell vanilla because the vanillin molecule ($C_8H_8O_3$) is rather small and volatile. Certain substances, such as the candle wax (paraffin, $C_{30}H_{62}$), have high molecular weight, low vapor pressure, and thus virtually no odor.

Measuring the Purity of Liquids: One can determine the amount of solutes dissolved in a solvent by measuring the vapor pressure or the boiling point elevation of the solution and applying Raoult's law or the boiling-point elevation equation $\Delta T_b = K_b m$.

Aerosols: Some products such as hair spray, paint, pesticides, and deodorants are dispensed using aerosol cans. In such systems, a substance with a very high vapor pressure is packaged with the product that is to be sprayed. Chlorofluorocarbons (CFC) were used as the primary propellant for many years because they had such a high vapor pressure. Unfortunately, CFCs were found to contribute to the breakdown of the protective ozone layer found in the stratosphere and had to be replaced with other propellants.

Humidifier: The surfaces of the respiratory passageways may dry and crack when the relative humidity is very low, such as frequently occurs in heated buildings in cold, dry weather. To minimize such problems, many people use humidifiers, machines that disperse tiny water droplets to increase the relative humidity of the air in a room.

4.3 FLUID PRESSURE

Lake Baikal in south central Siberia is truly one of the natural wonders of the world. It is the deepest lake in the world (1,637 meters, more than a mile) and holds one fifth of the world's fresh water, more than all of the Great Lakes (Superior, Huron, Michigan, Erie, and Ontario) combined. There are 52 species of fish in Lake Baikal, some of which are found nowhere else in the world. For centuries, fishermen have caught fish in the lake's frigid waters to provide food for their families and the tiny communities on the shores of the lake. Most of the fish caught are from the surface waters, but occasionally an angler will go after fish that live deep in the lake. Although these fish are not hurt by the great pressure they experience in the depths of the lake, they are hurt by the low pressure experienced near the surface. When brought to the surface, their eyes pop out, indicating their internal pressure is far greater than the external pressure at the surface of the lake.

Deep-sea divers encounter related problems if they rise to the surface too quickly. Occasionally a diver will panic, remove his or her weight belts, and ascend rapidly to the surface and experience a potentially lethal condition known as "the bends." Gasses normally dissolved in the diver's blood leave the blood and form bubbles in the same way carbon dioxide bubbles form when a pressurized soft-drink can is opened. These bubbles may cause excruciating pain throughout the body and may interfere with blood circulation by stimulating the formation of dangerous blood clots. To understand the "bends" and many other important and interesting phenomena, it is important to first understand the concept of fluid pressure.

A fluid is a substance that flows easily and takes the shape of its container. Both gases and liquids flow and are considered to be fluids. *The pressure of a fluid is defined as the product of its density (ρ), the acceleration due to gravity (g), and the height of the fluid column (h):*

$$P_{(fluid)} = \rho g h$$

Since the acceleration due to gravity is a constant ($g = 9.8 \text{m/s}^2$ at sea level), and the densities of most fluids ρ are relatively constant with depth, *the principle factor influencing fluid pressure is depth.*

The pressure at any level beneath the surface of a fluid is the same in all directions. If, for example, a balloon is submerged in water, it will assume a smaller spherical shape as water presses equally upon it in all directions, rather than a flattened shape as if someone sat on it (see Figure A). Centuries ago the French scientist Blaise Pascal noted this phenomenon and stated a principle that today bears his name: *A confined fluid transmits externally applied pressure uniformly in all directions.* The air in a submerged balloon transmits pressure equally in all directions so the balloon maintains a spherical shape.

Principles of fluid pressure are applied when sinking wells, building reservoirs, installing plumbing fixtures, constructing earth-moving equipment, designing automobile brakes, exploring the ocean, inspecting dams, searching for oil, constructing

A

waste-water treatment plants, generating electricity, and when scuba diving. The list of applications of fluid pressure could go on and on, but for now, let's get some hands-on experience.

4.3.1 Siphons

Concepts to Investigate: Fluid pressure, pressure differential, siphons, water levels.

Materials: Two beakers or similar containers (250 ml or larger), ruler, hose clamp, tubing (clear tubing works best).

Principles and Procedures: Rome had the most extensive aqueduct system of any city in the ancient world. Eleven aqueducts totaling 479 kilometers (298 miles) in length delivered water to the city. In 125 B.C. the Romans completed the Aqua Tepula, a major aqueduct constructed of clay pipes to siphon water over numerous hills on its way to Rome. *A siphon is a pipe filled with liquid and arranged so that a pressure differential causes fluid to flow from an intermediate level over a higher level to a lower level so long as no air is admitted to the upper arm of the siphon.* Today, siphons are used extensively in major aqueducts as well as in household plumbing.

Part 1. Siphon: To make a siphon, it is necessary that the tubing be filled entirely with water and that both containers be open to the atmosphere. Partially fill two containers with water and then fill a section of tubing by submerging it in a filled sink and kneading it until all air bubbles have escaped. Once it is completely filled, cover one end of the tubing with your finger and lift it out of the sink. Carefully submerge this end in one beaker, and the other end in a second beaker, and then release your finger. Slowly raise beaker #1 and notice that water moves to the lower beaker (Figure B). Raise beaker #2 above beaker #1 and notice that water flows back into beaker #1 (Figure C). Under what conditions, other than entry of air into the tube, will water stop flowing in the siphon? Using a 5-m section of tubing, determine if water will siphon between beakers if the barrier between them is 2 m high.

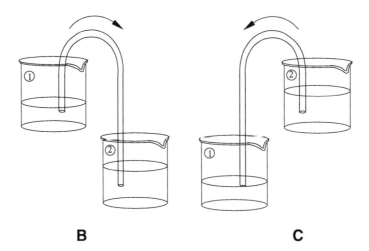

B   **C**

© 1994 by John Wiley & Sons, Inc.

Part 2. Carpenter's level: When experimenting with the siphon in Part 1, you may have noticed that water stops flowing through the tube when the levels in both containers are the same height above the ground. Under such conditions there is no net force on the water and it remains stationary. We can use this information to develop a device known as a level, sometimes used by surveyors and builders to detect slight differences in elevation. Fill a long (10 meter or longer) clear flexible tube with water, as described in Part 1. Drain water from approximately 50 cm of both ends of the tubing and hold these ends next to each other at the same elevation such that the meniscus of one tube is directly opposite the meniscus in the other tube. Stand a meter stick on end and note the height of the menisci above the floor. Carry one end of the tubing to the other end of the room. Raise or lower this end so the water in the stationary end of the tubing remains at the same height. Use a meter stick to measure the height above the floor of both menisci. If the free end is higher, then there is a greater distance between the water level and the floor in this corner of the room than in the reference corner, indicating that the floor is slanted down to this corner. Repeat this procedure to determine if the floor in your room is level. Figure D shows a room where one end of the floor is 7 cm lower than the other end.

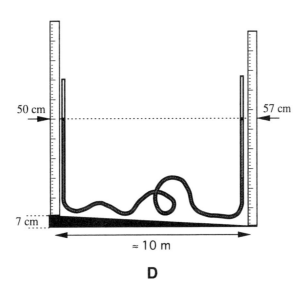

D

Questions

(1) Under what conditions will the water stop flowing in the siphon described in part 1?

(2) Use the concept of water pressure to explain how the water level described in part 2 works.

(3) Explain how a siphon works.

4.3.2 How Does Water Pressure Vary with Depth?

Concepts to Investigate: Pressure, water pressure and depth, pressure and fluid flow.

Materials: Two-liter soft-drink container, tape, pencil or glass rod, ruler, pliers, nail, burner, large pan.

Principles and Procedures: You may have felt pain or pressure in your ears when swimming near the bottom of a deep pool, but not when swimming near the surface. The pain you experience in deep water results from the pressure water exerts on your eardrums. Water pressure increases with depth according to the equation:

$$P_{(fluid)} = \rho g h$$

where ρ is the density of the fluid, g is the acceleration due to gravity, and h is the height of the water column above the point in question. Since the density of water is constant ($\rho = 1$ g/cm³) and the acceleration due to gravity at Earth's surface is constant ($g = 9.8$ m/s²), the only variable is depth. Thus, fluid pressure is directly proportional to depth. This can be tested using the apparatus shown in Figure E.

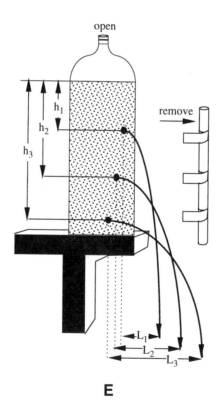

E

© 1994 by John Wiley & Sons, Inc.

Obtain a clear two-liter soft-drink container. While holding the head of a nail with pliers, heat the tip in the flame of a Bunsen burner and then use it to melt three holes of equal diameter in the container, as shown in Figure E. The holes should be slightly offset from each other as illustrated. Wrap the ends of three pieces of tape around a rod so they are spaced the same distance from one another as the holes in the container. Place the other ends of the tape over the holes. Fill the container with water, leave it uncapped, and mark the water level on the bottle. Measure the distance from the water level to each hole and record these in the table as h_1, h_2, and h_3. The initial pressure may be calculated using the equation $P = \rho g h$. To quickly calculate the pressure (measured in Pascals) multiply the depth (h, measured in centimeters) by 98 Pa/cm. Place the bottle at least one meter above a pan. Pull the rod away from the bottle so all three holes are opened simultaneously and record the maximum horizontal distance each stream of water moves before reaching the pan. From your data, does it appear as though the relationship between fluid depth and fluid pressure $P = \rho g h$ is valid? Explain.

	Depth (cm)	Initial Pressure (Pa)	Length of Water Stream (cm)
Upper hole	$h_1 =$ _____	$P_1 =$ _____	$l_1 =$ _____
Middle hole	$h_2 =$ _____	$P_2 =$ _____	$l_2 =$ _____
Lower hole	$h_3 =$ _____	$P_3 =$ _____	$l_3 =$ _____

Questions

(1) Do your data validate the pressure equation: $P = \rho g h$? Explain.

(2) Describe what would happen to a strong, flexible volleyball if you released it from a submarine at the bottom of the ocean.

(3) The Marianas Trench is the deepest known portion of the Earth's surface, with a maximum depth of 11,034 m (36,201 ft). In 1960, Jaques Piccard and Don Walsh descended to a depth of 10,912 m (35,800 ft) in the bathyscaph *Trieste*. Use the pressure equation to determine the approximate pressure in kiloPascals (1 Pascal = 1 newton/m² = 1 kg/ms²) experienced by the bathyscaph at this depth. Assume that ocean water has a density of 1 g/cm³ and that density does not vary with depth. How many times greater is the pressure at this depth than at the surface?

4.3.3 Pascal's Principle

Concepts to Investigate: Pascal's principle, fluid pressure, transmission of pressure in closed containers.

Materials: Small funnel or thistle tube, rubber tubing, glass U-tube, balloon.

Principles and Procedures: Pascal's principle states that fluids exert pressures equally in all directions. Thus, a diver experiences as much pressure from the water beneath her as from the water above her. In this investigation you will develop a pressure gauge to determine if water pressure is nondirectional. Construct a U-tube by bending a section of glass tubing as illustrated in Figure F. Alternatively, you may use two straight pieces of glass connected by an arc of flexible tubing. Add water to the U-tube until it is approximately half-full. Measure the height of the water in both arms and record in the table. Using a pair of scissors, cut a section from a large balloon big enough to fit over the opening of a small funnel or thistle tube. Stretch the material over the opening and secure it with rubber bands if necessary. Connect tubing to the end of the funnel and one end of the U-tube. Immerse the funnel in water and record any changes in the level of the water in the U-tube (Figure G). A rise in the column of water on the open side of the U-tube indicates an increase in pressure on the funnel membrane. Carefully measure the change in height within the tube and record it in the table. Invert the funnel, keeping the membrane at the same level, but facing the reverse direction. Again record the height of the water column (Figure H). Repeat the procedure, holding the funnel horizontally so that the middle of the funnel is at the same level. After completing three measurements at the same level, move the funnel deeper and take three additional measurements. What is the influence of depth on pressure? On the basis of your data, is fluid pressure directional? (Is pressure greater in one direction than another?) Are your data consistent with Pascal's principle?

  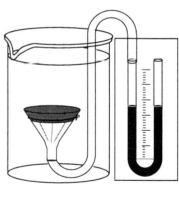

F   **G**   **H**

Depth (cm)	Orientation	Height Gain of Water Column (cm)		
Open Air	all directions	_____ cm		
10 cm	up	_____ cm		
10 cm	down	_____ cm		
10 cm	horizontal	_____ cm		
20 cm	up	_____ cm		
20 cm	down	_____ cm		
20 cm	horizontal	_____ cm		
_____ cm	up	_____ cm		
_____ cm	down	_____ cm		
_____ cm	horizontal	_____ cm		

Questions

(1) Are your data consistent with those predicted by Pascal's principle? Explain.

(2) Figure I illustrates the basic principle of hydraulic lifts used by automobile mechanics to lift vehicles. What force will be exerted on the piston in cylinder 2 if a force of 10,000 N is exerted on cylinder 1? The surface area of cylinder 1 is 0.1 m² while that of cylinder 2 is 1.0 m². Remember Pascal's principle states that the addition of pressure at one point results in an equal increase in pressure at all points. Also, remember that pressure is defined as force per unit area $p = F/A$. (3) Certain unusual fish live in the hadal (deepest) zones of the ocean where pressures are 1,000 times as great as atmospheric pressure. Why don't these fish collapse? What would happen to these fish if you "reeled" one in on a long fishing line?

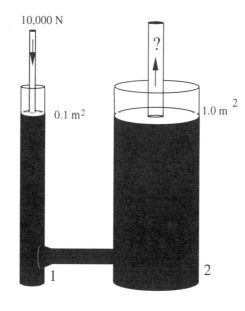

I

FOR THE TEACHER

The demonstration performed in 4.3.2 clearly illustrates the relationship between fluid depth and pressure, but if you desire to show it to an entire class, you may wish to develop a larger apparatus using large-diameter PVC (polyvinyl chloride) or ABS (ABS plastic is a copolymer of the monomers acrylonitrile, butadiene, and styrene) drain piping available at most hardware stores. Cap one end of an 8-foot section using a pipe cap, and drill three holes approximately one meter apart. Cover the holes with tape, fill the cylinder with water, and place the cylinder on top of a desk so the entire class can see. When the tape is removed, students will see a dramatic illustration of the dependence of fluid pressure on depth. Make certain you have pails placed to catch the water.

To determine if students understand the relationship between air pressure and water pressure you may wish to present the following counter-intuitive demonstration. Prepare a bottle as described 4.3.2. Find a single-holed rubber stopper that seals this bottle, and insert a hollow glass tube through the stopper. Lubricate the tube with glycerin or other lubricant so the tube slides smoothly through the stopper hole. Fill the bottle with water and position the glass tube so the lower end is above the water line. Remove the tape and note how the water flows out of the holes. Slowly move the tube down until it touches the surface of the water. At this point, all streams of water should slow because air is no longer flowing in through the tube to fill the void created as water exits. If you continue to move the tube downward to the first (Figure J), second (Figure K), and third holes (Figure L), you should note that the water stops flowing as soon as the tube reaches these levels. The flow through the holes ceases when the tube reaches their levels because the opening in the side

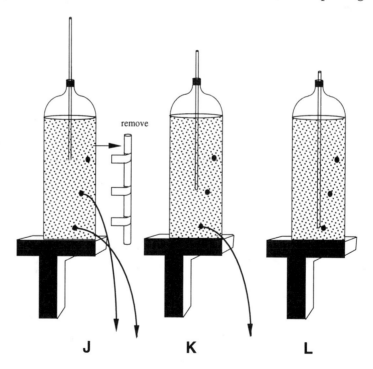

J   K   L

of the bottle and the opening in the glass tube are both exposed to the atmosphere, and there is no longer a pressure differential to force the water out.

4.3.1 Siphons

Discussion: For a siphon to function, there must be a difference in liquid pressure at the two ends of the tubing. In the siphon illustrated in Figure M, atmospheric pressure is approximately the same at both ends of the tube, but the liquid pressure is different. Liquid pressure can be calculated by multiplying the density of the fluid ($\rho = 1$ g/cm³ for water) by the acceleration due to gravity ($g = 9.8$ m/s²) by the height differential h. Thus, a 10-cm column of water exerts a pressure of approximately 1 kPa (1000 N/m²) and a 30-cm column of water exerts a pressure of approximately 3 kPa (3000 N/m²).

$$\text{Fluid pressure of column 1} = \rho g h = \left(\frac{1\text{g}}{\text{cm}^3}\right)\left(\frac{9.8\text{m}}{\text{s}^2}\right)(0.1\text{m}) \approx 1 \text{ kPa}$$

$$\text{Fluid pressure of column 2} = \rho g h = \left(\frac{1\text{g}}{\text{cm}^3}\right)\left(\frac{9.8\text{m}}{\text{s}^2}\right)(0.3\text{m}) \approx 3 \text{ kPa}$$

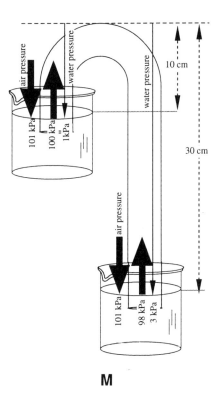

M

Thus, pressure at the bottom of the upper arm of the tube is 100 kPa (101 kPa of air pressure - 1 kPa of water pressure) while pressure at the bottom of the lower arm is only 98 kPa (101 kPa of air pressure - 3 kPa of water pressure). Since pressure at the bottom of the upper arm is greater than the pressure at the bottom of the lower arm, water will flow through the tubing to the lower beaker. The greater the difference in height between the two beakers, the greater the pressure differential, and the greater the flow of water.

Answers:(1) Water will stop flowing when the water levels of both containers are an equal distance above the ground. (2) If the water levels in two ends of a tube are at different heights, then a difference in fluid pressure exists. According to Newton's second law, the fluids will move until all forces are balanced, which occurs when the menisci are at equal heights and the pressure differential is eliminated. (3) See discussion.

4.3.2 How Does Water Pressure Vary with Depth?

Discussion: Fluid pressure is a function of density and depth. Since the density of water is relatively constant (1 g/cm³), the only factor determining pressure is water depth h. It is very important that this activity be performed on the edge of a table so that the water will make a full arc before hitting the ground, otherwise the length measurements L_1, L_2, L_3 may not provide meaningful information. When performing this activity as a demonstration, add food coloring to the water to increase visibility.

Answers: (1) Students should explain that the fluid moves farther under greater pressure, indicating that pressure at the bottom of the container is greater than pressure at the top. (2) The ball would probably collapse immediately under the pressure of the sea water, and would then gradually expand as it floated to the surface. (3) $P = \rho g h =$

$$\frac{1\ \cancel{g}}{\cancel{cm^3}}\ \left|\ \frac{kg}{1000\ \cancel{g}}\ \right|\ \frac{1\times 10^6\ \cancel{cm^3}}{m^3}\ \left|\ \frac{9.8\ \cancel{m}}{s^2}\ \right|\ 10{,}912\cancel{\,m} = \frac{1.07\times 10^8\,kg}{m{\cdot}s^2} = 1.07\times 10^5\,kPa$$

The pressure at the bottom of the Mariana's trench is approximately 1,050 times as great as the pressure at the surface!

4.3.3 Pascal's Principle

Discussion: Students should note that the pressure exerted by the water at any given level is the same, regardless of the orientation of the membrane. This substantiates Pascal's principle, which states that a confined fluid transmits externally applied pressure uniformly in all directions. They should also notice that pressure varies only with fluid depth.

Answers (1) See discussion. (2) 100,000 N. (3) Fluids in the bodies of these fish exert an equal and opposite pressure upon the water that surrounds them. If a fish from the hadal zone is rapidly brought to the surface it will probably rupture as a result of the tremendous pressure differential between its body and the surrounding environment.

Applications to Everyday Life

Aqueducts: Since the tenth century B.C., aqueducts have been used to carry water to population and agricultural centers. The Greeks and Romans improved upon the general design of aqueducts by employing pipes to siphon water over hills and mountains. Modern aqueducts use this same principle. The Owen's River aqueduct in California employs a siphon to carry water over the Sierra Madre mountains en route to Los Angeles. Since the source of the water in the Owen's Valley is higher than the destination in Los Angeles, the water siphons over the intervening mountains.

Emptying a Swimming Pool: It is easy to drain the water out of a swimming pool by establishing a siphon, as long as the hose is filled with water and the outlet is at a lower elevation than the bottom of the pool.

Hydraulic Lift: Many automobile repair shops use hydraulic lifts to raise cars so mechanics may work on them more easily. By applying a relatively small force to a small piston, hydraulic lifts generate a large force on a large piston (see Figure I). The hydraulic lift multiplies force at the expense of distance. The small piston must move farther than the large piston.

Hydraulic Press: The hydraulic press is a machine used for molding plastics or metals into specific shapes. It consists of two cylinders connected by a tube and filled with oi,l as illustrated in Figure I. As with most hydraulic devices, a low viscosity oil is used because it has protective and lubricating properties. By exerting a small force on a small piston, hydraulic presses produce a large force on the large piston that shapes plastic or metal in special molds. See the answer to question 2 in section 4.3.3 for an explanation.

Hydraulic Brakes: Automobiles have hydraulic brakes that multiply the force placed on the brake drums or disks. The small cylinder shown in Figure I is known as the master cylinder, and the large one is the slave cylinder. The brake pedal applies pressure on the master cylinder, causing an increase in pressure in the slave or wheel cylinder, which subsequently applies force on the brake shoes.

Dams: When designing dams, civil engineers must consider the water pressure a dam will experience as the reservoir fills. The fluid pressure equation $P = \rho g h$ indicates that pressure is directly proportional to depth. Because pressure increases with depth, engineers design the bases of dams much wider than the tops. At the base of hydroelectric dams you may see water exiting at great speed in dramatic contrast to water that tumbles slowly over the spillway. Water at the bottom of a tall dam is under great pressure and may be used to turn massive turbines and generate electricity.

Household Plumbing: Bathtubs, sinks, washing machines, dishwashers, and toilets discharge water into sewer lines. Bacteria, gasses, and vermin could reenter the house through drain pipes were it not for the "traps" installed in each drain. A trap is an "S" shaped turn in a drain line that holds water, preventing gasses and organisms from entering the house. When a sink is drained, the water column on the sink side becomes taller than the highest point in the trap, and water is forced through the trap and down the drain pipe. However, the draining water might create a siphon and evacuate the trap were it not for the relief piping system that provides a channel to equalize air pressure. On the roofs of homes you will generally see small pipes without covers. These are the relief pipes that prevent the siphoning of water out of the traps.

4.4 FLUIDS IN MOTION

In the eighteenth century, the Swiss scientist Daniel Bernoulli discovered the following relationship: *The pressure of a gas or liquid decreases as its velocity increases.* This statement might seem rather strange to anyone who has lived through a hurricane. Surely it is the vast pressure of the wind that causes such devastation, isn't it?

Residents of the southeastern United States are familiar with the devastating power of hurricanes. In August of 1969, Hurricane Camille hit the coast of Louisiana with a velocity of 172 miles per hour, leaving 256 people dead and millions of dollars of property damage. In 1989, Hurricane Hugo devastated much of Jamaica before hitting the shore of South Carolina with 135 mph winds. In the summer of 1992, Florida and Louisiana were hit by Hurricane Andrew; entire communities were destroyed and thousands were left homeless.

Hurricanes and typhoons are tropical cyclones with sustained winds of at least 120 km/h (75 mph). Storms in the Atlantic and eastern Pacific are known as hurricanes, while those in the western Pacific are known as typhoons, a Chinese word meaning "great wind." As water vapor in moist tropical air condenses, heat is released, providing the energy that spawns hurricanes and typhoons. These storms intensify as they pass over warmer water and weaken only when reaching cooler water or land.

Hurricanes and typhoons are cyclones, masses of air rotating around a low-pressure zone. The pressure in the center, or "eye," of a hurricane is often as low as 950 millibars and may get as low as 900 millibars (normal atmospheric pressure is 1,013 millibars). Winds surrounding the eye of a hurricane may exceed 180 miles per hour (300 km/h). According to Bernoulli, it is not only the force of the wind that causes property damage, but also the low pressure associated with the high winds. Bernoulli's principle suggests that air pressure outside a sealed house may drop so low that windows and doors are forced out because the pressure inside is so much greater than the pressure outside (there is a large pressure differential; Figures A and B). Meteorologists therefore warn residents to keep windows open during hurricanes, typhoons, or tornadoes so air pressure inside their homes will drop with atmospheric pressure, thereby preventing the development of dangerous pressure differentials.

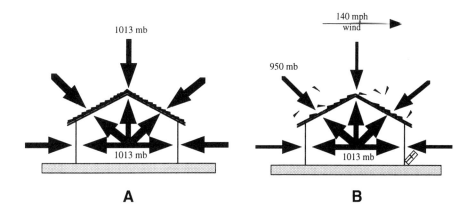

A   B

Bernoulli's principle helps us understand a wide variety of phenomena, from the flight of birds to the trajectory of a pitcher's curve ball. In the following activities you will investigate the properties of fluids in motion and learn how Bernoulli's principle applies to everyday life.

4.4.1 Bernoulli's Principle

Concepts to Investigate: Bernoulli's principle, manometer, atomizers, pressure differential.

Materials: Table-tennis balls, thread, tape, paper, straw, food coloring.

Principles and Procedures

Part 1. Air stream between two objects: Use tape to attach a piece of thread to each of two table-tennis balls and suspend them as shown in Figure C. Use a straw to blow between the two table-tennis balls and note the movement of each. On Figure C indicate the new positions of the balls and the regions of lower and higher pressure. On the same diagram indicate where one must blow so the table-tennis balls move in opposite directions. Try it. Once again indicate where the regions of lower and higher pressure must be and the direction of the net force on each ball.

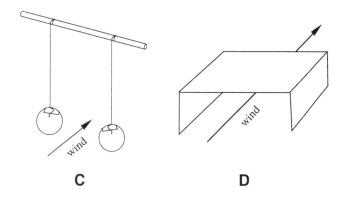

        C   **D**

Fold a sheet of notebook paper in half lengthwise and then fold down the ends as shown in Figure D to make a paper bridge. What do you think will happen if you place the "bridge" on your desk top and then blow under it? Try it and indicate on the diagram the regions of higher and lower pressure and indicate with an arrow the net force on the bridge.

Part 2. Measuring pressure with a straw-manometer: Will the level of water in the straw illustrated in Figure E change if you blow across its tip using another straw as shown? Try it. Was your prediction correct? Indicate on the diagram where the regions of lower and higher pressure must be to cause this result. Squeeze the tip of the horizontal straw and try it again. Is the result more pronounced? Why or why not?

When you are not blowing, the air pressure is the same (approximately 1,013 millibars) above the water in the straw and above the water in the beaker because both are open to the atmosphere. When you blow, air pressure above the straw decreases while air pressure above the water in the glass remains constant. You can determine the reduction in pressure by measuring the height of the water in the straw. Every centimeter the water rises represents a reduction of one millibar (about

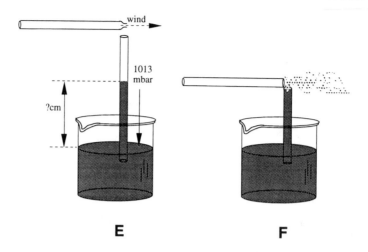

E   F

0.01 percent of normal atmospheric pressure). If, for example, water rose 10 centimeters, you could conclude that air pressure above the straw decreased by approximately 10 mbar. Determine how high the water will rise in the straw and calculate the accompanying air pressure above the straw. Compare your value to the class average. As a point of comparison, the air pressure on top of Mount Everest, the highest mountain in the world, is only about 340 mbar!

	Height of Water in Straw	*Reduction in Air Pressure*	*Air Pressure Above Straw*
No wind	0 cm	0 cm	1,013 mb
Maximum height	_____ cm	_____ mbar	_____ mbar
Class average	_____ cm	_____ mbar	_____ mbar

Part 3. Atomizer: Homeowners and gardeners spray fertilizers or pesticides on lawns and gardens using a sprayer attached to the end of a hose. As water is forced through a narrow point in the nozzle, pressure decreases and fertilizer or pesticide is drawn through a side arm from the bottle into the stream of water. You can make your own "atomizer" or garden sprayer simply by shortening the straw used in Part 2 so fluid rises to the top of the straw when blowing across its open end. Place a few drops of food coloring in a beaker and then use your atomizer to spray a mist of the colored water onto a sheet of white paper (Figure F).

Questions

(1) Given only two straws, how can you separate the suspended table-tennis balls without blowing on them? Explain.

(2) Evaluate this statement: "The table-tennis balls in part 1 were attracted to each other."

(3)   The reduction in fluid pressure is proportional to the square of the speed of the fluid. On the basis of this relationship, how much higher would water move in a straw if the velocity of the air across the top doubled?

(4)   How could you employ Bernoulli's principle to develop an anemometer, a device used to measure wind speed?

(5)   What are some devices that use Bernoulli's principle to atomize (to reduce into fine particles) and spray a liquid?

(6)   Hurricanes and tornadoes may cause houses to explode. Explain.

(7)   Why is it dangerous to stand near a fast-moving train?

(8)   Ships that pass close to each other run the risk of a sideways collision. Explain.

4.4.2 Lift

Concepts to Investigate: Lift, airfoil, flight, Bernoulli's principle, hydrofoil.

Materials: Pencil, paper, tape, 3″ × 5″ card, straight pin, funnel, straw, tubing, table-tennis ball.

Principles and Procedures: On November 2, 1947, industrialist Howard Hughes piloted a flying boat by the name of *Spruce Goose* to a height of 70 feet on a 3,000-foot test run in Long Beach Harbor, California. Although it never flew again, the 212-ton aircraft set the record as the largest and heaviest aircraft ever to fly. Newton's second law states that an object will accelerate only if there is a net force acting upon it. To fly, the *Spruce Goose* required a lifting force in excess of its 212-ton weight. How was such a force generated?

According to Bernoulli, fluid pressure decreases as speed increases. If a fluid travels more rapidly across the top of a wing than the bottom, the wing will experience a lifting force because the pressure on top will be less than the pressure on the bottom. An examination of the wings of birds and airplanes shows they have greater curvature on the top than on the bottom (Figure G). The relative speed of air moving over the wing is greater than the speed of air moving under the wing because it must travel a greater distance in the same length of time. Thus the pressure on top is less than the pressure on the bottom, creating a lifting force. If the lifting force is greater than the weight of the plane, the plane will climb (Figure H), but if the weight is greater than the lifting force, the plane will descend (Figure I).

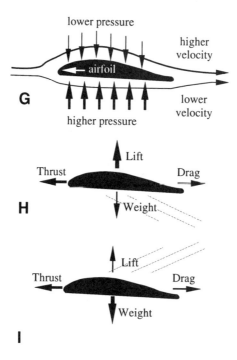

Part 1. Airfoil: Wings, rudders, and propeller blades are examples of airfoils, surfaces used to control the speed and direction of aircraft. In this activity you will examine the principle of lift as it applies to airfoils. Trim a piece of notebook paper to a width slightly less than the width of your pencil. Tape the paper to the pencil as illustrated and blow across the top surface of the paper (Figure J). Explain movement of the paper in terms of Bernoulli's principle. Draw a diagram of the airfoil and indicate regions of higher and lower pressure.

Part 2. Airstream: Cut a seven-cm square from a sheet of heavy paper or thin cardboard. Determine the center of the card by drawing diagonal lines and marking the point of intersection. Place a straight pen through the card at this point and tape its head to the card, as shown in Figure K. Place the tip in the end of a spool of thread, gently hold the card against the spool, and blow through the center of the spool. Remove your hand and report your observations. Explain the results in terms of Bernoulli's principle. Indicate on Figure K the regions of higher and lower pressure.

Part 3. Float valve: Cut a small section of drinking straw and connect it to a funnel, as shown in Figure L. You may need to use a piece of rubber tubing to connect the straw to the funnel. (The only reason for the straw is to ensure sanitation. Never touch your mouth directly to laboratory glassware as it may be contaminated.) Place a table-tennis ball in an upright funnel, tilt your head back, and blow steadily. Does the ball fly out or remain in the funnel? Now point the funnel down (Figure M), hold the table-tennis ball in the funnel, blow steadily through the funnel, and slowly remove your hand. Repeat until the ball remains in the inverted funnel while you are blowing. On Figure M indicate regions of lower and higher pressure and the direction of the resultant force upon the ball.

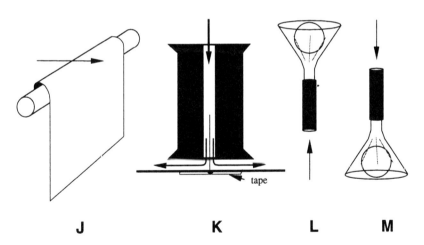

J   K   L   M

Questions

(1) What is the relationship between the speed of air across the paper and the amount of lift in part 1?

(2) Does it become easier or more difficult to remove the table-tennis ball from the funnel as the wind speed increases? Explain.

(3) The table-tennis ball in Part 3 acts like a valve. Is it a one-way or a two-way valve? Explain.

(4) Some race cars have elevated inverted winglike structures known as spoilers (Figure N). What effect may such spoilers have on a race car's performance?

(5) A hydrofoil is a boat that uses submerged wings (also known as hydrofoils) to raise the hull out of the water when traveling at high speeds. Sketch your own design for such a boat and explain how it functions.

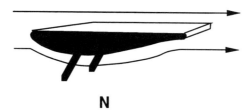

N

4.4.3 Streamlines and Air Drag

Concepts to Investigate: Streamlines, air drag, stability, Bernoulli's principle.

Materials: Paper, tape, candles, flexible straw, table-tennis ball.

Principles and Procedures: In 1934, Chrysler Corporation introduced the "Airflow," one of the first automobiles to feature a streamlined aerodynamic design. Today, auto manufacturers routinely use wind tunnels to study airflow patterns over cars in an effort to minimize air resistance or drag. A streamlined design is one that provides a smooth, nonturbulent flow of air across the surface of the vehicle.

Part 1. Air drag: Cut a note card into a 5-cm square and place lighted candles in front of it and to the sides, as shown in Figure O. Blow toward the card, and note which way each of the flames bend. Cut a piece of notebook paper into a rectangle 5 cm wide by 28 cm long, shape into a teardrop as illustrated in Figure P, and tape the ends. The widest portion of the "teardrop" should be 5 centimeters. Blow toward the paper and once again record the directions the flames move. Indicate on Figure P the regions of lower and higher pressure and the direction of the net force upon each flame. (Force is equal to the pressure multiplied by the surface area on which the pressure acts.) Does the flame behind the barriers move the same direction in both cases? Explain.

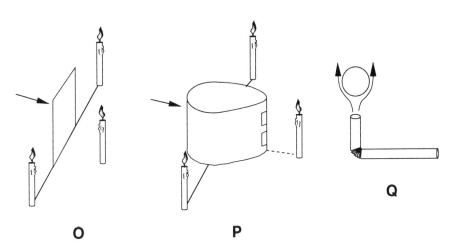

O   P   Q

Part 2. Balancing a ball in air: A streamline is the line a fluid particle follows as it flows. If an automobile is "streamlined," air molecules follow predictable streamlines as they flow over the surface of the car. If the car is not streamlined, air particles may flow in an unpredictable turbulent manner. You may have noticed people driving on a highway with a sofa or mattress strapped to the top of their car. Such objects cause turbulent airflow and reduce the stability of the vehicle. A passenger in a car carrying such a load may notice the car jerk erratically as it moves down the highway. The following investigation will help you understand stability.

Bend a flexible straw as shown in Figure Q. Take a deep breath and blow a slow, steady stream of air through the straw. Gently release the table-tennis ball over the stream of air and record the length of time you can keep it suspended. With a little experience you should be able to keep it aloft for five seconds or more. Repeat the process using a wad of paper of similar size and mass. Which is easier to keep aloft? Which object is more streamlined and stable?

Questions

(1) Use Bernoulli's principle to explain why the flames bend in different directions depending on the type of barrier.

(2) Explain why some freight trucks have large fiberglass or metal "bubbles" on top of the cab.

(3) Is it easier to keep a table-tennis ball or a wad of paper aloft in Part 2? Which object is more streamlined?

(4) Use Bernoulli's principle to explain how the ball can be balanced in midair.

FOR THE TEACHER

A formal statement of Bernoulli's principle is: *At any two points along the streamline in a nonviscous, incompressible fluid in steady flow, the sum of the pressure, the kinetic energy-per-unit volume, and the potential energy-per-unit volume has the same value.* Quite a mouthful, but really not as mysterious as it may sound.

Bernoulli used the laws of conservation of energy and mass to explain phenomena such as those observed in the activities of this chapter. Although most of these activities involve air, it is easiest to explain Bernoulli's principle using an ideal fluid, a hypothetical substance that is incompressible and flows in a perfectly streamlined fashion (no turbulence). According to the first law of thermodynamics (conservation of energy), the total energy of the fluid remains constant as it flows through a pipe (Figure R). The energy-per-unit volume of the liquid can be resolved into three components: the kinetic energy $1/2\rho v^2$, the gravitational potential energy ρgh, and the fluid pressure P. One may notice that the kinetic energy and gravitational potential energy terms are very similar to those terms for solids. For example, the kinetic energy of a moving solid object is $1/2mv^2$, where mass m occupies the same place that density ρ occupies in the Bernoulli equation. If the total energy-per-unit volume in the tube is the same at all points then we can write the following equation:

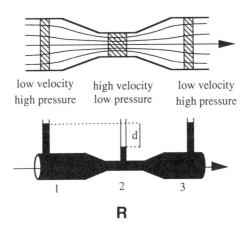

low velocity   high velocity   low velocity
high pressure   low pressure   high pressure

R

$$P_1 + 1/2\rho v_1^2 + \rho gh_1 = P_2 + 1/2\rho v_2^2 + \rho gh_2$$

Note that each term ($1/2\rho v^2$, ρgh, P) is an expression of energy-per-unit volume (that is, joule/liter). Since the pipe being considered in Figure R is level, the heights h_1 and h_2 are equal. In addition, the density ρ is unchanged and acceleration due to gravity g is constant so the gravitational potential energy terms ρgh_1 and ρgh_2 must be equal and cancel, leaving the equation:

$$P_1 + 1/2\rho v_1^2 = P_2 + 1/2\rho v_2^2$$

Since the density ρ of an ideal fluid is constant, the only variables remaining are the velocity v and pressure P of the fluid. If a unit volume is to pass points 1 and 2 in the same length of time, the volume passing point 2 must be moving faster. If velocity increases, pressure decreases because energy-per-unit volume must remain constant, as shown in the previous equation. The manometers in Figure R show how the pressure varies as a function of fluid flow. The height differential d in manometers 1 and 2 is a result of increased fluid velocity.

Although Bernoulli's equation is based on the behavior of ideal fluids, it can also be used to qualitatively describe the behavior of nonturbulent gasses. Each of the phenomena observed in the activities of this chapter can be understood if one identifies the location where the speed of gas is greatest as the region where pressure is lowest and the location where the speed of gas is least as the region where pressure is greatest. The resulting pressure differentials cause the observed phenomena.

Bernoulli's principle applies to fluids moving around stationary objects as well as objects moving through stationary fluids. Relative motion is the important factor. For example, your hair will blow the same whether you are riding a bicycle at 30 km/h through still air or waiting at a stoplight in a 30 km/h wind.

4.4.1 Bernoulli's Principle

Discussion: In all diagrams, students should identify low-pressure regions where fluid is moving fastest and high-pressure regions where fluid is moving slowest. For example, students should identify the region between the table-tennis balls in Part 1 as a low-pressure zone, and the regions to the sides of the balls as high-pressure zones. Assume the air pressure between the table-tennis balls were reduced to 1,000 mb as a result of increased velocity. Since the pressure on the outside of the balls remains at 1,013 mb (atmospheric pressure), there is a 13-mb pressure differential. This causes a net force on each ball that pushes it inward, as illustrated in Figure S.

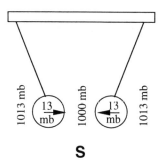

S

Demonstration 1. "Shower Curtains": You may wish to introduce Bernoulli's principle by asking students to predict the motion of a suspended table-tennis ball brought near to a stream of water (Figure T). Many will think the ball will be forced away, but actually it will be pulled into the stream in the same way a shower curtain is pulled into the stream of water. Air surrounding the stream is moving and is therefore at lower pressure than the air in the rest of the room. A pressure differential develops, and the ball or shower curtain is pushed into the stream of water.

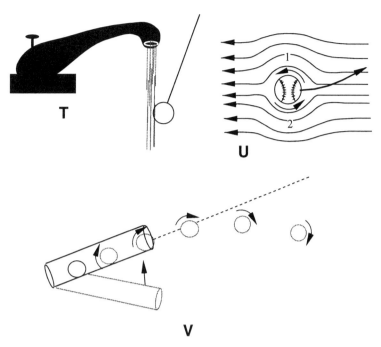

Demonstration 2. "Curve Balls": Baseball pitchers employ Bernoulli's principle when throwing a curve ball, and tennis players use it when giving the ball a top spin so it drops rapidly on the other side of the net. The stitches on a baseball or the fuzz on a tennis ball scoop a layer of air as the ball spins. On one side of the ball this air moves in the same direction as the air moving past the ball (side 1, Figure U), while on the other side it moves in the opposite direction (side 2, Figure U). The relative velocity on side 1 is greater, hence the pressure is less and the ball is pushed to this side. This "Bernoulli curve ball" can be illustrated by throwing a table-tennis ball out of a short cylinder such as a paper-towel tube or 2-inch-diameter PVC pipe (Figure V). Hold the tube horizontally and then move it rapidly in a lateral direction. The ball will exit the tube spinning and will curve away from the tube as shown. With a little practice you should be able to master the curve ball.

Answers (1) If you direct a stream of air to the outside of both balls, the pressure in those regions will fall and the balls will be pushed away from each other. (2) The balls were not attracted to each other, but rather pushed toward each other as a result of the pressure differential. See discussion for explanation. (3) If using an ideal fluid, it should rise four times as high, but since we are not the rise will be less. (4) The height to which water rises in an open tube is proportional to the square of the velocity of the air above the open end. The tube could be calibrated by relating the height of water in the tube to known wind speeds. (5) Perfume bottles, garden sprayers, airbrushes, automobile carburetors. (6) If wind velocity is great, as in a hurricane or tornado, the pressure differential between the inside of the house (approximately 1,013 mb) and the outside (900–950 mb) may be sufficient to blow out windows, doors, and sometimes entire walls. (7) As a train passes, a region of low pressure forms between you and the train while air pressure behind you remains constant. Since the pressure behind you is greater, you may be forced toward the train. (8) The velocity of water in the region between the ships is greater than the velocity of water on the other sides of the ships. A pressure differential develops and the ships are pushed toward each other.

4.4.2 Lift

Discussion: When blowing across the paper in Part 1, many students are surprised to see it rise. The paper rises because the wind creates a low-pressure zone above the paper. Since the atmospheric pressure below the paper remains constant, it exceeds the pressure on top and pushes the paper up. Make certain students understand that this principle allows birds to glide and airplanes to fly. Students may be equally surprised to see the card stick to the spool or the table-tennis ball stick in the funnel when air is blowing against them. Make certain they realize that the pressure in the region between the card and the spool or between the funnel walls and the table-tennis ball is relatively low because air is traveling fast. The pressure of the surrounding still air is greater than the moving air and pushes against the card or ball to keep it in place.

Answers (1) The greater the wind speed, the greater the lift. (2) As wind speed increases, the pressure in the space between the ball and the funnel decreases, resulting in a greater pressure differential that makes it more difficult to remove the ball. (3) This can be considered to be a one-way valve since the ball will form a seal if the direction of the fluid is reversed. (4) Air passing under the spoiler has a greater relative velocity than air passing over it. The resulting pressure differential acts to keep the tires in contact with the road, thereby improving traction and performance. Spoilers are of value only at race-track speeds and are of little value on cars used for personal transportation. (5) Students' pictures should show a submerged wing or hydrofoil that is fastened below the hull of the boat. The curvature of the top of the hydrofoil should be greater than the curvature of the bottom just as it is in the wing of an airplane, illustrated in Figure G. The velocity of water across the top of the hydrofoil is greater than the velocity of water across the bottom. Therefore, the pressure is greater beneath, and the foil and attached boat are lifted up.

4.4.3 Streamlines and Air Drag

Discussion: When wind hits the flat card illustrated in Figure O, it becomes turbulent and moves laterally in both directions, blowing the flames of the lateral candles away from the card. As the air moves laterally, a low-pressure zone is created to the left and right of the card and the flame behind the card is pushed forward by atmospheric pressure. Cyclists have set world-record speeds by traveling in the "draft" of a truck that acts like the card. When air hits the teardrop, it splits and moves around the obstacle in a streamlined manner and converges on the flame in the back, moving it away from the obstacle, or possibly extinguishing it. The flames to the left and right of the teardrop are pushed inward due to the pressure differential that results from the airstream moving around the paper.

Answers (1) See discussion. (2) Freight trucks have much wind resistance because of their large profile. A portion of their wind resistance is reduced when curved shields are placed in front of the cargo section, thereby promoting a streamlined flow of air around the vehicle. This reduces drag and increases performance and fuel efficiency. (3) The ball is more streamlined and thus easier to balance in the air stream. (4) As the ball moves to the right, the air flows by rapidly to the left of the ball, creating a low-pressure zone. The atmospheric pressure to the right remains relatively unchanged and thus pushes the ball back into the stream of air.

Applications to Everyday Life

Airplane Wings and Bird Wings: Airplane and bird wings are designed so upper surfaces are more curved than lower surfaces (see Figure G). As the wing moves, air forced over it will move faster than air forced under it because the distance from the leading edge to the trailing edge is longer on top of the wing than on the bottom. Since the airstream on top of the wing is faster than on the bottom, the pressure on the bottom is greater, and the net force on the wing will oppose gravity (provide lift).

Hydrofoil: A hydrofoil is a wing-shaped device designed to provide lift as a boat moves through water. The term *hydrofoil* is now applied to vessels fitted with hydrofoils. Alexander Graham Bell realized that boats could travel faster if their hulls were not in the water and designed a vessel fitted with a ladder of foils. As the boat accelerated, the lift increased and the boat rose out of the water until it was supported only by the bottom foils.

Curve Balls and Top Spins: A baseball pitcher can put a curve on a baseball by setting it spinning when it is released. The relative velocity of air in contact with the ball is dependent upon two factors, the translational movement of the ball through the air and the rotational movement of the ball on its axis. Although the translational velocity is the same on both sides of the ball, the rotational velocity is not. Thus, the air moves faster (pressure is lower) on one side, and the ball curves in this direction. The top spin used by a tennis player works in a similar manner.

Spoilers: Some race cars employ spoilers to provide stability (Figure N). A spoiler is essentially an inverted wing and creates a net downward force that keeps the wheels of the car firmly on the ground and ensures traction.

Air Drag and Automobile Design: If a vehicle has a flat frontal profile such as the note card (Figure O), it will leave a low-pressure zone immediately behind it. The vehicle will experience a "drag" as the high-pressure zone in front of the vehicle pushes the car back into this partial vacuum. Cars are aerodynamically designed to decrease drag and thereby increase fuel efficiency and performance.

Bicycle Racing: Bicyclists use the low-pressure "drag" zone when they are being "drafted" by the leader. The lead cyclist creates a drag zone and the second cyclist gets pushed into this partial vacuum in the same way the flame was pushed toward the card. The influence of drafting is clearly seen when one looks at the world-record speeds for bicycle racing. The record speed for an undrafted cyclist is held by Michael Hübner of Germany, with a speed of 72 km/h (45 miles/h). By contrast, the record speed for a cyclist being drafted by a vehicle is 245 km/h (152 miles/h) by John Howard of the United States.

Aerodynamics: Some vehicles, such as large freight trucks, inherently have much wind resistance because of their large profile. A portion of this wind resistance is reduced when fiberglass or aluminum bubbles are placed on top of the cab, in front of the cargo section, to promote a more streamlined flow.

Aspirators: Some science laboratories use water aspirators such as that illustrated in Figure W to produce a partial vacuum. Notice that the water passageway in the aspirator is very narrow, causing the water to increase in speed. As speed increases, pressure decreases, creating a partial vacuum at the point where the vacuum tube is connected. The vacuum is regulated by the rate water flows through the aspirator. Dentists use aspirators to remove excess saliva from the mouth.

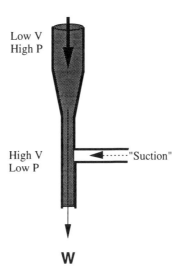

W

Energy and Momentum

5.1 Work and Power

5.2 Potential and Kinetic Energy

5.3 Momentum

5.4 Machines

5.1 WORK AND POWER

"School is too much work." "I have to work for a living." "All work and no play make Jack or Jane dull people." "Do it my way or it won't work!"

"Power can corrupt a person." "I have the power to finish this task." "This car has a really powerful engine." "The President of the United States is a powerful person."

Obviously the terms "work" and "power" are used to convey many different ideas. In science, work and power have very specific meanings. Work *is equal to force multiplied by distance: W = F × d*. The work done by a force acting on a body while the body undergoes a displacement is a scalar quantity defined by the product of the magnitude of the displacement and the component of the force in the direction of the displacement. Work is related to motion. If you push on a wall and it does not move, you have done no work. If you push on a stalled truck and it moves, you have done work on the truck equal to the force you exerted in the direction of the truck's motion multiplied by the distance the truck moved (Figure A). The component F_1 of your force parallel to the truck's displacement does work, but the component F_2 perpendicular to the displacement does not.

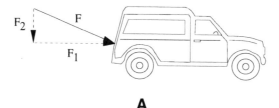

A

In the metric system newton-meter (N·m) is the unit of work called a joule (J), while in the Customary (British) system the unit of work is foot-pound (ft·lb). One joule is the work done by a constant force of 1 newton when the body on which the force is exerted moves a distance of 1 meter in the direction of the force. One foot-pound is the work done by a constant force of one pound when the body on which the force is exerted moves a distance of one foot in the direction of the force. One joule is approximately 0.74 ft·lb.

Suppose you lift a suitcase and then begin to walk with it. You did work lifting the suitcase vertically and you did work accelerating it horizontally to your walking speed (constant speed). However, as you continue to walk with the suitcase you are doing no work on it. Although it requires energy to support the suitcase, you are performing no work on it because you are not moving it against the force of gravity nor are you accelerating it in a horizontal direction. Note that time is not involved in the definition of work. The same work is done in raising a weight through a given vertical distance regardless of the time involved.

Suppose your friend lifts a suitcase to the same height in half the time you do. Both you and your friend perform the same amount of work lifting the suitcase the same distance against gravity, but your friend is more tired because he or she did the work faster and used more power. *Power is the time rate at which work is done. Power is the work done in a given time interval (P = W/t).* When work is measured in joules and time in seconds, power is expressed in watts (W). A watt is one joule per second: W = J/s. One kilowatt is 1,000 watts. When work is measured in foot-pounds (ft·lb) and time in seconds, power is expressed in ft·lb per second. One horsepower is 550 ft·lb/s which is approximately 0.75 kilowatt. You may believe there is something inherently electrical about watts and kilowatts, but this is not so. Electrical power could just as well be measured in foot-pound or horsepower units.

To understand rotational work and power, it is helpful to understand a unit of measurement known as a radian. You will find this unit of angular measure through-out your studies of science and mathematics, and you should become familiar with it. In order to define the angle of one radian we draw a circle of radius R and then rotate the line OX_1 about the center O to a position OX_2 so that the length of the arc X_1X_2 is R as shown in Figure B. The length of the arc X_1X_2 is equal to the length of the radius R. The angle generated is called a radian. Since there are 2π radii in the cir-cumference of a circle ($c = 2\pi R$), there are 2 radians in an angle generated by one complete revolution. Therefore, 2π radians $= 360°$, so 1 radian $= 180°/\pi = 57.3°$ and $1° = (\pi/180)$ radians $= 0.0175$ radian. When the radian is used to measure an angle its name is omitted. For example, an angle of $360°$ is equal to 2π or 6.28.

It is instructive to consider work done in rotational motion. Inspect the wheel shown in Figure C in which a force is shown acting at a right angle (tangent) to the radius. The angle theta θ shows the angular displacement of the wheel. The arc shown as d is the linear distance through which the force acts. Consequently the work done on the wheel is equal to the force F multiplied by the linear distance, d.

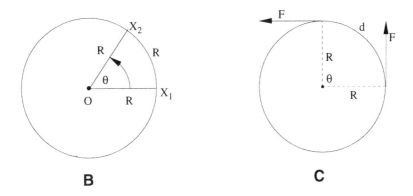

B   **C**

The arc d is equal to the angle θ measured in radians multiplied by the radius R of the wheel: $d = R\theta$ by definition of the radian. Consequently, the work done on the wheel is equal to the product of the force F, the radius R of the wheel, and the angle of displacement θ. $W = FR\theta$. But since torque τ is equal to FR, we have: $W = \tau\theta$. The work done in rotational motion can be computed by finding the product of the torque producing the motion and the angular displacement given in radians.

5.1.1 Measuring Work

Concepts to Investigate: Work, equation of work, units of work.

Materials: Flight of stairs, metric measuring tape, brick, spring scale, adhesive tape.

Principles to Investigate: Use the measuring tape to determine the vertical height of the flight of stairs in meters. Walk up the flight of stairs and determine the work performed by multiplying your weight in newtons (1 lb = 4.45 N) by the height of the stairs measured in meters (1 N·m = 1 J). Remember that work is equal to the force applied (your weight) multiplied by the distance through which the force acts (vertical height of the stairs). How much work would be performed if you ascended two flights of stairs? Three flights?

Measure and mark a distance of one meter on a floor or large bench. Place a brick or box on the flat surface one-half meter in front of the first mark. Attach a scale to one end of the object and pull horizontally so it travels at constant speed as it crosses the first and second marks (Figure D). Since there is friction between the brick and the surface, work must be done to move the brick at a constant speed. Calculate the work performed by multiplying the average reading on the scale during the marked distance by this distance $W = Fd$. Repeat the process at a higher but constant velocity. Does the amount of work depend upon the speed at which the object is moved?

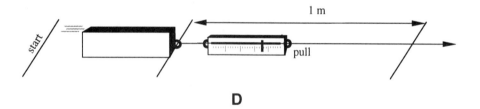

D

Questions

(1) If you weigh twice as much as your friend, you do twice the work when climbing stairs. Explain.

(2) Why do we use the vertical height of the stairs in computing work and not the distance from bottom step to top step?

(3) Impulse (see chapter on momentum) is the product of force and the time over which it acts. In this chapter we define work as force multiplied by the distance over which it acts. Clarify the difference between impulse and work.

(4) In which of the following cases is more work done: lifting a 2000-N object a vertical distance of 10 m or lifting a 1000-N object a vertical distance of 20 m?

(5) A flight of stairs is a type of simple machine known as an inclined plane. A smaller force through a longer distance on an inclined plane may perform the same amount of work as a larger force through a shorter distance lifted directly. Explain.

(6)   On the basis of your data with the moving block, does work depend on time? Explain.

(7)   If the radius of the wheel shown in Figure E is 0.5 m and the force *F* is 20 N, what work is done in half a revolution? In a complete revolution?

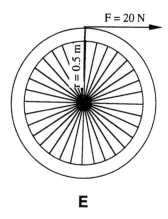

E

5.1.2 Measuring Power

Concepts to Investigate: Power, units of power, comparison of work and power.

Materials: Ramp, metric measuring tape, brick, spring scale, adhesive tape, stopwatch or digital watch.

Principles and Procedures: Power is the rate at which work is done ($P = W/t$). The traditional unit of work is the "horsepower," the equivalent of 550 foot-pounds per second. The SI unit for power is the watt, which is equal to one joule per second. One horsepower is approximately 746 watts.

A 1/100 horsepower (7.5 watt) motor is often used to power small clocks. A two-horsepower ($\approx$1,300 watt) engine is often used to power lawn mowers. Henry Ford used a 20-horsepower (15,000 watt) engine to power the famous Model-T that was dominant in the automotive market from 1914 to 1927. Today, some 8-cylinder automobile engines deliver 250 horsepower ($\approx$190,000 watt) or more. The world's most powerful motors are used in heavy industries and deliver more than 100,000 horsepower ($\approx$74,600,000 watt). How powerful are you?

Students with health problems should not perform the following activity. Determine your weight in newtons (1 lb = 4.45 N). Measure the height of a steep ramp and record in the table. Run up the ramp as fast as you safely can and use a stopwatch to record the elapsed time to the nearest tenth of a second. Calculate your power in both watts and horsepower (1 hp = 746 W). Compare the power you generated with the power generated by other students and the motors and engines listed above. If you do not have access to a ramp, you may perform this activity on a flight of stairs, but walk swiftly up the stairs, don't run.

Student	Weight (N)	Height (m)	Time (s)	Work (J)	Power (W)	Power (hp)

Questions

(1) If you ran up the ramp in half the time of another student of equal weight, you did the same work but used twice the power. Explain.

(2) Suppose the vertical height of the ramp or stairs were reduced by half. How would this affect the work and power required to climb the stairs?

(3) During times of dire emergency, people have been known to lift tremendous weights, such as the rear of a car to free a mechanic on whom the car has fallen. Is greater power necessary to perform such feats than when lifting the same car using a jack? Explain.

(4) How many gallons of water will be pumped from a well 30 feet deep by a 1/2 hp engine in 1 minute? (1 gallon weighs 8.34 pounds)

(5) What is the power in horsepower of a 100-watt light bulb? What is the power in kilowatts of a 200-horsepower engine?

5.1.3 Reading Your Electric Meter

Concepts to Investigate: Energy consumption; relation between power, work, and energy; power from electricity and gas.

Material: Electric meter.

Principles and Procedures: Each year the United States produces more than 2,500 billion kilowatt-hours of electric energy. Nearly 75 percent of this energy is produced by coal-, oil-, or gas-powered generators. The remainder is produced in roughly equal proportions by hydroelectric and nuclear power plants. Why do we need so much energy? Where does all this energy go?

Energy is the ability to perform work. Energy is used to perform the work required to open a garage door, power an air-conditioning compressor, or turn the hands of a clock. Household appliances, industrial equipment, vehicles, and machinery of every type consume energy as they perform work to simplify, enrich, and sometimes complicate our lives.

Wattage is used to measure the amount of power appliances such as toasters and light bulbs consume. The greater the wattage of an appliance the more rapidly it consumes energy. The longer the appliance is on the more energy it consumes and the more work it can do. One watt-hour is the amount of energy consumed in one hour by a device if it uses energy at the rate of one watt. The watt is too small a unit to measure energy consumption in everyday life. Instead we use a unit called kilowatt-hour (kW·h), which is 1,000 watt-hours. Note carefully that watt-hour and kilowatt-hour are units of energy or work and not of power. Your electric bill is computed on the basis of cost per kilowatt-hour. One kW·h is the energy consumed by a device working at a constant rate of 1 kilowatt for one hour. Since energy conversion is never 100 percent efficient, the work accomplished by such a device will always be less than one kW·h.

Figure F illustrates a meter used by utility companies to measure the amount of energy your household consumes each month. The dials of most gas meters look identical, so be sure you are looking at the correct meter when you perform the following activities. (1) The dials should be read from left to right. (2) Some of the dials read counterclockwise and some read clockwise. (3) When a pointer is between two numerals, the reading is the lesser of the two numerals. (4) When a pointer appears to be pointing exactly on a numeral, inspect the dial to the right. If the pointer on this dial is between 0 and 1, it has passed zero and the reading on the left dial is the numeral at which the pointer appears to be pointing. If the pointer on the right dial is between 9 and 0, it has not yet reached zero and the reading on the left dial should be read as one less than the numeral at which the pointer appears to be pointing. The right-hand dial reads in kilowatt-hours from 0 to 10, the second dial from the right reads by tens from 0 to 100, the third dial reads by hundreds from 0 to 1,000, and the fourth dial reads by thousands. The reading shown on the first meter is 1,641. What are the readings on meters two and three?

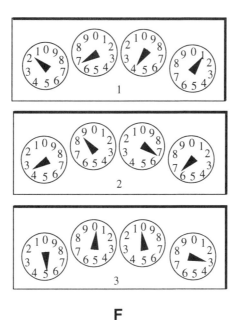

F

Part 1. Daily energy consumption: On a day spent at home, read your electric meter every two hours from the time you wake until the time you go to sleep, and construct a histogram (bar chart) indicating power consumption during each 2-hour block of time. The amount of energy consumed in the preceding 2-hour period may be calculated by subtracting the previous reading from the current reading. In addition, keep a record of all household appliances that are active during each 2-hour block. On the basis of your data, which appliances do you find consume the greatest amount of energy and probably perform the greatest amount of work?

Part 2. Weekly energy consumption: Read your electric meter at the same time each day during the week. Determine the amount of energy consumed in the preceding 24-hour period by subtracting the previous reading from the current reading. Create a histogram of daily energy consumption and offer explanations for differences in daily consumption.

Part 3. Yearly energy consumption: If granted permission, examine your family's electric bills during the past year. Construct a histogram showing the amount of energy consumed each month and offer explanations for monthly variations. Many homes are also supplied with natural gas to power furnaces, space heaters, water heaters, stoves, and clothes dryers. Utility companies charge customers by the number of cubic feet of natural gas consumed. Examine monthly utility bills and plot the energy consumption from natural gas on the same chart (1 cubic foot of gas releases approximately 170 kW·h of energy when burned).

Questions

(1) How much energy was used between time 2 and time 3 in Figure F?

(2) Read the electric meter at your home at the beginning and end of a billing period. Compare your readings to those shown on your electric bill. What might account for small differences in meter readings?

(3) Why might your graph of household energy consumption vary from day to day?

(4) Suppose the electric meter at your home read 5459 kW·h in January and 5793 kW·h in February. How much energy was used in the intervening time? If the cost of one kilowatt-hour was $0.07288, what was the cost for this energy?

5.1.4 Conserving Electricity

Concepts to Investigate: Energy consumption, energy conservation, power ratings.

Materials: Appliances commonly found in the home.

Principles to Investigate: Which appliance in your home consumes the greatest amount of energy? Is it the refrigerator? The television set? The toaster? The electric clock? You can find out by inspecting appliances in your home and determining the number of watts each consumes and multiplying this By the number of hours operated. By law, each electric device must specify power requirements, and these are generally recorded on a small tag located on the appliance or on the power cable connected to it. Inspect the following appliances in your home and record power requirements in the table. Some appliances are rated in amperes (amps). To determine watts for these, multiply the voltage indicated on the appliance by the amps indicated. For example, if the rating for a motor is 3 amps at 120 volts, the power is 3 amps × 120 volts or 360 watts.

Appliance	*Power Rating* *(W)*	*Time Used* *per Day* *(h)*	*Energy Consumed* *per Day* *(kW·h)*
Air conditioner (room)			
Clock radio			
Clothes dryer			
Color TV			
Compact-disc player			
Computer			
Drip coffee maker			
Electric alarm clock			
Electric can opener			
Electric toothbrush			
Iron			
Shaver			
Toaster			
Vacuum cleaner			
Washing machine			

Questions

(1) Compare and contrast "electric energy" and "electric power."

(2) Suppose you use a 1,500-watt hair dryer for 2 minutes to dry your hair and your friend uses a 600-watt microwave oven to heat a breakfast for 4 minutes. Who uses the most energy?

(3) Compare and contrast those appliances that have high power ratings such as an iron or toaster with those that have much lower ratings such as an electric toothbrush and an electric clock. What factors account for the great difference in consumption of energy?

(4) Mega (M) is a prefix in the metric system meaning one million. The electrical power output of power plants, for example, is commonly measured in megawatts (MW). What is the power output in kilowatts of a nuclear reactor that has a rating of 1,450 MW?

FOR THE TEACHER

5.1.1 Measuring Work

Discussion: Regardless of the force applied to an object, if the object does not move no work is done. Work is a scalar quantity defined as the product of the magnitude of the components of force and displacement. This may be a good time to review the concepts of scalars and vectors. A quantity that can be completely specified by magnitude is called a scalar quantity (that is, 20 meters, 60 joules, 40 liters). By contrast, a vector quantity also specifies direction (that is, displacement of two kilometers westward, momentum of 100 kilogram meter/second at an angle of 35 degrees). If the force is constant and always in the same direction as the displacement, then work is simply the product of force and distance: $W = F \times d$. It is important to note, however, that in most instances both the magnitude and direction of a force may vary along the path. Hence the more general expression for work is:

$$W = \int_{S_1}^{S_2} F_s ds$$

where F_s is the component of force F in the direction of the displacement ds. Work can be negative. For example, if a force is applied in a westward direction to retard the motion of a body already moving with a positive velocity eastward, the work is the negative of the product of the force and the displacement.

Answers (1) Work is equal to the product of force and distance. When climbing stairs, the force one must apply is equal to one's weight. If the weight is doubled the required force is doubled. (2) The vertical height of the stairs is the direction through which the force, equal to the climber's weight, acts. You might climb any number of stairs to reach a location. It is the vertical distance from the bottom of the stairs to this location through which the lifting force acts and that determines the amount of work done. (3) Impulse and work are different quantities. Time is not a factor in work but it is in impulse. Impulse changes the momentum of an object while work changes the displacement of an object. (4) The work done is the same: 2000 N × 10 m = 20,000 joules = 1000 N × 20 m. (5) Suppose there is no friction between the plane and object (Figure G). The work done pushing the object 2 meters up the incline to the top is the same as the work done lifting the object 1 meter vertically to the top; however, the force required is not the same. To push the object up the incline requires a force of only 0.5 N compared to 1.0 N required to lift it vertically, but the distance

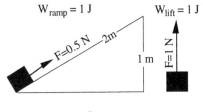

G

the object moves on the incline is twice the vertical distance. (6) Work is the product of force and distance. Students should note that both distance and force are the same, regardless of the velocity of the block. (7) $W = \tau\theta$. Torque $\tau = 20 \text{ N} \times 0.5 \text{ m} = 10 \text{ N·m}$. The angle θ in radians through which the wheel is rotated is 3.14 (180 degrees). $W = 10 \text{ N·m} \times 3.14 = 31.4$ joules. In one complete revolution the work done is 62.8 joules.

5.1.2 Measuring Power

Discussion: The faster a given amount of work is done, the more power is exerted. Horsepower is a unit of power commonly used in the United States. One horse-power *hp* was originally defined as the rate of work maintained by an average dray horse (horse used to pull a strong low cart or wagon without sides). One horsepow-er is 550 ft·lb/s = 33,000 ft·lb/min. From the relations between the newton, pound, meter, and foot it can be shown that 1 hp = 746 watts (W) or 0.746 kilowatt (kW). One kilowatt-hour is the work done in one hour by a device delivering one thousand watts. If a device performs 1,000 joules of work a second (1,000 watts), the work done in one hour is 3600 seconds × 1000 joule/second = 3,600,000 joules (3.6×10^6 joules). One horsepower-hour is 33,000 ft·lb of work each minute multiplied by 60 minutes = 1,980,000 ft·lb (1.98×10^6 ft·lb). A common misconception is that there is something inherently electrical about a watt and something inherently mechanical about a horsepower. Not true. The power of an automobile engine can be rated in kilowatts while the power consumption of a light bulb can be rated in horsepower.

Answers (1) Power is the rate of doing work. You did the same amount of work in half the time, so your power output was twice that of the other student. (2) The work required would be half, but the power would remain unchanged. (3) Yes. Power is the rate at which work is performed. A jack lifts a car very slowly and therefore requires less power. (4) One horsepower is 550 ft·lb/s = 33,000 ft·lb/min. A 1/2-hp engine can do 16,500 ft·lb of work in one minute. The weight of one gallon of water is 8.34 pounds. The distance through which this weight must be lifted is 30 feet. Work required to lift one gallon is 30 ft × 8.34 lb = 250 ft·lb. The number of gallons pumped in one minute is (16,500 ft·lb)/(250 ft·lb/gal) = 66 gallons. (5) 1 hp = 746 W, thus 100 W = 0.134 hp. A 200-hp engine = 200 hp x 0.746 kW/hp = 149 kW.

5.1.3 Reading Your Electric Meter

Discussion: Remind students that horsepower-hour and kilowatt-hour are units of work (energy), not power. The SI unit for energy or work is the joule, which is equiv-alent to 1 watt-second, 10 million ergs, 0.7376 foot-pounds, and 9.48×10^{-3} Btu (British thermal units). The variety of units used to measure work or energy may be very confusing to students and their teachers.

Students can learn much about work and energy consumption, conservation and the family budget by performing this activity, but be aware of the need to pro-tect privacy. This is a good opportunity to stress the need to conserve energy. Students should notice that energy consumption is greatest when heavy appliances such as air conditioners, washing machines, and dishwashers are running. When they examine their electric bills during the past year they may notice that energy consumption varies by a factor of 2 or 3 from month to month. Ask students to generate hypotheses explaining such variations. Factors such as weather, number of people at home, and time spent at home may greatly affect energy consumption.

Answers (1) 5003 kW·h – 3866 kW·h = 1137 kW·h. (2) You probably didn't read the meter at the same time of day as the meter reader. (3) Activities change from day to day. For example, a washing machine and clothes dryer may be used on only one day of the week, dramatically increasing energy consumption on that day. In addition, changes in weather may activate the thermostat and turn on the heater or air conditioner on some days, but not on others. (4) 5793 kW·h – 5459 kW·h = 334 kW·h. 334 kW·h × $0.07288/kW·h = $24.34.

5.1.4 Conserving Electricity

Discussion: Impress upon students the need to conserve energy of all types, not simply electrical. Have them compare the energy requirements of the appliances listed in the table and ask if they have suggestions for conserving energy. It's to be hoped that they will notice that those appliances that use electricity to heat or cool are those that consume the greatest quantities of electricity and will suggest that these appliances be used as little as possible.

We have provided a list of power ratings for common household appliances, but realize that these may vary substantially depending upon size, design, and manufacturer. Room air conditioner, 860W; clock radio, 10 W; clothes dryer, 4,900 W; color television, 144 W; compact-disc player, 10 W; computer, 120 W; drip coffee maker, 1,000 W; electric alarm clock, 5 W; electric can opener, 70 W; electric toothbrush, 1 W; iron, 1,100 W; shaver, 15 W; toaster, 1,050 W; vacuum cleaner, 630 W; washing machine, 510 W.

Answers (1) Electric energy is the amount of energy consumed, while electric power is the amount of energy consumed during a given period of time. (2) You do. 1,500 W × 2 min = 13,000 W·min, which is greater than 600 W × 4 min or 2,400 W·min. (3) The factor of greatest importance is conversion of electricity directly to heat (resistance of current by the heating element such as in a toaster or iron). (4) 1,450 MW × 1,000 W/MW = 1,450,000 W.

Applications to Everyday Life

Work and Power: Work is something difficult to avoid in one's everyday life. You do work in the scientific sense every time you lift a bag of groceries, wink your eye, brush your teeth, open a door, or turn on the TV set. Try to think of an activity in which you do not do work. Remember that energy is the capacity to do work. When you do work you expend energy. Power is the rate of doing work. The faster you lift that bag of groceries, wink your eye, brush your teeth, open that door, or turn on that TV set the more power you use.

Hydroelectric Power: The total power generated by the world's hydroelectric plants is more than 9×10^7 kW, totaling approximately 8×10^{11} (800 billion) kilowatt-hours of energy per year. The United States is the leader in electricity generation from falling water. Hydroelectric generators have grown from the 12-kW machines of 1882 to the 600,000-kW units at the Grand Coulee Dam in the state of Washington.

Lamps: Lighting consumes 25 percent of all electrical power in the United States. Incandescent lamps commonly found in the home contain a tungsten filament, and only 5 percent of the electricity that flows through the filament is converted to light while the remaining 95 percent is converted to heat. Fluorescent lamps are about three to four times more efficient in converting electricity into visible light and emit more light per watt than incandescent lamps. A novel lamp called the E-Lamp has no filament like conventional incandescent and fluorescent lamps and is not subject to burnout. It would last for about 14 years but is substantially more expensive than conventional bulbs. In an E-Lamp a magnetic coil inside an argon-filled globe generates high-frequency radio waves that convert the gas to a plasma or ionized state. The plasma emits invisible light that strikes a white phosphor coating on the inside of the bulb causing it to glow with visible light. The E-Lamp could save consumers between $50 to $100 over its 20,000-hour lifetime by using 75 percent less energy and by lasting longer.

Stereos: Stereos in the home and in vehicles are distinguished by the number of watts they provide per channel. Typical home stereo systems have amplifiers that provide 100 watts per channel. The loud "boom-boxes" often heard in passing cars or trucks require about 15 watts to produce those loud booms. Over the years efficiency of speakers has greatly improved so they require fewer watts to deliver high-quality performance.

Dynamometer: A dynamometer is an apparatus used to measure the power output of machinery and is commonly used to test the horsepower developed by electric motors and automobile engines. Dynamometers are used in some service stations to diagnose problems with your car and to measure the power output of the engine.

Solar Power: The largest solar electric-generating system in the world is the LUZ plant, located in the Mojave Desert in California. In 1993, the plant was producing

55,000 MW, with the goal of increasing production to 675 MW to provide enough power for one million people.

Annual Energy Requirements of Appliances: Estimated kW·h consumed annually by some selected appliances: coffee maker, 100; dishwasher, 360; toaster, 40; refrigerator/freezer (automatic defrost, 20 cubic feet and greater), 1,900; clothes dryer, 1,000; iron, 60; washing machine, 100; water heater, 4,200; fan, 40; hair dryer, 15; shaver, 0.5; toothbrush, 1.0; radio, 90; color television, 320; clock, 20; vacuum cleaner, 50.

TV Sets and Antennas: If the distance from transmitter to TV set is great, the image on the screen displays "snow" (noise) because random currents in the antenna rods are produced by motions of free electrons. Reception can be obtained from weak signals at distances of 30 miles, which means that images can be separated from the snow even if the power intercepted from the incoming radio wave is less than one trillionth of a watt. Because the power tube requires a power of about one watt to operate, the receiver must then amplify the signal power a trillion times.

Engines and Power: Engines are commonly rated in horsepower, but they could also be rated in watts or kilowatts. Ratings of today's automobile engines may range from 100 to greater than 300 horsepower.

Power Levels: Power levels produced by various devices cover a wide range. A laser may produce an intense beam of energy with a power of only 3 milliwatts; electrical input to a typical light bulb is 60–100 watts; power generated by a large automobile may be 1 megawatt; electrical power generated by a power station may be 1 gigawatt (GW).

5.2 POTENTIAL AND KINETIC ENERGY

Energy is a word you hear every day, but what exactly is it? Energy comes from the Greek root meaning "in work" and is the capacity for doing work. Energy exists in many different forms, and one form of energy can be converted into another. Energy and matter are related by the equation $E = mc^2$, where E is energy, m is mass, and c is the speed of light, 3×10^8 m/s. A nuclear-power plant transforms a small amount of matter into a huge amount of energy. If, for example, one kilogram of matter is completely converted into energy, 9×10^{16} joules are released, enough to supply all of America's energy needs for approximately 3.5 days. ($E = mc^2 = 1 \text{ kg} \times (3 \times 10^8 \text{ m/s})^2 = 9 \times 10^{16}$ joules $= 2.5 \times 10^{10}$ kW·h).

Our universe is composed of matter and energy. Matter has substance (it has mass and occupies space) and thus can be sensed by either smell, taste, touch, hearing, or sight. Energy, however, is more fleeting and is observed only when it is being transformed. When you turn the key to start a car or truck, chemical energy of the battery is transformed to electrical energy in the wires that is transformed into mechanical energy of the starter motor that sets the flywheel of the engine in motion. An electric spark from the spark plug ignites the fuel in the cylinders of the engine, and the chemical energy of the fuel is suddenly transformed into heat energy (rapid molecular motion), which moves the pistons.

Matter is rather easy to visualize because it has substance (we can touch and feel it), but energy is more elusive. *You can think of energy as something that can move matter. In every interaction of any kind, the total energy after the interaction is always the same as the total energy before the interaction. Energy is conserved.*

One of the tallest roller coasters in the world is the 70-meter (230 foot) high Moonsault Scramble at the Fujikyu Highland Park near Kawaguchi Lake, Japan. Many of us have experienced the thrill that comes when a car reaches the top of a coaster like the Moonsault and then plummets toward the ground at an ever increasing speed, rounding curves and ascending and descending decreasing rises until coming to an abrupt halt at the point of passenger departure. The car is pulled to the top of the highest part of the coaster shown in Figure A as point 1 by a chain or other device. After the car begins to move it accelerates to point 2 and then climbs the next hill to point 3. How is it possible for the car to ascend to point 3 on the tracks without being pulled up by the chain? As the car moves from point 1 gravity pulls it

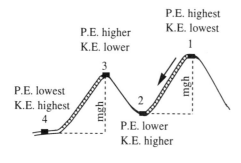

A

down the track, and its speed increases. Something else is also increasing—the energy of motion of the car. *Energy of motion is called kinetic energy.* When the car reaches the bottom of the track at point 2 its speed and kinetic energy are higher and its potential energy is lower. The kinetic energy of the car causes it to climb to point 3. As the car rounds the top at point 3 it again gains speed and kinetic energy for the trip to point 4. If it were not for frictional forces, the car could continue to climb and descend the rails forever. *Potential energy is energy of position, or stored energy.* As the car moves up and down the track, potential energy is alternately converted to kinetic energy and kinetic energy is alternately converted to potential energy.

Can you think of some things that possess potential or kinetic energy? A diver ready to jump from a diving board possesses potential energy relative to the surface of the water. As the diver rotates and somersaults toward the water, potential energy is converted to kinetic energy. When the diver hits the surface of the water, the kinetic energy is quickly converted to other forms of energy as it does work moving the water apart and as heat is generated by frictional interactions between the diver's body and the water. A coiled spring such as found in a watch possesses potential energy and is able to move the gears of the watch and subsequently the second, minute, and hour hands. As the pendulum of a grandfather clock swings from side to side potential energy is alternately changed to kinetic energy and kinetic energy back into potential energy.

Since energy is the capacity for doing work, we may use work units for measuring both potential and kinetic energy. Two factors must be considered in measuring work: the force applied and the distance through which the force acts. The amount of work done is equal to the product of the force times the distance: *Work = force × distance.* Remember that the potential energy of an object is a measure of the object's ability to do work. When an object is lifted a vertical distance against gravity, the work done on the object against gravity is equal to the product of force (weight) required to lift the object and the distance moved: work = force × distance (weight times height). According to Newton's first law, the weight of a body is equal to the mass of the body multiplied by the acceleration of gravity g. When you lift an object, work is changed into gravitational potential energy (*gravitational potential energy = weight × height = mgh*).

The kinetic energy of an object is the measure of the moving object's ability to do work. The faster the object moves the more work it is able to do. Suppose you throw a baseball straight up. As the ball rises, gravity opposes its motion, doing negative work and decreasing the ball's kinetic energy. When the kinetic energy is depleted (ball reaches its highest point) its potential energy is at a maximum. Now gravity does positive work on the ball, increasing its kinetic energy until the kinetic energy reaches a maximum just before the ball strikes the ground at its highest speed. Kinetic energy is transformed to potential energy and then potential energy is transformed to kinetic energy.

Kinetic energy can be of two types: translational and rotational. Suppose you throw a baseball to a friend. The ball possesses both translational and rotational energy. It moves through the air in a linear fashion (translational energy), but it also spins (rotates) about its center (rotational energy). The linear kinetic energy of an object is equal to $1/2mv^2$, where m is mass of the object and v is the speed of the object. The rotational kinetic energy of an object is equal to $1/2\ I\omega^2$, where I is rotational inertia and ω is angular velocity. *The total kinetic energy due to linear and rotational motion is expressed: $E_k = 1/2\ mv^2 + 1/2\ I\omega^2$.* If the mass is given in kilograms (kg) and the speed in meters per second (m/s), then the kinetic energy is given in Joules ($J = kg\cdot(m/s)^2$). Notice that the speed term v in the equation is squared. The effect of this squaring of the speed is important in understanding the magnitude of kinetic energy and will be considered in more detail in this chapter. Let's experiment with potential and kinetic energy.

5.2.1 Magnetic Potential Energy

Concepts to Investigate: Potential energy, kinetic energy.

Materials: Strong bar magnets, table or desk with smooth top.

Principles and Procedures: Place two bar magnets on a tabletop with the south poles facing each other (Figure B). Push the two poles toward each other until the magnets are touching. Energy is required to move the magnets together, some of which is stored as potential energy in the fields surrounding the magnets. When you release the magnets, they quickly separate, as magnetic potential energy is converted into kinetic energy (Figure C). Repeat the process using the two north poles. When is magnetic potential energy greatest? When is kinetic energy greatest? Turn one magnet around so its N pole is facing the S pole of another. You may obtain a qualitative indication of the magnitude of magnetic potential energy by rating the pull or push of the magnet upon your hand at a given distance. How should the magnets be positioned so potential energy is greatest? Try it and see if you are correct.

   Tie one end of a thread to a paper clip and the other to a fixed object and suspend the paper clip below a magnet, as shown in Figure D. The paper clip has magnetic potential energy that is converted to kinetic energy when the string is cut. When is magnetic potential energy greatest? When is kinetic energy greatest?

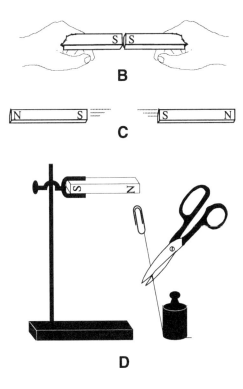

B

C

D

Questions

(1) Is the work used to push two like magnetic poles together lost? Explain.

(2) Potential energy depends on position or state relative to another position or state. Give an example.

(3) Describe the changes in potential and kinetic energy of the bob of a simple pendulum as it swings. At what point in the swing is the potential energy E_p greatest? At what point is the kinetic energy E_k greatest? At what point is the kinetic energy equal to the potential energy?

(4) Energy cannot be created or destroyed but may be transformed (changed) from one form to another. Give three specific examples to illustrate this important law of conservation of energy.

5.2.2 Kinetic Energy

Concepts to Investigate: Kinetic energy, $E_k = 1/2mv^2$, the mass and speed factors of kinetic energy.

Materials: Spherical lead fishing weights, glass marbles and wooden spheres of same diameter (you may substitute golf balls, solid rubber balls, and Ping-Pong balls of approximately the same diameter), pad of soft clay, graduated pipette, meter stick.

Principles and Procedures: Select three spheres (lead weight, glass marble, wooden sphere, golf ball, rubber ball, Ping-Pong ball, etc.) of similar diameter but different mass, and measure their masses on a balance. Hold the three spheres 0.20 meters above a pad of soft clay and drop them (Figure E). Observe that the three spheres of different mass hit the clay at the same time, so their impact speed must be the same. Using the kinematics equation ($v_f = \sqrt{2gd}$); where g is 9.8 m/s^2) we calculate this speed to be 2 meters/second. Visually rank the volume of the craters, or measure the volume of each by filling with water from a graduated pipette (Figure F). Record your observations in the table. The volume of the craters is related to the kinetic energy of the spheres. The greater the kinetic energy of the spheres when they hit the clay, the greater the work done on the clay, and the greater the volume of the craters created. Which sphere had the greatest amount of kinetic energy just before impact?

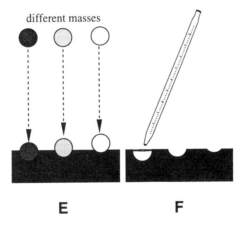

different masses

E   F

Repeat the procedure, dropping the balls from a height of 0.82 meters so they will have double the velocity (4 m/s) and 4 times the kinetic energy upon impact. Repeat from a height of 1.84 meters so they will have triple the velocity (6 m/s) and nine times the kinetic energy upon impact.

Draw a graph of crater volume as a function of mass, and another graph of crater volume as a function of impact speed. Are the shapes of the graphs different? On the basis of your observations, which factor, mass, or velocity has the greatest influence on kinetic energy? Explain.

	Drop Height = 0.20 m Velocity = 2 m/s		Drop Height = 0.82 m Velocity = 4 m/s		Drop Height = 1.84 m Velocity = 6 m/s	
Object	*Mass*	*Crater vol.*	*Mass*	*Crater vol.*	*Mass*	*Crater vol.*
Lead sphere	___g	___ ml	___ g	___ ml	___ g	___ ml
Marble	___g	___ ml	___ g	___ ml	___ g	___ ml
Wooden sphere	___g	___ ml	___ g	___ ml	___ g	___ ml

Questions

(1) Explain the relationship between the masses of the spheres, the kinetic energy of the spheres, the work done by the spheres, and the size of the craters created.

(2) Neglecting air friction, any objects, regardless of size, shape, or mass, dropped from the same height at the same time will hit the floor at the same time. Explain.

(3) On the basis of your data, which factor, mass, or velocity has a more significant influence upon kinetic energy? Explain.

5.2.3 Conversion of Potential and Kinetic Energy

Materials: Slinky®, stairway.

Concepts to Investigate: Gravitational potential energy, potential energy of springs, kinetic energy.

Principles and Procedures: Place a Slinky® on the first step of a flight of stairs. Make certain the stairs are not so wide that the top part of the Slinky® cannot flip over the edge of each step and then descend to the next step. Lift the top part of the Slinky® and pull it to a position above the second step and release it, as shown in Figure G. The Slinky® will walk down the stairs, uncoiling and coiling as it moves. The top of the Slinky® is pulled by gravity to the next step. As this end falls, potential energy is stored in stretched coils. The potential energy is converted to kinetic energy as these coils pull the trailing end of the Slinky® down. The trailing end of the Slinky® now possesses momentum and moves up and past the high point of the arc. Gravity then pulls it down to the next step and the process is repeated. The Slinky® repeats these movements, constantly changing gravitational and spring potential energy to kinetic energy, until it reaches the bottom of the stairs. Adjust your technique until the Slinky® consistently makes the journey from the top stair to the bottom stair. What conditions are necessary for the Slinky® to make the journey successfully?

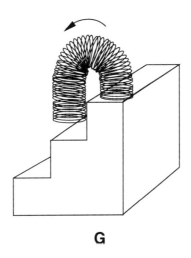

G

Questions

(1) Will a Slinky® walk up a flight of stairs? Explain.
(2) At what point is the kinetic energy of the Slinky® greatest? When is the potential energy of the Slinky® greatest?
(3) What variables must be adjusted so the Slinky® "walks" down the entire flight of stairs?

5.2.4 Conservation of Energy

Concepts to Investigate: Conservation of energy (First Law of Thermodynamics), elastic collisions, frame of reference.

Materials: Golf ball, Ping-Pong ball, basketball, measuring tape, superball.

Principles and Procedures: Determine the height to which a Ping-Pong ball will bounce when dropped 30 centimeters onto a hard, firm surface (Figure H). Now place a Ping-Pong ball on top of a golf ball so they are aligned and touching and drop them together from a height of 30 cm so they bounce *straight up* (Figure I). It may take a few minutes of practice to achieve a vertical "lift off." How many times higher does the Ping-Pong ball bounce when dropped with the golf ball than when dropped alone? Why does it bounce so high? Repeat the procedure, dropping the balls from different heights of your choice.

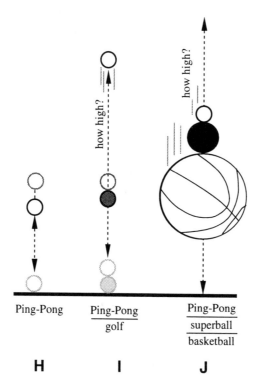

Ping-Pong	Ping-Pong	Ping-Pong
	golf	superball
		basketball
H	**I**	**J**

© 1994 by John Wiley & Sons, Inc.

    One of most important and firmly established laws of nature is the First Law of Thermodynamics, known also as the law of conservation of energy. This law states that *energy is neither created nor destroyed, but may be converted from one form to another.* Energy stored in gasoline or uranium is known as potential energy and is transformed into kinetic energy in the engine of a car or the core of a reactor. An object suspended above the ground has gravitational potential energy with respect to the ground. If it is released, this energy is transformed into kinetic energy. *Gravitational potential energy is defined as the product of an object's mass (m), acceleration due to gravi-*

ty (g), and height h *above the ground (E$_p$= mgh). Kinetic energy is defined as one half the product of mass and velocity squared (E$_k$=1/2 mv^2).* When a falling ball hits the ground, its gravitational potential energy is zero ($h = 0$, ∴ $mgh = 0$) and all energy is kinetic. By the time the ball bounces to its maximum height h, kinetic energy is zero and all energy is in the form of gravitational potential energy *mgh*. This potential energy is transformed into kinetic energy as the ball falls, and the resulting kinetic energy is transformed back into gravitational potential energy as the ball rebounds. This can be expressed by the following equation:

$$E_{p(top)} = E_{k(bottom)} \therefore mgh_{(top)} = \frac{1}{2}mv^2_{(bottom)}$$

By solving for h, the approximate height to which a ball will bounce can be expressed as a function of the speed v it attains before striking the floor:

$$h = \frac{v^2}{2g}$$

When they are released, the gravitational potential energy of the Ping-Pong ball and golf ball are transformed into kinetic energy and each attains the same speed (v, disregarding friction) before striking the ground. However, the golf ball (bottom ball) reverses direction an instant before the Ping-Pong ball (top ball) and approaches it with an equal speed in the opposite direction. As a result, the relative speed between the balls is $2v$ just as the relative speed of two cars driving toward each other at 50 miles per hour is 100 miles per hour.

In an elastic collision (one in which no kinetic energy is lost) the relative speed of objects is the same after collision as before. Before the Ping-Pong and golf ball collide, their relative speed is $2v$. Since the momentum of the Ping-Pong ball is much less than the golf ball, it bounces off it nearly the way it would bounce off a moving wall. Because the golf ball has much greater momentum than the Ping-Pong ball, it continues moving up after the collision with nearly the same velocity it had before the collision. Since the golf ball continues moving at speed v, and the Ping-Pong ball recoils from the surface of the golf ball with a relative speed of $2v$, the speed of the Ping-Pong ball with respect to the floor must be $3v$.

Since energy is conserved, the gravitational potential energy of the Ping-Pong ball at the top (*mgh*) of the bounce will equal its kinetic energy at the bottom. Thus, the height to which the Ping-Pong ball will bounce when dropped on top of the golf ball (upward speed of $3v$) is 9 times the height it bounces when dropped alone (upward speed of v):

$$h_{(dropped\ together)} = \frac{9v^2}{2g} \qquad\qquad h_{(dropped\ alone)} = \frac{v^2}{2g}$$

How much higher will the Ping-Pong ball bounce if dropped on top of a "super ball" that itself is dropped on top of a basketball? Try it (Figure J). For purposes of comparison, the Ping-Pong ball should fall the same distance before hitting the superball as the distance it falls to the floor when dropped alone. Although it is difficult to position the three balls so they fall and rebound in a straight line, you will notice that the Ping-Pong ball bounces much higher than when dropped on just one other ball.

	Drop Height 30 cm	Bounce Height (Average)	Drop Height (Your Choice)	Bounce Height (Average)
Ping-Pong ball alone	30 cm	cm	cm	cm
Ping-Pong on top of golf ball	30 cm	cm	cm	cm
Ping-Pong ball on top of super ball on top of basketball	30 cm	cm	cm	cm

Questions

(1) Compare the height bounced by the Ping-Pong ball when dropped alone with the height reached when dropped in combination with the golf ball.

(2) The theoretical height to which Ping-Pong balls may bounce is 9 times the height when dropped alone, but this is never attained. Explain.

(3) If there were no friction, and if the collisions were perfectly elastic, a light-weight ball could bounce 49 times the height of a regular bounce when dropped upon a massive ball that itself is dropped on an even more massive ball. Explain.

5.2.5 Linear and Rotational Kinetic Energy

Concepts to Investigate: First Law of Thermodynamics, linear kinetic energy, rotational kinetic energy.

Materials: Smooth board (preferably 2 meters or longer), books, collections of solid spheres with different radii (marbles, spherical lead fishing weights, solid balls), discs with different radii (sections cut from wooden or metal dowels), and hoops with different radii (sections cut from pieces of plastic or metal tubing).

Principles and Procedures: Galileo suggested that all falling objects experience the same acceleration in the absence of friction. After landing on the moon, American astronauts proved Galielo's principle by simultaneously dropping a feather and a moon rock and observing that they hit the surface at the same time. Although objects fall to the earth with the same acceleration, do they roll down ramps with the same acceleration? Let's find out.

Part 1. Do all objects roll at the same speed? Place two solid spheres made of the same material but with different radii (different masses) at the same level on a 10 percent inclined plane (the rise is 10 percent of the run), release, and record the time necessary to reach the bottom (Figure K). Repeat the activity, using other spherical objects with different radii and different composition (steel balls, marbles, lead fishing weights, etc.). Do all spheres accelerate at the same rate? Repeat the activity using a variety of discs (solid cylinders such as coins, sections of dowels, cans of semi-solid food such as cranberry sauce), and a variety of hoops (sections of pipe, tin cans with both ends removed). Do all discs reach the bottom of the ramp at the same time? All hoops? Is there any difference in the average time required for discs, spheres, or hoops to reach the bottom of the ramp? Repeat the procedure using a 20 percent ramp.

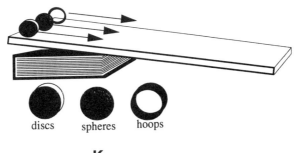

discs   spheres   hoops

K

Spheres			Discs			Hoops		
Mass	Diameter	Time	Mass	Diameter	Time	Mass	Diameter	Time
10% incline								
g	cm	s	g	cm	s	g	cm	s
g	cm	s	g	cm	s	g	cm	s
g	cm	s	g	cm	s	g	cm	s
g	cm	s	g	cm	s	g	cm	s
g	cm	s	g	cm	s	g	cm	s
20 % incline								
g	cm	s	g	cm	s	g	cm	s
g	cm	s	g	cm	s	g	cm	s
g	cm	s	g	cm	s	g	cm	s
g	cm	s	g	cm	s	g	cm	s
g	cm	s	g	cm	s	g	cm	s

When you drop objects, they possess only linear (translational) kinetic energy as they move toward the ground (assuming you provide no torque to set them spinning on their axis) and hit the ground at the same time. However, when you roll objects down an inclined plane they have two kinds of kinetic energy: linear and rotational. A spinning top is an example of an object with rotational energy but no translational energy—the top rotates on its axis but remains in one spot on the floor and therefore has no linear kinetic energy. By contrast, the wheel of a moving automobile has both linear and rotational kinetic energy. The wheel turns on its axle (rotational kinetic energy) as the axle moves along the road (linear kinetic energy). *The kinetic energy of an object is the sum of the energy due to linear motion and the energy due to rotational motion.* Since all the potential energy at the top of the ramp is converted into kinetic energy when it reaches the bottom, the only factor determining the transit time is the proportion of kinetic energy that is translational. The fastest object has the highest percentage of translational kinetic energy and the least amount of rotational kinetic energy, while the slowest object has the lowest amount of translational kinetic energy and the highest amount of rotational kinetic energy. You may have discovered that some shapes develop great linear velocity but little rotational velocity while others develop little linear velocity but great rotational velocity. What factors influence the rotational kinetic energy of an object?

Rotational kinetic energy depends not only on the mass of the object, but also on the distribution of mass around the axis of rotation of the object. The farther mass is from the axis of rotation, the greater the energy required to set the object in motion. Since the distribution of mass in a hoop is farther from the axis than in a disc of the same mass, it is more difficult to start and stop its rotation. Examine the shapes and explain why some have a higher percentage of rotational energy while others have a higher percentage of linear kinetic energy.

Part 2. Tin-can race: Obtain three cans of similar size, one filled with a liquid (juice, fruit nectar, etc.), one with a solid or semi-solid (cranberry sauce, tuna), and an empty can with the ends cut out. Which can will reach the bottom first when released on a ramp at the same time? Last? Test your predictions.

Questions

(1) Which shape in Part 1 reached the bottom of the incline first? Second? Third?

(2) Which can in part 2 (juice, cranberry sauce, empty) reached the bottom of the incline first? Last? Explain.

(3) If a car triples its speed from 10 kilometers per hour to 30 kilometers per hour, by what factor is the kinetic energy increased?

(4) In the 1970s, the United States' government issued a law limiting the maximum speed of vehicles to 55 miles per hour. Prior to that time, many states had limits of 70 miles per hour. Although the main reason for this law was to conserve fuel during the Arab oil embargo, many states retained the law after the federal law was rescinded, arguing that it resulted in a tremendous saving of life. Explain in terms of kinetic energy and work done in collisions.

FOR THE TEACHER

It is important that students understand that *energy can neither be created nor destroyed, but can be converted from one form to another. The principle of conservation of energy states that the total amount of energy in the universe is constant.* Use a variety of examples and activities to emphasize the concept of energy conversion. For example, discuss how gasoline can be burned in an internal combustion engine to produce heat energy that, in turn, produces kinetic energy (movement of the vehicle). It should also be noted that the process of energy conversion is never perfect, and some is inevitably lost as heat energy or sound rather than being converted to useful work.

Earlier in this section we told students that the kinetic energy of a moving object is equal to $1/2mv^2$ where m is the mass of the object and v is its velocity, but we did not explain how we arrived at this equation. We provide a simple derivation for you to pass on to your students if you choose. The gravitational potential energy of an object is mgh $E_p = mgh$. When an object falls, the total potential energy *mgh* lost must equal the kinetic energy E_K gained. From kinematics equations we know that the velocity of a freely falling body is equal to $\sqrt{2gd}$, where g is the acceleration due to gravity and d is the distance it has fallen $(v = \sqrt{2gd})$. Solving for d, we obtain: $d = v^2/2g$. Since the kinetic energy gained must equal the potential energy lost, we have: $E_K = mgh$. Substituting the value of d for h, we obtain:

$$E_K = mg \times \frac{v^2}{2g} \quad \text{or} \quad E_K = \frac{1}{2} mv^2$$

A sample problem is in order: calculate the kinetic energy of a baseball of mass 0.14 kg thrown by a pitcher with a velocity of 30 m/s:

$$E_K = \frac{1}{2} mv^2 \quad E_K = \frac{1}{2} \times 0.14 \text{ kg} \times (\frac{30m}{s})^2 = 63 \text{ J}$$

5.2.1 Potential Energy

Discussion: Playing with magnets helps students internalize the important relationships between potential energy, kinetic energy, and work. They will note that work is required to push two like poles of the magnets together. When the magnets are released they will see that the potential energy stored as a consequence of this work results in kinetic energy as the magnets move apart.

Answers: (1) The work required to push the magnets together is stored as potential energy in a magnetic field. When your hands are removed, the potential energy of this field is converted to kinetic energy as the magnets move apart. (2) A book resting on the top shelf of a bookcase has more gravitational potential energy relative to the floor than it does relative to the second shelf of the bookcase. (3) The speed of the bob at the bottom of its swing is equal to the speed of a bob dropped vertically from the same height. The bob will be moving at greatest speed and has greatest kinetic energy at the bottom of its swing, while it will have the lowest speed and greatest potential energy at the highest point of its swing. Kinetic and potential energy will be equal at half-height of the swing. (4) Student answers will vary. A good example is the pendulum, in which potential and kinetic energy are constantly being converted one to another. At some points in the swing all the energy in a pendulum bob is potential, while at other times it is all kinetic, and at locations in between a portion is kinetic and a portion is potential.

5.2.2 Kinetic Energy

Discussion: It is important that students understand that both mass and speed of a moving object determine its kinetic energy. Kinetic energy is directly proportional to the mass of the object: doubling the mass doubles the kinetic energy, tripling the mass triples the kinetic energy. Kinetic energy is directly proportional to the square of the speed: doubling the speed increases the kinetic energy by a factor of four, while tripling the speed increases the kinetic energy by a factor of nine. Impress on students the significance of the relationship between kinetic energy and speed. For example, if the car's speed doubles, the work required by the brakes to stop it quadruples because the kinetic energy has quadrupled ($E_k = 1/2\ mv^2$).

In this activity, students made indirect measurements of the relative magnitudes of the kinetic energy of falling objects by measuring or estimating the volume of craters they created. Ideally, a student graph of crater volume as a function of mass should be linear, while a graph of crater volume as a function of velocity should be exponential. Unfortunately, this technique does not produce such accurate results, but make certain students understand that their graphs can be calibrated if the kinetic energy of the falling objects is known. Using the kinetic energy equation ($E_k = 1/2\ mv^2$), students can determine the theoretical values and calibrate their graphs.

Answers (1) Kinetic energy is directly proportional to the mass of an object, and the square of its speed. Since all objects have the same speed upon impact when dropped from the same height (neglecting air friction), differences in kinetic energy are the result of differences in mass. If the mass is twice as great, the kinetic energy will be twice as great, the amount of work that can be done will be twice as great, and hence the crater should have roughly twice the volume. (2) If one object has twice the mass of a second, the gravitational force on the second is twice that on the first. Hence the ratio of force to mass is constant and is equal to the acceleration of gravity: $F/m = g$. (3) The graph of crater size as a function of speed was exponential while the graph of crater size as a function of mass was linear. This illustrates the relationship: $E_k = 1/2\ mv^2$. Changes in speed have a greater effect on kinetic energy than proportional changes in mass because the speed term is squared when determining kinetic energy while the mass term is not.

5.2.3 Conversion of Potential and Kinetic Energy

Discussion: Perhaps science educators have been remiss in not using simple toys such as the Slinky® to teach and reinforce important science concepts. In this activity, the Slinky® demonstrates interconversion of potential and kinetic energy. Yo-yos, super balls, or pogo sticks may also be used to illustrate this principle.

Answers: (1) No. For the Slinky® to walk up steps, potential energy would need to be created from nothing, a violation of the law of conservation of energy. (2) The kinetic energy of the Slinky® is greatest as it falls from one step to the next. The potential energy of the Slinky® is greatest when it is poised ready to fall from one step to the next. (3) Student answers will vary, but may include such variables as height to which Slinky® was raised, initial velocity given to one end of Slinky®, width of the steps, initial position of Slinky®, and so forth.

5.2.4 Conservation of Energy

Discussion: *In a perfectly elastic collision objects rebound from one another with no loss of kinetic energy.* If the collision of a ball with the floor were perfectly elastic and there were no air friction, a ball would continue to bounce indefinitely without loss in height. Make certain students understand that the collisions they witness are not perfectly elastic, which is one reason the balls never rise to their theoretical limits.

The result of this activity is startling and provides a wonderful discrepant event because students expect the Ping-Pong ball to rebound only to its original height. When it bounces 5 to 9 times higher, they are quite astonished. The activity can be performed with other balls, as long as the bottom ball is much more massive than the top ball (for example, baseball on top of a basketball).

You may want to perform the following demonstration to test for student understanding. Drop three balls of different masses together, as shown in Figure J. The direction of the bottom, large-mass ball is reversed the moment it hits the ground. A medium-mass ball falling with speed v above it collides with it at a relative speed of $2v$. If the collision is elastic and the medium ball is much less massive than the large ball, it will bounce away from the large ball with a relative speed of $2v$, and away from the ground with a speed of $3v$ since the massive ball is itself rebounding at speed v. When this medium-mass ball with speed $3v$ collides with a small-mass ball falling behind it at speed v, the relative speed is $4v$. As a result, the small-mass ball bounces away from the medium-mass ball with a speed of $4v$, but since the medium-mass ball is itself moving with a speed of $3v$, the small-mass ball must move away from the floor with a speed of $7v$. Since energy is conserved, the gravitational potential energy mgh of the small-mass ball at the top of the bounce will equal its kinetic energy $(1/2\ m(7v)^2)$ at the bottom. Thus the theoretical limit to which the small-mass ball can rise is 49 times the height it bounces when dropped alone $h = 49v^2/2g$.

Answers (1) When dropped separately, the Ping-Pong ball bounces to approximately the same height as the golf ball. When dropped in combination, the Ping-Pong ball may bounce as much as nine times its normal height. (2) The collisions are not perfectly elastic, so much energy is dissipated as heat. In addition, considerable energy is dissipated as heat due to the friction of the ball with the air. (3) See discussion.

5.2.5 Linear and Rotational Kinetic Energy

Discussion: Energy conservation requires that the objects reach the bottom in this order: spheres, disks (solid cylinders), and hoops (rings), regardless of their radii, masses, or the slope of the incline. The division of energy in a rolling object depends on its rotational inertia. If a hoop and a disk of equal mass and diameter roll down the same incline, the disk will experience greater linear acceleration. Its rotational inertia is less than that of the ring, thus its rotational kinetic energy is less. Its linear kinetic energy is therefore greater, and it acquires a higher linear velocity and reaches the bottom first.

The moment of inertia (I) determines the resistance of an object to rotational motion and depends on the total mass of the object and the distribution of this mass about its axis. The further the distribution of mass from the axis of rotation, the greater the moment of inertia. As shown in Figure L, the moment of inertia of a sphere is 2/5 *mr²*, where *m* is the mass of the sphere and *r* is the radius. The moment of inertia of a solid cylinder is $1/2\ mr^2$ and the moment of inertia of a hoop is mr^2.

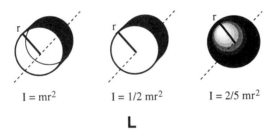

$I = mr^2$ $I = 1/2\ mr^2$ $I = 2/5\ mr^2$

L

The greater the moment of inertia, the greater the rotational kinetic energy acquired by an object rolling down an inclined plane. Hence, the hoop gains the greatest rotational kinetic energy, followed by the disk and the sphere. The more energy that goes into rotation, the less available for translation. Hence, the sphere reaches the bottom first because it has the lowest rotational kinetic energy and thus the highest translational kinetic energy (highest speed). The hoop reaches the bottom last because it has the highest rotational kinetic energy and thus the lowest translational kinetic energy (lowest speed).

We can show that the rate at which a sphere or other object rolls down an incline is independent of the mass and radius of the object. To do so we will consider a specific problem. Consider a ball rolling along a horizontal surface. The ball possesses both translational kinetic energy and rotational kinetic energy. The total kinetic energy of the ball at any time is given by the following equation:

$$E_K = \frac{1}{2}mv^2 + \frac{1}{2}I\omega^2$$

E_k is the total kinetic energy of the rolling ball. The translational kinetic energy is given by $1/2\ mv^2$ where *m* is the mass and *v* is the translational (linear) velocity. The rotational kinetic energy is given by $1/2\ I\omega^2$ where *I* is the moment of inertia and ω is the rotational (angular) velocity. Angular velocity is a measure of the rate of rotation of an object and is measured in units such as revolutions per second or radians per second. Note that the v in $1/2mv^2$ is the linear velocity of the center of mass of the ball as it moves across the floor. The linear velocity of a point on the surface of the ball is equal to the radius of the ball multiplied by the angular velocity: $v = r\omega$. The moment of inertia of a sphere is $2/5mr^2$. Substituting this value for I and v/r for ω in the equation gives:

$$E_K = \frac{1}{2}mv^2 + \frac{1}{2}(\frac{2}{5}mr^2)(\frac{v}{r})^2$$

$$E_k = \frac{7}{10}mv^2$$

Notice that the radius of the ball does not appear in the equation and thus does not effect kinetic energy. Suppose we place the ball at the top of an incline. Its potential energy E_p is mgh, where m is the mass of the ball, g is the acceleration of gravity, and h is the vertical distance through which the ball is raised, which is the vertical height of the inclined plane. Since $E_{K\ (at\ bottom)} = E_{P\ (at\ top)}$, we have:

$$mgh = \frac{7}{10}mv^2 \quad \text{or} \quad v = \sqrt{\frac{10gh}{7}}$$

The speed of the ball at the bottom of the incline is independent of the radius and mass. Substitute the appropriate values for a cylinder and hoop and you will find the speeds of these at the bottom of the ramp are also independent of radii and mass.

Answers: (1) The sphere reached the bottom of the incline first followed by the solid cylinder (disc) and hoop (ring). (2) A can filled with a solid will roll down the incline more slowly than a can filled with a liquid because the liquid does not have to rotate with the can and the potential energy of the liquid can go into linear, not rotational motion. The empty can will be last down the incline because the distribution of its mass from its axis is much greater than the filled cans, indicating it has the greater moment of inertia. (3) The kinetic energy of an object is proportional to the square of its speed. If the speed is increased from 10 km/h to 30 km/h (tripled), the kinetic energy is increased by a factor of nine ($3^2 = 9$). (4) Substituting the values of 55 MPH and 70 MPH into the kinetic energy equation shows that the kinetic energy of a vehicle moving at 70 miles per hour is 1.6 times as great as the kinetic energy of a vehicle moving at 55 miles per hour. Thus, a 27 percent increase in speed results in a 60 percent increase in kinetic energy. When the car crashes, kinetic energy is transformed into work that may damage the car and injure passengers.

Applications to Everyday Life

Racing: The wheels of a car possess both translational (linear) and rotational motion. The wheels turn on their axle as the car moves linearly over the road. The total kinetic energy of the car is part linear kinetic energy and part rotational kinetic energy. Lightweight "mag" wheels are used on race cars to improve linear acceleration. Suppose you have two cars of equal mass: One has a heavier chassis and lighter "mag" wheels and the other has a lighter chassis and heavier steel wheels. Given the same energy input from identical engines, the car with the "mag" wheels will accelerate more rapidly because less energy is required to rotate the wheels, leaving more energy available to provide linear motion (motion over the road).

Space Shuttle: The initial attempt of the crew of the space shuttle *Endeavor* to capture the stranded communications satellite, *Intelsat 6*, was unsuccessful. Astronaut Thuot was to grab the satellite using a specially designed "capture bar," which cost several million dollars, but was unable to do so because the satellite proved more sensitive to force than anticipated and spun away after each attempt. The translational energy of the satellite was the same as that of the *Endeavor* (both were moving linearly in an orbit at about 17,000 miles per hour). However, the satellite was rotating and it possessed rotational kinetic energy relative to the *Endeavor*. Thuot was not able to use the "capture bar" to stop the rotation. The three astronauts working together were able to capture the satellite with their gloved hands and stop its rotation. They attached a new rocket motor to the satellite that fired and boosted it into its proper orbit.

Automobile Air Bags: Air bags are becoming increasingly popular in cars, but some drivers find driving around with an explosive device 14 inches from the face rather unnerving. Auto makers, however, have designed sensors, electronic systems, and firing mechanisms for air bags striving to achieve a 99.999 percent rate of reliability, and there have been very few cases of accidental deployment of air bags. The purpose of an air bag is to absorb the energy of a rapidly moving human body involved in a head-on collision. The bag must quickly change the kinetic energy of the body to zero. The air-bag sensor must determine whether a crash is occurring in 8- to 9-thousandths of a second and order the air-bag firing mechanism to inflate the bag with a substance called sodium azide that gets hotter than steam and must be contained in order that it not burn the person the bag is supposed to protect. The air bag inflates in 0.2 seconds!

Driving: Watch your speed! Brakes must do work to stop a moving car. The faster the car is moving the greater its kinetic energy and the greater the work required to stop it. The table shows the stopping distance (from eye to brain to foot to wheel to road) required for each of these speeds. Remember that the kinetic energy of an object depends on the square of the speed. The brakes must do work to stop a moving car in that they must change the kinetic energy of the car ($1/2\ mv^2$) to zero. If the speed is doubled the breaking force required is quadrupled. Inspection of the table shows that the stopping distance required for a car moving at 90 km/h (55 miles per hour) is approximately three and one-half times that required at 40 km/h (25 miles per hour), which is about 70 meters versus 20 meters. Increasing the speed 125 percent results in a 250 percent increase in stopping distance. Obviously, braking distance is related to the kinetic energy of the car. Although this increase could not have been predicted solely on the basis of the kinetic energy formula (due to complexity of the system), it nonetheless suggests the importance of the v^2 term in kinetic energy.

Stopping Distance of Average Passenger Car	
Speed (v)	*Stopping Distance*
25 MPH (40 km/h)	62 ft. (19 m)
35 MPH (56 km/h)	106 ft. (32.3 m)
45 MPH (72 km/h)	162 ft. (49.4 m)
55 MPH (89 km/h)	228 ft. (69.5 m)
65 MPH (105 km/h)	306 ft. (93.3 m)

Sports and Games: All sports involve activities in which potential energy is converted to kinetic energy and kinetic energy is converted to potential energy. Some examples follow: *baseball*—the kinetic energy of pitched ball is converted to kinetic energy in the opposite direction by a bat or is rapidly brought to zero by the catcher's mitt; *football*—the kinetic energy of a running fullback is rapidly brought to zero by the tackle; *ice skating*—the rotational kinetic energy of a slowly twirling ice skater rapidly increases as the skater brings her arms in close to her body; *skate boarder*—the kinetic energy of the boarder rapidly changes to potential energy as the boarder moves to the top of a hill or track and then rapidly changes to kinetic energy as the boarder descends; *checkers*—yes, even games such as checkers involve conversion of energy when pieces that are at rest (zero potential energy) must be moved (kinetic energy) to another square.

Animal Locomotion: Have you ever tried to hop on a "pogo stick"? It's not easy to keep one's balance. The "pogo stick" has a coiled spring at its base, and when the stick hits the ground the spring compresses, changing kinetic energy to potential energy of the spring. The spring then expands as potential energy is converted to kinetic energy of your motion. Some animals such as the kangaroo also hop around, but they don't have springs. Animals have tendons (fibrous tissue connecting muscles to bones), which store potential energy as do springs. As animals walk, tendons alternately stretch (store potential energy) and then retract, providing some kinetic energy for movement. A kangaroo is an especially efficient hopper because it uses its entire body as a spring, bending far over when it lands and quickly straightening out as it pushes off for the next hop.

Amusement-Park Rides: Do most rides involve translational kinetic energy, rotational kinetic energy, or both? Let's name a few popular rides and then think about these questions. *Octopus*—each car moves in a circle (translational) and rotates on its axis (rotational); *tilt-a-whirl*—each car moves along the platform in a linear motion (translational) and rotates on its axis (rotational); *roller coaster*—each car moves along the track in linear motion (translational) as the wheels of the car rotate (rotational); *ferris wheel*—each car moves linearly in a circle (translational), and each car rotates on the supporting bar (rotational) as it moves in a circle.

5.3 MOMENTUM

One of the most famous American fantasy stories is *The Wonderful Wizard of Oz*, a story of a young farm girl from Kansas who dreams she is carried away by a tornado to a strange land called Oz. Although the story is purely fiction, many children and adults have experienced nightmares after watching the screenplay because they are familiar with the destructive power of such storms. Tornadoes are rapidly rotating columns of air hanging from cumulonimbus clouds. Known also as cyclones and twisters, these powerful storms can cause substantial damage. In general, wind speeds in tornadoes average 240 km/h (150 mph) or less, but speeds up to 800 km/h (500 mph) have been inferred from the damage left by very strong twisters. The largest outbreak of tornadoes in recorded history occurred on April 3 and 4 in 1974 in the Mississippi River Valley of North America. In a two-day period, 148 tornadoes struck, killing 300 people, injuring 6,000, and leaving swaths of destruction through many farms and towns. To understand tornadoes and many other important phenomena, one must understand momentum. Simply stated, *momentum is the product of mass and velocity, and, like energy, must be conserved*. If an object is moving, it has momentum. Consider the following phenomena that require an understanding of momentum to explain.

1. A pool ball approaches a second pool ball head-on. After collision, the first ball comes to an abrupt halt and the second ball moves off at the same rate as the original velocity of the first.

2. An ice skater spinning in one spot pulls her arms closer to her body and her rate of spin increases. She then moves her arms away from her body and her rate of spin slows. A spinning skater of the same mass as the first, but with much larger and longer arms, pulls her arms in close to her body and her rate of spin increases even faster than that of the first skater.

3. The captain of a large supertanker must cut the engines miles out to sea, while the skipper of a much smaller yacht moving at the same rate as the tanker does not need to reduce speed until the yacht is almost at dock.

4. The engineer of an Amtrak train applies the brakes long before the train arrives at the station to ensure the train will come to a halt at the station, while the engineer of the small-scale train at an amusement park applies the breaks just moments before entering the station.

5. A diver leaves the board and begins a slow somersault. She pulls her arms and legs into a tuck position and her rate of rotation increases. Just before entering the water she extends her legs and arms to slow the rotation. Another diver of the same mass but with much longer legs and arms performs the same dive and her rate of rotation is greater than that of the first diver.

Analysis of the events described illustrates that conservation of energy is insufficient to explain them. For example, conservation of energy suggests two possible outcomes for the colliding billiard balls (Figure A): (1) the first ball stops (no kinetic

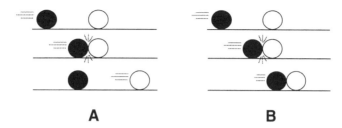

A   **B**

energy) and the second ball moves off in the same direction with the same velocity as the first, or (2) both balls move off in the same direction with half the original velocity of the first ball (Figure B). Why does the first result occur and never the second? Consider the spinning skater. Although the skater pulls her arms in toward her body, her mass is still the same. So why does she spin faster? The same question applies to the diver. Obviously there must be more involved in the phenomena described above than merely conservation of energy.

Momentum is a measure of mass in motion. Linear momentum is the product of the mass of an object and its velocity: momentum = mass × velocity. A supertanker is more difficult to stop than a yacht moving at the same velocity because the tanker has more mass and, consequently, more momentum. Note that we use the term, velocity, which indicates that momentum is a vector quantity. A short arrow is placed above a letter to indicate it is a vector quantity and has both magnitude and direction. For example, since velocity is a vector quantity, we write: $\vec{v}$. Consequently, for linear momentum we write: $\vec{p} = m\vec{v}$, where $\vec{p}$ is momentum, m is mass, and $\vec{v}$ is velocity. We will not normally use the arrows over vector quantities unless making a specific point concerning vector quantities.

In the absence of external forces such as friction, the linear momentum of a system is conserved, meaning it does not change. In the case of the two pool balls (Figure A; neglecting friction), momentum is conserved because the momentum of the black ball is mv before the collision and zero after the collision, while the momentum of the white ball is zero initially but is mv after the collision. Therefore, the change in momentum is zero ($mv - mv = 0$).

Just as a mass moving in a straight line has linear momentum, a mass moving in a circular path or rotating about an axis has rotational (angular) momentum. Angular momentum is defined as the product of the moment of inertia and angular velocity. If L represents angular momentum, I represents moment of inertia, and ω angular (rotational) velocity, then $L = I\omega$. *In the absence of external torques, the angular momentum of a system is constant.*

The rotating skater and diver posses angular momentum because they have mass and are rotating about an axis. When the skater pulls her arms in close to her body, the moment of inertia I is decreased. Since the law of conservation of angular momentum requires that L remains unchanged, ω must increase ($L = I\omega$). When the skater moves her arms out from her body, her moment of inertia I increases and her angular velocity ω must therefore decrease if angular momentum is to be conserved. The same arguments apply to the diver. The *expression, $\vec{p} = m\vec{v}$ for linear momentum is analogous to the expression, $\vec{L} = I\vec{\omega}$ for angular momentum.* The activities that follow will help you learn more about linear momentum, rotational (angular) momentum, and conservation of momentum.

5.3.1 Linear Momentum

Concepts to Investigate: Momentum, $\vec{p} = m\vec{v}$, mass and momentum, velocity and momentum.

Materials: Marbles and steel balls of the same diameter (ball bearings are available in auto-supply stores), 4-foot section of corner molding as shown in Figure C (molding is available in the lumber department of a home-improvement store; plastic 30-cm rulers with grooves down the center may be substituted if necessary), C-clamp, book or block to place under ruler to form inclined plane, soccer ball.

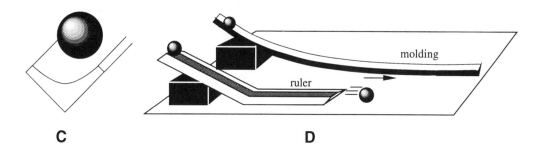

C   D

Principles and Procedures

Part 1. Mass is important in momentum: When a trash truck runs into a parked car it causes significantly more damage than a compact car traveling at the same speed does. The trash truck is more difficult to stop because it has greater momentum. What role does mass play in determining the momentum of an object?

    Make a track for balls by taping grooved rulers together end to end or by using corner molding as shown in Figure D. The corner molding is flexible and you may develop a curved ramp by nailing the center to a block of wood using finishing nails or by pushing the middle of the track into a clump of modeling clay. Place a book or block under one end of each track to give a vertical height of about 2 centimeters. Obtain two balls of similar diameter but different mass (e.g., a steel ball and a Ping-Pong ball, or a ball bearing and a glass marble). Place each at the same vertical height on the track, release, and measure the distance traveled after reaching the base of the incline. Do both balls hit the bottom of the ramp at the same time? Do they travel the same distance once off the ramp? Repeat several times and calculate the average distance traveled for each ball. The greater the momentum, the more difficult it is for friction to stop an object. Does the more massive or less massive ball have greater momentum?

Part 2. Velocity is important in momentum: Roll a soccer ball swiftly on a field and predict the direction the ball will travel when kicked gently at a right angle to the direction it is rolled. Try it and see if you were correct. Set up goals approximately 3 meters from the kicker at 30°, 60°, and 90° to the direction of the ball's roll (Figure E). Have your partner roll the ball swiftly and kick it at a right angle so it hits the

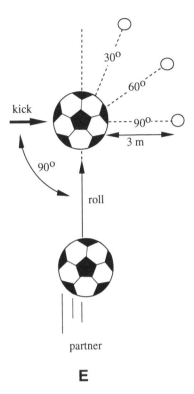

E

target at 30°. Roll the ball at the same speed and kick it at a right angle to its roll with sufficient force to hit the target at 60°. Is it possible to hit the target at 90° without changing the direction of the kick or the roll? Try it. The direction of motion of the ball after being kicked shows that momentum is a vector quantity (momentum possesses both magnitude and direction). The final momentum of the ball depends on the momentum of the rolling ball at the point immediately prior to being kicked plus the momentum given the ball when kicked (impulse).

Questions

(1) The momentum of a body can be increased by increasing its velocity, mass, or both. Explain.

(2) Describe the final momentum of the soccer ball (its speed and direction) if the speed of the roll is very slow and the force of the kick is very great.

(3) An object of mass 10 kg moving at twice the velocity of a mass of 20 kg has the same momentum but different kinetic energy. Explain.

(4) When a rocket explodes all the pieces may scatter in many directions, but the center of mass of the rocket continues to travel in the original path of the rocket. Explain in terms of linear momentum.

(5) The final velocity of the final stage of a multistage rocket is much greater than the final velocity of a single-stage rocket of the same total mass and the same initial fuel supply. Explain.

5.3.2 Elastic and Inelastic Collisions

Concepts to Investigate: Elastic collisions, inelastic collisions, conservation of linear momentum.

Materials: Swinging-ball apparatus as shown in Figure F (available at toy stores or novelty shops), Velcro® with adhesive.

Principles and Procedures: An elastic collision is one in which the total kinetic energy following a collision is equal to the total kinetic energy preceding it. By contrast, an inelastic collision is one in which kinetic energy is converted to other forms, principally heat and work. Consequently, the amount of kinetic energy following an inelastic collision is less than the amount preceding it. Two football players or two destruction derby drivers collide inelastically such that the total energy is conserved, but total kinetic energy is not. The motion of the football players or cars is halted (kinetic energy is reduced to zero) as kinetic energy is converted to heat or work (bending the players' padding or the frames of the cars).

   Perform each of the investigations illustrated in Figure F, then repeat after placing adhesive Velcro® pads to the balls. In the space provided, draw diagrams of what occurs following each collision. On the basis of your observations, does it appear as though the total momentum ($p = mv$) and kinetic ($E_k = 1/2 \, mv^2$) energy are conserved for a steel/steel collision? Is a steel/steel collision elastic or inelastic? Does it appear as though the total momentum ($p = mv$) and kinetic ($E_k = 1/2 \, mv^2$) energy are conserved for a Velcro/Velcro collision? Is a Velcro/Velcro collision elastic or inelastic?

Questions

(1) Do your results suggest that linear momentum and kinetic energy are conserved in the steel/steel collisions? The Velcro/Velcro collisions?

(2) A ball of mass 0.1 kg moving at 2 m/s strikes a stationary ball of mass 0.1 kg. Following the collision, the first ball stops while the second ball moves away with velocity 2 m/s. Was momentum ($p = mv$) conserved? Was kinetic energy ($E_k = 1/2 \, mv^2$) conserved? Was the collision elastic or inelastic? Explain.

(3) A ball of mass 0.1 kg moving at 2 m/s strikes a stationary ball of mass 0.1 kg. The colliding surfaces of both balls are covered with Velcro® so they stick together following the collision and move together at a velocity of 1 m/s. Was momentum ($p = mv$) conserved? Was kinetic energy ($E_k = 1/2 \, mv^2$) conserved? Was the collision elastic or inelastic? Explain.

(4) An inelastic collision occurred when two Velcro®-clad balls of equal and opposite velocity collided. Explain in terms of relative velocity of the balls before and after collision.

(5) How do the crumpled parts of cars that have been in a collision indicate the collision was inelastic?

	Draw the position of the balls following the collision.	
	Without Velcro	With Velcro

F

(6) Would a head-on collision between two automobiles be more damaging to the passengers if the cars bounced apart or stuck together?

(7) A 4,000-kg truck moving at 10.0 m/s strikes the rear of a 1,400-kg car at rest. If the bumpers lock (inelastic collision) what is the final velocity of the vehicles? Compare the original kinetic energy to the final kinetic energy. Was energy lost or converted to another form?

5.3.3 Conservation of Linear Momentum

Concepts to Investigate: Conservation of momentum, elastic collisions.

Materials: Two 30-cm plastic rulers with grooves down the center, collection of ball bearings or marbles of various sizes with at least six of the same size. Steel ball bearings work best and may be obtained from specialized auto-supply stores. It is possible to substitute curved corner molding for the rulers. Such molding (Figure C) is available in the lumber departments of most home-improvement stores and makes excellent ramps (Figure D). An alternative to the marbles and ruler is to use the apparatus shown in Figure G, which is commonly found in novelty stores.

Principles and Procedures: An elastic collision is one in which objects rebound from each other without a loss of kinetic energy. In the following activities you will investigate elastic collisions involving equal and unequal masses.

Part 1. Elastic collisions with equal masses: Make a track for balls by taping grooved rulers together end to end or by using corner molding, as shown in Figure D. Be certain to use the same size (mass) bearings or marbles and the same vertical position on the inclined ruler in the following activity. Place one marble on the inclined ruler and one marble on the flat ruler. Release the upper marble and carefully observe the motion of the marbles prior to, and following the collision. Now place one marble on the incline and two marbles, touching, on the flat ruler. Release the upper marble and record the number of marbles that move after the collision. Record the number of marbles that move following each of the collisions specified in part 1 of the table (Figure H).

© 1994 by John Wiley & Sons, Inc.

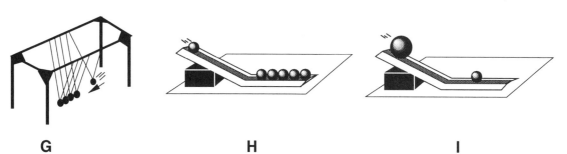

G   H   I

If you are using the swinging balls apparatus (Figure G), pull back one, then two, then three, and then four successively and note the results in each of the four cases. Finally, use your left hand to pull back two balls from the left side and your right hand to pull back two balls from the right side. Release the balls simultaneously and record what happens following the collision. The law of conservation of momentum states that the total momentum following a collision is equal to the total momentum before the collision. Are your findings consistent with this law? Explain.

Part 2. Elastic collisions with different masses: Obtain two sizes of marbles or steel spheres, one of which is approximately double the mass of the other. Investigate the following elastic collisions and record in part 2 of the table the speed and direction of the spheres following the collision. The original speed of the moving sphere is arbitrarily assigned a value of 3. If a sphere is stationary after the collision, circle 1. If it is moving more slowly than the speed of the original sphere, circle 2. If it is moving at approximately the same speed as the original sphere, circle 3; if it is going slightly faster, circle 4; and if it is going substantially faster, circle 5. If it continues in its original direction, circle "f" for forward, but if it reverses, circle "r" for reverse. Record your results for the following collisions in part 2 of the table.

1. Place a large sphere on the incline and a smaller sphere on the flat ruler. Release the large sphere and record the speed and direction of the spheres following the collision (Figure I).

2. Place the small sphere on the incline and the larger sphere on the flat ruler and repeat.

3. Place two large spheres a distance apart on the flat ruler and then roll them toward each other at the same speed.

4. Place two small spheres a distance apart on the flat ruler and then roll them toward each other at the same speed.

5. Roll large and small spheres toward each other at the same speed.

Part 1							*Part 2*				
#spheres on slope							*small sphere*		*large sphere*		
		1	2	3	4	5		Speed	Direction	Speed	Direction
#	1						1	1 2 3 4 5	f r	1 2 3 4 5	f r
spheres	2						2	1 2 3 4 5	f r	1 2 3 4 5	f r
on	3						3			1 2 3 4 5	f r
level	4						4	1 2 3 4 5	f r		
	5						5	1 2 3 4 5	f r	1 2 3 4 5	f r
Record the number of spheres that move following collision.							1 = stop; 2 = slow; 3 = original speed; 4 = fast; 5 = very fast f = continues in forward direction; r = reverses direction				

In these activities, you investigated momentum and elastic collisions. Momentum is conserved in collisions: The total momentum of a system of colliding objects is unchanged both before, during, and after the collisions because the forces that act on objects involved in the collision are internal forces. Two marbles approaching each other on the track constitute a system. When they strike, the forces of collision are internal to this system. The total momentum before collision is equal to the total momentum after collision. Gravity would be an example of a force external to the system of the two marbles. Gravity acts vertically on the marbles to hold them on the track, but has no component of force in the horizontal direction and does not affect the momentum of the marbles.

When a moving marble makes a head-on (straight line) collision with an identical marble at rest, the moving marble stops and the target marble moves off with almost the same velocity as the first marble. Although the individual velocities of the marbles have changed, the relative speed of the marbles is almost the same after the collision as before because this is an elastic collision. *In a perfectly elastic collision both momentum and kinetic energy must be conserved.*

In the introduction we made this observation: "A pool ball approaches a second pool ball head-on. After collision, the first ball comes to an abrupt halt and the second ball moves off at the same rate as the original velocity of the first." By applying the principles of conservation of energy and linear momentum, we can understand why this must occur. The following table shows momentum and energy data for two possible scenarios: case 1: both balls move off with half the velocity of the initial ball, and case 2: the first ball stops and the second moves away at the original velocity of the first. An analysis of the data for case 1 reveals that the total final momentum following the collision is the same as the total initial momentum, but the total final kinetic energy $E_{k(total)}$ is only one half the total initial kinetic energy. Thus, momentum is conserved, but kinetic energy is not. By contrast, case 2 satisfies both the principles of conservation of momentum and energy because the total energy and momentum following the collision are the same as the energy and momentum before the collision. Thus, case 2 is observed in the real world, but case 1 is not.

Case 1: Both balls move off with half the velocity of the first ball.				Case 2: First ball stops, second ball moves off with original velocity of the first ball.			
Before Collision		*After Collision*		*Before Collision*		*After Collision*	
Ball 1	Ball 2	Ball 1	Ball 2	Ball 1	Ball 2	Ball 1	Ball 2
$p_1 = p$	$p_2 = 0$	$p_1 = 1/2p$	$p_2 = 1/2p$	$p_1 = p$	$p_2 = 0$	$p_1 = 0$	$p_1 = p$
$KE_1 = E$	$KE_2 = 0$	$KE_1 = 1/4E$	$KE_2 = 1/4E$	$KE_1 = E$	$KE_2 = 0$	$KE_1 = 0$	$KE_2 = E$

Questions

(1)   When two marbles of the same mass but opposite velocities collide they move away in opposite directions with the same speed. Explain in terms of conservation of momentum.

(2)   When one marble strikes two touching marbles, one of the two touching marbles moves away with the same velocity as the incoming marble, rather than two marbles moving with half the velocity of the incoming marble. Explain in terms of conservation of momentum and kinetic energy.

(3) Two large marbles of the same mass are approaching head-on (in line), each with a speed of 5 m/s. After colliding, the marbles separate at a relative speed of 10 m/s. Explain in terms of elastic collisions.

(4) Suppose you throw a basketball while standing on a stationary skateboard. Describe your momentum and that of the ball. What will happen if you go through the motions of throwing but decide not to release the ball?

(5) A 2-kg cart moving at 10 m/s strikes a 1-kg cart moving at 5 m/s in the same direction. What is the final velocity of each cart assuming a perfectly elastic in-line collision?

5.3.4 Impulse and Momentum

Concepts to Investigate: Impulse, momentum, impulse-momentum equation (F∆ t = m∆v).

Materials: Balloons or eggs, hay or Styrofoam packing material.

Principles and Procedures: Bungee divers leap from great heights while tethered to a series of Bungee cords that are fastened to their body harness. The Bungee cords stretch as the diver falls, and then cause the diver to bounce back 10 or 15 times before coming to rest. Although Bungee divers may perform such stunts routinely, they might not survive a single fall if ropes were substituted for the Bungee cords. Although both Bungee cords and ropes bring the momentum of the jumper to zero, the Bungee cords do so over a longer time interval. The Bungee cord exerts a smaller force on the jumper for a longer time so the diver gradually decelerates rather than coming to an abrupt halt. By contrast ropes exert a greater force over a shorter time, causing an abrupt and hazardous stop.

Newton's second law states that the acceleration of a body is directly proportional to the force acting on the body and inversely proportional to the mass: $F = ma$, where F is force, m is mass, and a is acceleration. Since acceleration is defined as change in velocity with change in time (we use the symbol Δ to indicate a change), $F = m (\Delta v/\Delta t)$. Rearranging we obtain, $F\Delta t = m\Delta v$. *The quantity F∆t is called impulse.* Impulse is equal to change in momentum ($m \Delta v$) and is also equal to the product of force and the time interval over which the force acts ($F\Delta t$).

The momentum of a Bungee diver is brought to zero over a longer period of time (greater Δt) when using Bungee cords than ropes, and as a result the force applied to the diver's body is substantially smaller and less damaging. The impulse-momentum relationship can be used to analyze a variety of phenomena where momentum is increased or decreased.

Part 1. Water-balloon toss: Each lab group should fill a balloon with an equal amount of water and then exit the laboratory to a playing field. A member of each group should stand 2 meters away from his or her partner and gently toss the balloon so the partner will be able to catch it without it breaking. After each successful catch, take another step back and toss it again (Figure J). As the distance between partners increases, it is necessary to throw the balloon with greater velocity and momentum ($\Delta p = m\Delta v$). Since impulse equals the change in momentum ($F\Delta t = m\Delta v$), it is necessary to increase the time over which the halting force is applied if the momentum is to be reduced to zero without increasing the force applied on the balloon. Examine the technique used by the champion balloon tossers to see how they accomplish this. The winners often minimize the force on the balloon by extending their arms forward and, as the balloon lands, moving them backward so the balloon decelerates slowly.

Part 2. Gentle collisions: Roll an egg or water-balloon rapidly toward a concrete wall (Figure K). Place some hay or Styrofoam packing in a pile against the wall and roll an egg or water-balloon rapidly against the pile (Figure L). The momentum of the balloon or egg is brought to zero by both the concrete and the hay, but the damage is generally less severe when rolled against the hay. Explain in terms of impulse and momentum ($F\Delta t = m\Delta v$).

Part 3. Egg Drop: Design a device in which a raw egg can fall from a height of two stories onto concrete without breaking. When designing your device, remember that the egg will be less likely to break if its momentum is reduced to zero over a long period of time. Hold a contest with other lab groups to see whose design is most effective.

Questions

(1) Which technique is most effective in catching the water-balloon? Explain in terms of momentum and impulse.

(2) Does the wall or straw exert a greater force on the balloon in Part 2? Explain in terms of the momentum-impulse equation ($F\Delta t = m\Delta v$).

(3) When riding a horse, a jockey stands in the stirrups, legs flexing with each stride of the horse. Dirt-bike riders do the same as they travel over bumpy terrain. Explain in terms of impulse and momentum.

(4) When jumping off a wall or rock you should land with legs bent rather than straight. Why?

(5) A swimmer who jumps from a high diving board can enter the water and sustain no injury. The same person jumping from the same height and landing on concrete may not live to tell about it. Explain in terms of impulse and momentum.

5.3.5 Conservation of Angular Momentum

Concepts to Investigate: Angular momentum, conservation of angular momentum, stability, gyroscopes.

Materials: Coins (pennies and quarters), tin-can lid or other disk, "lazy Susan" or other turntable (available at hardware stores), bicycle wheel, handles (wood or plastic file handles designed to screw onto a file are inexpensive and may be purchased from a hardware store), small toy gyroscope available from most toy stores, top.

Principles and Procedures

Part 1. Angular momentum, torque and stability: Hold a coin horizontally, using thumb and first finger of one hand. Slowly move your fingers apart until the object falls. Unless you are agile enough to release both fingers from the coin at precisely the same instant the coin will flip as it falls because the last finger touching the coin acts as a pivot point and gravity acting at the coin's center of mass provides an external torque to rotate the coin about this axis (see Figure M). As the coin falls, it rotates around its center of mass. Again hold the coin between thumb and finger, but this time give the coin a twist in the horizontal plane while dropping it (Figure N). The angular momentum imparted to the coin will keep it in a horizontal position as it falls. Although gravity produces a torque as before, if one finger releases the coin before the other, the angular momentum will resist the resulting torque and the coin will remain in a horizontal position as it falls.

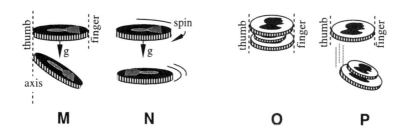

M   **N**   **O**   **P**

Place a penny between two quarters and hold them between your thumb and index finger as shown in Figure O. Position your other hand approximately 20 centimeters beneath this hand and release the lower quarter while holding onto the upper quarter (Figure P). Why does the quarter land on top of the penny even though it was originally positioned below it? What can you do, without changing the distance between your hands, so that order will be maintained and the penny will land on top of the quarter? Try it.

Part 2. Gyroscopic motion: Why is it easier to balance on your bicycle when moving than when still? Why will a rolling coin not topple until it has nearly stopped rolling? Why is it easier to balance on the tip of ice skates when spinning than when standing still? A physicist might answer "angular momentum" to each of these questions, but what is "angular momentum" and what influence does it have on the world around us?

To investigate angular momentum, construct your own gyroscope or use a purchased one. Remove the wooden or plastic handles from a file or other hand tool and screw them onto the axle of a front wheel that has been removed from a bicycle. Ask your partner to set the wheel spinning rapidly while you are holding both handles. Tilt the axle of the wheel upward and then downward while keeping the axle in a vertical plane (Figure Q). When you attempt to tilt the spinning wheel it exerts a torque on you, and to keep it in a vertical plane you must exert an equal and opposite torque on the wheel.

Hold the wheel by both handles in a vertical position while your partner again sets it spinning rapidly. Tilt the wheel both left and right and describe the effects (Figure R). The rotating wheel resists being tilted from any position, including an upright position, which explains why a moving bicycle is much easier to keep upright than a motionless one. When the wheel is spinning it has angular momentum, which helps maintain the axis (axle) of the wheel oriented in the same direction. When you attempt to tilt (exert a turning force) on the axle, you are exerting a torque on the wheel and the wheel will exert an equal and opposite torque (turning force) on you.

Q   R

Just as an external force is required to change the linear momentum of an object, an external torque is required to change the angular momentum of an object. The spinning wheel possesses angular momentum that has both magnitude and direction. The direction of the angular momentum is along the wheel's axis (axle). When you are standing or sitting on a turntable, you, the turntable, and the spinning wheel comprise a system, and the principle of conservation of angular momentum states that any change in angular momentum of this system must be accompanied by an opposite change elsewhere in the system so the net effect will be zero. To see this effect, carefully sit or stand on a stationary turntable while holding the axle (axis) of the wheel vertically (same direction as your axis and that of the turntable). Set the wheel spinning rapidly. Now tip the axle from the vertical until it is horizontal (Figure S). The torque that you supply to move the wheel from the vertical to the horizontal is internal to the system (the system being you, the wheel, and the platform). Since there is no external component of torque on the system about the

Which way will
turntable rotate?

S

vertical axis (force of gravity cannot supply such a torque because the lever arm is zero), the vertical component of angular momentum of the system must be conserved. You and the platform must supply this additional angular momentum about the vertical axis, meaning that you and the platform will begin to rotate about a vertical axis. Practice with the gyroscope and see how fast you can get the turntable to rotate by turning the spinning bicycle wheel.

Questions

(1) Explain why giving the coin or other object a sharp twist upon releasing causes it to fall toward the ground in a horizontal position.

(2) Were you able to ensure that the penny landed on the quarter rather than vice versa? Explain how you accomplished this.

(3) How must a quarterback throw a football so it does not tumble through the air? Explain in terms of angular momentum.

(4) Why are spinning bullets, footballs, and basketballs more stable than when not spinning? A basketball player wishing to balance the ball on his finger will be more successful if the ball is spinning than when it is at rest. Why?

(5) A girl rotating on a turntable has arms extended. She suddenly pulls her arms inward and her rotational velocity increases dramatically. Explain in terms of conservation of angular momentum.

5.3.6 Precession

Concepts to Investigate: Angular momentum, conservation of angular momentum, stability, gyroscopes, precession.

Materials: Front wheel of a bicycle, handles (wood or plastic file handles designed to screw onto a file are inexpensive and may be purchased from a hardware store), rope. Optional: Toy gyroscope, top.

Principles and Procedures: Construct the wheel gyroscope described in the previous exercise or obtain a toy gyroscope. Set the wheel spinning rapidly and hang it from two ropes as shown in Figure T. Cut one of the ropes (Figure U) and note that the wheel remains balanced and slowly precesses (rotates) in a circle about a vertical axis of the rope (Figure V). As the wheel slows, the axle will drop from the horizontal and the wheel will fall if not removed. See how many times you can get the wheel to precess before it falls.

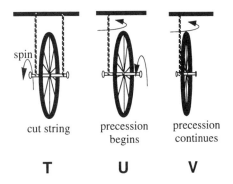

cut string   precession   precession
begins   continues

T   **U**   **V**

How can angular momentum be used to explain these nonintuitive observations? If the wheel were not spinning the torque produced by gravity acting at the center of mass would cause it to fall toward the ground. When the wheel spins, however, there is no torque pulling it down, but there is torque causing the axis to move. This movement of the axis is called *precession*. You may have played with a toy top (see Figure W) and realized that it would not remain upright unless spinning. If the top is not spinning, the force of gravity, mg, acting on its center of mass will topple it. However when the top is spinning, the force of gravity causes it to precess around (circle) the vertical axis. As the rate of spinning decreases, the rate of precession increases.

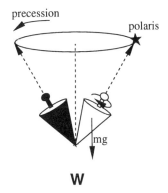

W

The Earth spins and precesses like a big top, but the rate of precession is very slow. The Earth completes a single precessional cycle in 26,000 years. Just as the Earth's gravity causes a top to precess, the gravitational pull of the sun on the Earth produces an external torque that causes the Earth to precess. The northern end of the Earth's axis is currently pointed toward Polaris, a star we identify as the "north star," but as the Earth precesses other stars will eventually become the "north star."

The axis of the Earth is titled 23.5 degrees, and this tilt is responsible for the seasons. In 13,000 years the Earth will have processed halfway through its cycle, the tilt will be in a direction opposite to what it is now, and the seasons as we know them now will be reversed. In time, precession will cause the months that are now winter to become summer.

Questions

(1) The bicycle wheel, if not spinning, will topple from its support, while a spinning wheel will rotate about this support. Explain in terms of torque and angular momentum.

(2) Explain how the Earth's precession will eventually change the time of the seasons as we know them now.

FOR THE TEACHER

Conservation of linear and angular momentum are among the fundamental conservation laws that include conservation of mass, energy, and electric charge. Make certain students understand that momentum, in the absence of external forces such as friction, is conserved. Conservation of linear and angular momentum can be used to explain many important scientific phenomena from the smallest to the largest scale—electrons to galaxies.

It is important that students understand that an external force is required to change the linear momentum of a body or system. For example, when a skyrocket or firecracker explodes the forces are internal. Although fragments move away from the center of mass of the firecracker and skyrocket, the positions of the centers of mass are not affected by these internal forces. If the skyrocket were moving through the air in a certain trajectory, its center of mass would continue along this trajectory after explosion. Gravity provides the external force to keep the center of mass of the skyrocket moving along this trajectory.

It is important that students understand that an external torque is required to change the angular momentum of a body or system. Remind students that the mass of a body can be considered to be concentrated at a point called the center of mass. Consequently, there can be no external torque of gravity on, for example, a diver executing a complicated dive involving spins and somersaults because gravity acts on the center of mass of the body and there is no lever arm. The diver is able to execute the spins and somersaults by constantly changing his moment of inertia by moving various parts of his body toward and away from his center of mass. There is, however, an external torque acting on the top and wheel (gyroscope) described in this section because both are resting on supports, and there is a lever arm from the center of mass to the point of support. Gravity acts on the center of mass of the wheel and produces a torque equal to the force multiplied by the length of the axle from the center of mass to the point of support that is the hand or rope.

In a perfectly elastic collision the relative speed of the colliding objects is the same before and after the collision. Both momentum and kinetic energy are conserved. In a perfectly inelastic collision (objects stick together) the relative speed after the collision is zero and there is a maximum loss of kinetic energy. In the "real world" of collisions the relative speed after collision is less than before collision, but not zero, and consequently collisions are somewhere between elastic and inelastic. If an object has momentum it must also have some kinetic energy.

5.3.1 Linear Momentum

Discussion

Part 1: Although both balls moved down the incline at the same velocity, the steel ball travels a greater distance after reaching the bottom because it has more mass and hence more momentum. Its greater momentum carries it a greater distance because more work (friction × time) is required to stop it. Since all other variables are controlled, this activity shows that momentum is dependent upon mass.

Part 2: This activity helps students understand the contribution of velocity to momentum. The diagrams in Figure X show how the resultant motion of the soccer ball depends on its initial momentum and the momentum imparted to it by the kick. To increase the momentum of an object, increase its velocity, increase its mass, or increase both mass and velocity.

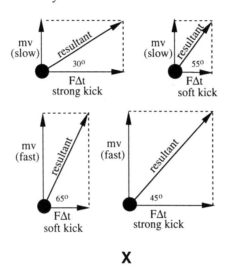

X

Answers (1) Momentum is the product of mass and velocity. Consequently, increasing mass, velocity, or both increases momentum. (2) If the speed is slow the momentum of the ball in the direction of the roll is small. If the kick is great then the momentum imparted to the ball in the direction of the kick is great. As a result, the ball moves at a small angle to the direction of the kick (see Figure Y). (3) Momentum is the product of mass and velocity, which is the same for both objects. By contrast, kinetic energy is proportional to the mass and the square of the velocity. The smaller mass is half that of the larger but its velocity is double. Thus, while they both have the same momentum, the kinetic energy of the smaller mass is twice that of the larger. (4) An external force is required to change momentum, but the explosive force is internal. Since momentum is conserved, the center of mass continues in its trajectory. (5) The fuel supplies the same total force for each rocket, but as each stage of the multistage rocket is jettisoned, mass decreases. Given the same force, a decrease in mass results in an increase in velocity.

5.3.2 Elastic and Inelastic Collisions

Discussion: This activity can be performed as an instructor demonstration if the hanging-ball apparatus is placed upon an overhead projector. Students should understand that in inelastic collisions the relative speeds of the colliding objects change as a result of the collision. Momentum is conserved, total energy is conserved, but kinetic energy is not. Some kinetic energy is converted to heat and some does work when the colliding objects are deformed.

Answers (1) Students should find that steel/steel collisions are elastic and both momentum and kinetic energy are conserved, but Velcro/Velcro® collisions are inelastic and momentum is conserved, but kinetic energy is not. (2) The collision was elastic and the total momentum and the total kinetic energy were conserved. (3) The total momentum was conserved, but the total kinetic energy was not, indicating that the collision was inelastic. (4) There was relative speed between the approaching balls but none following impact, so the collision was inelastic. (5) Crumpled parts indicate that work was done (energy was expended) on the car so kinetic energy was not conserved and the collision was inelastic. (6) In a front end collision, the bumpers and fenders of both cars crumple (kinetic energy is converted to heat and deformation) and "give" so the momentum of the cars is decreased over a longer period of time than would happen in an elastic collision. It is less damaging to the passengers if the cars stick together than if they bounce apart. If, for example, an object strikes a wall and sticks, the change in momentum is p, but if it strikes the wall elastically the change in momentum is $p - (-p) = 2p$. The greater the change in momentum, the more damaging the collision, indicating that elastic collisions are more hazardous than inelastic ones. (7) Since momentum must be conserved we have $(4000 \text{ kg})(10 \text{ m/s}) + (1400 \text{ kg})(0 \text{ m/s}) = (5400 \text{ kg})v_3$. The final velocity of the combined vehicles is $v_3 = 7.4 \text{ m/s}$. The original kinetic energy is $1/2 (4000 \text{ kg})(10 \text{ m/s})^2 = 200,000$ joules, but the final kinetic energy is only $1/2 (5400 \text{ kg}) (7.4 \text{ m/s})^2 = 150,000$ joules, indicating a loss in kinetic energy of 25 percent. The "missing" 50,000 joules of kinetic energy was converted into heat and work as the vehicles crumpled.

5.3.3 Conservation of Momentum

Discussion: These experiments may be performed as instructor demonstrations if clear rulers or the hanging ball apparatus are placed upon the overhead.

Part 1: To predict what will occur following the collisions specified in this activity, students must have an understanding of the conservation of energy and the conservation of momentum. Both momentum and kinetic energy must be conserved. Predictions based only upon conservation of momentum or conservation of kinetic energy may be inaccurate. For example, momentum is conserved when two balls of mass m collide with velocity v with five stationary marbles, and one marble leaves with momentum $m(2v)$, but kinetic energy is not conserved: $1/2 \, mv^2 + 1/2 \, mv^2$ is not equal to $1/2 \, m(2v)^2$. The single marble traveling away at velocity $2v$ would have twice the total kinetic energy of the incoming marbles—clearly a violation of the law of the conservation of energy. Be certain that students understand that both momentum and kinetic energy must be conserved in an elastic collision.

Part 2: Students should understand that if collisions are elastic, as can be assumed in these activities, there is no loss of kinetic energy and the relative speed of the marbles before and after collision is the same. When a massive marble collides with a small, stationary marble, they both move in the same direction, with the small marble moving faster. When a small marble collides with a massive stationary marble, the marbles move apart in opposite directions with the less massive marble moving at greater speed. In all cases both momentum and kinetic energy must be conserved.

Answers (1) The initial momentum of the system is zero, and so the final momentum must be zero. Therefore, $mv_1 + m(-v_1) = 0 = m(-v_1) + mv_1$. The quantity, $-v$, indicates a reversal in direction of a marble. (2) If two marbles move off with half the velocity of the incoming marble, momentum would be conserved, but not kinetic energy. If one marble moves off with the velocity of the incoming marble both momentum and kinetic energy are conserved. See discussion. (3) The relative speed of approaching marbles is 10 m/s and relative speed of separation is 10 m/s, showing that collision is perfectly elastic because both momentum and kinetic energy are conserved. (4) The momentum of the system (you and the ball) is zero. If you throw the ball in one direction, conservation of momentum indicates you will move in the opposite direction with the same momentum as the ball. If you push the ball away and then decide to retain it, all the horizontal forces on the ball are internal and there is no net change in momentum and no net movement of you in the opposite direction. (5) Momentum is conserved in the collision. Assuming that m_1 and v_1 are the mass and velocity of the 2-kg cart and m_2 and v_2 are the mass and velocity of the 1-kg cart, we have: $m_1v_1 + m_2v_2 = m_1v_1' + m_2v_2'$. Substituting known values we have: 25 kg·m/s = $2kg·v_1' + 1kg·v_2'$. Kinetic energy is conserved in the collision so we have: $1/2 (m_1v_1^2) + 1/2 (m_2v_2^2) = 1/2 m_1v_1'^2 + 1/2 m_2v_2'^2$. Substituting known values gives: 225 kg·m²/s² = $2kg·v_1'^2 + 1kg·v_2'^2$. Solving these two simultaneous equations using the quadratic equation yields: v_1' (velocity of 2-kg cart) = 6.7 m/s and v_2' (velocity of 1-kg cart) = 11.6 m/s.

5.3.4 Impulse and Momentum

Discussion: Impulse is force multiplied by the time it acts. The time during which a force acts (time required to bring momentum to zero) on a body may be used to explain many phenomena. The winners of the balloon-catching activity are the students who apply the least force to the balloon by bringing its momentum to zero in the greatest amount of time after the balloon makes contact with their hands. In a similar manner, the egg or balloon is less likely to break when rolled into a wall if straw is placed in front since the straw allows the momentum to be brought to zero over a longer period of time, and hence the balloon is topped with less force.

Answers (1) See discussion. (2) The wall exerts greater force because it stops the balloon or egg in less time. Since $F = (m\Delta v)/\Delta t$, the force is greatest when the time required to bring momentum to zero is smallest. (3) The jockey and the bike rider stand in the stirrups to lessen the force on their bodies by bending legs to increase the time over which each impact is absorbed (decreasing momentum over a longer time). (4) Bent legs act like a spring, increasing the time over which momentum is brought to zero and decreasing the jarring to your body. Those learning to skydive sometimes break their legs upon landing because they do not flex their legs and roll when landing. (5) The water decreases the diver's momentum over a much longer time than does the concrete, and as a result, the force applied to the diver's body is considerably less.

5.3.5 Conservation of Angular Momentum

Discussion

Part 1: It is difficult to release the coin simultaneously from your thumb and finger. The last point of contact with the fingers serves as a pivot point about which the coin will rotate as gravity acts on the center of mass. If you impart a quick spin to the coin before dropping, the coin's angular momentum will resist such a torque and the coin will fall in a horizontal position. This principle also applies when dropping the penny on top of the quarter, as illustrated in Figure P. Although other combinations of coins will work, the copper color of the penny contrasts with the silver color of the quarter, allowing you to make observations more easily.

Part 2: Please see the discussion in the following section on precession.

Answers (1) Angular momentum imparted to the coin resists any torque of gravity to rotate it just as a spinning bicycle wheel resists any attempt to change the orientation of its axle. (2) The penny and quarter will not flip if the quarter is given a twist when released. (3) A quarterback places a spin on the football when releasing it from his hands. This spin imparts angular momentum to the ball, which keeps it stable in the same way the spin keeps the coins stable in this activity. (4) Objects spinning about their major axes possess angular momentum, which helps them resist changes due to external torques. Rifling in the barrel of a gun imparts a spinning motion to the shell, giving it angular momentum that prevents spinning about its horizontal axis and prevents it from tumbling. Angular momentum of the football keeps it on track and prevents it from tumbling. Spinning a basketball before balancing it on a finger gives it angular momentum that resists the torque of gravity to topple it. (5) Angular momentum must be conserved. Angular momentum L is the product of angular velocity ω and the moment of inertia I. When the skater moves her arms in toward her body, her moment of inertia (distribution of mass) decreases, which means her angular velocity must increase if angular momentum is to be conserved.

5.3.6 Precession

Discussion: Gyroscopic motion is difficult to explain and understand, but since it finds application in a multitude of phenomena, we present a rather detailed explanation, some or all of which you may wish to pass on to your students. Figure Y shows the wheel and the various forces and torques that act on it.

Suppose the wheel is not spinning and is supported by two ropes, one attached to each end of the axle. The upward force exerted by each rope would be 1/2 *mg*, each supporting half the weight of the wheel. Suppose we cut one rope. The upward force at point O is 1/2 *mg*, and there is now no upward force supporting the other

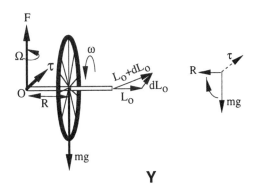

Y

end. Hence the resultant vertical force on the wheel is not zero and the center of mass experiences a downward acceleration and the wheel falls to the ground.

Suppose the wheel is spinning and is again supported by two ropes and again one rope is cut. The upward force at O, at the instant the rope is cut, is still $1/2\ mg$. Again the resultant vertical force is not zero, and the center of mass has an initial downward acceleration. At the same time, the wheel begins to precess (rotate about the rope). The result of this precession causes the end of the axle at point O to press down with a greater force on the rope so that the upward force exerted by the rope at point O becomes greater than mg, the weight of the wheel. The center of mass then begins to accelerate upward. Eventually the up-and-down oscillations, called nutation, become minimal and the wheel settles with its axle in a horizontal position.

Let's examine the spinning wheel in greater detail. The wheel is rotating about the pivot O and the spin axis remains horizontal. If the axis of the wheel were fixed in space, its angular momentum L would equal the product of its moment of inertia I about the axis and its angular velocity ω about the axis and would point along the axis. Because the axis itself is rotating about the pivot in a horizontal plane (such rotation is called precession) with magnitude Ω, the angular momentum vector no longer lies on the axis. However, if the angular velocity Ω of the axis is small compared with the angular velocity ω about the axis, the component of angular momentum resulting from rotation of this axis can be neglected, thus simplifying the analysis because we can assume the angular momentum points along the axis.

The angular momentum vector L_o, about point O, lies along the axis as shown. As the wheel and its axis rotate about O, its angular momentum vector rotates with it. The upward force F at the pivot point O exerts no torque because there is no lever arm. The resultant external torque is the product of the weight of the wheel mg and the lever arm R, $\tau = mgR$. The direction of τ is perpendicular to (into the plane of the paper) the axis of the wheel. Remember that torque is a vector and has both magnitude and direction. The direction of the torque can be determined from the right-hand rule that indicates the direction a right-handed screw would advance if located at point O if the force vector mg were rotated clockwise into the lever arm R, R also being a vector (see Figure Y). If the right hand is held so that the curled fingers follow the rotation of mg into R (the direction indicated by the curved arrow), the extended thumb will point in the direction of the torque vector τ, which is into the plane of the paper. Try it.

The torque is horizontal to the axis and can have no effect other than to rotate the axis about point O. In a very short time denoted by dt, this torque produces a change (dL_o) in the angular momentum that has the same direction as the torque τ. After this short time the new angular momentum is $L_o + dL_o$, the vector sum of $L_o + dL_o$, and has the same magnitude as the old, but a different direction. *The direction of the angular momentum vector changes with time, but the magnitude does not.* Inspection of Figure Y shows that the change (dL_o) in direction of the vector L_o moves it in the same direction as the torque vector τ. The angular momentum vector is, so to speak, chasing the torque vector.

Why does the wheel not topple? This is the question that most people ask, because it appears the spinning wheel is defying gravity. Not so. If the wheel is not spinning there is a net torque on the center of gravity and the wheel falls, but if the wheel is spinning sufficiently fast, the orientation of the torque changes so no net torque remains on the center of gravity. The upward force F exerted on the wheel by the rope is equal to the wheel's weight mg. Thus, the resultant vertical force is zero and there is no translational motion of the wheel. In other words, the vertical component of the wheel's linear momentum remains zero. The wheel is spinning, and the torque of gravity is directed into the plane of the paper as shown by τ. The wheel does not fall because there is no net force to move it in the vertical plane and no net torque to topple it.

Let's consider the case when the student grasped the handle of the rapidly spinning wheel and tilted it upward and downward. When the student tilted the wheel upward, it swerved to the one side. As we explained earlier, the weight of the wheel multiplied by the distance R produces a torque directed into the paper (to the left). But the student is now applying a force at the handle that acts on the distance R in an upward direction. Consequently, the torque is directed out of the paper to the right. When the wheel is tilted in the downward direction, the situation is reversed and the wheel swerves to the left. When the wheel is tilted by the student, the angular momentum, directed along the axis, is changed. The more rapidly the axis is tilted the more rapid is the change in angular momentum and the greater the resulting torque.

Finally, we explain the rotating platform. The total angular momentum of the system (person, wheel, and platform) must be conserved. The initial angular momentum of the system comes from the spinning wheel, the axis of which is being held in a vertical position parallel to the spin axis of the platform. The student now supplies the torque required to tilt the axis toward the horizontal. This torque is internal to the system as we have defined it. Since there is no external component of torque on the system about the vertical axis of the platform (gravity acts parallel to the axis and cannot exert such a torque), the vertical component of angular momentum of the system must be conserved. As the wheel is tilted from the vertical toward the horizontal, it contributes successively less and less of the vertical component of angular momentum required in the conservation of angular momentum. Consequently, the student and platform must supply the additional angular momentum about the vertical axes, and they begin to rotate about a vertical axis. If the wheel is spinning clockwise as viewed by the student holding it, then the platform will also rotate clockwise as viewed by the student.

Answers (1) When not spinning, the wheel has no angular momentum. Gravity acts on the center of mass to topple it. A spinning wheel has angular momentum, but the torque of gravity on the spinning wheel is directed parallel to the ground and therefore changes the direction of the axle in this plane. There is no unbalanced torque to topple the wheel. (2) The inclination of the Earth with its orbit (23.5 degrees) causes the seasons. Summer occurs in the northern hemisphere when the north end of the axis is inclined toward the sun, and winter occurs when it is inclined away from the sun. As the Earth precesses, eventually the north end of the Earth's axis will point toward the sun during the months of December to March, and the period we now identify as winter will be "summer."

Applications to Everyday Life

Transportation Safety: Airbags, seat belts, shock-absorbing bumpers, and padded dashboards all act to protect passengers in a collision by decreasing momentum of the passengers over the greatest time possible during a collision. This is advantageous since a smaller force acting for a longer time will cause less damage than a larger force acting for a shorter time.

Baseball: When catching a baseball, the player first moves his hands toward the ball so that when the ball arrives the hands may be pulled back to cushion the impact (decrease momentum over a longer time) and minimize the force. Baseball players swing hard at the ball, and the high speed of the bat means the time of contact will be small so the force will be large *(mΔv = FΔt)*. Players also follow through on their swings to maximize contact with the ball (maximizing impulse) to give it the greatest velocity possible.

Preventing Sea-Sickness: Many cruise ships employ large gyros in their hulls to stabilize the ship's motion. This dampens the rolling motion of the waves and helps prevent seasickness among the crew and passengers.

Bungee Diving and Rock Climbing: The rapid motion of a Bungee diver is arrested as the Bungee cords change the diver's momentum to zero slowly as the cords stretch. The cord increases the time of impact, thus decreasing the force on the diver. Rock climbers use nylon ropes that stretch to absorb the impact of a fall, bringing the climber's momentum to zero over a longer time and thereby reducing the injurious forces upon the body.

Jet Aircraft: Some people mistakenly think that after a plane has landed, the jet engines are reversed to slow the plane, but such a reversal would create internal stresses that would tear the engines apart. Instead, the pilot activates a movable metal shield, attached to each engine, which moves behind the engine in the path of the ejected exhaust, causing the exhaust to reverse direction. This provides a force to counteract the forward momentum of the plane and may be quite noticeable by the passengers if the pilot finds it necessary to reduce speed quickly.

Hurricanes and Tornadoes: The rapidly whirling tangential circulation of hurricane and tornado winds can be explained by conservation of angular momentum. Just as an ice skater rotates faster as she brings her arms closer to her body, so too does the air in a hurricane and tornado rotate faster as it moves from an area of high pressure in toward one of low pressure.

Pulsars: Astronomical objects know as pulsars are believed to be rapidly rotating objects. As they shrink, they spin faster, accelerating from a speed of one revolution per three weeks to several revolutions per second.

Earth-Moon System: The Earth and moon serve as a good example of how angular momentum is conserved in a system. They revolve around a common center of gravity (the center of gravity is actually located within the Earth because it is so much more massive than the moon), and each rotates on its own axis. The Earth's spin is gradually slowing down as a result of the influence of the tides. The loss of angular momentum from the Earth's rotation is transferred to the moon's orbit and causes the moon to slowly recede from the Earth about one centimeter per lunar month.

Guidance and Control Systems: A gyroscope acts according to the law of conservation of angular momentum and will resist any attempt to change the direction of the axis about which the rotor spins. Most communications satellites use large rotors for maintaining appropriate orientation. Airplanes and spacecraft, including the Shuttle, use gyros to provide both directional control and stability.

Muskets and Rifles: The musket was introduced in Spain in the mid-1500s and served as the key firearm for armies and militias for more than 200 years until the rifle was introduced. The term "rifle" was derived from "rifling," the shallow spiral grooves etched within the barrel. These etches impart a spin to the bullet in order to give it greater accuracy and stability than could be attained by a spherical musket ball.

5.4 MACHINES

In approximately 2500 B.C., Egyptian King Khufu ordered the construction of the Great Pyramid at Giza, the most massive monument ever built. The Great Pyramid, which was to become Khufu's tomb, measured 230 meters (756 feet) on each side at its base, and 147 meters (482 ft) in height. To build his tomb, Khufu mobilized nearly all of Egypt's male work force. Massive blocks were quarried at sites along the Nile and carried by barges on the river and by sleds on land to the construction site, but it remains a mystery as to how the Egyptians raised these massive blocks into position. It is obvious that machines must have been used; however, we are not certain what they looked like.

A machine is a device that enables work to be done easier or faster. *A machine is used to transform energy, transfer energy, multiply force, multiply speed, or to change the direction of a force.* However, a machine cannot multiply work or energy because the law of conservation of energy states that energy cannot be created or destroyed, meaning that the work output cannot exceed the energy or work input.

All compound machines such as automobiles, airplanes, and power shovels are combinations of the six simple machines: lever, pulley, wheel and axle, inclined plane, wedge, and screw (Figure A). The wedge and screw are themselves variations of the inclined plane, while the pulley and wheel and axle are variations of the lever. Neglecting friction, in any machine the output of work equals the input of work. Since work equals force multiplied by distance, the input (applied) force times input distance must equal the output force (resistance) times output distance ($F_i d_i = F_o d_o$). Solving for the output force we have $F_o = F_i d_i / d_o$. From this equation, it can be seen that the output force can be magnified if the input force F_i is moved through a great distance. A small force moved over a great distance will produce a large force moved over a short distance.

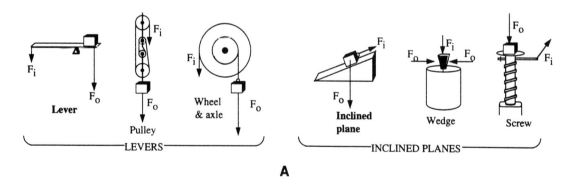

A

One of the simplest machines is the lever. When the fulcrum (pivot point) is nearer the load than the effort, a small input force will produce a large output force, because the input force moves through a greater distance than the output force. The great scientist Archimedes is reported to have stated that, given a sufficiently long lever and a strong fulcrum, he could lift the Earth. Do you agree or disagree with Archimedes?

Examine the six simple machines shown in Figure A. F_i is the input force (often called effort or applied force, E) and F_o is output force (often called resistance, R). Which would you most likely find on a door? Which would be used to split a log? Which would be used to slide a large crate from the street to the bed of a moving van? Which would you use to lift the engine from a car? Which would you use to lift a car to change a flat tire? Which would you use to pry the lid off a can of paint?

We use machines because they provide mechanical advantage that allows us to accomplish tasks otherwise beyond our capabilities. For example, you pull nails with a hammer, not your fingers, because the hammer multiplies the input force. You use a jack to lift a car for the same reason. *The mechanical advantage of a machine is the ratio of the force exerted by the machine to the force applied to the machine.* If you apply 100 N of force and the machine outputs 300 N of force, the mechanical advantage is 300N/100N = 3. In order to gain the mechanical advantage of three you must move the effort force three times the distance of the output force: $F_i d_i = F_o d_o$ = 100 N × 3 meters = 300 N × 1 meter. Once again it is clear that you can't get something for nothing, an expression of the law of the conservation of energy (first law of thermodynamics).

Make a list of ten items commonly found in the kitchen and note how many are machines. Keep track of the first ten things you do after arriving home from school and note which involve the use of machines. This simple activity will demonstrate that machines can be found in every aspect of our lives.

5.4.1 Levers

Concepts to Investigate: First-class levers, second-class levers, third-class levers, multiplying force, multiplying speed, mechanical advantage.

Materials: 2" × 4" beam, saw, ruler.

Principles and Procedures: A lever is a rigid bar free to turn about a fixed point called the fulcrum or pivot point. Figure B shows the three types of levers. The fulcrum f of a first-class lever is always between the input force F_i (effort force, E) and the output force F_o (resistance, R). A first-class lever can be used to multiply either force or distance, depending on the position of the fulcrum. The fulcrum of a second-class lever is always at one end of the lever, and the resistance is between the fulcrum and the effort. This lever can be used only to multiply force. The fulcrum of a third-class lever is also at one end of the lever but the effort is between the fulcrum and the resistance. Consequently, a third-class lever can be used only to multiply distance or speed.

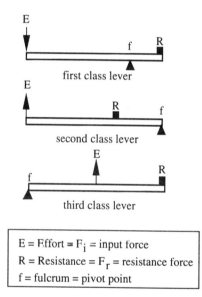

first class lever

second class lever

third class lever

E = Effort = F_i = input force	
R = Resistance = F_r = resistance force	
f = fulcrum = pivot point	

B

Part 1. Using a first-class lever to multiply force and speed: Place a stout beam on a support and position one end of the beam under the lip of a heavy desk as shown in Figure C. Try to raise the desk by pushing at point x, then at point y, and finally at point z. At what point was it easiest to lift the desk? Compare the distance your hand moves when pushing at each point on the beam with the distance moved by the desk. At which point is mechanical advantage greatest?

Now make a seesaw by placing the beam on the support at a point near the center. Push on one end of the beam while progressively moving the support toward the other end. Describe the motion of the other end of the beam. Where should the fulcrum be positioned to multiply force? Where should it be positioned to multiply speed?

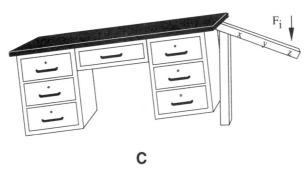

C

Part 2. Using a ruler as a first-, second-, and third-class lever: With your finger as a fulcrum, use the ruler as a first-class lever to lift the side of a book. Use the ruler as a second-class lever to lift the side of the book (the fulcrum will be one end of the ruler). Outside the classroom, use the ruler as a third-class lever to propel an object resting on one end of the ruler. Describe the relationship of the input force, output force, and fulcrum in first-, second-, and third-class levers. Draw diagrams illustrating how you used the ruler as a first-, second-, and third-class lever.

Questions

(1) A first-class lever can be used to multiply either force or speed depending on the position of the fulcrum, while a second-class lever can be used only to multiply force. Explain.

(2) Draw a diagram that shows how a beam can be used either as a first-class lever or as a second-class lever to lift a heavy box.

(3) If a machine is used to gain speed, the input force must be greater than the output force. If a machine is used to gain force, the input force is less than the output force. Explain.

(4) What are three methods to compute the mechanical advantage of a lever?

(5) What type of lever is each of the following: screwdriver used to pry the lid from a paint can, your forearm when throwing a baseball, the paddle of a canoe, a wheelbarrow?

5.4.2 Wheel and Axle

Concepts to Investigate: Simple machines, wheel and axle, mechanical advantage.

Materials: Double corrugated cardboard, string or fishing line, pins, lightweight objects such as clothespins, heavy-gauge wire or heavy-duty paper clips, nail, drawing compass.

Principles and Procedures

Part 1. The mechanical advantage of a wheel and axle: A wheel or crank attached to an axle (Figure D) is a form of a first-class lever with the axis of the axle acting as the fulcrum (Figure E). If you do not have a wheel-and-axle assembly available, you may construct one as follows. Use a compass to draw circles of 5-cm and 10-cm diameters on corrugated cardboard. Carefully cut out the wheels, making certain the edges are smooth. Use a nail to punch a hole in the center of the wheels and then glue them together, as shown in Figure D. Mount the assembly to a board using a nail as shown, enlarging the nail hole if necessary to ensure that the wheel turns freely. Press gently into the rim of each wheel with a blunt tool to make a groove. Wind string over each wheel and attach one end to the groove with a pin.

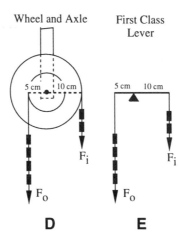

D   E

Attach four clothespins or other equal-weight objects to the free end of the string on the smallest wheel. Attach similar weights to the free end of the string on the larger wheel until the four clothespins are lifted. How many clothespins on the large wheel are required to lift six on the small wheel? How many are required to lift ten clothespins? Try other combinations of weights on the small and large wheels. You can see that a wheel and axle is actually a turning first-class lever and that it can move a load a greater distance than a standard lever because it can continue to revolve. The radius of the larger wheel is equivalent to the longer part of a first-class lever, and the radius of the smaller wheel is equivalent to the shorter part of a first-class lever. What is the theoretical mechanical advantage of the wheel and axle you designed? According to your calculations, what is the actual mechanical advantage (F_o/F_i; output force/input force)? Explain the difference between the theoretical mechanical advantage and the actual mechanical advantage.

Part 2. Cranks: Hold each end of a 15-centimeter piece of heavy metal wire between your thumb and forefinger and twist them in opposite directions as shown in Figure F. (You may use an unfolded heavy-duty paper clip if you have no wire.) Is it easier to spin the wire in one direction or the other? Why or why not? Now use pliers to bend the wire at a right angle about 2 cm from one end to form a crank as shown in Figure G. Grasp the "handle" with one hand and the straight end of the wire with the other hand and twist in opposite directions as before. Which hand "wins"? Now bend the wire approximately 4 cm from the straight end and repeat (Figure H). Which hand "wins" this time? Why? Why is a crank classified as a "wheel and axle"?

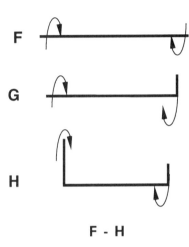

F - H

Questions

(1)   Explain why a wheel and axle is actually a turning first-class lever.

(2)   How many clothespins must be suspended on the large wheel to lift four clothespins on the small wheel? To lift six clothespins? To lift ten clothespins? Is there greater mechanical advantage when the effort force is applied to the wheel or to the axle?

(3)   If a weight of 12 N is suspended from the small wheel used in this activity, how many newtons of force would be required on the larger wheel to lift it? (Neglect friction.)

(4)   Automobile steering wheels, doorknobs, faucet handles, and cranks are examples of a wheel and axle. Explain.

(5)   What is the mechanical advantage of a screwdriver, used as a wheel and axle, if its blade is 0.90 centimeters wide and the handle is 3.6 centimeters in diameter?

(6)   What advantage would there be to applying effort to the axle rather than to the wheel? Give an example.

5.4.3 Pulleys

Concepts to Investigate: Simple machines, pulleys, block and tackle, mechanical advantage, machine efficiency.

Materials: Pulleys (or empty thread spools of the same size, wire coat hangers and string), broomsticks or heavy dowels, rope, spring balance.

Principles and Procedures: A pulley is a simple machine used to multiply and/or change the direction of an applied force. It consists of a wheel with a grooved rim in which a rope or chain is pulled and is used to raise many objects, including flags, awnings, venetian blinds, elevators, scaffolding, and automobile engines. Inexpensive pulleys are available at hardware stores, but if you are unable to obtain these you may construct your own using spools and wire coat hangers. Cut off both "shoulder wires" of a hanger about 20 cm from the hook, bend the wires at right angles, pass the ends through the spool, and bend them down (Figure I).

Part 1. Simple pulleys and block and tackle: Suspend one pulley as shown in Figure J and pass a length of string over it, tying a hook made of a paper clip or heavy wire to each end. Attach an object of known weight to one end of the string and a spring scale to the other end. Determine the force required to lift the weight. Repeat with a second object of different weight. Pull the string a distance of 20 centimeters and record the distance moved by the weight. Does the single pulley magnify force, multiply speed, or simply change the direction of the applied force?

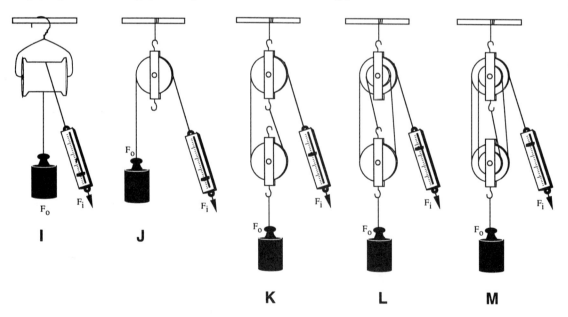

Position two pulleys in a block-and-tackle arrangement as shown in Figure K. Attach an object of known weight to the lower pulley and a scale to the string extending from the upper fixed pulley. Record the force necessary to lift the objects and the distance moved by the weight when the scale is moved 20 centimeters. Knowing that the efficiency of a machine is defined as the ratio of the work output to the work input, compute the efficiency and mechanical advantage for your block and tackle and compare it to the simple pulley. What is the relationship between distance moved by the scale and distance moved by the weight? What is the theoretical mechanical advantage of the combination of pulleys? Repeat the process with a three-pulley system (Figure L) and a four-pulley system (Figure M). Record your results in the table. What is gained each time a pulley is added to the system? What is lost?

Number of Pulleys	Scale Reading	Distance Scale Moved	Work Input	Weight	Distance Weight Moved	Work Output	Efficiency (work output)/(work input) × 100%	Mechanical Advantage
	F_i	d_i	$F_i \times d_i$	F_o	d_o	$F_o \times d_o$	E	F_o / F_i
1	N	m	N·m	N	m	N·m		
1	N	m	N·m	N	m	N·m		
2	N	m	N·m	N	m	N·m		
2	N	m	N·m	N	m	N·m		
3	N	m	N·m	N	m	N·m		
3	N	m	N·m	N	m	N·m		

Part 2. Broomstick pulleys: Tie one end of a rope to a broomstick and wrap the other end once around a second broomstick, as shown in Figure N. While your partners try to hold the sticks apart (Figure Q), try to pull them together by pulling on the free end of the rope. Wrap the rope around one more time (Figure O) and repeat. Is it easier or more difficult than before? Why? Wrap the rope again (Figure P) and pull again. How many times must you wrap the rope until you are able to overcome the force applied by your two partners? In which case is the mechanical advantage greatest?

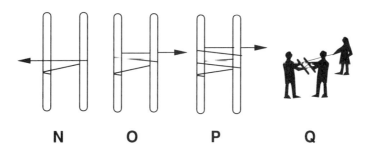

N   **O**   **P**   **Q**

Questions

(1) The top pulley hanging from the support produces only a change in direction of the effort force and not any mechanical advantage. Explain.

(2) Determine the relationship between the number of strands supporting a block and tackle and its mechanical advantage.

(3)   What is the mechanical advantage of the arrangement of pulleys shown in Figure M?

(4)   If there are sufficient loops of rope around the broomsticks (Part 2) the person pulling the rope is generally able to pull the sticks together no matter how hard the others try to keep the sticks apart. Explain.

(5)   A force of 510 newtons is exerted on the rope of a block and tackle, and the rope is pulled 9.1 meters, lifting a weight of 2,500 newtons 1.6 meters. What work was put into the machine? What was the work output? What was the efficiency? What was the theoretical mechanical advantage? The actual mechanical advantage?

5.4.4 Inclined Plane, Wedge, and Screw

Concepts to Investigate: Inclined plane, wedge, screw, mechanical advantage, conservation of energy.

Materials: Boards, smooth blocks of wood, books, pencil, paper, wagon, protractor.

Principles and Procedures: Inclined planes are used when we wish to increase the height or elevation of an object without exerting the force to lift it vertically. Inclined planes are very common: a road that climbs over a hill, a ramp extending from the back of a moving van, a ramp leading from one level of a parking garage to the next. A double-edged ax is a double-inclined plane, while a screw is an inclined plane wound upon a cylinder.

The work required to push an object up a frictionless ramp is dependent only upon the weight of the object and the vertical distance it is lifted $(W = f \times d)$. The work is the same whether the object is lifted vertically or pushed up a slope. The advantage of a gentle slope is that it decreases the required effort force by increasing the distance this force must move. Since work W is constant, the required force can be minimized by increasing the distance through which it moves.

Part 1. Inclined plane: Support one end of the wooden plank on bricks. With your partner sitting in a wagon, pull it up the incline. Place another layer of bricks on the first layer to increase the angle of incline and repeat the activity. Is it more difficult to pull the wagon? Why? Does it require more energy or just more force? Explain.

Part 2. Inclined plane and mechanical advantage: Construct an inclined plane as illustrated in Figure R. Determine the theoretical mechanical advantage *MA* of the inclined plane by dividing the length of the plane by the height. Attach a spring scale graduated in newtons to a heavy block with smooth, flat sides. Slowly pull the block to the top of the incline at a constant rate and read the scale. Place the block on the floor, attach the scale, and lift the block vertically at a constant rate (Figure S). Determine the actual mechanical advantage of the inclined plane by dividing the force required to lift the block vertically by the force required to pull it at constant speed up the incline. Why is the actual mechanical advantage less than the theoret-

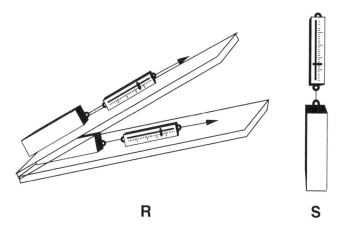

R   S

ical mechanical advantage? Repeat with various blocks and various angles of inclination.

The work required to pull the block to the top of the inclined plane is equal to the length of the plane multiplied by the force used. Compute this work using the reading on the scale when pulling the block up the incline. Compute the work required to lift the block vertically by multiplying the weight of the block by the height of the inclined plane. Do inclined planes multiply work?

Weight of Block	Angle of Incline	Applied Force	Actual MA	Theoretical MA Length/Height	Work: (theoretical)	Work: (calculated)
N	°	N			J	J
N	°	N			J	J
N	°	N			J	J
N	°	N			J	J

Part 3. Wedge: A wedge is a double-inclined plane shown in Figure T. Most cutting tools such as chisels, needles, axes, and can openers are wedges. Use a saw to cut two wedges from a block of wood, one 30 cm long and 5 cm high and the other 15 cm long and 5 cm high. Use a wedge to lift a heavy desk. Place a wedge under the leg of a heavy desk or table. Tap on the wedge with a hammer until the desk is raised to the height of the wedge (Figure U). Repeat with the other wedge. Which wedge must you strike harder to lift the table? Which wedge has the greater mechanical advantage? Why?

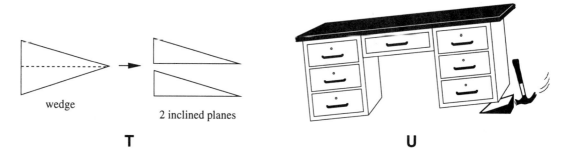

wedge   2 inclined planes

T   **U**

Part 4. A screw is an inclined plane: Cut out a sheet of paper in the shape of a right triangle and wind it around a pencil as shown in Figure V, beginning with a side of the triangle and rolling toward a point. Remove the paper from the pencil and then rewrap it, making the distance between the wrappings (threads) less (Figure W). You can see that a screw is actually an inclined plane wound upon a cylinder. Which screw, V or W, has the greatest mechanical advantage? What do you sacrifice as you increase mechanical advantage?

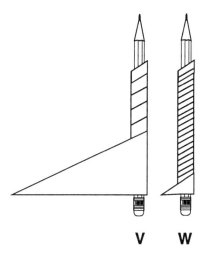

V   W

A screw is a machine that can provide great mechanical advantage and can be used to lift large weights such as when a bumper jack lifts the front of an automobile. The effort force may be applied by a screwdriver or wrench at the head of the screw. The distance d between the threads is called the pitch of the screw. If r is the length of the lever arm upon which the effort force acts, in one revolution the force will complete a circle of radius r and the screw will move a distance d. Consequently, the mechanical advantage of this lever arm-screw combination is $2\pi r/d$.

Questions

(1) What is the relationship among an inclined plane, a wedge, and a screw?

(2) Neglecting friction, what is the shortest plank that could be used to enable you to exert a force of 250 newtons parallel to the plank to push a barrel that weighs 1,250 newtons onto a platform 1.5 m high?

(3) A wedge is a modified plane in which the plane rather than the resistance is moved. Name several tools, such as a knife, that are actually wedges.

(4) Which of the "screws" in Figures V and W has the greatest mechanical advantage? Explain.

(5) A wrench is being used to tighten a bolt. The distance from the end of the handle of the wrench to the center of the bolt is 25 cm. A force of 100 newtons is exerted at the end of the wrench handle. If the pitch of the threads on the bolt is 6 threads to the centimeter, what is the mechanical advantage of this machine (wrench + bolt)? Neglecting friction, what effort force is required to provide a tightening force of 178,000 newtons?

5.4.5 Gears, Chains, and Belts

Concepts to Investigate: Gears, chains, belts, compound machines, gear ratios, mechanical advantage, multiplication of speed, multiplication of force.

Materials: Ten-speed bicycle.

Principles and Procedures: Gears are a series of levers and may be used to multiply force, multiply speed, or change direction. They are found in many compound machines (machines composed of more than one simple machine) including automobiles, bicycles, clocks, and photocopy machines.

If you do not have a set of commercial gears you may make some out of heavy cardboard or wood and mount them on a board with nails through their centers so they turn freely. One of the gears shown in Figure X has eight cogs, while the other has four. By applying force to the smaller gear as it turns the larger gear, a mechanical advantage of 2 is obtained. By applying force to the larger gear as it turns the smaller gear, a speed advantage of 2 is obtained. For every revolution of the larger gear there are two revolutions of the smaller gear. Mechanical advantage or speed advantage can be determined by calculating the gear ratio, the ratio of the number of cogs on the driven gear to the number of cogs on the driving gear, or the ratio of the number of revolutions of the drive gear to the number of revolutions of the driven gear. Speed is magnified when the gear ratio is low, while force is magnified when the gear ratio is high.

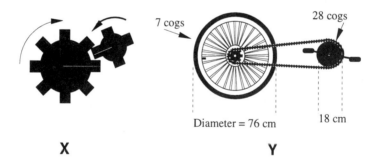

7 cogs   28 cogs

Diameter = 76 cm   18 cm

X   Y

When a car starts from rest in first gear, the gear ratio might be 3 to 1 (3:1) meaning that the crankshaft (connected to the engine) turns three times to turn the drive shaft (connected to the wheels) once. After the car gains some speed, the transmission is shifted into second gear, with a gear ratio of perhaps 2:1, meaning that the crank shaft turns twice to turn the drive shaft once. To increase speed, the car may eventually shift into high gear in which the gear ratio may be 1:1, indicating that the crankshaft turns once to turn the drive shaft once.

In some machines such as a bicycle, gears do not come into direct contact, and a chain or belt is used to connect them and transfer energy. Inspect Figure Y, which shows the rear wheel and the rear and front sprockets of a bicycle. Given 28 cogs on the drive gear (front) to 7 cogs on the driven (rear) gear, the bicycle will have a gear ratio of 1:4, meaning that for every revolution of the pedals, the rear wheel will make four revolutions (28/7 = 4). The effort supplied by the rider's foot moves $2\pi r$

= 2 × 3.14 × 18 cm = 113 cm, while the rear wheel moves 4 × 2πr = 4 × 2 × 3.14 × 38 cm = 955 cm. Thus, the wheel moves nearly 9 times as far as the foot in the same amount of time. In other words, the gears multiply speed by a factor of 9.

Ten-speed bicycles typically have a chain that can engage two gears (e.g., 52 and 39 cogs) at the pedals and five gears (e.g., 28, 24, 20, 17, 14 cogs) at the rear wheel for a total of ten combinations. If, for example, the 39-cog crank gear is connected to the 28-cog wheel gear, the gear ratio is = 1:1.4 (39/28 = 1.4), meaning that for every revolution of the pedals the rear wheel will make 1.4 revolutions, providing a small speed advantage.

Count the number of cogs on the front and rear gears of a bicycle and determine the speed advantage for each combination. Turn a bicycle upside down and mark a location on the wheel with a piece of tape. Slowly move the crank through one complete revolution and record the number of revolutions of the wheel during this same period. The observed gear ratio (the ratio of the number of revolutions of the pedal to the number of revolutions of the wheel) should be the same as the calculated gear ratio (ratio of the number of cogs in the driven gear to the number of cogs in the drive gear). If you have no access to a bicycle, use the following numbers to calculate gear ratios: cogs on drive gears 52, 39; cogs on driven gears: 28, 24, 20, 17, 14. Which gear combination provides the greatest speed? Which gear combination provides the greatest mechanical advantage for riding up steep hills?

Pedal Gear	Cogs	Wheel Gear	Cogs	Gear Ratio (calculated)	Revolution of Pedal	Revolutions of Wheel	Gear Ratio (observed)
1 (smallest)		1 (smallest)			1		
1		2			1		
1		3			1		
1		4			1		
1		5 (largest)			1		
2 (largest)		1 (smallest)			1		
2		2			1		
2		3			1		
2		4			1		
2		5 (largest)			1		

Questions

(1) Identify some devices in and around your home that include either belt- or chain-drive power transmission.

(2) Two gears in contact are actually a series of first-class levers. Explain.

(3) A gear with 16 cogs meshes with a gear of 32 cogs. If the first turns the second, what is the mechanical advantage? If the second turns the first, what is the mechanical advantage?

(4) Why do racing and mountain bikes provide 10 or more gear combinations?

5.4.6 Compound Machines

Concepts to Investigate: Compound machines, block and tackle (pulley), inclined plane, efficiency of compound machines.

Materials: Board, bricks, metric ruler.

Principles and Procedures: A combination of two or more simple machines is called a compound machine. *The total mechanical advantage of a compond machine is the product of the separate mechanical advantages of the simple machines of which it is composed.*

The mechanical advantage of an inclined plane is equal to the length of the plane divided by the height: $MA_{(plane)} = l/h$. The mechanical advantage of a hanging pulley is equal to the number of supporting ropes (those ropes that are attached to the pulley or its frame): $MA_{(pulley)} = \#$ supporting ropes. Therefore, the mechanical advantage of a compound machine made of a pulley and plane should equal the product of both mechanical advantages: $MA_{(compound)} = MA_{(plane)} \times MA_{(pulley)} = (l/h) \times (\#$ supporting ropes). Let's test this assertion.

Determine the weight of an object using a spring balance, as illustrated in Figure Z. Determine the force needed to pull the object up an inclined plane at constant speed (Figure AA) and the mechanical advantage of the plane by dividing the object's weight by this force. Determine the mechanical advantage of the pulley system illustrated in Figure BB by dividing the weight of the object by the force necessary to lift it using the block and tackle. Theoretically, the mechanical advantage of using both these machines together should be the product of their individual mechanical advantages. Compare this value with the mechanical advantage determined by dividing the weight of the object by the force necessary to move it up the inclined plane using the compound machine illustrated in Figure CC. Record your results in the table.

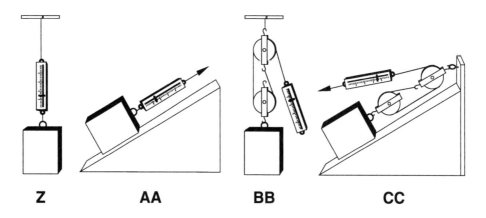

| Z | AA | BB | CC |

Weight of object	N	Weight of Object	N	Weight of Object	N
Force measured on inclined plane	N	Force measured on pulley	N	Force measured on plane-pulley	N
Mechanical advantage of plane		Mechanical advantage of pulley		Calculated Mechanical Advantage of plane-pulley	
Calculated Mechanical Advantage of Plane-Pulley_____ System				Measured Mechanical Advantage of Plane-pulley_____ system	

Questions

(1) Give some examples of compound machines used in your everyday life.

(2) The mechanical advantage of a compound machine is the product of the mechanical advantages of the simple machines of which it is composed. Explain and give examples.

(3) That is the theoretical mechanical advantage of the compound machine illustrated in Figure DD?

(4) The front sprocket of a bicycle has 32 cogs and the rear sprocket has 8. If the diameter of the bicycle wheel is 76 cm, how far forward does the bicycle move with one complete turn of the pedals? If the pedals revolve at the rate of 45 times per minute, what is the speed of the bicycle?

(5) A car weighing 18,000 newtons must be pulled up an inclined plane 6 meters in length onto a truck bed 1.2 meters high. A series of pulleys (block and tackle) in which 5 strands support the moveable block is attached to the car. If two students, each pulling with a force of 560 newtons, are required to move the car, what is the efficiency of the compound machine (inclined plane + pulleys)?

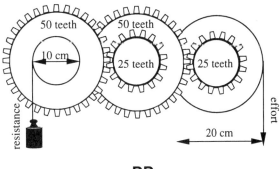

DD

FOR THE TEACHER

Impress upon your students that whenever they use even the most common of articles such as a comb, fork, nail clipper, or bicycle, they are using machines. Machines, both simple and compound, are ubiquitous. Machines make life easier for all of us. To convince students that machines are an essential part of their lives, ask them to carefully examine one room in their home, such as the kitchen or garage, and to identify all the devices that are applications of one or more of the machines studied in this chapter. All compound machines are combinations of simple machines, and all simple machines are variations of two basic machines, the lever and the inclined plane. A pulley and wheel and axle are modifications of levers, while the screw and wedge are modifications of the inclined plane. Thus, all complex machines, including automobiles, industrial robots, and household appliances are combinations of levers and inclined planes. Although they may include electrical and thermal elements, their mechanical components are based upon the principle of the lever or the inclined plane.

The wheel was certainly one of the greatest inventions in history. For our modern society, the crank, which is a variation of the wheel and axle, is a particularly important invention because, when used in conjunction with a connecting rod, it can convert linear motion of pistons to rotary motion of crankshafts. This process is used in the internal combustion engines that power most of the vehicles that travel the streets and highways of our world.

We use machines to provide mechanical advantage, multiplying either force or speed, but not both. When a simple machine magnifies force, the effort force must move through a greater distance than the output force. *For any simple machine, mechanical advantage equals (a) the resisting (output) force divided by the acting (effort) force, or (b) the distance the acting force moves divided by the distance the resisting force moves. Compound machines are combinations of two or more simple machines, and the net mechanical advantage is equal to the product of the separate mechanical advantages.* When a machine is used to magnify speed (distance traveled per unit time), an input force greater than the output force must be applied. Machines can be used to transfer energy, but they cannot multiply work. *Friction demands that work input into a machine is always less than the work output from that machine.* No machine is 100 percent efficient.

5.4.1 Levers

Discussion: Allow students to experiment with a wide variety of the three types of levers and have them give many examples of each. In what could be quite a dramatic classroom demonstration, show students that a long stout, pole can be used to lift a massive object if the fulcrum is sufficiently close to the object. Show students how a heavy desk can't be lifted if the d_i/d_o ratio (distance moved by the input force relative to the distance moved by the output force) is small, but can be lifted if the ratio is large. Request students to make a list of all the devices in their homes that are levers and to compare their lists. Make certain students understand that the efficiency of any machine is always less than unity (one) due to friction—the output work of a machine is always less than the input work. Encourage students to challenge Archimedes' claim that, given a sufficiently long lever he could lift the Earth. One of the problems students might suggest is that there is nothing that might serve as a fulcrum!

Answers (1) If the effort arm is shorter than the resistance arm, a first-class lever is used to gain speed, and if the effort arm is longer than the resistance arm, to gain force. In a second-class lever the resistance is always somewhere between the fulcrum and the effort, so the effort arm is always greater than the resistance arm, and the lever can multiply force, but not speed. (2) Student diagrams should resemble those shown in Figure B. (3) In the absence of friction, the input work must equal the output work. In other words, the product of the input force F_i and the distance this force moves d_i must equal the product of the output force F_o and the distance through which it moves: $F_i d_i = F_o d_o$. To gain speed, d_o must be greater than d_i, and consequently F_i must be greater than F_o. To gain force, d_i must be greater than d_o, and consequently F_o must be greater than F_i. (4) The distance moved by the effort and the distance moved by the resistance are proportional to the lengths of the lever arms upon which they act. Consequently, $d_i/d_o = d_{ea}/d_{ra}$, where d_{ea} is length of effort arm and d_{ra} is length of resistance arm. Hence, to find mechanical advantage of a lever, divide d_i by d_o, divide d_{ea} by d_{ra}, or divide F_o by F_i. (5) A screwdriver used to pry the lid from a paint can is a first-class lever; your forearm when throwing a baseball is a third-class lever; the paddle of a canoe is a third-class lever; a wheelbarrow is a second-class lever.

5.4.2 Wheel and Axle

Discussion: Use diagrams to show students that a wheel and axle is actually a lever with unequal arms. Ask them to locate pictures in various magazines and advertisements that show examples of the wheel and axle, such as doorknobs, crank can openers, electric mixers, and parts of compound machines such as lawnmowers, automobile engines, and bicycles. When the effort is applied to the wheel, force is magnified. When the effort is applied to the axle, speed is magnified.

Answers (1) An imaginary lever passes through the center of the wheel. One arm extends from the perimeter of the wheel to the center of the axle while the other extends from the perimeter of the axle to its center. The center of the axle serves as the fulcrum. See Figure E. (2) Student answers will differ depending on the frictional forces involved; however, the number of clothespins attached to the large wheel should always be less than the number attached to the axle (small wheel). If the diameter of the "wheel" is twice the diameter of the "axle" the machine will have a mechanical advantage of 2. As a result, only two clothespins hanging from the wheel should be required to lift four suspended from the axle, but frictional forces may necessitate that more be added. (3) The mechanical advantage of the wheel and axle is 2 (10 cm/5 cm). Hence 6 N (12 N/2) would be required. (4) Each of these has a larger wheel secured to a smaller wheel. (5) The mechanical advantage of a wheel and axle is determined by dividing the radius of the larger wheel by the radius of the axle. The mechanical advantage of the screwdriver is $r_1/r_2 = 1.8$ cm$/0.45$ cm $= 4.0$. (6) When effort is applied to the axle rather than to the wheel, speed is magnified at the expense of force. Such arrangements are used to turn the wheels of automobiles.

5.4.3 Pulleys

Discussion: A pulley system consists of one or more grooved wheels, called sheaves, revolving in a frame called a block, connected by a system of ropes known as a tackle, thus the familiar name, block and tackle. The pulleys constructed by your students are sufficient to show how pulleys operate, but there are significant frictional forces involved in their operation. Large commercial pulleys are available that you can use for demonstration purposes. By arranging and combining these in various ways, you can lift quite heavy loads showing students the effect of gaining significant mechanical advantage. You may use Figure EE to help students understand that a supported pulley is a second-class lever.

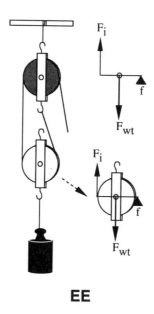

EE

Answers (1) The top pulley is a first-class lever with the fulcrum at the center. Since the effort arm d_i is equal to the resistance arm d_o, no mechanical advantage is possible, only a change in direction of the applied force. (2) The mechanical advantage of a block and tackle is equal to the number of supporting strands. (The strand to which force is applied is not a supporting strand.) (3) The movable block containing the two pulleys is supported by four strands, and its mechanical advantage is 4. The bottom block is actually a compound machine consisting of two simple machines of the same type—two pulleys. The mechanical advantage of a compound machine is the product of the mechanical advantages of the simple machines of which it is composed. Since the mechanical advantage of one movable pulley is 2, the mechanical advantage of the compound machine is $2 \times 2 = 4$. (4) Although the broomsticks do not actually turn, the rope wrapped around them moves as if they do. The broom-sticks represent a series of pulleys with significant mechanical advantage. The student pulling the rope has this mechanical advantage working for him or her, while the student pulling on the brooms does not. If there were 5 loops, there were 10 strands, and thus the person pulling had a mechanical advantage of 10, neglecting friction. (5) Work input = 510 N × 9.1 m = 4600 $N·m$ = 4600 J. Work output = 2500 N × 1.6 m = 4000 $N·m$ = 4000 J. Efficiency = work output/work input = 4000 J/4600 J = 0.87 = 87%. Theoretical mechanical advantage = 9.1 m/1.6 m = 5.7. Actual mechanical advantage = theoretical mechanical advantage × efficiency = 5.7 × 0.87 = 5.0.

5.4.4 Inclined Plane, Wedge, and Screw

Discussion: Inclined planes are simple machines that can be used to raise an object from one level to another. A wedge is an inclined plane in which the plane rather than the resistance is moved. A screw is an inclined plane wrapped around a cylinder and may have great mechanical advantage as seen in the jackscrew, which is used to lift autos and raise houses. Bring to class a collection of screws and bolts, vehicle jacks, C-clamps, faucets, and other gadgets representative of the many variations of the inclined plane. Ask students to identify additional examples of inclined planes used in their everyday lives.

Answers (1) A wedge and screw are modifications of an inclined plane. (2) Work input = work output: 250 N × (length of plank) = 1250 N × 1.5 m. Length of plank = 1250 N × 1.5 m/250 N = 7.5 m. (3) Answers will vary: ax, hatchet, nail, pin, needle, front tooth, chisel—any item that forces two surfaces apart. (4) The "screw" shown in W has the greatest mechanical advantage because it has the smallest pitch (distance between threads). (5) Since there are 6 threads to the centimeter, the pitch of the screw is 1 cm/6 turns or 0.17 centimeters per turn. The mechanical advantage = $2\pi r$/pitch = 2 × 3.14 × 25 cm/0.17 cm = 920. Effort force required is 178,000 N/920 = 193 N.

5.4.5 Gears, Chains, and Belts

Discussion: Gears can be either meshed directly or connected by chains. The fan belt on an engine is used to transfer energy from the crankshaft to the water pump, alternator, and air conditioner. Ask your students for other examples of belts and chains. Twisting a belt connecting two pulleys will change the direction of one pulley. This can be easily demonstrated by putting pencils into the loops of a rubber band that has been shaped into a "figure 8." Under such circumstances, a clockwise spin of one pencil induces a counterclockwise spin of the other.

Answers (1) Answers will vary: video cassette recorder, tape player, record turntable, lawnmower, rototiller, bicycle, automobile. (2) Use imaginary lines to extend the position of one cog across the gear wheel and it forms a lever (with fulcrum at the center of the wheel) intersecting the imaginary extension of a cog from the second gear wheel. (3) When the first turns the second, the mechanical advantage is 32/16 = 2. If the second turns the first, the mechanical advantage is 16/32 =

0.5. A mechanical advantage greater than one indicates force is multiplied, while a mechanical advantage less than one indicates speed is multiplied. (4) When climbing steep hills, mechanical advantage is required and the rider shifts to lower gears (high-gear ratios) to provide greater torque. When riding on flat terrain, speed can be achieved by shifting to higher gears (low-gear ratios).

5.4.6 Compound Machines

Discussion: Compound machines may have high mechanical advantage, but friction may lower their efficiency. Energy is dissipated with each machine. For example, if each of three simple machines that make a compound machine is 90 percent efficient, then the efficiency of the compound machine is 0.9 x 0.9 x 0.9 = 0.73. Bring compound machines such as axes (lever handle and wedge), push rotary lawn mowers (lever handle, gears, blades), and bicycles and ask students to identify the simple machines from which these are made. Bring a diagram of a large Earth-moving machine such as a power shovel and ask students to identify the many simple machines used in its construction.

Answers (1) Answers may vary and may include such things as a car, bus, truck, bike, motorcycle, airplane, power shovel, road grader, snowplow, food chopper, and so on. (2) If a compound machine is composed of three simple machines with mechanical advantages of 3, 4, and 5, then the mechanical advantage of the compound machine is 3 × 4 × 5 = 60. Some examples: using a crescent wrench to tighten a bolt, using a screwdriver to tighten a screw, using a movable pulley to drag a car up a ramp. (3) The mechanical advantage of the gear train is 4, while the mechanical advantage of the wheel and axle is 2. Therefore, the net mechanical advantage is 8. (4) In one complete turn of the pedals, the rear wheel will revolve 4 times and will move a distance of 4 × 3.14 × 76 cm = 960 cm = 9.6 m. 45 cycles/min. × 9.6 m/cycle = 430 m/min. = 26 km/h. (5) The mechanical advantage of the inclined plane is 6 m/1.2m = 5. The mechanical advantage of the block and tackle is 5. Consequently the theoretical combined mechanical advantage of the compound machine is 5 × 5 = 25. With this mechanical advantage 18,000 N/25 = 720 N should be required to move the car, but 1,120 N were actually required. The efficiency = 720N/1,120N = 0.64 = 64%.

Applications to Everyday Life

Roads: A road climbing an incline such as a hill or mountain is actually an inclined plane. Engineers are careful to make certain that the grade of a road, which is the ratio of the height of an incline to its length, is not so great that vehicles would not be able to climb it. A road that rises 5 meters in 100 meters has a grade of 5 percent. A grade of 3 percent is about the maximum for a good road. Such a road has a mechanical advantage of approximately 33.

"Perpetual-Motion Machines": For centuries people have been trying to develop a mechanical perpetual-motion machine that can continue moving forever once it is started. Such a device can never be built because dissipative forces such as friction ensure that the output work of a machine is always less than the input work. Lubricants may be used to reduce friction greatly, but will not eliminate it, indicating that a perpetual-motion machine can be approximated but never achieved. The closest thing to a perpetual-motion machine is a superconducting ring in which a direct current is established. Once established, the current continues relatively undiminished with time.

Tools: A simple tool is a machine used or worked by hand. A shovel used to lift and throw sand is a third-class lever while a shovel used to pry a rock from the ground is a first-class lever. A small hand-held pencil sharpener is a compound machine consisting of a wheel and axle (the pencil and pencil lead) and an inclined plane, the cutting blade.

Ancient Irrigation Systems: Irrigation is the process of artificially supplying water to land to sustain the growth of crops and was widely used in ancient times as it is at present. Water-lifting machines were developed to lift water from streams and canals to irrigate higher-lying fields. One such machine was a bucket and a counterweight attached to the ends of a pivoted pole in which the bucket was pulled down, filled by hand, and then lifted by the counterweight. The Persian wheel consisted of a chain of buckets that passed over a vertical wheel, turned by a horizontal wheel rotated by a draft animal. Archimedes invented a machine called "Archimedes' screw," which was a large hand-turned screw within a wooden cylinder. This screw lifts water on its wide threads from the end dipped in a source of water. Modern irrigation systems often use powerful electric pumps and a system of pipes to distribute water over great areas.

Human Body: Your body is a magnificent compound machine composed of a myriad simple machines. Your front teeth are wedges that can easily bite through a carrot because the jaw is controlled by strong muscles and acts as a third-class lever. When you munch the carrot on the back molars there is an even stronger force because the jaw is now acting as a second-class lever. When you stand on your tiptoes, your foot is acting as a second-class lever. When you lift an object upward with your hands, with the arms bending at the elbow, your forearms are acting as a third-class lever. When you throw a baseball overhand, your arm is acting as a third-class lever. When you turn your forearm at the elbow, you have a wheel and axle. If you relax your neck muscles, your head slumps forward, not backward, indicating your head is supported by a first-class lever. The trochlear muscle posterior to the eye acts as a pulley to raise your eyes. It is evident that simple or compound machines are found in virtually all internal and external body movements.

Transportation: Think carefully and you will realize it is impossible to move from one location to another without the use of a machine. Your body is a machine for walking and running. Bicycles, automobiles, trucks, buses, trains, and airplanes are machines to move about our world. Rockets and other spacecraft are machines to move beyond our world. Our economy, including industry, commerce, and tourism, could not exist without machines.

UNIT SIX

Waves

6.1 Waves

6.2 Sound

6.3 Transmission of Sound

6.4 Frequency and Wavelength of Sound

6.5 Wave Properties of Sound

6.1 WAVES

While traveling across the Pacific Ocean on a routine mission in February of 1933, the USS *Ramapo* encountered a hurricane with 68-knot winds. The winds from the hurricane helped form waves of 34 meters (112 feet) in height, the tallest sea waves ever recorded. Although the *Ramapo* waves were extremely large for sea waves, they were small compared to the largest tsunamis, or tidal waves. Tidal waves have nothing to do with the tides, but rather result from seismic activity such as volcanoes and earthquakes. In April of 1771 an 85-meter (278-foot) tidal wave appeared off the coast of Ishigaki Island in Japan, tossing an 830-ton block of coral more than 2.1 kilometers (1.3 miles). Tidal waves have been observed moving at a rate of 789 km/h (490 miles/h), and many possess great energy and may destroy entire coastal cities if they reach the coast before dissipating. Fortunately, relatively few people will ever see a tidal wave, but some of us will actively seek the "tamer" waves that routinely crash on our shores. Today, one of the premier locations for surfing is in Waimea Bay, Hawaii, where waves often reach the ridable limit of 9–11 meters (30–35 feet).

Winds can also produce waves in other media, sometimes with damaging effects. In 1940, winds produced devastating transverse waves in the Tacoma Narrows Bridge, one of the country's longest suspension bridges that linked the seaport of Tacoma with Washington's Olympic Peninsula. With time, the constant swaying of the bridge caused it to break apart, and portions fell into the water below. Anyone who has seen footage of the Tacoma Narrows Bridge's destruction is impressed by the energy of the waves that traveled through this steel and concrete structure.

What are waves? *A wave is a displacement or disturbance (vibration) that moves through a medium or space.* A wave involves some quantity or disturbance that changes in magnitude with respect to time at a given location and changes in magnitude from place to place at a given time. Common examples of waves are circular water waves produced when a stone is dropped and strikes the surface of a pond, or sound waves produced by musical instruments. A wave cannot exist only in one place but must extend from one place to another.

Waves transfer energy from one location to another, but they cannot transfer matter. Mechanical waves such as sound require a material medium such as air to propagate while electromagnetic waves such as light require no material medium. Light waves, for example, travel through empty space from the sun to the Earth, while the sound waves generated by the ongoing nuclear reactions in the sun cease when they reach the evacuated regions beyond the sun's surface. Although both mechanical and electromagnetic (light, radio, X-rays, etc.) waves require an energy source, only mechanical waves require an elastic medium for transmission. In this chapter we will investigate the characteristics and applications of mechanical waves.

6.1.1 Wave Characteristics

Concepts to Investigate: Wavelength, amplitude, frequency, period, crest, trough.

Materials: Small plastic or paper cup, string, sand or paint, rolls of white paper about 30 cm wide.

Principles and Procedures

Part 1. Picturing transverse waves: Use a nail to puncture a small hole in the bottom of a paper cup as well as two holes on opposite sides near the rim. (Alternatively, you may melt holes in a plastic cup with a nail that has been heated in the flame of a laboratory burner.) Tie a string through the upper holes as shown in Figure A and cover the bottom hole with a piece of tape. Fill the cup with dark sand or dilute paint. Place a sheet of white paper under the cup. Uncover the hole and swing the cup in a small arc. If the sand or paint does not leak fast enough to make an easily observable straight track on the sheet, increase the diameter of the hole until it does. The swinging cup is a pendulum, and if the arc (amplitude) is small it will undergo simple harmonic motion as discussed in the chapter on periodic motion.

Tie the cup to a support, unroll about one meter of white paper and position one end of this sheet perpendicular to the direction of the cup's swing. The middle of the sheet should be positioned directly under the resting cup. Pull the cup back to the edge of the paper, remove the tape over the hole, and allow the cup to swing as your partner slowly pulls the paper at constant speed in a direction perpendicular to the cup's swing, as illustrated in Figure A.

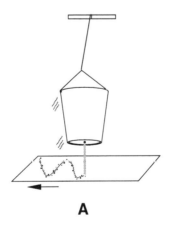

A

The trace left by the paint or sand will be a sine wave such as shown in Figure B. The amplitude of the sine wave represents the maximum displacement of the pendulum (cup) from its rest position. *The distance from crest (high point) to crest or from trough (low point) to trough is called the wavelength (λ).* How can you obtain a wave pattern with the same wavelength but with different amplitude? How can you obtain a wave pattern with the same amplitude but with a shorter wavelength? Experiment with the length of the pendulum and the speed at which the paper is moved until you obtain such wave patterns.

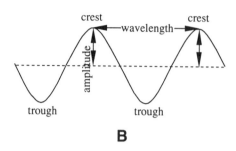

B

Frequency is a measure of the number of waves per unit time and in this activity is determined by how rapidly the pendulum swings. If the pendulum makes one complete swing in a second the frequency is 1 vibration/s, also known as one cycle per second or one hertz (1 Hz). The period is the time required to make one vibration. Since frequency is the number of crests or troughs passing a given point in unit time, and period is the time between the passage of two successive crests or troughs, the relationship between frequency f and period T is reciprocal: $f = 1/T$ or $T = 1/f$. How can you obtain a wave with a longer period? How can you obtain a wave with a higher frequency? Experiment with the length of the pendulum and the speed at which the paper is moved until you obtain such wave patterns.

Part 2. Transverse waves in water: Fill a rectangular pan with water to a depth of about 1.5 cm. Place the pan on a level surface. Cut a wooden dowel (2-cm diameter or thicker) to a length slightly less than the width of the pan and place the dowel in the water at one end. Touch a finger to the dowel and roll it back and forth once and observe the transverse wave move across the water's surface. Roll the dowel back and forth repeatedly and observe the train of waves moving across the water's surface.

The speed of a wave through a given medium is constant. Roll the dowel back and forth at a slow rate and note the length of the wave generated. Roll the dowel back and forth faster (increased frequency) and note that the wavelength is shorter. Roll the dowel even faster and note that the wavelength is shorter yet. These activities show that there is an important relationship between the speed of a wave and the frequency and wavelength of the wave: wave speed is the product of the frequency and wavelength (wave speed = frequency × wavelength). If v is speed, f is frequency, and λ is wavelength we have: $v = f\lambda$. This fundamental relationship is true for waves of any type propagating through any medium, even for electromagnetic waves such as light, which require no material medium for propagation.

Questions

(1) What is a wave? A crest? A trough?
(2) Describe the changes in the waves as you increased the amplitude of the pendulum's swing. Describe the change in the waves as your partner pulled the paper faster and faster when the pendulum's length was the same.
(3) Describe and distinguish between the following characteristics of a wave: frequency, period, amplitude, wavelength.
(4) How are the frequency and period of a wave related? In what units are frequency and period measured?

6.1.2 Transverse and Longitudinal Waves

Concepts to Investigate: Transverse waves, longitudinal waves, wave energy, amplitude, frequency, attenuation.

Materials: Wave demonstration spring (if not available, you may substitute a hose or rope, but the results will not be as striking), 3 or 4 Slinkys®, sandwich-bag twist-ties, rectangular glass tray such as a cake pan or aquarium, wooden dowel (≥2-cm diameter).

Principles and Procedures: Transverse waves displace particles perpendicular to the direction of wave propagation. You can produce transverse waves by fastening one end of a rope or wave spring to a wall or tree and shaking the free end up and down as shown in Figure C. By contrast, longitudinal waves displace particles parallel to the direction of wave propagation. You can produce longitudinal waves by quickly pushing one end of a Slinky® or similar spring back and forth as shown in Figure D.

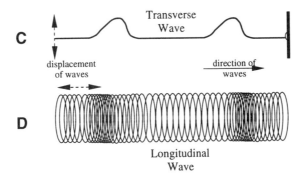

Part 1. Transverse waves: Obtain a demonstration wave spring or tie a series of Slinkys® together using twist-ties or small-gauge wire. While your partner holds one end of the spring firmly, produce one transverse wave by quickly shaking your end back and forth once. Observe the pulse move down the spring. Notice that the amplitude of the wave decreases (attenuates) as it moves because energy is lost due to frictional forces. Now generate a train of transverse waves by shaking your end of the spring back and forth while keeping the amplitude the same. Increase the frequency by shaking the spring more rapidly while keeping the amplitude (the height of the waves) the same. *The power (energy per unit time) transmitted by a mechanical wave is proportional to the square of the frequency.* Consequently, to double the frequency, it is necessary to quadruple the energy input. Does it seem as if you have to put in four times as much energy to double the frequency?

The power (energy per unit time) transmitted by a mechanical wave is proportional to the square of the amplitude. Shake the spring at various amplitudes keeping the frequency the same in each case. If the frequencies of two waves are the same, the wave of greater amplitude carries more energy. If the wave amplitude is doubled, the vibrational energy is quadrupled. Does it seem as if you have to put in four times as much energy to double the amplitude?

Part 2. Longitudinal waves: Fasten a series of Slinkys® together using twist-ties or small-gauge wire. Grasp one end of the spring while your partner grasps the other and produce a longitudinal wave by quickly pushing your end of the spring forward and then pulling it backward. Then produce a train of waves by repeatedly moving the end rhythmically forward and backward. The waves travel along the spring as a series of compressions (coils closer together) and rarefactions (coils farther apart). These compressions and rarefactions are analogous to the crests and troughs of a transverse wave (Figures E and F). The wavelength of a longitudinal wave is the distance between a compression and a rarefaction. Double the frequency of the longitudinal waves. Does it appear that four times as much energy is required to double the frequency?

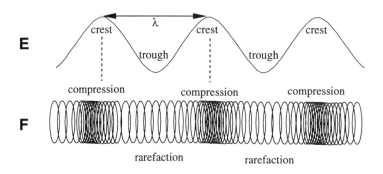

Questions

(1) What is a transverse wave? A longitudinal wave? How can you measure the wavelength of each?

(2) What is the relationship between the energy and amplitude of a wave? What is the relationship between the energy and frequency of a wave?

(3) What is the relationship between the velocity, frequency, and wavelength of a wave?

(4) If the amplitude and frequency of a wave are both increased by a factor of 3, by what factor is the energy of the wave increased?

(5) While sitting in your anchored boat, you notice that waves that you estimate to be of wavelength 2.3 meters pass the anchor chain at the rate of 36 waves every 30 seconds. What is the speed of these waves?

6.1.3 Superposition

Concepts to Investigate: Wave interaction, superposition, constructive interference, destructive interference.

Materials: Wave demonstration spring (a rope may be substituted, but the results will not be as dramatic).

Principles and Procedures: When an ocean wave hits the shore, a smaller reflected wave travels back to sea. When reflected waves meet incoming waves, a brief swell occurs in which the crest of the combined waves equals the sum of the heights of the two individual waves, causing a swimmer or body surfer to rise higher for a brief period of time. While such swells are normally small, they become quite significant when the surf is large. After the swell, one can see the reflected wave continuing out to sea and the incoming wave proceeding to shore, totally unaffected by each other. It is clear from such observations that *waves travel through media independent of each other*. This independence enables us to hear the sound of an individual trumpet in the midst of a marching band and allows our radio receiver to pick up a specific station amidst the variety of radio waves traveling through the atmosphere. From watching the ocean waves, it also becomes clear that *the displacement of water at any time is the vector sum of the displacements of the individual waves acting upon it*. We say that waves *superpose*. If, for example, two waves of magnitude 1 meter cross, the resulting swell will reach a height of 2 meters. Figure G shows the resultant wave (bold line) when two waves of different frequencies meet. Note that at all points, the height of the resultant wave y is the sum of the heights of the component waves y_1, y_2 at that instant.

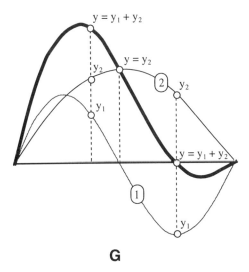

G

Stretch a long wave demonstration spring or rope across an open floor. Both partners should send single pulses with opposite polarity (their crests are on opposite sides of the spring). Do the crests disappear as they cross, as illustrated in Figure H? We refer to the addition of crests and troughs as destructive interference because the resultant wave form is smaller than either component.

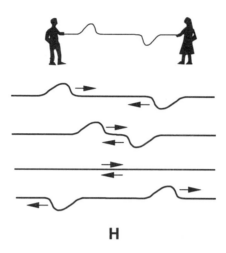

H

Now both partners should send single pulses with similar polarity (their crests are on the same side of the spring). Is the combined wave twice as high where the waves cross? Draw a diagram similar to Figure H that shows what happens as the two waves pass through each other. We refer to the addition of crests to crests or troughs to troughs as constructive interference because the resultant wave form is larger than either component.

Perform the following activity to study the interaction of two standing waves. One student should establish a standing wave while a second student holds the other end of the rope or wave spring, and a third student notes the locations of the nodes and loops and then draws the wave pattern. Although it is possible to create standing waves in the air, it is often easier to do so when the demonstration spring or rope is on the floor. After stopping the motion of the spring, the second student should generate a standing wave pattern of the same amplitude but twice the frequency of the first. The third student should draw this wave pattern, and then the team should predict the wave-form that will appear when both standing waves are generated at the same time (Figures I and J). Produce both waves simultaneously, draw the resulting wave-form, and compare it with the predicted wave-form. Were your predictions correct?

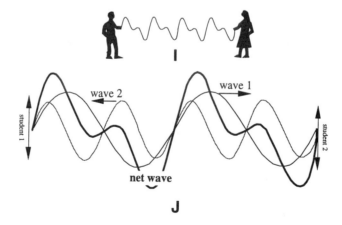

J

Questions

(1)   The French horn produces tones composed almost entirely of the fundamental and second harmonic. Draw the superposed wave on Figure K.

(2)   Why are you able to hear the sound of a single instrument such as a base guitar amidst the collection of sounds generated by a band?

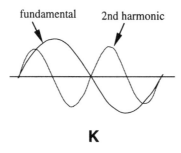

fundamental   2nd harmonic

K

6.1.4 Standing Waves

Concepts to Investigate: Standing waves, constructive interference, destructive interference.

Materials: Coiled spring (long demonstration springs are available from scientific supply firms) or rope, rectangular pan, pencils, tape or string.

Principles and Procedures: Shake one end of a spring or rope that is tied firmly to a wall or other unmovable support to produce a train of waves that moves down the spring, reflects from the end, and travels back in the opposite direction (Figure L). If you shake the rope in such a manner that wavelength, amplitude, and frequency remain constant, the incident and reflected waves will interact to form a standing wave as shown in Figure M. *A standing wave results when two identical waves move through the same medium in opposite directions. It is known as a "standing" wave because it does not move even though its component waves do.*

The points where no movement of the rope occurs are called nodes. The locations where super-troughs and super-crests successively appear are known as antinodes. A standing wave is formed because the waves moving in opposite directions interfere with each other, as shown in Figures N and O. When the crest of one wave overlaps the trough of another, destructive interference occurs and the waves cancel (Figure N). Though the energy-carrying waves are simultaneously passing the same point, there is no visible response of the spring (medium) at that point. When the crest of one wave overlaps the crest of another or the trough of one wave overlaps the trough of another, constructive interference occurs and the waves add (Figure O).

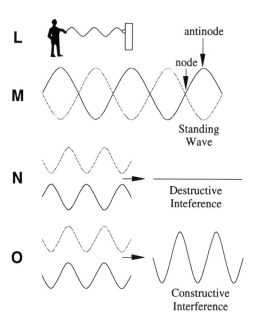

Part 1. Standing waves in a rope or coiled spring: Firmly attach one end of the spring or rope to a solid support and shake it up and down, adjusting the frequency to produce a standing wave of 1/2 wavelength as shown in Figure P. This is the natural frequency for this length of spring and is also referred to as the fundamental frequency. The fundamental frequency is the lowest possible frequency for the formation of standing waves. Shake the spring or rope with twice the frequency to set up a standing wave of 1 wavelength (Figure Q). Shake even faster to set up a wave of 1 1/2 and 2 wavelengths (Figures R and S). The wave patterns in Figures Q, R, and S are referred to as the second, third, and fourth harmonics respectively. Does it require more of your energy to establish the fourth harmonic than the second harmonic? Why or why not? What is the relationship between frequency and energy?

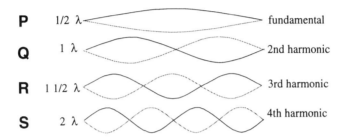

Part 2. Standing waves on the surface of a liquid: Place a clear rectangular tray on an overhead projector and fill with water to a depth of about 1.0 to 1.5 centimeters. Place a board in the pan and move it back and forth at a constant frequency and observe the wave patterns on the screen. Establish the fundamental frequency by adjusting the frequency of the board so that the oscillations just match the round-trip time of a reflected wave. Be patient, since it may take some practice to establish clear standing wave patterns. If you have a wave-generating machine adjust its frequency to establish the second, third, and fourth harmonics.

Part 3. Interference of waves on the surface of a liquid: Fasten two pencils together as shown in Figure T and repeatedly touch the surface of the water at a constant

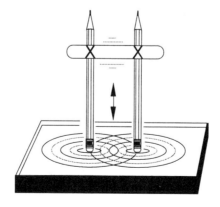

T

frequency. Observe the interactions of the waves. Can you see any evidence of constructive or destructive interference? Draw a diagram of the resulting interference pattern, indicating the nodal lines (where the water appears calm) and the antinodal lines (where the water oscillates up and down vigorously). If you have a wave-generating machine, double the frequency of the waves and draw the resulting interference pattern.

Questions

(1) Two waves that approach each other may undergo constructive or destructive interference. Explain.

(2) What is a standing wave? Explain.

(3) What are nodes? When and how are they produced?

(4) If you hold the base of a goblet to a table and move a moistened finger slowly in a circle around the rim, a distinct sound will be heard. Explain.

6.1.5 Wave Propagation and Interactions

Concepts to Investigate: Rectilinear propagation, wave energy, wave amplitude, angle of incidence, angle of reflection, wave equation $v = f\lambda$, wave speed, reflection, refraction, diffraction, aperture, interference.

Materials: Ripple tank, overhead projector, screen, wave generator, blocks of wood, small plates of glass.

Principles and Procedures: All wave phenomena, whether mechanical or electromagnetic, share the following common properties: rectilinear (straight-line) propagation, reflection, refraction, diffraction, and interference. Propagation refers to how waves move through a medium. Reflection refers to how waves bounce off barriers. Refraction refers to how waves change direction when traveling from one medium to another. Diffraction refers to how waves spread as they move through an opening. Interference refers to how waves add or subtract when passing through each other. In the following activities you will use a wave generator and a ripple tank to study these characteristics of waves. Your instructor can describe how to make an inexpensive wave generator if commercial generators are not available. You may also perform many of these activities simply by moving a dowel back and forth (to generate straight wave fronts) or the blunt ends of pencils up and down (to generate circular wave fronts) in a shallow pan of water, but the results may be more difficult to observe and interpret.

The water waves may reflect off all four sides of the pan rather than just the surface you wish to study. To dampen such reflections, construct a wave fence out of surgical gauze and wire mesh as illustrated in Figure U. Place a fence around all sides of the tank where you wish to prevent reflection.

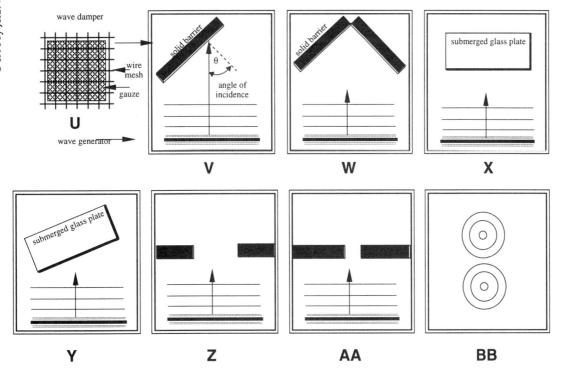

Part 1. Wave propagation, speed, and energy: Float a cork near the center of the tank. Generate a straight wave front with the wave generator and note that the cork moves up and down as the wave passes but does not move in the direction of the wave, showing that waves transmit energy but not matter. Touch the surface of water with the tip of a pencil and observe the circular wave moving out from the source. Again the cork moves up and down but not horizontally.

Start the electric motor of the wave generator at slow speed. When the image is projected down, the wave crests appear as parallel bright lines and the wave troughs are the parallel darker lines. The opposite is true when projected on an overhead screen. The portions of the water's surface in which particles are in the same phase of motion are called wave fronts. The wave moves in a direction perpendicular to these fronts. This is referred to as rectilinear (straight line) propagation.

Increase the speed of the motor and note the inverse relationship between wavelength and frequency—the greater the frequency, the shorter the wavelength. Increase the amplitude of the wave generator and note the increased brightness of the crests and darkness of the troughs, showing that the amplitude of the water waves has also increased. Greater energy is required to move the wave generator at larger amplitudes, and this energy is transferred to the water, creating larger waves with greater energy. The amplitude or height of a wave is a measure of its energy.

Part 2. Wave reflection: Generate a single straight wave in the tank by gently pushing a ruler or other straight edge and observe the reflection of the wave from the opposite wall. The incident wave is unrestrained so the reflected wave is not inverted and a crest is reflected as a crest and a trough is reflected as a trough. If an incident wave is restrained, as was the case when you sent waves down a spring tied securely to a wall earlier in this chapter, the incident wave is inverted and a crest is reflected as a trough while a trough is reflected as a crest.

Place a barrier in the ripple tank so advancing waves will strike it at an angle as shown in Figure V. Start the motor and note the angle at which the waves strike the barrier and the angle at which they are reflected. The angle between the incident wave and the normal (the normal is the line perpendicular to the interface) is called the angle of incidence, and the angle between the reflected wave and the normal is called the angle of reflection. Complete Figure V to show the result when waves reflect off the barrier. Change the position of the barrier and again start the motor. What can you conclude about the relationship between angle of incidence and angle of reflection?

Repeat using parabolic barriers, or barriers positioned at right angles (Figure W) and draw the resulting wave patterns, indicating the angle of incidence and the angle of reflection. Does the angle of incidence equal the angle of reflection?

Part 3. Change in wave speed: Place a thin rectangular pane of glass under the water at one end of the ripple tank as shown in Figure X. Start the motor and compare the wavelength and speed of the waves in the deep water with those in the shallow water. Complete Figure X to show the direction and wavelength of waves as they pass over the submerged glass. Recalling the wave equation $v = f\lambda$, are the waves traveling faster or slower in the shallow water? The shallow water is one medium and the deep water is another. Do your findings suggest that waves travel the same speed in all media? Do you suspect that sound travels at the same speed in steel as in air or that light travels the same speed in air as in glass? Why or why not?

Part 4. Wave refraction: Place the thin rectangular pane of glass under the water at one end of the ripple tank as shown in Figure Y so that an approaching straight wave will encounter it at an angle. Start the motor and note the direction of the approaching waves and the direction of the waves after they pass over the boundary. Complete Figure Y to show the direction and wavelength of waves as they pass over the submerged glass. Do waves bend toward or away from the normal (the line perpendicular to the interface) when they slow upon entering shallow water? Move the glass plate so it is under the wave generator. The waves will then begin in shallow water and move to deep water. Do waves bend toward or away from the normal when they accelerate upon entering deeper water?

Part 5. Wave diffraction: Position two barriers parallel to the wave front with an opening (aperture) that is much wider than the wavelength (Figure Z). Complete Figure Z to show the appearance of the waves as they emerge from the wide aperture. Now make the aperture progressively smaller until it is approximately the same width as the wavelength of the water waves and observe the results. Complete Figure AA to show the appearance of waves as they pass through an aperture of equal dimension to their wavelength. Does diffraction (spreading of the waves) increase or decrease as the width of the aperture is reduced to a width of approximately one wavelength? Slowly increase the speed of the motor and observe diffraction as the wavelength becomes smaller than the width of the aperture. Does the spreading of the emerging waves diminish or increase as the wavelength of the oncoming waves is decreased?

Part 6. Wave interference: Install two spherical probes on the wave generator. Slowly increase the speed and note the changes in the wave patterns. The bright and dark regions show increased amplitude where crests reinforce crests and troughs reinforce troughs in the process of constructive interference. Regions where crests and troughs meet in the process of destructive interference are shown by the nodal lines where the water is calm. Complete Figure BB to show the resulting wave pattern when circular waves meet.

Questions

(1) When a wave moved from the deep water to the shallow water above the immersed pane of glass, did the frequency increase or decrease? The wavelength? The speed?

(2) When a surface wave in a ripple tank strikes a straight barrier, the wave is unrestrained, the wave crest is reflected as a crest, and a trough is reflected as a trough. However, when you send a transverse wave down a rope that is firmly attached at one end the reflected pulse is inverted. Explain.

(3) Distinguish between wave refraction and wave diffraction. Give examples.

(4) The two point sources generated circular waves that constructively and destructively interfered. Which type of interference caused the nodal lines (nodes)?

(5) What generally happens to the speed of ocean waves as they approach the shore? Explain.

FOR THE TEACHER

Make certain students understand that electromagnetic waves such as light are able to travel through a vacuum as well as through certain materials, while mechanical waves travel only through matter. Point out that the waves students investigated using the ropes, springs, and ripple tank were two-dimensional waves, but that sound and light waves emitted from a point source are three-dimensional spherical waves. Whenever a transverse or longitudinal wave moves through a medium, individual particles of the medium are displaced but return to their equilibrium positions after the wave has passed, indicating that energy, but not matter, is transferred from one location to another. To illustrate this point, ask students to consider the movement of a seagull on an ocean wave or a duck on a swell in a lake. The birds move up and down, but not laterally, as the wave passes. *Waves moving in a medium travel independently as if other waves were not present. When passing through one another, waves may interfere constructively or destructively, producing standing waves if they are moving in opposite directions and have the same amplitude and frequency. If the amplitudes and/or frequencies of the waves are different, they will superimpose to form a wave whose shape can be determined by simply adding the amplitudes of both waves along their lengths.*

6.1.1 Wave Characteristics

Discussion: If the pendulum is swung at small amplitudes it will undergo simple harmonic motion as explained in the chapter on periodic motion. If the paper is moved perpendicularly under the swinging pendulum the resulting trace will be a sine curve that is a pictorial representation of a wave. The simplest type of regular wave train is a sinusoidal wave motion. Each time the pendulum makes a complete oscillation, the wave moves a distance λ in the direction of the wave and the wave speed is $v = \lambda/T$, where T is the period of oscillation. In terms of frequency the wave speed can be written as: $v = f\lambda$. These are important general relations and hold for sinusoidal wave motion of any type.

Answers (1) A wave is a disturbance that propagates through a medium or space. A crest is point of maximum upward displacement of a wave while a trough is point of maximum downward displacement of a wave. (2) The amplitude of the waves increased with the amplitude of the pendulum's swing. The wavelength of the waves increased as the paper was pulled faster. (3) Frequency is the number of vibrations per second. Period is time required for one complete vibration. Amplitude is the maximum displacement of a wave from its equilibrium position. Wavelength is the distance between corresponding parts of a wave such as crest to crest or trough to trough. (4) Frequency is the reciprocal of period $f = 1/T$. The SI unit of frequency is the hertz (Hz), which is equivalent to one cycle per second. A wave propagated at 30 cycles per second (30/s) has a frequency of 30 Hz and a period of 1/30 s.

6.1.2 Transverse and Longitudinal Waves

Discussion: If a transverse pulse is sent down a spring or rope whose end is free to move, the reflected pulse will not be inverted. This can be illustrated in class by tying the spring or rope to a ring that is free to slide up and down a ring-stand support, broom handle, or other pole. If, however, one end of the spring or rope is tied securely to a support, the reflected pulse will be inverted. The incident pulse exerts an upward force on the fixed support and the support, in turn, exerts an equal and opposite force on the rope that causes an inverted reflected pulse. Students will observe that water waves reflected from a barrier are not inverted because the incident wave is not restrained. (*Note:* A good substitute for a transverse wave-spring is a long, high-quality jump rope in which the rope is attached to the handles by freely pivoting hooks.)

Answers (1) A transverse wave is one in which the displacements of the particles of the medium are perpendicular to the direction of wave's propagation. A longitudinal wave is a wave in which the displacements of the particles of the medium are parallel to the direction of the wave's propagation. You can measure the wavelength of a transverse wave by measuring the distance between corresponding parts of the wave such as from crest to crest or trough to trough. You can measure the wavelength of a longitudinal wave by measuring the distance between corresponding parts such as from the midpoint of a compression to the midpoint of an adjacent compression. (2) The energy of a wave is proportional to the square of the wave amplitude and the square of the wave frequency. (3) The velocity of a wave is equal to the frequency multiplied by the wavelength $v = f\lambda$. (4) The energy of the wave is increased by a factor of 81 since energy is proportional to the square of amplitude (3^2) and the square of frequency (3^2): $9 \times 9 = 81$. (5) The frequency of the wave is 36 waves/30 seconds = 1.2 waves/s. Since $v = f\lambda$, the speed of the waves = 2.3 m × 1.2 waves/s = 2.8 m/s.

6.1.3 Superposition

Discussion: This activity can be used to illustrate the harmonic wave forms emanating from musical instruments. The quality of sound refers to the number of harmonics and their relative intensities. Figure J illustrates the superposition of second and fourth harmonics, which is the characteristic wave pattern of some trumpets. By contrast, the tones produced by French horns are composed almost entirely of the first and second harmonics.

Answers (1) See Figure CC. (2) The sound waves produced by the various instruments are unaffected by the other waves traveling through the air, eardrum, bones, middle ear, or inner ear. Thus, the sound waves from the base guitar are not diminished by the presence of sound waves from drums, synthesizers, or singers.

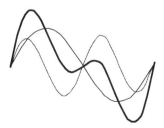

6.1.4 Standing Waves

Discussion: Standing mechanical waves occur in the tubes of wind instruments, in the strings of string instruments, and in the membranes or plates of percussion instruments. Standing electromagnetic waves occur in microwave wave guides, radio-transmitting antennas, and the glass coatings of optical instruments. Standing waves are produced when two sets of waves of equal frequency amplitude and wavelength pass through each other in opposite directions such that they are periodically in and out of phase. At specific locations known as "nodes" two identical waves traveling in opposite directions will interfere destructively so there is no displacement of the medium. Those points where the standing wave flips up and down with maximum displacement are called antinodes. Standing waves can be produced in either transverse or longitudinal waves.

Teacher demonstration: Standing waves can be illustrated and explained easily using the overhead projector. Draw identical sine waves in different colors on each of two overhead transparencies. Mark a third transparency with a series of alternating solid and dashed vertical lines spaced one quarter of a wavelength apart, as illustrated in Figure DD. Place this lined transparency on the bottom and the two other transparencies on top. Position the sine waves so they are in phase and their peaks are aligned with the solid vertical lines, as shown in Figure EE. Slowly move one sine wave to the left while moving the other to the right at the same rate. Students should observe simultaneous-troughs appearing on the solid vertical lines where simultaneous-crests previously appeared and vice versa (Figure FF). They should also note that nodes remain fixed on the dashed vertical lines.

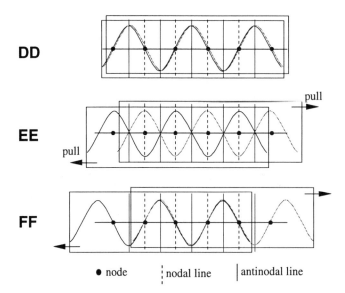

Answers (1) When a crest approaches a crest and a trough approaches a trough, they interfere constructively to create super-crests and super-troughs. When a crest approaches a trough they interfere destructively and the amplitude of the resultant wave will be reduced. (2) A standing wave is a stationary pattern caused by the interference of two wave trains of equal wavelength, amplitude, and frequency as they pass through each other in opposite directions. The medium moves up and down in a pattern, but the pattern itself does not move. (3) A node is a point of no disturbance in a standing wave and is produced when two waves moving in opposite directions continuously interfere destructively at the same point. (4) The friction of your finger on the rim establishes standing waves in the glass, producing sound in the same manner bowing a violin produces sound.

6.1.5 Wave Propagation and Interactions

Construction of a wave generator: If you have no access to a commercial ripple tank and wave generator you may construct one as described below. (Encourage students to devise their own designs for the most effective ripple tank.) Obtain a window (set in its frame) and seal the edges with aquarium silicone caulking to make it waterproof. Use the seats of two chairs to support the window in a horizontal position. To make the wave bar, cut a section of a triangular board a little shorter than the width of the window. Screw two eye-hooks equidistant from each end of the dowel and use thick rubber bands to hang the dowel from a support so it will rest horizontally on the surface of the water.

Obtain a miniature toy electric motor (one taken from a toy car will serve nicely) and a wooden dowel with a diameter greater than the diameter of the motor's shaft. Use a drill to make a hole in the end of the dowel slightly greater than the diameter or the shaft, place a small amount of white glue in this hole, and force it onto the shaft. When it has dried, screw a nut and bolt onto the end of the dowel, as shown in Figure GG. The bolt makes the assembly eccentric so it will vibrate when turning just like a clothes washer or drier will vibrate when loaded with a heavy blanket that is off center. By moving the nut in and out on the shaft of the bolt, it is possible to adjust the eccentricity of the assembly and the amplitude of the vibrations. Fasten the motor on top of the triangular bar with wire, twine, or tape, as illus-

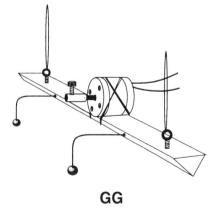

GG

trated in Figure GG. Connect the motor to a dry cell in series with a 10-ohm rheostat. If you do not have a rheostat, use a piece of nichrome wire and make connections using alligator clips. Sliding one clip down the length of the nichrome wire while the other is fixed will vary the resistance of the circuit and alter the speed of the motor and hence the frequency of the waves it generates. When studying straight waves, place the bar in the tank. You may study circular waves by gluing marbles or other spherical objects to the heads of nails and inserting the nails into the side of the dowel, as shown in Figure GG.

Place a shielded 200-watt clear light bulb above the ripple tank and a large white sheet of paper below, or place the entire assembly on an overhead projector. The light from the bulb will project through the water to the paper or screen. Wave crests will appear on the paper as bright regions, and troughs will appear as dark regions or vice versa depending on which way the image is projected. Fill the tank to a depth of about one centimeter. Repeatedly touch the surface of the water with a finger while adjusting the height of the light until projected crests and troughs are as bright and as dark as possible.

Discussion: A fundamental wave principal, originally proposed by Christian Huygens, states that every point on an advancing wave front acts as a source from which new waves continually spread. This principle is illustrated in the diffraction activity when the dimension of the aperture is approximately the same as the length of a wave. If you make a long barrier with a number of apertures you can illustrate Huygens' principle for an entire wave front. The answers to student activities are found in Figures HH–NN. Figure OO illustrates a detailed two-point interference pattern that you may wish to share with your students.

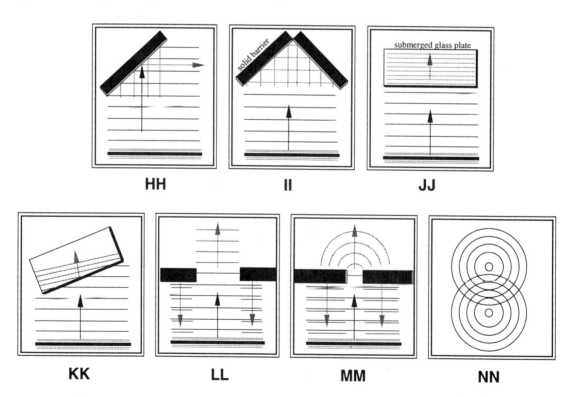

HH   II   JJ

KK   LL   MM   NN

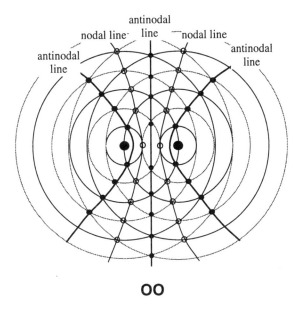

antinodal
nodal line· line ⌐nodal line
antinodal   ˎantinodal
line /   line ˎ

OO

Answers (1) Students will note that waves slow and wavelengths shorten as they move into shallow water; however, the frequency does not change because it is dependent only upon the frequency of the source, not the media through which the wave travels. The ratio of velocity to wavelength remains constant $f=v/\lambda$. Differences in water depth can be used to simulate different media when studying other wave phenomena such as light and sound. For example, the shallow water can represent glass and the deep water air when studying the behavior of light. (2) A wave traveling in a rope will invert when it reaches a fixed end because the upward force exerted by the wave is accompanied by an opposite and equal reaction force that causes the wave to invert. However, when a surface wave in a ripple tank encounters a barrier it is unrestrained (the medium is not attached to the barrier) and the reflected wave is consequently not inverted. (3) Refraction occurs when a wave travels obliquely (at an angle) from one medium to another. When the wave encounters a boundary at an angle, the part of the wave front striking the boundary changes speed before the other part of the wave front, causing the wave to bend toward or away from the normal and change direction. Diffraction occurs in the same medium and is the spreading of a wave disturbance into a region behind an obstruction. (4) Nodal lines were caused by destructive interference when the waves interacted to produce points of zero displacement. (5) Ocean waves slow as they approach shallow waters near the shore.

Applications to Everyday Life

Waves Are Everywhere: Waves transfer energy and are pervasive in our environment. Most information concerning our surroundings comes to us in the form of waves. It would indeed be a mind-boggling experience if all these various types of waves were visible. Waves from the sun travel through space and sustain life on our planet. You rely on light waves to see and sound waves to hear. You rely on waves to bring AM and FM radio and TV to your home. Sea waves are great for surfing, but if too large can cause damage to boats and coastal regions. High-energy microwaves cook your meals in microwave ovens while low-energy microwaves transmit messages between cellular phones. According to Einstein's theory of relativity, even gravity is transmitted as a wave, and neurologists routinely analyze waves emanating from patients' brains. Waves are everywhere. (*Note:* Not all waves mentioned in this paragraph are mechanical waves.)

Tidal Waves (Tsunamis—Seismic Sea Waves): Tsunamis are generated by seismic activity such as volcanoes, landslides, and earthquakes. The waves generated move at approximately 500 km/h (300 mph) with periods ranging from 5 to 60 minutes and can cross the ocean in several hours, inflicting great damage when they reach shore. Tsunamis in the open ocean may go unnoticed by seafarers because their amplitude is often less than 1 meter. However, like any swell or wave reaching a beach, their amplitude increases greatly as they approach land. In 1737, a 210-foot-high tsunami broke on the south tip of Kamchatka, and in 1896 a 93-foot-high tsunami struck the city of Miyako, Japan. In 1883, a 110-foot-high tsunami caused by the eruption of Krakatoa killed 36,000 people in the islands of modern-day Indonesia.

Animal Locomotion: Animals such as eels and snakes move as transverse body waves push against the water or ground. By contrast, earth worms are propelled by longitudinal waves as they rhythmically lengthen or shorten their body segments. Some one-celled animals send waves down whiplike flagella, thereby propelling themselves through their aquatic world.

Music: A standing wave is produced by the interference of two periodic waves of the same amplitude and wavelength traveling in opposite directions. The sounds produced by musical instruments are the result of such standing waves.

Earthquakes: Earthquakes generate seismic waves that travel through the earth. The P wave (primary wave) is a longitudinal (compressional) wave in which the particles vibrate parallel with the line of the wave's propagation. The S wave (secondary wave) is a transverse (shear) wave in which displacement is at right angles to the direction of wave propagation. P waves travel faster than S waves. A seismograph is an instrument used to measure the strength of an earthquake. By carefully timing the arrival of P and S waves, seismologists are able to determine the epicenter of an earthquake and the size and orientation of the active fault. Local monitoring of seismic waves created by detonation of underground explosives can help geologists identify potential sources or mineral and petroleum deposits.

Shock Waves and Sonic Booms: Shock waves may arise from the sharp and violent disturbances of a lightning stroke, explosions, or the steady supersonic flow of air over an aircraft. As an aircraft approaches the speed of sound, the sound waves produced overlap to form a wave barrier on the leading edges of the wings and body. Additional thrust is required by the engines to cross this barrier, but once crossed, the aircraft can fly faster than the speed of sound without encountering additional barriers. When an aircraft travels faster than the speed of sound, waves made by the aircraft cannot travel in front of it. The compacted sound waves still travel outward at the speed of sound, but a conical wave front forms behind the aircraft just as a bow wave is formed behind a speedboat. As the conical wave spreads, it reaches the ground, creating a continuous sonic boom that moves with the aircraft. The supersonic Concord aircraft was banned from flying in the United States because it generates intense sonic booms. Both the space shuttle and jet aircraft fly faster than sound and generate two booms, one caused by the compression of air at the leading edge of the wings and the other from the rarefaction of air at the trailing edge.

6.2 SOUND

The most massive trees in the world are the giant redwoods (*Sequoiadendron giganteum*) that grow in the Sierra Nevada Mountains of California. These trees may exceed 5,500 metric tons (6,000 tons), and may grow to a height of 99 meters (325 ft) with a diameter of nearly 9 meters (30 ft). In the latter part of the nineteenth century, loggers came into the mountains to cut these grand giants, but fortunately soon left because the trees did not yield high-quality lumber. Those who were present at the felling of the giant redwoods witnessed an ear-splitting roar when these massive trees crashed to the ground. Although the giant redwoods are now protected in Sequoia, Kings Canyon, and Yosemite National Parks, occasionally an ancient tree will crash to the ground, but only as a result of a strong wind or heavy snow, and not because of an ax or saw. If no one is around when such a tree falls, does it make any sound? You be the judge.

Sound is generated whenever an object vibrates and there is a medium such as air to transmit the sound waves. Your voice is formed by the vibration of your vocal cords. The howling sound of wind on a stormy night is caused by the vibration of air as it travels around rocks and trees. The sound of a jazz tune may be formed by the vibrating lips of a trumpeter and the vibrating reeds of a saxophone. Even the familiar chirping of crickets on warm summer evenings is caused by vibrations as these insects rub their wings together.

When a door is opened into a room, a pulse of pressurized (compressed) air moves across the room and may push curtains out an open window on the other side. A pulse of depressurized (rarefied) air is produced when the door closes, and the air outside the window pushes the curtains back into the room. If the door is repeatedly opened and closed, waves of compressed and rarefied air resembling sound waves are formed. *Sound is a series of compression and rarefaction waves.* Figure A shows how the expanding tongs of a tuning fork compress air, while Figure B shows how the retracting tongs leave a partial vacuum behind them. If the tuning fork is allowed to vibrate, a series of compression and rarefaction waves is established, as shown in Figure C. The wavelength (λ) of the resulting sound is the distance between successive rarefactions or compressions. If you put your hand next to the "woofer" (base membrane) of a stereo speaker you can actually feel the compression waves as they impact your hand.

Sound is a form of energy, but is weak when compared to other forms with which we are familiar. While engineers and scientists are busy at work learning how to tap the energy of wind, light, geysers, tides, and alternative fuels, no research is being conducted on harnessing the energy in sound because it is insignificant. However, our ears are extremely sensitive to sound and can detect waves with a power of only 10^{-12} watts per square meter.

You may have noticed a seagull riding waves at the ocean. The seagull moves up or down as the waves pass by, but is not moved toward or away from the shore. *Sound waves, like ocean waves, transmit energy without transporting matter.* Thus, you

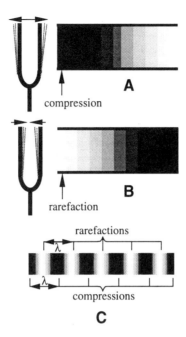

can hear people speaking even though the air expelled from their lungs never comes in contact with your ears. This makes it possible to listen from a distance to a person with a respiratory illness without necessarily contracting their illness. Although the sound energy may reach your ears, it is likely that the exhaled air and bacteria it carries may not travel that far. You will investigate the nature of sound in the following activities.

378

Unit Six: Waves

6.2.1 Sound is Caused by Vibration

Concepts to Investigate: Vibration, induced vibration, frequency.

Materials: Thin metal ruler, hacksaw blade, tuning fork.

Principles and Procedures: Vibrating materials create sound, but most objects vibrate so rapidly it is difficult to see their oscillations. A plucked guitar string, for example, appears only as a blur because its oscillations are too rapid and small for the human eye to resolve. It is possible to see the relationship between vibrations and sounds only if the vibrating material goes through sufficiently slow and large oscillations. By holding one end of a flexible metal ruler, hacksaw blade, or thin strip of sheet metal on the edge of a desk while bending and releasing the free end, it is possible to generate visible vibrations and accompanying audible sounds (Figure D). Change the position of the ruler to generate different sounds and determine the relationship between length, vibrational frequency, and pitch.

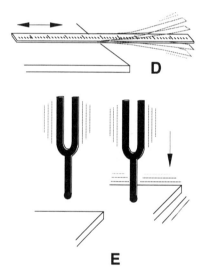

Objects may be forced to vibrate either when they are struck, stretched, or placed in contact with other vibrating objects. A "middle C" tuning fork vibrates 256 times per second, and when its base is placed upon a tabletop, the table is forced to vibrate at this frequency (Figure E). Notice that the amplitude of the note generated increases dramatically because the large surface area of the tabletop is set into motion. Place a vibrating tuning fork on a variety of objects to see which resonates the loudest. If you do not have a set of tuning forks, try the same procedure using the lids of various-diameter cooking pots.

Questions

(1) What is the relationship between the frequency of vibration and pitch?
(2) What is the purpose of the sounding boards (the wood front on a guitar or violin) found on stringed instruments?
(3) Why is the sound generated from a piano generally louder than that generated by a harp?

© 1994 by John Wiley & Sons, Inc.

6.2.2 Sympathetic Vibrations

Concepts to Investigate: Natural frequencies, resonance, sympathetic vibrations.

Materials: Miscellaneous objects (wrench, pencil, newspaper, etc.), tuning forks, one-holed rubber stoppers, two small wooden boxes, drill, two 2-liter soda bottles.

Principles and Procedures: Auto mechanics can determine whether they have dropped a screwdriver or a wrench solely on the basis of the sound it makes upon impact. When struck or dropped, objects vibrate at their own unique natural frequencies, allowing us to differentiate one from another. *The natural (resonant) frequency is the frequency at which the least amount of energy is necessary to cause the object to vibrate.* It is dependent upon the object's shape and elasticity and is largely responsible for the characteristic sounds associated with the object. Each wire in a piano, or each piece of metal in a xylophone has a specific natural frequency, and thus produces a specific note. In the same way, a tuning fork or a soft-drink bottle has a natural frequency. *If an object generates sound waves at the natural frequency of another object, the second one may start to vibrate even though it has not been struck. These induced vibrations are known as sympathetic vibrations.*

Part 1. Identifying objects by their natural frequencies: Close you eyes while your laboratory partner drops ten common objects (book, newspaper, basketball, wrench, etc.), one at a time, on the floor. Try to identify each of the objects by the sound of its impact. Record your results and determine the percentage of objects correctly identified.

Part 2. Induced resonance (sympathetic vibrations) in tuning forks: Construct two wooden boxes, each with an open side, as shown in Figure F. Fit identical tuning forks snugly into holes in the tops of the boxes and position the boxes opposite each other as shown. Strike one tuning fork and then slowly move the other box back and forth until it starts to hum "in sympathy" with the first. Does the induced (sympathetic) tone have a higher, lower, or identical frequency to the inducing (original) tone? Is the amplitude of the induced sound greater, smaller, or the same as the original? Why?

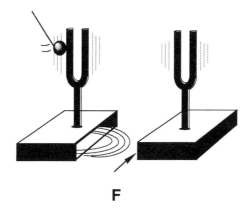

F

Part 3. Induced resonance in soda bottles: The principle of induced resonance can be illustrated using two soft drink bottles (Figure G). Blow across the mouth of one bottle to produce a constant sound while placing the mouth of the other bottle next to your ear as shown. The second bottle should start to hum "in sympathy" with the first. Is the induced (sympathetic) tone higher, lower, or the same as the inducing (original) tone? Is the amplitude of the induced sound greater, smaller, or the same as the original? Explain.

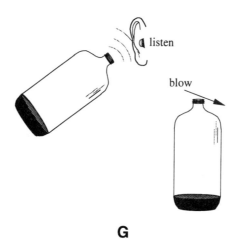

G

Questions

(1) What percentage of objects were you able to identify correctly solely upon the basis of their impact sounds? In general, what factors appear to be responsible for the natural frequency of an object?

(2) Why is the induced pitch in the second tuning fork or bottle the same as the pitch of the object that induced it?

(3) Place your head in a sink or shower stall and start humming. Change the pitch of your humming until you hit a frequency at which the volume increases dramatically. Explain the cause of the increased volume.

6.2.3 Sound Is a Form of Energy

Concept to Investigate: Sound energy.

Materials: Audio speaker, audio amplifier, (standard home stereo system); confetti, rice or poppy seeds.

Principles and Procedures: Energy is the capacity to do work (move objects against a force). For example, it takes energy to lift a set of barbells against the force of gravity. If there is energy in sound, it should be possible to use this energy to perform work. In this activity, you will see if the vibration energy in a loudspeaker membrane is able to move lightweight objects, such as confetti or rice, against the force of gravity.

Obtain an old loudspeaker from a household stereo system. Remove the protective grill on the front of the speaker to expose the "woofer" (large membrane for low sounds) and the "tweeter" (small membrane for high sounds). Place confetti, rice, or poppy seeds on the surface of the "woofer." Turn on the stereo and note the movement of the confetti (Figure H). Keeping the volume constant, use the tuner to play different songs and note how the movement of the confetti varies. The most energetic vibrations should send the confetti highest. Adjust the volume, treble (high frequency), and bass (low frequency) to determine their influence upon sound energy.

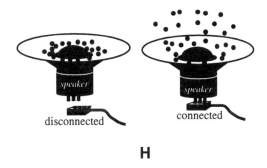

H

Questions

(1)   What is the relationship between volume and sound energy?
(2)   When traveling through air, sound is dissipated as heat. High frequencies are converted to heat more rapidly than low frequencies. Knowing this, explain why engineers design foghorns to generate deep sounds rather than high-pitched sounds.

6.2.4 Psychological and Physical Definitions of Sound

Concepts to Investigate: Sound (psychological and physical definitions), adaptation.

Materials: Stethoscope, tuning fork.

Principles and Procedures: At the beginning of this chapter we asked the question: "If a tree falls in the forest when no one is around to hear it, does it make any sound?" This question is difficult to answer because people have different definitions of "sound." Because they define "sound" on the basis of compression/rarefaction waves, many physicists would say that the falling tree makes sound regardless if anyone is around to hear it. By contrast, many physiologists and psychologists would say that the tree makes no sound because they define "sound" as a sense detected by an animal.

Place a stethoscope in your ears and clamp one tube, as shown in Figure I. Place a vibrating tuning fork near the membrane of the stethoscope and listen carefully as the sound begins to fade. (*Be careful not to touch the membrane with the tuning fork as it may hurt your ears.*) When the sound of the tuning fork is no longer audible, remove the clamp. Can you hear the tuning fork again? If so, why couldn't your first ear still hear the sound? Is human hearing an objective, quantifiable, and repeatable measure of sound?

clamp

I

Questions

(1) On the basis of your observations, is your sense of hearing a reliable indicator of the amplitude of sound? Explain.

(2) After listening to a steady sound for a prolonged period of time, your hearing adapts so that the sound no longer seems as loud. Give an example of another sense that illustrates such adaptation.

(3) If a tree falls in the forest when no one is around to hear it, does it make any sound? Explain.

FOR THE TEACHER

Sound is a wave phenomenon, transmitting energy but not matter. For example, two people can sit on opposite sides of a campfire and talk to each other through the smoke without the smoke moving one direction or the other. Compression waves move through air, smoke, steel, or other media without transporting the media itself. You can illustrate this concept to your students using a Slinky® or similar spring. Tape small pieces of paper at equal intervals over the length of a Slinky®. Grasp one end of the spring while a student grasps the other and produce a longitudinal wave by quickly pushing your end of the spring forward and then pulling it backward (Figure J). You can produce a train of waves by repeatedly moving the end forward and backward. The waves travel along the spring as a series of compressions (coils closer together) and rarefactions (coils farther apart). The coils vibrate, but do not accompany the energy as it moves down the length of the spring.

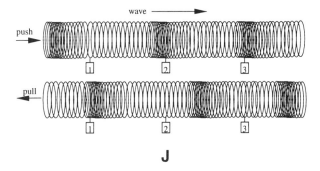

J

When students are first told that sound travels as waves, many envision transverse waves similar to the water waves with which they are familiar. In such waves, the oscillation of particles is transverse (at right angles) to the movement of energy. By contrast, sound waves are longitudinal, and the oscillation of particles is in the same direction as the movement of energy. Be sure to make this distinction between transverse and longitudinal waves.

Send pulses down the spring from both directions at the same time. Students should note that the waves pass through each other, unaffected by the presence of each other. This explains why you can hear two or more people talking at the same time and why, when listening to a symphony or rock band, you can hear the sound of an individual instrument. You can also use the Slinky® to illustrate the principle of an echo by tying one end of the spring to a fixed object and then watching the reflection of pulses back to the sender. Echoes occur when sound waves reflect at the interface between two media.

6.2.1 Sound Is Caused by Vibration

Discussion: An advancing object forces the air in front of it together, creating a pulse of compressed air, while a pulse of rarefied air (partial vacuum) is left behind it. When an object vibrates, pulses of compressed air alternate with pulses of rarefied air, producing longitudinal waves. In such waves, particles within the medium vibrate back and forth in contrast to the perpendicular vibration in transverse waves.

Answers (1) Pitch is directly proportional to the frequency at which an object vibrates. The greater the rate of vibration, the higher the pitch. (2) The string in a piano or guitar has a relatively small surface area and hence is not capable of generating a loud sound. To magnify the volume, these instruments have sounding boards that are forced to vibrate just as the tabletop is forced to vibrate when touched with the base of a vibrating tuning fork. (3) Pianos generate louder sounds than harps because they have larger sounding boards.

6.2.2 Sympathetic Vibrations

Discussion: When two objects have the same natural frequency, vibrations in one may induce lower amplitude vibrations of the same frequency in the other. In this activity, both bottles and both tuning forks were constructed identically so their natural frequencies were identical. When one vibrated, it produced sound waves that forced the other to vibrate sympathetically (in synchrony). The concept of natural frequency may be understood by analogy to a playground swing. If the frequency at which a child pumps his or her legs is similar to the natural frequency of the swing, there will be a significant increase in amplitude and the child will swing quite high. If, however, the child does not synchronize his or her legs with the natural frequency of the swing, the child will not move. The natural frequency of a swing is dependent only upon its length: $f = 1/(2\pi \sqrt{L/g})$, where L is the length of the pendulum, and g is the acceleration due to gravity, 9.8 m/s^2.

Answers (1) Size (frequency decreases as size increases) and material (highly elastic materials such as steel produce higher-pitched sounds than inelastic materials such as plastic) help determine the natural frequency. (2) The pitch of both objects should be identical since they have the same shape and elasticity and hence the same natural frequencies. (3) When you hum at the natural frequency of the shower or sink, the walls are forced to vibrate at that frequency, thereby increasing the overall amplitude of the sound. Sinks and showers are closed tubes and will resonate at odd quarter-wavelength intervals.

6.2.3 Sound Is a Form of Energy

Discussion: A loudspeaker converts electrical energy into mechanical energy. Movable magnets are attached to the backs of the "woofer" and "tweeter" diaphragms and are made to move when magnetic fields are induced in nearby coils. When the user turns up the volume dial, the voltage in the coils is increased, and consequently the amplitude of membrane vibration and resulting sound waves is increased. Students will note that the rice or confetti jumps in synchrony with the music. Large-amplitude vibrations of the membrane are more energetic than small, and therefore generate louder sounds and send the rice or confetti flying higher. At full volume, rice or confetti may be sent more than a meter high.

Answers (1) An increase in volume reflects an increase in sound energy. (2) The foghorns of lighthouses and ships are designed to transmit sound at low frequencies because such sounds travel very far since little of their energy is dissipated as heat. If you are a long way from a thunderclap, you will hear only a dull, low rumble because the higher frequencies are converted to heat before they reach your ears.

6.2.4 Psychological and Physical Definition of Sound

Discussion: All the senses are subject to a phenomenon known as adaptation. For example, when you enter a bakery you immediately smell the aroma of baking bread, but after a few minutes this sensation wanes. In the same way, you adapt to noise so that after prolonged exposure to a constant frequency, the apparent volume is attenuated. Because the second ear was not exposed to the sound, it did not adapt. Hence, when the clamp was released and sound waves were allowed to travel to this ear, the sound once again became audible. The general range of human hearing is from 20 Hz to 20,000 Hz, but this varies from person to person. You can demonstrate variations in the range of hearing by connecting a frequency generator in series with an audio-amplifier and a loudspeaker. Ask students to raise their hands when they can hear a pitch and lower them when they cannot hear it. As you gradually move the dial from 0 to 30,000 Hz, you will notice variations in the ranges of hearing of your students, and if you are significantly older than your students, you will probably also notice that your range of hearing is less than theirs.

Answers (1) Your hearing is not a reliable indicator because it is unquantifiable, variable from person to person, and subject to adaptation. This activity illustrates adaptation, the apparent attenuation of a sense with continued exposure to a constant stimulus. (2) All senses are subject to adaptation. For example, you can feel a wristwatch when you first put it on, but after a while the sensation disappears. Similarly, if you stare at a colored light for a long period of time, you will be less able to see that color when you look away. (3) Student answers will vary depending on whether they adopt a physical or psychological definition of sound. A physical definition of sound requires that there be a source of sound and a medium through which it travels. By comparison, a psychological definition requires that there also be a receiver.

Applications to Everyday Life

Diagnosing Car Problems: Sounds are produced when objects vibrate. Unusual automobile sounds may indicate that nuts, bolts, rods, or bearings are vibrating because they are loose or out of alignment. By experience, a mechanic learns to identify loose or damaged parts by the natural frequencies at which they vibrate.

Music: All musical instruments produce sound by vibrating an object that in turn vibrates air. Percussion instruments vibrate plates, string instruments vibrate wires, wind instruments vibrate air columns, and electronic instruments vibrate speaker diaphragms.

Mufflers: Internal-combustion engines generate compression waves of great magnitude. Mufflers fractionate sound waves so their energy is dissipated as heat and smaller amplitude sound waves.

Foghorns, Thunder, and Rock Concerts: Sound energy is dissipated as heat as it travels through the atmosphere. High-frequency waves are converted to heat more rapidly than low-frequency waves, so low-pitch sounds travel farther. If you are a considerable distance from an explosion, a thunderclap, a marching band, or a loud stereo, you will hear only the lowest frequencies. Foghorns give off low frequencies so the sound may be heard at much greater distances.

Microphones: Compression waves increase the pressure on the quartz crystal element within a microphone. Quartz and other substances demonstrate piezoelectricity (pressure-electricity) and generate voltage in proportion to the strain placed upon them. Compressions produce positive voltages while rarefactions produce negative voltages. Pressure changes in sound waves can therefore be translated into electrical signals and processed accordingly.

Earthquake Alert: Earthquakes release energy as different types of waves. The primary (P) waves travel fastest (8 km/s) and precede the destructive sheer (S) waves by a period of time that varies with distance from the epicenter. Like sound, P waves transmit energy as alternating waves of compression and rarefaction and can be detected by infrasonic devices. Engineers and seismologists have developed alarms that are triggered when P waves are detected, giving people a few seconds to run for cover prior to the arrival of the sheer waves. P waves have a frequency in the 0.5 to 25 Hz range and can sometimes be heard as a deep rumble prior to the arrival of the damaging S wave. (*Note:* The lower threshold for human hearing is 20 Hz.)

6.3 TRANSMISSION OF SOUND

On October 14, 1947, U.S. Air Force Captain Charles Yaeger became the first man to travel faster than sound and thus break the "sound barrier." Yaeger's mission was daring because prior attempts to break the sound barrier ended in disaster as aircraft disintegrated from the intense vibrations accompanying the transition from subsonic to supersonic speed. As Yaeger's Bell X-1 research plane reached the speed of sound (Mach 1), it generated forward-moving compression waves faster than they were conducted away. As a result, compression waves piled up and formed a shock wave known as a "sonic boom." Fortunately, the designers of the Bell X-1 understood the physics of sound transmission and streamlined and stabilized the plane so it did not disintegrate when breaking the sound barrier. Today, numerous aircraft routinely travel faster than the speed of sound. The Concorde Super Sonic Transport (SST) carriers 125 passengers at Mach 2 (twice the speed of sound) from New York to London in approximately 3 hours, and NASA's space shuttle travels at Mach 25 (25 times the speed of sound) when it first reenters Earth's atmosphere.

Aerospace engineers are not the only people who must understand properties of sound transmission. Musicians, conductors, acoustic engineers (those who design such things as concert halls and noise abatement devices), ornithologists (those who study birds and their songs), and audiologists (those who prescribe hearing aids) are but a few of the many professionals who use principles of sound transmission daily.

Sound will travel through any substance that returns to its original shape after being disturbed. Sound is transmitted when energetic molecules transfer energy to their neighbors through collisions, and then return to their original positions. Gasses, solids, or liquids conduct sound if they transmit compression waves with minimal loss of energy. Most terrestrial creatures communicate using atmospheric sound waves, while aquatic organisms use water to transmit sound. Dolphins, for example, emit high-frequency sounds and determine the location of obstructions and prey on the basis of echoes that return to them through the water.

The speed of sound is dependent upon properties of the media through which it travels. Sound travels fastest in incompressible media of relatively low density. In iron, sound travels approximately 5130 m/s (≈3 miles a second), while in rubber, which is substantially more compressible, sound travels only 54 m/s (≈0.03 mile per second). Although air has a low density, sound travels slowly through it because air is very compressible. Among common substances, sound travels fastest through granite (6,000 m/s) because it is very incompressible and yet has a density lower than most similar incompressible solids. *The speed of sound is independent of frequency.* For example, when you listen to a marching band on a football field, the high notes of the flutes and piccolos arrive at the same time as the low notes from the trombones and sousaphones.

Stereo hearing allows humans to locate the origins of sounds. Because our ears are located on opposite sides of our heads, sound reaches them at different times. Our brains determine the direction of a sound source on the basis of differences in volume, as well as the time delay required to reach the ear farthest from the sound. When an object is emitting sound directly in front of the observer, the sound waves are received simultaneously. If the difference in path length to both ears is 25 centimeters, the observer will receive sound in the first ear approximately 0.0007 second prior to the second ear. Although this time delay is small, it is sufficient for your brain to determine which ear is closest to the sound source. You will investigate the principles of sound transmission in the following activities.

6.3.1 Can Sound Travel in a Vacuum?

Concepts to Investigate: Sound transmission, experimental treatment, control, vacuum.

Materials: Laboratory burner or hot plate, ring stands, flasks, one-holed stoppers, rubber bands, thread, glycerin, glass rods, "jingle bells" or electronic buzzers and batteries (available from electronic-supply companies), goggles, hot mitt.

Principles and Procedures: In June of 1962, Edward White became the first American to walk in space. On the third orbit of the mission, White maneuvered outside the *Gemini 4* spacecraft. During his 21-minute walk in space, White communicated extensively with his fellow astronauts inside the spacecraft by radio, even though he was only a few feet away from the spacecraft. Why couldn't he simply talk back and forth with them as he could on Earth?

Space is a vacuum, a region devoid of matter. Although it is possible to see in space, it is not possible to hear because sound requires a medium for transmission whereas light does not. In this activity we will compare the volume of a buzzer or bell enclosed in an evacuated container with one enclosed in an air-filled container.

Using glycerin as a lubricant, slowly twist glass rods through two rubber stoppers until approximately 5 centimeters protrudes through the other end. Suspend a "jingle bell" or electronic buzzer (with battery) by thread from each rod, securing the thread to the rod with rubber bands, as shown in Figure A. *Do not* place the stopper assembly in the flask at this time.

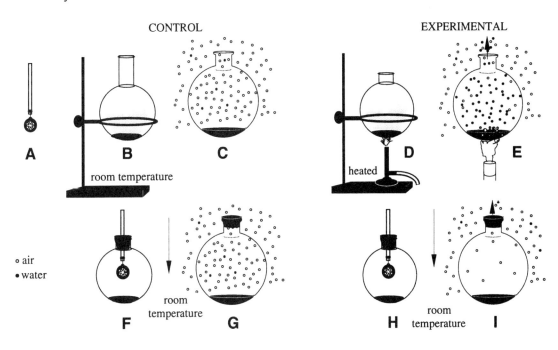

Place approximately 20–30 ml of water in each of two open flasks. Allow one flask to stand at room temperature (Figure B) and boil the other (Figure D). NEVER HEAT A SEALED CONTAINER! The flask at room temperature is referred to as the control, while the heated flask is known as the experimental treatment. When performing experiments, it is necessary to compare experimental treatments against a control to determine the effect of the treatment. Figures C and G show that the concentration of water and air molecules remains relatively unchanged when an unheated flask is sealed. Figure E shows that air escapes when the flask is heated and is replaced by water vapor from the boiling water. When sealed and cooled, water vapor condenses (Figure I), leaving a vacuum within the flask. Given such a vacuum, one can determine if sound requires matter for transmission, as we asserted earlier.

Before all the water is evaporated, remove the experimental flask from the heat source and immediately seal it and the control flask with the stopper/bell apparatuses (Figures F and H). Wrap a cloth around the heated flask for protection in case the flask should crack while cooling. As the gasses inside the experimental flask cool, water vapor condenses, leaving a partial vacuum (Figure I). You may accelerate the cooling of the flask by pouring cold water over the outside. Immersing the flask in ice water for 5 minutes will produce an excellent partial vacuum. Compare the noise made by the buzzer or bell in the evacuated flask (Figure H) with the noise produced in the control flask (Figure F). Is there any difference in volume? Do your data suggest that sound requires matter for transmission?

Questions

(1) Under which of the following conditions was the sound produced by the bell loudest: (a) control (air); (b) immediately after sealing the experimental flask; (c) after allowing the experimental flask to cool in air; (d) after allowing the experimental flask to cool in the ice-water bath? Explain your results.

(2) On the basis of your observations, is sound transmitted through a vacuum? Explain.

(3) Some scientists have advocated we develop settlements on the moon. Would noise pollution near a spaceport on the moon be a concern as it is near an airport on Earth? Explain.

6.3.2 Determining the Speed of Sound in Air

Concepts to Investigate: Speed of light, speed of sound, indirect measurement.

Materials: Binoculars, hammer, large field (approximately 400 meters in length), digital watch or metronome.

Principles and Procedures: While watching the half-time show at a football game, you may notice that the motions of the conductor or drum major are not synchronized with the music produced by the band. While the visual (light) signals of the conductor reach you almost instantaneously, the auditory (sound) signals reach you significantly later since sound travels at approximately only one millionth the speed of light. The farther away you are from the source of a sound, the greater the time delay between the visual and auditory signals. In this activity you will use the time delay between light and sound to indirectly measure the speed of sound in air.

The air must be still and quiet when this activity is performed. Practice hammering on a metal trash-can lid or old metal pot until you can consistently strike at precisely one second intervals (Figure J). Synchronize your strikes with a digital watch, chronometer, or metronome.

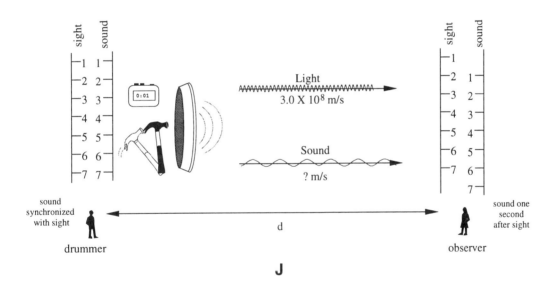

J

A second student (the observer), equipped with a pair of binoculars, should stand approximately 200 meters away. When the first student (drummer) starts pounding, the observer will note the sound is not synchronized with the pounding. The light reflected from the hammer reaches the observer almost instantaneously, but the sound produced by the hammer does not. The observer should then walk away from the drummer, repeatedly making observations. Eventually, the observer will find that the sound is synchronized with the pounding, but will hear one additional beat precisely one second after the drummer stops pounding ($t = 1$ second). At this distance d, the sound from the previous beat reaches the observer's ears at the same instant light from the current beat reaches his or her eyes (Figure J). Thus, the observer can assume that sound has traveled this distance in the time *t* between strokes (1 second).

The observer should mark this location and pace off the distance (d) between him or her and the drummer. The velocity of sound can now be calculated as *d/t*. Repeat this procedure three times and determine an average value for the observed speed of sound in air.

Trial	*Distance*	*Time*	*Velocity*
1	_____ m	1.0 s	_____ m/s
2	_____ m	1.0 s	_____ m/s
3	_____ m	1.0 s	_____ m/s
average	_____ m	1.0 s	_____ m/s

Questions

(1) According to your calculations, what is the approximate speed of sound in air?

(2) Park ranger Roy Sullivan of Virginia holds the dubious distinction of being the only human to have been hit by lightning seven times. How could he determine the distance between himself and nearby lightning so that he could seek cover the next time the lightning was getting too close?

(3) Approximately how far away is lightning if you hear thunder 3 seconds after seeing the flash?

(4) Why might those at the end of a long marching band be out of step with those in the front?

(5) On July 20, 1969, Neil Armstrong became the first person to set foot on the moon and proclaimed: "That's one small step for [a] man, one giant leap for mankind." Those watching the landing of the *Eagle* heard his statement less than one and a half seconds after he spoke it. How can this be true if the moon is approximately 240,000 miles (386,000 km) from Earth?

6.3.3 Sound Transmission in Solids and Liquids

Concepts to Investigate: Media for sound transmission, quality of sound.

Materials: Watch, spoon, fishing line or string, aquarium or large bucket, block of wood.

Principles and Procedures: Does sound travel more efficiently (farther) in solids, liquids, or gasses? In which media is least energy lost to heat and most transmitted as sound? Perform the following simple activities to determine the answer.

Part 1. Sound transmission in solids: (a) Hold a ticking watch at arm's length from your ear. Subsequently, place the watch on a tabletop, press you ear to the table, and listen. Which is more efficient at conducting the sound, the air or the tabletop? Which produces a "richer" sound with a greater range of frequencies? (A richer or higher-quality sound has more harmonics or overtones.) (b) Find two adjacent rooms that both have sinks. While your partner taps on the faucet in one room, listen in the other room, first with your ear placed on, and then off the faucet. Is sound traveling more efficiently through the pipes or through the air? (c) Tie a spoon or other utensil to the middle of a string, as illustrated in Figure K. Wrap the loose ends of the string around your index fingers and place your fingers in your ears. Swing the spoon so it strikes a tabletop and compare the volume and quality of the sound received with that received directly through the air. Does sound travel better through the string or through the air?

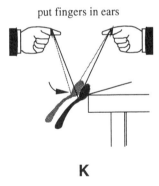

put fingers in ears

K

Part 2. Sound transmission in liquids: (d) Float a block of wood in an aquarium or large bucket. Place the base of a vibrating tuning fork on the wood while your ear is pressed to the wall of the container. Repeat with your ear an equal distance from the tuning fork, but above the container so no glass or water is in the way. Is sound conduction more efficient in water or air? (If a tuning fork is unavailable, use a pencil to tap lightly on the block of wood.) For activities a–d, record your results in the table, circling the media in which sounds were transmitted with greater volume and richness (timbre, quality, number of overtones).

	Volume (Which is loudest?)	*Timbre* (Which is richest?)
(a)	air / table	air / table
(b)	air / pipe	air / pipe
(c)	air / string	air / string
(d)	air / water	air / water

Questions

(1) Are solids or air more effective in transmitting sound? Explain your conclusion.

(2) Are solids or liquids more effective in transmitting sound? Explain your conclusion.

(3) As a child you may have made a "telephone" by connecting two tin cans with a long string. Explain how such a "telephone" works.

6.3.4 Speed of Sound in Different Media

Concepts to Investigate: Speed of sound in different media.

Materials: Hammer, sidewalk or long hallway.

Principles and Procedures: The speed of sound varies as a function of the elastic and inertial properties of the substance through which it moves. In iron, for example, sound moves at a speed of 5,130 meters per second, while in lead it travels at only 1,230 meters per second. Although both substances are metals, lead is less elastic (more easily deformed) and has greater inertia (is denser), causing sound waves to travel more slowly. In this demonstration you will compare the speed of sound in a solid such as concrete with the speed of sound in air.

Two students should stand at opposite ends of a long, quiet sidewalk or hallway (>50 meters). One student should press his or her ear to the sidewalk while the student at the other end strikes the sidewalk with a hammer (Figure L). The blow of the hammer will initiate sound waves though the air as well as through the sidewalk. If the speed of sound is the same in both media, the listener will hear only one sound. If, however, sound travels at different rates, the listener will hear two sounds in rapid succession. The greater the distance between the hammer and the listener, the greater the time interval between the arrival of the two sounds. One can compare the rate of sound transmission in steel and air by repeating this procedure using abandoned railroad tracks. Repeat the procedure until you can clearly identify which sound is reaching you first. If the two sounds seem to arrive simultaneously, move farther apart and repeat.

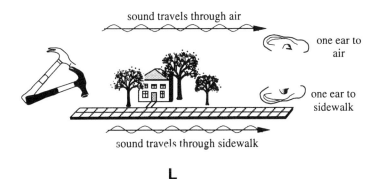

sound travels through air

one ear to air

one ear to sidewalk

sound travels through sidewalk

L

Questions

(1) On the basis of your investigations, does sound travel at the same rate in concrete and steel as it does in air? If not, specify the media in which it travels fastest and how you determined this.

(2) Which would be noticed first, the sound or tremor (shaking) of a distant explosion? Explain.

6.3.5 Locating the Source of Sound

Concepts to Investigate: Stereo hearing, temperature and speed of sound.

Materials: Ring stand, clamps, thread, pencil, ear plug, vacuum-cleaner hose (garden hose or other flexible tubing may be substituted).

Principles and Procedures

Part 1. Locating sound source: One student should be blindfolded, *slowly* spun in a *few* circles, and placed in the middle of a quiet room. A second student should use a pencil to gently tap at different locations around the perimeter of the room while the first student tries to locate the tapping sound by pointing. Using a protractor, measure the angle between the student's estimated direction and the true direction to the sound source. Plug one ear and repeat the procedure, reporting your results in the table provided. Does stereo (two-ear) hearing provide a better sense of directionality than mono (one-ear) hearing?

Part 2. Stereo hearing: Obtain a vacuum-cleaner hose or similar tube. Place a mark at the center of this tube and suspend it from a ring stand, as shown in Figure M. One student should close his or her eyes and place the two ends of the hose over opposite ears, listening while the other student *gently* taps the tube with a pencil. Start tapping in the center and then move toward one end until your partner can identify which ear is closest to the sound. Record the smallest distance from the center of the tube d that the listener can consistently differentiate. Record the Celsius temperature T at which the activity is performed and determine the velocity of sound at this temperature using the following formula:

$$v_T = v_o + (0.6\text{m/s})(T°\text{C})$$

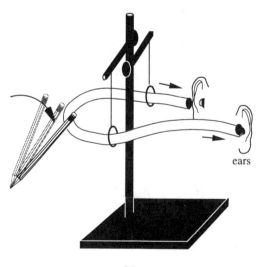

ears

M

© 1994 by John Wiley & Sons, Inc.

where v_T is the velocity at the measured temperature T, and v_o is 331.3 m/s, the velocity of sound at 0°C. Knowing the minimal differentiable distance, and the velocity of sound, calculate the difference in time required for the sound impulse to travel to both ears d/v_T. Record your results in the table. What is the minimum time required between sounds so that you may detect them as separate?

	1	2	3	4	Average
Angle of error using both ears	____°	____°	____°	____°	____°
Angle of error using one ear	____°	____°	____°	____°	____°
Temperature T	____°C				
Velocity v_T	____(m/s)				
Distance difference d	____m				
Time difference	____s				

Questions

(1) Is there any improvement in your ability to locate the source of sound when both ears are used in part 1? Explain.

(2) Our brains use the delay between the time sound reaches our first and second ears to determine the direction of a sound source. Measure the distance between your ears and determine the maximum time delay you have to use in this process.

(3) What other auditory factor(s) could help you determine the location of a sound source?

(4) Sound travels at approximately 340 m/s through air at room temperature and approximately 1,445 m/s in water at the same temperature. Would it be easier to identify the location of a sound source in water or in air? Why?

FOR THE TEACHER

Sound waves will be produced only if there is a source that can initiate a mechanical disturbance, and an elastic medium through which the disturbance can be transmitted. The first activity in this section indicated that sound requires a material medium for transmission. To make this point clearer, you may wish to perform a classic demonstration that uses a doorbell or electronic buzzer suspended in a bell jar that is connected to a vacuum pump. As the jar is evacuated, the sound of the bell or buzzer slowly decreases until it completely disappears. Once the vacuum pump is turned off and air is allowed to reenter the bell jar, the sound of the buzzer once again becomes audible. This same phenomenon will be encountered as you increase in elevation. The higher in the atmosphere, the lower the density of air, and the less efficient the transmission of sound. When you enter the vacuum of space beyond the limits of the atmosphere, sound is no longer transmitted.

6.3.1 Can Sound Travel in a Vacuum?

Discussion: Although virtually no sound will be transmitted through the rarefied air in the flask or bell jar, students may detect a slight sound due to energy transmitted through the string supporting the noisemaker. Although this procedure works well with Erlenmeyer flasks, we recommend using round-bottom flasks because they distribute pressure more evenly and are less likely to implode as the vacuum is established.

Answers (1) The bell will sound loudest under control conditions. The pressure in the control (air) is approximately 760 mm Hg (1 atmosphere). When the flask is sealed and cooled, a partial vacuum develops, dropping the pressure to about 5 mm Hg (at 0°C), or less than 1 percent of normal. As the distance between molecules increases, transduction of energy becomes less efficient, resulting in a decrease in the amplitude of the sound. (2) Sound is not transmitted through a vacuum. Although the flask is not a perfect vacuum, so little energy will be transmitted that the observer will not be able to hear it. (3) Sound pollution would not be a problem because there is no atmosphere on the moon and hence nothing to transmit sound to the observer.

6.3.2 Determining the Speed of Sound in Air

Discussion: Sound travels at approximately 340 m/s at 20°C. To obtain a one-second time delay, the observer must be 340 meters (1,115 feet) away, or approximately 3.7 times the length of a football field. This is a good activity to introduce estimation of distance using the pace. Students can calculate their pace simply by dividing a given length (e.g., a football field = 300 feet) by the number of paces required to walk that distance. Emphasize to your students that to obtain accurate results, they should walk normally, not exaggerating or minimizing their strides. This activity should be conducted in a quiet, still (no wind) area because background noise will make data collection difficult.

Answers (1) Sound travels at approximately 340 m/s at 20°C and increases approximately 0.6 m/s per degree Celsius. (2) Since light travels at 3×10^8 m/s, we can assume that the observer sees lightning almost instantaneously. However, the sound of thunder travels at a slower rate ($\approx$340 m/s). By multiplying the time delay observed between lightning and thunder by the speed of sound at the appropriate temperature, it is possible to calculate the distance of an observer from a lightning strike. (3) 3s(340m/s) = 1,020m = 3,346 feet = 0.63 miles. Student answers will vary depending upon their measured speed of sound. (4) Members in the back of a long marching band attempt to play in "auditory" synchrony with those in the front. Because of the distance, they must lag slightly behind those in front in order to achieve this effect. Since they synchronize their marching with the rhythm they hear, their cadence will be slightly out of phase (behind) those in the front. (5) Astronauts communicate with Earth through radio waves that travel at the speed of light. Inform students that when they talk on the telephone, sound is converted to electric, optic, and/or microwave signals (depending on the route of the call) that travel at approximately the speed of light, making communication nearly instantaneous. The receiver of the phone converts these signals back into sound so they may be heard.

6.3.3 Transmission in Solids and Liquids

Discussion: Most solids and liquids conduct sound better than air because their closely packed molecules provide more rapid and efficient transfer of energy. Students should report that sounds transmitted through solids and liquids are louder and richer (wider range of frequencies) than those same sounds transmitted through air.

Answers (1, 2) Solids and liquids transmit sounds more efficiently than gasses because individual molecules don't oscillate for as great of distances before colliding with others to transfer their energy. (3) If the string is taut, the vibrations induced in the "speaker can" will cause the string to vibrate. Because the "telephone line" is essentially two dimensional, most of the energy will be transmitted down its length to the "receiver can." The "receiver" has a larger surface area than the string, allowing more sound energy to be transmitted back to the air so it may be heard by the listener.

6.3.4 Speed of Sound in Different Media

Answers (1) Sound travels faster through concrete or steel than through air, so the observer hears sound through these media immediately prior to sound in the air. The greater the distance between the origin of a sound and the listener, the greater the time delay between the two pulses. (2) An observer will generally feel the ground shake immediately prior to hearing an explosion because shock waves traveling through the Earth propagate at over 10 times the rate of those in air.

6.3.5 Locating the Source of Sound

Discussion

Part 1: Students should be able to point to the source of a sound with greater accuracy when using both ears because they receive the benefit of stereo reception. To obtain best results, average and analyze the data from the entire class.

Part 2: Most students should be capable of distinguishing between sounds when the pathway difference is 10 cm or more. At 10 cm, sound is detected by the first ear 0.0003 second (0.3 millisecond) prior to the second ear.

Answers (1) Stereo reception improves localization skills by providing clues through differences in volume and time. (2) The maximum distance between both ears is approximately 25 cm, allowing for a time delay of approximately 0.7 milliseconds. (3) The auricle (outer ear) has a lateral and anterior orientation, providing best sound reception from the side and front. If the brain detects a greater voltage from the left auditory nerve than from the right, it will interpret the sound as coming from the left. Sounds from behind the head will seem softer than those from the front because of the anterior orientation of the auricles. (4) It is easier to detect the origin of sound in air than in water because sound travels slower in air, providing for a greater differential in the time required to reach both ears.

Applications to Everyday Life

Sound Insulation: Sound will not propagate in a vacuum. Acoustic engineers use this principle when designing soundproof barriers. By evacuating the space between two walls, it is possible to restrict sound transmission to only those locations where the walls are connected, thereby greatly reducing the amount of sound that passes through the barrier.

Measuring Distances: You can determine the distance between you and another object by the following equation: $d = (t_{echo} \times v_{sound})/2$, where t_{echo} is the time required for an echo and v_{sound} is the velocity of sound ($\approx$340 m/s at 20°C). Mountaineers use this principle to determine the width of valleys, while exploration geophysicists use it to determine the depth of oil wells.

SONAR: SOund NAvigation and Ranging is a system for detecting the location of underwater objects on the basis of an acoustic echo. Developed by the Allies in World War I, SONAR was used to detect the location of enemy submarines. Sonar devices emit pulses of sound, which echo off underwater objects and return to SONAR devices for interpretation. The time elapsed between transmission and reception indicates the distance to the object. Today, commercial fisherman use SONAR to locate schools of fish.

Determining the Epicenter of Earthquakes: Earthquakes generate massive compression waves known as P (primary) waves similar to those of sound, in addition to S (secondary) waves that move rock transversely in a shearing fashion. Since the velocities of both are known, it is possible to calculate the distance between the epicenter and an observer on the basis of the time differential between P and S waves. The greater the differential, the farther away the quake. If three or more laboratories record the time differential simultaneously, it is possible to determine not only the distance to the epicenter, but also its precise location by the process of triangulation.

Explosions: Because compression waves travel faster through rock and soil than through air, an observer will detect a tremor in the ground prior to hearing the sound of a distant explosion.

Stereo Hearing: Sound travels relatively slowly, creating a measurable difference in the time required to reach both ears. The brain uses this time delay to determine the location of the sound source.

Probing Shipwrecks: On April 9, 1940, Hitler's most formidable destroyer, the "unsinkable *Bluecher*" was sunk by artillery fire from a Norwegian island. The *Bluecher* sank in the cold waters of the fjord and took with it approximately 1,300 tons of fuel. In the years since the sinking of the *Bluecher*, oceanographers and environmental biologists have become increasingly concerned about the possibility of a major leakage of fuel into the ocean. To locate the fuel without disturbing the ship and causing a leak, scientists launched a robotic submarine that aimed low-frequency sound waves at the *Bluecher*. Sound waves travel differently in oil than in water or steel, and echoes from the *Bluecher*'s fuel yielded data that were used to locate the aging fuel tanks.

6.4 FREQUENCY AND WAVELENGTH OF SOUND

You have probably noticed dogs in your neighborhood howling when an emergency vehicle drives past with its siren blaring. Although the sound of a siren is unpleasant to the human ear, it is painful to dogs because they hear a piercing high-pitched noise we can't detect. Capitalizing on this feature of dogs' hearing, engineers have developed harmless "anti-bark" dog collars to silence noisy dogs by emitting high-pitched noises whenever the dog barks.

The pitch (how high or low) of a sound is related to its vibrational frequency. Middle C, for example, is defined as a series of compression/rarefaction waves with a frequency of 256 or 264 cycles per second, depending upon the scale used. If the strings of a violin, or the air column in a trombone, vibrate 256 times each second, the resulting note is middle C. The average frequency of an adult male voice is 120 Hz, while that of an adult female is 250 Hz, or approximately twice as high. The lowest note on a piano is 27.5 Hz, while the highest note is approximately 4,186 Hz. The range of human hearing extends from 20 to 20,000 Hz, and frequencies above 20,000 Hz are termed ultrasonic (above the range of hearing), while those below 20 Hz are known as infrasonic (below the range of hearing). Although some humans can detect the full range of sound from 20 to 20,000 Hz, others cannot, particularly as they grow older. Children, for example, can generally detect an extremely high-pitched noise associated with electronic equipment such as stereos or computer monitors, while many adults cannot. While the upper limit of human hearing is 20,000 Hz, dogs can hear sounds in excess of 30,000 Hz, explaining why they respond to noises from dog whistles and sirens that are inaudible to us. Numerous other small mammals including mice, shrews, and bats are capable of detecting frequencies above the limit of human hearing. Bats, for example, emit and hear sounds in the 100,000 Hz range. By listening to echoes from these squeaks, they determine the location of obstructions or prey.

The frequency of sound depends on the relative motion of the source and receiver (Doppler effect). You may have noticed the pitch of a train whistle, motorcycle rumble, or car horn increase as it approaches and then drop as it passes by. Figures A and B illustrate the sound waves stationary observers hear from the horns of stationary and moving motorcycles. By comparing Figures A and B, you can observe that the pitch heard by the observer in front of a moving motorcycle is higher than that received from the stationary source because waves are received closer together (more waves per second). By contrast, the pitch heard by the observer in back of a moving motorcycle is lower than that received from the stationary source because waves are received farther apart (fewer waves per second).

The frequency of sound is inversely proportional to its wavelength, as expressed by the equation $f = v/\lambda$ where λ is the wavelength, v is the velocity of sound, and f is the frequency. As the wavelength increases, the frequency and pitch decrease. Musicians change the pitch of their music by adjusting their instruments to emit sounds of different wavelengths. *The frequency at which a string vibrates is inversely proportional to its length and directly proportional to the square root of its tension.* Thus, a guitar player can create a higher sound either by pressing down on a fret (shortening the string),

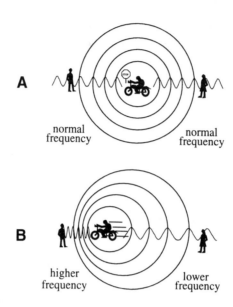

or by tightening the string as when tuning the instrument. Wind instruments generate different pitches when the length of the air column is changed. If, for example, a trombone player moves his or her slide so the air column is twice as long, the frequency will be halved. *The wavelength of a closed tube, such as found in some musical instruments, is approximately four times its length, while that of an open tube is approximately twice its length.* In this chapter you will perform a variety of investigations relating to the frequency and wavelength of sound.

6.4.1 Vibrational Frequency and Pitch

Concepts to Investigate: Pitch, frequency, wavelength.

Materials: Hacksaw blades (or other strips of thin, elastic sheet metal), block of wood, hammer, nails, needle, tape, candle and pane of glass (or flour and flour spreader).

Principles and Procedures: It is difficult for deaf individuals to learn to talk because they cannot hear or imitate the words spoken by others. Although the deaf may not be able to hear the sounds they or others produce, they may be able to imitate vibrations associated with those sounds. Some have learned to modulate the pitch of their voice by imitating the vibrations they feel in the larynx of their speech therapist. Place your hand on your own larynx (lower, front side of your neck) and hum a range of notes. Can you determine the relationship between pitch and vibrational frequency? If you are very observant, you may feel the rate of vibration increasing as the pitch of your voice increases, and decreasing as your pitch drops.

You can visualize the relationship between frequency and pitch by observing a vibrating hacksaw blade. Hold one end of the blade firmly against the tabletop. With your other hand, pull back and release the free end. Adjust the position of the blade so the portion hanging over the edge varies. Does the pitch increase or decrease when the length of the vibrating end is shortened?

Construct the apparatus illustrated in Figure C. Using screws or nails, attach hacksaw blades to opposite sides of a block of wood. One blade should extend approximately 10 cm while the other about 20 cm. Set the blades in motion and note the pitch created by each. Tape pins or sewing needles to the ends of the blades so their points just reach the surface. Light a candle and let it burn under a pane of glass until a layer of soot accumulates on the surface. Invert the glass and position the hacksaw-blade apparatus so the needles just touch the surface of the smoked glass. As the needles vibrate, they will leave a trace in the soot. (Alternatively, you may use a flour spreader to create a thin layer of flour on the surface of a table.)

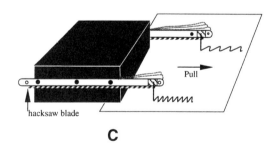

hacksaw blade

C

Start both blades vibrating at the same time with the same amplitude and then quickly but steadily pull the apparatus across the recording surface. The vibrating needles should scratch sine waves on the surface of the smoked glass, as illustrated in Figure C. Count and compare the number of wavelengths λ over a given distance.

The relative frequencies of the vibrations are directly proportional to the number of waves measured in the same distance. What is the relationship between frequency and pitch?

Questions

(1)   What is the relationship between frequency and pitch?
(2)   What is the difference between frequency and pitch?
(3)   Can an object vibrate, but have no pitch?

6.4.2 Doppler Effect

Concepts to Investigate: Frequency, pitch, Doppler effect.

Materials: 9-volt battery, 9-volt piezoelectric buzzer (available at radio/electronic supply stores, frequency in the 500- to 1,500-Hz range), heavy-duty plastic cup or tub, rope, tape.

Principles and Procedures: When a sound source approaches a listener, the waves in front of the source are crowded together so the listener receives more waves per unit time and thus detects a higher pitch than when there is no movement (Figures A and B). When the sound source moves away from the listener, the reverse is true and the pitch is lower. This change in frequency due to relative motion between the source and the receiver is known as the Doppler effect. In this activity you will investigate the Doppler effect using the device illustrated in Figure D.

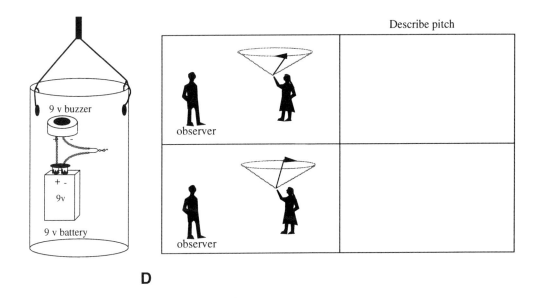

D

    Tie approximately 3 meters of nylon cord through holes in the side of a heavy-duty plastic container. Secure the container so there will be no danger of its slipping off when you swing it. Place the buzzer-and-battery assembly in the bottom of the container and *carefully* swing it in a circle over your head. Your partner should stand a safe distance in front of you and listen for any differences in pitch accompanying the buzzer's orbit. Is the pitch higher when the buzzer is approaching you or when it is moving away? Record your observations in the table provided. Is the Doppler effect more noticeable at slow speeds or high speeds?

Questions

(1)   At what point in the swing was the pitch of the buzzer highest? Why?

(2)   Calculate the speed of the buzzer. (The speed of the buzzer may be determined by dividing the circumference of a swing $2\pi r$ by the time required per revolution. To determine the time required for one revolution, measure the time required for 10 revolutions and divide by 10.)

(3)   The pitch observed by a person standing in front of the moving buzzer can be calculated by the following equation:

$$f_o = f_b \frac{v}{v - v_b}$$

where f_o is the frequency observed, f_b = frequency of the buzzer, v = velocity of sound (340 m/s at 20°C), and v_b is the velocity of the buzzer. If you know the frequency of the buzzer and its speed (see question 2), calculate the frequency heard by the observer.

6.4.3 Determining the Wavelength of Sound

Concepts to Investigate: Wavelength of sound, resonance, fundamental mode, harmonics, speed of sound.

Materials: Tuning forks, 1-liter graduated cylinder or equally deep sink or container, 1"- or 2"-diameter PVC or glass pipe, hacksaw, demonstration spring or rope.

Principles and Procedures: The length of an ocean wave is defined as the distance between the crests or troughs of two successive breakers. In a similar fashion, the length of a sound wave λ is defined as the distance between two compression or rarefaction pulses (Figure E). Although it is possible to measure the wavelength of ocean waves as they approach the shore, it is impractical to measure sound waves because they travel fast (340 m/s at 20°C) and are invisible. When, however, two waves of the same amplitude and wavelength travel in opposite directions, a "standing wave" is established providing the opportunity to make measurements. Standing longitudinal waves may be understood by analogy to standing transverse waves as occur in vibrating springs or ropes. In Part 1 we will examine standing transverse waves, and in Part 2 we will determine the wavelength of sound using standing longitudinal waves in an open pipe.

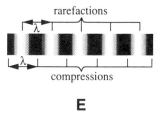

E

Part 1. Standing transverse waves: Secure one end of a wave demonstration spring or rope to an immovable object and move the other end in an oscillating fashion, as illustrated in Figure F. Some portions of the rope will appear to stand still (nodes), while other portions move rapidly back and forth (loops). In an open pipe such as a trumpet or trombone (Figure G), air molecules oscillate (move back and forth) rapidly at the loops, but not at all at the nodes. The fundamental mode is defined as the mode in which only one node exists (Figures F and G) and represents the lowest frequency, or tone, the instrument can produce. Move the free end of the rope more rapidly. When two nodes appear, the third harmonic has been established (Figures H and I). A "harmonic" is a whole number multiple of the fundamental frequency and can be generated given the same string or tube length as that producing the fundamental frequency. The pitch produced by a nonelectronic instrument is never pure, but contains one or more harmonics. These harmonics are responsible for the "quality" or "timbre" of a sound. Increase the frequency of the rope or spring again until first the fifth and then the seventh harmonics are produced. Listen carefully and notice that the loops in the rope generate a "whooshing" sound while the nodes remain silent. Draw pictures of both the fifth and seventh harmonics for a spring and an open pipe, identifying the nodes and loops in each.

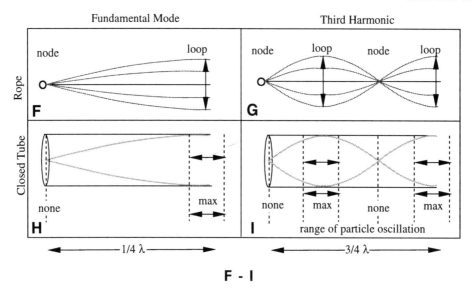

Fundamental Mode | Third Harmonic

F - I

Part 2. Standing longitudinal waves: Like the transverse waves in Part 1, standing sound waves also develop quiet nodes and noisy loops. The closed end of a tube acts like the fixed end of a rope, reflecting waves back toward their source. If the length of the tube is one quarter the wavelength (1/4 λ) of the sound, a loop will appear at the mouth of the tube, just as a loop appears in your hand in the fundamental mode of an oscillating rope or spring (Figures F and G). At this loop, there will be a maximum oscillation of particles, just as there was a maximum transverse oscillation of

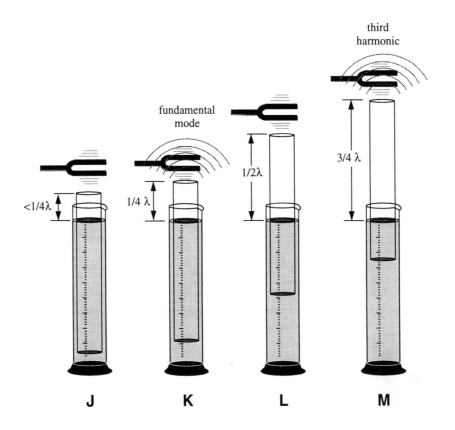

the rope. Consequently, the sound will reach a maximum volume and the tube is said to resonate or reverberate.

Use a hacksaw to cut a section (length ≥ 50 cm) of Plexiglas, PVC, or ABS pipe (diameter ≥ 2.5 cm) and immerse in an upright position in a large graduated cylinder or other deep container. Hold a vibrating middle-C (261.6 Hz) tuning fork above the cylinder (Figure J) and slowly raise the pipe until it resonates and the amplitude of the sound increases significantly (Figure K). The shortest length at which the pipe resonates is known as the fundamental mode and is one quarter the length of the sound wave. Measure the length of the air-filled pipe (l) and multiply by four to determine the wavelength λ of sound generated by the tuning fork. Continue raising the pipe and note that the volume decreases (Figure L) before it increases again at the third harmonic (Figure M). Record the length of the third harmonic. Is it three times the length of the first harmonic? Repeat this process, using other tuning forks in the octave scale and record your results in the table provided. Determine the relationship between frequency and wavelength by plotting your data. The wave equation states that $v = f\lambda$. Knowing this, calculate the speed of sound for each tuning fork. Is the speed of sound dependent upon its frequency?

Note	f $(1/s)$	l	λ $(4 \times L)$	$v_{(sound)}$ $(f \times \lambda)$
C	261.6			
D	293.7			
E	329.6			
F	349.2			
G	392.0			
A	440.0			
B	493.9			
C	523.3			

© 1994 by John Wiley & Sons, Inc.

Questions

(1) The speed v of sound is equal to its wavelength multiplied by its frequency $v = f\lambda$. Calculate the speed of sound produced by three tuning forks. Is the speed of sound dependent upon its wavelength ? Explain.

(2) How can one determine the fundamental mode?

(3) Does the pitch increase, decrease, or remain the same as the wavelength increases?

(4) If you have ever hummed while standing in a stairwell or shower, you may have noticed that certain frequencies cause the walls to vibrate. Explain why and when this will occur.

6.4.4 Resonant Frequency and Pitch

Concepts to Investigate: Frequency, resonance, pitch, scales.

Materials: Test tubes (15–20-cm long tubes work best), test-tube rack, Pasteur pipette or medicine dropper.

Principles and Procedures: The largest and most complex of all musical instruments is the pipe organ found in many large churches and concert halls. Pipe organs consist of a set of pipes connected to an air-supply system and controlled by a keyboard. Despite their magnificence, these grand instruments work on the same principle as the panpipes, an ancient instrument made from tubes of varying length. Even today, variations of the panpipes are used by musicians of China, South America, and Southeast Asia. Panpipes and pipe organs create different pitches using pipes of different lengths.

Part 1. Panpipes: In this activity you will create a simple set of closed-end panpipes and determine the relationship between the length of an air column and the pitch it generates. Place eight test tubes in a rack and fill with water, as shown in Figure N. Select a test tube and blow across its opening, adjusting your lips until you produce a resonant frequency (the point at which it "hums" loudest). Determine the lowest resonant frequency (fundamental frequency) for each of the tubes. Which test tube generates the lowest sound? Which test tube generates the highest sound? What relationship exists between the length of an air column and its fundamental frequency ?

Part 2. Developing a musical scale: You can develop an eight-note scale (do, re, mi, fa, so, la, ti, do) by adjusting the depth of the water in each tube until the tone matches a pure tone produced by a pitch pipe or tuning fork (Figure O). Use a Pasteur pipette or medicine dropper to adjust the water level in each tube. Once you have completed your scale, test it by playing a simple tune such as "Row, Row, Row Your Boat."

© 1994 by John Wiley & Sons, Inc.

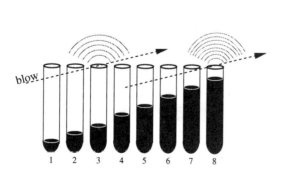

N

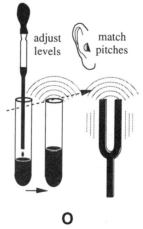

O

Questions

(1) Describe the relationship between the length of an air column and its associated pitch.

(2) Organists create different pitches by directing air into tubes of differing lengths. What enables trumpet players to play different pitches?

(3) Why is the range of notes from a sousaphone lower than those of a trumpet?

6.4.5 Laws of Strings

Concepts to Investigate: Laws of strings, law of length, law of tension.

Materials: Piano wire (high-test fishing line will suffice), spring scales, angle molding, 1m² sheet of plywood, nuts, bolts, weights.

Principles and Procedures: The first law of strings states that the frequency at which a string vibrates is inversely proportional to its length: f/f′ = l′/l; where f = original frequency, $f′$ = new frequency, l = original length, and $l′$ = new length. Thus, one can play a higher note on a guitar, banjo, violin, or other stringed instrument by shortening the length of the string plucked or bowed. To facilitate this, such instruments are equipped with narrow lateral ridges underneath the strings known as frets. The musician presses the wire against these frets to shorten the length of the string that is plucked. Construct your own stringed instrument by assembling the apparatus illustrated in Figure P. Hang equivalent weights on both lines and adjust the "frets" so the strings are as long as possible and produce the same pitch. Now shorten the length of one string to half by moving the position of the fret (Figure P). Does the pitch of the string increase as the law of length indicates?

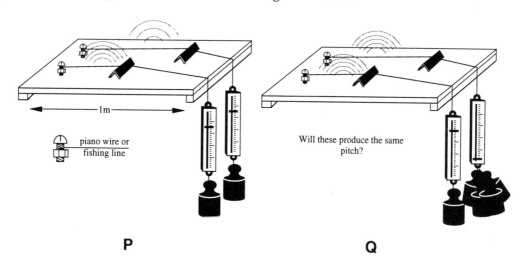

piano wire or
fishing line

Will these produce the same
pitch?

P   **Q**

A second law of strings states *that the frequency of a string is directly proportional to the square root of its tension: f/f′ = $\sqrt{T}/\sqrt{T′}$,* where T represents tension. Thus, if the tension on a string is quadrupled, the frequency of the string is doubled $f′ = (f\sqrt{T′})/\sqrt{T}$. Quadruple the tension on a string by quadrupling its weight (add three more equivalent masses) and pluck the string. Does the pitch of the string increase with tension as the law of tensions suggests?

The law of tensions states that frequency is inversely proportional to the length of the string, while the law of frequency states that it is directly proportional to the square root of its tension. Therefore, two strings should produce the same note if one has twice the length and four times the tension of the other. Try it and see if this is true (Figure Q).

Questions

(1) Does the pitch increase or decrease as the length of the vibrating portion of a string is increased?

(2) Guitar players make use of the law of lengths, but do they use the law of tensions? Explain.

(3) In addition to length and tension, the diameter and density of strings will affect their frequency. Look inside a piano and you will notice certain wires have very large diameters. What influence does this have upon the frequencies they produce?

FOR THE TEACHER

To increase student interest, ask them to bring musical instruments to class when studying the concepts discussed in this chapter. Whenever possible, use an oscilloscope to visually illustrate the principles of sound. To do so, connect a microphone, amplifier, and oscilloscope in series. The output from the amplifier becomes the input for the oscilloscope. Compare the complex wave patterns produced by human voices, stringed instruments, and wind instruments with those produced by a synthesizer. Unlike natural instruments and human voices, the synthesizer will produce clear, precise tones. To illustrate the relationship between frequency and pitch, connect a wave generator to the input port of an amplifier and an oscilloscope and loudspeaker in parallel on the output port. Students can then hear and see the relationship between frequency, wavelength, and pitch. *Note:* Make sure to read the owner's manuals of your electronic equipment before making connections.

6.4.1 Vibrational Frequency and Pitch

Discussion: Because many students have difficulty detecting changes in the frequency of vibrations in their larynx, you may wish to show the relationship of frequency and pitch in another manner. For example, if you have a multispeed fan, increase its speed (frequency) and have students note the accompanying increase in pitch.

Answers (1) Pitch is directly proportional to vibrational frequency. (2) Frequency is an objective measure of how rapidly something is vibrating. Pitch, however, is an interpretation of frequency by the listener. For example, a tone-deaf individual may be unable to discern between two pitches, but can use instruments to illustrate differences in their vibrational frequencies. (3) Infrasonic and ultrasonic vibrations have no pitch because human ears cannot detect them.

6.4.2 Doppler Effect

Discussion: The pitch of a moving object as observed by one standing in front of it can be calculated by the following equation:

$$f_o = f_x \; \frac{v}{v - v_x}$$

where f_o is the frequency observed, f_x = frequency emitted, v = velocity of sound (340 m/s at 20°C), and v_x is the velocity of the source. When the observer is behind the moving object the equation is

$$f_o = f_x \; \frac{v}{v + v_x}$$

If the velocity of the sound source v_x is small relative to the velocity of sound v, the observed frequency f_o may be indistinguishable from the emitted frequency f_x. If you know the frequency of the buzzer, you may ask your students to calculate the frequencies observed in front of and behind the can. The speed of the can can be determined by dividing the circumference of a swing $2\pi r$ by the time required per revolution. Students should note that the Doppler effect is more pronounced at higher speeds.

Answers (1) The pitch of the buzzer is highest when it is approaching the observer because the sound waves are being received at closer intervals. (2) Student answers will vary. (3) Student answers will vary.

6.4.3 Determining the Wavelength of Sound

Discussion: The wavelength of a fundamental tone (lowest resonant frequency) is approximately four times the length of a closed tube $\lambda \approx 4 \times l$. Experimentation, however, shows that the diameter of the tube also influences the frequency. When the diameter of the tube is considered, the equation becomes $\lambda = 4(l - 0.4d)$. Use this formula for more precise measurements and predictions.

This activity can easily be modified to study the effect of temperature on the speed of sound. The wave equation $v = f\lambda$ states that speed v is the product of frequency f and wavelength λ. Ask your students to determine the speed of sound at room temperature, then ask them to remeasure the speed of sound outside on a hot day and again on a cold day. The speed of sound is 331.5 m/s at 0°C and increases with temperature about (0.6 m/s)/°C.

The table in this section includes the frequencies of tuning forks for an equal-tempered scale. Some schools may have tuning forks tuned to the diatonic scale with the following frequencies: C, 256 Hz; D, 288 Hz; E, 320 Hz; F, 341.3 Hz; G, 384 Hz; A, 426.7 Hz.

Answers (1) No. The speed of sound is the same, regardless of frequency. If not, you would hear the sound of the piccolos in a marching band before the sound of the sousaphones, or vice versa. (2) The fundamental mode will be the shortest distance at which the pipe resonates. (3) As the wavelength increases, the pitch decreases. (4) A shower or stairwell has a natural frequency just as an open pipe does. Therefore, when you hum at this frequency, there will be resonant amplification.

6.4.4 Resonant Frequency and Pitch

Discussion: Students should note that the frequency of a closed pipe is inversely related to its length. The greater the length, the lower the frequency and pitch. You may wish to distribute tubes to each student and then serve as their conductor for a given tune. You may substitute soda bottles, PVC pipe, or Plexiglas tubes for the test tubes.

Answers (1) Pitch is inversely proportional to the length of the column. As the length of the air column increases, the pitch decreases. (2) The trumpet, like most brass instruments, has valves that redirect the flow of air. As valves are depressed, air is diverted to paths of differing lengths. If the length is longer, the note is lower, and if it is shorter, the note is higher. (3) The length of the tubing in a sousaphone is much greater than in a trumpet, so the range of resonant frequencies is much lower.

6.4.5 Laws of Strings

Discussion: The frequency of a string is dependent upon four factors, two of which the students examined in the activity. In addition, frequency is inversely proportional to string diameter and the square root of string density. An increase in either diameter or density will therefore decrease its pitch. You can illustrate the law of diameters by comparing the pitch produced by equal lengths of different-diameter (different test strength) fishing line, or guitar strings. This activity can also be used to introduce the concept of beats, amplitude pulsations that occur when two frequencies are slightly different. Musicians fine-tune their instruments by eliminating instrument-pitch-pipe beats.

Answers (1) As the length increases, the frequency decreases. (2) Yes. Musicians employ the law of strings when tuning their stringed instruments. By increasing the tension on the strings, frequency and pitch increase. (3) The frequency of a string is inversely proportional to its diameter if all other factors are constant: $f/f' = d'/d$. Large-diameter piano wires will therefore vibrate at lower frequencies than small-diameter wires.

Applications to Everyday Life

Ultrasonic Cleaning of Jewelry and Teeth: Jewelers use high-frequency sound to shake deposits off jewelry. Dentists and dental hygienists use ultrasound to remove plaque from teeth.

Ultrasonic Animal Communication: Dolphins produce a series of ultrasonic squeals to communicate danger and other basic messages. Bats use reflected ultrasound to locate insects and obstructions.

Removing Kidney Stones and Gallstones with Ultrasound: Kidney stones may form as a result of infection, disease, or metabolic disorder. Traditionally such calcium oxalate stones could be removed only by surgery, but now high-intensity ultrasonic waves are used to fracture them into small, harmless pieces that are subsequently eliminated through the urinary tract. In a similar fashion the gallstones (calcium, cholesterol, and bilirubin deposits) of the gall bladder can be shattered by ultrasound.

Ultrasonic Medical Diagnoses: Low-intensity ultrasonic waves are used to observe internal organs as well as the development and movement of children still in the womb. The high-frequency waves bounce off the organ or child and produce a video image physicians can interpret. Physicians can monitor heartbeat and blood flow using information provided by ultrasonic Doppler shifts.

Doppler-Shift Burglar Alarms: Numerous security devices employ the Doppler shift to detect intruders. By analyzing the frequency of reflected ultrasound, such alarms detect motion. If there has been no change in frequency, then there has been no motion in the room. An increased frequency indicates motion toward the sensor, while a decreased frequency indicates motion away from the sensor.

Wind Instruments and Resonance: All wind instruments rely upon the principles of resonance. By shortening the length of the resonating air column, the frequency may be increased. To increase the pitch, trombonists pull the slide in, trumpeters press valves to redirect the air through shorter passages, flutists open valves directly to the air, and organists, through keys on the console, select shorter pipes.

Musicians and the Laws of Strings: All stringed instruments rely upon the four laws of strings. Musicians can increase the desired pitch by shortening the length of the string (e.g., pressing down on the fret of a banjo), increasing the tension (e.g., tightening the strings to tune a violin), decreasing the diameter of the string (e.g., striking the thin strings on the right side of a piano), or decreasing the density.

Timbre and the Quality of Sound: The quality of a sound depends upon the number of harmonic frequencies produced and their relative intensities. Musicians pluck or bow stringed instruments near one end of the strings because this produces the greatest number of harmonics and consequently the richest sound.

6.5 WAVE PROPERTIES OF SOUND

The Hollywood Bowl in Los Angeles, California, is one of the world's most famous outdoor amphitheaters. It derives its name from a very large acoustically designed shell located behind the stage that reflects sound from the orchestra to the audience. Without the bowl, sound would rapidly dissipate, but with it the sound is sufficiently focused to provide excellent acoustics for the audience. Loudspeakers share a similar design, using a parabolic bowl to reflect sound waves toward the listener. *Sound is a wave phenomenon and reflects from surfaces just as light reflects from a mirror, or water waves reflect from a breakwater.* In addition to reflection, sound exhibits other properties characteristic of waves, including diffraction, interference, and refraction.

Diffraction is the bending of waves around obstacles. Sound waves bend around doorways and windows, enabling you to hear conversations in adjacent rooms, even though those speaking are not in a direct line of sight. Without diffraction, it would be much more difficult to eavesdrop on other peoples' conversations.

Interference is the interaction of wave trains that results in regions of reduced and enhanced amplitude (volume). When the crests of two waves meet, sounds are amplified, but when the crest of one meets the trough of another, sounds are diminished. Interference of sound is rarely observed because reflected sounds generally mask the interference pattern.

Refraction is the bending of waves that occurs as they pass obliquely (at an angle) from one medium, or layer, into another in which their speed is different. When waves slow down, they bend (refract) toward the normal (line perpendicular to the interface of two media), but when they speed up, they bend away from it. Sound travels faster in water than in air, while light travels faster in air than in water, and as a result, sound waves bend away from the normal when they enter water while light bends toward it. If you stand on a dock or on the side of a swimming pool and want to shout to a submerged friend, it is therefore best to aim your voice below your line of sight (see Figure A).

In this section you will have the opportunity to investigate reflection, diffraction, interference, and refraction of sound.

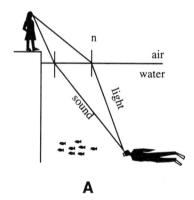

A

6.5.1 Reflection of Sound

Concepts to Investigate: Reflection, law of reflection, echo, superposition.

Materials: Buzzer or other sound source, poster board, funnel, large balloon (most plastic films will work well), candle.

Principles and Procedures: Just as ocean waves reflect off breakwaters and light waves reflect off mirrors, so sound waves reflect (echo) off various surfaces. If the reflecting surface is far enough from the source, such as a distant wall of a canyon, the reflected sound will return with sufficient delay and be heard separate and distinct from the original. Although sound reflects off virtually any surface, we rarely hear distinct echoes either because the reflecting surface is uneven or too close. When a surface is uneven, portions of the sound waves are reflected at different times and at different angles so the sound becomes garbled. When the reflecting surface is too close to the source, the sound returns too early to be distinguished from the original.

Part 1. Reflecting sound: Investigate the reflective properties of sound by holding a broad, flat board in back of an electronic noisemaker, ticking watch, or other sound-producing device. Slowly alter the angle of the board (Figure B) until the sound is loudest. Describe the angle θ of the board (relative to the sound source and your ears) at which the volume is maximum and the angle at which it is minimum and explain why this is so. Our ears are shaped in such a way as to reflect sound waves into the auditory canal to amplify sound. By cupping your hands around your ears you can reflect additional sound into your ears and thereby amplify sound even more. Cup your hands around your ears so they face your instructor while he or she is talking. Now cup them so they face away from your instructor. Do you hear the reflected sound of your instructor off the back wall of the room? The earliest hearing aid, known as the ear trumpet, used this principle to collect and amplify sound waves. Using poster board or other suitable material, develop your own "ear trumpet" hearing aid. Compare your design with that of other laboratory groups to determine which design amplifies sound the most.

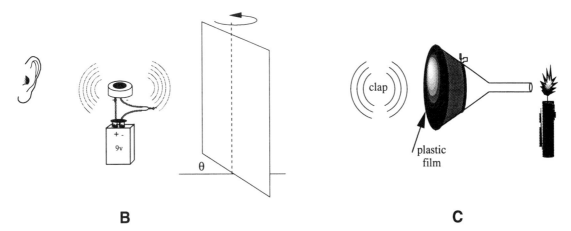

B   **C**

Part 2. Funneling sound: You can visualize the effect of reflected waves using the apparatus shown in Figure C. Stretch a piece of balloon or plastic film over the end of a funnel and aim the end at a lighted candle. Try to extinguish the flame by clapping in front of the funnel as illustrated. Determine the maximum distance from the candle that you can extinguish the flame by clapping, both with and without the funnel, and record your results. Draw a picture to illustrate how the funnel is used to amplify the sound waves through reflection.

Questions

(1)   Why might a teacher be more likely to strain his or her voice when presenting a lecture outdoors as opposed to indoors? Explain.

(2)   How do oceanographers use the principle of sound reflection to determine the depth of the oceans?

(3)   What was the maximum distance from the candle that you could extinguish the flame by clapping, both with and without the funnel? Explain how the funnel apparatus assists in extinguishing the flame.

(4)   Sound waves transmit energy without transporting matter. Explain how the funnel/candle demonstration illustrates this principle.

(5)   Concert halls are designed to provide a moderate amount of sound reflection. What effect does this have upon the quality of music heard by the audience?

(6)   The law of reflection states that the angle of incidence (the angle between the incoming wave and the normal) is equal to the angle of reflection (the angle between the reflected wave and the normal). Draw a diagram that illustrates how sound reflects in this way as it passes through the funnel.

6.5.2 Diffraction of Sound

Concept to Investigate: Diffraction.

Materials: 3000–4000-Hz electronic buzzer (available at electronic- and radio-supply stores), pitch pipe or tuning fork (available at music stores), fan, board.

Principles and Procedures: When a sound wave hits an obstacle, part is reflected while part may bend around the obstruction in a process known as diffraction. The relationship between wavelength and diffraction can be observed by noting the decrease in volume as the sound source moves behind a barrier. If there is much diffraction, the volume will not change significantly because the sound waves will bend around the edges and still reach the listener. If there is little or no diffraction, a significant change in volume will be observed. Obtain an electronic buzzer (available from most radio- and electronic-supply stores) that generates a high-pitched sound in the 3000–4000 Hz ($\lambda \approx 0.1$m) range. Place the buzzer on a tabletop in a box that has both ends removed. Face an open end toward you, as shown in Figure D. Note changes in the intensity of the sound as you gradually lower your head until it is well below the level of the table (Figure D). Repeat the procedure, listening to the constant tone of a pitch pipe, tuning fork, or hum, in the middle range of the scale (264–528 Hz; $\lambda \approx 1.3$–0.6m). Which diffracts more around the bench top (maintains the most constant volume), the high- or the moderate-frequency sound?

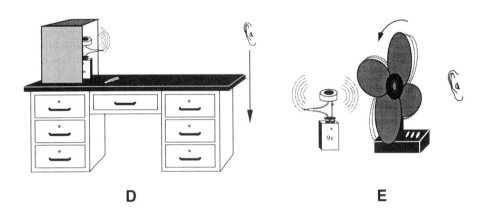

D   **E**

Obtain a fan and place the high- and moderate-pitch sound sources on the intake side, one at a time, while you listen on the output side (Figure E). When the fan is turned on, it will cut the path between the sound source and you. If the sound does not diffract, it will be cut into pulses, creating a warbling sound. If, however, the sound diffracts significantly, you will detect a constant tone because sound will bend around the edges of the fan to fill in the gaps. Which diffracts more through the fan (maintains the most constant volume), the high- or moderate-frequency sound?

Questions

(1) Which frequencies of sound (high or low) can you hear better around a corner?

(2) Does the high- or moderate-frequency sound diffract more around the desk? Through the fan? Explain.

(3) The sirens on many emergency vehicles emit a wide range of frequencies. What is one advantage of the low frequencies?

6.5.3 Interference of Sound

Concepts to Investigate: Interference, constructive interference, destructive interference, nodal lines (minima), antinodal lines (maxima).

Materials: 3000–4000-Hz electronic buzzer (available at radio- or electronic-supply stores), 2"-diameter PVC pipe (available from hardware stores) or large mailing tube or carpet tube.

Principles and Procedures: While standing at the shore of the ocean you may notice that waves momentarily increase in height when a wave reflected from the shore encounters an incoming wave. Both waves add together in a process known as constructive interference, creating a taller wave. When waves reflect off breakwaters or other obstructions, the same amplification process is observed, creating larger waves popular with surfers. When, however, a reflected wave encounters an incoming trough, the wave may momentarily disappear because the trough cancels the crest in a process known as destructive interference. In a similar manner, air is twice as compressed when the compression pulses of two sound waves meet, twice as rarefied when two rarefaction pulses meet, and normal when a compression and rarefaction pulses meet.

For audio interference to be observed, two sound sources must have the same frequency. To accomplish this, you will split the sound waves emanating from an electronic noisemaker by placing it in the middle of a 100-cm tube (carpet tube, PVC pipe, Plexiglas tube, or mailing tube work well). If the tubing is thin, wrap carpet, newspaper, or other sound-absorbing substance around its length so sound will be allowed to exit only from the ends of the tube. Hold the tube in a horizontal position with one end pointing directly at the listener, who is sitting approximately 3 meters away. As the pipe is rotated, the listener should observe fluctuations in the volume corresponding to the maxima (antinodal lines) and minima (nodal lines) resulting from interference (Figure F). Slowly rotate the pipe 180° and count the number of maxima. Collect data for tubes of 80-, 60-, and 40-cm lengths by cutting off portions of the tube. Does the number of antinodal lines (maxima) change as the length of the tube is shortened? Record your data in the table.

Tube Length	# Maxima	# Minima
100 cm	_____	_____
80 cm	_____	_____
60 cm	_____	_____
40 cm	_____	_____

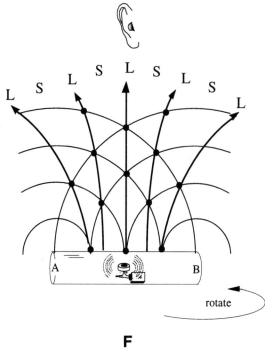

F

Questions

(1) Did you hear more or fewer maxima when the tube was shortened? Explain.

(2) Would maxima and minima from a P.A. (public address) system be more noticeable in a stadium or in an open field? Explain.

6.5.4 Refraction of Sound

Concepts to Investigate: Refraction, lenses, focal point.

Materials: 3000–4000-Hz electronic buzzer (available at radio- or electronic-supply stores), balloon, CO_2 source (dry ice, compressed CO_2, or vinegar and baking soda).

Principles and Procedures: When light passes from air into glass, it slows and bends toward the normal (line perpendicular to surface). This process, known as refraction, is used to design lenses for a wide variety of applications including eyeglasses, microscopes, telescopes, and photocopy machines. Because sound is a wave, it also refracts when passing through media with different propagation speeds. Carbon dioxide ($MW = 48$) has greater mass than equal volumes of either oxygen ($MW = 32$) or nitrogen ($MW = 28$), the principle components of air. Greater mass means carbon dioxide also has greater inertia and is slower in transmitting sound waves. Thus, if sound moves from a standard atmosphere into one of pure carbon dioxide, it will encounter greater molecular inertia and will slow down. By filling a balloon with carbon dioxide, it is possible to make a lens for focusing sound.

Fill the balloon with carbon dioxide in one of the following ways:

1. Fill the balloon directly from a cylinder of compressed carbon dioxide.
2. Crush dry ice and use a funnel to place it into a deflated balloon. As the dry ice sublimes, the balloon will fill with carbon dioxide gas.
3. Mix vinegar with baking soda (sodium hydrogen carbonate) in an Erlenmeyer flask. A few seconds after the bubbling begins, cap the flask with the balloon.

Most of the air is displaced during the initial seconds, so the gas that subsequently fills the balloon will be enriched in carbon dioxide. Method 1 is best.

Place the buzzer on a table approximately 4 meters away from your ear. Cover the buzzer with towels until it is barely audible at the 4-meter distance. Move the balloon back and forth between you and the buzzer and locate the position at which the sound is loudest (Figure G).

When the sound waves strike the carbon dioxide in the balloon, they decelerate and bend toward the normal so that the angle of refraction *r* is less than the angle of incidence *i*. When the sound waves reach the far side of the balloon, they pass into a media (air) with lower inertia than carbon dioxide, so the angle of refraction will be greater than the angle of incidence, and the wave front will bend away from the normal (Figure H). As a result of the geometry of the balloon, the sound will be focused at a location known as the focal point. The distance between your ear and the center of the balloon is known as the focal length of your "sound lens." What is the focal length of your balloon? How could you make sound lenses with longer or shorter focal lengths?

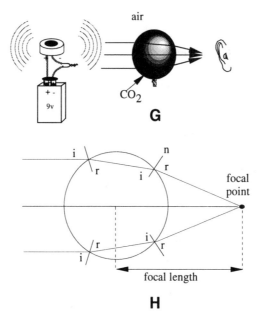

G

H

Questions

(1) What was the focal length (the distance required to focus the sound) of the balloon filled with carbon dioxide?

(2) The balloon focuses high-frequency sound better than low-frequency sound. Why?

(3) Which would focus sound better, a balloon filled with helium or one filled with xenon?

(4) Fill a second balloon with your breath and drop it at the same time as you drop the balloon filled with carbon dioxide. Which appears to be denser? Explain.

FOR THE TEACHER

All wave phenomena share certain properties: reflection, diffraction, interference, and refraction. While the first three are easily observable with sound, refraction is much more difficult to observe. Sound waves refract, or bend, when they pass between media with differing acoustic properties. For instance, as sound travels from air to water it speeds up and bends away from the normal (the normal is the line perpendicular to the surface at the point of incidence), and when it moves from water to air it slows down and bends toward the normal. Although the refraction of sound is relatively unimportant in the terrestrial environment in which we live, it is very important when studying the propagation of sound through large bodies of water. Propagation speed is affected by temperature and pressure, both of which vary greatly with depth. When generating profiles of the ocean floor, oceanographers rely upon reflected sound waves to determine relative depth. If scientists fail to account for refraction due to changes in speed associated with depth, their maps will be grossly inaccurate.

6.5.1 Reflection of Sound

Discussion: Sound reflections are ubiquitous and taken for granted, but are very helpful to teachers who talk with large numbers of students each day. The walls of the classroom reflect your voice back to students, thereby reducing the amplitude necessary to communicate effectively. You may have noticed you speak much louder when conducting an outdoor field trip because you are compensating for the lack of reflection. Teachers who have chronic laryngitis will aggravate their speech problems if they lecture out of doors or in large lecture rooms where reflection is minimal. Make sure students understand the law of reflection: that sound will reflect from a surface at an equal angle to the angle it approaches the surface, just as a handball bounces off a wall at an equal angle to the angle it approaches the wall.

Answers (1) When lecturing outdoors, there is no barrier to reflect sound back to the audience, so volume is diminished. People compensate for this lack of reflection by raising their voices, and this subsequently tires them. (2) Given the speed of sound in water, oceanographers can calculate depth using the following equation: $d = vt_{echo}/2$, where d is the depth, v is the velocity of sound in water, and t_{echo} is the time required for the echo. The value is divided by 2 because sound has traveled twice the depth by the time it returns to the sender. (3) Students will find there is a dramatic difference in distance. Sound reflects off the walls of the funnel such that the angle of incidence equals the angle of reflection. Because the funnel walls are sloped, the sound reflects back toward the center line. As the funnel becomes narrower, the energy becomes more concentrated. According to the principle of superposition, when waves intersect, the magnitude of the resultant wave is the sum of all involved. As a result, the compression and rarefaction pulses become great. When the rarefaction pulse hits the candle, there is little oxygen and the flame is easily extinguished. (4) The membrane was located between the clap and the flame, yet the flame was extinguished, indicating that energy was transferred to the candle even though matter was not. (5) A moderate amount of reflected sound contributes to the clarity and brightness of music. If the walls are excessively reflective, however, reverberations (reechoes) occur, distorting the quality of the music. (6) Student diagrams.

6.5.2 Diffraction

Discussion: Waves spread beyond an opening in a barrier in a process known as diffraction. The spreading of waves is greatest when the length of the wave is approximately the same as the width of the opening. Visible light is composed of wavelengths of approximately 4 x10^7 m to 7 x 10^{-7} m, while the wavelengths of human speech are in the 1– 4-meter range. Since the wavelengths of human speech are comparable to the dimensions of doors and windows, a substantial amount of diffraction occurs enabling you to hear people who are talking even though they may be standing around a corner or outside a door. Because the wavelength of visible light is so small compared to the dimensions of doors and windows, little diffraction of light occurs, making it impossible to see individuals if they are standing around a corner, even though you may hear them speak.

Answers (1) Low frequencies. (2) Low-pitched sounds provide the most constant volume both around the edge of the desk and through the fan, indicating that they experience the greatest degree of diffraction. (3) Low frequencies (long wavelengths) diffract more around large obstructions such as buildings and cars, making it easier for drivers who are not in the line of sight of an emergency vehicle to hear its siren.

6.5.3 Interference

Discussion: This activity works well as a classroom demonstration. Have your students hold their hands up when they hear a maxima, and put them down when they hear a minima. As you slowly rotate the tube, students will indirectly see waves of maxima and minima rotating as students alternately raise and lower their hands. The diffraction pattern is dependent upon the frequency of the sound source. If the frequency of the sound source is low, the wavelengths will be long and the number of interactions between waves will be reduced. For this reason, interference patterns in short pipes ($\leq$1 m) are best observed when the frequency of the buzzer is rather high (3000–4000 Hz). The angles along which maxima are located can be calculated by the equation $sin\theta = n\lambda/d$, where θ is the diffraction angle, n is the order of the maxima, λ is the wavelength of the sound, and d is the distance between the ends of the tube. You may ask your students to conduct experiments to verify this relationship.

Answers (1) When the tube is shortened, there will be fewer maxima. The number of orders of maxima can be determined by dividing the distance between the two sound sources by the wavelength of the sound. A 3000-Hz sound has a wavelength of 0.11m. Therefore, it will produce approximately 9 orders of maxima when placed in a 1-meter tube. (2) If a P.A. system has two speakers, it is possible to detect an interference pattern in an open field, but virtually impossible in a stadium because the reflection of sound waves from the walls of the stadium mask the interference pattern.

6.5.4 Refraction

Discussion: It is possible to make a lens with a longer focal length simply by diluting the carbon dioxide in the balloon. If you fill the balloon half full with carbon dioxide and then fill the rest with your breath, you will create an environment in which the propagation speed is less than air, but greater than the pure carbon dioxide. This lens will be less dense and possess a longer focal length.

Answers (1) The focal length of this lens will probably be between 0.3 and 1.0 meters. (2) Low-frequency sounds will diffract around the balloon. (3) Xenon. The balloon filled with helium would not be able to focus sound because helium (AW = 4) is less dense than either oxygen or nitrogen. As a result, sound would travel faster through the helium and diverge rather than converge. Xenon (AW = 54) is more massive than the other components of air and therefore serves as a better "sound lens" than carbon dioxide. (4) The balloon filled with carbon dioxide is denser and will fall faster since the force-to-air-friction ratio is greater.

Applications to Everyday Life

High-Tech Fishing: Fishing fleets often use SONAR (*Sound Navigation and Ranging*) to detect schools of fish. Sound waves reflected off schools of fish are distinct from those reflected off the ocean bottom, allowing fishermen to locate good areas in which to spread their nets.

Nondestructive-Materials Testing: Minute flaws in machinery can be detected using reflected ultrasound since minute cracks and other defects alter the angle of reflection. Technicians examine ultrasound reflections (as translated on video screens) to locate material defects.

Loud Car Stereos: Low frequencies diffract easily through car windows and around obstacles, explaining why it is more common to hear the low notes (bass) than the high notes from the stereo of a passing car.

Eavesdropping: The "eavesdrop" is the location where water drips from the eaves of a roof. Eavesdropping gets its name from people who stand under the eaves of a house to listen secretly to the private conversation of others. Eavesdropping is possible because sound diffracts through doorways and open windows, while light does not. This allows the eavesdropper to listen without being seen.

Acoustic Shadows: Diffraction is greatest when wavelength approximates the dimensions of the opening or obstruction through which, or around which, it is diffracted. For this reason, diffraction of sound around a book is significant (the book casts virtually no acoustic shadow), while diffraction around a building is minimal (the building casts a large acoustic shadow).

Interference in Outdoor P.A. Systems: A two-speaker public-address system will create nodal lines (where sound is softer) and antinodal lines (where sound is louder). These soft and loud locations are noticeable only when reflected sound is eliminated.

Ocean Cartography and Marine "Shadows": The velocity of sound in an ocean varies with depth and temperature. Sound bends as it descends into the cold pressurized water, making it difficult to receive reflected sound from certain zones of the ocean floor. For this reason, "shadow" areas exist, hidden beyond the realm of SONAR detection. Cartographers need to use other techniques to map these sections of the ocean floor.

Light

7.1 Reflection

7.2 Refraction

7.3 Interference and Diffraction

7.4 Polarization

7.5 Optics

7.6 Color

7.1 REFLECTION

In 1948, American scientists and engineers inaugurated the Hale telescope on top of Mt. Palomar, California. Since its construction, the Hale telescope has produced a wealth of information about our solar system, galaxy, and universe. The critical component in this massive instrument is a 200-inch-diameter concave mirror that gathers light and magnifies its intensity nearly 1,000,000 times. Although the Hale telescope is still quite useful, it must examine the stars through an atmosphere that is increasingly subject to air and light pollution. To avoid atmospheric interference, engineers designed the Hubble Space Telescope and launched it into orbit on the NASA Space Shuttle in 1990. The Hubble Space Telescope uses a 94-inch-diameter mirror and cost approximately 1.5 billion dollars. This 12-ton instrument was designed to see objects 50 times fainter than those seen by earthbound telescopes. While astronomers have begun to send telescopes into orbit, they have not abandoned the drive to perfect terrestrial telescopes. The Keck Observatory atop 4,205-m (13,796-ft) Mauna Kea in Hawaii became the world's largest telescope when it opened in 1992. This massive instrument has a 394-inch mirror, composed of 36 separate segments fitted together to produce the correct curvature.

Although instruments like the Keck Observatory, the Hubble Space Telescope, and the Hale Telescope are extremely expensive and sophisticated devices, they rely upon a principle that has been known for centuries: reflection. The phenomenon of reflection was probably first observed in still ponds and lakes. The ancient Egyptians developed the first solid mirrors using the reflective mineral selenite, and the Romans later improved the technology by placing reflective metal sheets behind glass plates. In 1835, the German chemist Justus von Liebig developed a process for depositing silver on glass that is still used in the manufacture of household mirrors. In addition to telescopes and the household vanity, mirrors are used in cameras, dental tools, automobiles, projectors, head lamps, and many other devices. One wealthy Swiss man was so enamored with mirrors that he built a mirrored maze in his hometown of Lucerne. The reflections are so confusing that many tourists need maps of the maze to escape.

Scientists believe light is composed of tiny packets of energy known as photons. When a photon strikes a surface, it can either go though it (transmit), stop (be absorbed), or bounce off (reflect). A mirror is an excellent reflector because nearly all the photons bounce off it, while black paint is a poor reflector (good absorber) because nearly all the photons stop when they hit it. You can see this page because photons from the sun or other light source reflect off it and proceed to the retina of your eye where they are absorbed. *All light follows the law of reflection: the angle of incidence (the angle light rays strike the surface) is equal to the angle of reflection (the angle the rays bounce off the surface).* All angles are defined with reference to the normal, a line perpendicular to the surface at the point of incidence (the point where light strikes the surface). An angle of incidence of 90° is parallel to the surface, while an angle of incidence of 0° is perpendicular to the surface. The law of reflection can be easily observed by watching the bounce passes of basketball players (Figure A). The larger the angle of incidence, the larger the angle of reflection.

The law of reflection applies to a wide variety of wave and particle phenomena. Ocean waves reflect off breakwaters, radio waves reflect off the ionosphere, and handballs reflect off court walls. Can you describe how the law of reflection is used in the following sports: basketball, baseball, racquetball, tennis, billiards?

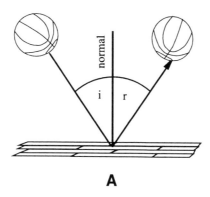

A

7.1.1 Law of Reflection

Concepts to Investigate: Law of reflection, mirror images, angle of incidence, angle of reflection.

Materials: Large mirror (approximately 2' × 3'), string, 5 or more small mirror tiles (available from home-improvement stores), masking tape, small blocks of wood, butcher paper.

Principles and Procedures

Part 1. Law of reflection: The law of reflection states that the angle of incidence (i) must equal the angle of reflection *r*. To investigate this law, mount a large mirror (approximately 2' × 3') at eye level in the center of a classroom wall (Figure B). Using chalk, draw a line normal (perpendicular) to the wall on the floor, aligned with the center of the mirror, as shown. Arrange six students in a symmetrical row an arbitrary distance from the mirror, as shown. Attach a piece of tape to the center of the mirror and ask each student to focus on that piece of tape and report the name of the person they see in the mirror. If the angle of incidence is equal to the angle of reflection, then pairs of students should be mutually visible. For example, if student 1 can see only student 6, then student 6 should be able to see only student 1. Tape the center of a piece of long string to the center of the mirror and hand one end to each student in a pair. The participating students should hold the strings against their noses while a third student uses a protractor to measure the angle of incidence and the angle of reflection at the mirror. Repeat for each pair of students. Do your data support the law of reflection? Repeat the procedure at different distances from the mirror.

© 1994 by John Wiley & Sons, Inc.

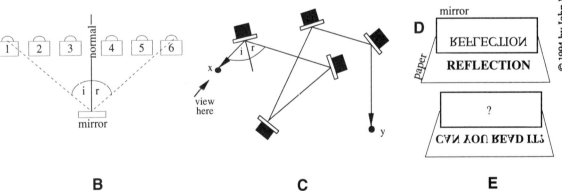

B	**C**	**E**

Part 2. "Hide and seek" with mirrors: Roll out butcher paper on a large table and identify two arbitrary positions on the edge as *x* and *y*. Attach small mirrors to wooden blocks or the sides of milk cartons. Use a water-soluble pen to draw a small circle in the middle of each mirror. One student should crouch down so his or her nose is directly above *x*, while the other student does the same at *y*. Position the mirrors such that you can see the other student through the reflections of all five mirrors (see Figure C). Adjust the mirrors so all dots line up, trace their location on the

butcher paper, and use a meter stick to trace the light path from the center of one mirror to the center of the next. Use a protractor to measure the angles. Does the angle of incidence equal the angle of reflection in each case? Repeat the activity using two different locations for *x* and *y*.

Part 3. Mirror images: Have you ever tried to trim your hair while looking in a mirror? It's not easy because the image you see is a "mirror image." Hold a page of written text up to a mirror and note that it is difficult to read because images are reversed (Figure D). What would happen if you held up a page of reversed text? Would the mirror unscramble the image? Write a message on a sheet of paper using large, bold lettering. Place the paper on a window and trace the outline of the lettering as seen from the back. Hold this reversed image up to the mirror. Can you read your message (Figure E)? Draw a ray diagram of a reflected letter to illustrate that "mirror images" are a result of the law of reflection (ray diagrams are discussed in section 7.5).

　　　If an object is made of two "mirror images" we say it has bilateral symmetry. To show the bilateral symmetry of a person, obtain a picture of someone's face from a magazine. Cut the picture in half down the midline. Hold the picture up to a mirror to recreate the face. The image may appear rather unusual because faces of humans do not exhibit perfect symmetry. It is the subtle asymmetrical features in human faces that help us recognize people.

Questions

(1) 　When looking in the rearview mirror of a car, a driver sees only the forehead of a passenger in the back seat. Can the passenger see the eyes of the driver?

(2) 　How many ways are there of arranging the mirrors so both students can see each other (part 2)?

(3) 　Does the angle of incidence equal the angle of reflection when there are multiple mirrors?

(4) 　How could you design a periscope, such as those used on submarines? Draw a ray diagram illustrating how it would work.

7.1.2 Creating Illusions with Reflections

Concepts to Investigate: Law of reflection, image.

Materials: Two candles, pane of glass.

Principles and Procedures: In the past two hundred years, "magic" shows have become a popular form of entertainment, as crowds are baffled by the illusions, sleight of hand, and trickery of "magicians." During the nineteenth century, illusionists developed a variety of marvelous tricks using electromagnets, unusual stage lighting, and a variety of optical devices. In this activity you will investigate a classic illusion based on the principle of reflection.

Place a lighted candle approximately 15 centimeters in front of the center of a pane of glass. Position a second candle behind the glass such that it is aligned with the reflection of the flame of the first one when viewed in front (Figures F, G). The rear candle appears to be lit because the reflected rays from the flame align with the direct rays from the rear candle (Figure H). To enhance the impact of the illusion, place your hand above the unlit candle so that your hand appears to be in the flame when viewed from the front. Now place the unlit candle in a beaker of water so it appears to be burning under water when viewed from the front. It may be necessary to adjust the room lighting to obtain the optimal illusion.

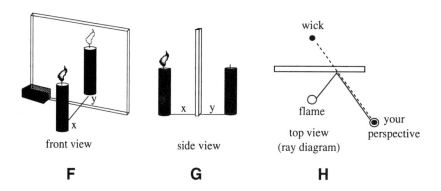

front view   side view   top view
                                                         (ray diagram)

   F   G   H

© 1994 by John Wiley & Sons, Inc.

Once you have determined the precise location at which the unlit candle appears to be burning, measure the distances between the candles and the mirror x, y. Move the lighted candle to a distance of 20 cm from the mirror and adjust the unlit candle so it appears to be burning once again. How would you describe the relationship between an object and the apparent position of its image in the mirror?

Questions

(1) What is the relationship between the position of the flame and the apparent position of its image?

(2) If you double the distance between an object and a mirror, where is the apparent position of the image?

(3) From what angles does the unlit candle appear to be burning?

7.1.3 Multiple Images

Concepts to Investigate: Images, multiple reflections, lasers, coherent light.

Materials: Two mirrors (preferably made of steel or plastic), tape. Optional: drill.

Principles and Procedures: Tape two mirrors together so they are connected like the binding of a book and position them so they are at an angle of approximately 140° to each other. Place a marking pen, candle, or other object in front of the mirrors and count the number of images (Figure I). Decrease the angle between the two mirrors and use a protractor or polar-coordinate graph paper to measure the maximum and minimum angles for a given number of images. What is the angular range in which three images appear? Four images? Five images? In the table provided, record the range of angles at which the specified number of images can be seen. What will happen to the number of images as the angle between the mirrors approaches zero?

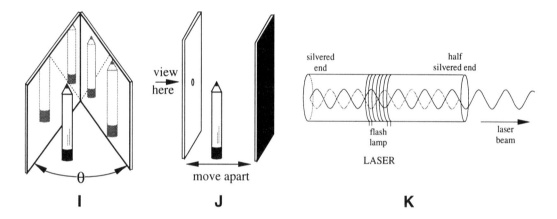

Separate the mirrors and position them so they are parallel. (If the mirrors are made of steel or plastic, you may drill a viewing hole in the center of one.) Look through the viewing hole or across the top of one of the mirrors and observe the series of "shrinking" images. Position the mirrors so you can obtain as many images as possible (Figure J). What is the maximum number you can see?

Parallel mirrors are widely used in lasers such as the ruby laser shown in Figure K. A xenon flash lamp excites electrons in the ruby crystal. As electrons return from their energetic state, they emit light of a standard wavelength. A standing light wave is established as light bounces off the mirrored ends of the tube. (This is analogous to a standing sound wave in the pipe of an organ.) One end of the tube is only half-silvered, allowing some light to escape. All the radiation in this beam of light has the same wavelength and phase relationship and is said to be coherent. Lasers are also made using glass, liquid, gas, or plastic and have a wide variety of industrial applications. They are used to scan bar codes at the supermarket, guide aircraft for instrumentation landings, repair detached retinas in the eyes, send telephone messages across fiber-optic cables and read music and data from compact discs. Without the simple principle of reflection, these and many other "high-tech" applications would not exist.

Number of Images										
	3	4	5	6	7	8	9	10	11	12
Maximum angle										
Minimum angle										

Questions

(1) What is the range of angles between the mirrors that creates four images? Five images? Six images? Seven images?

(2) Many photocopiers include a reducing feature. Although this is typically achieved using lenses, how might it be achieved using mirrors? Explain.

7.1.4 Total Internal Reflection

Concepts to Investigate: Total internal reflection, critical angle.

Materials: Aquarium, slide projector or flashlight with focusable beam, cooking oil, rubbing alcohol, food coloring, beaker.

Principles and Procedures

Part 1. Critical angle for water/air interface: The higher the optical density of a substance, the farther toward the normal light it will bend (higher index of refraction, see section 7.2). Although light may enter a material of high optical density, it is not always possible for it to leave. There is a critical angle above which light will no longer pass through the interface, but will instead be entirely reflected internally. In this investigation you will determine this angle for a water/air interface.

Tape a protractor on the side of an aquarium filled with water. Darken the room and project a light beam from a slide projector or focusable flashlight up through the water, as illustrated in Figure L. Adjust the angle of the light and determine the angle at which it is entirely reflected at the water/air interface, as indicated by the decrease in light falling on the card (Figure M). The angle at which the light is no longer transmitted is known as the critical angle.

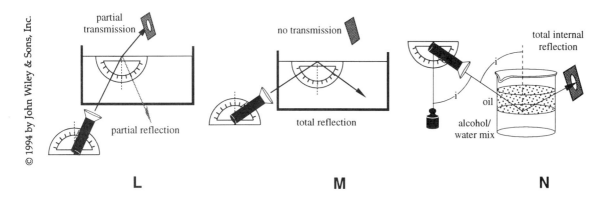

Part 2. Critical angle for oil/alcohol: Fill a beaker half full with a 33 percent alcohol mixture (2 parts water to 1 part isopropyl alcohol by volume). Place a few drops of food coloring in this mix. Slowly fill the top half of the beaker with vegetable oil. Oil is less dense than the alcohol/water mix, and will float on the surface. Although oil has a lower mass density, it has a higher optical density. Darken the room and shine the light on the oil water interface (Figure N). If the angle of incidence is small, the light will refract (bend) through the oil/water interface and illuminate the lower liquid, revealing its color. If, however, the angle of incidence is high, the light will be totally reflected and will not enter the oil. Record the critical angle for this interface. (Any angle greater than the critical angle will result in total internal reflection.)

Repeat this experiment using a 67 percent alcohol mixture (1 part water to 2 parts isopropyl alcohol). Put the food coloring in the oil, put the oil in the beaker first and then layer the alcohol/water mix on top. Does light reflect off the interface as before? Explain.

Questions

(1) Are you able to see the color of the food dye when the angle of incidence is greater than the critical angle?

(2) Describe the appearance of the oil/water interface when illuminated from a large angle of incidence.

(3) Is it possible to have total internal reflection when light travels from a material of low optical density (such as alcohol) into a material with high optical density (such as oil)? Explain.

(4) Why is a diamond brilliant? Relate your explanation to the findings of this investigation.

7.1.5 Fiber Optics

Concepts to Investigate: Total internal reflection, fiber optics.

Materials: Plastic soda bottle, burner, tongs, nail, high-intensity focusable flashlight or 35-mm projector, aluminum foil, goggles, glass rod, flashlight.

Principles and Procedures: Fiber optics is a technology with an immense number of industrial applications. Optical fibers made of glass or other transparent materials conduct light while copper and other metals conduct electricity. Fiber optics permit the transmission of superior video and sound messages and are not subject to electromagnetic interference as are metal wires. In this activity you will investigate some of the concepts behind fiber optics.

Part 1. "Pouring light": Use tongs to insert the tip of a nail in the flame of a laboratory burner. Remove the nail from the flame and melt one hole in the side of a plastic soft-drink bottle, as illustrated in Figure O. When the plastic is cool, cover the hole with a piece of transparent tape. After wrapping the bottle in aluminum foil, make a small window over the hole in the bottle, as well as a large one on the opposite side of the container. Fill the bottle with water, darken the room, position a flashlight as illustrated, and then remove the tape over the hole (Figure P). Does the light travel in a straight line, or does it follow the stream of water?

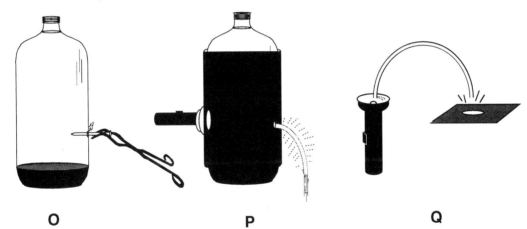

O   P   Q

Part 2. Fiber Optics: (CAUTION: Wear goggles and do not touch sections of glass that have been placed in the flame until they are cool.) Use a flame spreader to gently bend glass stirring rods to form the following shapes: "L", "U", and a "loop." The curves should be arcs, not right angles. When cool, place one end of the glass rod on the lens of the flashlight and examine the other end (Figure Q). If there is sufficient internal reflection, the end of the tube will glow. Does light reflect around bends? Loops? Experiment with other shapes to determine which transmit light best.

Questions

(1) Where does the beam of light emerge from the stream of water?
(2) Which conducts light better, glass bent at an abrupt right angle or glass bent in a gradual arc? Explain.
(3) Traditional telephone cables are made of copper, while fiber-optic cables are made of glass. Which type of cable would be better suited for telephone lines near an electrical power station? Why?

FOR THE TEACHER

This unit on electromagnetism includes chapters on reflection, refraction, diffraction, polarization, optics, and color. For visibility and convenience, most of the activities use visible light, and this may give students the false impression that the information learned does not apply to other forms of electromagnetism. Impress upon your students that visible light is but one portion of the electromagnetic radiation spectrum and that other forms of electromagnetism, including power, radio (long wave, AM, short wave, TV, FM, microwaves), infrared, ultraviolet, X-rays, gamma, and cosmic, also exhibit the phenomena discussed.

7.1.1 Law of Reflection

Discussion: The activity in Part 1 is a good classroom demonstration because all students can participate simultaneously. Make an overhead transparency of a scale drawing of your seating chart and ask each student whom they see. Then draw appropriate ray diagrams on the transparency to illustrate the law of reflection. Part 2 lends itself nicely to a classroom game. After selecting positions for x and y, the teacher can challenge students to arrange the mirrors in as short a time as possible to achieve the desired objective. Besides the motivational value, this will help develop an intuitive understanding of the law of reflection.

Answers: (1) No. You can see another person's eyes only if they are able to see yours. (2) There is an unlimited number of ways to arrange the mirrors. (3) Yes, the principle is universal. (4) The ocular mirror of a periscope is positioned at a 45° angle to the observer. The objective mirror is parallel but opposite to this mirror, causing light to reflect through two right angles before reaching the observer (see Figure R).

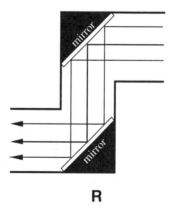

R

7.1.2 Creating Illusions with Reflection

Discussion: This activity makes an excellent classroom demonstration because it is relatively independent of the viewing angle. Lighting, however, is critical. If the lighting is too bright, you will be unable to see the reflection of the flame in the glass, and if the lighting is too dim, you will be unable to see the unlit candle. For classroom demonstrations, a distance of 30 cm works well.

Answers (1) The image created by a planar mirror will appear to be located the same distance behind the mirror as the object is in front. (2) Doubling the distance between object and mirror doubles the apparent distance to the image. This is easily checked by placing the unlit candle where it appears to be lit and measuring the distance. (3) Nearly all.

7.1.3 Multiple Images

Discussion: The number of images increases as the angle between the mirrors decreases. The minimal angle θ for a given number of images n is given by the equation: $\theta = 360°/n$. Thus, if you want to get 20 images, the angle between the mirrors must have a value between 18.0° and 18.9° ($360°/20 = 18.0°$; $360°/19 = 18.9°$). As the angle approaches zero, n approaches infinity. Thus, to achieve an infinite number of images, the mirrors must be precisely parallel. This is a good activity to introduce the mathematical concept of limits.

Answers (1) 4 images: 90°–120°; 5 images: 72°–90°; 6 images: 60°–72°; 7 images: 51°–60° (2) Each time an image is reflected, it is also reduced. An image can be reduced by increasing the net length of a ray's path either by adding more mirrors or by increasing the distance between mirrors.

7.1.4 Total Internal Reflection

Discussion: Alcohol and water are both polar solvents and are thus miscible with each other, but immiscible with the nonpolar oil. Vegetable oil (corn oil) is less dense than water, but more dense than alcohol, thus a dilute alcohol/water mixture will sink while a concentrated mixture will float on the oil. If you perform this activity as a teacher demonstration, it is essential to have a narrow, intense beam of light such as a laser, slide projector, or light-beam pointer so all students in the class will be able to see the effect.

Answers (1) If the angle of incidence is greater than the critical angle, all light will be reflected at the interface. Since the flashlight is the only source of light in the room, the food dye will not receive any illumination and will not be seen. (2) The interface will appear shiny when the angle of incidence is greater than the critical angle. This shininess results from total internal reflection and may resemble a silvered mirror. (3) No. As light enters material of high optical density it bends toward the normal, rather than away from it. (4) The oil in this activity appeared bright because light was reflected back to the surface. Diamonds possess a very high index of refraction ($n = 2.42$) and thus reflect substantially more light than the oil in this experiment. The cut of the diamond is designed to promote extensive internal reflection. It is the ability of diamonds to internally reflect light that makes them the most brilliant of gemstones.

7.1.5 Fiber Optics

Discussion: Fiber optics depend upon total internal reflection of light within glass and/or plastic fibers. This can be illustrated with a "fiber glass" fountain (available at many novelty stores). These "fountains" are made of numerous glass or plastic fibers bound together at the bottom and free at the top. A small light illuminates these fibers at the bottom, and the free tips subsequently glow, showing that light has reflected through the bends in the fibers.

Answers (1) The light beam emerges at the point where the stream breaks up. (2) Gradual turns are necessary for continued transmission of optical signals. If a turn is too abrupt, light will hit the interface at less than the critical angle and exit the glass rather than reflect. (3) Glass telephone cables are superior to copper cables whenever there are strong electrical or magnetic fields. Copper is an excellent conductor of electricity, and as a result, copper lines are susceptible to electromagnetic interference, while glass lines are not.

Applications to Everyday Life

Flashlights and Searchlights: Flashlights, automobile headlights, and searchlights are designed to project a beam of light with minimal dispersion. To accomplish this, the light bulb is positioned at the focus of a parabolic mirror. Light rays emanating from the focus will reflect off the parabolic mirror parallel to the parabola's axis and emerge as a parallel beam.

Moon, Planets, and Comets: The moon does not emit any light of its own and would be invisible if it did not reflect the sun's light. Planets, moons, comets, and interstellar dust are seen only because they reflect the light of stars.

Periscopes, Photoperiscopes: A periscope employs two mirrors to reflect light rays through two 90° angles. Submarines use periscopes to view the horizon without surfacing, and archeologists use photoperiscopes to photograph ancient tombs and other archeological digs to avoid disturbing the contents.

Reflecting Microscopes: A reflecting microscope employs an objective composed of one convex mirror and one concave mirror. Because mirrors are used, rather than lenses, reflecting microscopes are not subject to chromatic aberration (the nonfocusing of light of different wavelengths). Although simple in design, reflecting microscopes have very small tolerances and are therefore more expensive and less popular than refracting microscopes.

Reflecting Telescopes: Reflecting telescopes can be made larger than refracting telescopes because large lenses are exceedingly difficult to make and often warp under their own weight.

Multiple-Mirror Reflecting Telescope: The Whipple Observatory at Mount Hopkins, Arizona, uses 600 3-inch mirrors simultaneously to collect light. The light-gathering ability of this scope is equivalent of a single 176-inch mirror.

Solar Collectors and Furnaces: Concentrating solar collectors are made from parabolic mirrored troughs or dishes. Light is focused on a central tube to boil water for heating or steam generators. Solar furnaces use an array of mirrors and may concentrate enough light to melt steel. The largest solar furnace in the world, "Solar I" near Barstow, California, is constructed of approximately 2,000 concentrically arranged mirrors.

Telecommunications: The principle of total internal reflection has made possible the field of fiber optics. Traditionally, telephone messages have been sent on copper wires, but today an increasing percentage are being sent on optical fibers. Optical fibers are superior to copper wires because they offer a wider bandwidth, are lightweight, and exhibit low attenuation of signals. They are also nonconducting with respect to electricity and are therefore not susceptible to electromagnetic interference.

Microsurgery; Endoscopes: Optical fibers have revolutionized surgery by allowing physicians to see into the body without making major incisions. Small optical fibers are used to reflect light into the body while additional fibers reflect video images back to the surgeon. While viewing on the endoscope, the surgeon can watch the action of his or her instruments as they are inserted through additional small incisions.

Measuring the Thickness of the Antarctic Ice Cap: The continent of Antarctica is covered with a sheet of ice, more than a mile thick at some locations, making it very difficult to determine the topography of the land underneath. To determine the depth of ice, scientists aim radio waves at the ice cap and measure the time required for the echo. Since radio waves penetrate ice, but not rock, they reflect (echo) off the underlying rock. The thickness of the ice is directly proportional to the time required for the echo to be received.

7.2 REFRACTION

In 1271, at the age of 17, Marco Polo set out on a journey with his father and uncle from Venice to China. Upon returning to his home in Italy in 1295, he wrote the classic *Travels of Marco Polo,* a book that gave Europeans their first glimpse of the wonders of Asia and inspired future explorers such as Christopher Columbus. One of the most formidable obstacles in Marco Polo's travels was the massive Gobi Desert of central Asia. In Mongolian, the name "Gobi" means "place without water," an apt description for a region whose rainfall is often less than 76 mm (3 inches) per year. In the summer, the temperatures may reach 50°C (113°F), and the Polos were often faced with the threat of dehydration or heat exhaustion. In traveling across the desert sands, the Polos would often see what appeared to be oases, but as they eagerly approached, the water would vanish from sight. Such mirages have disappointed many hot and thirsty desert travelers. Mirages and other elusive phenomena such as rainbows and moon halos result from the fact that light bends (refracts) as it moves from one medium to another. The lakes the Polos thought they saw were actually refracted portions of the blue sky above.

Mirages deceive us because our experience tells us that light always travels in a straight line, when in fact it does not. *The speed of light, like the speed of all wave phenomena, is dependent upon the media in which it travels*. This dependence upon media can be visualized by rolling a wagon off a sidewalk onto a lawn at an oblique angle as shown in Figure A. When the first wheel hits the lawn, it slows down, pulling the wagon toward the grass. Try this activity with a wagon, skateboard, or other four-wheeled object. What will happen if the wagon is rolled from the lawn to the pavement? The angle of incidence *i* is the angle between the approaching wagon (or wave front) and the normal (line perpendicular to interface). The angle of refraction *r*, is the angle between the wagon (or wave front) in the new medium and the normal.

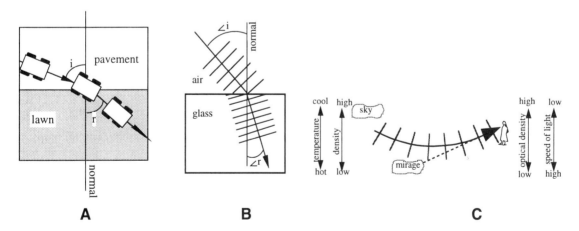

A   **B**   **C**

Light does not travel the same speed in all media. Light travels 299,792 km/s in a vacuum, 299,729 km/s in air, 225,407 km/s in water, and 197,231 km/s in glass. A medium in which light travels relatively fast (such as air) is described as having a low optical density, while one in which it travels relatively slowly (such as glass) is described as having a high optical density. *When light passes from a substance with low optical density into one with high optical density, it slows and bends toward the normal.* In the same way, the wagon changes direction when one of its wheels rolls off the pavement onto the grass. The reverse is also true—when light passes from a substance with a high optical density into one with a low optical density, its speed increases and it bends away from the normal. Did the wagon or skateboard bend away from the normal when you rolled it from the grass back onto the pavement? Figure B shows how the direction of light changes as it enters glass. Because light travels significantly more slowly in glass than in air, it bends toward the normal when it strikes glass at any angle less than 90°. Glass is used to bend light rays in eyeglasses, telescopes, microscopes, and cameras.

While it is easy to see how light will bend at the interface between air and glass or air and water, it is somewhat more difficult to see how it bends in air only, as it does in a mirage. It should be noted that mirages occur only when the air next to the ground is significantly warmer than the air above. Light travels faster in warm air than in cold air, creating an effect similar to a glass/air interface. (Warm air has a lower mass density and a lower optical density than cold air.) Figure C shows how light rays from the sky travel more slowly in the higher, cooler air, than in the lower, warmer air. As a result, light from the sky travels fastest near the surface and subsequently bends upward toward the observer. The blue coloration of a mirage is therefore nothing more than refracted light from the blue sky above.

The principle of refraction is essential for understanding such diverse phenomena as vision, microscopes, telescopes, sunsets, rainbows, bird coloration, gem identification, and fiber optics. The following activities will give you "hands-on" experience with refraction.

7.2.1 Refraction

Concepts to Investigate: Refraction, index of refraction.

Materials: Opaque cup (or beaker and aluminum foil), water, coin.

Principles and Procedures: The Arawak are a group of culturally diverse Indian peoples who live in the tropical rain forests of South America. The Arawak, like other natives of the Amazonian basin, have learned to survive on the resources found in the jungle. Many have become excellent at fishing, being able to strike fish with a single toss of their spears. How would you aim a spear if your dinner depended upon it? At the fish, above it, or below it?

Place a coin in the bottom of an opaque cup or can and position it so it is just out of view (Figure D). Slowly add water to the cup and record the height at which the coin first becomes completely visible (Figure E). Repeat the process using cooking oil and rubbing alcohol (isopropyl alcohol, 2-propanol).

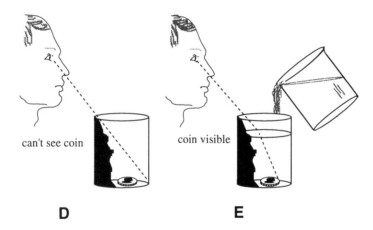

| D | E |

Light bends when it travels between media with differing optical densities. As light reflected from the coin strikes the water/air or oil/air interface, it speeds up and bends away from the normal. Thus, while the coin is initially out of sight (Figure D), the addition of water makes it visible (Figure E). Which of the liquids tested has the highest refractive index (bends light the most)? Which has the lowest refractive index (bends light the least)? Record your results in the table.

	Height	*Relative Index of Refraction*
Water	_____ cm	_____
Oil	_____ cm	_____
Alcohol	_____ cm	_____

Questions

(1) In which liquid does light travel slowest? Explain.

(2) Would the addition of water help you see the coin if light traveled faster in water than air? Explain.

(3) Cormorants are birds that have been domesticated by fishermen of the Orient. When cormorants see a fish, they dive swiftly into the water, pierce it with their long, sharp bills, and bring it to their masters. At what angle must these birds hit the water to minimize distortion due to refraction?

(4) An Amazonian spear fisherman spots a fish in the water. How must he aim his spear to ensure he hits the fish? Explain.

7.2.2 Index of Refraction

Concepts to Investigate: Index of refraction, angle of incidence, angle of refraction, Snell's law, optics.

Materials: Glass plate, pins, cardboard or Styrofoam sheet. Optional: aquarium, sheet of Plexiglas.

Principles and Procedures: The Dutch astronomer Willebrord Snell (1580–1626) stated that each transmitting substance has a constant index of refraction n, which is expressed as the ratio of the sine of the incident angle (i, the angle at which light falls on a surface relative to the normal) to the sine of the refraction angle (r, the angle at which light travels in the new medium relative to the normal). Later investigations showed that the index of refraction represents the ratio of the speed of light in these two media. To provide a standard, all indices are measured in a vacuum, but since the speed of light in air is nearly equal to the speed of light in a vacuum, indices determined in air approximate standard values.

$$n = \frac{\sin i_{(vacuum)}}{\sin r_{(medium)}} = \frac{\text{speed of light in vacuum}}{\text{speed of light in medium}} \approx \frac{\sin i_{(air)}}{\sin r_{(medium)}}$$

Every light-transmitting substance has a unique index of refraction that can be used as an identifying "fingerprint." By measuring the index of refraction, scientists can determine if a gem is real or synthetic, or whether the oil in a salad dressing is made from corn or safflower. In this activity you will make your own "refractometer" and measure the refractive indices of two substances.

Trace the outline of a rectangular pane of glass with a pencil and place a pin x adjacent to the pane, as illustrated in Figure F. Draw a line perpendicular (normal) to the glass at this point, and then place another pin w on a line that is approximately 30° from the normal. Crouch down so one eye is at table level and pin w is blocking your view of pin x (Figure F). Looking through the glass lengthwise, place two pins on the other side such that the shafts (not the heads) of all four appear to be in a straight line (Figure G).

Remove the glass plate and draw line segments to connect all four pins, as illustrated in Figure H. Using a protractor, measure the angle of incidence i, and the angle of refraction r, and calculate the refractive index of glass $n=\sin i_{(air)}/\sin r_{(glass)}$. Repeat this activity using a sheet of Plexiglas. To determine the index of refraction of water use a filled aquarium, and substitute long, thin wooden dowels for the pins.

Questions

(1) What was the index of refraction of glass? Plexiglas? Water?

(2) How might the following professionals make use Snell's of law? (a) Gemologist, (b) Food scientist, (c) Environmental Protection Agency (EPA) investigator.

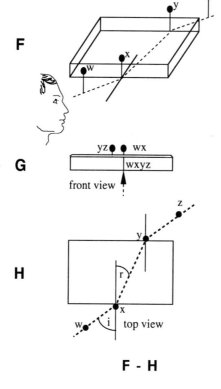

F

G

front view

H

top view

F - H

7.2.3 Refraction and Distortion

Concepts to Investigate: Refraction, ray diagram, distortion.

Materials: Pencil, beaker, water.

Principles and Procedures: Place your hand in a beaker of water. Does it appear larger or smaller than normal? What causes this distortion?

Place a pencil, pen, or straw on the side of a filled beaker, as illustrated in Figure I. As the pencil is submerged, it appears to "break" in two. The ray diagram in Figure J illustrates how the image *i* of the submerged pencil is at a different location from the real pencil *p*. Move the pencil throughout the beaker until you locate the position at which the two halves of the pencil appear to be farthest apart as well as the location at which the two halves are in line. Indicate the positions of the pencil *p* and image *i* in each of these cases and draw the appropriate ray diagrams. (Ray diagrams are discussed in section 7.5.)

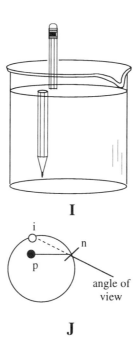

I

J

Questions

(1) Under what conditions does the pencil appear not to split? Explain.
(2) Under what conditions does the pencil appear to be split most? Explain.
(3) Would the number of hours of daylight be longer or shorter if the Earth had no atmosphere? Explain.
(4) Atmospheric refraction distorts the position of stars. Under what conditions will the stars appear in their true positions? Explain.

7.2.4 Total Internal Reflection

Concepts to Investigate: Refraction, total internal reflection, critical angle.

Materials: Aluminum foil, beaker, water, cooking oil.

Principles and Procedures: In this activity you will determine how refraction can be used to hide objects that would otherwise be visible. Make a lid for a beaker from aluminum foil, as illustrated in Figure K. Place the beaker on top of a coin and view from the angle indicated. Slowly add water through a hole in the aluminum foil cap while continuing to view the coin from the same angle. Stop adding water the moment the coin completely disappears and record the height of the water. Repeat the procedure using cooking oil.

Initially the content of the beaker is air, the same medium in which it is viewed. Under such conditions (Figure L) light reflected from the coin exits the glass walls of the beaker at the same angle it enters them. If the walls of the beaker are thin, the degree of distortion is minimal, just as in a household window. When, however, the beaker is filled with water or oil (Figure M), light reflected from the coin does not bend significantly when striking the inner wall of the beaker because the optical density of the liquid is similar to the optical density of the glass. When it passes from the glass to the air, it will bend away from the normal. If the angle of incidence is large enough, the angle of refraction will be 90° and the light rays will be reflected at the glass/air interface rather than transmitted (Figure M). This process is known as total internal reflection. The minimum angle at which all light rays reflect is known as the critical angle.

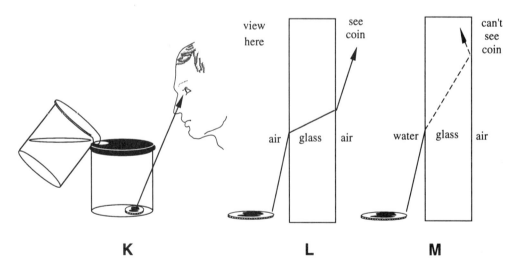

K   L   M

Questions

   (1)   In which liquid was the coin concealed best? Why?

   (2)   Some zoos have large aquariums where visitors can look eye to eye with sharks, dolphins, and other large marine animals. Occasionally, such animals will position themselves so they cannot see the ogling crowds. Draw a diagram to show how total internal reflection might hide the crowds from view.

7.2.5 Magnification

Concepts to Investigate: Magnification, refraction, optical density.

Materials: Cardboard (or other suitable material), beaker, water, plastic wrap.

Principles and Procedures: The speed of light increases when it passes from glass (or other substances with high optical density) to air (or other substance with low optical density). As its speed increases, it bends away (diverges) from the normal. If the interface is convex, light rays will diverge upon leaving the glass, causing objects to appear larger than they actually are. This is the basic principle behind all magnifying lenses.

Cut a rectangle from cardboard, a piece of wood, sheet metal, or other suitable material, as illustrated in Figure N. The rectangle should be approximately 1.5 times as high as the beaker and one third as wide. Carefully measure the bottom width d_1 and then remeasure its apparent width d_2 after submerging one end in water, as shown in Figure O. Move the rectangle back and forth. Does the apparent width of the submerged end of the rectangle d_2 vary with position? At what position in the beaker does the object appear largest? Figure P shows how the bending of light rays makes the width of the object d_2 appear larger than the actual width d_1. The magnification of a lens is the ratio of an object's apparent size when viewed through the lens to its actual size d_2/d_1. Determine the maximum magnification of this "beaker-lens."

A simple convex magnifying lens is made when a drop of water rests on a water-repellent surface. Cover a page of printed material with a sheet of plastic wrap, sprinkle with a few drops of water, and determine the magnification of these "water-lenses" (Figure Q).

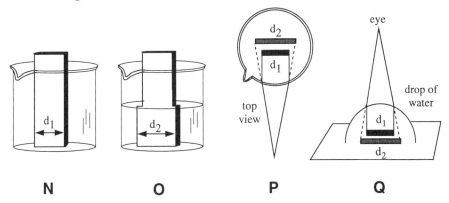

N   **O**   **P**   **Q**

Questions

(1) Does the object appear widest when it is closest to the viewer, in the middle of the beaker, or farthest from the viewer? Use diagrams to explain.

(2) Will fish appear larger in a rectangular aquarium or in a spherical fishbowl? Explain.

(3) Light travels more slowly in vegetable oil than in water. Will an object appear larger or smaller if the beaker is filled with oil rather than water?

**7.2.6 Refraction and Transparency:
Disappearing Act**

Concepts to Investigate: Index of refraction, optical density, transparency.

Materials: Test tubes, beakers, vegetable oil (Wesson® regular).

Principles and Procedures: We can tell that a sliding glass door is open either because it reflects or refracts light. Reflected light produces a glare and refracted light produces a mild distortion, both of which provide clues to the observer that glass is present. Reflection and refraction occur at the interface between two surfaces. Light refracts when it passes between two materials that have different optical densities. But what if they have the same optical density (same index of refraction)?

The index of refraction is 1.47 for Pyrex® (borosilicate) glass, 1.33 for water, 1.00 for air, and 1.47 for Wesson® oil. Given these refractive indices, do you think you would be able to see an air-filled test tube in an air-filled beaker? An oil-filled test tube in an oil-filled beaker? Investigate each of the combinations listed in the table and rank from most visible to least visible (Figure R). Which is least visible? Why?

			Refractive Indices		
	A	*B*	*C*	*D*	*E*
Beaker	glass; 1.47	glass; 1.47	glass; 1.47	glass; 1.47	glass; 1.47
Beaker contents	air; 1.00	water; 1.33	oil; 1.47	oil; 1.47	oil; 1.47
Test tube	glass; 1.47	glass; 1.47	glass; 1.47	glass; 1.47	glass; 1.47
Tube contents	air; 1.00	water; 1.33	air; 1.00	water; 1.33	oil; 1.47
Results:					
5 = most visible	———	———	———	———	———
1 = least visible					

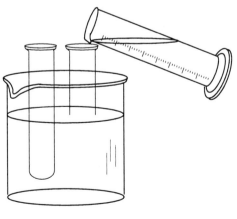

R

Questions

(1) Under which conditions is the test tube "invisible"? Explain.

(2) Which of the following substances would be least visible in water? Substance X ($n = 1.74$); Y, ($n = 1.3$); Z, ($n = 1.57$)? Explain.

(3) H. G. Wells, author of the science-fiction classics *The Time Machine* and *The War of the Worlds,* also wrote the intriguing novel entitled *The Invisible Man.* What physical characteristics would a person need to be invisible?

(4) Why can you see ice cubes in a glass of water if both ice and water are made of the same substance?

FOR THE TEACHER

If students have difficulty understanding the wagon analogy for refraction introduced at the beginning of the chapter, you may wish to use an analogy of a platoon of soldiers marching forward in a line, as illustrated in Figure S. While marching on the same surface, the line remains straight, but if some encounter more difficult terrain such as a marsh or bog, they will slow down and the line will bend as illustrated. You may wish to have your class hold hands and walk across a football field at an oblique angle to the goal line. Instruct students to slow their pace when crossing the goal line, the line will bend as illustrated. Request your students to draw a ray diagram of this activity. For more information on ray diagrams, refer to section 7.5.

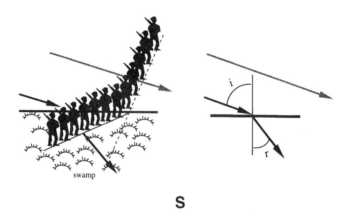

S

7.2.1 Refraction

Answers (1) The oil bends light more than water does, allowing you to see the coin earlier. This indicates oil has a higher index of refraction, and hence light moves through it more slowly. (2) If light traveled faster in water than in air, light from the coin would bend toward the normal (away from the observer) and make it more difficult to see the coin. (3) Refraction is reduced to zero at an angle of incidence of 0° (90° to the surface of the water). Observers will note that fish-eating birds hover directly over their prey and then plunge directly into the water. (4) The fish will appear farther from the shore than it is, so the fisherman must correct for refraction and aim his spear closer than the fish appears.

7.2.2 Index of Refraction

Discussion: While it is simple to measure the refractive indices of solids, it is difficult to accurately measure the indices of liquids because a container is required to hold them. The aquarium used in this activity adds an element of error to the calculation of the refractive index of water, but it is minimal if the glass is thin relative to the width of the aquarium. This activity is excellent for tracking the course of a beam of light. If lenses are substituted for the pane of glass, one can easily draw ray diagrams and determine focal points.

Answers (1) The indices of refraction for most types of glass range between 1.46 and 1.52. Plexiglas (methacrylic acid) has an index of refraction of 1.43, while water has an index of 1.33. (2) Each gem has a unique index of refraction, which gemologists use to verify its composition. For example, a quick analysis with a refractometer will determine if a stone is diamond ($n = 2.42$) or glass ($n = 1.50$). Food scientists examine the refractive index to determine types of oils and fats used in foods. Environmental scientists identify organic solvents and other pollutants by their refractive indices.

7.2.3 Refraction and Distortion

Discussion: The position of objects immersed in water is distorted by the bending of light that occurs at the air-water interface. To illustrate such distortion, place a meter stick into a water-filled aquarium. When looking at the stick from above, the stick appears to bend.

Answers (1) The pencil will not appear split if it is in the exact center of the beaker. Light reflected from the pencil at this position will strike the surface of the beaker at the normal angle (angle of incidence = 0°). When the angle of incidence i is 0°, the angle of refraction r must also be zero. (2) The pencil appears to be split most when positioned against the left or right side of the container. In this position, the angle of incidence i is greatest, and consequently the angle of refraction must also be greatest. (3) The atmosphere bends light and allows us to see the sun after it has dipped below the horizon in the same way that the water in this activity allows us to see the coin that is out of the line of sight in air. Refraction of light in the Earth's atmosphere allows us to see the sun for several minutes longer than if the Earth had no atmosphere. (4) The apparent position of the stars is distorted by refraction of light by the atmosphere. The only stars whose apparent positions coincide with their actual positions are those directly overhead. The light rays from these stars come directly through the atmosphere with an angle of incidence equal to 0°, preventing any distortion due to refraction.

7.2.4 Total Internal Reflection

Discussion: The addition of fluid to the container hides the object because the fluid changes the direction of light rays so they exit at an angle different than the original angle. If light strikes the surface at an angle of 48.5°, it will refract at 90.0°, parallel to the surface. At this angle, none of the light escapes from the flask, and hence the object in the container is hidden. This angle is known as the critical angle and can be calculated as: $i_c = \arcsin(1/n)$. For water, $n = 1.33$ and $i_c = 49°$. For vegetable oil, $n = 1.47$ and $i_c = 43°$. Since the critical angle of oil is less than the critical angle for water, objects will be hidden more easily in oil.

Answers (1) The oil will do a better job of hiding the coin because the critical angle for oil is approximately 6 degrees less than for water. While the coin can be seen if viewed from an angle of ± 49° from the normal in water, it can be viewed only from an angle of ±43° in oil. (2) Student diagrams.

7.2.5 Magnification

Discussion: Refraction has been used to magnify images for centuries. Ask your students to generate a list of devices that use refraction to magnify images. Microscopes, refracting telescopes, telephoto lenses, and magnifying lenses all use the refractive properties of glass to magnify images.

Answers (1) The object will appear widest when it is farthest from the viewer. (2) Fish will appear larger in a spherical fishbowl than in a rectangular aquarium because the curvature of the bowl creates a diverging (magnifying) lens. (3) The index of refraction of vegetable oil exceeds that of water, so the angle of refraction for light leaving an oil-filled container will exceed the angle of refraction for light leaving a water-filled container. As a result, the object will appear slightly larger in oil than in water.

7.2.6 Refraction and Transparency: Disappearing Act

Discussion: A dramatic "magic" trick can be performed as follows. Prior to class submerge a Pyrex or Kimax (borosilicate) test tube in a beaker of oil. When students are present, take a similar test tube, wrap in a cloth and crush it with a hammer. Pour the pieces into the oil, and then use tongs to remove the intact tube. Because all glass submerged in the oil is invisible, it will appear to students as though the broken test tube was somehow reassembled in the oil.

Answers (1) The test tube will be nearly invisible when filled with oil and resting in a beaker filled with oil. Under these conditions, visual clues caused by refraction and reflection are minimized because all materials have the same refractive index. (2) The degree of distortion increases as a function of the difference in refractive indices. The material with a refractive index of 1.34 would be least visible in water because its refractive index nearly matches the refractive index of water (1.33). (3) To be invisible, the person must be transparent, colorless, reflect no light, and have a refractive index equal to air. (4) Most ice has air trapped inside it, giving it a different refractive index than pure water.

Applications to Everyday Life

Refracting Telescopes: In the early seventeenth century, Galileo Galilei used a refracting telescope to discover the moons of Jupiter, lunar mountains, Saturn's rings, and that the Milky Way is composed of many stars. Refracting telescopes remain the telescope of choice for planetary studies and astrometric work requiring precise measurements.

Light Microscopes: Shortly after the invention of the telescope, the Dutch biologist Antoni van Leeuwenhoek used refractive lenses to examine living systems and in 1683 reported the discovery of protists (single-celled organisms). Today, light microscopes are still the most widely used microscopes for instruction and medical diagnostics.

Eyeglasses: Eyeglasses use refraction to counter refractive errors of the eye. If the lens of the eye is too close to the retina, a person will be farsighted (hyperopia), and if it is too far the person will be nearsighted (myopia). Concave lenses are used to correct hyperopia while convex lenses are used to correct myopia. Approximately half of all Americans wear eyeglasses or contact lenses.

Moon Halos: On cold, humid nights it is common to see a ring of light around the moon. This halo results from the refraction of light from the moon by ice crystals suspended in the Earth's atmosphere.

Identifying Chemicals: The index of refraction is an identifying characteristic of a substance. Using a refractometer, chemists can identify a wide range of substances, from kerosene to sapphires.

Prisms and Rainbows: Sunlight is composed of a wide variety of electromagnetic radiation with wavelengths varying from 400 to 700 nanometers. The index of refraction for these varies as a function of the wavelength (color) of the light. In most ordinary media the refractive index increases as the wavelength becomes shorter. As a result, short wavelength light, such as violet and blue, bends more than long wavelength light, such as red and orange. When light enters glass or water at an oblique angle, the different wavelengths of light bend differently and disperse, creating the colorful spectrum with which we are familiar.

Salinometer: The refractive index of water varies as a function of the amount of dissolved solutes. Scientists can determine the salinity of water samples by determining their refractive indices. Salinometers are used to monitor the quality of ground water in coastal areas subject to sea water intrusion.

Twinkling Stars and Hot Automobile Hoods: Hot air has a lower mass density and a lower optical density than cool air. As a result, light bends away from the normal when passing from cool air to warm, and bends toward the normal when passing from warm air to cool. The difference in light speed in warmer and cooler air accounts for the twinkling of stars and the blurry, vaporlike appearance of the air immediately over the hood of your car on a hot day. Since the temperature of the air is not uniform, light rays bend at different angles, producing a "twinkling" or blurry image.

7.3 INTERFERENCE AND DIFFRACTION

In 1779 Captain James King observed Hawaiian natives engaged in a "most perilous and extraordinary sport" known as "Amo amo iluna ka lau oka nalu." This sport, which we know as surfing, has advanced since the early days of riding palm-tree trunks and is now popular along the coasts of Hawaii, California, New Zealand, Australia, Peru, and Brazil. One exciting, but potentially treacherous place to surf, is the "Wedge" in Newport Beach, California. The breakwater of Newport Harbor is positioned such that waves reflect off it and head toward the shore where they meet other incoming waves (Figure A). *The principle of superposition states that the resultant wave is the sum of the waves present.* Thus, where wave fronts intersect, the resultant crests may be twice as high (solid circles), and the troughs twice as low (open circles) as their component waves. While it may be a thrill to ride a double-height crest, it may be unnerving when double-deep troughs expose bare sand.

Perhaps you have noticed waves reflecting off the shore of a lake or ocean and returning with reduced height. As these waves intersect incoming waves, there is a brief surge followed by a brief lull. When the crests of both waves are aligned (constructive interference; Figure B) the water surges to a height equal to the sum of both crests. When, however, the crest of one wave intersects the trough of another (destructive interference; Figure C) the resultant wave is reduced.

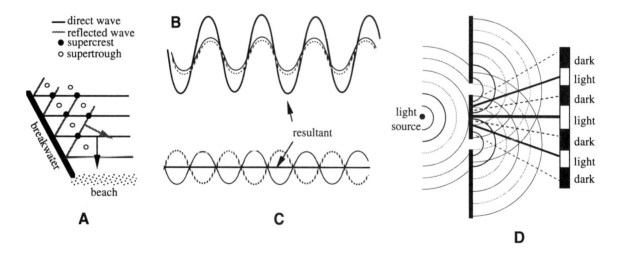

If light is actually a wave phenomenon, then it must demonstrate all characteristics of waves, including constructive and destructive interference. By projecting monochromatic (single color) light through a screen with a double slit (Figure D), the English physicist Thomas Young demonstrated interference, lending credibility to the wave theory of light.

To repeat this classic experiment, first take a picture of a solid red or green surface using 35-mm slide film. After developing the slide, place it in a projector and aim it toward a sheet of aluminum foil in which you have cut two parallel slits (about 1 mm apart) with a razor blade. If the room is darkened, an interference pattern may be observed by placing a sheet of paper on the opposite side of the foil. Where crests intersect, the light is bright (constructive interference), but where crests and troughs intersect, it is dark (destructive interference). Although it wasn't until 1801 that the principle of light interference was explained, people have appreciated its effects for centuries in such things as the brilliant colors of peacock feathers and the beautiful iridescence of abalone shells.

When waves meet obstructions, they spread out, or diffract. The diffraction of water waves around rocks, AM radio waves around buildings, or sound waves around doorways is easily observable, but the diffraction of light is rarely seen. *Diffraction (spreading of waves) is greatest when the dimensions of the obstruction or opening are comparable to the wavelength.* Hence, light will be seen to diffract only when it encounters very small obstructions or slits. In this chapter you will have the opportunity to study the diffraction of light by making your own diffraction slits as well as using specially manufactured surfaces known as diffraction gratings. Principles of diffraction are used in such fields as photography, holography, radio broadcasting, chemistry, microscopy, astronomy, and ornithology. The following activities will help you understand the basic principles of interference and diffraction and illustrate a variety of ways in which these principles are applied in everyday life.

7.3.1 Interference in Thin Films

Concepts to Investigate: Constructive interference, destructive interference, interference patterns, complementary colors.

Materials: Light machine oil, black paper, glass, colored cellophane (red, green, or blue), flashlight, bubble soap and bubble wand (available at toy stores), two sheets of Plexiglas (approximately 20 cm x 20 cm).

Principles and Procedures: Have you ever noticed a brilliant array of colors on the oily pavement at a service station following a gentle rain, or on the surface of the water of a polluted harbor or lake? Perhaps you have seen similar brilliant colors when opening a new pack of microscope slides, examining a piece of heated metal, looking at the surface of a compact disc, or looking at the surface of soap bubbles in your kitchen sink. These brilliant displays have captured the attention of people for years and archeologists recently discovered references to these patterns on 3,000-year-old clay tablets of the Assyrians. We now know that these colorful patterns are created by the interference of light waves reflecting from two surfaces of a thin film.

   Oil and water do not mix, so when oil is placed on water, it spreads out in a thin film. When light strikes the air/oil interface, a portion is reflected, and a portion is transmitted (Figure E). When the transmitted portion strikes the oil/water interface on the other side, more light is reflected. The second reflection may interact with the first in much the same way as the reflected ocean waves do at the "Wedge," discussed earlier. Those colors of light whose wavelengths are reflected in phase with one another will be brighter as a result of constructive interference (Figure F), while those that are 180° out of phase ($\pm 1/2\lambda$) will be dimmer as a result of destructive interference (Figure G). If blue light is eliminated by destructive interference, the film will appear yellow since blue and yellow are complementary colors (see chapter on color). The other complementary color pairs are: red/cyan, orange/greenish-blue, green/magenta, and violet/greenish-yellow. Different colors of light are eliminated by different thickness of film, so the colors you see are a function of film thickness (distance *d*, Figures F and G).

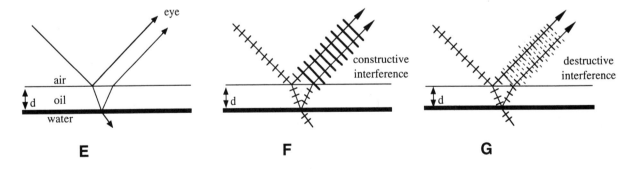

E   F   G

Part 1. Interference in oil films: Place a Petri dish, microscope slide, or similar plate of glass on a nonreflective black surface (black construction paper works well). Place a thin layer of water on the glass and add a few drops of light machine oil or kerosene to the surface. Darken the room, illuminate the surface of the oil with a bright beam from an angle as shown in Figure H, and observe the colorful patterns.

How can you change the patterns? Place a sheet of red, green, or blue cellophane (glass or plastic) in front of the light and observe the patterns again. Describe how the patterns look different when viewed through the colored filter. Make a drawing of the interference patterns you observe.

Part 2. Interference in soap films: Blow bubbles using a toy bubble kit and examine their colors in direct sunlight. Dim the room lights and reflect light off the surface of a bubble using a bright light source such as a focusable flashlight or a slide projector (Figure I). Place a colored sheet of cellophane in front of the light and note that the interference patterns on the bubbles are now monochromatic. Remove the bubble wand from the soap solution and allow it to stand vertically. Describe changes in the color pattern of the film over time until the film breaks. Why does the color pattern change?

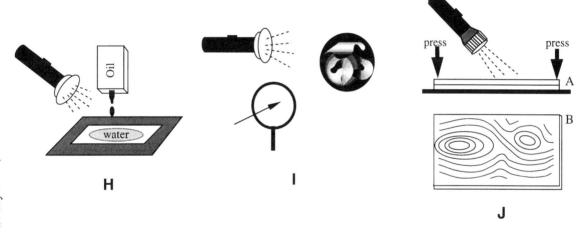

Part 3. Interference in air films: Just as oil forms a film on the surface of water, or soap forms a film in air, so air forms a film when trapped between two solids. In this activity you will trap a minute film of air in the space between two clean scratch-free sheets of Plexiglas. The Plexiglas sheets should be cleaned with rubbing alcohol (isopropyl alcohol) and dried with a lint-free soft cloth. Tape the Plexiglas sheets together with black electrician's tape and attach a sheet of black construction paper to the back of one of the plates. Place the apparatus in bright light and draw a picture of the interference patterns you observe (Figure J). Gently squeeze the sheets in different locations and describe changes in the interference patterns. Place a sheet of colored cellophane, plastic, or glass in front of the light beam and describe the appearance of the interference patterns.

Questions

(1) Explain how you can alter the colorful interference patterns seen in a thin film of oil on water.

(2) When red cellophane is placed in front of the light source, the interference pattern is seen only as red and black stripes. Explain.

(3)   When a soap film in a bubble wand is allowed to stand, the interference pattern gradually changes so there becomes one wide band at the top and many narrow bands near the bottom. Explain what might cause this change in pattern.

(4)   Why does the interference pattern between two Plexiglas plates change when these plates are squeezed together?

(5)   Instruments known as interferometers are used to measure the thickness of various films. Explain how they might work.

(6)   Explain how interference patterns create "topographical maps" of a film.

7.3.2 Single Slit Diffraction

Concepts to Investigate: Interference, diffraction.

Materials: Two pencils, tape, candle or other small, bright light source.

Principles and Procedures: While sitting in a classroom, you can hear people in the hall even though you can't see them. Sound diffracts or bends through the doorway and window openings, allowing you to hear noises that are not in a direct line with the openings. In a similar manner, radio waves diffract around and between buildings and trees, allowing you to pick up signals from stations that are not in the line of sight. If light is actually a wave phenomenon, then it also should diffract or bend around obstructions and through openings, but why don't we observe this? While sound and radio waves bend around corners, light doesn't, otherwise we would always be able to see the people we hear talking in the hallway.

While all waves diffract, the amount of diffraction is related to the size of the opening or obstruction in relation to the wavelength of the wave. When the opening or obstruction has approximately the same dimensions as the length of the waves, diffraction is maximum. Light is not observed to diffract under normal circumstances because its wavelengths are much smaller than openings or obstructions with which we are familiar. To observe the diffraction of light, it is therefore necessary to create an opening with a diameter of approximately the same dimension as a wavelength of light. This can be done using two pencils or other straight edges, as illustrated in Figure K. Place a piece of tape around the shaft of one pencil to provide a spacer between them and then place them side by side as illustrated. Darken the room, peer through the slit between the pencils, and observe a candle flame at a distance of 2 meters. With practice you should be able to observe an interference pattern roughly resembling that shown in Figure L. Rotate the pencils and describe changes in the interference pattern. Increase and decrease the pressure on the pencil shafts to alter the width of the gap and describe changes in the interference pattern.

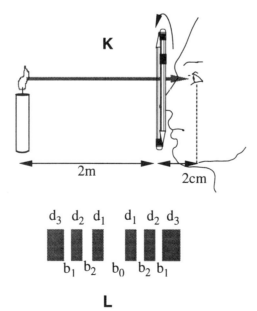

Questions

(1) How does the interference pattern change when the pencils are squeezed together? Explain.

(2) In examining the interference pattern, you may have noticed colored bands on both sides of the white lines. What is the color of the band that appears to be farthest from the light source? What does this indicate about the angle of diffraction for this color of light?

(3) Describe the change in orientation of the interference pattern as you rotate the pencils.

7.3.3 Diffraction by Gratings and Particles

Concepts to Investigate: Diffraction, diffraction gratings, diffraction by particles, spectroscopes, spectral identification.

Materials: Diffraction-grating (available from scientific supply houses), aluminum foil, unfrosted light bulb and socket, mailing tube, razor blade, pair of glasses or pane of glass.

Principles and Procedures

Part 1. Diffraction gratings: Interference patterns can be created by multiple slits as well as by single and double slits. A sheet of glass or plastic containing numerous, closely spaced parallel slits is known as a diffraction grating and is capable of creating interference patterns resembling patterns created by prisms. A simple spectroscope (a device used to resolve and analyze light spectra) can be made using a mailing tube or wrapping paper tube, as illustrated in Figure M. Cover both ends of the tube with aluminum foil, and make a window for the diffraction grating at one end and a 2-millimeter wide viewing slit in the other end. The slits in the diffraction grating and the viewing slit should be positioned so they are parallel. Look at an unfrosted light bulb through your spectroscope and note the variety of colorful images present. Which colors appear to diffract least (are closest to the original light source)? Which colors appear to diffract most (are farthest from the light source)? Is it possible to position the diffraction grating in another orientation so that the positions of the colors are reversed? Although diffraction gratings create a spectral display similar to that created by prisms, the manner in which they do so is quite different. Prisms separate light on the basis of refraction (light of different frequencies travels at different speeds through glass) while diffraction gratings separate light on the basis of interference (certain wavelengths are eliminated due to destructive interference, and the energy is redistributed).

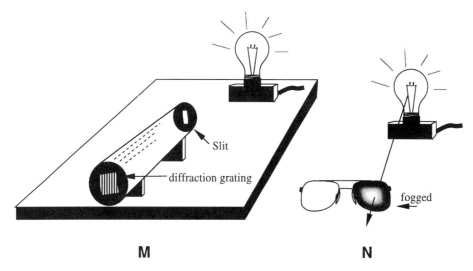

M   **N**

Diffraction gratings, like prisms, allow us to analyze the composition of light. While an incandescent light bulb releases a continuum of light in a manner similar to the sun, other light sources do not. Examine the light from a neon tube, a mercury vapor lamp (blue-tinted street lamps), sodium vapor lamp (yellow-tinted street lamp), and Bunsen burner (methane gas) through a diffraction grating, and describe and record the differences in the spectra.

Part 2. Diffraction by particles: Waves diffract when they encounter the sides of a particle just as they do when encountering the sides of a slit. Very fine particles, such as the water droplets in fog, diffract light and create a faint, colorful, circular interference pattern known as a corona. When you look at the moon, street lamps, or any other bright light source on a foggy or very humid night, you may see a colorful "halo" around the light source. By exhaling on a sheet of glass or a pair of glasses, you can deposit a series of similar sized water droplets that mimic the water droplets in fog. Darken the room and stare at an unfrosted light bulb through the fogged glass (Figure N). Which color diffracts most (is farthest from the light source) and which color diffracts least (closest to the light source)?

Questions

(1)   Which color diffracts most? Which color diffracts least? Explain.

(2)   Astronomers use diffraction gratings to determine the composition of stars. Explain.

(3)   The distance between slits in a diffraction grating (d, grating constant) determines the spacing of the spectral lines. How might the size of the droplets in a mist alter the spectral lines?

FOR THE TEACHER

The phenomenon of interference can be demonstrated by placing two overlapping combs on an overhead projector as illustrated in Figure O. The dark bands resulting from the overlap of the teeth represent the "super-crests" that result from constructive interference.

O

To improve students' understanding of diffraction and interference, it is helpful to introduce Christian Huygens' wave principle: *Every point on a wavefront acts as a source of a circular-shaped wavelet that moves forward in the same direction and at the same speed as the wave front. The tangent line drawn between the leading edges of these wavelets represents the new wavefront.* When students understand this concept of wave propagation, they may find the diffraction of waves through openings more understandable.

7.3.1 Interference in Thin Films

Discussion: Part 2 can be performed as a classroom demonstration by reflecting light off a soap film and focusing it on a projection screen. A bubble frame can be made by punching a hole in the bottom of a large, opened tin can. A film will form across the open end when placed in soap solution, and the hole will allow for pressure equalization across the film. Once a bubble is formed, secure the can to a ring stand so the soap film is at a right angle to the ground. Dim the room lights and shine a bright, focusable light (a 35-mm slide projector works well) at an angle on the surface of the film. Use a Fresnel lens (many overhead projectors have a Fresnel lens immediately beneath the glass plate) or a large convex lens to focus the reflected light on the screen. Colored sheets of cellophane can be placed in front of the light beam to create monochromatic interference bands.

Answers (1) Different thicknesses of film result in the elimination of different colors of light by the process of destructive interference. By tilting the glass, adding more oil, or stirring the liquid you can alter the thickness of the oil. This changes the wavelengths that will be eliminated and consequently the complementary colors that appear. (2) Red cellophane, like red glass or plastic, allows only red light to pass through. In those regions where the thickness of the film is such that red light is reflected 180° out of phase with the first reflection, destructive interference will occur. A black band will appear since no red light is present and no other colors of light transmit through the red cellophane. These black bands do not appear when viewed without the filter because white light is composed of a range of frequencies, no two of which experience total destructive interference at the same film thickness. (3) As the soap film is allowed to stand in a vertical position, its mass is redistributed by gravity. While the top becomes relatively thin and uniform, the bottom becomes increasingly thick. Few, wide interference bands are seen at the top because the film is relatively uniform in thickness, but numerous bands are found near the bottom because the film's thickness changes rapidly there. (4) When the Plexiglas sheets are squeezed, the volume of air trapped between them decreases, changing the thickness of the air film and the associated interference patterns. (5) Isaac Newton determined that the colors of an interference pattern were related to the thickness of the film reflecting the light. Interference occurs when the thickness of a film is a multiple of whole or half wavelengths. Blue light, with a short wavelength, experiences interference at smaller thicknesses than red light which has a longer wavelength. Engineers who design interferometers correlate thickness scales with color. (6) A topographic map uses continuous lines to identify positions with equivalent elevations. Because color is a function of film thickness, a particular color interference band identifies all locations where a film is equally thick.

7.3.2 Single Slit Diffraction

Discussion: Students find single-slit diffraction more difficult to conceptualize than double-slit diffraction. They may be able to better understand it if they consider each half of the wave in the slit to be a separate source just as the two slits in Figure D can be considered as separate sources. When the difference in distance between these two sources is half a wavelength, they will be out of phase, destructively interfere, and produce a dark band.

A variation of this demonstration follows. Position an unfrosted light bulb in a darkened room and ask students to squint and draw the diffraction patterns they see. If diffraction patterns are not seen, rotate the light bulb so it is parallel with the floor. The space between the eyelids serves as the diffraction slit for this activity.

Answers (1) As the pencils are squeezed, the slit is narrowed and the interference bands spread. Destructive interference occurs when the crest of one wave is momentarily canceled by the trough of another. If two sources (the two sides of the slit) are close together, a larger angle will be required to put them out of phase with each other, and thus the bands will be farther apart. (2) Blue bands are closer to the light source while red bands are farther. This indicates that long waves (red) bend more than short waves (blue). (3) The interference pattern (line of dark and light spots or lines) is always at right angles to the length of the slit.

7.3.3 Diffraction by Gratings and Particles

Teacher demonstration: The diffraction grating constant (d, the distance between slits), the diffraction angle (θ, the angle of the n order image), and the wavelength of light λ are related by the equation: $\lambda = (d \sin\theta)/n$. Students can use this equation to determine the wavelength of monochromatic light. This is best done by projecting a laser through a diffraction grating in a darkened room, measuring the first order ($n = 1$) diffraction angle (θ, angle between the central image and the first order image), and solving for λ. Diffraction gratings come with a specification sheet that gives the value of the diffraction grating constant d.

Answers (1) Red light diffracts most as indicated by the fact that the red image is farthest from the source. Violet light diffracts least as indicated by the violet image always being closest to the source. (2) Astronomers can match the spectral emissions of starlight with the spectra of known elements and thereby infer the composition of the stars. (3) The size of the spectral lines is determined in part by the size of particles in the mist. Scientists can therefore use diffraction patterns to determine the particle size of various mists and fogs.

Applications to Everyday Life

Color of Butterfly Wings and Abalone Shells: The iridescence of abalone shells and some butterfly wings is created by a double reflection from the upper and lower surfaces of a transparent coating. This causes a colorful interference pattern similar to those seen in soap and oil films.

Holograms: Holograms are special photographs that display three-dimensional characteristics such as depth and parallax (change in appearance with change in perspective). To make such "whole" (holo-) pictures (-grams), coherent light is split into two beams, one of which reflects off the object before reaching the photographic plate. When the resulting interferogram is illuminated by a reference beam, a 3-D image is created. Many banks now use holograms on credit cards to help prevent counterfeiting.

Lens Coatings: The lenses of most cameras and binoculars are coated with a film that is one quarter the average wavelength of visible light. Light reflected from the inner surface of the film is one-half wavelength out of phase with that reflected from the outer surface, resulting in destructive interference and the elimination of reflective glare. Light that would otherwise be reflected as glare is transmitted, increasing the amount that reaches the film or viewer.

Measuring Small Distances: The colors in the interference patterns produced by thin films are directly related to the thickness of the film. Interferometers are used to measure the thickness of extremely thin objects on the basis of the interference patterns they produce.

Color of Bird Feathers: The ridges in the feathers of such birds as the peacock act as diffraction gratings, creating highly colorful interference patterns.

Colorful Patterns in Laser Discs and Compact Discs: The data on laser discs and CDs are etched in "pits." These pits behave like mist or other fine particles, causing the light to diffract and form colorful interference patterns.

Radio Reception: Diffraction is helpful in spreading radio signals into areas beyond obstructions. AM signals have long wavelengths (186–560 meters) and diffract around large obstructions such as office buildings and hills. FM signals have shorter wavelengths (2.8 to 3.4 m) allowing them to diffract around smaller obstructions such as tunnels and overpasses. This helps explain why AM signals appear to die when you go through a tunnel or under a bridge, while FM signals fade when you drive behind hills or mountains.

Microscopes: Diffraction limits the magnification obtainable with a microscope. Tiny objects in a specimen diffract light rays and thereby produce fuzzy images. While the practical limit for light microscopes is approximately 1000X, electron microscopes can produce clear images at substantially higher powers because electrons have much smaller wavelengths than visible light and thus do not diffract except when the detail is exceedingly small.

Element Identification: Transmission diffraction gratings are used in spectroscopes to split light into its constituent wavelengths. Spectroscopes are used to identify elemental composition by comparing unknown emission spectra with known spectra. Astronomers have determined that the composition of the sun is approximately 87 percent hydrogen and 10 percent helium on the basis of spectral analysis. Helium was first discovered in the sun by its spectral emission, hence its name (-helios means "sun").

Crystal Identification: The German physicist Max von Laue (1912) believed that the regular rows of atoms in a crystal should diffract short wavelength X-rays in the same manner that parallel slits diffract longer wavelength visible light. Von Laue was correct, and now X-ray diffraction is a standard identification technique for a wide variety of powdered materials. X-ray diffraction patterns have helped biochemists determine the structures of complex molecules such as hemoglobin and DNA.

7.4 POLARIZATION

When a honeybee returns to her hive after a successful foraging venture, she communicates information to other bees about the food source through a fascinating symbolic dance. The direction to the food source is indicated by the orientation of her dance while the distance is indicated by the number of times she "waggles" her body from side to side. If she dances vertically on the wall of the hive, the food is in the same direction as the sun, while a dance to the right or left of vertical communicates an angle to the right or left of the sun. The sun is a good reference on cloudless days, but how do bees navigate when it is overcast? To unravel this mystery, entomologists (those who study insects) have studied bees in great detail and have determined that they possess special sensory organs that are sensitive to the polarity of light. Since light scattered by the atmosphere is polarized, it is possible that bees can determine the location of the sun by examining the polarity of such light, even on overcast days. Although humans do not have such abilities, we have developed numerous devices and technologies that use polarized light.

All electromagnetic radiation (gamma, X-ray, ultraviolet, visible light, infrared, radio, and power) is transmitted as waves that possess electric and magnetic components. *Most light sources release waves in every possible orientation, but interaction with matter may cause certain wave orientations to be selectively absorbed, reflected, refracted, or scattered. If the vibrations of the resulting radiation are confined to parallel planes, the light is said to be polarized.* Although most metallic surfaces reflect light in all possible orientations, most nonmetallic surfaces polarize light, as shown in Figure A. The incident radiation is propagated in all planes (represented by crossed arrows). When light hits a surface such as a concrete road, the wave components parallel to the road (represented by the double arrows) are reflected while others are absorbed.

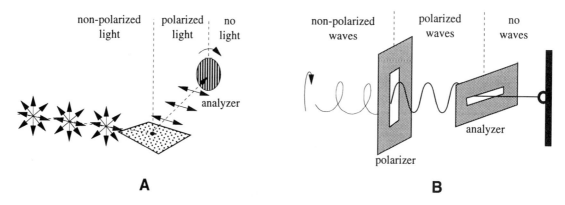

A   **B**

In the 1920s a college student named Edwin Land became fascinated with the potential technological applications of polarization and set out to develop a filter that could polarize light. In 1928 he invented the first polarizing sheet by successfully embedding micro crystals of quinine iodosulfate in a thin plastic sheet. During the 1930s he learned how to apply this new technology to produce antiglare automobile head lamps, camera filters, reduced-glare sunglasses, and three-dimensional motion pictures. Land was not only a great scientist, but also an industrialist who understood the potential benefits of scientific knowledge. The Polaroid Corporation, which he founded, is a monument to his efforts in the fields of polarization and single-step (instant) photographic development.

The glaring light reflected from lakes, snow fields, and roadways is polarized. Land understood that this glare could be eliminated using a filter that blocked waves of the appropriate polarity. The idea of such a polarizing filter can be understood by experimenting with the apparatus shown in Figure B. Both sheets are made of cardboard or wood, with a slit to allow transverse waves in a single plane. By twirling the end of a rope or "wave spring," it becomes apparent that the first sheet polarizes by transmitting only waves in a single plane. The second sheet (filter) eliminates these waves completely when rotated 90° to the first. The first sheet may represent anything that polarizes light, such as the atmosphere (through scattering), the surface of the ocean (through reflection), a crystal (through refraction), or a filter (through selective transmission). The second sheet may represent a polarizing filter such as those found in sunglasses, camera filters, microscope filters, or "3-D" glasses. In this chapter we will investigate the interesting properties and applications of polarized light. A few pairs of Polaroid® sunglasses and some simple household items are all you need.

7.4.1 Cross Polarization

Concepts to Investigate: Polarization, cross-polarization, polarization by selective transmission.

Materials: Three pairs of polarizing sunglasses or three small polarizing sheets.

Principles and Procedures: Certain crystals transmit light in only one plane. If such "dichroic" crystals are embedded in an orderly fashion, as in a polarizing filter, the entire filter assumes the property of the individual crystals and transmits light in only one plane. The crystals polarize light by selective transmission. What happens when we attempt to pass light through two successive filters? How must the filters be oriented so light will be transmitted? How must the filters be oriented so light will be blocked? Test your hypotheses using two pairs of polarizing sunglasses.

Look at the horizon though a pair of polarizing sunglasses while rotating the lens of another pair in front, as shown in Figure C. (Alternatively, you may use polarizing sheets, as shown in Figure D.) Determine the angle at which light is totally blocked (Figures E and F). Holding the first two sunglasses in this position, orient a third lens between them, as shown in Figures G and H. Is all light still blocked? Is this what you expected? Remove the center pair and place it behind the other two. Is all light blocked? Record your results.

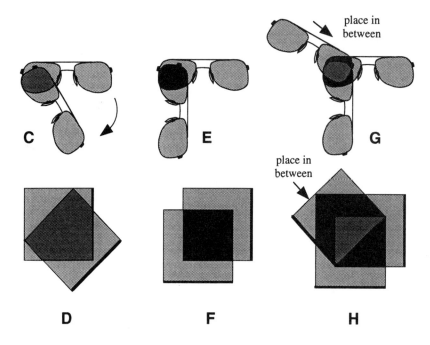

Questions

(1) How must the polarizing filters be positioned so no light is transmitted? Explain.

(2) What is glare? Do you think all polarizing sunglasses are designed with the same plane of polarization? Explain your reasoning.

(3) Explain how insertion of the middle lens allows light to pass when no light was allowed to pass without it (Figures G and H).

(4) Would addition of the third polarizing lens allow light through if it were placed behind the two mutually perpendicular lenses? Explain.

7.4.2 Polarization by Reflection

Concepts to Investigate: Polarization by reflection, Brewster's angle.

Materials: High-intensity focusable flashlight, pane of glass, string, protractor, polarizing sunglasses or filters, black paper.

Principles and Procedures: Truck drivers know that the reflective glare from water on the road or from the windows of other vehicles can be annoying and even dangerous. Fortunately, such light is polarized and can be selectively reduced by polarizing glasses. As a result, many long-distance drivers routinely wear polarizing glasses.

The English physicist Sir David Brewster discovered that *the degree of reflective polarization is dependent upon the reflecting material and the angle of incidence.* Brewster observed that polarization is maximum when the reflected and refracted rays are oriented 90° to each other (Brewster's angle ϕ). This angle is related to the index of refraction n as follows: $\tan \phi = n$. In this activity you will investigate reflective polarization and determine Brewster's angle for glass.

Place a pane of glass on a piece of black paper and aim a light beam from a flashlight or slide projector at the glass, as illustrated in Figure I. Darken the room and place a polarizing lens from a pair of sunglasses in front of the reflected beam. Rotate the lens to determine the position where the most light is blocked and then maintain the filter in this position while you alter the angle of the incident light beam.

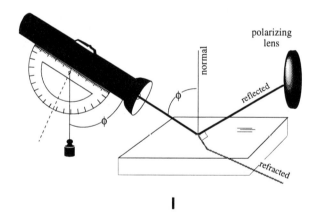

I

Slowly change the angle of the flashlight and observe the amount of light transmitted through the polarizing filter. The angle at which the least light passes through the filter is the angle at which the most light is polarized (Brewster's angle). Measure this angle by taping a protractor to the flashlight and hanging a weighted string as shown. As the angle of the flashlight is changed, you should notice a distinct reduction in the intensity of the beam somewhere between 30° and 70° from the normal. This is Brewster's angle. Record this angle, repeat twice, and calculate an average value.

Questions

(1) What was the angle of greatest polarization (Brewster's angle) for glass?

(2) Brewster's angle for water is 53°. At what time(s) of day would a fisherman's sunglasses be most effective in reducing glare from the lake? (Sunrise, midmorning, noon, midafternoon, sunset?) Explain.

7.4.3 Polarization by Scattering

Concepts to Investigate: Scattering of light, polarization by scattering.

Materials: Large beaker or small aquarium, powdered dairy creamer, focusable flashlight ("Maglite"), polarizing sunglasses.

Principles and Procedures: At the beginning of this chapter we discussed how bees communicate with one another through elaborate dances. These dances describe the direction and distance to potential food sources, but require that other bees are able to orient with respect to the plane of polarization of light scattered by the atmosphere. In this activity we will investigate the polarization that occurs when light is scattered by molecules or particles in air or water, and we hope to gain an understanding of how bees determine the direction of the sun on overcast days.

Visible sunlight is composed of innumerable shades of red, orange, yellow, green, blue, indigo, and violet light. Blue light vibrates at a frequency approximately equivalent to the resonant frequency of the nitrogen and oxygen molecules in the atmosphere. Thus, a high percentage of blue light is absorbed and reradiated, but not necessarily in its original direction. Since the atoms in the atmosphere possess no specific orientation, the light they reemit is scattered. We see a blue sky because we see the blue light scattered by atmospheric nitrogen and oxygen.

Particulate matter, such as dairy creamer dispersed in water, scatters light in a similar manner. Fill an aquarium or large beaker with water, darken the room, and shine a flashlight through the container, as shown in Figure J. Slowly mix powdered dairy creamer into the water until a beam from a focusable flashlight becomes clearly visible when viewed from the side. Rotate a pair of polarized glasses in front of the beam, as shown. If the light scattered by the particulate matter in the aquarium is polarized, the intensity of the beam should vary as the lens is rotated. Is the scattered light polarized? How does the plane of polarization change as the angle of the flashlight changes? Shine the light from above or below, as illustrated in Figure K. Is the plane of polarization the same or different from before? Bees can determine the position of the sun on the basis of the plane of polarized light scattered by the sky.

© 1994 by John Wiley & Sons, Inc.

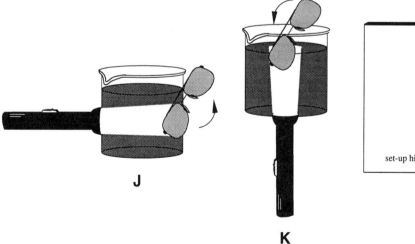

J

K

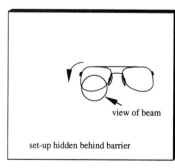

view of beam

set-up hidden behind barrier

L

Can you determine the position of the flashlight on the basis of the plane of polarized light scattered by the creamer? Cut a hole in a sheet of cardboard and position it so your partner can see only a section of the beam, as shown in Figure L. Position the light at 0°, 45°, and 90° to the tabletop and ask your partner to determine the angle. Repeat until both of you can consistently determine the angle of the light beam solely on the basis of the plane of polarized light scattered by the dairy creamer.

Questions

(1)   Is the light scattered by the dairy creamer polarized? Explain.
(2)   Polarizing sunglasses reduce reflective glare. Are they of value in reducing glare from scattering? Explain.
(3)   Which color of light is scattered most by smoke? Explain.

7.4.4 Polarization by Refraction

Concepts to Investigate: Polarization, polarization by refraction, double refraction.

Materials: Calcite crystal (Iceland Spar).

Principles and Procedures: Calcite (a form of calcium carbonate) is a common mineral found in igneous, metamorphic, and sedimentary deposits. A rather rare form of calcite, known as Iceland Spar, is transparent, and although it looks somewhat like glass, it behaves quite differently. When light passes through glass, it produces a single image, but when it passes through Iceland Spar, it produces two images. Place a crystal of Iceland Spar on a section of large print and note that two images are formed (Figure M). Light from the print splits into two beams as it refracts through the crystal enroute to the observer. Thus, the observer sees a double image of the print.

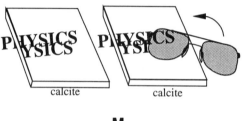

calcite   calcite

M

© 1994 by John Wiley & Sons, Inc.

Iceland spar is a doubly refracting medium and has two different indices of refraction. A ray of unpolarized light will be split into two refracted rays, polarized at right angles. Rotate a polarizing filter over the calcite crystal and observe changes in the intensity of the two images. Images will disappear only if they are made of polarized light oriented at right angles to the polarity of the filter. Are both images made of polarized light? Are the images polarized at right angles to each other?

Questions

(1) Are both images formed by polarized light? Explain.
(2) Are both images polarized in the same plane? Explain.

7.4.5 Analyzing Physical Stress with Polarized Light

Concepts to Investigate: Polarization, stress analysis.

Materials: Clear, hard plastic (such as disposable utensils, CD or audio-cassette case, clear plastic ruler), two polarizing filters (polarizing sunglasses work well).

Principles and Procedures: One of the worst air disasters occurred when an engine fell off a passenger jet upon take-off from Chicago's O'Hare International Airport. After months of investigation it was determined that a simple metal pin was at fault. The Federal Aviation Administration ordered an investigation of other similar jets and found many had pins that were experiencing substantial stress and might have similar problems. As a result of the findings, the manufacturer of the jet was ordered to retrofit all similar jets with new, stronger pins to ensure that a similar disaster would not occur. To ensure that these pins were sufficiently strong, the manufacturer subjected them to a series of stress tests and installed only those pins that passed. In this activity you will learn how such stress tests are performed.

One of the major industrial applications of polarized light is in photoelastic stress analysis. Scale models of the object to be analyzed are made of a transparent plastic that polarizes light when stressed. Each wavelength of light is polarized at its own angle, creating a colorful display when viewed through a polarizing filter. Engineers can determine locations of greatest stress by examining these colorful patterns. Large monochromatic (single-color) bands are associated with regions of low stress, while numerous narrow bands of different colors are associated with regions of high stress.

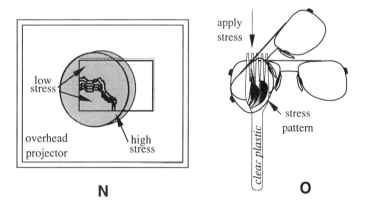

N   **O**

Place a piece of clear, hard plastic between two polarizing filters. (The clear plastic found in disposable utensils, audio-cassette cases, and CD boxes works well.) Hold the assembly up to the window or place it on an overhead projector. Gradually rotate the filters and note the colorful stress patterns (Figure N). Flex the plastic and note changes in the stress patterns (Figure O). Draw a picture of the stress pattern while the plastic is not being flexed and indicate regions of high and low stress. Draw a second picture illustrating the stress pattern when the plastic is flexed. Indicate where you think the plastic is most likely to break if flexed excessively.

Questions

(1) How can you determine if the light creating the stress patterns is polarized?
(2) What types of industries might use this stress-analysis technique?
(3) Does stress seem to be greater at sharp corners or in the middle of large flat areas?

7.4.6 Polarization of AM Radio Signals

Concepts to Investigate: Polarization of radio waves, radio transmission.

Materials: Portable AM radio, compass, city map.

Principles and Procedures: Light is only one form of electromagnetic radiation. It differs from X-rays, radio waves, and other radiation on the basis of frequency. All forms of radiation are transverse waves and experience reflection, refraction, diffraction, and polarization. Polarization filters allow us to visualize polarized light, but how can we observe polarized radio waves?

Radios receive radio waves and translate them into audio signals. Some inexpensive portable AM radios contain an internal loop antenna that picks up the magnetic component of the radio wave. If the radio is oriented so its loop is in line with the radio wave's oscillating magnetic field, it will pick up the signal. If, however, it is at a right angle to the field, it will pick up very little of the signal.

Keep the external antenna retracted so the radio uses only the internal, planar antenna. Tune to an AM station and slowly rotate the radio (Figure P). You should note two locations where the signal is weakest as well as two locations where it is strongest. Take a compass bearing of the radio's orientation when the signal is weakest. Locate the position of the AM station's transmitting antenna on a local map and determine the relationship between the radio's orientation and the antennae (call the radio station for location if you don't know where it is). Tune to a second AM station and repeat the procedure and predict the direction to the antennae. Call the station to find the location of the antennae and see if you are correct.

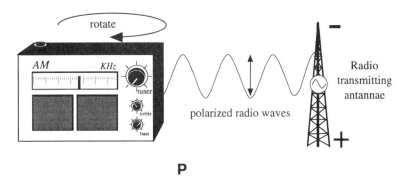

P

Questions

(1) Are AM broadcast signals polarized? How can you tell?

(2) Describe the orientation of the radio when the signal is weakest. If possible, open the radio to examine the orientation of the internal loop antenna. (Make certain to unplug it first.)

(3) It is not difficult to reorient a portable radio to get the best signal, but this would be a real problem for an automobile radio. How might an automobile radio be designed differently to receive signals equally in all directions?

FOR THE TEACHER

Light was thought to be a longitudinal wave until the work of Thomas Young and Augustin Fresnel in the early nineteenth century. Fresnel noted that light falling on Iceland Spar (calcite) produces two separate beams, but although these beams are coherent, they produce no interference fringes. Such observations could not be explained if light were a longitudinal wave, leading Young to propose that light is a transverse wave. In longitudinal waves, vibrations are in the same direction as wave movement. By contrast, the direction or directions in which vibrations occur in transverse waves are at right angles to the direction of wave movement. Figure B shows how transverse waves are polarized by filters that absorb light with a specific transverse orientation. Using this same apparatus and a wave spring, you can demonstrate to students that longitudinal waves cannot be polarized. Hold a section of a wave spring tightly together and then release it so that a pulse travels down the spring (Figure Q). Students will see that the longitudinal pulse is unaffected by the polarization filters. Only transverse waves can be polarized, which gives support to Young's hypothesis that light cannot be a longitudinal wave.

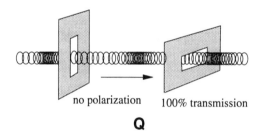

no polarization   100% transmission

Q

For students to grasp the concept of polarization, it may be necessary to introduce vector concepts as they relate to light. Figure R illustrates how the electric vector of a wave train can be resolved into two mutually perpendicular components, E_x and E_y. In this example, E_y is parallel to the polarizing direction of the filter and will be transmitted, while E_x is perpendicular to the polarizing direction and is therefore absorbed. Figure S shows a situation in which no light will be transmitted because the entire electric component of the wave train is at right angles ($E = E_x; E_y = 0$) to the polarizing direction of the filter. By contrast, Figure T illustrates the situation in which the entire electric component of a wave-train is parallel to the polarizing direction of the filter ($E = E_y$) allowing 100 percent transmission of the light. Taken together, these diagrams can be used to explain how an analyzer will transmit all light when aligned with a polarized wave train (Figure T), transmit progressively less as the angle is rotated from 0 to 90 degrees (Figure R), and transmit none when it is oriented at 90 degrees (Figure S).

It is important to note that not all sunglasses are polarized. Some sunglasses are simply made of dark glass that removes all polarities of light equally. Inform your students that such sunglasses will not work for any of the activities described in this chapter.

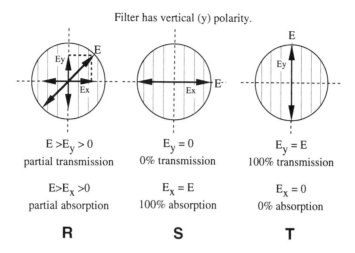

Filter has vertical (y) polarity.

$E > E_y > 0$	$E_y = 0$	$E_y = E$
partial transmission	0% transmission	100% transmission
$E > E_x > 0$	$E_x = E$	$E_x = 0$
partial absorption	100% absorption	0% absorption
R	**S**	**T**

7.4.1 Cross Polarization

Discussion: The entire class can view cross polarization when this activity is performed on an overhead projector in a darkened room. Although many students expect the two filters to block light when positioned at right angles, nearly everyone is surprised when insertion of an intermediate filter allows light to pass through once again. If the plane of polarization of the middle filter is not at right angles to the plane of polarization of the first filter, some light will be rotated and will pass with a new, oblique polarity. This light is not perpendicular to the final filter and will subsequently be partially rotated to pass it as well.

Answers (1) Light is completely blocked when two polarizing filters are held at right angles. It is assumed that the planes of polarization for both sunglasses are the same, so when the second is rotated 90 degrees, it effectively blocks the light transmitted through the first. (2) Glare is reflected light that has a plane of polarization parallel to the surface from which it is reflected. To effectively eliminate glare, the plane of polarization of sunglasses must be at right angles to this plane. Thus, one might assume that sunglasses are designed with a plane of polarization at right angles to the surface or to the earth. (3) See discussion. (4) No light will pass through two successive mutually perpendicular polarizing filters, so the addition of a third filter behind or in front will have no effect on the amount of light transmitted.

7.4.2 Polarization by Reflection

Discussion: When light strikes glass, the component lying in a plane parallel to the incident surface is largely reflected, while the component perpendicular to the surface is largely refracted (Figure U). The reflected and refracted beams are partially polarized, and the degree of polarization changes with the angle of incidence. The polarization angle (Brewster's angle, ϕ) is the angle at which polarization of reflected light is complete (100 percent), and is the arc tangent of the index of refraction ($\phi = \tan^{-1} n$). For glass, $n = 1.5$, and Brewster's angle is 56°. Before Land invented the polarizing sheet, polarizing devices were constructed of a series of glass plates posi-

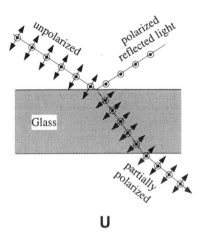

U

tioned in a tube such that light struck each successive glass plate at the polarizing (Brewster's) angle. With this technique it was possible to obtain a transmitted beam that was 99 percent polarized.

Answers (1) $n_{(glass)} = 1.5$; $\phi = \tan^{-1} n = 56°$. Student values may vary depending on the type of glass used. (2) Sunglasses will be most effective in reducing glare when the sun is 37° above the horizon (90° - 53° = 37°). This often occurs in the mid-morning or mid-afternoon but varies with latitude and season.

7.4.3 Polarization by Scattering

Discussion: This demonstration can also be used to show why the sky is blue and sunsets and sunrises are red and orange. The sky will appear bluest to observers who are at right angles to the light rays because blue light is scattered much more than other colors. The sky will appear red or orange when looking directly at the incident rays because blue light has been scattered. The time least dangerous to look toward the sun is at sunrise or sunset because at these times light passes through the greatest amount of atmosphere, and thus many of the damaging rays have been scattered or absorbed. (*Note:* Never look directly at the sun.) The higher-frequency light (blue, indigo, and violet) is scattered the most, leaving the lower-frequency light (yellow, orange, and red) to come through.

   If you perform this activity as a demonstration and your students have difficulty seeing the effect, you may wish to try the following alternative procedure. Obtain two pieces of cardboard large enough to cover the bottom of an aquarium or similar container and cut a 3-cm hole in each. Place one sheet of cardboard on the overhead projector and then place two wooden blocks on top. Place the second piece of cardboard on top of the blocks so the holes are aligned and then place the aquarium on top of it and fill it with water. If the two holes are aligned and positioned toward the front of the aquarium, a visible cylindrical beam will be produced. Dim the room and turn on the overhead projector. Slowly add the powdered creamer until a bluish beam appears.

Answers (1) Yes. The intensity of unpolarized light appears the same regardless of the orientation of the sunglasses. The intensity of the light scattered by the creamer changes as the polarizing filter is rotated. (2) Yes. Scattered light, like most reflected light, is polarized. Thus, polarizing filters will be helpful in reducing its glare. (3) Blue. Smoke tends to have a bluish tint, indicating that it scatters blue light more than other frequencies.

7.4.4 Polarization by Refraction

Discussion: Use an overhead projector to display to the entire class the double refraction of light by Iceland Spar. Write on a transparency sheet and place the crystal over a portion of the writing. The light transmitted through the crystal will be split into two images while the light bypassing the crystal will produce a single image.

Iceland Spar is a doubly refracting crystal. Upon entering the crystal, light is split into two polarized beams (Figure V). One beam is composed of light vibrating in a plane parallel to the surface and shows a constant index of refraction of 1.66, while the other beam is composed of light vibrating in a plane perpendicular to the surface and shows an index of refraction that varies between 1.49 and 1.66, depending on the angle of incidence. If the index of refraction for the beam that does not obey Snell's law is low (close to 1.49), then the images will be widely spaced, but if it is high (near 1.66), the observer may see only one image. The difference in refractive indices indicates that light travels at different speeds through the crystal, depending on the plane of polarization. It should be noted that early experiments with Iceland Spar by the French physicist Agustin Fresnel confirmed the hypotheses of Thomas Young, that light is a wave phenomenon.

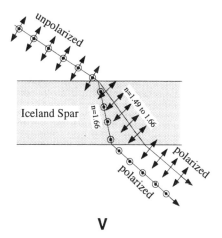

V

Answers (1) You can determine that both images are made from plane polarized light because they change in intensity as the polarizing lens is rotated. (2) The two images are polarized in mutually perpendicular planes. By rotating the polarizing lens 90°, one image can be made to disappear and the other to reappear, indicating that they are produced by polarized light rays that are mutually perpendicular.

7.4.5 Analyzing Physical Stress with Polarized Light

Discussion: This activity can be clearly seen by the entire class using the overhead projector. Place one polarizing filter on the overhead and rotate the other one while you apply stress to the plastic. The plastic divides light into two perpendicularly polarized waves much the way that the calcite crystal did in the previous activity. These two waves have different indices of refraction, indicating that they are traveling at different speeds. As the waves recombine upon exiting, each color possesses its own unique polarization. As the filter is rotated, some colored regions will disappear while others appear.

A dramatic stained-glass window effect can be made by placing portions of cellophane tape or clear cellophane at different angles on a plate of glass and inserting this glass between the two polarizing filters. The high-quality, nonyellowing clear plastic tapes do not work well for this activity, while the inexpensive cellophane-based tapes do. Project the image on a screen, and rotate the upper filter to create beautiful visual effects.

Answers (1) We know that the light of the stress patterns is polarized because it can be filtered out by rotating the analyzer (second polarizing filter). (2) Stress analysis is a standard technique used by mechanical and structural engineers. For example, aerospace engineers can examine the stresses on a new airplane wing design by making a model of the wing and subjecting it to the rigors of a wind tunnel, while mechanical engineers may use the technique to study the structural integrity of a new bolt design. Materials engineers examine stress patterns and suggest appropriate materials for given levels of stress. (3) Stress generally appears to be greatest at sharp corners or in regions where the plastic has been stamped.

7.4.6 Polarization of Radio Signals

Discussion: This is an effective demonstration for illustrating that different forms of electromagnetic radiation share common wave characteristics. This activity does not work well with FM signals because most FM radios possess circuitry that automatically boosts signals when they become weak. Radio antennae produce plane polarized radio waves because charge vibrates up and down their axes, as shown in Figure P.

Answers (1) AM signals are polarized, as shown by the directional response of an AM radio to a radio signal. When it is aligned with the magnetic component of radio waves, the internal-loop antenna picks up the signal, but when it is at right angles, it doesn't. Vertical AM transmitting antennae broadcast vertically polarized radio waves (electric field has a vertical orientation). (2) When the signal is weakest, the plane of the internal loop antenna is perpendicular to the line between the radio and the transmitting station. At this point it experiences the least magnetic flux and hence the weakest reception. (3) Automobile radios rely more heavily upon vertical antennae that are less sensitive to direction than the planar internal-loop antennae found in many portable AM radios. Car radios exhibit directionality if the external antenna is removed.

Applications to Everyday Life

Antiglare Devices: Polarizing lenses are effective in reducing reflective glare from nonmetallic surfaces. As a result, they are used widely in sunglasses, camera filters, and microscope lenses. Fishermen wear polarizing sunglasses to see fish through the surface of the water that would otherwise be hidden by the glare.

3-D Movies: Traditional movies appear two dimensional (flat) because only one perspective (the camera's) is displayed, while we are accustomed to receiving information from two perspectives (both eyes). To make a movie appear three dimensional, cinematographers must imitate human stereoscopic vision by taking simultaneous footage from two slightly different locations. Both images are projected on the screen, but at opposite polarities. The viewer wears glasses equipped with lenses with opposing polarities so the left eye can see only the footage taken by the left camera and the right eye can see only the footage taken by the right camera. You can make your own 3-D 35-mm slide by taking two pictures of a subject from approximately 10 cm apart. When projected through opposite polarity filters to the same location and viewed through lenses of opposite polarity, the image will appear three dimensional.

Animal Navigation: The light scattered by the atmosphere is polarized and the degree of polarization is dependent upon the position of the sun. It is believed that bees and certain migratory birds use the sun as a reference for navigation and on overcast days determine the sun's location by the degree of polarization of light scattered in the atmosphere.

Interstellar Matter: The gas and dust between stars is known as interstellar matter. Astronomers have determined that light transmitted through such matter is polarized, indicating that interstellar dust is probably made of elongated particles aligned by large-scale magnetic fields.

Medical Diagnosis: Gouty arthritis results from a metabolic disorder in which excess uric acid from the blood becomes deposited in the joints. White blood cells ingest these crystals but then release enzymes that stimulate an inflammatory response. Another disease of the joints, known as pseudogout, mimics the symptoms of gout by producing crystals of calcium pyrophosphate. Because the polarization properties of the two crystals are different, physicians can analyze the crystals and diagnose the actual condition.

Chemical Identification: Certain chemicals are "optically active" in that they rotate the plane of polarized light. In 1815 the French physicist Jean Baptiste Biot noted that certain organic substances, such as sugar and turpentine, are optically active regardless of whether they are in a solid, liquid, gaseous, or dissolved form. Compounds that rotate polarized light to the right are termed D-rotary (dextro, right), while compounds that rotate it to the left are termed L-rotary (levo, left). For example, D-glyceric acid and L-glyceric acid have the same formula ($C_3H_6O_4$) but rotate light differently based upon a difference in the specific location of the hydroxyl (-OH) group. Such compounds are known as stereoisomers and can be identified by analyzing the angle at which they polarize light.

Liquid Crystal Displays: Certain materials do not melt directly to the liquid phase, but first pass through a partially ordered paracrystalline stage in which they have the optical properties of solid crystals. Such materials are known as "liquid crystals" and are widely used in the displays of calculators, automobile stereos, and portable computer monitors. Liquid crystals polarize light. If you rotate a polarizing filter in front of a liquid crystal display, you will notice positions in which all of the characters on the screen disappear.

7.5 OPTICS

"Optics," from the Greek "optikes," originally referred to the study of the eye and vision, but today refers to the study of all phenomena related to light. In this chapter we focus on geometric optics, dealing with the formation of images by reflection and refraction of light. We can see images only when light from the object is focused on the light-sensitive tissue at the back of our eyes known as the retina (Figures A and B). The retina sends signals through the optic nerve to the back of the brain where they are interpreted as visual scenes. People may temporarily lose their vision when hit in the back of the head, not because of damage to their eyes, but rather due to damage to the portion of the brain that interprets messages received from the eyes.

Images appear clear when focused at the retina (Figure A), but are blurry when focused behind (Figure C) or in front (Figure E) of the retina. The thirteenth-century English scientist Roger Bacon is credited with the invention of eyeglasses to compensate for such refractive errors in the eye, and today more than half of all Americans wear eyeglasses or contact lenses to correct their vision by refocusing light on their retinas.

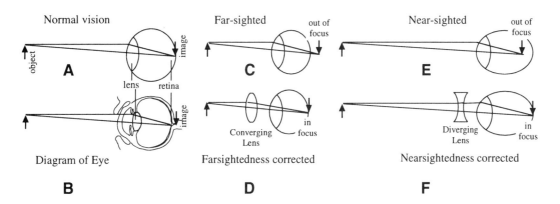

People who are farsighted (hyperopic) cannot focus on close images because an abnormally short eyeball causes light to focus behind the retina (Figure C). Farsightedness can be corrected with converging lenses (thicker in the center, thinner on the sides) that bring images forward to the plane of the retina (Figure D). By contrast, people who are nearsighted (myopic) cannot focus on distant images because an excessively long eyeball causes light to focus in front of the retina (Figure E). Nearsightedness can be corrected with diverging lenses (thinner in the center, thicker on the sides) that bring images back to the plane of the retina (Figure F).

By looking though a lens of a pair of glasses, you can determine if the owner is nearsighted or farsighted. Look at a distant object while holding the pair of glasses at arm's length. The object will appear smaller if the glasses have diverging lenses (owner is nearsighted), but larger if the glasses have converging lenses (owner is farsighted). Nearsightedness is more common than farsightedness among adults because eyes generally elongate with age. Determine if the people you know who wear glasses are farsighted or nearsighted by looking through their glasses. Is near-sightedness more common than farsightedness among the adults you know who wear glasses? Which is more common among the teenagers or children you know?

In addition to myopia and hyperopia, many people suffer from astigmatisms in which their lenses are not spherically uniform and consequently create distorted images on the surface of the retina. By using lenses with "reverse warping," it is possible to correct astigmatisms. You can determine if a person has an astigmatism by rotating his or her glasses through a 360° circle. If the image viewed through a lens changes shape while rotating the lens, then the person probably has an astigmatism. You can test yourself for astigmatisms by examining Figure G with one eye covered. If either the horizontal or vertical sets of lines appears darker than the other, then you may have an astigmatism.

One of the central principles in geometric optics is the law of rectilinear propagation, which states that *light will travel in a straight line in an optically uniform medium. When, however, light passes obliquely from one medium to another it will bend (refract).* In the first activity you will see how images can be generated by straight rays using a pinhole, and in subsequent activities you will examine how glass, water, plastic, and other transparent media can be used to create images by refraction. As you study geometric optics you will learn how optical systems are used to create interesting and useful images.

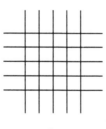

G

7.5.1 Law of Rectilinear Propagation

Concepts to Investigate: Law of rectilinear propagation, pinhole optics, silhouettes, real images.

Materials: Light-tight box, aluminum foil, tape, pin or needle, film, blanket, note card.

Principles and Procedures: The law of rectilinear propagation states that *light travels in a straight line when moving through a uniform medium.* The straight beam from an automobile headlight, or the sharp shadow cast by a tree at sunrise are evidence that light indeed travels in straight lines.

Part 1. Pinhole camera: Although modern cameras employ glass or plastic lenses to focus light on a sheet of photographic film, the first cameras used only a simple pinhole. Figure H shows how straight beams of light from an object will pass through a pinhole and create an inverted real image on the other side. To make your own pinhole camera, cut or drill a 1-centimeter-diameter hole in the end of a shoe box or other similarly shaped container. Tape a piece of foil over the opening and punch a very small hole in the center using a straight pin or needle. Cover the hole with a piece of opaque tape until the time you wish to take a picture. To load film into the camera, it is necessary to have "pitch black" conditions. If you don't have a darkroom, you can work at night and cover the box with a heavy blanket. In the dark, unroll a section of film as long as the box is wide and secure it to the inside of the box using paper clips. Seal the box with black electrician's tape to ensure that no light enters it. On a bright, sunny day, aim the camera at a large, distant object such as a tree or church tower. Remove the tape from the pinhole and expose the film for approximately 5 seconds. Return to the dark room to advance the film for a second exposure. Repeat the process using 15-, 30-, 45-, and 60-second exposure times. Faster films (ASA 400, 1000) may require less exposure time, while slower films (ASA 100) may require more. Rewind the film in the darkroom and send it to the developers. What was the most appropriate exposure time for the scenery you photographed?

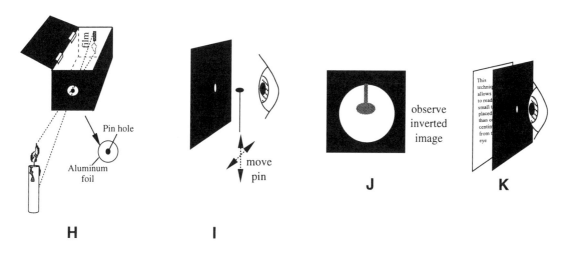

Pin hole

Aluminum foil

move pin

observe inverted image

H   **I**   **J**   **K**

Part 2. Inverted shadows: Punch a hole in the center of an opaque 3″ × 5″ card using a straight pin. Position the card approximately 4 cm from your eye and look through the hole. Direct the hole toward a well-lighted region and slowly move the head of the pin back and forth between your eye and the card, as illustrated in Figure I. Note that a shadowy, enlarged, and inverted image of the pin appears in the pinhole (Figure J). Which direction does the shadow move when you move the pin to the right? Which direction does it move when you move the pin down? Explain the behavior of the shadow using ray diagrams and the principle of rectilinear propagation.

Part 3. Pinhole "magnifier": Punch a hole in the center of an opaque 3″ × 5″ card using a straight pin. Place the hole close to your eye and try to read text placed less than 1 centimeter from your eye on the other side of the hole (Figure K). Without the pinhole it is impossible to focus on objects that are this close because overlapping rays from the object blur the image. The pinhole restricts the rays that hit the retina, thereby clarifying the image. The image is actually not magnified, but simply clarified so you can observe it at extremely close range.

Questions

(1) Is the image projected on the film in your pinhole camera right side up or upside down? Explain.

(2) What disadvantages and advantages are there to using pinhole photography as opposed to lens photography?

(3) What is "fast film" ?

(4) Why does the shadowy image of the pin in Part 2 appear upside down while the pin appears right side up?

7.5.2 Magnification

Concepts to Investigate: Magnification, objective lens, ocular lens, inversion of images.

Materials: Magnifying lens, ruler, lined paper, test tubes, stoppers.

Principles and Procedures: Magnifying lenses are commonly used in microscopes, telescopes, and telephoto camera lenses. Light microscopes employ two magnifying lenses in series to enlarge images up to 1,000 times. Note that the power of each microscope lens is inscribed on its barrel. A 4× objective lens (the lens nearest the specimen) combined with a 10× ocular (the lens nearest the eye) will produce a 40× magnification (10 × 4 = 40), while a 100× objective combined with a 10× ocular will produce a 1000× magnification. Using 1000× magnification, a 1-micrometer-wide object (1×10^{-6}m) will appear to be 1 mm wide (1×10^{-3}m). What magnifications are available on the microscopes in your laboratory?

Part 1. Determining the power of a lens: The power of a hand-held magnifying lens can be determined by comparing the dimensions of an image created by the lens with the actual dimensions of the object being viewed. Move a magnifying lens over the surface of a piece of lined paper until lines of the image are aligned with lines from the unmagnified paper (see Figure L). If there are two lines on the sheet of paper for every one line viewed through the lens, then the lens is doubling the size of the image, and is 2× power. What is the greatest power attainable with the lens you are using?

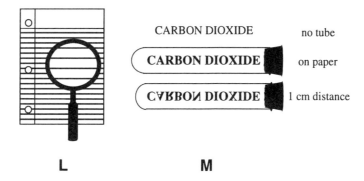

L   **M**

Part 2. Homemade magnifying lenses: Any cylindrical glass container can be used as a magnifying lens, but for simplicity we suggest test tubes for this activity. Fill a glass test tube with water and seal it with a stopper. Type CARBON DIOXIDE in capital letters on a 3″ × 5″ card, and view it through the test tube, as illustrated in Figure M. Observe the appearance of the phrase when the tube is positioned 0, 1, 2, and 10 centimeters away from the card. Are the images of both words inverted when viewed from a distance of 1 centimeter or more? Why or why not?

Questions

(1)   What is the power of the magnifying lens in Part 1?

(2)   Is the magnified image seen in Part 2 real (one formed by actual rays of light) or virtual (one that only appears to be formed by rays of light)? Explain.

(3)   Draw a simple ray diagram to illustrate why the magnified image is upright when the tube rests on the paper, but inverted when the tube is moved away.

(4)   Can a magnifying lens invert images? If so, under what conditions?

7.5.3 Real Versus Virtual Images

Concepts to Investigate: Real images, virtual images.

Materials: Magnifying lens (available at stationery and department stores).

Principles and Procedures: *A real image is one formed by rays of light, while a virtual image is one that only appears to be formed by such rays.* An image is real if it can be projected onto a surface.

Cover all the windows in a room with blinds or dark paper. Create a narrow opening for light in one window and position a magnifying glass parallel to this window, as shown in Figure N. Slowly move a piece of paper or cardboard backward and forward behind the lens until an image is clearly seen on the paper. This is a real image because it can be projected onto a surface. Describe the orientation and size of the image relative to the object being viewed.

Unlike real images, virtual images cannot be projected onto a surface. Use a hand-held magnifying lens to examine some written text, as illustrated in Figure O. The magnified image is "virtual" since it is not possible to project it on a surface. Describe the orientation and size of the virtual image.

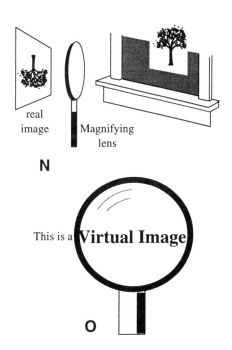

Questions

(1) Why is it necessary to darken the room when projecting an image of the scenery outside a window?

(2) How is a real image in this activity oriented with respect to the object?

(3) Is the image projected in a movie theater real or virtual? Explain.

(4) Is the image seen through binoculars real or virtual? Explain.

7.5.4 Focal Length

Concepts to Investigate: Focal length, focal point, ray diagrams, refraction, optical center, principal axis.

Materials: Magnifying lens, paper, assorted lenses, straight pins, cardboard or Styrofoam block.

Principles and Procedures

Part 1. Using the focal point of a lens to start a fire: The light rays from the sun are essentially parallel when they strike the surface of the Earth. Converging lenses are able to focus such parallel rays of light to a specific point known as the focal point. Since ancient times, people have known how to position dry leaves or wood shavings at the focal point of glass chips to start fires. Your objective is to determine the focal length of a lens by noting the location of the focal point.

Position a magnifying lens as shown in Figure P and move a sheet of paper backward and forward until the dot of light is smallest. This is the focal point *f*. If you leave the paper in this position long enough, the paper will probably start to burn. The distance between the focal point and the center of the lens is the focal length. Determine the focal lengths of a variety of lenses. What is the relationship between the curvature of these lenses and their focal lengths?

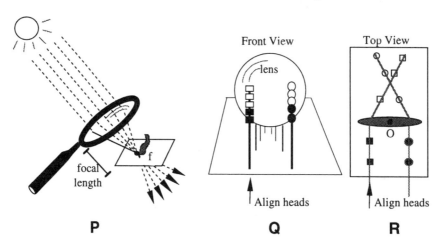

Part 2. Determining the focal point by tracking rays: When looking through a microscope, you may have noticed that a specimen appears to move to the right as you move it to the left, and that it appears to move down when you move it up. Lenses such as those in a microscope may produce results you find confusing until you understand how lenses bend light. In this activity you will see how a beam of light that appears straight from one perspective is actually bent when viewed from another perspective.

Position a converging (biconvex) lens in an upright position on a cardboard or Styrofoam platform, as shown in Figure Q. Align two pins to the left of center in front of the lens so they form a line perpendicular to the lens. While looking through the lens, position additional pins behind it so they appear to be in a straight line with the pins in front. After placing four pins on the other side, view from above and note how the light rays bend as they pass through the lens (Figure R). Repeat this procedure for a ray on the other side of the lens. Finally, position pins in front of the lens so they form a line perpendicular with the optical center O (the principal axis). While looking through the lens, place additional pins on the other side to continue the principal axis. Does the principal axis bend like the other two rays? Draw an outline of the lens on the cardboard or Styrofoam base and then use a ruler to connect the dots formed by the pins of the principal axis and the two parallel rays. *The point at which light rays parallel to the principal axis converge is known as the principal focus or focal point.* The focal length is the distance from the center of the lens to this position. Compare your measurements with those obtained in Part 1.

Questions

(1) What is the focal length of the magnifying lens measured in Part 1?
(2) Fire investigators have often cited old soda-pop bottles as the cause of brush fires. Explain.
(3) Is there any way you can position the first two pins in Part 2 so the pins behind the lens will be in a straight line with those in front? Explain.

7.5.5 Practical Uses of Lenses

Concepts to Investigate: Optical bench, lens equation, practical uses of lenses, principal rays.

Materials: Meter stick, small electric light (25 watts or less), small cardboard or plastic container, utility knife, lens, modeling clay, 3″ × 5″ cards.

Principles and Procedures: A lens can have a variety of applications, depending upon its position relative to the object viewed. In this activity you will alter the relative positions of the lens and object to investigate the various applications of lenses. All arrangements shown in Figure T can be investigated using the simple optical bench shown in Figure S. Although a candle may serve as a light source for this activity, it is difficult to accurately measure the height of the flame for calculations. If possible, use a low-wattage bulb on a simple mount, as illustrated in Figure S. Obtain a small cardboard can or box and cut out an arrow using a sharp utility knife. When positioned over the light bulb, the arrow will serve as a bright object whose height h_o is easily measured.

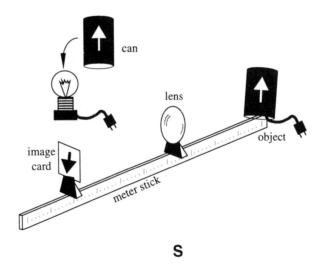

S

Figure T illustrates ray diagrams for six different applications of converging lenses. The black arrows represent objects, and the white arrows represent images of these objects. The lines emanating from the tips of the object arrows represent rays that have easily identified paths. These rays are known as the principal rays and are used to predict the locations of images. Those rays traveling parallel to the principal axis always pass through the focal point f, while rays traveling through the optical center of the lens do not bend. The location where these two principal rays intersect is the location of the image.

Determine the focal length f of your lens using the technique described in the previous activity. Using a piece of clay or other support, position the lens in the middle of the meter stick and identify with tape the positions of f and $2f$ on both sides of the lens. Darken the room and place the light source beyond $2f$ (case 2). Move a 3″ × 5″ card on the opposite side of the lens until you obtain a clear image of the arrow. The image is reduced, inverted, and positioned between f and $2f$ as illustrat-

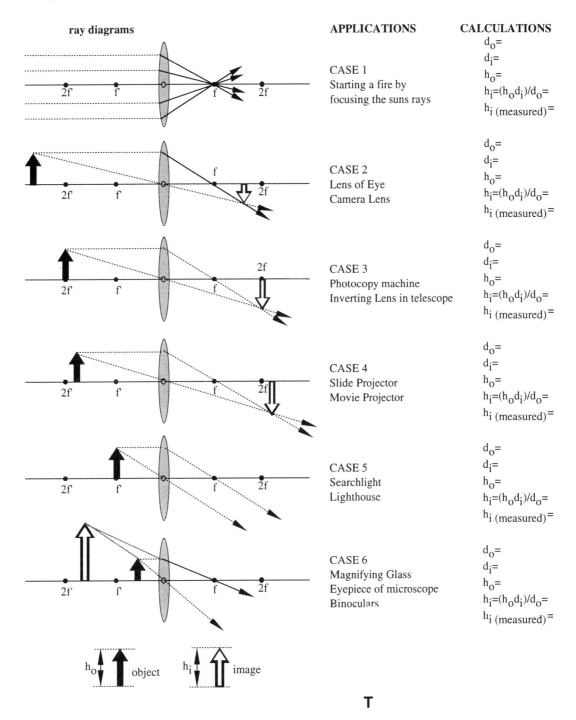

ray diagrams   **APPLICATIONS**   **CALCULATIONS**

CASE 1
Starting a fire by
focusing the suns rays

$d_o=$
$d_i=$
$h_o=$
$h_i=(h_o d_i)/d_o=$
$h_i \text{ (measured)}=$

CASE 2
Lens of Eye
Camera Lens

$d_o=$
$d_i=$
$h_o=$
$h_i=(h_o d_i)/d_o=$
$h_i \text{ (measured)}=$

CASE 3
Photocopy machine
Inverting Lens in telescope

$d_o=$
$d_i=$
$h_o=$
$h_i=(h_o d_i)/d_o=$
$h_i \text{ (measured)}=$

CASE 4
Slide Projector
Movie Projector

$d_o=$
$d_i=$
$h_o=$
$h_i=(h_o d_i)/d_o=$
$h_i \text{ (measured)}=$

CASE 5
Searchlight
Lighthouse

$d_o=$
$d_i=$
$h_o=$
$h_i=(h_o d_i)/d_o=$
$h_i \text{ (measured)}=$

CASE 6
Magnifying Glass
Eyepiece of microscope
Binoculars

$d_o=$
$d_i=$
$h_o=$
$h_i=(h_o d_i)/d_o=$
$h_i \text{ (measured)}=$

h_o object h_i image

T

ed in Figure T (case 2). Just as the image is focused on the card, so too is light in the human eye focused on the retina and light through a camera focused on the film. Measure the height of the image on the card h_i, the distance from the center of the lens to the object d_o, and the distance from the center of the lens to the image d_i.

The lens equation states the ratio of the height of an image to the height of an object is the same as the ratio of the distance to the image to the distance of the object

$h_i/h_o = d_i/d_o$. Therefore, $h_i = (h_o d_i)/d_o$. Measure the height of the image h_i as shown on the card and compare this with the height of the image as computed by the equation. Investigate cases 3–6 in the same way you investigated case 2. Is the lens equation a good predictor of image height? Report your findings in the table adjacent to Figure T.

Questions

(1) Calculate the percentage error between the computed and measured values of h_i for each case. The formula for percentage error is:
$$((h_{i(measured)} - h_{i(calculated)})/h_{i(measured)}) \times 100\%.$$

(2) At what location in a projector must a slide be positioned if it is to be projected clearly on a screen?

(3) Which of the six lens arrangements illustrated in the table produces a virtual image? Explain.

(4) At what location should the light source of a searchlight be placed? Explain.

(5) Photocopy machines typically produce an inverted image. What would be necessary to make a photocopy produce an upright image?

FOR THE TEACHER

Broadly speaking, optics is the study of the generation, propagation, transmission, and detection of electromagnetic radiation extending from long-wave X-rays to short-wave radio waves. In this chapter we have addressed only the domain of geometric optics, namely the study of light rays and their imagery through optical systems such as lenses and pinholes. With the exception of pinhole optics, everything in this chapter is based upon the concept of refraction, so it is important that students understand this principle before attempting these activities.

7.5.1 Law of Rectilinear Propagation

Discussion: Although the pinhole camera is an interesting demonstration of the law of rectilinear propagation, it is rather difficult to perform as a classroom demonstration because of the time and conditions required. The "camera" can be modified for demonstration purposes simply by replacing the film and the back panel with a sheet of translucent white tissue paper, wax paper, or onion-skin paper. Darken the classroom and aim the camera through a small opening in the blinds. If the room is sufficiently dark, students will see a dim, reduced, inverted image on the tissue paper covering the back of the box.

Pinhole optics can be used to view solar eclipses. Make a pinhole in a 3" × 5" card and position the card at right angles to the sun's rays. Place a white piece of paper in the shade below the card and move it up and down until a disc-shaped image of the sun comes into focus (Figure U). As the moon moves in front of the sun, the image of the sun will appear as a crescent. Check your local newspaper for the specific time of the next solar eclipse in your area.

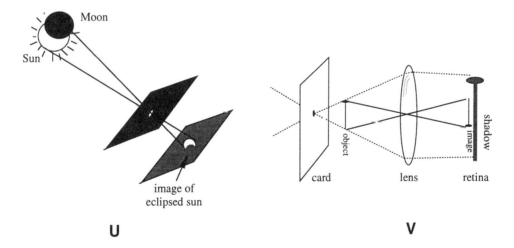

U

V

Answers (1) The image will be inverted, as rays from the top of the object expose the bottom of the film after passing through the pinhole, while rays from the bottom of the object expose the top of the film. (2) Pinhole cameras require long exposure times because the only light available to expose the film comes through the tiny pinhole. Pinhole cameras have a much broader depth of focus, allowing objects to be in focus even though they are great distances apart. (3) The faster the film, the less time required to obtain an adequate exposure. ASA 1000 is a fast film and requires substantially less exposure time than ASA 100. Unfortunately, fast film produces grainy images. (4) Both an image and a silhouette of the pin are formed on the retina. The image, like normal scenes viewed through the eye, is inverted by the lens and projected upside down on the retina. The brain, however, on the basis of experience, interprets the image as being right side up. The silhouette of the pin is formed as light passing through the pinhole is blocked by the pin en route to the lens. The pinhole acts as a point source, but since it is so close to the eye, rays forming the silhouette strike the lens at angles too great to be inverted prior to reaching the retina (Figure V). The silhouette of the pin is therefore cast upright upon the retina, but inverted by the brain. Thus, the image of the pin appears upright, but the silhouette of the pin appears inverted.

7.5.2 Magnification

Discussion

Part 1: This activity can be performed as a classroom demonstration by placing a lined transparency on an overhead projector while carefully positioning a magnifying lens above.

Part 2: With the following modifications, the activity described in Part 2 can be used to help students learn to make observations and generate hypotheses. Prepare 3″ × 5″ cards in which CARBON is typed in uppercase black and DIOXIDE in uppercase red letters. Ask students to make observations and generate hypotheses. They will note that the word CARBON inverts, while DIOXIDE does not appear to invert. (Of course the word DIOXIDE also inverts, but appears unchanged due to the symmetry of its letters.) Students may suggest a variety of reasons why CARBON inverts while DIOXIDE does not, including differences in refraction due to the different colored ink. Ask students to test their hypotheses until they realize that the entire text is indeed inverted.

Answers (1) Student answers will vary depending on their lenses. (2) The magnified image is virtual, because although it is seen by the eye, it cannot be projected on a piece of paper. (3) Student diagram. (4) A regular magnifying lens will invert images if placed at a sufficient distance from the object. The radius of curvature of a magnifying lens is substantially greater than that of a test tube, and so distances must be greater before the inversion will occur.

7.5.3 Real Versus Virtual Images

Discussion: Students often have a difficult time understanding where real images are located when there is no screen present. For example, if a slide projector casts images on a screen, where is the image if the screen is removed? The following activity can be used to help students better understand real images. Focus a slide projector on a flat screen and then remove the screen. As you move a pointer, meter stick, or other such object rapidly through the beam in the plane where the screen once was, students will see the original image appear in "thin air" (Figure W). The image was always there, but simply not visible until something reflected the light to their eyes. Although the pointer is very thin, they can see the entire picture because visual images on their retinas persist until the stick returns. You can create a variety of interesting projections by moving the rod in arcs or cylinders.

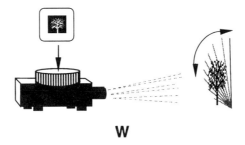

W

Students should understand that the lens of the human eye projects a real image of the environment on the retina of the eye. The image is reduced and inverted, just as was the image created in Part 1 of this activity. Many students have performed dissections of cow or sheep eyes, and have extracted the lens. Although the lens of a preserved eye is less transparent than a living lens, it is still possible to observe how it projects an inverted and reduced image of the world around it. Ask students to look at the horizon through such a lens and note that the ground appears on top and the sky appears on the bottom.

Answers (1) Stray light will illuminate the paper and "wash out" any image you are trying to project. (2) The image is inverted relative to the original scene. (3) The movie projector in a theater focuses light beams on the screen, creating a real image. (4) Binoculars produce a virtual image. There is no place in which you can position a screen on which its image may be projected.

7.5.4 Focal Length

Discussion: Camera lenses are given f-number ratings to describe their ability to gather light. A low f-number indicates that a lens is very efficient at gathering light and therefore can be used under low-light conditions. The f-number is the ratio of the focal length of a lens to its effective diameter. A rating of $f/4$ indicates that the focal length is 4 times the diameter of the lens. You can have your students determine the f-number of the lenses they use simply by dividing the observed focal length by the measured diameter of the lens. The time required for an exposure increases as the square of the f-number. The procedure in Part 2 can be used to create ray diagrams for diverging lenses, prisms, and mirrors.

Answers (1) The values students obtain are dependent upon the lenses used. (2) Cylindrical bottles can serve as converging lenses. If dry leaves or grass are positioned at the focal point of this "lens," it is possible they can be ignited when the solar radiation is intense. (3) A straight line will be obtained only if the first two pins are aligned with the optical center of the lens.

7.5.5 Practical Uses of Lenses

Discussion: The optical lab bench is a superb teaching tool. In this activity we used it to illustrate the six basic cases concerning a convex (diverging) lens. Stress the applicability of the lens arrangements to various technological applications, as mentioned in Figure T. You may wish to introduce the second lens equation

$$1/f = 1/d_o + 1/d_i$$

and show that it is predictive of where images will form. When discussing this equation, remind students that distances are positive for real images, negative for virtual images, and that f is positive for converging lenses, but negative for diverging lenses.

Answers (1) Student values will differ. (2) The slide must be positioned between the focal length and twice the focal length. (3) Case 6 produces virtual images such as those seen in magnifying lenses. The image appears large and upright, but there is no place in which you can place a screen on which such an image can be projected. (4) The bulb should be positioned at the focal point to project parallel rays. This is the reverse of case 1 in which parallel rays focus at the focal point. (5) An inverting lens (case 3) reverses the image. A second inverting lens could be placed at 2f to reinvert the image (case 3).

Applications to Everyday Life

Human Vision: The human eye contains a flexible lens. The ciliary muscles change the shape of the lens to alter its focal length so it can focus images of objects that are near or far. As people age, the lens becomes less flexible, making it difficult to refocus the eyes from close objects to far objects. People with such problems are often advised to use bifocals or trifocals to aid in the refocusing process.

Squinting: Many near-sighted people squint to view distant objects if they don't have their glasses. Squinting places pressure upon the lens of the eye and assists the intrinsic muscles as they reshape the lens when viewing distant objects. Squinting may bend the lens enough so that it will bring the real image into focus on the retina. Squinting may also be helpful to persons who have misplaced their reading glasses.

"Water Burns" (focal point): Many broad-leafed plants will suffer damage if their leaves are watered by a sprinkler on a hot, clear day. The droplets of waters serve as converging lenses for the sunlight and can focus light energy so it kills cells within the leaves.

Correcting Vision: Nearsightedness is corrected by placing diverging lenses (lenses thicker around the side than in the center) in front of the eye. Farsightedness is corrected using converging lenses (lenses thicker in the center).

Compound Microscope: The compound microscope, invented by Zacharias Janssen in 1590, uses an objective lens to produce an enlarged real image (case 4), which is then magnified as a virtual image (case 6) by the eyepiece.

Refracting Telescopes: Refracting telescopes use three lenses in series. The objective lens is large, to collect as much light as possible. It produces a reduced, inverted image (case 2), which a second lens (placed at the $2f$) reinverts (case 3). Finally, the eyepiece creates an enlarged virtual image of this upright real image (case 6).

Projectors: Slide, movie, and overhead projectors are designed with lenses positioned so enlarged images will be projected onto a distant screen (case 4).

Lighthouses, Searchlights, Fresnel Lenses: The beam from a lighthouse or searchlight will be effective only if it is projected as a focused, parallel beam, which can be achieved by placing the light source at the focal length (case 5). Unfortunately, large lights demand lenses that are very large, heavy, and difficult to make. The French physicist Augustin Fresnel realized that the critical factor in image formation was not the thickness of the lens, but rather the curvature of its surfaces. Fresnel therefore designed lenses for the French lighthouse commission that retained the curvature, but eliminated the mass of the lens. Figure X shows how a Fresnel lens compares with a standard lens with the same focal length. Such Fresnel lenses are widely used where light-gathering capability must be maximized and lens mass minimized.

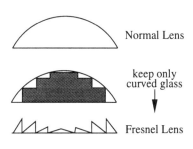

X

7.6 COLOR

When people look at a painting do they all perceive the same colors? When you look at a flower do you see the same patterns and colors as the insect or bird that pollinates it? Does a mouse appear the same color to a rabbit as it does to a rattlesnake preying upon it? Recent findings indicate that the answer to all of these questions is no.

While some people are capable of distinguishing as many as 10,000,000 colors, others are incapable of distinguishing red from green. For the 4 percent of the population who are "color blind," the red and green lights in a traffic signal are distinguishable only on the basis of their position. While there is a wide variety of color vision among humans, there is an even greater variety of color perception among animals. Most birds see very well in the red portion of the spectrum and are frequently seen pollinating red flowers or foraging on red berries. In contrast, honey bees are unable to distinguish such targets, but are adept at locating yellow, blue, or violet flowers.

The retina of the human eye is sensitive to electromagnetic radiation of wavelengths in the 400- to 700-nanometer range (1 nanometer = 1 billionth of a meter). Inspection of Figure A shows that our eyes are sensitive to only a small portion of the electromagnetic spectrum. Such forms of radiation as gamma rays, X-rays, microwaves, and radio waves are invisible to us. Radiation in the 700-nm range produces a sensation that we identify as "red," while waves in the 400-nm range evoke a sensation we call "violet." Between these two extremes are the colors of orange, yellow, green, blue, and indigo. Although humans cannot see "colors" of wavelengths shorter than 400 nm or longer than 700 nm, other creatures can. For example, numerous insects see ultraviolet light and are attracted to ultraviolet markings on flowers that are not visible to us. Special "bug zapper" lights capitalize on this fact by emitting light in the violet to ultraviolet range, thereby luring unsuspecting insects toward their fatal high-voltage electrodes.

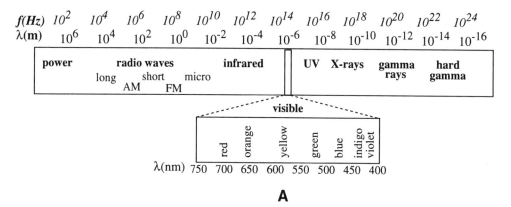

A

Rattlesnakes can see light of lower energy than red (longer wavelength, infrared radiation). Infrared radiation is the heat radiation we feel when facing a campfire or heat lamp. Rattlesnakes possess a special structure known as the pit organ, located midway between their nostrils and eyes, sensitive to infrared radiation the way our retinas are sensitive to red, green, and blue light. The pit organ allows the snake to see temperature variations of as little as a thousandth of a degree Celsius, much as we might notice variations in the colors of a rainbow. While to us a gray mouse appears hidden against a gray desert soil, to a snake it may stand out as a different shade of infrared if its body temperature is different from that of its surroundings.

Color is the sensation one receives when light stimulates the retina of the eye. Since color sensitivity varies from individual to individual, it is more objective to classify light on the basis of its wavelength or energy than on color. Figure A shows that light of 470-nm wavelength produces a sensation we call blue, while 690 nm produces red.

The frequency of light is equal to its speed divided by its wavelength ($f = c/\lambda$). Since the speed of light ($c = 3 \times 10^8$ m/s) is constant, the frequency of light is inversely related to its wavelength. As the wavelength increases, the frequency decreases. It is also known that the energy of a photon (quantum or packet of light energy) is directly proportional to its frequency: $E = hf$, where h is Plank's constant (6.63×10^{-34} J·s). *Thus the energy of light is inversely proportional to its wavelength: $E = hc/\lambda$.* Since blue light has a shorter wavelength than red, it also has a higher energy. In this chapter you will have the opportunity to investigate properties of color, wavelength, and frequency.

7.6.1 The Visible Spectrum

Concepts to Investigate: Wavelength, frequency, color, prisms, solar spectrum, polychromatic light, dispersion of light, recombination of light.

Materials: Prisms (or microscope slides, clear tape and modeling clay), light source with focused beam (slide projector or focusable flashlight).

Principles and Procedures: Light from the sun appears white, but when it travels through the prisms of a chandelier, the facets of a diamond, or the water droplets in the sky it is separated into its many colors, producing a brilliant display known as the visible spectrum. In the 1600s, Sir Isaac Newton demonstrated that the "color" white is merely the sensation our minds generate when we receive the full spectrum of colors found in a rainbow. Each wavelength (color) of light has its own unique speed when traveling through media such as glass or water, and each will have its own unique angle of refraction upon striking an oblique surface. Violet light refracts (bends) most and comprises one end of the spectrum while red light refracts least and is found at the other (see chapter on refraction). Newton argued that since it is possible to disperse white light into its constituent colors, it must be possible to recombine these colors to produce white light once again. In this activity you will test this hypothesis.

To disperse white light into the spectrum requires one prism, and to recombine the spectrum to produce white light requires a second prism. Glass prisms may be obtained from optical-supply companies or from an old pair of binoculars. If you do not have access to glass prisms, you can make glass/water prisms with microscope slides, tape, and modeling clay. Tape the joints of the slides together as illustrated in Figure B, and seal one end with modeling clay. After filling the triangular container with water, seal the other end with clay. Position the prisms as illustrated in Figures C or D.

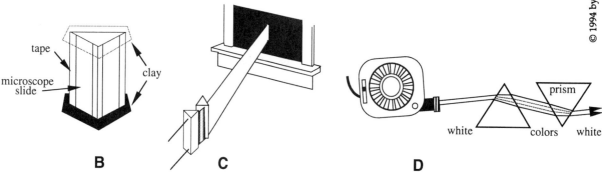

B   C   D

Spectral displays are best observed under very dark conditions. Place cardboard or other material over the windows of your room. If light is shining upon a window, you may use it as a light source simply by cutting a hole in the cardboard on that window (Figure C). If this is not possible, you can generate an intense "pencil beam" of light using a 35-mm slide projector. Place electrician's tape or other opaque tape over an old slide and then make a hole in the center with a hole puncher. When this slide is placed in the projector it will generate a narrow beam of light and produce a clear spectrum when projected through a prism. Position the prisms with respect to the light source, as illustrated in Figure D. Adjust the positions of both prisms so the light dispersed from the first prism is recombined to produce white light by the second. Trace and identify the positions of the prisms as well as the positions of the various bands of color on a piece of white paper.

Questions

(1) What colors can you identify in the spectrum?

(2) Which color travels fastest in the prism? Explain how you can determine this based upon the spectrum from a single prism.

(3) Is it possible to recombine the spectrum into a single beam of white light with the prisms oriented in the same direction? Explain.

7.6.2 Infrared Radiation

Concepts to Investigate: Electromagnetic radiation spectrum, infrared light.

Materials: Prism, thermometer.

Principles and Procedures: Visible light represents only one portion of the electromagnetic radiation spectrum (see Figure A). Radiation more energetic than violet is known as ultraviolet (ultra-; above), while radiation less energetic than red is known as infrared (infra-; below). Although we cannot see infrared light, we can feel it. If you have ever stood next to a campfire on a cold night, you may have noticed that one side of your body was heated while the other side remained quite cold. The fire heats primarily by emitting infrared radiation—heating of the air is minimal. When your body and clothes absorb infrared radiation, they become warmer. Sunlight, like firelight, has an infrared component.

Find a window upon which sunlight is shining. Cover the window with black construction paper or other opaque material. Using a single-sided razor blade or utility knife, cut a small slit (approximately 5 mm × 15 mm) in the paper to allow light to pass through. Place a prism in front of the beam, as illustrated in Figure E. Although glass prisms work best, it is possible to use prisms made from microscope slides, tape, and clay as described in the previous activity.

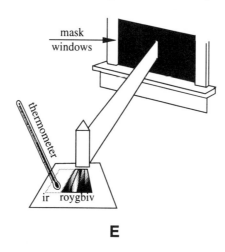

E

Record the temperature of the room by placing the thermometer far away from the spectrum, then place the thermometer in the visible region of the spectrum (red, orange, yellow, green, blue, indigo, violet) and read the temperature after three minutes. After measuring the visible portion of the spectrum, move the thermometer to the portion immediately beyond the red region. Is the dark region beyond red light hotter or colder than the visible spectrum? Explain.

Questions

   (1)   Why might the region beyond red be hotter than portions of the visible spectrum?

   (2)   Certain types of photographic film are sensitive to infrared radiation. When infrared film is developed, it allows you to "see" infrared radiation. What would an infrared picture of a recently driven automobile look like? (Describe key features.)

   (3)   Fluorescent light fixtures are more efficient than incandescent light bulbs because they emit less infrared radiation. Explain.

7.6.3 Absorption and Transmission

Concepts to Investigate: Absorption, transmission, monochromatic light.

Materials: Light source, prism, colored cellophane (transparent, colored report covers work well).

Principles and Procedures: Monochromatic light is light composed of a single color. A plant grown in monochromatic red light can survive while one grown in monochromatic green light soon becomes sick and dies. Why? While chlorophyll pigments in plants absorb and use red light in the vital process of photosynthesis, they cannot absorb or use green light. Thus, plants grown in monochromatic green light cannot produce sugars because no photosynthesis occurs. Since green light is not absorbed, it is either reflected and/or transmitted, producing the green color of trees and shrubs.

Part 1. Selective absorption: This activity requires a bright light source such as a 35-mm slide projector or the natural light coming though a sunlit window pane. Produce a narrow beam of light either by punching a hole in a 35-mm slide that has been masked with black tape (Figure F) or by cutting a slit in a piece of opaque paper with which you are covering the window pane (Figure E). Darken the room and place a prism in the path of the beam, as illustrated in Figure F or E. Place a piece of red cellophane or a red transparent plastic report cover between the prism and the screen. What colors does the red filter allow through? Repeat the procedure using green and blue filters. Record your results.

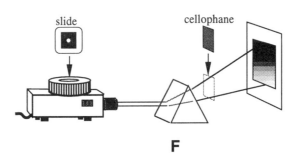

slide   cellophane

F

Part 2. "Secret code": Things look different when viewed through a colored filter. Look at colorful photographs in a magazine through a red cellophane or plastic filter and notice that blue skies and green trees appear black, while red cars remain red. The pigment in the filter selectively absorbs all colors except red, allowing red to be transmitted to produce the red color we see.

Use red- and green-colored markers to write the word "physics!" (Figure G). Draw "h", "i" and "!" in green, and the other letters in red. When you examine the writing through the red filter, you should be able to see only the word "hi!" (Figure H). The light from the green letters was absorbed by the filter, leaving a black silhouette against the red background. The white background reflects all wavelengths of light, but appears red when viewed through the filter because all other colors are

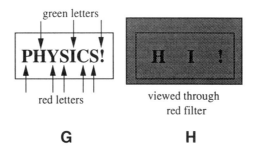

G   H

absorbed by the filter. Red letters blend with this background and seem to disappear, leaving only those written in green. Develop your own secret coding system using a different combination of colored inks and filters.

Questions

(1) In what color(s) does a multicolored picture appear when viewed through a red filter? Explain.

(2) How will a multicolored picture appear when viewed through both a red and a blue filter at the same time? Try it.

(3) Before polarized lenses were popular, opticians sold sunglasses made of green-tinted glass. Describe potential problems with such glasses.

7.6.4 Primary Colors

Concepts to Investigate: Additive properties of light, primary colors.

Materials: Red, green, and blue lights (use Christmas lights for a small-scale investigation and floodlights for a classroom demonstration), electric drill (any rapidly spinning spindle will work), bolt, nuts, washer, disk, paints or markers (red, green, and blue).

Principles and Procedures: Examine a color computer or television monitor using a magnifying lens and note that the screen is composed of numerous pixels (picture cells) that occur in triplets. Each triplet has a red, a green, and a blue dot. By illuminating different combinations of these dots at varying intensities, the monitor produces a wide range of colors. Red, green, and blue light are considered the primary colors because they can be projected in different combinations to produce all other colors. Some restaurants have large-screen projection monitors on which they broadcast sports events. By casting beams of red, green, and blue light onto a screen these monitors generate enough colors to produce a lifelike effect. In this activity you will make your own "big-screen" monitor.

Part 1. Additive colors: Darken the room and adjust the red, green, and blue lights so they shine on the same white surface, as illustrated in Figure I. Note that the screen appears white where the three beams overlap. Now turn on just the red and the blue lights and describe the color produced. Place an object close to the screen and note the color of the two shadows. Repeat with the red and green lights followed by the blue and green lights. Now turn on all three lights and place an object such as your hand or a ball in front of the beams, as shown in Figure I. Since the object is illuminated from three different locations, it will cast three separate shadows. Where red is blocked, the shadow will be composed of only blue and green light. What color is produced when blue and green light are combined? Where green light is blocked, the shadow will be composed of red and blue light. What color is produced when red and blue light are combined? Where blue light is blocked, the shadow will be composed of red and green light. What color is produced when red and green light are combined? Record your findings.

© 1994 by John Wiley & Sons, Inc.

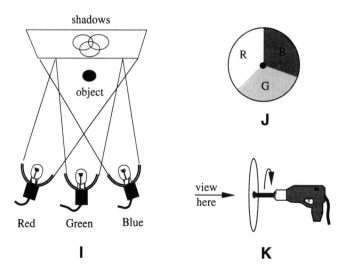

Part 2. Color wheel: The image on a computer monitor is created as a beam of electrons moves rapidly back and forth across the screen in rows from top to bottom. Phosphorous zones on the screen glow when they are hit by electrons and remain black when they are not, creating an image from a series of bright and dark dots. The electron beam sweeps back and forth across the screen so rapidly that our eyes cannot detect that the glowing dots are actually turning on and off, so the picture appears smooth and continuous to our eyes. In a similar fashion, the spokes of a rapidly spinning bicycle wheel appear to blend into a smooth blur. If a disk painted in the three primary colors is spinning rapidly, will we be able to see all the colors distinctly, or will they blend into a composite image? If they blur together, will they combine to form white light the way red, green, and blue dots do on a computer screen?

Cut a circular disk from a piece of heavy cardboard or thin plywood. Divide it into three equal sections and paint these red, green, and blue, as illustrated in Figure J. Drill a hole in the center of the disk and mount it on a long bolt using lock washers and nuts. Tighten the nuts securely so they will not loosen while the bolt rotates. Tighten the bolt in the chuck of the drill and turn it on (Figure K). View the disk in bright light and note its appearance. Can you see the three colors, or do they blend together into gray or white?

Questions

(1) What color is produced by mixing green and blue light? Red and blue? Red and green?
(2) How was the green shadow produced? The red shadow? The blue shadow?
(3) What is the color of the background? Why?
(4) Why must big-screen projection monitors be viewed in dimly lit rooms?
(5) Do the colors on the rotating disk (Part 2) blend into white? Explain.

7.6.5 Complementary Colors

Concepts to Investigate: Complementary colors, additive properties of light.

Materials: Broad marking pens or paints, bright light, 3″ × 5″ card, string.

Principles and Procedures

Part 1. Retinal fatigue and complementary colors: The previous activity showed that the simultaneous projection of the three primary colors (red, green, and blue) produces white light. However, if only the green and blue were projected, the color appeared cyan (bright greenish-blue). If the red light was then turned on, the screen once again appeared white, showing that cyan and red are complementary colors, meaning that they add together to produce white light. *Any two colors that combine to produce white light are known as complementary colors.*

If you have been photographed with a camera equipped with a strobe (electronic flash), you may have noticed a dark after-image of the strobe long after the flash of light was gone. The flash was so intense that it fatigued photoreceptive cells in your retinas so they were temporarily unresponsive to light. As a result, a black image of the flash appeared in your vision. Your retinas may also fatigue after staring at colored objects for long periods of time. When you look away toward a white surface, however, you will not see a black after-image, but rather one that is the complementary color of the object you were staring at. For example, if you stare intensely for one minute at a red dot and then turn your eyes toward a sheet of white paper, you will see a cyan (the complimentary color of red) after-image of the dot. Light reflected from white paper normally stimulates the red, green, and blue cones (photoreceptive cells) of the retina, but if you have first fatigued the red cones by staring at a red object, these cells temporarily will not respond to red light. As a result, only the green and blue cones in that region of the retina are stimulated, causing the image to appear cyan (the combination of green and blue), the complementary color of red.

Draw a solid red circle on a white sheet of paper using a marker or paintbrush. Cover one eye, place the circle in bright light, and stare at it. At the end of one minute, quickly refocus on a well-lit sheet of white paper. What color is the after-image of the circle? Repeat this process with green and blue dots and examine your results. What are the complementary colors of green and of blue?

Using a 3″ × 5″ card, color the flags, as illustrated in Figure L. Stare at each of these flags in bright light for one minute, then shift your gaze to white paper. Record the after-image of these flags in the spaces provided in Figure M. Can you identify the countries or states represented by these flags? Take another 3″ × 5″ card and draw the flag of the United States in its complementary colors. Stare at it in bright light, then turn your eyes to white paper to see if it resembles the actual colors of the flag.

Part 2: Complementary color disk: Yellow light is formed by the combination of green and red light. When yellow light is mixed with blue light, all three primary colors (red, green, blue) are present and the combination appears white. We say that

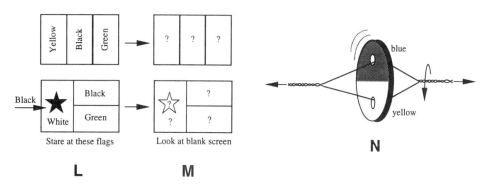

L   M

yellow and blue are complementary colors because they produce white light when combined. In this activity you will investigate complementary colors using a rapidly spinning disk that is painted with complementary color pairs.

Construct a small disk from cardboard or other suitable material and paint one half blue and the other yellow, as shown in Figure N. Place a string through the two holes and then twist the ends of the strings until they are fully wound. Pull on the ends of the strings and the disk will begin to spin rapidly. As the disk spins, regions of your retina alternately receive blue and yellow light in rapid succession. However, since yellow light is made of red and green light, your retina is actually receiving all three primary colors, and so the disk appears white.

Repeat the procedure using a disk painted green and magenta, and then one using red and cyan. Does the spinning disk appear white in each case? Explain.

Questions

(1) According to your findings in part 1, what is the complementary color of green? Of red?

(2) What color after-image appears after staring intensely at a red dot and then moving your eyes to a blank sheet of white paper? After staring at the green and blue dots?

(3) What colors do the flags appear after staring at them and then refocusing your eyes on blank white paper? Why do they appear these colors? What countries do these flags represent?

(4) With repeated washing, white garments tend to yellow. To combat this problem, some detergent manufacturers put a blue dye in their detergent. You may also purchase a special blue dye known as "blueing" to accomplish this same result. Explain.

7.6.6 Scattering of Light

Concepts to Investigate: Scattering, absorption, reemission, color of the sky, color of sunsets and sunrises.

Materials: Aquarium or other transparent container, slide projector or other high-intensity light source, powdered nonfat milk or dairy creamer.

Principles and Procedures: Microwave ovens heat moist foods by emitting microwaves that are then absorbed by the hydrogen-oxygen bonds in water molecules, causing them to vibrate rapidly. In much the same way, the bonds in atmospheric nitrogen and oxygen molecules vibrate when exposed to blue light. These molecules may then release energy by emitting blue light in all directions. Thus, while longer-wavelength red and yellow light pass through the atmosphere unaffected, blue light is scattered (absorbed and reemitted) in all directions, making the sky appear blue.

When blue and violet light are removed by scattering, the remaining sunlight has a higher proportion of green, yellow, orange, and red. Of these, the long-wavelength red light is scattered least. As a result, the sky is red when you look toward the sun (never look directly at the sun), particularly when looking through a substantial portion of the atmosphere as occurs when the sun is on the horizon at sunrise or sunset.

Fill an aquarium or other transparent container with water. Shine a bright, focusable beam through the aquarium, as illustrated in Figure O. (To obtain a narrow beam, you may wish to mask an old 35-mm slide with black electrician's tape, punch a hole in it, and place it in a projector, as illustrated in Figure F.) Slowly add and mix nonfat powdered milk or dairy creamer into the container. Report the color of the transmitted light (color that appears on the screen) and scattered light (color of the beam when viewed from the side) as the powder dissolves. Are the colors the same or different? Explain.

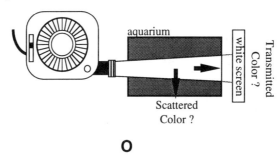

O

Questions

(1) What color does the beam appear when viewed from the side? The screen? Explain.

(2) Does the entire length of the beam appear the same color when viewed from the side after much powder has been dissolved? Explain.

(3) What color would the sky appear directly overhead when viewed at noon on a clear day from the top of Mount Kilimanjaro, the tallest mountain in Africa (19,340 feet, 5899 meters). Explain.

(4) The sky appears bluer when air is dry than when humid. Explain

(5) The sky appears bluer after a rain than immediately before. Explain.

7.6.7 Determining the Wavelength of Light

Concepts to Investigate: Wavelength of light, diffraction, diffraction angle, principal image, first-order image, diffraction grating equation.

Materials: Diffraction grating (available from scientific-supply companies), meter sticks, light socket with cord, 25-watt clear tubular showcase lamp, two meter sticks.

Principles and Procedures: Light displays all properties common to waves, including diffraction, the spreading of light into a region beyond an obstruction. In this activity you will measure the angle of displacement of a first-order diffraction image in order to calculate the wavelength of given colors of light.

Place a 25-watt clear tubular showcase lamp, or other similar lamp with a long, straight filament, in a socket at the junction of two meter sticks positioned at right angles, as shown in Figure P. Look at the lamp through a diffraction grating at a distance of one meter from the lamp. The diffraction grating will disperse the light into a series of spectrums. The central spectrum is called the principal image, and the spectrums to both sides are called the first-order images (Figure Q). Upon locating the first-order image of red light, request your partner to move a pencil laterally along the second meter stick until it appears in line with the red image (no parallax). Your partner should record this distance as *y* in the table provided. Repeat this procedure for the orange, yellow, green, blue, indigo, and violet bands. If you find it difficult to resolve differences in the measured distances for the various colors *y*, increase the distance between the diffraction grating and the light source *x*.

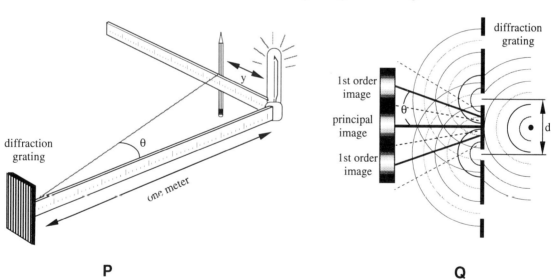

P   **Q**

The wavelength of light can be calculated using the grating equation: $n\lambda = d \sin\theta$, where λ is the wavelength, d is the diffraction grating constant (distance between slits), θ is the angle to the diffraction image, and n is the order of the image. The grating constant, d, can be determined as the inverse of the number of lines per unit length. For example, if the diffraction grating contains 600,000 lines per meter, then $d = 1/600,000$ or $d = 1.7 \times 10^{-6}$m. Determine the wavelength for each color of light. Which color has the shortest wavelength? Which has the longest?

Color	x	y	θ arctan (y/x)	λ $d \sin \theta$
Red	1.00 m			
Orange	1.00 m			
Yellow	1.00 m			
Green	1.00 m			
Blue	1.00 m			
Indigo	1.00 m			
Violet	1.00 m			

Questions

(1) What wavelength did you obtain for red light? Orange? Yellow? Green? Blue? Indigo? Violet?

(2) If you heat rock salt in a Bunsen-burner flame, a bright yellow color is produced. If you examine the light of this flame through the diffraction grating you will notice a bright yellow band. Do you think that the wavelength determined from this monochromatic source would be the same as that determined from the lamp? In other words, does light of a given color have the same wavelength regardless of its source?

FOR THE TEACHER

In art class, students learn that the three primary colors are blue, red, and yellow. When they take a science class and learn that the three primary colors are red, green, and blue, they often are quite confused. Help your students understand that red, green, and blue are the *additive primary colors of light,* while their complementary colors, cyan, magenta, and yellow (commonly called blue, red, and yellow), are the *subtractive primary pigments.* A close examination of a color television or computer monitor will convince students that red, green, and blue are additive primaries, because by mixing these three colors of light, the monitor can generate virtually any desired color. For example, when blue and green light are present at the same time, our eyes interpret it as cyan.

While light is additive, pigments are subtractive. A pigment appears a particular color because of what is reflected after other wavelengths or light are absorbed. While a mixture of the primary colors of light produces white light (a combination of all wavelengths), a mixing of the primary pigments produces a black pigment because all the wavelengths are absorbed, leaving none to be reflected to the eye. To illustrate the subtractive nature of pigments, set up a series of beakers with water. Add different colors of food coloring to each, and to the last beaker mix a variety of pigments until it appears black. Place all the beakers in direct sunlight for a few hours and monitor their temperatures (Figure R). The black beaker will register a higher temperature because the net absorption of light by all the pigments in it is greater than the absorption of any one pigment alone.

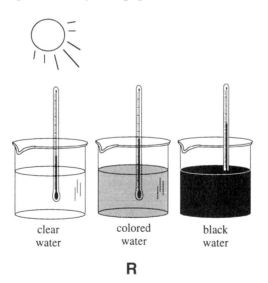

clear   colored   black
water   water   water

R

Cyan, magenta, and yellow are the complementary colors of red, green, and blue. When used as pigments, these colors can be mixed to produce a wide range of colors. A cyan pigment absorbs all wavelengths except that which is necessary to produce cyan, namely green and blue (Figure S). A yellow pigment absorbs all wavelengths except that which is necessary to produce yellow, namely green and red (Figure T). If yellow and cyan pigments are mixed together, the yellow pigment will absorb the blue light normally reflected or transmitted by the cyan pigment, and

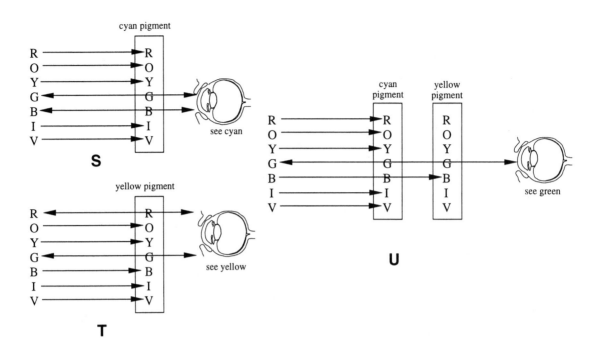

the cyan pigment will absorb the red light normally reflected or transmitted by the yellow pigment. Since green is the only color of light reflected or transmitted by both pigments, a mixture of cyan and yellow pigments will appear green (Figure U).

7.6.1 The Visible Spectrum

Discussion: This demonstration is difficult to perform if the room is not dark, or if the beam of light is diffuse. The beam of light should not spread beyond the sides of the prism. Although the microscope slide prisms work well in separating light, they are much more difficult to use than glass prisms when recombining the colors to produce white light. If using a projector for a light source, punch as small a circle as possible, or use a razor blade or utility knife to make a tiny rectangular slit in the slide.

Answers (1) Red, orange, yellow, green, blue, indigo, and violet (roygbiv). (2) Red light diffracts (bends) least, while violet light diffracts most. Since the angle of refraction of light is inversely proportional to the speed of light in a medium relative to its speed in a vacuum, red light must travel fastest through the prism while violet light travels slowest. (3) No. It is necessary that the second prism be inverted relative to the first, otherwise the colors will spread even farther on emerging from the second prism.

7.6.2 Infrared Radiation

Discussion: Infrared radiation is located in the spectrum between red light and radio waves. It was discovered in 1800 by the English physicist Sir William Herschel, who performed this same experiment and noted that the area beyond red showed the most heating although no radiation was visible. Half a century later, Armand Fizeay and Jean Foucault of France showed that infrared light, although invisible, behaves like visible light and can produce interference patterns as well as other wave phenomena.

Answers (1) Infrared light is found in the region beyond red. Most objects readily absorb infrared light, thereby resulting in a temperature increase. (2) The hotter an object, the more infrared radiation it releases. Photographs taken with IR film allow us to see temperature variations. An IR photograph of a recently driven car will show a bright (hot) engine and exhaust system, and a relatively dark (cool) cabin. (3) Incandescent fixtures release more infrared light than visible light, and while this may be nice if you are trying to heat your house, it is very inefficient if you are trying to provide lighting for your house. Fluorescent fixtures emit a higher percentage of radiation in the visible spectrum and are thus more efficient for lighting applications.

7.6.3 Absorption and Transmission

Discussion: Most filters are not monochromatic. A filter may appear green, but may transmit some blue and yellow light. As a result, students will probably see more than one color when the light from a prism is directed through a colored filter.

Answers (1) A multicolored picture will appear in red and black when viewed through a red filter. Light of various wavelengths (colors) may be reflected from the picture, but only the red will pass through the filter, while all other colors are absorbed. Where there is no red light, the image will appear black. (2) If the filters are ideal (monochromatic), everything will appear black, because no light will be transmitted. The red filter absorbs all wavelengths but red light, which the blue filter subsequently absorbs. (3) The green filter will reduce light intensity to the eye by removing all wavelengths but green light. Unfortunately, this creates a monochromatic environment where everything appears either green or black, making it more difficult to discern such things as the color of a traffic light.

7.6.4 Primary Colors

Discussion: The activity described in part 1 makes an excellent classroom demonstration. In order to produce images large enough for the entire class to see, separate the red, green, and blue floodlights by approximately 2 meters. You can create a shadow simply by walking in front of the screen. This demonstration is most dramatic when the room is very dark and the screen is highly reflective.

Most students are confused when they learn that red, green, and blue are the primary colors. Because of their experience with paints, they believe that red, yellow, and blue are the primary colors. Clarify to your students that light, such as that present in a monitor, is additive, while pigments are subtractive. The addition of the three primary colors of light will produce white light. By contrast, pigments are subtractive and appear the color of the wavelength that is reflected. Red paint appears red because it absorbs all wavelengths but red light, which it reflects. Blue and yellow pigments both absorb red light, and so when mixed together with red will eliminate the reflection of red light, causing the pigment mixture to appear black (the absence of any color).

Answers (1) Green and blue light produce cyan (greenish-blue), red and blue produce magenta, and red and green produce yellow. (2) The green shadow occurs where both the blue and red lights are blocked, leaving only the green to shine through. Similarly, the red shadow occurs where the green and blue are blocked, and the blue occurs where the red and green are blocked. (3) The background appears white because all three primary colors (red, green, and blue) are present. It will appear bright white only if the filters represent true primary colors. (4) Under bright light, images will disappear because all wavelengths of light will be present, creating a totally white image. (5) As you focus on the disk, regions of your retinas alternately receive pulses of red, green, and blue light. If the disk is spinning sufficiently fast, red and green cones will still be active when the blue cones are stimulated. When all three cones are simultaneously active, our minds interpret the color as white. The disk may appear gray if it is not painted with pure primary colors.

7.6.5 Complementary Colors

Discussion: Many scientific supply houses sell 35-mm projection slides of the primary colors (red, green, and blue) and their complements (cyan, magenta, and yellow). To illustrate the principle of complementary colors, project color pairs simultaneously from two slide projectors. As with the student activity, the result will appear bright-white only if the hues of the slides are precise.

If all three primary colors are projected in overlapping circles, as shown in Figure V, a Venn diagram is created. Students can see that yellow is the result of green and red light, and when added together with blue produces white. Even if you are unable to produce such an image in your class, a discussion of this diagram will help students understand the principles of primary and complementary colors.

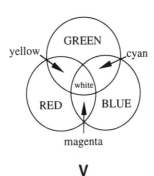

V

The activity discussed in Part 1 may be performed as a classroom demonstration by projecting the images from an overhead projector in a darkened room. Allow students to stare at the images for one minute, and then quickly remove the transparencies so students now stare at a blank screen. Most students will immediately see the after-image of the object appearing in its complementary colors.

To make the flag of the United States in complementary colors, draw black stars on a yellow field with cyan (blue will work) and black stripes. The activity in Part 2 can be a classroom demonstration simply by painting a large disk and attaching it to an electric drill or other rotary device. It should be shown in a well-lit room.

Answers (1) The complementary color of green is magenta, and the complementary color of red is cyan. (2) You will see cyan after staring at red, magenta after staring at green, and yellow after staring at blue. (3) The flags will appear red, white, and blue, which are the complements of green, black, and yellow, respectively. The first is the flag of France, and the second is the flag of Texas. (4) Blue is the complementary color of yellow. By reflecting more blue from a yellowing fabric, a whiter color will be achieved.

7.6.6 Scattering of Light

Discussion: This demonstration is a model of the scattering of light that occurs in the atmosphere. Initially, the transmitted beam will appear white on the screen and will be invisible when viewed from the side. This is analogous to the environment on the moon where there is no atmosphere to scatter light. As the powder dissolves, the beam turns a dark-blue color (when viewed from the side), similar to the appearance of the sky at high altitudes where there is little air to scatter the blue light. As additional powder dissolves, it scatters more light and the beam becomes bluer when viewed from the side and redder on the screen. If the particulate size is too large, colors other than blue will be scattered and the beam may appear white or gray when viewed from the side, similar to the appearance of the sky when there is much dust or smog present. You may also perform this activity by mixing 40 grams of sodium thiosulfate per liter of water and then adding a few drops of sulfuric acid while stirring. The fine particles that are produced will scatter the light.

Answers (1) The beam appears blue when viewed from the side because the dissolved powder scatters blue light more than red light. The beam appears red when viewed from the end because red light is scattered least and therefore transmitted most. (2) The beam will appear blue-white near the light source and red-yellow at the other end. This illustrates that blue light is scattered immediately, leaving only the longer wavelengths of light in the beam. (3) The sky will appear navy blue/black because there is very little nitrogen or oxygen at that altitude to scatter the light. The "sky" appears black on the moon because there is no atmosphere to scatter light. (4) Water in the sky scatters a wide range of colors, creating a white appearance. When there is no water in the atmosphere, only blue light is scattered. (5) Dust and particulate matter scatter red, orange, and yellow light, giving the sky a gray, white, or brown appearance. Rain washes dust and particulate matter from the atmosphere, so only blue light is scattered in large amounts.

7.6.7 Determining the Wavelength of Light

Discussion: If you have a laser, this activity can be performed as a classroom demonstration. Instead of viewing a light source through a diffraction grating, shine the laser through the grating in a darkened room. (Make certain the laser is always shining away from the eyes of your students.) On the opposite wall you will see the first-, second-, and third-order diffraction images. Measure the angle as before and calculate the wavelength of light emitted by the laser. The helium/neon laser commonly used in classrooms emits red light with a wavelength of approximately 680 nm.

Answers (1) Average values should be approximately: red 680 nm (6.80×10^{-7}m), orange 620 nm, yellow 580 nm, green 520 nm, blue 470 nm, indigo 430 nm, violet 410. (2) Yes, a color will always have the same average wavelength, regardless of its source.

Applications to Everyday Life

Color Vision: The retina of the human eye has two types of photoreceptive cells, the rods and cones. Rods are much more sensitive than cones, but cannot discern colors. As a result, scenery viewed under low light conditions appears only in black and white. The cones are stimulated by higher light intensities and are sensitive to either red, green, or blue light. A red stop signal produces light in the 700-nm-wavelength range and causes the red cones to send a signal to the brain that we interpret as the color red.

Color Blindness: Approximately 8 percent of men and 0.4 percent of women are classified as "color blind," but in reality most are merely color deficient because they cannot distinguish certain colors such as red and green. Color blindness results if one set of cones (red, green, or blue) is defective.

Stage Lighting: Stage managers use a variety of colored gelatin filters to create desired color effects. An actor's yellow clothes can instantly turn black if stage lighting is changed from white to blue. Yellow, the complementary color of blue, reflects only red and green light and thus appears black when illuminated by pure blue light.

Chemical Identification: Every chemical absorbs some wavelengths of light and reflects others. A spectrophotometer is an instrument that identifies chemicals on the basis of their absorption spectra. A good spectrophotometer can distinguish between approximately 4,000,000 colors of visible light.

Department-Store Lighting: Fluorescent fixtures emit a high percentage of short-wavelength (high-frequency) light, generating a cool, bluish color. Department stores often install incandescent (light-bulb) fixtures in clothing departments because such lighting is more representative of natural sunlight and will give a more accurate representation of the true colors of clothing.

Emergency Vehicle Coloration: The solar spectrum is richest in the yellow-green zone. This is also the region in which our retinas are most sensitive. As a result, many airport emergency vehicles are painted yellow-green, providing maximum visibility for incoming planes, particularly in foggy conditions.

Blue Eyes: Brown eyes result from a dark pigment known as melanin. The irises in blue eyes contain no melanin, but scatter blue light the same way it is scattered in the atmosphere, giving eyes a blue coloration.

Color Monitors: Color computer and television monitors have screens that emit the three additive primary colors: green, red, and blue. By mixing these three colors, they can produce the spectrum of colors necessary for "real-life" color.

Painting: Painters mix the three subtractive primary pigments (magenta, cyan, and yellow; often called red, blue, and yellow) to produce a wide range of colors by the process of color subtraction.

Military Surveillance: Unlike snakes, humans cannot see infrared radiation unless they are equipped with special infrared-sensitive goggles. The military uses such goggles at night to see warm objects such as vehicles and personnel. Scouting teams often use special infrared lamps to illuminate their surroundings because such light is invisible to everyone except those wearing appropriate eyeware.

Electricity and Magnetism

8.1 Electrostatics

8.2 Circuits

8.3 Magnetism

8.4 Electromagnetism

8.1 ELECTROSTATICS

Approximately 100 lightning bolts strike the Earth every second. Although general-ly associated with rainstorms, lightning may also accompany snowstorms, sand-storms, or volcanic eruptions. Images from the *Voyager I* spacecraft suggest that lightning may also occur on Jupiter. The most massive lightning strikes, known as "positive giants," release enough energy in a fraction of a second to power an aver-age household for most of a year. Although the central core of a lightning bolt may be only 1/2-inch wide, it may reach temperatures in excess of 54,000°F (30,000°C, hotter than the surface of the sun) and generate a glowing corona envelope 20 feet in diameter and up to 4 miles in length.

In 1752 Benjamin Franklin demonstrated that lightning was an electrical phe-nomenon akin to the common static shock one gets after walking across a rug and touching a metal faucet or door frame. Franklin illustrated this by flying a metal-tipped kite in a thunderstorm. Fortunately for Franklin, lightning did not strike the kite, but the voltage differential between the clouds and the ground was sufficient to charge the string and cause all its fibers to stand on end the way hair does after being brushed or combed on a dry day. Although the famous kite experiment helped earn Franklin a position in the Royal Society and the French Academy of Sciences, it proved fatal for the next two researchers who tried to verify his findings. Don't try this activity.

Today, physicists recognize *electricity (electromagnetism) as one of the four funda-mental interactions (forces) of the universe.* It is believed that all motion in the universe results from electromagnetism, gravity, weak nuclear forces, strong nuclear forces, or some combination of these. *Objects with like charge repel each other, while those with unlike charge attract.* Two positively charged objects move away from each other while a positively charged object will move toward a negatively charged object.

Atoms, the smallest particles of elements, are composed of positively charged protons, neutral neutrons, and negatively charged electrons. When the number of electrons in an atom is equal to the number of protons, the atom is electrically neu-tral. When there are more electrons than protons, it is negative, and when there are more protons than electrons it is positive. *An object is electrically positive if the positive charges outnumber the negative charges, and is negative if the negative charges outnumber the positive charges.*

Normally your body is electrically neutral because the number of electrons pre-sent is roughly equivalent to the number of protons. When, however, you scuff your shoes across a new carpet in dry weather, your body builds a net negative charge by removing electrons from the carpet. The charge that develops may be released through an electrostatic discharge (spark) as you approach an uncharged or posi-tively charged object (Figure A). In a similar manner, portions of clouds can devel-op charges opposite from the ground or other regions within the cloud. If the elec-tric potential is sufficient, a major electrostatic discharge, known as lightning, will jump between the cloud and the ground (Figure B) or between two regions within the cloud. *The principle of conservation of charge states that electrical charge, like energy and momentum, is never created or destroyed, but simply redistributed.* The massive electrical discharge in lightning or the simple electrostatic shocks you receive in dry weather result not from the formation of charge, but rather from the redistribution of existing charge.

In this set of activities you will investigate electrostatics, the study of charges at rest. The activities in this section will help you understand a variety of important natural phenomena and inventions, including lightning, photocopiers, computer monitors, air pollution control devices, electron microscopes, chemical bonds, and static cling.

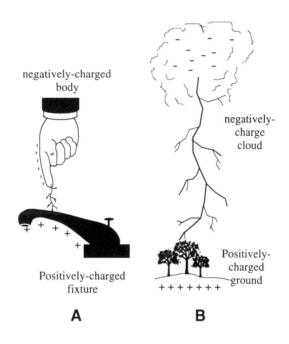

8.1.1 Electroscopes

Concepts to Investigate: Electroscopes, electrostatic repulsion, electrostatic induction, charging by conduction.

Materials: Flask, one-holed stopper, copper wire, wool or flannel, silk, glass rod, hard-rubber rod (vulcanite, Lucite, ebonite, or some plastics) or hard-rubber black comb, gold leaf (available from art-supply stores) or very thin aluminum foil.

Principles and Procedures: Electricity is invisible, so to study it we must develop instruments that allow us to observe its effects. One such instrument, an electroscope, can be easily constructed in the science classroom or at home. Obtain a flask or jar that can be fitted with a one-holed rubber stopper. Place a heavy-gauge copper wire through the stopper, as shown in Figure C, and seal it in place with paraffin (candle wax) or other nonconducting material. Place the round end of a hollow metal curtain rod over the exposed end of the wire. If such a ball is not available, you can solder a circular piece of copper sheet metal to the end of the wire, or fashion a ball from aluminum foil. Bend the other end of the copper wire and carefully fold a rectangular piece of gold leaf or thin aluminum foil over the end as shown, keeping the surfaces from touching. Gold leaf works best because it is very thin and very conductive. If you must use another metal for the vanes, use as thin a piece of foil as possible.

   After placing the stopper assembly in the flask, the metal vanes should hang straight down because they are uncharged and affected only by gravity. Rub a plastic rod or hard-rubber comb vigorously with a wool or flannel cloth. As you rub, the rod removes electrons from the fabric and develops a net negative charge. As you move the charged rod toward the metal ball, electrons in the metal are repelled and migrate toward the vanes, where a net negative charge is established. The charged rod induces a charge separation in the electroscope, as shown in Figure C. Since both vanes now possess a negative charge, they experience electrostatic repulsion and move apart. The higher the induced charge, the farther apart the vanes will move. Move the rod away and the vanes will collapse (Figure D). Again move the rod toward the ball, but this time touch it (Figure E). Electrons will flow from the rod to the vanes, and the vanes will move apart and remain apart even after the rod has been removed (Figure F). You have charged the electroscope by conduction.

   Rub the glass rod vigorously with a silk garment and repeat the activity. In this case, the silk obtains a negative charge, leaving the rod with a positive charge. Approach the tip of the electroscope wire with the positively charged glass rod. Do the vanes move in a different way? Why or why not? What happens if you touch the electroscope with the charged rod and then remove it?

© 1994 by John Wiley & Sons, Inc.

Questions

(1) Do the vanes separate any farther if you rub harder? Explain?

(2) Why do the vanes collapse after the charged rod is pulled back without touching the electroscope?

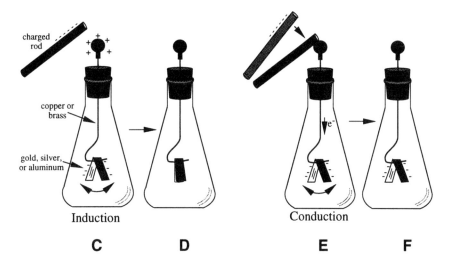

charged rod

copper or brass

gold, silver, or aluminum

Induction

C

D

Conduction

E

F

(3) Plastic has a net negative charge after being rubbed with wool, while glass has a net positive charge after being rubbed with silk. Do they produce the same or different effect when brought close to the head of the electroscope? Explain.

(4) Why do the vanes remain separated after the rod has touched the ball and been removed?

8.1.2 Electric Charges

Concepts to Investigate: Positive charge, negative charge, electrostatic repulsion, electrostatic attraction, transfer of charge, identification of charge.

Materials: Electroscope, glass, silk, hard-rubber comb or rod, wool or flannel, thread.

Principles and Procedures

Part 1. Determining charge with an electroscope: Rub a hard-rubber comb (or vulcanite or Lucite rod) vigorously with a wool or flannel garment. The rod or comb will acquire a negative charge by removing electrons from the fabric. While touching the ball or plate of an electroscope with one hand, position the charged rod next to it (but not touching it) with the other. The negative charge of the rod will repel electrons away from the electroscope and they will flow into your body (Figure G). When you remove your hand and the charged rod (Figure H), the vanes spread apart, indicating that the electroscope is now positively charged due to a loss of electrons. Bring the charged rod close to the electroscope once again (Figure I) and note that the vanes collapse as negative charges are repelled from the top of the electroscope and move into the vanes where they neutralize the positive charge. When the rod is removed (Figure H), the vanes will once again separate.

Knowing that the electroscope has a net positive charge, we can determine the charge on other objects. If, for example, an object with a positive charge is brought near to the head of a positively charged electroscope, electrons will move from the vanes toward the object. This will leave a larger positive charge on the vanes, causing them to separate farther (Figure J). By contrast, when a negatively charged object approaches the head of an electroscope, it repels electrons into the vanes. The positive charge in the vanes is then neutralized, and the vanes collapse. Charge glass and plastic rods using a variety of fabrics (wool, silk, flannel, animal fur) and determine their resulting charge using the electroscope.

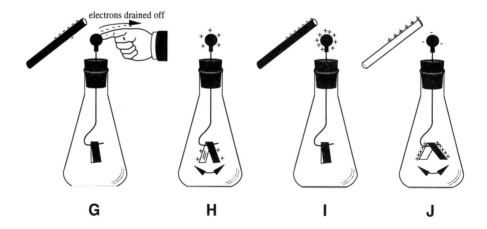

electrons drained off

G   H   I   J

Part 2. Determining charge using a suspended rod: Tie and tape both ends of a thread around the ends of a vulcanite, Lucite, or other hard-rubber or plastic rod. Charge the rod by rubbing it with wool or flannel (Figure K) and suspend it as shown in Figure L. Charge another rod in the same fashion. This second rod can now be used to "chase" the first rod since both have the same charge and like charges repel (Figure L). Now approach the suspended rod with the portion of the fabric on which the rod was rubbed (Figure M). Does it repel or attract the suspended rod? Explain.

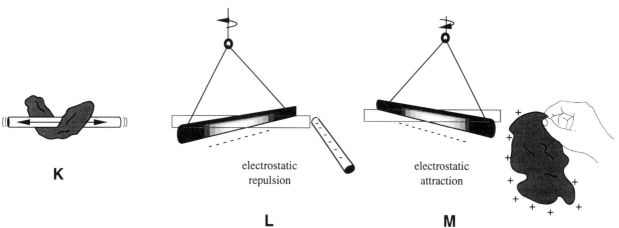

K

electrostatic
repulsion

L

electrostatic
attraction

M

Questions

(1) Will the vanes of the electroscope collapse or separate if both have the same charge? Explain.

(2) To establish a lasting charge on an electroscope by the process of induction, it is necessary to place your finger on the electroscope when charging it (Figure G). Explain.

(3) Under what conditions did you obtain maximum separation of the vanes? Explain.

(4) How can you place a negative charge on the electroscope by the process of induction? Try it.

(5) Why does the cloth attract the suspended rod while the rod that was rubbed with the cloth repels it (Part 2)?

8.1.3 Electrostatic Attraction

Concepts to Investigate: Molecular polarity, electrostatic attraction.

Materials: Comb, wool, faucet, paper, balloons.

Principles and Procedures

Part 1. Electrostatic attraction of water: When a hard-rubber comb or plastic rod is rubbed vigorously with a wool or flannel rag, it pulls electrons from the fabric and acquires a negative charge. This negatively charged comb can be used not only to attract positively charged objects, but electrically neutral objects as well. Adjust a faucet so it releases the smallest continuous stream of water possible. Bring the charged comb near the stream and note that it shifts the flow by means of electro-static attraction (Figure N). Water molecules are polar, meaning that one end is slightly negative and the other is slightly positive. If these molecules are subjected to the electric field of a negatively charged comb, they will reorient so the positive poles of the molecules are closest to the negatively charged comb (Figure O). Although the negative pole of the molecule is repelled by the negatively charged comb, the posi-tive pole is attracted. Since the force of an electric field decreases as the inverse square of the distance between two charged objects, the repulsion of the negative pole will be less than the attraction of the positive pole and the stream of water will be attracted to the comb. Will a stream of water be attracted if approached with a positively charged rod? Charge a glass rod with silk and try it.

© 1994 by John Wiley & Sons, Inc.

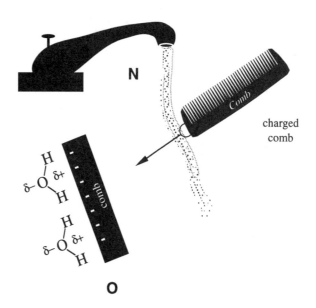

Part 2. Electrostatic attraction of paper: Tear a page of newspaper into small bits approximately one centimeter in diameter. Rub a hard-rubber comb with wool to give it a negative charge and record the maximum paper bits you can pick up with it (Figure P). Repeat the process using a glass rod that has acquired a positive charge by rubbing it with silk. Are you able to pick up the paper with either a positively or negatively charged rod? If so, which is more effective?

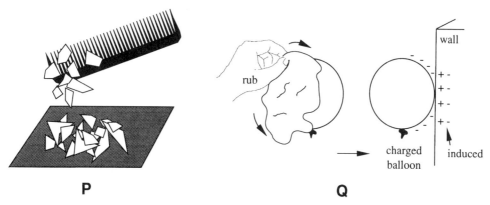

P   **Q**

Part 3. Hanging balloons with electrostatic forces: Inflate a balloon and then briskly rub one side of it on your hair. Place this surface of the balloon toward a wall or door and release it when it appears to be sticking. Upon rubbing, the balloon develops a static charge that can induce a reorientation of polar molecules in the wall (Figure Q). If, for example, the balloon acquires a negative charge, the molecules in the wall will reorient so that the positive poles face the balloon while the negative poles face the wall. The positive poles of the molecules in the wall are closer to the negatively charged balloon than are the negative poles. Thus, the attractive forces exceed the repulsive forces and the balloon sticks to the wall. Try sticking the balloon to other surfaces and record your findings. What can you conclude about the nature of the surfaces to which the balloon sticks?

Questions

(1) After drying clothes in a clothes dryer, you may notice that they stick together. Explain this "static cling."

(2) Will there be more "static cling" if all the clothes in the dryer are of the same or different materials?

(3) In the early days of the internal combustion engine there were a few disastrous gasoline-delivery truck explosions. Shortly after these disasters, gasoline-delivery trucks were equipped with chains that dragged on the road. What was the purpose of these chains?

(4) Why does the hair on your head stand up when you comb it with a hard-rubber comb on a dry day?

8.1.4 Induction

Concepts to Investigate: Induction, conduction, electrostatic attraction and repulsion, Coulomb's law.

Materials: Glass plate (or Petri dish), small bits of newspaper, Cheerios® or pith balls, thread, hard-rubber comb (or vulcanite or Lucite rod), wool (or flannel, or fur), glass rod, silk, Van de Graaf generator. (*Note:* Like all electrostatic investigations, this activity works best when the relative humidity is low.)

Principles and Procedures: An object may be charged by placing it in the electric field of another charged object. This phenomenon is known as induction and, unlike conduction, requires no physical contact and no movement of electrons between objects.

Part 1. Jumping paper: Tear a sheet of newspaper into small bits approximately one-half centimeter in diameter. Place the paper bits under a glass plate supported by two books. Rub the glass vigorously with silk and notice how the paper jumps up to the glass (Figure R). Alternatively, this activity can be performed by placing the paper under an inverted Petri dish. What attracts the paper to the glass? Why doesn't it stay attached to the glass?

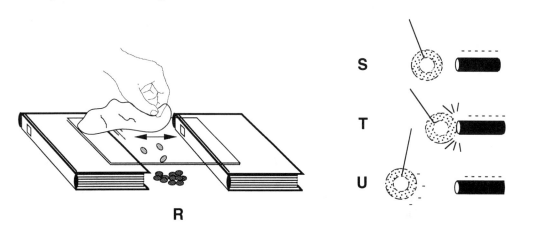

R   S   T   U

Part 2. Attraction and repulsion of Cheerios® or pith balls: Use a 50-centimeter piece of fine thread to support a bob made from a Cheerio® or pith ball. (Many other objects can be substituted, including Styrofoam packing material and puffed-wheat cereal). Charge a hard-rubber comb, Lucite rod, or other suitable hard plastic by rubbing with wool, flannel, or animal fur. The rubber or plastic will remove electrons from the surface of the fabric or fur and develop a negative charge. When approached by the negatively charged rod, the bob will first be attracted to it (Figure S), then contact it (Figure T), and then be repulsed by it (Figure U). The bob was attracted by induction, but it then acquired a similar charge by conduction when it contacted the rod, and was subsequently repulsed. At this point you should be able to "chase" the bob with the charged rod. Try it. Holding on to the thread, carry the charged bob near to your hand or the wall and note that it is attracted by induction. When it contacts your hand or the wall, it is neutralized because your body or the wall drains off the excess charge by conduction.

Drain the charge from the bob by touching it with your hand and charge a comb or Lucite rod by rubbing it with wool, fur, or flannel. Place the charged rod in your right hand and an uncharged glass rod in your left hand. Approach the bob from both sides with the two rods. With a little experience, you should be able to get the bob to bounce back and forth between the two rods twenty or thirty times (Figures V–Y). Why does the bob continue to swing back and forth?

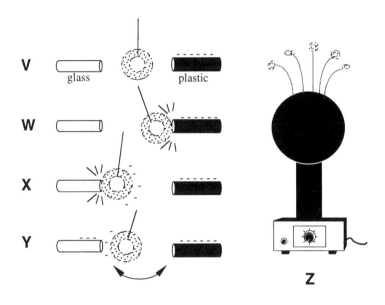

Part 3. Electrostatic levitation: Coulomb's law states that the repulsion between two charges is directly proportional to the product of the magnitude of their charges, and inversely proportional to the square of the distance between them. If two charges are large, of like sign, and close, the repulsive force can be significant. In this activity you will "levitate" Cheerios®, paper bits, or similar objects using a Van de Graaf generator (a high-voltage electrostatic generator). Place Cheerios® or paper bits on the dome of an uncharged Van de Graaf generator. Turn the generator on and watch the Cheerios® fly into the air (Figure Z). Pick the Cheerios® off the ground and place them once again on the dome. Do they remain? Why or why not? Repeat this activity with a variety of different objects and determine which fly highest. With practice, it may be possible to levitate a lightweight silk or wool cloth above the generator. Place the fabric on the center of the dome, turn on the power, and watch it slowly lift off.

Questions

(1) Why does the paper "jump" up to the glass in part 1?

(2) Why are some of the paper bits eventually repelled by the glass in part 1?

(3) Why does the bob bounce back and forth between the charged plastic rod and the uncharged glass rod in part 2?

(4) Why do the Cheerios® fly up when the Van de Graaf generator is turned on (part 3)?

(5) If the hair on your hands and arms stands up during an electrical storm, it may indicate that lightning is about to strike very soon. Explain.

8.1.5 Distribution of Charge

Concepts to Investigate: Charge distribution, lightning rods, electrostatic repulsion, plasma.

Materials: Van de Graaf generator, metal rod.

Principles and Procedures: All charged objects are surrounded by electric fields that exert an electric force upon other charged objects. In conductors, electrons move freely in response to external electric fields, redistributing so that the net electric field within the conductor is zero.

Electrostatic repulsion causes like charges to move away from each other to the perimeter of a conductor, as shown in Figure AA. If the conductor has an irregular shape, charges will collect at sharp curves and points where they are as far away from the majority of similar charges as possible (Figure BB). As a result, charge density in conductors is greatest at points and corners.

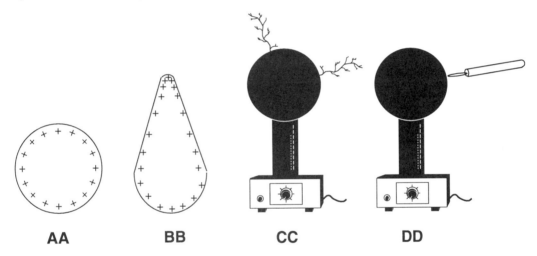

AA   **BB**   **CC**   **DD**

Where charge density is highest, the conductor is most likely to exchange electrons with the surrounding air. Benjamin Franklin used this principle in developing the lightning rod. A lightning rod has one end in the ground and another in the air with a sharp metal tip that continually exchanges charge with the surrounding atmosphere. Because charge is exchanged between the ground and the clouds, the potential difference between the ground and the clouds remains relatively low and the likelihood of a lightning strike is minimized. If lightning does occur, the current is directed through the rod into the ground, and not through the building it is protecting.

Darken the room, turn on a Van de Graaf generator, and record the frequency (number of sparks per minute) of electrical discharges emanating from the dome (Figure CC). Does the frequency of electrical discharges increase or decrease as you slowly approach the dome of the generator with a metal rod (Figure DD)? Is the metal rod acting as a lightning rod? If the room is very dark, you can see a tiny blue beam of ionized air between the end of the rod and the dome of the generator. This air is known as plasma and is capable of conducting an electric current. As long as this stream of ionized air continues to flow, the electrical potential between the dome and its immediate environment stays small, and spark discharges are unlikely to occur.

Questions

(1)   What is the tiny blue beam at the end of the metal rod?
(2)   What is the purpose of a lightning rod?
(3)   The wings of many airplanes are equipped with metal points that face backward. What is the purpose of these points?

8.1.6 Electrostatic Separators

Concepts to Investigate: Electrostatic attraction, electrostatic separation, electrostatic copiers (photocopiers), electrostatic induction.

Materials: Hard-rubber comb (or a plastic, Lucite, or vulcanite rod), pepper, salt, Petri dish, silk, wool, microscope slide.

Principles and Procedures: It is often said that "necessity is the mother of invention." People who need to perform a task faster, more accurately, or more efficiently may start dreaming of machines that could fulfill these needs. When such dreams are accompanied by ingenuity and hard work, an invention is sometimes produced that changes the way we live. The jet airplane, computer, and microwave oven are but a few of the inventions that have dramatically altered life in the last century.

In 1934, while pursing a career as a patent lawyer, Chester Carlson began looking for a fast, inexpensive way of making copies of drawings to submit to the patent office. After four years of experimenting, he developed the first successful electrostatic dry-copying process known as xerography. The Haloid company bought rights to the commercial development of his process and changed its name to the Xerox Corporation. Today, the xerography (photocopy) business is a multibillion-dollar industry and produces products that simplify work for people in nearly all walks of life. In the following activities you will experiment with the principles that helped make xerography a reality.

Part 1. Separation of salt and pepper by electrostatic attraction: Mix salt and pepper in a cup and spread the mix out on a flat surface. Charge a comb or plastic rod with wool, fur, or flannel and then hold it approximately one centimeter above the surface of the mixture. Which component, salt or pepper, is attracted to the rod by induction (Figure EE)? Explain.

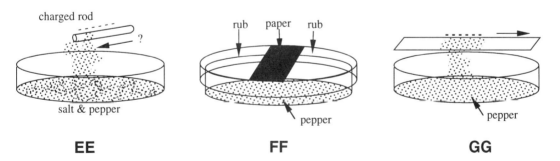

EE   **FF**   **GG**

Part 2. Electrostatic copier: Photocopy machines employ the principle of electrostatic induction to attract toner dust to the surface of a sheet of paper. The toner is then heated and fused to the paper to produce a copy of the original. You can understand how photocopiers work by performing the following activity. Place pepper or tiny pieces of paper in the bottom of a Petri dish. Cover the dish and tape a piece of paper across the top portion of the dish, as shown in Figure FF. Rub the surface of the dish vigorously with a piece of silk. Is the pepper attracted to the charged regions (exposed) or to the uncharged regions (covered by the paper)? Draw a design of your choice, tape it to the lid with double-stick tape, and repeat the process. Are you able to produce a pepper-copy of the original? Rub the center of a microscope slide vigorously with a piece of silk and then move the slide above a pile of pepper, as shown in Figure GG. Is the pepper attracted to the charged or uncharged region(s)?

Questions

(1) One way to separate salt from pepper is by using the principle of electrostatic induction described in part 1. Can you think of another method?

(2) Large electrostatic filters are used in the automobile-painting industry to clean the air after a car has been sprayed with paint. Explain how they might work.

(3) Why is pepper attracted only to those areas not covered by the paper in Part 2?

8.1.7 Electric Potential

Concepts to Investigate: Electric potential, fluorescent lamps.

Materials: Van de Graaf generator, fluorescent tube.

Principles and Procedures: Many businesses and industries illuminate their buildings with fluorescent lamps, rather than incandescent light bulbs, because of their high light output per watt and their long life. A fluorescent lamp produces nearly six times as much light per watt and lasts more than ten times longer than a similar wattage incandescent bulb. Fluorescent tubes are filled with a metal vapor that glows when subjected to high voltage. Is it possible to light a fluorescent tube even when it is not in its socket? Find out.

A typical 25-centimeter-diameter Van de Graaf generator is capable of generating a 200,000-volt potential difference that can cause gases in a fluorescent tube to fluoresce or glow. Darken the room, turn on the generator, and slowly move a fluorescent tube toward the generator and observe that it starts to glow. Does the tube glow best when positioned at right angles to the surface of the dome or when placed tangent to it. Move your hand back and forth down the length of the tube when it is positioned as shown in Figure HH. Why does only the portion of the tube between your hand and the generator glow? How could you turn on the fluorescent lights in your home without using the light switch?

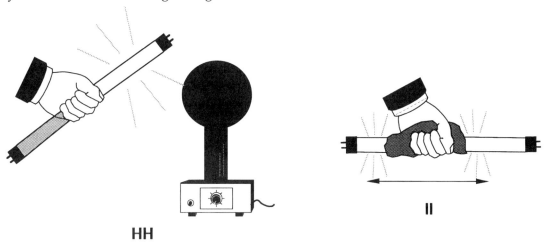

HH   II

Earlier in this chapter we noted that an electric potential can be generated by rubbing glass with a fabric such as silk. In a totally dark room, rub a fluorescent tube vigorously with silk and note the faint glow of the gases inside (Figure II). Repeat the process with other fabrics such as wool and flannel to see which builds the greatest potential difference and causes the tube to glow brightest.

Questions

(1) Why does the fluorescent lamp glow when placed near the generator?

(2) Why does the tube not glow as brightly when positioned tangential to the surface of the dome?

(3) When pointing the fluorescent tube at the Van de Graaf generator, what factor determines the length of the tube that will glow? Explain.

(4) The typical Van de Graaf generator in your laboratory may generate 200,000 volts. If you get too close to the generator you will feel a strong electric spark, but will not be harmed. Why are you not harmed by the Van de Graaf generator when you could be severely injured by touching a standard 110-volt power line in your house?

8.1.8 Capacitance

Concepts to Investigate: Capacitance, electrophorus, Leyden jar.

Materials: Styrofoam plate, pie tin, pencil, thumbtack, wool rag, plastic or hard-rubber comb, paper clips, plastic film canister or equivalent, aluminum foil, neon glow tube (optional).

Principles and Procedures: The electric eel, *Electrophorus electricus*, may develop a potential difference of 650 volts and deliver one ampere of current to stun its prey. The term "electrophorus" is Greek for "charge carrier" and aptly describes the electric eel. In 1775, the Italian physicist Alesandro Volta developed an instrument called an "electrophorus" because it too could carry charge from one place to another. In this activity you will develop your own electrophorus and use it to transfer charge to a device that stores charge and is known as a Leyden jar (a type of capacitor). As with all electrostatic experiments, this activity works best when the air is very dry.

Part 1. Electrophorus: Push a thumbtack through the base of a metal pie tin and into the eraser of a pencil. Be certain the tack does not contact either the pencil lead or the metal eraser bracket. Impart a negative charge to a Styrofoam plate by vigorously rubbing it with wool (Figure JJ). Place the pie tin on the charged Styrofoam plate and touch the pie tin with your hand, as illustrated in Figure KK. Because the metal pie tin is a conductor, electrons (e^-) will migrate from the negatively charged Styrofoam plate and will be drained off by your hand, leaving the pie tin with a net positive charge. By holding the electrophorus (pie tin and pencil) by the pencil, you can now carry charge to another location. Turn off the room lights and watch the electric spark that appears when you discharge the electrophorus by bringing it near to your lab partner's hand. You can also use your charged electrophorus to light a neon tube. Hold one lead from the neon glow tube with your fingers while you touch the other lead to the charged pie tin. In a dark room, you will clearly see the red-orange glow characteristic of ionized neon.

JJ

KK

Part 2. Leyden jar: In 1745, the Dutch scientist Pieter van Musschenbroek discovered that he could store electric charge in a jar whose inner and outer surfaces were lined with metal foil. The Leyden jar, which Musschenbroek first demonstrated at the University of Leyden, was the forerunner of the capacitor now used in circuits for storing electric charge.

Press sheets of aluminum foil on the inside and the outside of a drinking glass or plastic tumbler, making certain that neither sheet comes within the top centimeter of the vessel walls. Place a plastic or hard-rubber comb across the top of the container and from the comb suspend a chain of paper clips that reaches the foil in the bottom (Figure LL). This Leyden jar can now be charged by touching the electrophorus to the top paper clip while touching the aluminum foil on the outside of the glass with your other hand (Figure MM). If the electrophorus is positively charged, electrons will flow from the inner foil, through the paper clips, to the electrophorus. This will leave a positive charge on the inside foil, which will then attract electrons from your hand to the foil on the outside of the container. Because of the insulating walls, the Leyden jar retains a negative outside and a positive inside when the electrophorus and hand are removed.

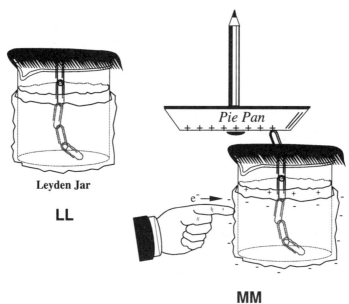

Leyden Jar

LL

Pie Pan

e⁻ →

MM

Charge the Leyden jar repeatedly with the electrophorus and then discharge it by touching the outer foil with one finger and the paper clips with another. Charge the Leyden jar again. Connect one lead of a neon glow tube to the aluminum foil and the other to the chain of paper clips. Compare the brightness of the resulting flash with that produced by the electrophorus alone.

Questions

(1)   Which has a greater affinity for electrons, Styrofoam or wool?

(2)   What causes the spark when the electrophorus or Leyden jar is discharged?

(3)   How can you charge the Leyden jar in reverse so that the foil is positively charged and the nail is negatively charged?

FOR THE TEACHER

It is important to realize that all activities in this chapter work best when the relative humidity is very low. If you live in a cold climate, it is easy to create a dry environment in the winter simply by shutting the windows and turning up the heat. You can demonstrate the influence of humidity on the dissipation of static charge by boiling water while performing any of these activities. The steam will help drain charge and minimize the effect of static electricity.

Although most of the activities in this chapter rely on very simple materials, we have included two that require a Van de Graaf generator because students find these activities particularly intriguing. The Van de Graaf generator is a high-voltage electrostatic machine in which electric charge is carried from a ground to a high-voltage terminal by way of an insulating belt (Figure NN). Electrons are transferred to the belt as it contacts negatively charged brushes in the base of the generator. At the other end, another set of brushes removes this charge and distributes it to the dome above. A dome of 25-cm radius can be raised to a potential of 400,000 volts. Although Van de Graaf generators, Wimhurst generators, and other static machines can develop large voltages, they are not able to store a significant quantity of charge and are therefore not able to deliver a large current. Since it is the current that injures, not the voltage, a static machine is relatively harmless. By contrast, a 110- or 120-volt circuit in your home is very dangerous because there is nearly an endless supply of electrons that can flow through your body if you should short-circuit the wires.

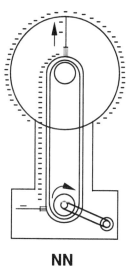

NN

8.1.1 Electroscopes

Discussion: The authors included this activity because we feel students understand concepts more fully if they construct their own equipment. However, for demonstration purposes, you may wish to purchase a commercial rotating dial electroscope since it will be visible to students throughout the classroom. When discussing electroscopes, make certain students understand that electrons move, but positive charges do not. Thus, the vanes of an electroscope become positive, not because positive charges flow into them, but because negative charges (electrons) flow out of them.

Answers (1) Charge is transferred between the fabric and the rod as a result of contact between two surfaces with differing affinities for electrons. Up to a point, the more the two surfaces are rubbed together, the more charge is transferred, the greater the induced charge on the vanes, and the greater the separation between them. (2) The net charge on the electroscope remains zero if the charged rod has not touched it. If a negatively charged rod approaches the ball of the electroscope, electrons in the ball will be repelled toward the vanes. Both vanes will now contain an excess of electrons and repel each other. When the rod is removed, electrons will flow again to reestablish neutrality throughout the wire, and the neutral vanes will collapse under the force of gravity. (3) In both instances, the vanes will move apart. A negatively charged rod repels electrons into the vanes, giving them both a net negative charge and causing them to repel each other. A positively charged rod attracts electrons, leaving a net positive charge in both vanes, once again causing them to repel each other. (4) When the rod touches the ball, electrons are transferred by conduction. The entire electroscope, including the vanes, now has a net charge. Since the vanes are free to move, they will continue to repel each other.

8.1.2 Electric Charges

Discussion: These investigations illustrate that objects can acquire a positive or negative charge. Charge is acquired as electrons flow into or away from an object, leaving it negative or positive. The transfer of charge can be shown in Part 2, where the charged rod repels the suspended rod while the portion of the cloth on which it was rubbed attracted the rod. Electrons were transferred from the cloth to the rod, leaving the rod negatively charged and the cloth positively charged.

Answers (1) The vanes will separate because like charges repel each other. (2) Your hand provides a ground, or an escape pathway to the earth. Without your hand or other "grounding device," charge cannot escape, so the electroscope will remain uncharged. (3) The vanes achieve maximum separation when a charged rod is brought near to the electroscope with like charge. As a result, additional electrons move within the electroscope, increasing the net charge upon the vanes and causing them to move farther apart. (4) Rub a glass rod with silk to generate a positive charge. Place your hand on the electroscope and bring the charged rod close to the electroscope. The positive charges in the rod will attract electrons from your hand into the electroscope. When you remove your hand, the electroscope is left with a net negative charge. (5) The rod strips electrons from the cloth. As a result, the rod and cloth have opposite charges and therefore produce opposite results.

8.1.3 Electrostatic Attraction

Answers (1) Clothes made of different fabrics have different affinities for electrons. When these clothes rub together, electrons migrate from one fabric to the other giving the fabrics opposite charges that causes them to attract (static cling). (2) There will be more static cling if the clothes are made of different materials because a charge differential will develop only if the fabrics have differing affinities for electrons. If they are both made of the same material, there will be little transfer of electrons and little attraction between them. (3) As vehicles move they accumulate charge as a result of friction with the air. Originally, truck tires were made of nonconducting rubber, so such electric charge could not be drained off to the road. If such trucks accumulated sufficient charge, an electrostatic discharge (spark) could occur and possibly cause an explosion if gasoline fumes were also present. After such calamities, truckers started dragging metal chains to drain off charge and reduce the potential of spark formation. Today, all gasoline-tanker trucks are equipped with conductive tires so chains are no longer necessary. (4) As a hard-rubber comb moves through your hair, it removes electrons and leaves your hair with a net positive charge. Since like charges repel, the positively charged hairs will move as far away from each other as possible, which in this case is accomplished by standing straight up.

8.1.4 Induction

Discussion: The paper in Part 1 will bounce back and forth between the charged glass plate and the table top for the same reason the Cheerios® move back and forth between the glass and Lucite rods. The charged surface attracts the paper or Cheerios® by induction, then imparts a like charge to them by conduction and subsequently repels them. As the paper or Cheerios® contact the uncharged surface, they lose this charge and are then attracted by induction once again to the charged rod.

Even an inexpensive Van de Graaf generator will levitate the Cheerios® or puffed wheat in Part 3. You can use this demonstration to introduce the concept of electric fields and field lines. Show your students that the objects travel according to the electric field lines, which start at the dome of the generator and move to the base. If you try to place the charged Cheerios® back on the generator, they will bounce off because both still have the same charge. This is a very amusing and interesting activity.

If a strong generator is available, place a stack of pie pans on its dome and watch them hop off one at a time. If available, place an animal fur (skin side down) on top of the generator's dome. The fur will become charged and will stand on end as individual hairs repel each other. If the generator produces sufficient voltage, the fur will levitate and fly off, creating a dramatic and rather unusual spectacle. Finally, you can place one hand on the generator and then turn it on. If the air is very dry and you are not grounded (stand on a rubber mat), the hair on the top of your head will stand straight up.

Answers (1) After rubbing with silk, the glass is left with a positive charge. This induces polar molecules in the paper to reorient so their negative poles are closer to the glass while their positive poles are farther away. The electrostatic attraction between the negative poles and the glass is therefore greater than the electrostatic repulsion between the positive poles and the glass, causing the paper to be attracted to the glass. (2) The paper has an excess of electrons, some of which are transferred to the glass upon contact. The paper becomes positively charged through loss of these electrons and then is repelled by the glass because like charges repel. (3) It is attracted to the charged plastic rod by induction (Figure V). It then acquires a negative charge by conduction (Figure W) and is repelled. It is then attracted to the glass rod by induction (Figure X), but is repelled once the rod acquires the same charge by conduction (Figure Y). (4) As the belt of the Van de Graaf generator moves, a substantial charge builds up on the generator's dome. The Cheerios® acquire the same charge as the dome by conduction. Once charged, they experience electrostatic repulsion and fly off. (5) Prior to an electrical storm, a strong positive charge builds on the undersides of clouds while a strong negative charge builds on you and the earth beneath the clouds. Since all your hairs acquire the same charge, they experience electrostatic repulsion and move as far from each other as possible, causing them to "stand up."

8.1.5 Distribution of Charge

Discussion: The stream of plasma at the end of the metal rod is clearly visible only when the room is very dark. If you are unable to illustrate this at night, then consider performing it in a closet. Don't stay in the closet for any length of time, however, because the process produces ozone, a strong oxidant. The distinctive odor you smell around the Van de Graaf generator is ozone (O_3).

Answers (1) The tiny blue beam is plasma, a high-temperature ionized gas consisting of electrons and positive ions. The charges in plasma allow it to conduct an electric current. (2) Lightning rods continually drain electrons from the clouds to the earth. They thereby reduce the potential difference between clouds and the earth and reduce the threat of lightning. If lightning does strike, it will strike the lightning rod rather than a building. (3) The metal points on airplane wings exchange charge between the airplane and the air in the same way that lightning rods and conductive truck tires exchange charge with their environments. This reduces the potential difference between the airplane and the air and reduces the likelihood of a lightning strike.

8.1.6 Electrostatic Separators

Discussion: Part 1 of this activity is effective in illustrating the differences between compounds and mixtures. Mixtures, such as salt and pepper, can be separated by a physical process such as electrostatic attraction, while compounds, such as water, cannot. Additionally, you can show how iron filings can be separated from sulfur powder using a magnet, or how sand can be separated from gravel using a sieve. You may wish to mix some salt and pepper and ask your students to discover a quick method of separating the two.

Answers (1) The pepper and salt mixture could be placed in water. The pepper will float on the surface and can be skimmed off. The salt will dissolve in the water and can subsequently be recrystallized by evaporating the water. (2) The filter is charged and attracts paint particles by induction, much the way the pepper is attracted by induction in this activity. (3) The paper prevents contact between the silk and glass. Thus, charge can build up on the exposed regions, but not on the protected regions.

8.1.7 Electric Potential

Discussion: The Van de Graaf generator is capable of producing very high voltages. The potential difference may be very high, but the total amount of charge or electric energy is not very high, producing a brief and low amperage current when discharged. If you have a strong generator, it can produce painful sparks and you should supervise its use with great caution.

Answers (1) The generator produces a strong electric field. When the tube is positioned such that the two ends are different distances from the generator, a potential difference across the tube is created and the gas glows. (2) In a tangential position, the potential difference between the two ends of the tube is insufficient to stimulate molecular activity inside the tube. (3) The gasses in the tube will fluoresce only in the region between the electrode nearest the generator and your hand. (4) Please see the introduction to this section.

8.1.8 Capacitance

Discussion: Encourage students to experiment with different designs for Leyden jars and determine which is capable of storing the most charge as measured by the intensity of a neon-glow-tube discharge. The Leyden jar can also be charged by connecting one terminal of a Wimhurst generator to the paper clips, and the other to the outer foil. The Leyden jar was the first method developed for storing electric charge and was the predecessor of the modern-day capacitor.

Answers (1) Styrofoam has a greater affinity for electrons. The Styrofoam plate acquires a negative charge when rubbed with wool because it has a greater affinity for electrons than wool does. (2) An electrostatic discharge occurs as electrons move through the air from an electron-rich region to an electron-poor region. These electrons ionize the air, which then emits light and sound. (3) The polarity of the Leyden jar can be reversed by touching the electrophorus to the aluminum foil on the outside while touching the nail with your finger. Alternatively, you could charge the electrophorus with a negative charge by rubbing it with a plastic bread bag and touching it to the nail as originally described.

Applications to Everyday Life

Electrically Conductive Truck Tires: Tire manufacturers produce electrically conductive tires. Such tires are able to drain charge from trucks that otherwise would acquire static charge as a result of friction with passing air. With conducting tires there is little danger of electrostatic discharges (sparking), which might prove catastrophic for trucks carrying explosive fuels.

Air Purification: Many heavy industries release a large amount of air pollutants into the atmosphere. Much of the fine dust can be eliminated by passing exhaust through electrostatically charged plates and grates that attract electrically charged smoke particles. Some air-conditioning systems use this technique to remove pollen, dust, and cigarette smoke from the air.

Lightning Safety: You are relatively safe from the danger of lightning in a metal airplane or a car because the field inside an electrically conducting container is zero.

Electrostatic Shocks by Scuffing Your Feet: Under ideal conditions it is possible to build up a 20,000-volt potential on your body by scuffing your feet across a new carpet. This charge can ionize the air at the tip of your fingers as you approach an object of lower potential, such as a door knob.

Cathode Ray Tubes; Monitors: A computer or television monitor contains a cathode that emits electrons upon heating. The electrons stream past two sets of electrostatically charged parallel plates. Electrons are deflected by electrostatic attraction or repulsion and are thereby directed to the portion of the screen to be illuminated.

Particle Accelerators: Large electrostatic generators such as the Van de Graaf device are capable of establishing electrical potentials of many million volts. Such potentials can accelerate charged particles in vacuums to nearly the speed of light and are of use in the study of particle physics.

Photocopiers: Most electrostatic copiers expose a photoconductive selenium drum to a corona discharge and then to a document. An electrostatic "image" of the original is established on the drum, which then attracts the toner. The toner is then transferred from the drum to the paper by direct contact and then fixed by heat.

Lightning: Lightning occurs when high voltage electrostatic fields are established. The bottoms of clouds generally develop large negative charges that can discharge to the positively charged upper surfaces of the clouds or the positively charged ground.

Chemical Bonds: Both ionic and covalent bonds are the result of electrostatic attractions. For example, in a covalent H-H bond, the attraction between the positively charged nuclei and negatively charged electrons of separate atoms provides the force that binds the hydrogen atoms together in the hydrogen molecule (H_2). In an ionic bond, such as is found in table salt (Na^+Cl^-), the electrostatic attraction between positively and negatively charged ions binds crystals together.

Electron Microscope Lenses: Electron microscopes use electrons, rather than light, to produce images. Electrons possess a negative charge and are focused by electrostatic "lenses." These "lenses" consist of well-designed electrostatic fields that direct the electrons by the force of electrostatic attraction and repulsion.

Computer Protection: The components of a computer or other electronic device are sensitive to electrostatic fields and discharges and are often housed in metal boxes to shield them from electric fields. To avoid damaging electrostatic discharges, computer technicians ground themselves before working on computers.

8.2 CIRCUITS

In 1880, the Electric Light Company of Rochester, New York, opened the world's first electric power station and began providing electricity to the residents of the surrounding neighborhood. From such humble beginnings, the production and delivery of electric power has grown to become one of the world's largest industries. Electricity has become an essential form of energy throughout most of the world, particularly within industrialized nations. Nearly 40 percent of the energy generated in the United States is converted to electricity, and interruption in the delivery of electric power can cause significant problems. On the evening of November 9, 1965, a massive power failure occurred across much of the northeastern United States and southeastern Canada, cutting off electricity to nearly 30 million people, and bringing commercial, civic, and industrial activity to a virtual standstill. Elevators, electric trains, electric buses, and subways ceased to function, leaving people stranded. Street lights, signal lights, railroad crossing guards, and parking garage gates stopped working, stalling vehicular traffic. Communication systems were interrupted as radio, television, and phone services were suspended. Markets, restaurants, and other businesses became chaotic as lights, cash registers, electric doors, and computers failed. For those fortunate enough to be at home when the blackout occurred, daily routines were interrupted as the electric controls and components of ovens, refrigerators, toasters, clocks, heaters, air conditioners, washing machines, dryers, and water heaters failed. The infamous 1965 "blackout" clearly illustrated how dependent industrialized societies are upon electric power.

In the years since 1965 our thirst for electric power has continued to grow as industries introduce an ever-widening array of electric-powered consumer goods, including everything from electronic encyclopedias to automatic pet-food dispensers. In 1990, Americans consumed nearly 10,000 kW·h of electricity per person, approximately 30 times as much as the average citizens of developing nations. From where does all this electric power come?

Approximately 73 percent of all electric power produced in the United States is generated by the burning of fossil fuels (natural gas, oil, and coal). Thus, an electric golf cart appears to be pollution-free only because fuel was first burned and smog produced at a distant generating plant. Approximately 14 percent of our electric power is produced by nuclear power plants and 13 percent by hydroelectric power plants. Since both fossil fuels (coal, gas, oil) and nuclear fuels (uranium, plutonium) are limited and will eventually run out or be too costly to obtain, there is great concern that we may eventually face a major energy crisis with symptoms not unlike those of the 1965 "blackout." Because we are dependent upon electric power, scientists and engineers are very interested in generating electric power by alternative, renewal means. Today, there are numerous small power plants that deliver electricity generated by the conversion of solar, geothermal, tidal, or wind power. By tapping the energy in sunlight, geothermal vents and geysers, ocean tides, and daily winds, engineers hope to be able to produce electric power to meet the needs of an ever-increasing world population. In this section you will investigate basic electric circuitry to gain an appreciation for, and understanding of, this form of energy we often take for granted—electricity.

8.2.1 Electric Current

Concepts to Investigate: Current, conductivity, galvanoscope, galvanometer, calibration, open circuit, closed circuit, Ohm's law.

Materials: Magnetic compass, 1.5- or 3.0-volt flashlight bulb, flashlight battery to power bulb, bulb socket, 5 meters of insulated wire (20 to 26 gauge).

Principles and Procedures

Part 1. Galvanoscope: The Danish physicist Hans Christian Oersted was convinced there was no relationship between electricity and magnetism and repeatedly illustrated this to his students by placing a current-carrying wire at right angles over a magnetic compass and noting that the needle did not deflect. In 1822, while he was lecturing to his students, he accidentally placed the compass such that the needle was parallel to the wire and noticed that the compass needle moved when the current flowed through the wire. Oersted's accidental discovery was one of the most important discoveries of all time and led to the development of a variety of electromagnetic devices, including generators, motors, and electric meters.

In this activity we will make use of Oersted's discovery to develop a galvanoscope, an instrument used to monitor electric current. *Electric current is the rate of flow of charge past a given point in a circuit.* Electric currents are necessary to power all electrical devices, from the toaster in your kitchen to the robotic arms on the space shuttle. Electric currents are used to accomplish work. The greater the current, the greater the amount of work that can be done.

Use a compass to determine the direction of Magnetic North (Figure A). Wrap approximately 30 turns of thin-gauge insulated copper wire around this compass in a north/south direction, and connect it to a 1.5-volt light bulb that is connected to a 1.5-volt battery, as illustrated in Figure B. (You may substitute different bulbs and batteries as long as the bulbs are of similar voltage to the battery.) When the circuit is closed, a current will flow, the lamp will glow, and the needle will move (Figure C). The brightness of the light and the angle of needle deflection are a function of

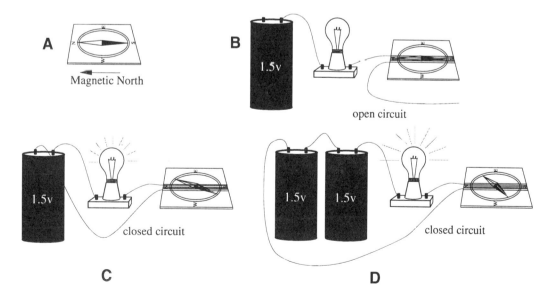

A

Magnetic North

B

open circuit

C

closed circuit

D

closed circuit

the magnitude of the electric current in the wire. This simple galvanoscope can be used whenever you want to detect the presence of small currents. Most current meters (ammeters) are based upon variations of this design. What effect will reversing the connection of the wires have upon the direction the needle moves when the circuit is closed? Will the needle move if the wire is wound in an east-west direction? Will the sensitivity of the galvanoscope increase if you increase the number of turns of wire? Design your own experiments to answer these questions.

Ohm's law states that the current (I) in a closed circuit is directly proportional to voltage (V), and inversely proportional to the resistance (R): I = V/R. According to Ohm's law, the current will increase, the lamp will glow brighter, and the needle of the compass will move farther if the voltage is increased. Record the needle deflection and the brightness of the bulb resulting from one, two, and three dry cells or batteries added in series (Figure D). Are your findings consistent with Ohm's law? (If the needle of the galvanometer does not turn appreciably, increase the number of turns of wire around it and repeat. If it is too sensitive, decrease the number of turns.)

The device you have constructed is known as a galvanoscope rather than a galvanometer because it is not calibrated to measure current. To calibrate your instrument so that it measures current, position the galvanoscope so it points to magnetic north, place it in series with a galvanometer, and measure needle deflection as you increase the number of batteries (Figure E). Plot needle deflection as a function of known amperage to develop a calibration curve that allows your instrument to serve as a galvanometer (Figure F).

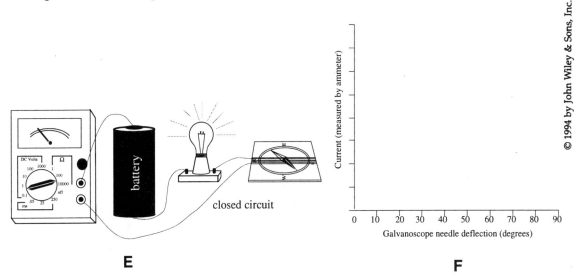

closed circuit

E   **F**

Part 2. Electrical conductivity: The bottoms of expensive pots and pans are often made of copper, while the sides are made of stainless steel and the handles are made of a heat-resistant plastic. Since copper is an excellent conductor of heat, energy is transferred efficiently from the stovetop to the food. Stainless steel is a less efficient conductor, and consequently less heat is lost through the sides of the cookware than would be lost if they were also made of copper. Plastic is a very poor conductor of heat and therefore is used for handles so the cook doesn't get burned.

Thermal and electrical conductivity both depend upon the transport of energy by electrons. This suggests that materials having large numbers of free electrons, such as copper, will be excellent conductors of both heat and electricity, while materials such as plastic that have virtually no free electrons will be poor conductors. To test this hypothesis, examine the electrical conductivity of copper, steel, and plastic by observing the deflection of the galvanoscope needle when equal-sized pieces of copper, steel, or plastic are substituted for the light bulb shown in Figure C. Test a wide variety of materials such as wool, paper, brass, chalk, tap water, salt water, and aluminum and determine if these are conductors or insulators.

Questions

(1) On the basis of your observations in Part 1, describe the relationship between voltage and current. Is this data consistent with Ohm's law? Explain.

(2) Why must the coils be parallel to the needle before connecting the wires of the galvanoscope?

(3) On the basis of your findings, does there appear to be a relationship between electrical conductivity and thermal conductivity? Explain.

(4) Rank the substances tested from high to low electrical conductivity.

(5) Salt water is a better conductor of electricity than fresh water, although it is not a better conductor of heat. Explain.

8.2.2 Electrical Energy from Chemicals

Concepts to Investigate: Electrochemical cell, wet cell, electrodes, electrolyte, potential energy, potential difference, voltage, resistance, galvanic skin response.

Materials: Citrus fruit, two different metals (aluminum, zinc, nickel, iron, copper, or silver), volt-ohm-milliammeter (or galvanoscope made in previous activity), wire leads with alligator clips, 0.5-volt lamp (available from electronic-supply stores), beaker, dilute sulfuric acid, sandpaper or steel wool.

Principles and Procedures: In 1780, Italian anatomy professor Luigi Galvani was washing some frog legs when one of them spontaneously twitched. Needless to say, Galvani was quite surprised to see the leg of a frog move hours after the frog had died. Galvani was fascinated by this event and tried to create conditions in which it could be repeated. After careful study, he noted that the leg would contract whenever it was simultaneously touched by two different metals such as iron and copper. Although Galvani thought he had discovered a phenomenon he termed "animal electricity," he had in fact discovered the basic principle that is now employed to start our cars, power our flashlights, and run our watches. Galvani had discovered the electrochemical cell.

The electrochemical cell may be understood by comparing it to a hydroelectric power plant. The Grand Coulee Hydroelectric Plant on the Columbia River in the state of Washington is one of the world's largest producers of electricity, providing nearly 11,000 megawatts of electric power, enough to provide lighting for 40 million homes. The water standing behind the dam has a higher potential energy than the water in the river bed below. As a result, gravitational potential energy is eventually converted to electric energy as water falls past the turbines in the dam. Just as hydroelectric power plants tap the gravitational potential energy of water, so electrochemical cells and batteries tap the electrochemical potential energy between dissimilar metals.

The energy of valence (outermost) electrons in iron is greater than the energy of valence electrons in copper, just as the potential energy of water behind a dam is greater than the potential energy of water in the river bed below. Placing the two different metals in an appropriate electrolytic media such as the fluid of a frog leg, an orange, or a jar of sulfuric acid allows chemical reactions to occur and electrons to flow, just the way opening a flume in a hydroelectric plant allows water to flow through the turbines. *As electrons flow from a position of higher electrochemical potential energy in iron to a position of lower electrochemical potential energy in copper, a usable electric current (flow of electrons) is generated.*

Part 1. Simple wet cell: All electrochemical cells require two electrodes made of different conductors, an electrolyte solution (a solution that conducts electricity) that reacts with the electrodes, and a conductive wire through which electrons may flow. Roll a lemon, orange, grapefruit, or other citrus on a firm surface to break the internal membranes. Cut strips (approximately 4 cm × 1 cm) of copper and zinc sheet metal and insert these in the fruit so they are approximately 1 centimeter apart. Attach the test wires of a volt-ohm-milliammeter (VOM) to the strips and measure the electric potential and the current (Figure G). Reverse the leads and note that the voltage changes sign while the current remains constant. The copper/zinc wet cell

© 1994 by John Wiley & Sons, Inc.

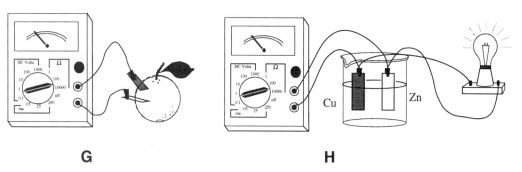

G   **H**

you have created should generate a potential difference of approximately 1.1 volts. Will the voltage of your wet cell change if you change the size of the electrodes? Try it! Will the voltage change if you construct the cell using different electrodes? Construct cells using electrodes made of any two of the following metals: aluminum, zinc, nickel, iron, copper, or silver. Try a variety of different electrode combinations and determine which produces the greatest voltage.

The previous activity described how you can make your own galvanoscope (current detector) using nothing more than a magnetic compass and copper wire. Once you have made such an instrument, you can use it in place of the commercial VOM specified in this activity. Another method of detecting current is to place a low-voltage light bulb (less than 0.5 volt) in place of the VOM.

Part 2. Voltaic cell: Wear goggles, gloves, and a lab coat to protect yourself in case of a sulfuric acid spill. Obtain pieces of zinc and copper and polish them with steel wool to remove any oxides. Carefully fill a beaker two thirds full with dilute sulfuric acid solution prepared in advance by your instructor. Use alligator clips to attach test wires to copper and zinc electrodes and suspend them in the beaker as shown in Figure H. Set your voltmeter to the 1- or 2-volt range and record the voltage of the cell. Use another set of test wires to connect a low-voltage lamp (0.5 volts or less) in parallel with the voltmeter as shown in the diagram. Repeat this procedure with electrodes made of any two different metals (aluminum, zinc, nickel, iron, copper, or silver). Try a variety of different electrode combinations to determine which produces the greatest voltage.

How long will your voltaic cell generate electricity? What factors determine the life of your voltaic cell? Determine the longevity of your voltaic cell by recording the length of time a bulb will remain lit. How will the following factors affect the longevity of a cell: electrode size, cleanliness of electrodes, freshness of electrolyte solution, voltage rating of bulb? Design an experiment to test the influence of each of these variables.

Part 3. Human cell (lie detector): Use alligator clips to connect test leads to sheets of copper and aluminum that have been polished with steel wool. Place the metal sheets on a nonconductive surface such as wood or linoleum, and attach the leads to a voltmeter. Adjust the meter to the 1-volt range, place your hands on the plates, and record the voltage and current (Figure I). Now dip your hands in water and repeat the process. Is there any difference in the voltage or current? Why or why not?

The electrons in aluminum are more energetic than those in copper, and as a result, electrons flow freely from aluminum through the wire to the copper plate.

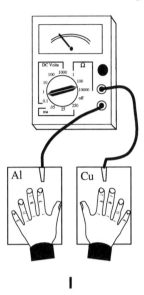

Here electrons are drained off through a reduction reaction with ions in your sweat, leaving the copper electrode with a positive charge. Meanwhile, negative ions in your sweat release electrons to the aluminum plate, giving it a net negative charge. The copper/body/aluminum system now behaves as a wet cell, producing a tiny electric current (flow of electrons).

Thoroughly dry your hands, turn the VOM to the resistance scale and record the resistance (opposition to electric current) of the copper/body/aluminum system in ohms (one ohm equals one volt per ampere). Now perform a vigorous exercise (running, push-ups, etc.) for ten minutes and once again record the resistance. Is your resistance greater or smaller after running? Why? Finally, wet your hands and measure your resistance one more time. When do you obtain the lowest resistance?

It is clear that the resistance of your skin changes as a function of moisture. Psychologists have noted that skin moisture (sweating) changes as a function of emotion and stress and have realized that the amount of sweating can be accurately assessed by monitoring changes in the electrical resistance of your skin. This process, known as galvanic skin response, is an important part of most lie detectors (polygraphs). Although no longer acceptable in courts of law, evidence suggests that people sweat more when they lie than when they tell the truth. Thus, a rapid reduction in skin resistance in response to a question may indicate that a defendant is lying.

Questions

(1) What influence does the size of the electrodes have upon the voltage and life of a cell?

(2) Of the metal pairs tested in Part 1, which pair generates the highest potential difference? Which generates the lowest potential difference?

(3) Why do batteries eventually run down?

(4) A typical 12-volt automobile battery has lead (Pb) and lead oxide (PbO_2) electrodes immersed in a solution of sulfuric acid. Explain why it is possible to test the degree of discharge of such a battery by measuring the density of the sulfuric acid solution.

8.2.3 Electric Energy from Heat

Concepts to Investigate: Conservation of energy, thermoelectricity, Seebeck effect, Peltier effect, thermocouple, thermopile, calibration.

Materials: Beakers, ice, galvanometer (or sensitive VOM), copper wire, iron wire, matches.

Principles and Procedures: The principle of conservation of energy states we can neither create nor destroy energy, but simply convert it from one form to another. Other forms of energy are converted to electric energy by means of electromagnetic (generators), photoelectric (photocells), piezoelectric (microphones), chemical (batteries), or thermoelectric (thermocouples) processes. In this activity you will investigate thermoelectric conversion, which is the transformation of heat energy directly into electric energy.

Part 1. Thermocouple (Seebeck effect): On March 9, 1979, the *Voyager 2* spacecraft was launched from Cape Canaveral, Florida, on the grandest space exploration mission ever attempted. *Voyager 2*, designed by NASA's (National Aeronautics and Space Administration) Jet Propulsion Laboratory in Pasadena, California, traveled for ten years before leaving the solar system. During this time, *Voyager 2* sent back a wealth of images and data on the planets Jupiter, Saturn, Uranus, and Neptune. Previous spacecraft relied heavily upon solar panels to convert sunlight into the electricity needed to run the spacecraft's instrumentation, but scientists realized that the intensity of solar radiation would be far too weak to power the spacecraft by the time it reached Jupiter. Consequently, NASA engineers designed a supplemental system that generated electricity from the heat produced by the decay of radioactive elements. Their thermoelectric generator relied upon a principle discovered by the German physicist Thomas Seebeck in 1821. *The Seebeck effect refers to the generation of electricity in a circuit composed of two wires whose junctions are at different temperatures.* In this activity you will have the opportunity to make your own thermoelectric generator.

Create thermocouple junctions at both ends of a section of iron wire by twisting the ends together with copper wires, as shown in Figure J. Place one copper/iron junction in a beaker filled with ice water while leaving the other junc-

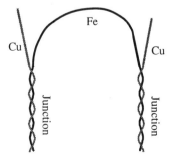

Thermocouple

J

tion outside (Figure K). The two remaining ends of the copper wires should be connected to a sensitive VOM, galvanometer, milliammeter, or similar current detector such as the one constructed in activity 8.2.1. Heat the exposed junction with a Bunsen burner or match and record the current. Does the current increase or decrease if the heat source is removed? Is the change in current immediate? Why or why not?

Part 2. Thermopile: When two or more batteries are placed in series (one after another; negative pole to positive pole), as in a flashlight or electric toy, a higher voltage is generated and more current is produced. Can the voltage and current of a thermoelectric system be increased by adding two or more thermocouples in series? Try it. Connect an additional thermocouple in series with the first, as illustrated in Figure L. Be sure one junction of this new thermocouple is in the water while the other is in the flame. Repeat with three and four thermocouples in series. Describe the relationship between the number of thermocouples in series and the current generated. You may wish to bundle the thermocouple wires together with string so the resulting thermopile is easier to manage.

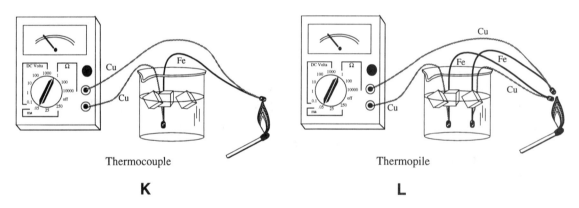

Thermocouple

K

Thermopile

L

Part 3. Thermometer: The current produced by a thermocouple or thermopile is directly related to the temperature difference between junctions. Because of this relationship, it is possible to develop a thermoelectric thermometer. Calibrate a thermopile or thermocouple by plotting the amperage measured on a galvanometer as a function of the temperature registered on an accurate mercury or alcohol thermometer. Place a reference junction in a beaker filled with ice water and the measuring junction in a second beaker. When the second beaker is filled with ice water there should be no flow of electricity since both junctions are at the same temperature. Gradually warm the second beaker until it boils, plotting the amperage of the circuit as a function of temperature (Figures M and N). Once you have completed the calibration curve, measure the temperature of various things using your new thermoelectric thermometer. Many of the thermometers used in hospitals and scientific laboratories are similar in design to your thermoelectric thermometer.

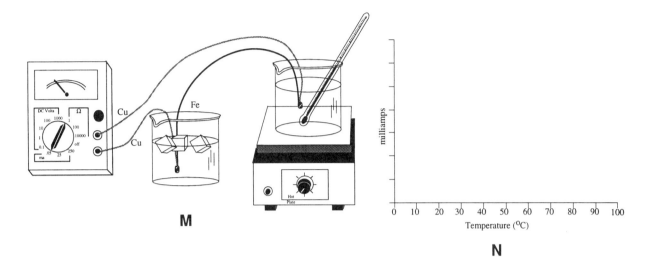

M   **N**

Questions

(1) What is the relationship between the temperature difference of the two junctions of a thermocouple and the resulting current?

(2) Explain why the current generated by the thermocouple does not change instantly when the heat source is removed.

(3) A thermopile is a group of thermocouples placed in series. Based upon your measurements, describe the relationship between the number of thermocouples and the resulting current.

(4) Settlers in remote regions of Siberia use thermoelectric generators to produce electricity from burning wood or kerosene. How might you design such a device to produce a current large enough to meet household needs?

(5) What advantages are there to a thermoelectric thermometer compared with a mercury or alcohol thermometer?

(6) The Seebeck effect describes the generation of an electric current when a temperature differential exists between the two junctions of a thermocouple. The reverse situation is known as the Peltier effect, in which an electric current generates a temperature difference between the junctions of a thermocouple. Describe possible uses of the Peltier effect.

8.2.4 Cells in Series and Parallel

Concepts to Investigate: Series circuits, parallel circuits, batteries, electrodes, anodes, cathodes, schematic diagrams, voltage, amperage.

Materials: Citrus fruit, volt-ohm-milliammeter, electrodes (most dissimilar metals will work well).

Principles and Procedures: Some companies advertise "new, improved, long-lasting" batteries that may power a child's toy for three months or a wristwatch for five years. While manufacturers continue to make improvements, the basic technology has been around for a long time, and long lasting batteries have too. In 1840, two British scientists, Watlin and Hill, constructed a zinc-and-sulfur battery that rang a small bell continuously for more than 150 years. In this activity you will investigate how batteries are made.

Part 1. Cells in series (batteries): A battery is a set of cells connected in series such that the positive electrode (anode) of one cell is connected to the negative electrode (cathode) of the next cell. What is the advantage of using a battery composed of many cells as opposed to a single cell? Perform the following investigation to find out.

The citric acid in lemons or oranges provides an excellent electrolyte solution for a simple wet cell (see activity 8.2.2). After rolling the fruit firmly on a table to rupture its internal membranes, insert two electrodes made of different metals, as illustrated in Figure G, making certain the electrodes do not touch. Nails may serve as iron electrodes, pre-1980 U.S. pennies or stripped electrical wire may serve as copper electrodes, pre-1965 U.S. dimes, silver jewelry, or silver utensils may serve as silver electrodes, and pre-1965 U.S. nickels may serve as nickel electrodes. Record the voltage across the electrodes of a single cell using a voltmeter (Figure G). Add a second and then a third similar "fruit cell" in series with the first cell and record the voltages (Figure O). Figure P, known as a schematic, is a diagram of this circuit. Repeat the activity, substituting a 1-volt lamp for the VOM. Continue adding cells until the light is brightly lit (Figures S and T). What is the advantage of adding cells in series?

Part 2. Cells in parallel: Many circuits are designed with cells or batteries in parallel such that anodes are connected to anodes and cathodes are connected to cathodes. What is the advantage of such parallel arrangements? Record the voltage across the electrodes of a single cell using a voltmeter (Figure G). Add a second and then a third similar "fruit cell" in parallel with the first one and record the voltages (Figures Q and R). What influence does each additional cell have upon the voltage of the system? Repeat the process, substituting a 1-volt lamp for the VOM (Figures U and V). Will you ever be able to light the lamp brightly by placing additional cells in parallel? Repeat the process measuring the amperage (current) through an individual cell as more cells are added in parallel. Does the amperage through a single cell increase, decrease, or remain the same as other cells are added in parallel? Of what advantage is this?

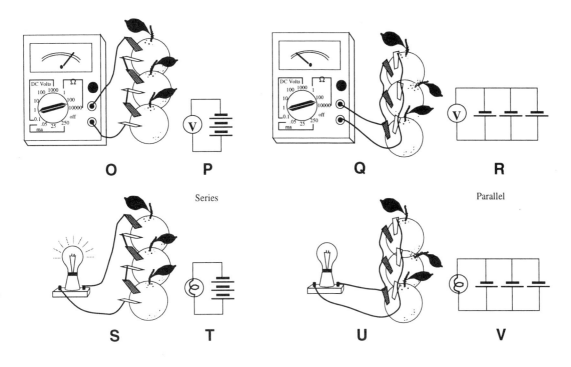

O   P

Series

Q   R

Parallel

S   T

U   V

Questions

(1) Which metals did you use for your electrodes? What is the voltage of a single cell?

(2) How does the number of cells in a series affect the voltage of the system?

(3) A portable drill requires 6 volts to operate. How many 1.5 volt "C" batteries would be required to power this drill? How must the batteries be arranged?

(4) How does the addition of identical cells in parallel affect the voltage of a system? How does it affect the amperage through an individual cell? How does the addition of cells in parallel affect the longevity of the cells? Explain.

(5) Manufacturers recommend that 1.5-volt dry cells not deliver more than 0.25 amps of continuous current. A HAM radio requires 0.75 amps in a 3-volt circuit. How should 1.5-volt dry cells be arranged to power the radio?

8.2.5 Ohm's Law

Concepts to Investigate: Ohm's law, resistors, resistance, factors affecting resistance.

Materials: Volt-ohm-milliammeter, 1.5-v light bulb and socket, 6-v battery, different-diameter mechanical pencil leads.

Principles and Procedures: The German physicist Georg Ohm discovered that in a closed circuit the ratio of the electromotive force to the current is constant. Ohm termed this constant the resistance and developed an equation to describe this principle. *Ohm's law states that $R = V/I$, where V = the potential across a circuit measured in volts, I = current measured in amps, and R = the resistance measured in ohms.* The equation is commonly expressed as $V = IR$. Electrical resistance is analogous to the opposition water experiences as it flows through a pipe. The smaller the pipe, or the greater its length, or the more obstructions in it, the greater the resistance and the smaller the flow of water. In a similar fashion, a reduction in the width of a conductor, an increase in the path length, or a decrease in the mobility of electrons will lead to an increase in resistance and a decrease in current.

Part 1. Resistance: A resistor is an electrical component that opposes the flow of current in a circuit. Since pencil "lead" is made of carbon (graphite), an element frequently used in resistors, we shall use it in our studies of resistance. Connect a flashlight bulb (1 to 2 volts) in series with a pencil lead and a 6-volt lantern battery, as illustrated in Figure W. (You may substitute different bulbs and batteries as long as the voltage rating of the battery is significantly higher than the voltage rating of the bulb.) Turn off the room lights and observe the brightness of the bulb. Move one wire contact along the length of the pencil lead and observe changes in the intensity of the light (Figure X). What effect does the length of the resistive path (the length between the two wire/graphite connections) have upon the total resistance? Repeat the activity with a pencil lead of a different diameter. What influence does the diameter of the resistor have upon the net resistance?

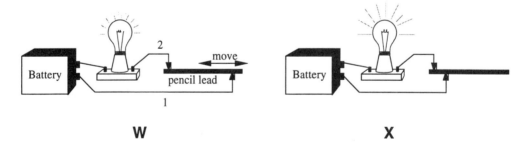

W   **X**

Part 2. Ohm's law: Ohm's law can be investigated using the set-up described in part 1 and a volt-ohm-milliammeter. Measure the voltage by attaching the wire leads of a VOM to locations 1 and 2 in Figure W and measure the current by placing the meter in series anywhere in the circuit. Calculate the resistance of the circuit from the equation $R = V/I$. Now measure resistance with the ohmmeter by disconnecting the battery and connecting the wires at points 1 and 2 and compare this value with the value given by Ohm's law. Change the length of the pencil lead resistor and repeat this procedure. What is the percentage error of your calculated values? Do your results agree with Ohm's law?

$$\text{percentage error} = \left(\frac{\text{calculated value - measured value}}{\text{measured value}}\right)100\%$$

Questions

(1) According to your observations, what influence do the length and diameter of the resistive path have upon the total resistance?

(2) Potentiometers and rheostats are variable resistors used to adjust such things as the volume of a stereo or the intensity of a lamp. On the basis of your observations, explain how such devices might work.

(3) Discuss your findings from Part 2. Do your results agree with Ohm's law? Explain.

8.2.6 Heating Effects

Concepts to Investigate: Fuses, short circuits, circuit breakers, resistive heating, overloading.

Materials: 1.5-volt dry cell, 6-volt lantern battery, flashlight bulbs and sockets, wire leads, steel wool or picture-frame wire.

Principles and Procedures: As electrical energy passes through a resistor, some is converted into heat. The amount of energy released as heat is directly proportional to the current. Many electric stoves, hair dryers, or space heaters are equipped with rheostats (variable resistors) to control temperature by adjusting the current to the heating element. If current through the heating element is reduced, the temperature drops, but if it is increased, the temperature rises. In addition to current, the resistance of the heating element also influences the percentage of electrical energy that will be transformed into heat. If you look in a toaster you will notice nichrome wires of the heating element glow red while the copper wires that deliver electricity to the toaster don't glow at all. Nichrome is 70 times more resistant to the flow of electrons than copper, and therefore transforms substantially more electricity into heat. Nichrome is used for the heating elements in a toaster because of its high resistivity (much electric energy is converted to heat), while copper is used for the wires that deliver electricity to the toaster because of its low resistivity (little electric energy is converted to heat).

The English physicist James Joule determined that the amount of energy released as heat Q is equal to the product of the square of the current I^2, resistance R, and duration of the current $Q = I^2Rt$.

Although the copper used in household wiring has a much lower resistivity than the nichrome wire used in a toaster or the tungsten filaments used in an incandescent light bulb, Joule's equation suggests that it also will heat if the current through it is sufficiently great. The heating effect in the main copper wire feeding three 1-amp appliances will be 9 times the heating effect if just one such appliance is connected ($(3amps)^2Rt$ versus $(1amp)^2Rt$). Because the heating effect in wires increases as the square of the current passing though them, the addition of a few high-amperage appliances (electric heaters, air conditioners, irons, etc.) to a circuit may cause the copper wire delivering the current to overheat and possibly cause a fire.

Part 1. Fuse: Thomas Edison recognized the danger of excessive current and developed a device known as the fuse to protect circuits, people, and homes from this threat. Although fuses have been replaced by circuit breakers (an electromechanical device) in most homes, they are still widely used in automotive electric systems and within household appliances. To make your own fuse, obtain a strand of iron wire either from a wad of steel wool or from unwound picture hanger wire. Using test wires equipped with alligator clips, connect the thin wire to a battery as shown in Figure Y, and note how the iron strand heats and eventually melts, breaking the circuit.

Part 2. Short-circuits: Excessive current can result either from a short-circuit or from an excessive load (too many appliances). *A short-circuit results when wires on opposite* *sides of the load touch, creating a low resistance pathway that allows current to bypass the appliance (load).* Current increases dramatically when a short-circuit occurs $I = V/R$. Since heating of a conductor increases as a square of the current $Q = I^2Rt$, the wires in a short-circuit rapidly overheat and may cause a fire. A fuse is a thin wire placed in a circuit to protect it against such problems. If the current is excessive, the fuse melts, opening the circuit and stopping the current.

Strip portions of the two wires so copper is exposed (Figure Z). Attach these wires in series with a flashlight bulb, a fuse made from a strand of iron picture frame wire or steel wool, and a battery or series of batteries of sufficient voltage to light the bulb. While the light is glowing, press the two bare sections of wire together as shown. Does the fuse melt when the circuit is shorted? Does the light go out? How does a fuse help prevent electrical fires when a short-circuit occurs?

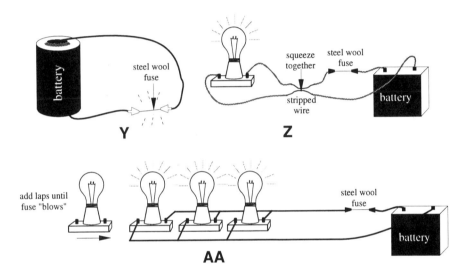

Part 3. Overloading a circuit: The sockets in household circuits are arranged in parallel, providing each appliance the full 120 or 240 volts characteristic of a house circuit. Each extra appliance that is plugged into the circuit provides an additional pathway for the current, thereby reducing the resistance and increasing the current in the circuit. If too many appliances are plugged in, the line may draw excessive current and the fuse may melt or the circuit breaker may be tripped. Most household circuits use 10- or 15-amp fuses or circuit breakers, and any current in excess of these limits melts the fuse or "throws" the breaker and opens the circuit. You can study circuit overloading using the harmless currents provided by a 6-volt lantern battery. Using the fuse developed in Part 2, continue to add lamps or other load-bearing devices in parallel with the first lamp until the fuse melts (Figure AA). How many bulbs were required to melt your fuse?

Questions

(1) The fuse boxes of some older houses were not designed to carry the loads required by modern appliances. To avoid continuously replacing fuses, some

people replaced fuses with copper pennies. Explain why this is extremely dangerous.

(2) Why do your electrical appliances stop when a circuit breaker is tripped or when a fuse is blown?

(3) How can you determine the amperage rating of the fuses constructed in this section? What is the amperage rating for a single strand of steel wool?

8.2.7 Series and Parallel Circuits

Concepts to Investigate: Series circuits, parallel circuits.

Materials: 6-volt battery, flashlight bulbs, lamp bases, wire leads.

Principles and Procedures: You may have noticed that an entire string of old Christmas lights goes out if one bulb burns out or is removed. By contrast, if a bulb in a chandelier burns out or is removed, the remainder of the lights continue to burn. What is the difference in the way these lights are wired?

Part 1. Series circuits: Connect one bulb in series with a battery and note its brightness. Now connect a second and third bulb in series with this bulb, as illustrated in Figure BB. Is there any change in the brightness of the first bulb when the second and third bulbs are added? Once all bulbs are lit, remove one of the bulbs. What happens to the brightness of the others?

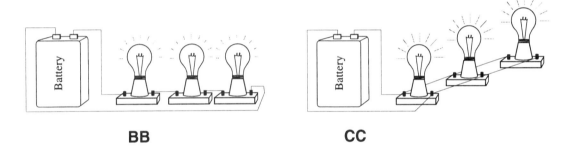

BB **CC**

Part 2. Parallel circuits: Connect one bulb to a battery and note its brightness. Now connect a second and third bulb in parallel with this bulb, as illustrated in Figure CC. Is there any change in brightness of the first bulb when the second or third ones are added? Once all bulbs are lit, remove one. Is there any change in brightness of the remaining bulbs?

Questions

(1) Is there any change in the brightness of a bulb when a second bulb is placed in series with it? Is there any change in the brightness of a bulb when a second one is placed parallel to it? Explain.

(2) Is there any change in the brightness of a bulb when another bulb in a series circuit is removed? Is there any change in the brightness of a bulb when another bulb in a parallel circuit is removed? Explain.

(3) Is the voltage across a bulb changed when a similar bulb is placed in series with it? In parallel with it? Explain.

(4) Are the outlets in your home arranged in parallel or series? How do you know? Why are they designed in this manner?

(5) At the beginning of this activity we discussed some observations regarding old Christmas lights and a chandelier. On the basis of these observations, which one is wired in parallel and which is wired in series?

FOR THE TEACHER

The transformation of available energy into electric energy may be accomplished by chemoelectric, thermoelectric, photoelectric, piezoelectric, or electromagnetic processes. The first four mechanisms represent direct conversion of one form of energy into another. Electromagnetic conversion represents a dynamic multiple-step process in which energy from burning fuels, falling water, or nuclear-fission reactions is used to turn generators that in turn supply the electric energy. In this chapter we discuss only the production of electricity by direct conversion. Dynamic conversion is covered in section 8.4 following a discussion of electromagnetic induction.

The following rules describe the behavior of series and parallel circuits and should be introduced to your students as necessary:

Series Circuits
1. The sum of all the potential drops in a series circuit is equal to the applied electromotive force: $E = V_1 + V_2 + V_3 + ...$
2. The current in all portions of a series circuit is equal: $I_t = I_1 = I_2 = I_3 = ...$
3. The total resistance of a series circuit is equal to the sum of all separate resistances: $R_t = R_1 + R_2 + R_3 + ...$

Parallel Circuits
1. The magnitudes of the potential drops across all branches of a parallel circuit are the same: $V = V_1 = V_2 = V_3 = ...$
2. The total current in a parallel circuit is the sum of the currents in all separate branches: $I_t = I_1 + I_2 + I_3 + ...$
3. For resistances in parallel, the reciprocal of the equivalent resistance is equal to the sum of the reciprocals of all separate resistances: $1/R_{eq} = 1/R_1 + 1/R_2 + 1/R_3 + ...$

8.2.1 Electric Current

Discussion: To illustrate the galvanoscope to the entire class, use an overhead projector and a compass with a clear plastic back. You can also use this set-up to illustrate electrical conductivity. In Part 1, students should find that the galvanoscope deflects the opposite direction if the leads are reversed. They should also find that the galvanoscope does not work when wound in an east-west direction, and that the degree of needle deflection is directly proportional to the number of turns or wire. In Part 2 they should find that copper is a better conductor than steel, which is better than plastic. They should also determine that wool, paper, and chalk are insulators, while brass and salt water are conductors.

Answers (1) Ohm's law states that the voltage in a circuit is equal to the product of the current times the resistance $V = IR$. Students should find a direct relationship between voltage and current as measured by the deflection of the galvanoscope needle. (2) The magnetic field of the coil generates maximum torque on the needle when it is in this position. This position can be considered the "zero point" of the galvanoscope, indicating no current. (3) Students should find a direct relationship between thermal and electrical conductivity. (4) Many substances such as wool and chalk will show no conductivity. Among metals, order of conductivity is as follows: silver>copper>gold>aluminum>iron>tin. (5) Salt water is conductive, not because of the mobility of free electrons, as in metals, but rather because of the mobility of charged sodium (Na^+) and chloride (Cl^-) ions. The reason it is a good conductor of electricity is therefore unrelated to its thermal conductivity.

8.2.2 Electrical Energy from Chemicals

Discussion: The citrus cell is a simple example of an electrochemical cell, but unfortunately, many students make the same mistake Galvani did, believing that the source of electricity is the fruit, rather than the difference in potentials of the two electrodes. The fruit is simply a source of electrolyte. By measuring the voltage of cells made with the same types of electrodes, but different fruits, students will see that the voltage is relatively independent of the electrolyte.

The potential difference (voltage) of an electrochemical cell is dependent upon the difference in affinity the two electrodes have for electrons. In the case of the zinc/copper cell, copper has a stronger affinity for electrons. Consequently, electrons flow from the zinc electrode to the copper electrode, creating current. The voltage of a cell can be predicted by adding the standard electrode potentials:

$$\begin{array}{ll} \text{Zn} \rightarrow \text{Zn}^{++} + 2e^- + 0.76v & E^o = 0.76v \\ \underline{\text{Cu}^{++} + 2e^- \rightarrow \text{Cu} + 0.34v} & E^o = 0.34v \\ \text{Zn} + \text{Cu}^{++} \rightarrow \text{Zn}^{++} + \text{Cu} + 1.10v & E^o = 1.10v \end{array}$$

Students can use a VOM to measure the potentials of cells made from common electrode materials such as aluminum, zinc, iron, nickel, tin, silver, and copper. The following table lists the standard electrode reduction potentials. It should be noted that many substances you may use for electrodes are alloys, and thus will show different reduction potentials from those listed in the table. For example pre-1965 dimes and quarters were 90 percent silver and 10 percent copper. Since that time, they have a face of 75 percent copper and 25 percent nickel over a core of 100 percent copper. While pre-1980 pennies were nearly 100 percent copper, newer pennies are made of brass, an alloy of zinc and copper. The dilute sulfuric acid solution required for Part 2 can be prepared by adding 1 part concentrated sulfuric acid to 9 parts water.

Half Reaction	Electrode Potential	Source
$Al^{+++} + 3e^- \rightarrow Al$	-1.71v	aluminum sheet metal; aluminum foil
$Zn^{++} + 2e^- \rightarrow Zn$	-0.76v	zinc sheet metal; wall of dry cell
$Ni^{++} + 2e^- \rightarrow Ni$	-0.28v	nickel sheet metal; pre-1965 nickels
$Fe^{+++} + 3e^- \rightarrow Fe$	-0.04v	paper clips; nails
$H^+ + e^- \rightarrow H$	*0.00v*	*S.H.E., standard hydrogen electrode*
$Cu^{++} + 2e^- \rightarrow Cu$	+0.34v	pre-1980 U.S. pennies; electric wire
$Ag^+ + e^- \rightarrow Ag$	+0.80v	pre-1965 U.S. dimes, quarters, and half dollars

Answers (1) Although the voltage of a cell is independent of the size of the electrodes, larger electrodes are capable of providing electricity for a longer period of time. (2) Student answers will vary depending upon the combinations of metals tested. The farther apart the electrodes appear in the table, the greater the potential difference. For example, an aluminum/silver cell will deliver 2.51 volts (0.80v-(-1.71v)), while a copper/silver cell will deliver only 0.46 volts (0.80v-0.34v). (3) Batteries produce an electric current as a result of chemical reactions that occur at their electrodes. When either of the electrodes or the electrolyte solution are depleted due to these reactions, the battery ceases to function. (4) The density of the sulfuric acid decreases as the sulfuric acid is consumed through reactions with the electrodes. Low density indicates the battery may be depleted.

8.2.3 Electric Energy from Heat

Discussion: These activities focus on the Seebeck effect, the generation of an electric current in a circuit where junctions of dissimilar metals are in environments of differing temperature. Although we suggest the use of iron and copper wires, many combinations of metals will work. Bailing wire is a form of iron wire, while electric wire is a good source of copper wire. Iron/copper junctions are generally used to measure temperatures up to approximately 275°C, while platinum/rhodium junctions are used for temperatures up to 1600°C.

The Peltier effect is the reverse of the Seebeck effect, releasing heat at one junction and absorbing it at the other when electricity is passed through the circuit. Some students may be able to feel Peltier heating or cooling when a thermocouple is attached to a 9-volt battery. You can illustrate to your class that the temperatures of the junctions reverse when the polarity of the wire leads are reversed.

Answers (1) The greater the temperature differential, the greater the resulting current. (2) The current in a thermocouple is dependent upon the difference in temperature of the two junctions. Since a junction cools gradually upon removal of the heat source, the current will decrease gradually. (3) In general, the current will increase linearly as a function of the number of thermocouples. (4) These activities show that electric current is dependent upon the temperature differential between junctions as well as the number of thermocouple junctions involved. To produce sufficient current, the generator should be made of a thermopile with a large number of junctions, one set of which is as cold as possible, while the other set is as warm as possible. (5) Thermoelectric thermometers can be made much smaller than standard mercury or alcohol thermometers and can therefore be used to measure temperatures in very localized positions, such as a particular group of cells or a specific crystal. Since it is easier to accurately read small variations in amperage using a galvanometer than it is to read variations in height on a thermometer, thermoelectric thermometers can be read more precisely. (6) The Peltier effect can be used to heat or cool localized regions. Peltier coolers are used to cool transistors, lasers, and light detectors in sensitive electronic circuits. Portable food coolers that plug into the lighter-socket in your car also employ the Peltier effect. The largest Peltier-cooling systems in the world are used to provide air conditioning on U.S. Navy submarines.

8.2.4 Cells in Series and Parallel

Discussion: To demonstrate this activity to the entire class, darken the room so students can clearly see the influence of the number and arrangement of cells upon the intensity of the light. As with other activities in this chapter, a variety of metals may be used and the theoretical voltage of an individual cell will be the difference in the voltages of the half reactions (see section 8.2.2). We recommend a zinc/copper system because it produces a convenient voltage of approximately 1 volt.

If cells are arranged in series, the same quantity of charge must flow through each cell, and as a result, the energy added to these charges will be the sum of the energy added by each individual cell. Thus, the electromotive force (*emf*) of a battery is equal to the sum of the *emf*s of the individual cells, and the current through any individual cell is equal to the current through all other cells. By contrast, if equivalent cells are added in parallel, charges will be energized only by the cell through which they pass. Thus, the electromotive force (measured in volts) of a system is unchanged if equal cells are placed parallel to each other. The total current in a parallel system is the sum of the currents in each individual path.

Answers (1) Student answers may vary. The voltage of a single cell can be determined by calculating the difference in the half-reactions of the electrodes used. (See teacher section for 8.2.2) (2) The total *emf* of a series circuit is the sum of the *emf*s of the individual components. (3) A 6-volt circuit can be created by adding four 1.5-volt batteries in series. (4) Adding additional similar cells in parallel does not affect the voltage of a system, but it does reduce the current through each cell and thereby prolongs its life. (5) To achieve 3.0 volts, two 1.5-volt cells must be added in series. To reduce the amperage in the cells to 0.25 amps from 0.75 amps, three sets of cells must be added in parallel. Thus, this radio will require a total of 6 cells arranged in three parallel sets of 2 serial cells each.

8.2.5 Ohm's Law

Discussion: Ohm's law states that resistance is the ratio of the electromotive force of the source to the current in a closed circuit $R = E/I$. The resistance in a circuit is the sum of the resistance in the conductor, the resistance of the load (light, resistor, appliance, etc.) and the internal resistance of the source of *emf*. In order to simplify this activity, we have introduced Ohm's law as it applies to the portion of the circuit excluding the power source, $R = V/I$. This simplification avoids the need to discuss internal resistance and produces an easy verification of Ohm's law.

Answers (1) Resistance increases as path-length increases and path-diameter decreases. (2) Resistance is most easily adjusted by increasing the length of the resistor. The dials of rheostats and potentiometers alter circuit resistance by adjusting the length of the resistor through which the current flows. (3) Resistances calculated from Ohm's law should agree closely with those measured directly with the ohmmeter.

8.2.6 Heating Effects

Discussion: To introduce students to fuses, you may wish to use the "balloon fuse" illustrated in Figure DD. Tape a strand of steel wool or steel picture-frame wire on an inflated balloon and connect both ends of the strand to a battery with wire test leads. In a short time the fuse will heat and pop the balloon. You may also desire to turn off the room lights and place a wad of steel wool across the terminals of a 6-volt lantern battery. Soon, many of the strands will glow, dramatically illustrating how a fire can start from an overheated wire.

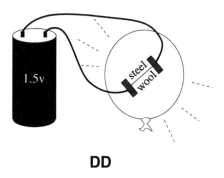

DD

Answers (1) Fuses are designed to melt when the current exceeds a given amperage. If a fuse is replaced by a copper penny the circuit will not break even when amperage is dangerously high. As a result, excessive current may travel through the circuit, overheating wires and perhaps starting a fire. (2) A fuse or circuit breaker acts like a switch. When the current exceeds the allowable limit, the circuit is opened, the current stops flowing, and the appliances immediately stop. (3) It is possible to rate the fuse by placing an ammeter in series with the fuse and recording the amperage at which the fuse melts as the current is slowly increased. Fuse ratings will vary depending upon the thickness of the steel wool used.

8.2.7 Series and Parallel Circuits

Discussion: If you want to demonstrate these activities to your class, we suggest that you attach ring-stand poles (any iron or copper rods will suffice) to the terminals of a 12-volt automobile battery. You may then suspend lights in parallel and serial arrangements between these poles, using copper wire. With this set-up, the entire class can easily view the demonstration and see the differences between serial and parallel circuits. We suggest that you review the basic equations for series and parallel circuits when performing this activity.

Answers (1) A bulb will dim when another bulb is placed in series with it, but will be unaffected when one is placed parallel to it. In a series circuit, the resistance of one bulb limits the current available for other bulbs. As a result, the bulbs get dimmer each time an additional bulb is added. By contrast, bulbs in a parallel circuit simply offer additional pathways for electrons and don't add to or detract from the voltage available to other bulbs. (2) The same current exists in all bulbs in a series circuit. As a result, when one bulb in a series is removed, the others stop glowing because the circuit has been broken. By contrast, removal of a bulb from a parallel circuit leaves the others unaffected. (3) Kirchoff's second law states that the algebraic sum of all the changes in potential occurring in a complete circuit is equal to zero. Each bulb added in series contributes resistance to the circuit and thus contributes to the potential drop, leaving less potential difference for the remaining bulbs. By contrast, bulbs placed in parallel do not affect the voltage across other bulbs as evidenced by the fact that the addition of more bulbs in parallel does not alter the intensity of those already in the circuit. (4) The outlets in houses are arranged in parallel so that a constant, predictable voltage will be available for each additional appliance added. If they were arranged in series, an appliance would work only if all other appliances in the circuit were on. In addition, the voltage supplied to an appliance in a series circuit would be unpredictable and dependent upon the other loads in the circuit. (5) The Christmas lights are wired in series, and the chandelier is wired in parallel.

Applications to Everyday Life

Painful Fillings: Dentists sometimes fill cavities with either gold or silver. Such fillings may cause pain if they come in contact with a metal fork or spoon. A simple wet cell may be created with a steel spoon serving as one electrode, the filling as the other electrode, and the saliva as the electrolyte solution. The minor current may cause pain by stimulating nerves in the region.

Long-life Batteries: Products such as portable calculators, hearing aids, and cellular phones have fostered a need for batteries with long lives and a high energy-to-weight ratio. Chemists and physicists are constantly exploring new combinations of electrodes and electrolytes. The nickel-cadmium battery, in which cadmium serves as the cathode and nickel oxide as the anode, is a highly efficient battery now in common use.

Electric Vehicles: The conventional lead acid battery used to start vehicle engines has too low an energy-to-weight ratio to be feasible in powering electric automobiles. New lithium batteries with high energy-to-weight ratios are being developed to solve this problem.

Cooling Systems: U.S. Navy submarines are equipped with climate-control systems that work on the Peltier effect. If electricity is forced through a thermopile, one set of junctions cools while the other one heats. By reversing the current in the thermopile, navy personnel can turn their air-conditioning system into a heating system. Portable coolers/heaters that operate on electricity from your car battery use this same principle.

Measuring Extreme Temperatures: Mercury and alcohol thermometers are suitable only for a narrow range of temperatures. Thermocouple and thermistor-type thermometers can be used over a much wider range of temperatures and can monitor temperatures inside ovens and cryogenic devices (devices used in the study of extreme cold).

Electrical Safety: The handles of most tools are made of nonconducting materials such as plastic to insulate workers from possible electric hazards.

Semiconductors: Certain materials such as germanium and silicon are known as semiconductors because they have a higher resistivity than conductors, but a lower resistivity than nonconductors. Transistors are made of semiconductors and act as electronic valves. A relatively large current between two regions of a semiconductor can be controlled by a small current or voltage applied to an intermediate region. The development of transistors in 1948 ushered in a new era of solid-state electronics and made possible the miniaturization of circuits that has revolutionized the world of electronics.

Volume Controls: Variable resistors known as potentiometers are used to control the volume of music in loudspeakers. When the volume control is turned clockwise, the resistance of the potentiometer is decreased, the current to the loud speakers is increased, and the volume therefore increases.

Electric Heating: Electric energy is transformed into heat when passed through materials with high resistivities such as tungsten and nichrome. Toasters, electric skillets, waffle irons, electric blankets, heat lamps, space heaters, hair dryers, irons, freezer defrosters, window defoggers, and hot-dog cookers are but a few of the devices that rely upon resistive heating.

Household Wiring: Most houses are built with three or four electric circuits, each of which is controlled by a 15-amp fuse or circuit breaker. Rooms that have appliances requiring much electricity (bathrooms, kitchens, and laundry rooms) are generally on different circuits to avoid overloading any one circuit when multiple appliances are in use.

"High-Tech" Christmas Lights: Traditionally, Christmas lights have been arranged in series, so when one bulb goes out the entire line goes out, making it difficult to locate the bad bulb. To deal with this problem, manufacturers produce lamps that short-circuit across the filament when it breaks, thereby offering virtually no resistance to the line. As a result, the remainder of the line stays lit. However, there is now a higher voltage across each remaining bulb because of the removal of bulbs from the system. If the offending bulbs are not replaced, the remaining bulbs may burn out prematurely due to excessive voltage.

Flashlights: It is possible to increase the *emf* in a circuit by adding batteries in series. For example, 6-volt flashlight bulbs can be powered by four 1.5-volt batteries added in series.

8.3 MAGNETISM

The carrier (homing) pigeon has a remarkable ability to return to its home after being transported long distances. Since the time of Christ, travelers have used carrier pigeons to deliver messages to their homes, and military spies have used them to report enemy positions to their leaders. Today, the raising and racing of homing pigeons is a popular hobby, and pigeon clubs sponsor races of distances in excess of 800 kilometers (500 miles). For years scientists have studied the homing instincts of carrier pigeons and have concluded that, among other things, pigeons can detect variations in the magnetic field of the Earth and use this information to orient themselves as they navigate their way home.

Recent research has revealed the presence of minute amounts of magnetite (magnetic iron oxide) in the human brain, causing some physiologists to hypothesize that magnetic fields may exert minor influence upon humans, but it is unclear as to what such influence might be. Although we do not have specialized sensory organs for detecting magnetic fields such as homing pigeons possess, we have developed numerous products that make use of magnetic fields. Electric generators, motors, loudspeakers, telephone receivers, audio-tape players, video cameras, computer monitors, microwave ovens, electric clocks, washing machines, mixers, circuit breakers, doorbells, automatic switches, junkyard cranes, computer disk drives, hearing aids, and metal detectors are but a few of the devices that require magnetic fields to operate. How would your life be different if inventors and engineers of the past had not applied the principles of magnetism to the development of practical products?

The ancient Greeks first noted that certain stones from the region of Magnesia in Asia Minor were capable of attracting iron. These stones became known as "magnetite," and their unusual property was termed "magnetism." Fascinated with the attractive force of magnetite, Ptolemy Philadelphos of Egypt plated the entire surface of a temple with it, vainly hoping to suspend an iron idol of himself in mid-air. By the twelfth century, it was noticed that magnetite oriented in a north/south direction, and inventors in both China and Italy capitalized on this property to develop the magnetic compass, one of the key inventions that made the Age of Exploration possible and forever changed the course of history. By the 1500s, Europeans employed compass navigation as they set sail to explore and colonize Africa, Asia, Australia, North America, South America, and the islands of the Pacific.

Although magnetism was first believed to be a fundamental force, physicists of the nineteenth century inferred that *magnetism results from the motion of electric charges and should therefore be considered as part of a larger phenomenon now known as electromagnetism. A magnetic field (a region where magnetic force may be detected) is produced by the movement of electric charges. Magnetism results when electrons spin on their axes or when electrons flow through conductors. If there is no movement of electric charge, there is no magnetic field.*

Magnetic fields are formed as electrons spin on their axes, but such fields are generally canceled by fields associated with electrons with opposing spins. The electrons of aluminum and copper pair precisely so their magnetic fields cancel, causing these metals to show no permanent magnetic properties. By contrast, 2 of the 26 electrons in iron do not pair, but rather maintain their north poles fixed rigidly in the same direction. The unpaired spins of these two electrons create a magnetic field around each iron atom. *If the atoms in a piece of iron are randomly arranged, the magnetic fields will cancel, but if aligned in the same direction, a magnetic field will exist.* This is what occurs in a permanent magnet.

Magnetic fields are also formed when electrons move through conductors. As electrons flow through the coils in the electromagnet of a junkyard crane, a magnetic field is created and cars are lifted. When, however, the current is terminated, the magnetic field collapses and the cars are dropped.

Although electric charges can exist in isolation, it appears that *magnetic poles always occur in pairs.* Thus, a north pole is always accompanied by a south pole, and vice versa. *Just as opposite electric charges attract and like charges repel, so opposite magnetic poles attract and like poles repel. While scientists can describe such forces, they cannot explain why they occur.* In this chapter you will have the opportunity to investigate magnetism for yourself.

8.3.1 Magnetic Domains

Concepts to Investigate: Magnetic domains, magnetization, demagnetization.

Materials: Test tube, stopper, iron filings (or steel wool), strong bar magnet, compass.

Principles and Procedures: Certain metals, such as iron, nickel, cobalt, gadolinium, and dysprosium are classified as "magnetic" because they experience a force when placed in a magnetic field. Evidence suggests that the magnetic properties of such metals result from the orbiting and spinning of their electrons. In nonmagnetic elements these fields cancel, but in magnetic elements they do not.

Although atoms of iron, nickel, cobalt, gadolinium, and dysprosium are magnetic, chunks of these metals are not always magnetized. The domain theory of magnetism was introduced to explain why materials made from magnetic atoms may exist either in magnetized or nonmagnetized form. *This theory posits that all ferromagnetic substances (materials strongly attracted to magnets) consist of many small regions of atoms known as magnetic domains.* Although the atoms within a magnetic domain have the same magnetic orientation (Figure A), each domain may differ from those around it. *If the domains are randomly arranged (Figure B), the fields cancel, leaving no net magnetic field. If, however, the domains are aligned (Figure C), the magnetic fields add, creating a magnetic field.* In this activity you will investigate the domain theory of magnetism using a magnet made from iron filings. For purposes of analogy, each filing may be considered as a magnetic domain. (In reality, each filing may be composed of many domains with diameters of approximately 0.01 mm).

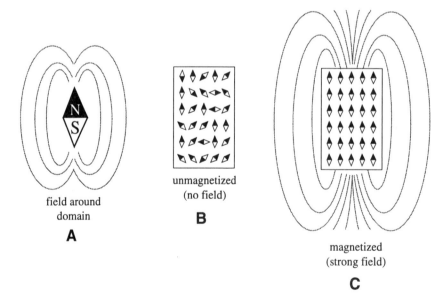

field around
domain

A

unmagnetized
(no field)

B

magnetized
(strong field)

C

Fill a test tube two thirds full with iron filings or shredded steel wool and approach the north and then the south end of a compass needle with the end of the tube, as shown in Figure D. Is one end of the needle more attracted than the other? Record the maximum angle to which the needle is deflected. Repeat these observa-

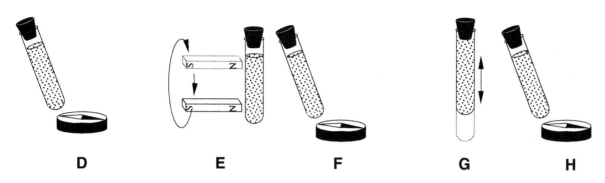

tions after stroking the tube 50 times with a permanent magnet (Figures E and F) and again after shaking the test tube vigorously for one minute (Figures G and H). In which situation was the test tube most highly magnetized? Why?

Questions

(1) Under which conditions did the test tube behave like a magnet? Explain.

(2) Did the tube's magnetic field increase or decrease after shaking? Why?

(3) Magnet manufacturers do not warranty their products against dropping. Why?

(4) How can you demagnetize a "permanent" magnet? Explain.

8.3.2 Magnetization

Concepts to Investigate: Earth's magnetic field, Curie temperature, magnetic compass, magnetic induction, demagnetization, making permanent magnets.

Materials: Hammer, compass, Bunsen burner, large nails, permanent magnet, thread, tongs or pliers.

Principles and Procedures: The first permanent magnets were fashioned from naturally occurring magnetite (Fe_3O_4). Today permanent magnets are made from alloys and compounds of ferromagnetic materials including iron, nickel, cobalt, gadolinium, dysprosium, samarium, neodymium, and boron. The strong magnets in loudspeakers, for instance, are made of Alnico, an alloy of aluminum, nickel, and cobalt. Whether naturally occurring magnetite, or artificial Alnico, all permanent magnets are made by exposure to an external magnetic field. The external field induces alignment of magnetic domains so their magnetic fields add rather than cancel.

Part 1. Magnetization by heating and cooling within a strong magnetic field: If a "permanent" magnet is heated above a critical temperature, domains disappear and it loses its ferromagnetic properties. This temperature is called the Curie temperature, discovered by Pierre Curie, in the early 1900s. If a metal is allowed to cool after being heated to the Curie temperature, new magnetic domains form and align with the existing magnetic field.

Use insulated tongs or pliers to heat a nail in the hottest part of the flame (the tip of the internal light-blue flame) until it glows. Remove the nail from the flame and place it lengthwise on a permanent bar magnet, as illustrated in Figure I. After the nail has cooled, measure its magnetic strength by determining the number of small paper clips that can be suspended in a chain from one end (Figure J). Compare the magnetic strength of this nail with the strength of one that was not heated, but rested on the permanent bar magnet for an equal length of time. Record your findings in the table.

Part 2. Magnetization by exposure to the Earth's magnetic field: In Part 1 it was shown that magnets form when ferromagnetic materials cool within strong magnetic fields. Is it possible that such metals will magnetize as they cool when exposed only to the weak magnetic field of the Earth? Heat two nails and allow one to cool in a north/south direction, and the other in an east/west direction on a ceramic or glass sheet, far away from any permanent magnets. Position a third nail in an east/west direction, and a fourth nail in a north/south direction on a hard, nonmetallic surface. Gently but firmly strike these unheated nails with a hammer three times (Figure K). Suspend all four nails by thread, allow them to hang in still air for 10 minutes, and compare their orientations with that of a magnetic compass (Figure L). Which nails act as compasses? Why? Compare the magnetic-field strength of these nails with the strength of the nails in Part 1 by comparing the number of paper clips each can support. Report your results in the table. Which method (Part 1 or 2) creates the strongest magnets? Will the magnetized nails still act as compasses if they are struck with a hammer while oriented east/west? Try it.

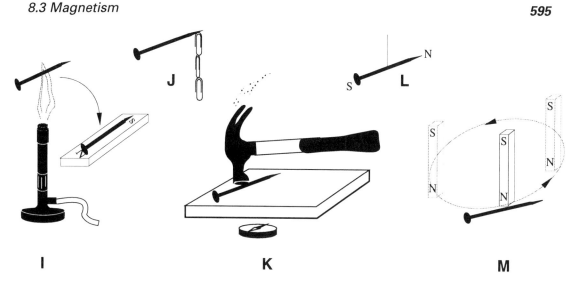

Part 3. Magnetization by stroking with a permanent magnet: A third way to make magnets is by stroking them with a permanent magnet, as illustrated in Figure M. Stroke a nail 30 times in the same direction with a strong bar magnet, removing the magnet from the nail between strokes. Qualitatively determine the strength of the nail's magnetic field by determining the number of small paper clips it can support in a chain and report your results in the table. How does the strength of this magnet compare with the strength of those made in Parts 1 and 2?

Part	Treatment	Does it act as a compass?	Number of Paper Clips Supported
1	Heated; cooled on bar magnet	_____	_____
1	Unheated; rested on bar magnet	_____	_____
2	Heated; cooled in N/S direction	_____	_____
2	Heated; cooled in E/W direction	_____	_____
2	Struck with hammer in N/S direction	_____	_____
2	Struck with hammer in E/W direction	_____	_____
3	Stroked with permanent magnet	_____	_____

Questions

(1) How many more paper clips can the heated nail of part 1 support than the unheated nail? Why does it have greater magnetic strength?

(2) Which orientation produces a stronger magnet in part 2? Explain.

(3) How can a nail be magnetized when struck with a hammer?

(4) Upon completion of the construction of an iron ship, the builders place a plaque in the bridge that records the orientation in which the ship was made. Why do they bother?

(5) Every iron atom in a nail is a miniature magnet, but not all nails are magnetized. Explain.

(6) Geologists believe that the core of the Earth is made largely of iron and nickel. Knowing that the Curie point is 770°C for iron and 358°C for nickel and that the temperature of the Earth's core is 4500°C, is it possible that the Earth's core acts as a large iron/nickel bar magnet? Explain.

8.3.3 Magnetic Poles

Concepts to Investigate: N- and S-poles; magnetic attraction and repulsion; magnetic dipoles, magnetic levitation.

Materials: Compass, strong bar magnet, circular ring magnets, glass or plastic funnel, iron or steel wire, Bunsen burner, sewing needle, thread, wire cutters.

Principles and Procedures: Magnets usually have well-defined poles at which their field strengths are greatest. If a magnet is suspended by a thread (Figure L), it will orient with respect to the Earth's magnetic field. The pole of the magnet that points toward the geographic north pole is considered to be the "north-seeking," or N-pole, while the other end is considered to be the "south-seeking," or S-pole.

Part 1. Forces between magnetic poles: Note that the N-pole of a compass is repelled by the N-pole of a permanent magnet, but attracted by the S-pole. Simple observations such as this illustrate that like poles repel and unlike poles attract. Suspend an unmagnetized steel sewing needle and approach the tip first with the N-pole and then with the S-pole of a permanent magnet (Figure N). In each case, is the needle attracted or repelled? Magnetize the needle by stroking it 30 times in the same direction with a permanent magnet, as illustrated in Figure M (Activity 8.3.2) and again approach the tip with the N- and S-poles of the bar magnet. Contrast the movement of the unmagnetized needle with the movement of the magnetized needle. How should you stroke the needle so the tip becomes N?

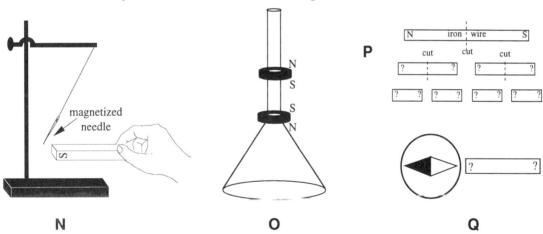

N   **O**   **Q**

Part 2. Magnetic levitation: In the 1980s, engineers in Japan and Europe developed trains that are lifted above the tracks and propelled forward by magnetic forces. Such maglev (magnetic levitation) trains travel at speeds in excess of 200 km/h and provide passengers with a comfortable, nearly vibration-free ride. To levitate a train it is necessary that the track have the same polarity as the base of the train. If it is possible to levitate a train by facing like poles toward each other, then it must certainly be possible to levitate simple magnets as well. Place a strong ring-shaped magnet over the tube of an inverted funnel (Figure O). Then slide a second magnet over the tube such that like poles of the two magnets face each other. Is the second magnet levitated by the interaction of its magnetic field with the field of the first magnet? Determine the maximum number of magnets that can be levitated in this fashion.

Part 3. Dipoles or monopoles: What happens to the polarity of a magnet if it is cut in half? Does one half become the N-pole and the other the S-pole, or do both halves contain N- and S-poles as the original? To answer this question, magnetize a section of iron wire using either the heating or stroking techniques described in the previous activity. Test the polarities of the wire by approaching each end with a compass. An N-pole will repel the N-pole and attract the S-pole of a compass. After determining the polarity of the wire, cut it in half with a pair of wire cutters and test the polarities of each half (Figures P and Q). Continue cutting each remaining section in half until the resulting pieces are too small to handle and test. Upon the basis of your observations, does it appear that magnets exist as monopoles, or that they always have both an N and a S-pole?

Questions

(1) How must you stroke a needle so that the point becomes a N-pole (Part 1)?
(2) Does the magnet in part 1 exert a greater, equal, or lesser force upon the suspended needle than the needle exerts on the magnet? Explain.
(3) How high above the base magnet was the first magnet levitated in Part 2? How could you achieve greater levitation?
(4) Based upon your observations in Part 3, do magnets exist as monopoles or dipoles? Explain.

8.3.4 Magnetic Fields

Concepts to Investigate: Magnetic lines of flux, magnetic fields, magnetic flux density, monopoles, magnetic attraction, magnetic repulsion, magnetic field interaction.

Materials: Bar magnet, horseshoe magnet, sewing needle, cake pan, Styrofoam or cork, plastic sheet, iron filings or old steel-wool pads, jar, salad oil.

Principles and Procedures: One of the dangers of space travel is cosmic radiation, composed of nuclei of various atoms that travel through the universe at speeds approaching that of light. Fortunately, these charged particles are deflected by or trapped within Earth's magnetic field and therefore rarely reach us. In 1958, data collected by the American satellite *Explorer I* confirmed the existence of large belts of high-energy protons and electrons trapped in two sets of doughnut-shaped rings 3,000 and 15,000 kilometers above Earth. Although it is comforting to realize that magnetic fields are protecting us from damaging radiation, just what are magnetic fields and what are their properties and characteristics?

Part 1. Magnetic lines of flux: *A magnetic field is a region in which a magnetic force can be detected. A magnetic field can be illustrated by magnetic lines of flux, which are lines that imaginary N-monopoles would follow if placed within a magnetic field.* Although we cannot create N-monopoles, we can illustrate their behavior by floating a dipole in water such that the N-pole is much closer to the magnet than the S-pole is. To give the tip of a needle a N polarity, stroke it from head to tip 30 times with the S-pole of a permanent magnet. Check the polarity of the sewing needle with a compass to ensure it is correct. The tip of the needle is N if it repels the N-pole of a compass. Stick the needle through a thin, flat, round piece of cork or Styrofoam. Place a strong bar magnet under a glass cake pan or other transparent container and fill the container with water so the tip of the needle floats approximately 1 millimeter above the bottom (Figure R). Release the needle in the locations specified in Figure S and draw the paths it travels. On your diagram indicate where field strength is greatest (where field lines are closest together) and where it is least (where field lines are farthest apart). To study the movement of N-monopoles around the poles of a magnet, polar-

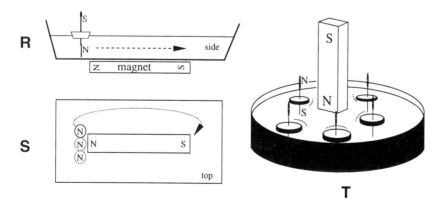

ize the needles so the exposed ends are N-poles and examine their movement, as illustrated in Figure T. Do N-monopoles move toward or away from N-poles?

Part 2. Magnetic fields in two dimensions: Place a strong bar magnet under a clear sheet of glass, Plexiglas, or plastic. (Transparent report covers and overhead transparencies work well.) Position the transparent sheet so it is level and then repeatedly tap a beaker filled with iron filings so they fall evenly over the surface (Figure U). If clumps of filings remain, tap the sheet gently to redistribute them. The iron filings should align themselves with the magnetic lines of flux (Figure V). The points where lines appear to converge represent locations of greatest magnetic flux density. *Magnetic flux density is a measure of magnetic force and is defined as the number of flux lines per unit area.* Is magnetic flux density greatest near the middle of the bar magnet or near the ends? Use the same procedure to examine and draw the magnetic fields of bar magnets and horseshoe magnets positioned as shown in Figures W, X, and Y. Do the patterns show that like poles repel and unlike poles attract? In addition to examining magnetic fields with iron filings, you may also examine them with compasses. Place a number of small compasses around a magnet as illustrated in Figure Z and draw a diagram showing the orientation of the needles. (If you have only one compass, simply move it from location to location until you can complete your diagram.)

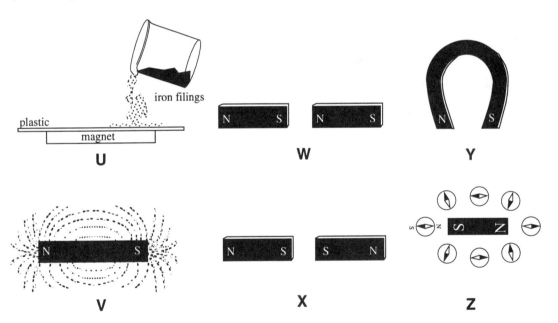

© 1994 by John Wiley & Sons, Inc.

Part 3. Magnetic fields in three dimensions: The three-dimensional aspect of magnetic fields may be examined using the set-up illustrated in Figure AA. Place iron filings in the bottom of a glass jar and fill 90 percent of the remainder of the jar with salad oil. (If you don't have iron filings, you may create iron shreds by rubbing two pieces of steel wool together rapidly.) Shake the container vigorously until the iron filings are evenly distributed throughout the container and then expose the jar to the magnetic fields of bar magnets as shown. Allow time for the iron filings to align with the magnetic field. Draw a diagram of the field lines when the S-pole of one magnet is opposite the N-pole of another, as illustrated in Figure BB.

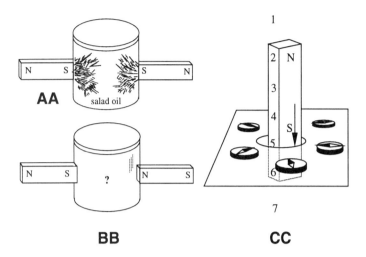

Alternately, you may generate a three-dimensional representation of the field surrounding a bar magnet by drawing diagrams showing the direction of the compass needles surrounding the magnet at each of the seven stations illustrated in Figure CC. Examine the three-dimensional nature of the field by placing all seven diagrams in sequence.

Questions

(1) Compare your field diagrams for the bar and horseshoe magnets. Which appears to possess the stronger magnetic field? Explain.

(2) Examine the field diagram for the case in which the S-poles of two bar magnets face each other. Do the field lines from the two magnets connect? What does this suggest?

(3) Examine the field diagram when the N-pole of one bar magnet faces the S-pole of the other. Do the field lines from the two magnets connect? What does this suggest?

(4) Draw a diagram of the Earth's magnetic field. Where is magnetic flux density greatest?

(5) Charged particles moving through a magnetic field experience greatest deflection when they move at right angles to field lines, and least deflection when they move parallel to field lines. Are you more likely to encounter harmful cosmic radiation (high-energy charged nuclei) at the poles or at the equator? Explain.

8.3.5 Magnetic Force

Concepts to Investigate: Magnetic force, magnetic induction, residual magnetism, retentivity, Coulomb's law of magnetism, inverse square law.

Materials: Strong bar magnet, ring stand and clamp, paper clips, toothpick, rubber bands, monofilament fishing line or suitable substitute, black-and-white TV or oscilloscope.

Principles and Procedures: A cyclotron is a device used to study the basic nature of protons and other fundamental particles. Protons (hydrogen nuclei) are accelerated to extreme speeds and then collided with other particles. Surprisingly, the world's strongest magnets are required to keep these infinitesimally small particles orbiting in their spiral paths. *Magnetic forces, like all forces, are capable of altering the motion of objects.* The stronger the force, the greater its ability to alter an object's motion. In these activities you will examine magnetic force.

Part 1. Magnetic force and magnetic induction: When the N-pole of a magnet is brought near a piece of iron, the magnetic domains within the iron reorient so their S-poles face the magnet's N-pole. This reorientation occurs because unlike poles attract. If enough domains reorient, the block of iron develops a measurable magnetic field of its own opposite to the field of the magnet that induced it. The stronger the magnetic field, the greater the degree of magnetic induction within the iron. You can test the field strength of a bar magnet by suspending paper clips along its length, as illustrated in Figure DD. The number of paper clips that can be suspended in a line is directly related to the field strength. Where along the length of the magnet is magnetic force greatest? Where is it least? Compare the strengths of a variety of different bar and horseshoe magnets.

   If you carefully remove a chain of paper clips you may notice that some retain their magnetic attraction to each other (Figure EE). This indicates that many of the magnetic domains within the iron have retained the orientation they received while

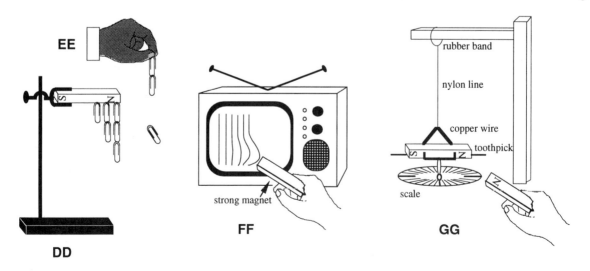

EE

DD

rubber band

nylon line

copper wire

toothpick

scale

strong magnet

FF

GG

in the field of the permanent magnet. This phenomenon is known as residual magnetism and varies as a function of the retentivity of the material of which it is made. *If a material is highly retentive it maintains its magnetism well in the absence of an external magnetic field.* Should permanent magnets be made from materials with high or low retentivity?

Part 2. Magnetic force on moving electrons: Televisions, computer monitors, and oscilloscopes contain cathode ray tubes in which a beam of electrons is aimed at a phosphorescent screen. Electrons are negatively charged and are pushed or pulled by magnetic fields in a direction perpendicular to the direction of their motion. Place a magnet on the screen of an *old* black-and-white monitor, television screen, or oscilloscope (Figure FF). (DO NOT use a color TV or monitor because the magnet can permanently magnetize the grid that sits immediately beneath glass.) Where is the distortion greatest? How does distortion vary with distance from the magnet? If you are able to generate a vertical or horizontal test pattern on the screen, you can measure the deflection of the lines and see if it follows the inverse square law discussed in the following activity.

Part 3. Coulomb's law of magnetism (inverse square law): Coulomb's law of magnetism states that:

$$F = k \; \frac{M_1 M_2}{d^2}$$

where F is the force between poles, k is a constant, M_1 and M_2 are the strengths of the poles, and d is the distance between them. Like the law of electrostatics and the law of gravitation, the law of magnetism shows that force decreases as the square of the distance between two poles. If, for example, the distance between two poles is reduced by half, the force between them increases four times, and if the distance between two poles is tripled, the force between them is reduced by a factor of nine. It is possible to investigate Coulomb's law of magnetism using the torsion balance illustrated in Figure GG. Suspend a magnet from a wooden support with a nylon fishing line and a cradle made of copper or another nonferromagnetic material. Both the top and the bottom of the line must be anchored with stiff rubber bands to provide resistance. Tape a toothpick to the magnet to facilitate making measurements on the protractor scale below. Position the N-pole of another magnet of equal strength 20 centimeters from the N-pole of the hanging magnet and record the angle of deflection using the scale. Move the magnet 1 centimeter closer and once again record the deflection. Record the deflection for every centimeter interval from 20 centimeters to 1 centimeter. Plot your results on graph paper. Do your results agree with the inverse square law?

Questions

(1) Where is the magnetic force greatest around a bar magnet? Where is it least? How do you know?

(2)   A chain of paper clips can hang at the end of the N-pole of a magnet as a result of magnetic induction. These paper clips may continue to hang together by induction after being removed from the magnet. Will the paper clips separate if the top clip is approached with the S-pole of a magnet? Explain.

(3)   The strongest permanent magnets are made of cobalt-samarium or iron-neodymium-boron. Do the compounds in these magnets have high or low retentivity? Explain.

(4)   A TV or computer screen is composed of thousands of picture cells (pixels) that glow or remain dark depending on whether they are struck by a beam of electrons. The beam of electrons that illuminates the screen does so many times a second. How is the electron beam directed to the various portions of the screen?

(5)   How much more does the torsion balance rotate when the distance between like poles is cut in half? In quarter?

8.3.6 Magnetic Shielding

Concepts to Investigate: Magnetic shielding, magnetic flux density, magnetic permeability.

Materials: Strong bar magnet, paper clip, thread, "tin" cans of various sizes, compass, paper or plastic cups of various sizes.

Principles and Procedures: Whenever a nuclear weapon is detonated, it releases a brief, intense electromagnetic pulse (EMP) that propagates for thousands of kilometers and can cause serious damage to electronic equipment. It is believed that a single high-altitude detonation over the central part of the United States could seriously damage the nation's communications system and make it difficult to respond to the attack. Military analysts have warned that our electronic communication and computer systems are extremely vulnerable to an EMP attack and have therefore encouraged manufacturers to shield important electronic components from intense magnetic fields. But how can you shield something from a magnetic field? Perform the following activities to find out.

Part 1. Magnetic "floating": Support a bar magnet as illustrated in Figure HH. Attach a thread to a paper clip and suspend it below the magnet as shown. Adjust the thread to locate the position farthest from the magnet where the paper clip will still "float." Given no disturbances, the paper clip will remain positioned in space indefinitely due to magnetic lines of force between the magnet and the paper clip. Slide a small sheet of paper in the gap between the paper clip and the magnet, being careful not to touch either. Does paper interfere with the magnetic field? Repeat the process using a sheet of plastic, aluminum foil, and the lid of a "tin" can ("tin" cans are made mostly of iron). Which, if any of the above, interfered with the magnetic field and allowed the paper clip to fall?

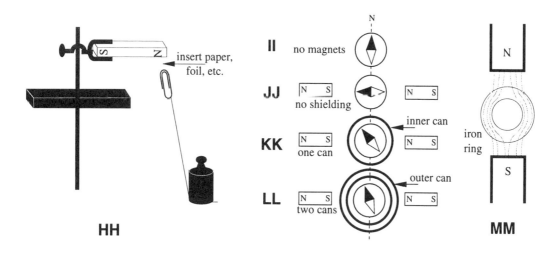

Part 2: Magnetic shielding: Cut the bottoms from two paper cups of different sizes, two plastic cups of different sizes, and two iron ("tin") cans of different sizes. Place a compass on a table and record the direction of magnetic north (Figure II). Now place two bar magnets 7 centimeters to the east and west of the compass so that the N-pole of one magnet faces the S-pole of the other (Figure JJ) and record the angle of deflection. Remove the magnets, place a tin can over the compass, replace the magnets, and again record the angle of needle deflection (Figure KK). Remove the magnets, place a second can around the first, replace the magnets, and again record the angle of compass-needle deflection (Figure LL). Does iron interfere with the magnetic field? Repeat the process using paper or plastic cups. Which of the substances best protects or shields the compass from the magnetic field of the bar magnets? Do two iron cans or cups provide better shielding than one alone? Figure MM illustrates how shielding material alters the magnetic lines of force and can protect instrumentation from magnetic fields. The material illustrated is known to have a high magnetic permeability because field lines permeate it more easily than the surrounding atmosphere. Which of the materials you tested has the highest magnetic permeability?

Questions

(1) How do paper and plastic affect magnetic fields?
(2) Which material provides the best shielding from external magnetic fields?
(3) Which of the materials tested in Part 2 has the highest magnetic permeability? Explain.

8.3.7 Geomagnetism

Concepts to Investigate: Earth's magnetic field, magnetic declination, magnetic dip (magnetic inclination), magnetic north and south poles.

Materials: Compass, knitting needle, washers, thread, sewing needle, cork.

Principles and Procedures: Although the Earth behaves as a giant magnet, the magnetic N- and S-poles are rather mobile and do not coincide with geographic north and south poles. By comparing maps made during the past 100 years, you will notice that the location of the magnetic N- and S-poles tend to wander. At times the magnetic north pole has been located on Bathurst Island, and at other times it has been located in the waters between the islands in Canada's Northwest Territories. Figure NN shows that the magnetic axis of the Earth is slightly different from the axis of rotation.

When using a compass to orient a map, it is important to realize that the magnetic north pole is actually located 1,800 kilometers from the geographic North Pole, in the direction of Chicago, Illinois. If you live in Chicago, you will not need to correct for this difference because magnetic north and true north are on the same longitudinal line that goes through Chicago. If, however, you live in Vancouver, British Columbia, magnetic north is 24 degrees to the east of true north, and so you must compensate by shifting the angle of your map 24 degrees to the west to align with true north. Compensating for the angle of magnetic declination is extremely important for sailors, backpackers, aviators, and others who navigate using a map and compass. Use a globe to estimate the angle of magnetic declination for your city and compare this value with the value printed on a topographic map of your region.

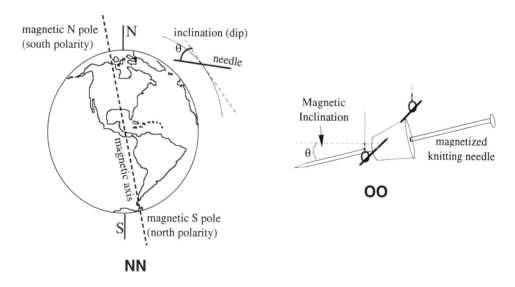

The strength of the Earth's magnetic field varies like that of a bar magnet, strongest at the poles and weakest at the equator. In addition, the angles of magnetic flux lines vary across the surface of the Earth, vertical at the magnetic poles and tangential to the Earth's surface at the magnetic equator. Consequently, the angle of the magnetic flux lines are correlated with the strength of the magnetic field. The steeper the angle of magnetic dip, the greater the magnetic strength. If the field lines in your area are inclined at 90°, then you must be standing immediately over a pole where the field strength is greatest. If the field lines are parallel to the surface of the Earth, the inclination is zero and you must be near the equator, where magnetic fields are weakest. It is possible to measure the angle of magnetic dip and make inferences about field strengths using the magnetic dip (inclination) needle shown in Figure OO.

To make a magnetic dip needle, push an unmagnetized knitting needle through a cork and a sewing needle at right angles to it, as illustrated. Balance the apparatus between the rims of two glasses or from suspended washers, as shown. The apparatus should be arranged so the tip of the knitting needle points toward the magnetic north pole. Carefully push the knitting needle back and forth through the cork until it is balanced in a horizontal position. Use a carpenter's level to determine if it is horizontal. Now magnetize the knitting needle by stroking it with a permanent magnet. Starting from the cork, stroke toward the tip using the S end of the magnet. After stroking this half 30 times, stroke the other half an equal number of times with the N-pole of the magnet, moving from the cork to the head of the needle. By stroking the needle in this fashion, the tip acquires a N polarity while the head acquires a S polarity. Place the apparatus back on its supports and allow it to stabilize. Use a protractor to measure the angle of dip (the difference between the current angle and the horizontal position, Figure OO).

Questions

(1) The magnetic north pole is currently located on Bathurst Island in Northern Canada. Use a globe to determine where the magnetic south pole is located.

(2) Does a compass point toward the S-pole if you are in Australia or Argentina? Explain.

(3) Determine the angle of magnetic declination of your city either by examining a topographical map of your area (the declination is printed on the bottom), or by using a protractor and a globe. Magnetic declination is the angle between true north and magnetic north.

(4) What is the angle of magnetic dip at your city measured with the device you built?

(5) The N-poles of compasses point towards what is commonly called the magnetic north pole, but we know that like poles repel each other. How can this be? What must be the actual magnetic polarity of the magnetic north pole?

FOR THE TEACHER

Magnetism is a force produced by the movement of charges, particularly electrons. Electrons orbit the nuclei of atoms and also spin on their axes the way the Earth spins on its axis. *It is the spinning of electrons, not their orbiting, that contributes to the properties we associate with permanent magnets.* Electrons can spin in either of two directions, + ("clockwise") or − ("counterclockwise"). Electrons spinning in opposite directions tend to form pairs, neutralizing their magnetic character. The ferromagnetic materials (materials strongly attracted by magnets) are characterized by a spin imbalance. In iron, for example, 24 of the 26 electrons pair, leaving 2 spinning in the same direction. It is these 2 electrons that give iron atoms their magnetic properties.

Whenever charges move, a magnetic field is generated. Although many students can visualize the translational movement of electrons that causes electromagnetism, they often have difficulty understanding permanent magnetism because there is no apparent movement of electrical charge in a standard bar or horseshoe magnet. It is at this point that the atomic theory of matter should be re-introduced. Students should understand that it is the rotational movement of electrons that causes permanent magnetism, while the translational movement of electrons in a conductor causes electromagnetism.

The atomic theory suggests that negatively charged electrons constantly orbit positively charged nuclei within "electron clouds" of various shapes. Apparently, the magnetic fields of electrons in most elements cancel each other except when subjected to an external magnetic field, in which case their paths are altered to generate a magnetic field opposing the applied field. This weak repulsive property is known as diamagnetism and is not addressed in the activities.

Students should understand that all forms of magnetism (ferromagnetism, diamagnetism, paramagnetism, ferrimagnetism, antiferromagnetism, and electromagnetism) result from the movement of charges. It should also be made clear that all electric and magnetic phenomena are united by a single theory of electromagnetism expressed in mathematical form in Maxwell's equations.

8.3.1 Magnetic Domains

Discussion: This activity can be demonstrated to the entire class using an overhead projector and a compass with a transparent base. When a ferromagnetic material is placed in a magnetic field, magnetic domains may align with the field, or favorably oriented magnetic domains may increase in size at the expense of adjacent domains. If a large percentage of domains retain their alignment after the external field is removed, the material is considered to be "permanently magnetized." Certain materials such as soft iron rapidly lose their magnetic properties after external fields are removed and are therefore useful in the cores of electromagnets where it is necessary to "turn off" magnetic fields. Other materials, such as the aluminum/nickel/copper alloy Alnico retain their magnetic fields for longer periods and are therefore widely used in "permanent" magnets.

Answers (1) Originally, the tube attracted both the north and south poles, indicating that it was not magnetized. After stroking, it attracted one pole and repelled the other, indicating that it was now magnetized. Stroking the tube with a magnet aligned the magnetic fields of the individual filings and thus produced a larger magnetic field. (2) Shaking the test tube randomizes the magnetic orientation of the individual iron filings, and thus decreases the field strength of the tube. (3) Dropping a magnet will have a similar effect to shaking the test tube of iron filings. The individual domains or filings reorient and the net magnetic field decreases. (4) Permanent magnets can be demagnetized by striking them with a hammer in the absence of an external magnetic field. The domains settle in a random fashion, so the material is no longer magnetized.

8.3.2 Magnetization

Discussion: Although all three methods magnetize iron, the technique mentioned in Part 1 is most effective due to the mobility of magnetic domains and the strong magnetic field surrounding the permanent magnet. An impressive display of the Earth's magnetic field can be made if all students suspend magnetized nails by threads from the ceiling. Request students to magnetize all nails such that the tips of the nails are N and the heads are S. You can then show disturbances in the magnetic field by walking under the nails with a powerful permanent magnet.

Answers (1) When heated to the Curie temperature, the domains in a ferromagnetic material disappear. When the material cools, the domains re-form and align with the external magnetic field. The magnetic domains in the unheated nail maintain a more random orientation because their domains cannot easily reorient with the external field. (2) The nail oriented in a north/south direction will have a stronger magnetic field because the domains along its entire length, rather than just its width, align and reinforce each other. (3) Striking a nail disrupts magnetic domains, allowing them to align with the Earth's magnetic field as they re-form. (4) The iron in a ship is repeatedly struck by hammers and rivet guns during the process of construction. The magnetic domains in the iron of the ship are thereby disrupted, and when they re-form they align with the Earth's magnetic field. As a result, the ship becomes a permanent magnet possessing a field that must be accounted for when taking compass bearings. (5) If the iron atoms are not aligned, their magnetic fields will cancel and the nail will not possess a magnetic field. (6) Above the Curie point, magnetic domains disappear and ferromagnetic materials cannot act as permanent magnets. Consequently, the magnetic field of the Earth must be produced by a different process, perhaps as a result of electric currents surrounding the Earth's core.

8.3.3 Magnetic Poles

Discussion: All these activities may be performed as teacher demonstrations. By suspending bar magnets by threads, and approaching them with other bar magnets, students can easily see the effect of the forces between magnetic poles. Students are fascinated by magnetic levitation. If you are unable to find ring-shaped magnets, you can perform this same demonstration using solid-disc magnets in a graduated cylinder or Plexiglas tube. The internal diameter of the tube should be only slightly larger than the magnets or they may invert and attract rather than repel and levitate.

The activity discussed in Part 3 illustrates that magnets exist as dipoles rather than as monopoles. Figure PP shows that the polarity of domains within the original magnet ensures that each magnet produced by cutting has N- and S-poles. It should be noted, however, that some physicists believe that magnetic monopoles exist and that their discovery would help substantiate the Grand Unification Theory that seeks to unify all of physics within a single comprehensive framework. Despite their efforts, however, only one report of a monopole is found in the literature, and their existence is therefore highly suspect.

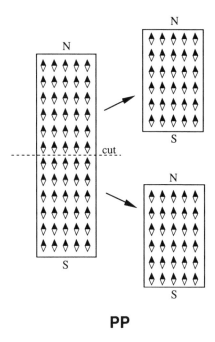

PP

Answers (1) The needle will develop a N-pole at the point if it is stroked with the S-pole of a permanent magnet from the head to the tip, or with the N-pole of permanent magnet from the tip to the head. (2) Newton's third law states that for every action force, there is an equal and opposing reaction force. Therefore, the needle and magnet exert forces of equal magnitude on each other. (3) Greater levitation can be achieved if a higher percentage of the domains in either magnet are aligned, resulting in a stronger magnetic field and greater repulsion. (4) Regardless of the number of cuts, the pieces always have one N-pole and one S-pole, suggesting that all magnets exist as dipoles.

8.3.4 Magnetic Fields

Discussion: Magnetic fields can be demonstrated to the entire class by performing the activities discussed in part 2 on an overhead projector. If you wish to preserve these field diagrams, you may do so by sprinkling iron filings onto a sheet of wax paper that rests on the sheet of glass that is positioned over the magnet. Once a field diagram is created, place the glass plate and wax paper on top of a hot plate (Figure QQ). Slowly heat until the wax melts and the iron filings become imbedded. Upon cooling, students will have a permanent record of the magnetic fields they investigated.

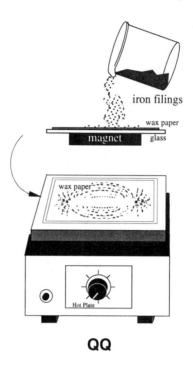

iron filings

wax paper

magnet   glass

wax paper

QQ

Answers (1) The magnetic flux density is greater between the poles of a horseshoe magnet than a bar magnet, indicating the horseshoe magnet has a greater magnetic field. (2) The field lines from two similar poles do not meet, suggesting that the fields repel each other. An imaginary N-monopole released near the N-pole of one magnet will move to the S-pole of the same magnet and will never reach the other magnet along these lines. (3) The field lines are continuous between opposing poles of the two magnets, suggesting that opposite poles attract. An imaginary N-monopole released on the field lines near the N-pole of one magnet will travel to the S-pole of the other magnet. (4) The magnetic field of Earth is similar to the field of a bar magnet tilted at a slight angle. The flux densities will be greatest at the magnetic north and south poles. (5) Cosmic radiation is greatest at the magnetic poles where field lines emanate from, or return to the Earth. Cosmic rays entering at this angle are parallel with the flux lines and are therefore not repelled into space.

8.3.5 Magnetic Force

Discussion: Display two metal bars and ask students if they can determine which is magnetized, using nothing other than the bars themselves. Eventually they may suggest you arrange the bars in a "T" formation. The two bars will stick together only if the magnetized bar forms the trunk of the "T" (Figure RR). It temporarily magnetizes the center of the metal bar by induction so that it has opposite polarity to the permanent magnet and is thereby attracted to it. If the magnet forms the crossbeam of the "T," there will be no attraction and the trunk will fall (Figure SS).

Answers (1) The magnetic force is greatest at the ends of the bar magnet because this is where the longest chain of paper clips is supported. Magnetic forces are least in the middle because few, if any, paper clips are supported there. (2) The paper clips

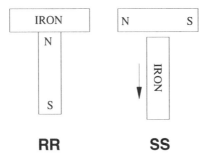

will separate as the S-pole of the magnet approaches the top clip. The magnet reverses the polarity of the top clip so it is N on top and S on the bottom. Since the top of the second clip still has a S polarity due to residual magnetization, it is repelled by the S-pole of the upper paper clip and the chain is broken. (3) Strong permanent magnets have high retentivity. Retentivity indicates the amount of time a substance will maintain its magnetic properties after an external magnetizing field is removed. (4) Electromagnets surrounding the tube quickly change polarity and magnitude in order to direct the electron beam across the screen. (5) If the torsion balance is accurate, students should observe the inverse square relationship between force and distance. As the separating distance is halved, the force is quadrupled and the needle moves approximately four times as far. If the separating distance is cut to one quarter, the force and needle displacement should be approximately 16 times as great.

8.3.6 Magnetic Shielding

Discussion: The activity in Part 1 makes an excellent classroom demonstration because students are fascinated to see paper clips suspended in space. In addition to illustrating the effect of magnetic shielding, this activity also illustrates magnetic fields. Position a number of paper clips around the magnet and note that they align with the magnetic lines of flux. It the field of the bar magnet is sufficiently strong, it is possible to "float" paper clips in a horizontal position.

Magnetic shielding can be easily demonstrated using either of the activities discussed in this section. In addition, you may wish to show the field lines by using the set-up described in Part 2 and then sprinkling iron filings over the entire surface. The iron will align with the magnetic lines of flux around the perimeter of the can, but within the can the iron will remain randomly arranged. By placing this set-up on the overhead projector, your students can clearly see the effect of magnetic shielding.

Answers (1) Interposing either of these materials in a magnetic field has no effect on the field strength or lines of flux. (2) Of the materials tested, the tin can provides the best magnetic shielding. "Tin cans" are made of iron with a thin coat of tin. (3) Iron alters magnetic lines of flux more than the other substances, indicating it has the greater magnetic permeability.

8.3.7 Geomagnetism

Discussion: Hikers and backpackers use topographic maps when venturing into wilderness. These maps indicate detailed topographic features and indicate the angle of magnetic declination so they may be correctly aligned with a magnetic compass. Show students how to orient such maps. Topographic maps may be obtained from sporting goods stores or directly from the United States Geological Survey (USGS).

Answers: (1) The magnetic south pole is located just off the coast of Antarctica, due south of Adelaide, Australia. (2) The field lines of the Earth are continuous from pole to pole just as are the field lines of a bar magnet. Thus, a compass continues to point to the magnetic north pole regardless of its position on the Earth's surface. (3) Angles of declination for major North American cities are: Halifax, 24°W; Boston, 15°W; New York, 10°W; Richmond, Virginia, 5°W; Chicago, 0°(on the agonic line; the line of zero declination); St. Louis, 5°E; Austin, 10°E; San Diego, 15°E; Los Angeles, 18°E; Portland, 20°E; and Vancouver, 25°E. (4) The angle of magnetic dip (or inclination) is 25–30° for most of the United States, Canada, Japan, and Europe. It is 0° along the magnetic equator in portions of Peru, Nigeria, Sri Lanka, and Thailand. (5) Magnetically, the magnetic north pole of the Earth is a S-pole. This is confusing for most students. Some of this confusion can be avoided if we consider the N-poles of compasses and magnets to be "north-seeking" poles rather than "north" poles.

Applications to Everyday Life

Videotapes, Audio Tapes, and Computer Disks: Videotapes, audio tapes, and computer disks contain a layer of a magnetic material (iron oxide, Fe_3O_4) imbedded in plastic. The recording head of a video camera, tape recorder, or computer-disk drive stores information on magnetic media by orienting magnetic domains of iron oxide. For example, the magnetic head on a computer disk drive may store the binary ASCII code for the letter "A" (01000001) as SNSSSSN, where "S" represents magnetic domains with a south orientation, and "N" represents domains with a north orientation. When the head reads this portion of the tape it detects the magnetic polarity of the individual domains and translates these into a signal that appears as an "A" on the computer monitor.

Magnetic Levitation Trains: A number of countries are developing maglev (magnetic levitation) trains supported and propelled by magnetic forces. When the "tracks" and the bottom of the train have the same magnetic polarity, the train is repelled and levitated. The train is accelerated by magnetic forces when the track in front has opposite polarity to the front of the train, and the track in back has like polarity to the back of the train.

Protecting Electronics: Sensitive electronic equipment is often placed inside iron or steel containers to protect it from strong magnetic fields. Iron and steel have high magnetic permeability, and as a result, magnetic field lines are redirected through the box, effectively bypassing the sensitive instruments inside.

Aging of Magnetic Tape: Videotapes, audio tapes, and computer diskettes slowly degrade as a result of exposure to magnetic fields. Information that is to be kept for archival purposes should therefore be shielded from magnetic fields, periodically transferred to other magnetic media, or transferred to an optical format such as compact discs.

Biomagnetism: Certain bacteria contain grains of magnetite that appear to serve as internal compasses. These magnetite grains align with the Earth's magnetic field and provide a sense of direction that the bacteria apparently use in locating food supplies. As discussed earlier, homing pigeons have special magnetite-containing tissues that are connected by nerves to various portions of their brains and apparently are involved in navigation. In 1992, researchers discovered the presence of magnetite in the human brain, but they don't yet know its function.

The Northern Lights: The violent thermonuclear reactions of stars release high energy atomic nuclei known collectively as cosmic rays. Some of these charged particles are captured in a portion of the Earth's magnetic field high above us. Occasionally, there are disturbances in the Earth's magnetic field and these particles dip into the atmosphere, striking molecules in the air and causing them to glow much the way gaseous molecules do in a fluorescent lamp. This colorful glowing is known as the

Aurora Borealis, or Northern Lights and can be seen during the night in northern regions such as Norway and Alaska.

Determining the Structure of Planets: German geologists have drilled the world's deepest well, 13.8 km (8.6 miles), in Bavaria, as part of a major geological investigation. Although this may seem deep, it is minuscule when you consider the Earth has a radius or "depth" of 6,371 km (3,960 miles). How then, can geologists predict the composition of the core or the Earth? The magnetic field or absence of a magnetic field provides some clues. The absence of a significant magnetic field around the moon, for example, has led scientists to believe it does not have a metallic core like the Earth.

Magnetic Fields Around Stars and Planets: The magnetic field of Jupiter is 4,000 times as strong as Earth's. The sun's magnetic field appears to reverse every 22 years and may be linked to the annual sunspot cycle that occurs every 11 years. The moon has no magnetic field.

Reversal of the Earth's Magnetic Field: Magnetite is an igneous, ferromagnetic rock. As magnetite grains cool, many align with the Earth's magnetic field, providing a record of the Earth's magnetic past. The field of paleomagnetism (study of ancient magnetic fields) suggests that the locations of Earth's magnetic poles have changed periodically. In other words, at certain times during the Earth's history a compass would have pointed south instead of north.

Security Cards: Many banks provide customers with magnetic cards to access electronic-teller and -payment machines (ATMs) at banks, shopping malls, and service stations. Such cards are equipped with a magnetic code linked with a personal identification number that the user must provide. Many hotels provide customers with magnetic cards to activate the locks to their rooms. When the customer checks out, the magnetic code of the key and lock are immediately changed, providing inexpensive access-security for the next customer.

Home Alarms: Some homes and businesses are equipped with magnetic alarms. A magnet is placed on the frame of a window and an electronic sensor placed opposite it on the window sill. If the window is opened, the sensor detects a change in magnetic flux and a signal is sent to activate the alarm.

8.4 ELECTROMAGNETISM

The past three centuries have witnessed a great number of political revolutions significantly influencing the course of world history. The American Revolution of 1776, the French Revolution of 1789, the Russian Revolution of 1917, and the Chinese Cultural Revolution of the 1960s are but a few of the political revolutions that have profoundly influenced our world. Important as these revolutions were, their influence has not been as pervasive as the peaceful, although sometimes painful, process known as the Industrial Revolution. While political revolutions have altered governmental systems, the Industrial Revolution has affected the way we work and live.

The Industrial Revolution, the process by which industrial productivity is increased by the substitution of machines for human and animal muscle power, began in England in the eighteenth century and continues to spread to virtually every society on the face of the Earth. The machines that began the revolution were powered by water or steam, but as the revolution progressed, electrical machines became increasingly popular.

In the early 1800s, the only devices capable of generating the electromotive force (*emf*) necessary to drive electric currents were voltaic cells. Since these cells could not generate much electric power, the first electric machines were mere novelties. Imagine trying to run an industry or even your household on dry cells and batteries alone. During the nineteenth century scientists discovered the principles of electromagnetism and developed the electric generator, a device capable of delivering large amounts of electric energy inexpensively. The generator fueled the Industrial Revolution and today produces nearly all of the world's electric power. The principles of electromagnetism also led to the development of electric motors now used in a wide variety of labor-saving devices.

Two nineteenth-century scientists, Michael Faraday and Joseph Henry, discovered *that electric current can be produced by changing the magnetic field in a conductor.* This phenomenon, known as electromagnetic induction, provides electricity to power the light by which you are reading, the printing presses that made this book, and the looms that made the fabric in the clothes you wear. Nearly everything you "plug in" uses electricity produced by electromagnetic induction. Generators convert mechanical energy into electric energy by moving coils of wire through a magnetic field. Mechanical energy may come from falling water (turbines in hydroelectric plants), expanding gas (coal burning electric-generation plants or gasoline-powered generators), steam (geothermal-power plants and nuclear-power plants), wind (windmills), or muscles (hand-crank magnetos). *When mechanical energy turns a coil in a magnetic field, an electric current is generated (generator effect). If the process is reversed and a current is sent through the coil, a magnetic field is created that interacts with the external magnetic field to turn the coil (motor effect).* Thus, the same device may serve as a generator or a motor.

The generators in power plants produce electric current that ultimately turns motors in our vacuum cleaners, fans, computer-disk drives, garage-door openers, electric-can openers, electric knives, and blenders, as well as the machines that manufacture the goods we consume. In this section you will investigate the principles and practical applications of electromagnetism.

8.4.1 Electromagnetic Fields

Concepts to Investigate: Electromagnetism, magnetic fields, Ampere's rule for straight conductors, galvanometer.

Materials: Dry cells, compasses, test leads with alligator clips, copper wire, iron filings.

Principles and Procedures: Scientists often learn much from accidents and bungled experiments. In 1896, the French physicist Antoine Becquerel discovered radioactivity after observing a photographic plate that had been ruined after sitting in the dark next to a rock containing uranium. In 1928, the English microbiologist Alexander Fleming discovered that a *Penicillium* mold that had accidentally contaminated a bacterial culture stopped the bacteria's growth. Fleming later showed the mold's antibacterial substance, penicillin, was effective in battling bacteria harmful to humans. In 1820, the Dutch physicist Hans Christian Oersted discovered that current-carrying wires generate a magnetic field while trying to demonstrate to his students just the opposite effect. The impact of such accidental discoveries is significant. Becquerel's discovery opened the way for the development of nuclear medicines, nuclear power plants, and nuclear warheads. Fleming's discovery led to the development of antibiotics and disease control. And Oersted's discovery led to the development of electrical power generation and the amazing array of electrical devices that fill our homes and businesses. In this activity you will perform Oersted's original "bungled" demonstration and study the magnetic fields that accompany current-carrying wires.

Part 1. Oersted's "unexpected" experimental results: To demonstrate to his students that there was no relationship between electricity and magnetism, Oersted routinely placed a wire at right angles to a compass needle, briefly connected it to a dry cell, and showed his students that the needle did not move. During one lecture he accidentally closed the circuit while the wire lay parallel to the compass needle, and to his and the student's surprise, the needle moved.

Repeat Oersted's experiment by positioning a wire at various angles to a compass needle and briefly connecting the wire to a dry cell (Figures A and B). The dry cell will run down very quickly if the wires are attached for more than a moment. At what angle relative to the needle must the wire be placed so needle deflection is greatest? At what angle is deflection least? Place two dry cells in series and see if increasing the current has any effect upon the magnitude of needle deflection. Is there a change in the direction of needle deflection if you change the direction of current through the wire by reversing the leads?

Since the degree of needle deflection is related to the magnitude of the current in the wire, an instrument for measuring electric current can be constructed by wrapping wires around a compass in a north/south direction. Directions for making such an instrument (galvanometer) are described in section 8.2.1.

Part 2. Magnetic fields around current-carrying wires: The magnetic field surrounding a current-carrying wire can be observed by noting the pattern iron filings

© 1994 by John Wiley & Sons, Inc.

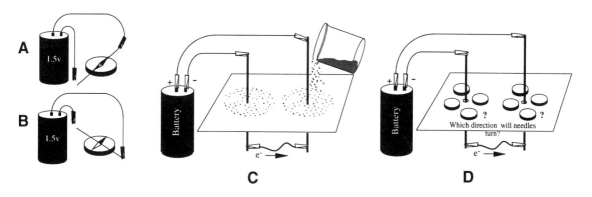

form when scattered around the wire. Punch two holes in a sheet of cardboard and place copper wire through these holes as illustrated in Figure C. Connect the wires to the terminals of a dry cell and gently tap a beaker containing filings to distribute these around the wires. If a pattern of concentric circles does not appear, gently tap the cardboard while the dry cell is connected and/or place an additional dry cell in series with the first. Although the orientation of iron filings helps us visualize magnetic lines of force, it does not allow us to determine the direction of these lines. To determine the direction, place compasses around the vertical wires as illustrated in Figure D and briefly connect the dry cell. Electrons flow through wires from negative electrodes to positive electrodes. Ampere's rule for straight conductors states that the magnetic flux lines (lines used to give a quantitative measure of magnetic field strength) are positioned in a plane perpendicular to the electron current. This can be visualized using Ampere's "left-hand rule" for straight conductors: If you grasp the wire with your left hand such that your thumb points in the direction of the electron current, your fingers will circle the wire in the direction of the magnetic flux (Figure E). That is, the N-poles of compasses will point in the direction your fingers point. If Ampere's rule is correct, the compass needles should point in a clockwise direction around one of the wires and in a counterclockwise direction around the other. Draw diagrams showing the orientations of the needles and determine if your results are consistent with Ampere's rule. How will the orientation of the needles change if the current is reversed? Switch the leads and find out. In what area is the field strength greatest? Position the compasses at varying distances from the wire to find out. To perform this activity with one compass, simply move the compass to different positions and record the deflection of the needle at each location on a piece of paper.

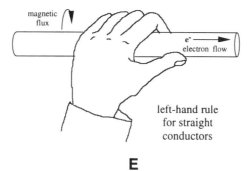

E

Questions

(1) What angle between the current-carrying wire and the compass needle produces the least deflection? The greatest deflection? Explain these observations in terms of Ampere's rule for straight conductors.

(2) Describe the relationship between voltage and needle deflection.

(3) Describe the relationship between the number of turns of wire and needle
deflection.

(4) Describe the relationship between direction of current and the direction of
needle deflection. (Remember that electrons flow through wires from the
negative electrode to the positive electrode.)

(5) Do the compass needles move in a clockwise or a counterclockwise direction
(when viewed from above) around the left wire in Figure D? Around the
right wire? Do your results agree with Ampere's rule?

(6) Do the compass needles change direction if the wires to the dry cell are
reversed?

8.4.2 Electromagnets

Concepts to Investigate: Electromagnets, solenoids, magnetic permeability, Ampere's rule for solenoids, electromagnetic attraction, electromagnetic repulsion.

Materials: Dry cells, test leads with alligator clips, nails, copper wire, compass, paper clips.

Principles and Procedures: In 1825, the English inventor William Sturgeon developed the first electromagnet and employed it to lift heavy iron materials. An electromagnet contains a soft-iron core magnetized by passing a current through a coil of wire wound on the core. Today, Sturgeon's invention is employed in a myriad devices including computer screens (electron beams are directed at the screen by electromagnets), circuit breakers (excessive current increases the magnetic strength and pulls a switch that breaks the circuit), magnetic-resonance imagers (MRI machines detect cancerous tumors by exposing the body to strong magnetic fields and examining how energy is absorbed), and doorbells (pushing the button completes a circuit in an electromagnet that attracts an iron arm to strike the bell).

Part 1. Electromagnetic attraction and repulsion: The French physicist André Ampère noticed that forces exist between parallel conductors in an electrical circuit. Ampère further noticed that wires attract or repel, depending upon the relative directions of the electric currents in the wires. In this activity you will repeat Ampère's famous experiment and determine the conditions for attraction and repulsion.

Cut two 10-cm × 1-cm strips of thin aluminum foil and balance these on pencils so their broad surfaces face each other approximately 0.5 cm apart (Figure F). Use test leads with alligator clips to stabilize the foil in this position. Alternatively, you may set the ends of the aluminum strips in small mounds of modeling clay. Obtain a voltage source in the 7.5-v to 12-v range, connecting batteries together in series if necessary. Briefly close the circuit. Do parallel conductors attract or repel when current through them is in the same direction (Figure G)? Repeat the activity with the wiring pattern shown in Figure H. Do parallel conductors attract or repel when current through them is in opposite directions?

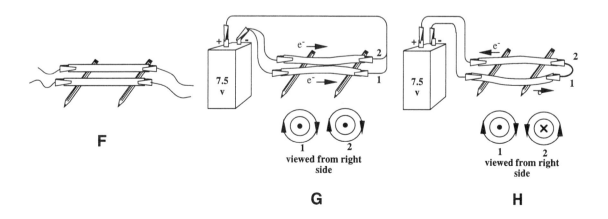

F

viewed from right side

G

viewed from right side

H

Part 2. Electromagnets: In Part 1 you learned that parallel conductors attract if the currents in each are in the same direction. It is logical to assume that the strength of the magnetic field (magnetic flux density) increases further if additional conductors with similarly directed currents are placed parallel to them. One way of achieving this additive effect is to wind a single wire into the shape of a coil. In a coil, each turn represents a conductor, and these conductors are parallel and their currents are in the same direction. Coils, also known as solenoids, have the magnetic properties of bar magnets. Wrap a strand of insulated copper wire 10 times around a nail, briefly connect it to a battery, note the deflection of a compass needle (Figure I), and determine the number of small paper clips that can be lifted (Figure J). Repeat the activity, winding an additional 10 coils around the nail. What is the relationship between the number of turns and the strength of the magnetic field? With the tip of the nail facing the compass, reverse the leads attached to the dry cell. What influence does this have upon the polarity of the electromagnet? Reverse the leads while supporting a chain of paper clips. Do they stay attached or fall?

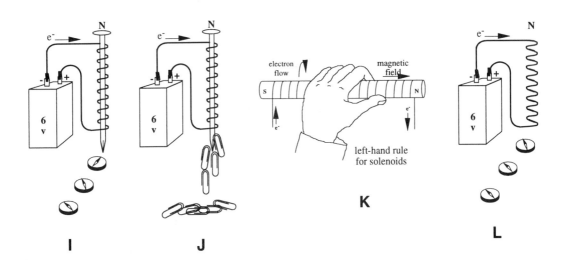

I J K L

Ampère's rule for a solenoid states that when you grasp the coil in your left hand so your fingers circle the coil in the direction of electron flow (the current), your extended thumb will point in the direction of the N-pole of the core (Figure K). (Remember that electrons flow through wires from negative to positive electrodes). Use a magnetic compass to test Ampère's rule. Remember that the N end of a compass will point to the S end of the solenoid because opposite poles attract.

The electromagnet you constructed has an iron core. Iron is known to have high magnetic permeability (great capacity to increase magnetic flux density). To test the influence of iron's magnetic permeability, remove the nail and repeat the activities described here. Is the coil with an air core stronger or weaker than the coil with an iron core (Figure L)?

Questions

(1)   Under what conditions do parallel conductors attract? Repel?

(2)   Figures G and H include diagrams of the direction of magnetic flux around the conductors. The dot indicates current is moving toward the viewer, and the "×" indicates it is moving away from the viewer. Do parallel conductors attract or repel if their magnetic field lines are pointed in opposite directions in the region between the two wires? If they point in the same direction?

(3)   Junkyard cranes with huge electromagnets lift entire cars. How do such cranes release these cars?

(4)   What are three ways to increase the strength of an electromagnet?

(5)   How does the strength of a solenoid with an iron core compare to the same solenoid with an air core?

(6)   Super-conducting electromagnets such as those used in a cyclotron are immersed in liquid helium (–232° C). At this temperature, electrical resistance in the niobium-titanium coils is virtually eliminated. Why is this decrease in resistance accompanied by an increase in the strength of the electromagnet?

8.4.3 Electromagnetic Induction (Generators)

Concepts to Investigate: Electromagnetic induction, generators, AC current, Lenz's Law.

Materials: Copper wire, VOM (volt-ohm-milliammeter), strong bar magnet, strong horseshoe magnet.

Principles and Procedures: After Oersted's experiments demonstrated that electric current could be used to produce magnetic fields, scientists began to wonder if magnetic fields could be used to produce electric current. Scientists were interested in this possibility because of its implication for the generation of inexpensive electric power. The physicist Michael Faraday spent many hours trying to generate an electric current, but met with failure after failure. One day, perhaps by accident, he moved a magnet through a coil of wire and detected a small current. Although Faraday's observation may seem rather trivial, it was one of the most important discoveries of all time. American physicist Joseph Henry performed similar experiments to show that electric current can be generated in a circuit whenever the total magnetic flux linking the circuit is changing, meaning that electric current can be produced in a wire simply by moving a magnet in or out of a coil of wire, or by moving the coil back and forth across the magnet. Faraday's and Henry's discoveries made possible the development of electric generators and transformers that now provide most of the electricity in the world.

Part 1. Electromagnetic induction: *The generation of electric currents by the relative movement of conductors and magnetic fields is known as electromagnetic induction.* In this activity you will induce an electric current by repeating one of Faraday's early experiments. Connect a length of copper wire to a VOM, as illustrated in Figure M. Move the wire up and down in a vertical direction and record the magnitude of any induced voltage and current. Now move the wire back and forth in a horizontal direction such that the movement is parallel with magnetic lines of force and again examine the induced voltage and current (Figure N). On the basis of your observations, is more electric current produced when a conductor crosses or parallels magnetic field lines? Repeat both activities, moving the wire back and forth as rapidly as possible. How does the speed of the conductor (relative to the magnetic field) affect the magnitude of the induced current?

© 1994 by John Wiley & Sons, Inc.

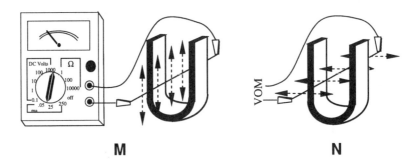

M   **N**

Part 2. Generators: Suspend a loop of insulated wire from a wooden support, as illustrated in Figure O. Connect the leads from the loop to a current detector and then move a strong permanent magnet back and forth through the loop. As the number of loops in the coil is increased, so too is the energy you must expend pushing the magnet into the coil. As the magnet moves through the coil, it induces a current in the circuit detected by a VOM. This current travels through the coil (solenoid) and produces a magnetic field opposing the motion of the magnet. Note that the coil is always repelled by the advance of a magnet, regardless of which pole of the magnet faces the coil. Investigate the influence of each of the following factors upon the magnitude of the induced current: (a) number of turns of wire; (b) speed of the magnet; (c) position of the magnet (inside vs., outside the loop); and (d) integrity of the circuit (closed circuit as shown in Figure O vs. open circuit as shown in Figure P). Remember to change only one variable at a time. If, for example, you change the number of loops and the speed of the magnet at the same time, you will be unable to determine which variable was responsible for the change in the induced current.

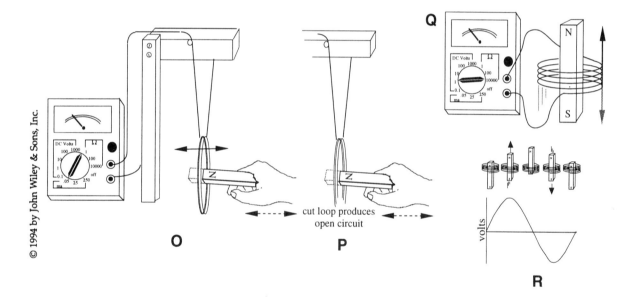

cut loop produces
open circuit

O   P

volts

R

Part 3. Alternating current: In Part 2 you discovered that electric current is induced when a magnet is moved through a coil of wire in a closed circuit. Is it possible to generate a current by moving the coil rather than the magnet? Experiment, using the setup displayed in Figure Q. If you are using a volt-ohm-milliammeter (VOM), switch the dial to the voltage scale and notice that the voltage oscillates between a positive value (as the coil moves one direction) and a negative value (as the coil moves the other direction, Figure R). This oscillation in induced voltage indicates that the current reverses direction. *This reversing current is called alternating current (AC) and is the form in which electric power is delivered to homes and businesses.* Although the design of an AC generator is different from that described here, the principles are the same.

Questions

(1) In order to induce an electric current, must a conductor cross or avoid magnetic field lines (Part 1)?

(2) Why is it more difficult to push a magnet through a coil when the number of loops is increased?

(3) What influence do the (a) number of turns of the coil, (b) speed of the magnet, (c) position of the magnet, and (d) integrity of the circuit (closed or open) have upon the magnitude of the induced voltage or induced current?

(4) Can a current be induced either by moving a conductor through a magnetic field or by moving a magnetic field past a conductor? Explain.

(5) Based on the observations from all three activities, state several methods of increasing the magnitude of induced current.

8.4.4 Motors

Concepts to Investigate: Motor/generator relationship, motor effect, armature, commutator, field magnets, rotor, brushes, alternating current, direct current, galvanometer (or VOM).

Materials: Magnet wire, speaker wire, nails, test tube, 6-volt source of *emf* (battery or series of batteries), copper foil, clay, super glue.

Principles and Procedures: In 1821, Michael Faraday developed the first electric motor, and by late 1800s DC (direct current) motors were widely used in industry. In 1888, the American physicist and inventor Nikola Tesla patented the first AC (alternating current) motor. Since utility companies provide alternating rather than direct current, the motors found in homes and business are generally AC. By contrast, motors that are run by batteries, such as those in toys and vehicles, are DC because batteries deliver direct current. In these activities you will investigate the motor effect and will build your own DC motor.

Part 1. Motor/generator relationship: *A generator transforms mechanical energy into electric energy, while a motor transforms electric energy into mechanical energy.* The same device may serve as a generator when mechanical energy is supplied, or as a motor when electrical energy is provided. To investigate the relationship between generators and motors, construct the apparatus shown in Figure S. The coils should be made of small-gauge insulated magnet wire (#28 gauge or smaller) so they will be very lightweight. Form the coils by wrapping approximately 100 turns of magnet wire around a jar or can with a diameter approximately 50 percent greater than the width of the arms of the magnets. Remove the coils from the can and use tape to bind them tightly together. Suspend both coils from wooden supports in a closed circuit, as illustrated. The wires connecting the coils should cross each other without touching. Pull back and release one of the coils. As this coil moves through the field of its magnet, a current is induced (generator effect). This current then induces a magnetic field in the other coil, which is then attracted or repelled by its stationary magnet (motor effect). A current is now induced by the motion of the second coil through the field of its stationary magnet (generator effect), and this serves to generate a magnetic field in the first coil that causes it to be attracted to or repelled by its magnet (motor effect). The process is repeated and the coils swing back and forth until their motion is slowly halted by friction. This activity illustrates that a motor can serve as a generator, and a generator as a motor. Determine the length of time the generator/motor apparatus will continue to swing on its own power. Place a galvanometer in series and determine whether the current generated is alternating (AC) or direct (DC).

Part 2. Motor effect: Position a thin copper wire within a horseshoe magnet, as illustrated in Figure T. The ends of the wire should rest on a relatively friction-free surface. Briefly connect the wire to a 9- or a 12-volt battery (or series of batteries) and note the direction of wire movement. Reverse connections and again note the direction of wire movement. The movement of a current-carrying wire within a magnetic field is known as the motor effect and is used to turn electric motors. As electric-

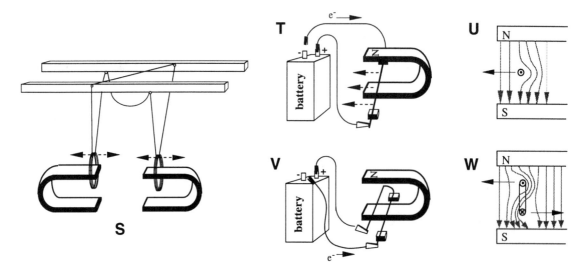

ity flows through the wire, a magnetic field is created in accord with Ampère's Law for straight conductors. This magnetic field opposes the magnetic field between the poles of a horseshoe magnet, and the wire is pushed out (Figure U).

Repeat the activity using a "U"-shaped wire (Figure V). Because electricity is flowing in opposite directions in the two sides of the "U," the distortion in the magnetic field will cause a torque and the wires will rotate (Figure W). The "U"-shaped wire is called the armature of a motor. Does it rotate in the opposite direction if the wires are reversed? How can the power of the motor be increased? Does the armature experience greater torque if the voltage is increased by adding batteries in series? Experiment and find out.

Part 3. DC motors: The purpose of an electric motor is to transform electrical energy into mechanical energy. Construct your own DC motor using the plans illustrated in Figure X. The two outer nails serve as electromagnets (field magnets). The two short nails anchor the wires. The long inverted nail in the center serves as a pivot for an inverted test tube. A block of clay serving as the rotor is molded to the outside of the test tube, and a nail serving as the core of the armature is imbedded in this clay. Using an appropriate adhesive, position two equal rectangles of copper foil on the outer wall of the test tube such that a 5-mm gap exists between them on both sides. These sheets serve as the commutator, which is a split ring, each segment of which is connected to one end of a corresponding armature loop. The commutator segments change from one brush to the other, causing the current in the armature to reverse. The "brushes" are exposed ends of the copper speaker wire that have been bent to provide contact with the commutator.

As electrons flow from the cathode (negative terminal) through the wire wrapped around the first nail, an electromagnet is formed in which, according to Ampère's rule for solenoids, the head becomes the N-pole and the point becomes the S-pole (Figure X). The electrons flow through the brushes to the commutator, and a magnetic field is formed in the horizontal nail (armature) such that the head is the N-pole and the point is the S-pole (Figure Y). The repulsion of like magnetic poles causes the armature to spin. When the brushes are not in contact with the commu-

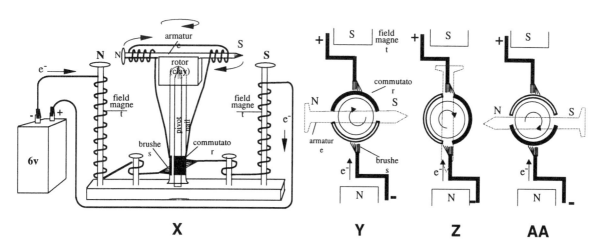

X   Y   Z   AA

tator plates, the electromagnetic field in the commutator collapses (Figure Z), but the momentum of the rotor causes it to continue spinning until the brushes contact the opposite commutator plates (Figure AA). At this point the current in the armature is reversed so the point is now the N-pole and the head is the S-pole. As a result, both ends of the armature are again repelled by local field magnets and attracted to distant field magnets, causing the armature to continue spinning. The polarity of the armature is reversed every 180° so that each end is always repelled by the local field magnet and attracted by the distant field magnet.

The motor is designed so that the portion of the armature closest to the field magnet's N-pole always has a N polarity, while the portion nearest the field magnet's S-pole always has a S polarity. Thus, magnetic repulsion from local poles and attraction to distant poles spins the rotor. To summarize, current from the battery produces two magnetic fields, one in the field magnets and one in the armature. The poles of the field magnet attract and repel those of the armature with sufficient force to rotate the armature. In certain positions the armature won't start spinning because there is no torque, and it may be necessary to give it a push. Determine the location of these neutral positions. Adjust the angle and position of the brushes to maximize the speed of the motor.

Questions

(1) For centuries, inventors have attempted to create a perpetual-motion machine (one that runs forever without external energy). It seems as if the generator/motor built in Part 1 might be a good candidate since the electricity produced by one coil is used to drive the other one and vice versa. Explain why this device can't swing forever.

(2) How will the movement of the wire in Figure T be affected if the direction of the electron current in the wire is reversed?

(3) Why are the armatures of most DC motors and generators designed with a large number of coils oriented at different angles rather than with a single coil?

(4) What factors influence the amount of torque a motor can develop?

8.4.5 Mutual Inductance (Transformers)

Concepts to Investigate: Mutual inductance, transformers, primary coil, secondary coil, step-up transformers, step-down transformers, alternating current.

Materials: Nail, insulated copper wire, voltmeter, galvanometer, strong bar magnet.

Principles and Procedures: Although major electrical transmission lines may carry voltages of approximately 1,000,000 volts, these lines must deliver power to households that use only 110 volts as well as businesses such as the National Electrostatics Corporation at Oak Ridge, Tennessee, that use 32,000,000 volts. Although most households in the United States receive power at 110 volts, small household appliances such as telephone-answering machines require only 13 volts. How can a utility company use a single set of transmission lines to provide power to meet such diverse needs?

In the previous activities it was shown that a voltage is induced in a conductor when the magnetic field around the conductor changes. Voltage is induced when a conductor moves through a magnetic field, or when a magnetic field moves through a conductor, meaning that voltage is induced when a wire is physically moved past a magnet or when a magnet is physically moved past a wire.

Relative motion of magnetic field and conductor can be created not only by the physical movement of conductors or magnets, but also by the expansion or collapse of the magnetic field itself. A current in a coil induces a magnetic field that builds from zero to a steady-state value determined by the number of turns of wire in the coil. When the circuit is opened and the current stops, the magnetic field collapses from this steady-state value to zero. Repeated connection and disconnection of the leads of a dry cell to a coil causes repeated expansion and collapse of a magnetic field, which induces a voltage in a conductor, even though neither the conductor nor the magnet are moving. It is the relative motion between conductor and magnetic field that induces a voltage, so *whenever a moving, expanding, or collapsing magnetic field crosses a conductor, voltage is induced.*

Part 1. Mutual inductance: Wrap 50 turns of insulated wire around a large nail and 10 turns of a second wire on top of the 50-turn coil (Figures BB and CC). Connect the leads of the 10-turn coil to a voltmeter, then connect the leads of the 50-turn coil to a dry cell and read the maximum induced voltage. After a few seconds disconnect the leads from the battery and once again measure the maximum induced voltage. Reverse the leads so the voltmeter is connected to the 50-turn coil and the dry cell is connected to the 10-turn coil and again measure peak voltages as the dry cell is briefly connected and then disconnected. Which arrangement induces the greatest voltage? Repeat the process, substituting a galvanometer or milliammeter for the voltmeter. Which arrangement induces the greatest current? *The coil connected to the source of emf (dry cell) is known as the primary, and the coil in which current is induced is known as the secondary. Together, these coils are a transformer because voltage is transformed from one value in the primary to a different value in the secondary.* A step-up transformer produces a higher voltage in the secondary than in the primary. A step-down transformer produces a lower voltage in the secondary than in the primary.

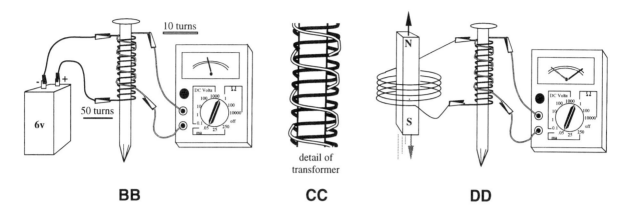

detail of
transformer

BB   **CC**   **DD**

Part 2. AC transformer: The activity in Part 1 showed that a variable voltage can be induced in a secondary coil as the magnetic field in the primary changes (expands and collapses). American and Canadian utility companies generate current that alternates 60 times per second (60 Hz), and magnetic fields expand and collapse so frequently that the current induced in the secondary is relatively constant. Because the standard 110-v, 60-Hz AC household current can be dangerous, this activity uses a weak alternating current induced by moving a magnet rapidly back and forth through a solenoid attached to the primary coil.

Construct a solenoid with a diameter 50 percent larger than the width of a strong bar magnet by wrapping wire around a broom handle or small jar. Use tape to hold the solenoid together and then connect it to either coil on the transformer. Rapidly move the magnet back and forth through the solenoid and record the maximum induced *emf* (Figure DD). Why does the *emf* alternate between positive and negative? If it were possible to move the magnet back and forth through the solenoid 60 times a second, a 60-Hz AC current would be induced in both the primary and secondary coils of the transformer.

Questions

(1) Would your transformer work as well if it were wrapped around a pencil rather than a nail? Explain.

(2) Step-up transformers are used to increase voltage. Based upon your experiments must there be more turns in the primary or the secondary coil in order to step up the voltage?

(3) A fax machine requires 15 volts AC, but the household current is 110 volts AC. Must there be more coils in the secondary or the primary in the transformer?

(4) You often see cylindrical transformers on telephone poles. What is their purpose?

(5) Why is alternating current, rather than direct current, used in power transmission?

FOR THE TEACHER

Faraday expressed the phenomenon of electromagnetic induction in a principle now known as "Faraday's Law": *An electric field is induced whenever a magnetic field is changing. The induced electric field is always at right angles to the changing magnetic field and directly proportional to the rate at which the magnetic field changes.* Later, the Scottish physicist James Clerk Maxwell realized that the reverse was also true: *A magnetic field is induced whenever an electric field is changing. The induced magnetic field is always at right angles to the changing electric field and directly proportional to the rate at which the electric field changes.* Make certain students understand that relative motion between conductor and magnetic field induces voltage. It makes no difference whether the wire or the magnetic field is moving.

In this chapter we described and used Faraday's and Maxwell's principles to explain solenoids, electromagnets, generators, and motors, but these principles also help explain the phenomenon of electromagnetic radiation. All electromagnetic radiation (hard gamma rays, gamma rays, X-rays, ultraviolet, optical, infrared, microwaves, TV, FM, short wave, AM, long wave, and power waves) is composed of periodic disturbances of magnetic and electric forces known as electromagnetic waves. The energy in these waves is equally divided between electric and magnetic fields. These fields are perpendicular to each other and to the direction of wave propagation. Students may be interested to learn that the principles governing the generator and motor effects are useful when explaining the nature of light.

8.4.1 Electromagnetic Fields

Discussion: To demonstrate these activities to the entire class, use compasses with transparent bases, substitute a sheet of Plexiglas or an overhead transparency for the cardboard, and place these on the overhead projector. When discussing the relationship between the strength of magnetic fields and the distance from the conductor, you may wish to introduce the equation for magnetic induction. Magnetic flux density (strength of the magnetic field) is a measure of the magnetizing force at any point in a magnetic field. Magnetic flux density B is directly proportional to the current I in a conductor, and inversely proportional to the radial distance r from the center of the conductor: $B = 2kI/r$, where k is a constant. This equation indicates that magnetic flux density increases as the current increases and the distance to the conductor decreases. Magnetic flux density B is measured in newtons per ampere meter, which is equivalent to webers per square meter or teslas, the tesla being the SI unit. An earlier unit for B that still enjoys widespread use is the gauss: 1 tesla = 10^4 gauss.

Answers (1) There is no deflection when the wire is at right angles to the needle. Deflection is maximum when the wire is parallel to the needle. Ampère's rule states that magnetic flux lines travel in a plane at right angles to the flow of electrons. If the needle is already at right angles to flux lines, there will be no torque and no further deflection. (2) Increasing the voltage increases the current $I = V/R$. Increased current produces a stronger magnetic flux density $B = 2kI/r$, and thus greater deflection of the needle. (3) Students will see a direct (but probably not linear) relationship between the number of coils and the degree of needle deflection. (4) The activity illustrated in

Figure D shows Ampère's left-hand rule for conductors. If you grasp the wire with your left hand so your thumb points in the direction of electron flow, the magnetic flux, as indicated by the direction of N-poles on the compasses, will be in the direction in which your fingers are curled. (5) As viewed from above, the compass needles will point in a counterclockwise direction around the left wire and a clockwise direction around the right wire, in agreement with Ampère's rule. (6) If the wires are switched, the compass needles will reverse and move clockwise around the left wire and counterclockwise around the right wire.

8.4.2 Electromagnets

Discussion: Ampère's experiment can be shown to your entire class using an overhead projector. If you desire a more dramatic attraction or repulsion, place additional dry cells in series to increase the voltage, current, and magnetic flux density (magnetic field strength) surrounding the aluminum foil. Ampère noticed that the attractive and repulsive forces between parallel conductors was directly proportional to the current. Knowing this, he was able to develop a precise method of measuring electrical current, and the unit of electrical current we now use bears his name. One ampere (amp) is defined as the current in each of two parallel conductors, spaced one meter apart, that produces a magnetic force of 2×10^{-7} newton per meter of the conductor's length.

Answers (1) Parallel conductors attract if their currents are in the same direction, and repel if their currents are in the opposite direction. (2) If magnetic flux lines between two parallel conductors point in opposite directions (Figure G), the wires attract, but if they point in the same direction (Figure H), the wires repel. (3) By reversing the polarity of a junkyard electromagnet, the magnet develops an identical polarity to that previously induced in the car. Since like poles repel, the car disengages from the magnet and falls. (4) The strength of an electromagnet may be increased by increasing the number of turns of wire, by increasing the permeability of the core, and by increasing the current. (5) Iron has a high magnetic permeability. When placed in the core of a solenoid, it dramatically increases the magnetic flux density at both poles of the coil, thereby increasing the strength of the magnet. (6) The strength of an electromagnet is dependent upon the number of ampere-turns. If the resistance in the coil is decreased, the current (amperage) increases and so does the resulting magnetic flux density.

8.4.3 Electromagnetic Induction; Generators

Discussion: Students noticed that the hanging coil (solenoid) is repelled by the approaching magnet. The solenoid produces a magnetic field that always opposes the field of the moving bar magnet. You can use this fact to introduce *Lenz's Law, which states that an induced current always flows in a direction that opposes the change that induced it.* Stated another way, a current induced in a moving conductor always is directed such that it produces a magnetic field that opposes the motion of the conductor. The faster the magnet is plunged through the solenoid, the greater the induced *emf*, the greater the accompanying magnetic field, and the greater the electromagnetic repulsion. It is more difficult to hold the solenoid still when the magnet moves faster than when it moves slower. This suggests that the more current a generator induces, the more electromagnetic repulsion it encounters, and the harder it is to spin. This observation is an example of the conservation of energy—you don't get something for nothing. Lenz's law may also be demonstrated with a hand-cranked magneto connected to a light bulb or other load. Students will notice that the faster they spin the armature, the more difficult it becomes to turn the crank.

The strength of an induced voltage depends on the number of magnetic lines cut per second. We can increase the rate at which lines are cut by increasing the strength of the field magnet, increasing the speed of the coil through the magnet's field, or increasing the number of turns in the coil. The magnitude of the *emf* induced in a coil can be expressed by the following equation:

$$emf = -N\frac{\Delta\Phi}{\Delta t}$$

where N represents the number of turns in the coil, $\Delta\Phi$ represents the change in magnetic flux linking the coil, and Δt represents the time interval. You may want to illustrate how this equation is derived using the observations made from activities presented in this section. The magnitude of the induced *emf* (and current) can be increased by increasing the number of turns in the coil N, increasing the number of field lines cut $\Delta\Phi$, and increasing the speed at which they are cut (decreasing the time interval, Δt).

Answers (1) In order to induce an electric current, a conductor must move across field lines. (2) The induced current creates an electromagnet that repels the magnet you are pushing through the coil. The magnitude of the induced current is a function of the number of coils, so the more coils, the more work must be expended to push the magnet through the coil. (3) The induced current is directly proportional to the number of turns of the solenoid and the speed of the magnet. The induced current is greatest when the magnet passes through the center of the coil, because this causes the greatest number of magnetic field lines to be crossed. For an electric current to be induced, the conductor must form a complete (closed) circuit. (4) Yes. Electromagnetic induction depends upon the relative motion of conductors and magnetic fields. It does not matter which component is moving and which is stationary. (5) The induced current can be increased by increasing the number of turns of the solenoid, increasing the relative speed of the conductor and magnet, and moving the magnet or conductor in a manner such that the greatest number of field lines are crossed.

8.4.4 Motors

Discussion: The generator/motor discussed in Part 1 is an excellent way to show that the difference between these devices is one of function, not structure. Stress that both motors and generators have field magnets, armatures, and commutators, and that motors can act as generators and vice versa. The motor described in Part 3 uses electric current to create the magnetic field in the stator (fixed field magnets of the motor) as well as the rotor (moving magnet). To demonstrate the operation of a generator, replace the battery with a galvanometer, substitute a horseshoe magnet for the two field magnets (outer nails), and rotate the armature with your hand to generate a current.

Answers (1) No machine is 100 percent efficient. Energy is always lost to friction, heat, or sound. Even if the machine is 99.9 percent efficient, it will gradually run down and stop. (2) The direction of motion will also be reversed. (3) The torque on an armature varies depending on its orientation with respect to the field magnet. By employing a number of armatures, it is possible to eliminate the "dead spots" and obtain more constant torque throughout the cycle. (4) The torque developed by a motor is a function of the current, the number of loops in the armature, the strength of the field magnet, and the orientation of the armature with respect to the external magnetic field.

8.4.5 Mutual Inductance, Transformers

Discussion: Demonstrate to your students the importance of the relative positions of the primary and secondary coils in a transformer by wrapping the primary coil at one end of a nail and the secondary at the other end. Measure the maximum current induced in the secondary and show students that it is substantially less than the current induced when the coils are wrapped around each other. Point out to students that transformers should be designed with closest coupling of the coils to achieve the most efficient transfer of energy. The efficiency of most commercial transformers is 95–99 percent.

Most commercial transformers are designed with a closed (circular) core to provide a continuous path for magnetic flux, which ensures that the secondary cuts all of the flux lines generated by the expanding and collapsing field of the primary. Assuming no losses in power, the voltage of the secondary can be calculated using the following equation:

$$V_s = \frac{V_p N_s}{N_p}$$

where V_p represents voltage in the primary, V_s represents voltage induced in the secondary, N_p is the number of turns in the primary, and N_s is the number of turns in the secondary. Students may mistakenly believe the ability of a transformer to increase voltage allows one to get something for nothing. Remind them that the law of the conservation of energy requires the energy output to be no greater than the energy input. Therefore, if a transformer increases voltage, the current must be decreased. The following equation illustrates this:

$$I_s = \frac{N_p I_p}{N_s}$$

where I represents the current. Thus, the greater the ratio of turns in the secondary to the primary, the greater the voltage, but the smaller the current.

Answers (1) No. The magnetic domains in the nail's iron align with the magnetic field of the coil (iron has a greater magnetic permeability than wood), thereby increasing the magnetic field of the primary. If there is a greater magnetic flux in the primary, more flux lines will be cut by the secondary and a greater current induced. (2) To step up voltage, it is necessary that the secondary have more turns than the primary. (3) To step down the voltage, the secondary must have fewer turns than the primary. (4) These are step-down transformers that reduce voltage so it is appropriate for homes and businesses. (5) It is much more efficient to transmit electricity at high voltage and low current than at low voltage and high current. However, homes and business require only 110 or 220 volts rather than the high voltage carried by transmission lines. Transformers provide a simple and inexpensive way to step down AC voltage to appropriate levels, but there are no comparable devices for stepping down DC voltage.

Applications to Everyday Life

Health Hazards Associated with Electromagnetic Fields: You may have read headlines in your local newspaper such as "Is My Electric Blanket Killing Me?" "Can Power Lines Cause Leukemia?" or "Students Removed from Classroom over Electromagnetic Concerns." Some researchers believe that low-level electromagnetic fields may increase risk to childhood cancers, adult leukemia, and brain tumors, but the research is inconclusive. Electromagnetic fields are produced by all electrical appliances and by power lines. Although no one is certain if electromagnetic fields may cause health problems, experts are suggesting that people minimize their exposure to strong fields whenever possible. You can reduce exposure to magnetic fields by keeping your distance from those machines that produce the greatest fields. The following table shows how magnetic-flux density, measured in milligaus, decreases rapidly with distance from the device that produces it (1 milligaus = 10^{-7} tesla = 10^{-7} webers per square meter).

	Magnetic Flux Density *(milligaus)*		
	at 1 inch	at 1 foot	at 1 yard
blow dryer	145	2	-
electric can opener	3,500	72	4
color TV	46	4	-
microwave oven	210	16	2
refrigerator	5	2	-

Source: Southern California Edison Customer Technology Application Center

Automatic Sprinklers and Heaters: Automatic sprinklers are used to water lawns, gardens, and crops in arid and semi-arid regions. Each water line is controlled by a solenoid valve connected to an electronic timer. At specified times the timer directs a small current to the solenoid. The resulting magnetic field moves the iron core which activates a valve, allowing water to flow through the line. When the current to the solenoid ceases, the magnetic field collapses and the valve closes. Household gas heaters operate on the same principle. When the thermostat sends current to the solenoid in the gas line, gas flows and is ignited by the pilot light. The "clicking" sound that precedes the flow of water or gas occurs when the electromagnet opens the valve.

Loudspeakers and Telephone Receivers: Loudspeakers and telephones employ a fixed magnet and a movable magnet. The movable magnet consists of a coil that is energized by an electrical signal from the amplifier. As the signal to the movable coil varies, so does its magnetic polarity, and it is alternately attracted to or repelled from the fixed magnet. This coil is linked to a diaphragm that subsequently vibrates and recreates the original sound.

Metal Detectors: During the 1970s terrorists hijacked a number of airplanes at gunpoint. In an effort to stop firearms from being carried on board airplanes, airports installed metal detectors. As you walk into the boarding area of an airport, you pass through a coil that is positioned in a weak magnetic field. Because of its high magnetic permeability, the iron in a revolver or knife changes the magnetic flux and induces a current in the loop, and an alarm is triggered. Metal detectors are now being used to increase safety in schools. People also use metal detectors to search for buried utility lines, coins, and other metal items.

Traffic-Signal Triggers: To gauge and regulate traffic, metal loops are installed underneath the pavement in traffic lanes. The rectangular etchings that appear in traffic lanes immediately before intersections indicate that signal triggers have been installed. As vehicles pass over these loops, the flux of the Earth's magnetic field through these loops changes because of the magnetic permeability of the iron in the car. A brief current is induced, and a signal is sent to microprocessors that monitor these signals and adjust the traffic lights to promote an efficient flow of traffic.

Seismometers: Geophysicists use seismometers to measure the magnitude of earthquakes, determine if nations are performing underground nuclear tests, and study the structure of the Earth in response to detonations when engaged in mineral exploration. One type of seismometer employs a massive magnet suspended by a spring inside a solenoid. When the ground shakes, the solenoid moves up and down, while the magnet remains relatively motionless because of its great inertia. The current induced in the solenoid is proportional to the relative motion of the magnet and coil and can be interpreted as an indication of the magnitude of Earth movement.

Generators and Alternators: DC generators rotate conductors through a stationary magnetic field, while AC generators (alternators) rotate magnetic fields past stationary conductors. AC generators provide the vast majority of electric power used throughout the world.

Magnetohydrodynamic Power: New superconductor technology has made possible the generation of direct current in magnetohydrodynamic (MHD) generators. High-speed-charged particles stream through the field of a superconducting electromagnet. Positively charged particles move in one direction in the field, while negative particles move in the opposite direction, creating a direct current between the two electrodes. American and Russian scientists and engineers collaborated to build the first commercial MHD power plant in the former Soviet Union.

Appliances: Power companies deliver alternating current, so AC motors are found in household appliances such as clocks, clothes washers, clothes dryers, vacuum cleaners, mixers, and fans. Automotive batteries deliver direct current, so starter motors, windshield washer motors, and windshield wiper motors have DC motors.

Electric Power Transmission: The resistance in transmission lines is directly proportional to their length $R = \rho \, l/A$, where R is resistance, ρ is resistivity, l is length, and A is cross-sectional area. The power lost due to resistance is directly proportional to resistance and the square of the current $P = I^2 R$. Thus, to minimize resistive power loss in long power lines, it is necessary to maintain a low current. This can be done by maximizing the voltage of the lines. If power is kept constant, the current can be decreased by increasing the voltage $P = IV$. Thus, step-up transformers are needed at power stations to increase the voltage and minimize the current. Transformers are used to step up the voltage to 1,330,000 volts for the 1,224-mile Pacific Inter-tie line in the western United States.

Magnetos: The small gasoline engines (1- to 10-horsepower) found in many machines, including lawnmowers, tillers, mulchers, cement mixers, and outboard engines use magnetos to supply electric energy to the spark plug. A simple generator consists of a coil rotated in the magnetic field of a permanent magnet. To obtain greater electrical output we may employ a magneto that uses a larger coil rotated in the field of several permanent magnets. When you pull the rope to start a small gasoline engine, the magneto provides a high voltage to the spark plug, and as the engine runs the magneto continues to supply this voltage.

Battery Chargers: Plug-in battery chargers (those little black boxes that accompany cordless power tools) are used to charge cordless products containing a permanent battery such as found inside the handle of an electric drill. These chargers contain a transformer that steps down the voltage and amperage of household electricity so the output of the device produces the appropriate voltage and current to charge the battery. In addition, the charger may contain a rectifier that converts AC current to DC current. A typical plug-in battery charger used to charge small appliances converts 120-volt household electricity to 5–7 volts at 150–300 milliamps.

DC-AC Adapters: These adapters work on the same principle as the plug-in battery chargers. They include transformers and rectifiers that step down voltage and convert AC to DC current appropriate for the electronic device being used. Most portable (notebook) computers come with an adapter that will run the computer while at the same time charging the battery.

Appendix

TABLE 1: PHYSICAL QUANTITIES AND THEIR UNITS

Physical Quantities and Their Units

Physical Quantity	Quantity Symbol	Measurement Units	Unit Symbol	Unit Dimensions
length (distance)	$l\ (d)$	**meter**	**m**	**m**
mass	m	**kilogram**	**kg**	**kg**
time	t	**second**	**s**	**s**
electric charge	Q	**coulomb**	**C**	**C**
temperature	T	**kelvin**	**K**	**K**
amount of substance	n	**mole**	**mol**	**mol**
luminous intensity	l	**candela**	**cd**	**cd**
acceleration	a	meter per second squared	m/s^2	m/s^2
area	A	square meter	m^2	m^2
capacitance	C	farad	F	C^2·s^2/kg·m^2
density	D	kilogram per cubic meter	kg/m^3	kg/m^3
electric current	I	ampere	A	C/s
electric field intensity	E	newton per coulomb	N/C	kg·m/C·s^2
electric resistance	R	ohm	Ω	kg·m^2/C^2·s
emf	ξ	volt	V	kg·m^2/C·s^2
energy	E	joule	J	kg·m^2/s^2
force	F	newton	N	kg·m/s^2
frequency	f	hertz	Hz	s^{-1}
heat	Q	joule	J	kg·m^2/s^2
illuminance	E	lux (lumen per square meter)	lx	cd/m^2
inductance	L	henry	H	kg·m^2/C^2
luminous flux	F	lumen	lm	cd
magnetic flux	ϕ	weber	Wb	kg·m^2/C·s
magnetic flux density	B	tesla (weber per square meter)	T	kg/C·s
potential difference	V	volt	V	kg·m^2/C·s^2
power	P	watt	W	kg·m^2/s^3
pressure	p	pascal (newton per square meter)	Pa	kg/m·s^2
velocity	v	meter per second	m/s	m/s
volume	V	cubic meter	m^3	m^3
work	W	joule	J	kg·m^2/s^2

Fundamental Units (rows: length through luminous intensity)

Derived Units (rows: acceleration through work)

TABLE 2: METRIC SYSTEM PREFIXES

Factor	Decimal Representation	Prefix	Symbol
10^{18}	1,000,000,000,000,000,000	exa	E
10^{15}	1,000,000,000,000,000	peta	P
10^{12}	1,000,000,000,000	tera	T
10^{9}	1,000,000,000	giga	G
10^{6}	1,000,000	mega	M
10^{3}	1,000	kilo	k
10^{2}	100	hecto	h
10^{1}	10	deka	da
10^{0}	1		
10^{-1}	0.1	deci	d
10^{-2}	0.01	centi	c
10^{-3}	0.001	milli	m
10^{-6}	0.000 001	micro	μ
10^{-9}	0.000 000 001	nano	n
10^{-12}	0.000 000 000 001	pico	p
10^{-15}	0.000 000 000 000 001	femto	f
10^{-18}	0.000 000 000 000 000 001	atto	a

TABLE 3: GREEK ALPHABET

Letter		Name	Letter		Name
A	α	alpha	N	ν	nu
B	β	beta	Ξ	ξ	xi
Γ	γ	gamma	O	o	omicron
Δ	δ	delta	Π	π	pi
E	ϵ	epsilon	P	ρ	rho
Z	ζ	zeta	Σ	σ	sigma
H	η	eta	T	τ	tau
Θ	θ	theta	Y	υ	upsilon
I	ι	iota	Φ	ϕ	phi
K	κ	kappa	X	χ	chi
Λ	λ	lambda	Ψ	ψ	psi
M	μ	mu	Ω	ω	omega

TABLE 4: SI AND CUSTOMARY UNITS AND CONVERSIONS

Quantity	SI Unit	Symbol	Customary Unit	Symbol	Conversion
Length	meter	m	foot	ft	1 m= 3.280 ft
Area	square meter	m²	square foot	ft²	1 m²=10.76 ft²
Volume	cubic meter	m³	cubic foot	ft³	1 m³= 35.32 ft³
Speed	meter per second	m/s	foot per second	ft/s	1 m/s = 3.281 ft/s
Acceleration	meter per second per second	m/s²	feet per second per second	ft/s²	1 m/s²= 3.281 ft/s²
Force	newton	N	pound	lb	1 N = 0.2248 lb
Work(energy)	joule	J	foot-pound	ft·lb	1 J = 0.7376 ft·lb
Power	watt	W	foot-pound per second	ft·lb/s	1 W = 0.7376 ft·lb/s
Pressure	pascal	Pa	pound per square inch	lb/in²	1 Pa = 1.450 x 10⁻⁴ lb/in²
Density lb/ft³	kilogram per cubic meter	kg/m³	pound per cubic foot	lb/ft³	1 kg/m³ = 6.243 x 10⁻²

TABLE 5: COMMON CONVERSIONS

Quantity	Customary Unit	Metric Unit	Customary/ Metric	Metric/ Customary
Length	inch (in)	millimeter (mm)	1 in = 25.4 mm	1 mm = 0.0394 in
	foot (ft)	meter (m)	1 ft = 0.305 m	1 m = 3.28 ft
	yard (yd)	meter (m)	1 yd = 0.914 m	1 m = 1.09 yd
	mile (mi)	kilometer (km)	1 mi = 1.61 km	1 km = 0.621 mi
Area	square inch (in²)	square centimeter (cm²)	1 in²= 6.45 cm²	1 cm² = 0.155 in²
	square foot (ft²)	square meter (m²)	1 ft² = 0.0929 m²	1 m² = 10.8 ft²
	square yard (yd²)	square meter (m²)	1 yd² = 0.836 m²	1 m² = 1.20 yd²
	acre (acre)	hectare (ha)	1 acre = 0.405 ha	1 ha = 2.47 acre
Volume	cubic inch (in³)	cubic centimeter (cm³)	1 in³ = 16.39 cm³	1 cm³ = 0.0610 in³
	cubic foot (ft³)	cubic meter (m³)	1 ft³ = 0.0283 m³	1 m³ = 35.3 ft³
	cubic yard (yd³)	cubic meter (m³)	1 yd³ = 0.765 m³	1 m³ = 1.31 yd³
	quart (qt)	liter (L)	1 qt = 0.946 L	1 L = 1.06 qt
Mass	ounce (oz)	gram (g)	1 oz = 28.4 g	1 g = 0.0353 oz
	pound (lb)	kilogram (kg)	1 lb = 0.454 kg	1 kg = 2.20 lb
	ton (ton)	metric ton (t)	1 ton = 0.907 t	1 t = 1.10 ton
Weight	pound (lb)	newton (N)	1 lb = 4.45 N	1 N = 0.225 lb

TABLE 6: UNITS OF PRESSURE

Unit	Definition	Pascal Equivalents	When It Is Used
Pascal (Pa)	N/m^2	1	Standard SI Unit. Used when mass is measured in kg and area in meters.
kiloPascal (kPa) gaseous,	$1000\ N/m^2$	1000	Practical metric unit of measuring fluid, or mechanical pressure (Pa is generally too small).
bar	$10{,}000\ N/m^2$	100,000	Practical metric unit of measuring atmospheric pressure. One bar is approximately 1 atmosphere.
millibar (mb) maps mb	$100\ N/m^2$	100	Weather reports. Note: Some weather drop the first two digits (e.g., 1013.3 may be reported as 13.3).
barye (dyne/cm²) ters and	$0.1\ N/m^2$	0.1	Standard CGS unit. Used when measurements are made in centime- grams.
torr a	1/760 of standard atmospheric pressure	133.3	Used when pressure is measured with mercury manometer or barometer.
mm Hg Standard	Pressure required to support a column of Hg 1 mm in height	133.3	Blood pressure measurements. blood pressure is 120/80 (systolic/diastolic)
cm $H_2 0$ using ter.	Pressure required to support a column of water 1 cm in height	98.1	Used when pressure is measured simple water barometer or manome-
atmosphere (atm)	Atmospheric pressure at sea level	101,325	Used when a comparison to standard atmospheric pressure is desired.
PSI sures	lb/in^2	6,894	Common measurement in mechanical and structural engineering. Tire pres- are rated in PSI.

TABLE 7: RELATIVE HUMITIDY FROM WET AND DRY BULB THERMOMETER

t= drybulb temperature; t'=wet bulb temperature, Δt=difference in temperature

Difference in temperature Δt

t→	0.2	0.4	0.6	0.8	1.0	1.2	1.4	1.6	1.8	2.0	2.2	2.4	2.6	2.8	3.0	3.2	3.4	3.6	3.8	4.0	4.5	5.0	5.5	6.0	6.5	7.0	7.5	8.0	8.5	9.0	9.5	10.0
-1	96	92	88	84	81	73	69	66	62	58	54	51	47	43	40	36	33	29	26	17	8											
0	96	92	89	85	81	74	71	67	64	60	57	53	50	46	43	40	36	33	29	21	13	5										
1	97	93	90	86	83	76	73	70	66	63	59	55	53	49	46	43	40	36	33	25	17	10										
2	97	93	90	87	84	78	74	72	68	65	62	58	55	52	49	46	43	40	37	29	22	14	7									
3	97	94	91	88	84	79	76	74	70	67	65	61	58	55	52	49	46	43	40	33	26	19	12	7								
4	97	94	91	88	85	80	77	75	72	69	64	62	60	57	54	51	48	45	43	36	29	22	16	12	5							
5	97	94	91	89	86	80	77	76	73	69	65	63	61	58	56	51	49	48	45	39	33	26	20	16	9							
6	97	94	92	89	86	81	78	76	74	70	67	64	63	60	58	55	53	50	48	41	35	29	24	17	13	7						
7	97	94	92	90	87	82	79	77	75	72	68	65	64	61	59	57	54	52	51	44	38	32	26	21	17	11	5					
8	97	95	92	90	87	82	80	78	76	73	69	67	65	63	61	58	56	53	51	46	40	35	29	24	19	14	10					
9	98	95	93	90	88	83	81	79	77	74	71	68	66	64	62	60	58	55	54	48	42	37	32	27	22	17	14	5				
10	98	95	93	91	89	83	81	80	78	75	72	69	67	65	63	62	60	57	55	51	44	39	34	29	24	20	15	8				
11	98	95	93	91	89	84	82	80	78	76	73	71	68	66	65	64	62	59	56	53	46	41	36	32	27	22	18	13	6			
12	98	96	93	91	89	85	82	81	79	77	74	72	69	68	66	64	62	60	58	54	48	43	38	34	30	25	21	16	12	5		
13	98	96	94	92	90	85	83	81	79	77	75	73	71	69	67	65	63	61	59	56	50	45	41	35	32	28	23	19	15	11		
14	98	96	94	92	90	86	84	82	80	78	76	74	72	70	68	66	64	62	60	57	51	47	42	38	34	30	26	22	18	14	10	7
15	98	96	94	92	90	86	84	82	80	78	76	74	73	71	69	67	65	63	61	58	53	48	44	40	36	32	27	24	22	16	13	10

Difference in temperature Δt

t→	0.5	1.0	1.5	2.0	2.5	3.0	3.5	4.0	4.5	5.0	5.5	6.0	6.5	7.0	7.5	8.0	8.5	9.0	9.5	10	10.5	11	11.5	12	12.5	13	13.5	14	14.5	15	16	17	18
16	94	90	85	81	76	71	67	63	58	54	50	46	42	38	34	30	26	23	19	15	12	8	5										
17	94	90	86	81	76	72	68	64	60	55	51	47	43	40	36	32	28	25	21	18	14	11	8	5									
18	94	91	86	82	77	73	69	65	61	57	53	49	45	41	38	34	30	27	23	20	17	14	10	8	5								
19	94	91	87	82	78	74	70	66	62	58	54	50	46	43	39	36	32	29	26	22	19	16	13	10	7								
20	96	91	87	83	78	74	70	67	63	59	55	51	48	44	41	37	34	31	28	24	21	18	16	12	9	7							
21	96	92	87	83	79	75	71	68	64	60	56	53	49	46	42	39	36	32	29	26	23	20	17	14	12	9	7						
22	96	92	87	83	79	75	71	68	64	61	57	53	50	46	44	40	37	34	31	28	25	22	19	16	14	11	8	6					
23	96	92	88	84	80	76	72	69	65	62	58	55	52	48	45	42	39	36	33	30	27	24	21	19	16	13	11	8	6				
24	96	92	88	84	80	76	72	69	66	62	59	56	53	49	46	43	40	37	34	31	29	26	23	20	18	15	13	10	8	5			
25	96	92	88	85	80	77	74	70	66	63	60	56	53	50	47	44	41	39	36	33	30	28	25	22	20	17	15	12	10	8	5		
26	96	92	88	85	80	77	74	71	67	63	60	57	54	51	48	45	43	40	37	34	32	29	26	24	21	19	17	14	12	10	8	5	
27	96	92	89	85	81	78	74	71	67	64	61	58	54	52	49	46	44	41	38	36	33	30	28	26	23	21	19	16	14	12	10	7	5
28	96	93	89	85	81	78	75	72	68	65	62	58	56	53	50	47	45	42	40	37	34	32	29	27	25	22	20	18	16	13	11	9	6
29	96	93	89	86	82	79	75	72	69	66	63	60	57	54	51	49	46	43	41	38	36	33	31	28	26	24	22	19	17	15	13	11	8
30	96	93	89	86	82	79	76	73	69	66	63	60	57	55	52	50	47	44	42	39	37	35	32	30	28	25	23	21	19	17	14	12	10
31	96	93	89	86	83	80	77	73	70	67	64	61	58	56	53	51	48	46	43	40	38	36	33	31	29	27	25	22	20	18	16	14	11
32	96	93	90	86	83	80	77	74	71	68	65	62	59	57	54	51	49	47	44	41	39	37	34	32	30	28	26	24	22	20	17	15	13
33	97	93	90	87	84	80	77	75	72	69	66	63	60	57	55	52	50	48	45	42	40	38	35	34	31	29	27	25	23	21	19	17	14
34	97	93	90	87	84	81	78	75	72	69	66	64	61	58	56	53	51	49	46	44	41	39	37	35	32	30	28	26	24	23	20	18	15
35	97	94	90	87	84	81	78	75	73	70	67	64	61	59	56	54	52	49	47	44	42	40	38	36	34	31	29	27	25	24	21	19	16
36	97	94	90	87	84	81	78	76	73	70	67	64	62	59	57	54	52	50	48	45	43	41	39	37	35	32	30	28	26	25	22	20	18
37	97	94	91	88	85	82	79	76	74	70	68	65	63	60	58	55	53	51	48	46	44	42	40	38	36	34	32	30	28	26	23	21	19

TABLE 8: WRITING STYLE GUIDELINES

CAPITALS:

Units: When written in full, all units begin with a lower case letter.
Correct: kelvin, farad, newton, joule, hertz, degree
Incorrect: Kelvin, Farad, Newton, Joule, Hertz, Degree

Symbol: The first letter in a unit symbol is uppercase when the unit name is derived from a person's name. The following is a list of units that are named after famous scientists. Note that the unit name is not capitalized, but the unit symbol is.

ampere	A	André Ampère: discovered basic principles of electrodynamics.
coulomb	C	Charles Coulomb: discovered law of force between charged bodies.
farad	F	Michael Faraday: pioneered research in electricity and magnetism.
henry	H	Joseph Henry: discovered electromagnetic induction and self-induction.
hertz	Hz	Heinrich Hertz: discovered radio waves.
joule	J	James Joule: pioneered research in thermodynamics.
kelvin	K	William Thomson (AKA Lord Kelvin): developed absolute temperature scale.
newton	N	Isaac Newton: pioneered work in calculus, optics, and gravitation.
ohm	W	Georg Ohm: discovered relationship between current, voltage, and resistance.
pascal	Pa	Blaise Pascal: discovered basic principles of hydrostatics.
tesla	T	Nicola Tesla: developed AC motor and high voltage transformers.
volt	V	Allesandro Volta: invented first battery.
watt	W	James Watt: developed the steam engine as a practical power source.
weber	Wb	Wilhelm Weber: performed early research in electricity and magnetism.

The following units are not named after people, and therefore their symbols are not capitalized: meter, m; kilogram, kg; second, s; mole, mol; candle, cd; lux, lx; degree, $^\circ$.

Prefixes: The symbols for all prefixes representing powers less than one million are never capitalized (a, f, p, n, μ, m, c, d, da, h, k). The symbols representing powers greater than or equal to a million are always capitalized (M, G, T, P, E). Please see table 2.

PERIODS: Periods are never used after a symbol, except at the end of a sentence.

DECIMALS: For numbers less than 1, a zero is written before the decimal point.
Correct: 0.03256   0.5234
Incorrect: .03256   .5234

COMPOUND UNITS: A centered dot is used to indicate when a unit is the product of two or more units.
Correct: N·m $kg \cdot m/s^2$
Incorrect: N·m $kg \cdot m/s^2$

When writing the name for a compound unit, a hyphen is recommended. A space is permissible, but never a centered dot; for example, newton-meter or newton meter.

DIFFERENTIATING QUANTITY SYMBOLS AND UNIT SYMBOLS: By convention quantity symbols are italicized but unit symbols are not. Quantity symbols represent a physical quantity such as time, mass, and length, while unit symbols represent specific measures of those quantities, such as seconds, kilograms, and meters.

Quantity symbols (italicized)	Unit symbols (not italicized)
time, t	seconds, s
mass, m	kilograms, kg
length, l	meter, m
heat, Q	joule, J

Index of Concepts
to Investigate

absolute humidity, 4.2.6

absorption, 7.6.3, 7.6.6

AC, 8.4.3, 8.4.4, 8.4.5

acceleration, 2.3, 2.3.2, 3.1.3

    due to gravity, 2.3.1, 2.3.5, 2.4.3

    greater than gravity, 2.3.5

    angular, 2.2.5

    centripetal, 2.3.2, 2.3.3

    constant, 2.3.1

    law of , 3.1.3

    negative, 3.1.3

accelerometer, 2.3.2

accuracy, 1.1.1

adaptation, 6.2.4

additive properties of light, 7.6.4, 7.6.5

air drag, 4.4.3

air pressure, 4.1

    and breathing, 4.1.5

    magnitude of, 4.1.1

air resistance, 3.1.6

airfoil, 4.4.2

alternating current, 8.4.3, 8.4.4, 8.4.5

amperage, 8.2.4

Ampere's rule for solenoids, 8.4.2

Ampere's rule for straight conductors, 8.4.1

amplitude, 2.4.1, 6.1.1, 6.1.2, 6.1.5

aneroid barometers, 4.1.6, 7.1.1, 7.2.2

angle of reflection, 6.1.5, 7.1.1, 7.2.2

angle of slip, 3.3.2

angular acceleration, 2.2.5

angular momentum, 5.3.5, 5.3.6

    conservation of, 5.3.5

angular velocity, 2.2.5

anodes, 8.2.4

antinodal lines, 6.5.3

aperture, 6.1.5

Archimedes' principle, 3.2.1, 3.2.5

armature, 8.4.4

atmospheric pressure, 4.1.1, 4.1.6

    and boiling, 4.2.2

atomizers, 4.4.1

attenuation, 6.1.2

attraction, electromagnetic, 8.4.2

attraction, magnetic, 8.3.4

axle, wheel and, 5.4.2

balanced torque, 3.4.1, 3.4.2, 3.4.3

ballast, 3.2.2

barometers, 4.1.6

    aneroid, 4.1.6

    water, 4.1.6

barometric pressure, 4.2.2, 4.1.6

base of support, 2.1.2

batteries, 8.2.4

belts, 5.4.5

Bernoulli's principle, 4.4.1, 4.4.2, 4.4.3

block and tackle (pulley), 5.4.3, 5.4.6

boiling, 4.2.2

boiling point elevation, 4.2.5

boundaries, phase, 4.2.3

breathing, 4.1.5

Brewster's angle, 7.4.2

brushes, 8.4.4

buoyancy, 3.2.2, 3.2.4, 3.2.5

    of different materials, 3.2.3

    regulation of, 3.2.2

buoyant force, 3.2

buoyant force, calculation of, 3.2.3

calibration, 8.2.1, 8.2.3

capacitance, 8.1.8

Cartesian diver, 3.2.2

cathodes, 8.2.4

cells in parallel, 8.2.4

cells in series, 2.8.4

center of mass, 2.1, 2.1.1, 2.1.2, 2.1.3, 2.3.5, 3.3.1

    and friction, 3.3.1

    external, 2.1.1

    internal, 2.1.1

    motion of, 2.1.4

    of composite objects, 2.1.3

centripetal acceleration, 2.3.2, 2.3.3

    motion in horizontal circle, 2.3.3

    motion in vertical circle, 2.3.4

centripetal force, 2.3.3, 3.1.5

chains, 5.4.5

charge, 8.1.2

    distribution, 8.1.5

    identification of, 8.1.2

    negative, 8.1.2

    positive, 8.1.2

    transfer of, 8.1.2

charging by conduction, 8.1.1

charging by induction, 8.1.1

circuit breakers, 8.2.6

circuits, 8.2

    closed, 8.2.1

    open, 8.2.1

    parallel, 8.2.4

    series, 8.2.4

short, 8.2.6
closed circuit, 8.2.1
coefficient of sliding friction, 3.3.3, 3.3.4
coefficient of static friction, 3.3.2, 3.3.3, 3.3.4
coherent light, 7.1.3
coil, 8.4.5
 8.4.5
 8.4.5
collisions, 5.2.4, 5.3.2, 5.3.3
 elastic, 5.2.4, 5.3.2, 5.3.3
 inelastic, 5.3.2
color, 7.6, 7.6.1
 complimentary, 7.3.1
 primary, 7.6.4
 sky, 7.6.6
commutator, 8.4.4
compass, magnetic, 8.3.2
complementary colors, 7.3.1, 7.6.5
composite bodies, 2.1.3
compound machines, 5.4.5, 5.4.6
 efficiency of, 5.4.6
conduction, 8.1.4
 charging by, 8.2.1
conductivity, 8.2.1
conductors, Ampere's rule for, 8.4.1
conservation laws
 angular momentum, 5.3.5, 5.3.6
 energy, 5.2.4, 5.4.4, 8.2.3
 linear momentum, 5.3.2, 5.3.3
 momentum, 5.3.3
constant acceleration, 2.3.1
constructive interference, 6.1.3, 6.1.4, 6.5.3, 7.3.1
control, 6.3.1
Coulomb's law, 8.1.4
Coulomb's law of magnetism, 8.3.5
crest, 6.1.1
critical angle, 7.1.4, 7.2.4
cross polarization, 7.4.1,
Curie temperature, 8.3.2
current, 8.2.1
 alternating, 8.4.3, 8.4.4, 8.4.5
 direct, 8.4.4

deceleration, 3.1.3
declination, magnetic, 8.3.7
demagnetization, 8.3.1, 8.3.2
density, 3.2.5, 3.2.6
 fluid, 3.2.5
density, optical, 7.2.5, 7.2.6
destructive interference, 6.1.3, 6.1.4, 6.5.3, 7.3.1

diffraction, 6.1.5, 6.5.2, 7.3, 7.3.2, 7.3.3, 7.6.7
 angle, 7.6.7
 by particles, 7.3.3
 grating equation, 7.6.7
 gratings, 7.3.3
 single slit, 7.3.2
 sound, 6.5.2
dimensions, 1.1.1
dip, magnetic, 8.3.7
direct current, 8.4.4
dispersion of light, 7.6.1
displacement, 3.2.1
 method of measuring volume, 1.2.2
 water , 3.2.3
distortion, 7.2.3
distribution of charge, 8.1.5
distribution of mass and rotational inertia, 2.2.6
domains, magnetic, 8.3.1
Doppler effect, 6.4.2
double refraction, 7.4.4
drag, air, 4.4.3

Earth's magnetic field, 8.3.2, 8.3.7
echo, 6.5.1
efficiency of compound machines, 5.4.6
effort, 3.4.1, 3.4.2, 3.4.3, 3.4.4
elastic collisions, 5.2.4, 5.3.2, 5.3.3
electric
 charges, 8.1.2
 current, 8.2.1
 energy from chemicals, 8.2.2
 energy from heat, 8.2.3
 meter, 5.1.3
 potential, 8.1.7
electricity, conservation of, 5.1.4
electrochemical cell, 8.2.2
electrodes, 8.2.2, 8.2.4
electrolyte, 8.2.2
electromagnetic
 attraction, 8.4.2
 fields, 8.4.1
 induction, 8.4.3
 radiation spectrum, 7.6.2
 repulsion, 8.4.2
electromagnetism, 8.4, 8.4.1
electromagnets, 8.4.2
electrophorus, 8.1.8
electroscopes, 8.1.1
electrostatic
 attraction, 8.1.2, 8.1.3, 8.1.4, 8.1.6

copiers, 8.1.6

induction, 8.1.1, 8.1.4, 8.1.6

repulsion, 8.1.1, 8.1.2, 8.1.4, 8.1.5

separation, 8.1.6

electrostatics, 8.1

energy, 5.1.3

conservation of, 5.2.4, 5.44

conservation, 5.1.4,

consumption, 5.1.3, 5.1.4

conversion of, 5.2.3, 8.2.3

kinetic, 5.2, 5.2.1, 5.2.2

potential, 5.2, 5.2.1, 8.2.2

sound , 6.2.3

vaporization, 4.2.1

wave, 6.1.2, 6.1.5

equilibrant, 3.1.2

equilibrium, 3.1.2, 3.4.1, 3.4.2, 3.4.3

evaporative heat loss, 4.2.1

experimental treatment, 6.3.1

external center of mass , 2.1.1

fiber optics, 7.1.5

field magnets, 8.4.4

fields, electromagnetic, 8.4.1

fields, magnetic, 8.3.4, 8.4.1

first class levers, 3.4.1, 5.4.1

first law of thermodynamics, 5.2.4, 5.2.5

first order image, 7.6.7

flight, 4.4.2

fluids, 4.1.3

density, 3.2.5

flow, 4.1.4, 4.3.2

motion, 4.4

pressure, 4.1.3, 4.3, 4.3.1, 4.3.3

fluorescent lamps, 8.1.7

flux density, 8.3.6

flux, lines of, 8.3.4

focal length, 7.5.4

focal point, 6.5.4

focal point, 7.5.4

force, 3.1, 4.1.2

buoyant, 3.1

centripetal, 3.1.5

determining buoyant force, 3.2.3

equal and opposite, 3.1.4

equilibrant

friction, 3.2

lift, 4.4.2

magnetic, 8.3.5

resultant, 3.1.2

Foucault pendulum, 2.4.4

frame of reference, 5.2.4

free fall, 2.3.1

frequency, 2.4.1, 6.1.1, 6.1.2, 6.2.1, 6.4.1, 6.4.2, 6.4.4, 7.6.1

natural, 6.2.2

sound, 6.4

friction, 3.2

equation, 3.3.4

coefficient of static, 3.3.2

factors affecting , 3.3.4

independence of surface area , 3.3.4

sliding, 3.3.1, 3.3.3

static, 3.3.1, 3.3.3

forces, 3.3.2

forces, ranking of, 3.3.2

fulcrum, 3.4.2, 3.4.3, 3.4.4

fundamental mode, 6.4.3

fuses, 8.2.6

g, 2.3.3, 2.4.3

galvanic skin response, 8.2.2

galvanometer, 8.2.1, 8.4.1

galvanoscope, 8.2.1

gear ratios, 5.4.5

gears, 5.4.5

generators, 8.4.3

geomagnetism, 8.3.7

geometric center, 2.1.1

geometric optics, 7.5

gravitational potential energy, 5.2.3

gravity, 2.3.1, 2.3.5, 3.1.6

determining acceleration of, 2.4.3

specific, 3.2.6

gyroscopes, 5.3.5, 5.3.6

harmonics, 6.4.3

hearing, stereo, 6.3.5

heating effects, 8.2.6

heating, resistive, 8.2.6

horizontal circle, motion in, 2.3.3

humidity 4.2.6

absolute, 4.2.6

relative , 4.2.6

hydrofoil, 4.4.2

identification of charge, 8.1.2

illusions, 7.1.2

image, 7.1.2, 7.1.3

first order, 7.6.7

principal, 7.6.7
    inversion of, 7.5.2
    multiple, 7.1.3
    real, 7.5.1, 7.5.3
    virtual, 7.5.3
implosions, 4.1.1
impulse, 5.3.4
incidence, angle of, 6.1.5, 7.1.1, 7.22
inclination, magnetic, 8.3.7
inclined plane, 5.4.4, 5.4.6, 5.44
index of refraction, 7.2.1, 7.2.2, 7.2.6
indirect measurement, 1.2, 6.3.2
    distance, 1.2.1
    mass, 1.2.3
    volume, 1.2.2
induced vibration, 6.2.1
inductance, mutual, 8.4.5
induction, 8.1.4
    electromagnetic, 8.4.3
    electrostatic, 8.1.1, 8.1.6, 8.2.1
    magnetic, 8.3.2
inelastic collisions, 5.3.2
inertia, 2.2, 2.2.1,
    effects of, 2.2.1
    fluid/solid systems, 2.24
    linear, 2.2.3
    liquids, 2.2.4
    rotational, 2.2.5, 2.2.6
infrared radiation, 7.6.2
interaction, law of, 3.1.4, 3.2.4
interaction, of waves, 6.1.3
interference, 6.1.5, 6.5.3, 7.3, 7.3.2
    constructive, 6.1.3, 7.3.1, 6.1.4
    destructive, 6.1.3, 6.1.4, 7.3.1
    patterns, 7.3.1
    sound, 6.5.3
    thin film, 7.3.1
internal center of mass, 2.1.1
inverse square law, 8.3.5
inversion of images, 7.5.2

kinetic energy, 5.2.1, 5.2.2, 5.2.3
    linear, 5.2.4, 5.2.5
    rotational, 5.2.5
    mass factor, 5.2.2
    speed factor , 5.2.2
lasers, 7.1.3
latitude, determination of , 2.4.4
law of...
    acceleration, 3.1.3

interaction, 3.1.4, 3.2.4
    length, 6.4.5
    of strings, 6.4.5
    rectilinear propagation, 7.5.1
    reflection, 6.5.1, 7.1.1, 7.1.2
    tension, 6.4.5
length, law of, 6.4.5
lens equation, 7.5.5
Lens's law, 8.4.3
lenses, 6.5.4
    objective, 7.5.2
    ocular, 7.5.2
    practical uses, 7.5.5
levers, 3.4.1, 3.4.2, 3.4.3, 3.4.4, 5.4.1,
    comparison of, 3.4.4
    everyday life, 3.4.4
    first class, 3.4.1, 5.4.1
    multiplying force with, 3.4.1,3.4.2
    multiplying speed, 3.4.1, 3.4.3
    second class, 5.4.1, 3.4.2
    third class, 5.4.1, 3.4.3
Leyden jar, 8.1.8
lift, 4.4.2
light, 7
    absorption of, 7.6.3, 7.6.6
    additive properties, 7.6.4
    coherent, 7.1.3
    color, 7.6
    diffraction of, 7.3.2
    dispersion of, 7.6.1
    frequency of, 7.6.1
    infrared, 7.6.2
    monochromatic, 7.6.3
    polarization of, 7.4
    polychromatic, 7.6.1
    primary colors of, 7.6.4
    propagation of, 7.5.1
    ray diagrams, 7.5.4
    recombination of, 7.6.1
    refraction of, 7.2, 7.2.3, 7.5.4
    scattering, 7.4.3, 7.66
    speed of, 6.3.2
    transmission of, 7.6.3
    wavelength of, 7.6.1, 7.6.7
lightning rods, 8.1.5
linear inertia, 2.2.2, 2.2.3
linear kinetic energy, 5.2.4, 5.2.5
linear momentum, 5.3.1, 5.3.2
linear momentum, conservation of, 5.3.2
liquid, inertia of, 2.2.1

longitudinal waves, 6.1.2

machines, 5.4
    efficiency, 5.4.3
    compound, 5.4.5, 5.4.6
magnetic
    attraction, 8.3.3, 8.3.4
    compass, 8.3.2
    declination, 8.3.7
    dip, 8.3.7
    dipoles, 8.3.3
    domains, 8.3.1
    field interaction, 8.3.4
    field of earth, 8.3.7
    fields, 8.3.4, 8.4.1
    flux density, 8.3.4, 8.3.6
    force, 8.3.5
    inclination, 8.3.7
    induction, 8.3.2, 8.3.5
    levitation, 8.3.3
    lines of flux, 8.3.4
    north and south poles, 8.3.7
    permeability, 8.3.6, 8.4.2
    poles, 8.3.3
    potential energy, 5.2.1
    repulsion, 8.3.3, 8.3.4
    shielding, 8.3.6,
magnetism, 8.3
magnetism, residual, 8.3.5
magnetization, 8.3.1, 8.3.2
magnification, 7.2.5, 7.5.2
manometer, 4.4.1
mass, 2.2.1
    influence on momentum, 5.3.1
maxima, 6.5.3
measurement, 1.1.1
    indirect, 1.2, 6.3.2
mechanical advantage, 3.4.1, 5.4.1, 5.4.2, 5.4.3,
    5.4.4, 5.4.5
media for sound transmission, 6.3.3
minima, 6.5.3
mirror images, 7.1.1
molecular polarity, 8.1.3
molecular size, 4.2.4
momentum, 5.3, 5.3.1, 5.3.4
    angular, 5.3.6
    conservation of, 5.3.3, 5.3.2
    impulse and, 5.3.4
    linear, 5.3.1
    mass and, 5.3.1

    velocity and, 5.3.1
monochromatic light, 7.6.3
monopoles, 8.3.4
motion
    vertical circle, 2.3.4
    irregular objects, 2.1.4
    center of mass, 2.1.4
    fluid, 4.4
    periodic, 2.4, 2.4.1
motors, 8.4.4
    motor effect, 8.4.4
    motor/generator relationship, 8.4.4
multiple images, 7.1.3
multiple reflections, 7.1.3
multiplication of force, 3.4.1, 3.4.2, 5.4.1, 5.4.5
multiplication of speed, 3.4.1, 3.4.3, 5.4.1, 5.4.5
mutual inductance, 8.4.5

N-pole, 8.3.3
natural frequencies, 6.2.2
negative charge, 8.1.2
neutral buoyancy, 3.2.2
Newton's Laws, 2.2.2, 3.1.3, 3.1.4, 3.1.5, 3.2.4,
    first law, 2.2.2
    law of interaction, 3.2.4
    second law, 3.1.3, 3.1.5
    third law, 3.1.4, 3.2.4
nodal lines, 6.5.3

objective lens, 7.5.2
ocular lens, 7.5.2
Ohm's law, 8.2.1, 8.2.5
open circuit, 8.2.1
opposite and equal forces, 3.1.4
optics, 7.2.2, 7.5
    optical bench, 7.5.5
    optical center, 7.5.4
    optical density, 7.2.5, 7.2.6
    optics, fiber, 7.1.5
orbital velocity, 3.1.5
overloading, 8.2.6

parabolic trajectories, 2.3.6
parallel circuits, 8.2.4, 8.2.7
Pascal's law, 4.1.3, 4.3.3
Peltier effect, 8.2.3
pendulum, 2.4
    comparison of simple and physical, 2.4.2
    equation, 2.4.3
    Foucault, 2.4.4

periods of, 2.4.2
physical, 2.4.2
simple, 2.4.1
period, 2.4.1, 6.1.1
periodic motion, 2.4, 2.4.1
periods of pendulums, 2.4.2
permanent magnets, 8.3.2
permeability, magnetic, 8.3.6, 8.4.2
phase boundaries, 4.2.3
photocopiers, 8.1.6
physical pendulum, 2.4.2
physical stress analysis, 7.4.5
pinhole optics, 7.5.1
pitch, 6.4.1, 6.4.2, 6.4.4
pitch and frequency, 6.4.1
pivot, 3.4.1
plane, inclined, 5.4.6, 5.4.4
plasma, 8.1.5
point of support, 2.1.3
polarization, 7.4, 7.4.1, 7.4.4, 7.4.5
    by reflection, 7.4.2
    by refraction, 7.4.4
    by scattering, 7.4.3
    by selective transmission, 7.4.1
    cross, 7.4.1
    of AM radio signals, 7.4.6
polychromatic light, 7.6.1
positive charge, 8.1.2
potential energy, 5.2.1, 5.2.3, 8.2.2
    conversion of, 5.2.3
    gravitational, 5.2.3
    magnetic, 5.2.1
    of springs, 5.2.3
potential difference, 8.2.2
power, 5.1, 5.1.2, 5.1.3, 5.1.4
    from electricity and gas, 5.1.3
    measurement of, 5.1.2
    ratings, 5.1.4
    units of, 5.1.2
precession, 5.3.6
precision, 1.1.1
pressure, 4.1.2, 4.3, 4.3.2
    air, 4.1
    atmospheric, 4.1.1
    definition of, 4.1.1
    differential, 4.1.4, 4.1.5, 4.3.1, 4.4.1
    equation, 4.1.1, 4.1.2
    fluid flow, 4.3.2
    transmission of, 4.3.3
    vapor, 4.2

primary coil, 8.4.5
primary colors, 7.6.4
principal axis, 7.5.4
principal image, 7.6.7
principal rays, 7.5.5
prisms, 7.6.1
projectile motion, 2.3.6
    influence of gravity on, 2.3.6
    projectile and target, 2.3.6
propagation, of waves, 6.1.5
propulsion, 3.1.4
psychrometry, 4.2.6
pulleys, 5.4.3

quality of sound, 6.3.3

radio, 7.4.6
    signals, polarization of, 7.4.6
    transmission, 7.4.6
ratios, 1.2.3, 1.3.1
ray diagram, 7.2.3, 7.5.4
rays, principal, 7.5.5
re-emission, 7.6.6
real images, 7.5.1, 7.5.3
recombination of light, 7.6.1
rectilinear propagation, 6.1.5
reference frame, 5.2.4
reflection, 6.1.5, 6.5.1, 7.1
    angle of, 6.1.5, 7.1.1
    illusions, 7.1.2
    law of, 7.1.2
    multiple, 7.1.3
    polarization by, 7.4.2
    sound, 6.5.1
    total internal, 7.1.4, 7.1.5
refraction, 6.1.5, 6.5.4, 7.2, 7.2.1, 7.2.3, 7.2.4, 7.2.5,
        7.5.4
    angle of, 7.22
    distortion, 7.2.3
    index of, 7.2.1, 7.2.2, 7.2.6
    polarization by, 7.4.4
    sound, 6.5.4
    transparency, 7.2.6
regulation of buoyancy, 3.2.2
relative humidity, 4.2.6
repulsion
    electromagnetic, 8.4.2
    electrostatic, 8.1.1, 8.1.3, 8.1.5
    magnetic, 8.3.4
residual magnetism, 8.3.5

resistance, 3.4.1, 3.4.2, 3.4.3, 3.4.4, 8.2.2, 8.2.5
    factors affecting, 8.2.5
resistance, air, 3.1.6
resistive heating, 8.2.6
resistors, 8.2.5
resonance, 6.2.2, 6.4.3, 6.4.4
resonant frequency and pitch, 6.4.4
resting weight, 3.1.3
resultant, 3.1.2
resultant forces, 3.1.2
retentivity, 8.3.5
rotation of earth, 2.4.4
rotational inertia, 2.2.5, 2.2.6
rotational kinetic energy, 5.2.5
rotor, 8.4.4

S-pole, 8.3.3
scalars, 3.1.1
scales, 6.4.4
scaling, 1.3
scaling down, 1.3.2, 1.3.3
scaling in living systems, 1.3.3
scaling up, 1.3.1, 1.3.2, 1.3.3
scattering, 7.6.6
    of light, 7.4.3, 7.6.6
    by polarization, 7.4.3
schematic diagrams, 8.2.4
screw, 5.4.4
second class levers, 3.4.2, 5.4.1
secondary coil, 8.4.5
Seebeck effect, 8.2.3
series circuits, 8.2.4, 8.2.7
shielding, magnetic, 8.3.6
short circuits, 8.2.6
silhouettes, 7.5.1
similar ratios, 1.2.1
similar triangles, 1.2.1
simple machines, 5.4, 5.4.2, 5.4.3
simple pendulums, 2.4.1
    factors affecting, 2.4.1
single slit diffraction, 7.3.2
siphons, 4.3.1
sliding friction, 3.3.1, 3.3.3
    coefficient of, 3.3.3, 3.3.4
slip, angle of, 3.3.2
Snell's law, 7.2.2
solar spectrum, 7.6.1
solenoids, 8.4.2
solute, 4.2.5
solution, 4.2.5

vapor pressure of, 4.2.5
solvent, 4.2.5
sound, 6.2, 6.2.4
    diffraction of, 6.5.2
    energy, 6.2.3
    frequency of, 6.4.1, 6.4.2, 6.4.4
    frequency, 6.4
    in solids & liquids, 6.3.3
    influence of temperature on speed, 6.3.5
    interference of, 6.5.3
    locating source of, 6.3.5
    physical definitions, 6.2.4
    pitch of, 6.4.1, 6.4.4
    psychological definition 6.2.4
    quality of, 6.3.3
    reflection of, 6.5.1
    refraction of, 6.5.4
    resonance, 6.4.4
    scales, 6.4.4
    speed of in different media, 6.3.4
    speed of, 6.3.2, 6.3.4, 6.4.3
    timbre, 6.3.3
    transmission media, 6.3.3
    transmission, 6.3.1, 6.3.3
    wave properties of, 6.5
    wavelength, 6.4, 6.4.1
specific gravity, 3.2.6
spectral identification, 7.3.3
spectroscopes, 7.3.3
spectrum, solar, 7.6.1
spectrum, visible, 7.6.1
speed
    light, 6.3.2
    sound, 6.3.2, 6.4.3
    sound in air, 6.3.2
    sound in different media, 6.3.4
spring, potential energy of, 5.2.3
stability, 2.1.2, 2.1.3, 4.4.3, 5.3.5, 5.3.6
standing waves, 6.1.4
static friction, 3.3.1, 3.3.3
    coefficient of, 3.3.3, 3.3.4
step-down transformers, 8.4.5
step-up transformers, 8.4.5
stereo hearing, 6.3.5
streamlines 4.4.2, 4.4.3
stress analysis, 7.4.5
strings, law of, 6.4.5
sunsets and sunrises, 7.6.6
superposition, 6.1.3, 6.5.1
surface area, 4.1.2

surface area and vaporization, 4.2.3
surface area to volume ratio, 1.3.2, 1.3.3, 4.2.3
surface interactions, 3.3.2, 3.3.3
swim bladders, 3.2.2
sympathetic vibrations, 6.2.2

temperature and speed of sound, 6.3.5
tension, law of, 6.4.5
thermocouple, 8.2.3
thermodynamics, first law of, 5.2.4, 5.2.5
thermoelectricity, 8.2.3
thermopile, 8.2.3
third class levers, 3.4.3, 5.4.1
timbre, 6.3.3
torque, 3.4
    balanced, 3.4.1
total internal reflection, 7.1.4, 7.1.5, 7.2.4
trajectory, parabolic, 2.3.6
transfer of charge, 8.1.2
transformers, 8.4.5
    step-down, 8.4.5
    step-up, 8.4.5
transmission, 7.6.3
transmission of pressure, 4.3.3
transmission of sound, 6.3, 6.3.1
transparency, 7.2.6
transverse waves, 6.1.2
trough, 6.1.1

units, 1.1

vacuum, 4.2.2, 6.3.1
vacuum, and sound transmission, 6.3.1
vapor pressure, 4.2
vapor pressure of solutions, 4.2.5
vaporization, 4.2.4
    energy, 4.2.1
    influence of molecular structure, 4.2.4
    influence of surface area on, 4.2.3
vector addition, 3.1.1, 3.1.2
vectors, 3.1.1
velocity, 2.2.6
    angular, 2.2.5

influence on momentum, 5.3.1
    orbital, 3.1.5
vertical circle, motion in, 2.3.4
vibration, 6.2.1
    induced, 6.2.1
    sympathetic, 6.2.2
    frequency and pitch, 6.4.1
virtual images, 7.5.3
viscosity, 2.2.4
visible spectrum, 7.6.1
volatility, 4.2.4
voltage, 8.2.2, 8.2.4

water barometers, 4.1.6
water levels, 4.3.1
water pressure and depth, 4.3.2
wave, 6.1
    amplitude, 6.1.5
    characteristics, 6.1.1
    energy, 6.1.2, 6.1.5
    equation, 6.1.5
    interaction, 6.1.3
    longitudinal, 6.1.2
    propagation, 6.1.5
    properties of sound, 6.5
    speed, 6.1.5
    standing, 6.1.4
    transverse, 6.1.2
wavelength, 6.1.1, 6.4.1, 7.6.1
    light, 7.6.7
    sound, 6.4, 6.4.3
weather forecasting, 4.1.6
wedge 5.4, 5.4.4,
weight, 2.2.1, 3.1.6, 3.2.4
    resting, 3.1.3
weightlessness, 2.3.4
wet cell, 8.2.2
wheel and axle, 5.4.2
work, 5.1, 5.1.1 5.1.3
    and power, 5.1, 5.1.2
    equation of, 5.1.1
    measurement of, 5.1.1
    units of, 5.1.1